MORE DIRTY LOOKS

More Dirty Looks

Gender, Pornography and Power

2nd Edition

Edited by
Pamela Church Gibson

 Publishing

For Roma Gibson. With love and gratitude.

This edition first published in 2004 by the
British Film Institute
21 Stephen Street, London W1T 1LN

The British Film Institute is the UK national agency
with responsibility for encouraging the arts of film and
television and conserving them in the national interest.

Cover design: Ketchup
Cover image: *Untitled #115 (Measuring Tape)* (© Jeff Burton, 2000)

Set by Fakenham Photosetting Limited, Fakenham, Norfolk
Printed in the UK by The Cromwell Press, Trowbridge, Wiltshire

British Library Cataloguing-in-Publication Data
A catalogue record for this book is available from the British Library

ISBN 0–85170–939–7 (pbk)
ISBN 0–85170–936–2 (hbk)

Contents

Preface: Porn Again? Or Why the Editor Might Have Misgivings

Pamela Church Gibson

In July 2002, while reviewing a new biography of Lenin for the the *London Review Of Books*, Žižek stated, categorically, that 'the left has undergone a shattering experience' and is now, therefore, compelled 'to reinvent its whole project'.[1] As this is such a precise description of the situation in which Left-leaning members of the Anglo-American academy find themselves, some might suggest that time spent re-examining the debates around pornography and censorship is time wasted. They might think that, rather than commission fresh essays around over-contested terrain, the source of so much wrangling within feminism for so long, it might be better to expend the same energy on examining – for example – current forms of counter-cinema, or women directors in third cinema, or whatever. And some will doubtless cavil at the inclusion, in this second edition, of male contributors.

Nevertheless, I feel that there *is* a need for this second collection – and the inclusion of male contributors was, in fact, my own suggestion. The rationale for both moves seemed straightforward enough. Firstly, in the increasingly sexualised atmosphere of Western society, where cinema censorship seems to be relaxing and sexually explicit images are to be found everywhere from the pages of fashion magazines to the advertising of alcoholic drinks, the relevant debates, within feminism and elsewhere, have certainly not been resolved. Indeed, given the conference flyers and course proposals that I see, they have been reinvigorated – particularly by the ever-growing activities on the internet. Cyberspace, of course, was originally perceived as a lawless frontier town – a Dodge City for the new millennium – and any form of consistently effective legislation still seems an impossibility, despite frequent attempts by various regulatory bodies and the introduction of on-line surveillance.

Secondly, many aspects of the debates around pornography are predicated upon assumptions that concern consumer behaviour. Since the majority of consumers are usually presumed to be male – whether gay or straight – and some surveys do seem to substantiate this belief, it seemed sensible to give male writers some voice in this second volume. Some, of course, may still be wary of encroaching on what they perceive as territory guarded by feminist critics, or as forming part of a gay and lesbian agenda. In 2001, in a paper at the Society for Cinema Studies annual conference, I rather flippantly used the expression 'male heterosexual beast' when discussing issues of consumption within the genre. Interestingly, in the plenary discussion, every questioner who felt that he might fall into that unappetising category felt it necessary to acknowledge this fact, rather fearfully, before saying anything else.

Academic discourse around 'feminism' seems, sadly, to have become disassociated from political activity – while the term itself has been questioned, re-examined, dismissed by some as outmoded, obsolete, irrelevant. In the early 70s, of course, when second-wave feminism and leftwing politics were seen as inextricably intertwined and the doors of the academy were not yet open to the former, public spaces rather than conference halls, seminar rooms and the pages of journals were the forum for action, taking to the streets the way to make the feminist presence felt and grievances known. Now that feminism is safely ensconced within the very heart of the academy, on both sides of the Atlantic and elsewhere, it sometimes seems as if it has been imprisoned there, by a terrible irony, and thus disempowered, leaving practical questions unresolved and the spaces of the streets available to new occupation.

Certainly, in Britain and the States, there now seems to be a three-pronged use of public space for political purposes. Firstly, rightwing groups are active once again, and standing up – or marching along – to be counted. Secondly, there is a new use of public space for a display of shared emotion – or histrionics – that's often worryingly nationalistic. The massive ranks of Middle Englanders who lined the streets for the funeral of Princess Diana developed a taste for street theatre; on both sides of the Atlantic, tub-thumping patriotism and flag-flying are back on the agenda. And lastly, there are those demonstrations that involve new modes of coalition. Over the past twenty-odd years, new age travellers have joined forces, from time to time, with the local bourgeoisie and the politically virginal to protest against road-widening schemes and other attacks on the environment. But recently, there have been larger excursions and more significant alliances. In October 2002, there was the first of two massive protest marches against a war with Iraq – organised jointly by the 'Stop the War' Coalition and the Muslim Council of Great Britain – glossed over here in Britain and virtually ignored in America. Yet, just one week earlier, when a different type of coalition force – the rural establishment – took to the streets of London, with dukes on the march and coaches ferrying up contingents from public schools, as well as bringing farriers and their families from small villages, all eager to defend their right to hunt with hounds, every newspaper and television channel had that march as a lead story. It was heralded as 'the biggest demonstration since the Chartist Marches' – and *Vogue* magazine even ran a two-page spread on what chic pro-hunting marchers were wearing. It seems that the press is still the best censor for which a rightwing government could hope.

This was surely one particular march where no overtly 'feminist' banners were to be glimpsed, although feminists – whether self-proclaimed or not – have played their part in most on-street activities over three decades. Nevertheless while large-scale, all-women processions might seem to many to be a thing of the past, there is one issue which still motivates women in particular to take up a stance – and to confront each other, rather than unite and fight in that bygone spirit of communality. That single issue is, of course, pornography.

The lines are still drawn up and the divide as clear as ever – increasing liberalisation only increases the tensions, while adding new factors to the equation.

I hope this introduction will make that clear and that a tale of four shops, offered up as illustration, may complete the picture.

The first 'shop snapshot' will take the reader back to the 80s when the growing debates around pornography, now so divisive, were in fact seen by many as a way of rallying women behind a single cause. The anti-pornography campaign extended its range to include attacks on the sex industry in general – and places which sold what are called 'sex accessories' or 'toys' were targets. In Oxford, the first sex shop was, bizarrely enough, situated opposite the East Oxford Women's Centre. From day one, it was picketed. Men – and I stress men, for it was assumed that the shop existed for the gratification of the male libido – who ventured in and out were captured on video by women from across the street. The windows of the shop were thoughtfully lined with brown paper, to spare the humiliation of the said men while they made their purchases. It looked gloomy, unwelcoming and thoroughly seedy. Today, the shop is still there, but the brown paper has gone and the gloom seems to have lifted – while the Women's Centre looks less busy than before, and rather dilapidated. This could figure as a kind of trope.

Whatever attitudes women have adopted towards pornography, whatever actions they may have taken in the past, the industry itself, of course, has flourished – a huge, multifaceted industry which has continued to grow and develop, utterly unmoved by debates, demonstrations or, more significantly, economic crises. For since pornography is an industry where the overheads can be minimal, the profits enormous and demand is continuous, it is not hindered in any way by the usual laws of market forces or touched by recession-related problems.

Concurrently, across the last three decades, British society has become increasingly sexualised. Far from feminism being able to prevent the objectifying and fragmentation of the female body, there's been a general commodification of the body *per se* – and the male body is now to be seen everywhere. Vast billboards display men clad in the latest designer underpants, overly muscular torsos decorate magazine covers – while recently, the admen have wheeled out their first full-frontal naked man, to publicise the new aftershave marketed by Yves St Laurent. His picture is thoughtfully cropped for display in bus shelters. Ten or more years ago, when freedom of expression seemed under threat, the anti-censorship campaign in Britain led to the formation of Feminists Against Censorship . The organisation had some strange bedfellows. Tuppy Owens, organiser of the Sex Maniac's Ball and editor of the *Sex Maniac's Diary*, was an enthusiastic supporter of the campaign, keen to explain how 'empowering' both ball and the diary were for women. The word 'empowerment' would be later heard again and again in discussions around pornography and the sex industry.

The second shop story involves women, on both sides of the widening divide, who clashed openly when the feminist bookshop Silver Moon took the decision to stock Della Grace's book of photographs, *Love Bites*, in 1993. Many of the photographs were of London 'leather lesbians', some overtly sadomasochistic. A speedily organised demonstration – by women – outside the bookshop demanded that it remove the volume from its shelves. One woman's 'imaginary domain', to quote Drucilla Cornell, is another woman's source of outrage. Silver Moon has since closed its doors and now occupies only a section of Foyle's – that too is significant. For it seemed, sadly, that this early feminist enterprise could only survive financially through appropriation by a middle-brow bookseller.

With the blurring of boundaries over the past decade, the cinema followed the pattern set elsewhere in the media. The British Board of Film Censors has become increasingly liberal. Cinematic footage of a sexually explicit nature – provided the film which contains it can be labelled 'art-house' – has, increasingly, been granted certification and can be viewed within mainstream cinema.

Catherine Breillat's film *Romance* (France, 1998) was one of the first to show an erect male penis, which belonged to the porn star, Rocco Siffredi. In *Romance* and in her second film *À ma soeur* (France, 2002) Breillat shows sex as utterly joyless, indeed punitive, for women. Andrea Dworkin and Catharine MacKinnon cannot be too affronted. However, they might cavil at the French film *Baise-moi* (Virginie Depente, 2002) where the two girls who play the lead roles are in fact former porn actresses. Far from being, as Linda Ruth Williams suggested, a feminist road movie that could be called 'Thelma and Louise Get Laid',[2] it's a grim picture of two women who embark, for no real reason, on a spree of random and seemingly motiveless murders. One heroine begins by strangling her flatmate when the flatmate asks – not unreasonably – that the hero-

ine clear up the flat a bit, rather than lie around in the sitting-room masturbating and smoking dope. The killings are interspersed with energetic couplings where the women do seem to exert a kind of power, but the only scene that depicts unalloyed pleasure shows them dancing together, in their underwear, on a hotel bed, well away from the company of men, who are treated throughout with near-contempt.

As pornography filters into the mainstream, its place on the feminist agenda seems, for a number of very good reasons, whether practical or theoretical, to be both assured and important. This does not mean that former contradictions have been resolved – indeed, there is often a new degree of ambivalence among those opposed to censorship. Within the academy, the study of pornography may form part of a gender studies programme, while within some institutions it is studied as part of film and media, despite the legal problems and moralistic concerns, to be examined as another genre, as a vast industry, and as a topic for raising questions around gender and sexuality. Within the realms of high theory, where certain feminist scholars are attempting to move beyond the fixed binaries of Western patriarchal thought and to create new modes of specifically feminist thought, the subject has particular resonance. Judith Butler devoted a chapter of *Excitable Speech: A Politics of the Performative* to an examination of the rhetoric of Catharine MacKinnon – and interestingly, begins by stating firmly, 'One might well agree that a good deal of pornography is offensive'.[3] For to her 'pornography is the text of gender's unreality, the impossible norms by which it is compelled', and she calls for a feminist reading of pornography 'different from the conventional liberalisation' – rather, the feminist must read it 'instead for the incommensurabilities between gender norms and practices that it seems compelled to repeat without restriction'.[4] For Butler what pornography delivers is 'a text of insistent and faulty gender relations that will not disappear with the abolition of the text itself'.[5]

Drucilla Cornell, Professor of Women's Studies and Law at Rutgers University, confronted and raised practical and social problems in her book, *The Imaginary Domain: Abortion, Pornography and Sexual Harassment*.[6] She makes it abundantly clear that to be anti-censorship is not to be uncritical of all current activity within the sex industry. Nevertheless, 'to deny a person their life as a sexual being, as they have imagined it through their own sexual imago and lived it as persona, is to deny them a fundamental part of their identity'.[7]

Her chapter, 'Pornography's Temptation', begins with a succinct sketch of the current situation:

> The pornography debate portrays its contestants within sex and gender stereotypes, its contenders drawn in the broad outlines of Harlequin romance. Rapacious men with libidos of mythological proportions heartlessly brutalise innocent women as the hopeless victims of their lust, while the anti-porn feminist poses herself as the sacrificial victim, the barrier to a tide of male sexuality that threatens violence. Meanwhile there thrives an 8 to 13 billion dollar a year industry, churning out hundreds of low-budget videos every month. If pornography was once a powerful political tool, produced in secret places by revolutionary groups, it is now also big business.[8]

The question she then poses should be recognised as the crux of the pornography debate: 'How can we both recognise the reality of the industry and the suffering it can impose on its workers at the same time that we affirm the need for women to freely explore their own sexuality?'.[9]

Cornell makes it clear that what concerns her is mainstream heterosexual pornography – the obvious inequity of power, the fact that coercion can be the basis of desire and a woman 'stripped completely of her personhood' in a way that doesn't happen in lesbian pornography. It's the form that has tried to create what she calls 'a predetermined lens' for all other types of pornography. Her extensive interviews with the porn star and director Ona Zee, who fought in the early 90s to unionise porn stars – she failed and was blackballed – are quoted throughout the text. Zee observes drily 'No little girl wakes up one morning and decides she's going to have sex for money.'[10]

Cornell discusses the logistical difficulties of trying to improve the quality of life for porn actresses. She argues that within the industry itself the difficulties are compounded not only by the high turnover of workers but by the inescapable fact that the industry is male dominated. She doesn't come up with any easy solutions, but she does work through the problems – something usually done only by those who want to advocate censorship.

Cornell also discusses something often unacknowledged – or avoided – by those in the anti-censorship camp. She asks what could be done to prevent many women, such as herself, feeling increasingly oppressed by the weight and number of sexual images that surround them. She suggests that possibly zoning – as a form of 'display regulation' – might be the solution, although difficult to implement. Why, she asks, should women be subjected to a non-stop enforced viewing of what she calls their 'sexed selves'? Women, she argues, 'need to have their imaginary domain protected, precisely so that they may continue the arduous journey of "finding the words to say it", to develop richer descriptions of their "sex" '.[11]

Cornell raises in this chapter many uncomfortable questions which others who oppose censorship might choose to ignore. It does seem that some of the unease and ambivalence which has arguably been exacerbated by recent social change is perhaps reflected within the academy. But there are those – in the world outside the academy, in the marketplace – who would have no truck with any notion of oppression, any suggestion that women might find this proliferation of imagery in any way burdensome. Among them are the English women who have opened new, very upmarket, sex shops, which look exactly like small high-fashion shops and have prices that are similar. Chic shops selling expensive underwear with designer labels and prohibitive price tags did very well in the London of the 90s – in fact, although sales of womenswear in general are steadily falling, what retailers refer to as 'lingerie' has had a dramatic rise in sales. Presumably this trend suggested to the entrepreneurially minded the idea of widening the remit of such shops. For though the purchasing of 'toys' and 'accessories' has always been a highly profitable part of the sex industry, the shops themselves have been rather sleazy, even disreputable in their décor, with a penchant for neon lights that, quite literally, reflect the lurid colours of the articles on display, while the actual quality of these goods would not win any Design Council awards. However, moves have now been made to bring notions of 'design' and 'good taste' into this particular sector of the marketplace. Whether or not they have actually read Bourdieu, three women entrepreneurs have become extremely rich through their understanding of how important it is for the professional middle classes to parade that awareness of 'taste' which he describes.[12] They have translated it into retailing reality and reconfigured the notion of the 'sex shop'.

The final 'shop snapshots' show in detail two of these new, women-owned businesses. Myla, founded by two women who used to work in the city, is situated in the affluent part of Notting Hill. Surrounded by small, expensive shops selling clothes and shoes, it blends in perfectly, while its 'concessions' within Selfridges and Liberty also merge seamlessly into their new context. Its press release claims that 'Sex Is the New Black' and although MYLA mainly sells costly underwear, there are plenty of accessories to be found. Most notable, here, is the recruiting of Tom Dixon, the 'creative director' of Habitat and pillar of society (the catalogue proudly reminds its readers that he is 'Tom Dixon OBE'). At Myla's request, Dixon designed a vibrator, called 'Bone'. Made from 'handcrafted black resin', it costs £199, is described as an 'art object', and has found its way into British *Vogue*. A full-page advertisement appeared in the December 2002 issue, strategically placed among the advertisements for Dior, Chanel and Gucci. It also appeared in the annual Christmas catalogue published by Liberty – that respected emporium, self-styled pioneer of 'taste' and one obvious place for the middle classes to buy their presents – amid the pictures of silk scarves and scented candles. There were illustrations of various Myla products – the oils, the potions and that same *objet d'art*, Bone, which can be so evasively described.

In Covent Garden, there is another new and equally successful shop, Coco de Mer. Altogether more extravagant than Myla, it sells negligees trimmed with genuine ostrich feathers, and silk crotchless knickers edged with mink. In fact, the advertising agency Saatchi & Saatchi was so impressed by what retailers call the 'proposition' presented by Coco de Mer's founder – which it saw as 'being in tune with the *zeitgeist*', to quote a press officer – that it greatly reduced its fee to provide the ad campaign for the fledgling business. Now Saatchi & Saatchi has received an award for its images. The founder of Coco de Mer is a young woman, Sam Roddick, who told me in an interview of her desire to 'enable women to enjoy their own sexuality'.[13] Her window displays are always tasteful – no-one need feel embarrassed to go in – and so is the decor. The walls are lined with gilt Züber wallpaper, the paint-

work is a kind of dusky aubergine, and the changing rooms have cunning peep holes and carved chairs. The overall effect is that of a set for *La Traviata*, the apartment of a successful courtesan, enhanced by the profusion of cushions and sofas. However, a closer look at the cushions reveal that they are printed with images of heterosexual couples busily engaged in sexual activities. The negligees hanging up turn out not just to be very expensive (average price £200–£350) but cunningly designed. Gaps, slits, frills could fly up to reveal breasts and slip aside to facilitate access. A toile-de-jouy printed gown turns out to have had the print cunningly altered, so that the bucolic but innocent men and maidens in the original rustic scenes are now replaced by images of couples hard at it. There are some expensive bondage accessories, including an elaborately carved chastity belt in solid silver and bejewelled cuffs. But the most interesting change from the Ann Summers chain is that the vibrators on offer here, rather than being garish in hue and made of ridged rubber, are, instead, smooth and sculptural, and the colours are described as 'onyx, ecru, and crushed strawberry'. Lastly, it is interesting to speculate what genuine London prostitutes might think of a halter-necked top on sale for £350. It is made up of endless little cards like those seen in telephone kiosks, where London prostitutes describe their attractions and detail their services. The cards have been reprinted on hard plastic rectangles and are now held together by silver chains. It does seem to me that this particular garment is a perfect example of what Drucilla Cornell calls the 'sentimentalisation' of the porn industry. Roddick describes herself as a 'post-feminist' and her customers she would include in the same category. She is almost as messianic, in her own way, as Dworkin and MacKinnon – but, I presume, far richer. As these feminist 'venture capitalists' conquer the world of glossy magazines, reap enormous rewards and, moreover, claim to do so under the problematic, tarnished standard of 'post-feminism', there is surely no further proof required of the need for a new anthology.

NOTES

1. Slavoj Žižek, *London Review of Books*, July 2002, p. 3.
2. Linda Ruth Williams, Review of *Baise-moi*, *Sight and Sound*, May 2002.
3. Judith Butler, *Excitable Speech: A Politics of the*

Performative (Routledge: London, 1997).

4. Ibid., pp. 70–3.

5. Ibid., p. 73.

6. Drucilla Cornell, *The Imaginary Domain: Abortion, Pornography and Sexual Harassment* (Routledge: New York and London, 1995).

7. Ibid., p. 8.

8. Ibid., p. 95.

9. Ibid., p. 96.

10. Ibid., p. 116.

11. Ibid., p. 153.

12. Pierre Bourdieu, *Distinction: A Social Critique of Taste* (London: Routledge, 1984).

13. Sam Roddick, Interview with Pamela Church Gibson, 2002.

Acknowledgments

First and foremost, I should like to thank Roma Gibson, the dedicatee of this anthology; the first collection of essays was entirely her idea, and it was she who invited me to work with her on the project.

Secondly, I'd like to thank Andrew Lockett of BFI Publishing, with whom I have really enjoyed working over the years – he is an editor who combines good humour and sense of humour in equal parts, and I am very grateful for both. Sophia Contento is another person at the BFI who must be thanked for her help – her expertise and hard work, her commitment and her patience should not go unmentioned.

Jeff Burton's photograph has provided the book with a wonderful cover and he has been extremely helpful throughout. Many thanks to Sadie Coles for making this possible.

Before I thank the contributors, I should first thank those with whom I work on a daily basis. Christopher Breward has changed the intellectual climate of the institution where we are both employed; I am very grateful to him for his comments on my work past and present, and for including me in his latest research venture. Actually in the trenches themselves is Adam Briggs, whose appointment has completely transformed the lives of the cultural studies staff, and for whose informed interest in this and other of my projects I am very grateful. He has also enabled me to combine research with teaching, and his unfailing kindness to all his staff is unusual in the changed climate of higher education. Jan Miller is also to be thanked, not only for bacon-saving but for her constant good-natured support.

The contributors have been helpful in every way – and patient beyond belief. I would like to thank Jane Gaines for her enthusiastic response both to this anthology and for the other projects on which we have worked. Jane Juffer, whom I enjoyed meeting at SCS, gave me an opportunity there to test the water-temperature in the States – while Stacy Gillis provided me with a similar opening nearer home. Paul Willemen and Ed Buscombe are also to be thanked for putting their heads above the parapet in this particular war of attrition. Lastly, I would like to thank my family and my friends – in particular, those women whose presence over the years has sustained me in so many ways.

Notes on Contributors

Edward Buscombe has lectured and published in Britain and America for over thirty years. He is a particular expert on the Western and has written monographs on *Stagecoach* (BFI, 1992) and *The Searchers* (BFI, 2000); his latest publication is *Cinema Today* (Phaidon, 2003).

Rich C. Cante is Associate Professor of Film at the University of North Carolina. He is the co-author of 'The Voice of Pornography' in *Keyframes: Popular Film and Cultural Studies* (Routledge, 2001) and 'The Cultural Aesthetic Specificities of All Male Moving Image Pornography' in *Porn Studies* (Duke University Press, forthcoming). He is currently researching gay male AIDS and US Culture.

Richard Dyer is Professor of Film Studies at the University of Warwick. He is the author of many books and articles on the cinema, among which are *Stars* (BFI, 1998) and a volume on *Brief Encounter* in the BFI Film Classics series (1993).

Jane Gaines is Professor of English and Literature and the Director of the Program in Film and Video at Duke University. She is the co-editor of *Collecting Visible Evidence* (University of Minnesota Press, 1999) and the author of *Fire and Desire: Mixed Race Movies in the Silent Era* (University of Chicago Press, 2001) and *Fictioning Histories: Women Film Pioneers* (University of Illinois Press, forthcoming).

Pamela Church Gibson is Senior Lecturer in Contextual Studies at the London Institute. She has published on film and fandom, history and heritage and is the co-editor of three anthologies including *The Oxford Guide to Film Studies* (Oxford University Press, 1998). She is currently working on the relationship between cinema and consumption in the post-War period.

Stacy Gillis is a Research Fellow in Cyberculture at the University of Exeter and also works at the Institute of Feminist Studies. She has co-edited *Third Wave Feminism* (Palgrave, forthcoming) and is currently working on an anthology of essays on *The Matrix* trilogy.

Henry Jenkins is the Director of MIT's Comparative Media Studies Program. He is the author of *Textual Poachers: Television Fans and Participatory Culture* (Routledge, 1992), co-editor (with Justine Cassell) of *From Barbie to Mortal Kombat: Gender and Computer Games* (MIT Press, 1998) and a contributor to *The New Media Book* (BFI, 2002).

Jane Juffer is Assistant Professor of English and Women's Studies at Pennsylvania State University. She is the author of *At Home with Pornography: Women, Sex and Everyday Life* (New York University Press, 1998) and 'Sexual Technologies/Domestic Technologies' in *Culture and Everyday* (Sociology Press, forthcoming).

Laura Kipnis is Associate Professor in the Department of Radio, Film and Television at Northwestern University, Chicago. She has published extensively and her books include *Bound and Gagged: Pornography and the Politics of Fantasy in America* (Grove Press, 1996) and *Against Love: A Polemic* (Pantheon Books, 2003). She is also a video artist and filmmaker whose work has been shown worldwide.

Chuck Kleinhans is Associate Professor in the Department of Radio, Film and Television at Northwestern University, Chicago. He has published widely on film and is the editor of *JumpCut*.

Gertrud Koch is a Professor of Film Studies at the Freie Universität Berlin. She has published widely and is co-editor of the journals *Babylon* and *Frauen und Film*.

Liz Kotz is Assistant Professor in Cultural Studies and Comparative Literature at the University of Minnesota. Formerly, she was a critic and curator and has written on film, video and visual arts for *Art Forum*, *Art in America*, *After Image* and other journals. She has co-edited an anthology of lesbian writing for *Semiotext(e)*.

Royce Mahawatte completed his PhD in Victorian literature at Wadham College, Oxford and has taught there and in London. He is currently working on Victorian popular fiction and studying on the Creative Writing MA at UEA.

Anne McClintock is the Simone de Beauvoir Chair of English and Women's Studies at the University of Wisconsin. She is the author of *Imperial Leather: Race Gender and Sexuality in the Colonial Contest* (Routledge, 1995). She is the editor of numerous collections of essays on post-colonial theory including *Queer Transexions of Race, Nation and Gender* in *Social Text* (1997). She is currently working on a collection of essays on commercial sex, provisionally entitled *Screwing the System*.

Lynda Nead is Professor in the History of Art at Birkbeck College, University of London. She has published widely and her books include *Myths of Sexuality: Representations of Victorian Women in Britain* (Blackwells, 1988) and *The Female Nude: Art Obscenity and Sexuality* (Routledge, 1992) and *Victorian Babylon: People, Streets and Images in Nineteenth-Century London* (Yale, 2000).

Alistair O'Neill completed his MA at the Royal College of Art and is currently a research fellow and lecturer at the London Institute. For some years he has curated and worked within the London gallery context.

Angelo Restivo is Associate Professor of Film at the University of East Carolina. He is the co-author of 'The Voice of Pornography' in *Keyframes: Popular Film and Cultural Studies* (Routledge, 2001) and 'The Cultural Aesthetic Specificities of All Male Moving Image Pornography' in *Porn Studies* (Duke University Press, forthcoming).

Lynne Segal is Professor of Psychology and Gender Studies at the University of London. She is the author of *Why Feminism? Gender, Psychology, Politics* (Polity Press, 1999), *Straight Sex: The Politics of Pleasure* (Virago, 1994) and editor of *Sex Exposed: Sexuality & the Pornography Debate* (Virago, 1992) She is currently working on a book addressing what remains of feminist attachments in the 21st century.

Chris Straayer is Associate Professor in the Department of Cinema Studies at NYU. She is the author of *Deviant Eyes, Deviant Bodies: Sexual Re-orientations in Film and Video* (Columbia University Press, 1996) and has contributed to *Jump Cut*, *Afterimage* and *Camera Obscura*.

Amy Villarejo is Assistant Professor in Film Studies and Program in Women, Gender and Sexuality at Cornell University. She is the co-author of *Queen Christina* (BFI, 1995), co-editor of *Keyframes: Popular Film and Cultural Studies* (Routledge, 2001) and author of *Lesbian Rule* (Duke University Press, forthcoming).

Jennifer Wicke is Professor and Director of Graduate Placement in the Department of English at the University of Virginia. She is the author of *Advertising Fictions: Literature, Advertisement and Social Reading* (Columbia University Press, 1988) and co-editor of *Feminism and Postmodernism* (Duke University Press, 1994).

Paul Willemen is Professor of Film Studies at the University of Ulster, Coleraine. His publications include *Looks and Frictions* (BFI, 1994) and he is the co-editor of *The Encyclopaedia of Indian Cinema* (BFI, 1994). He is currently writing a book on action cinema.

Linda Williams is a professor in the departments of Film Studies and Rhetoric and Director of the Program in Film Studies and of the Center for New Media at the University of California, Berkeley. She is the author of *Hard Core: Power, Pleasure and the Frenzy of the Visible* (University of California Press, 1989) and *Figures of Desire: A Theory and Analysis of Surrealist Film* (University of Illinois Press, 1981)

Foreword: So You Want to Teach Pornography?

Henry Jenkins

So you want to teach pornography?

Good for you, but you had better be prepared for some of the challenges of integrating sexually explicit media into the classroom. I had taught porn in my classes at MIT for almost a decade without complaint or controversy. I didn't realise I was performing without a net.

For me, it started with a phone call by a *Boston Globe* reporter who was doing an article about a controversy that had erupted on a neighbouring campus and wanted some yardstick for understanding what might constitute a responsible way of dealing with sexually explicit materials. I answered a few questions but the reporter wanted more 'dirt'. At one point he asked, 'Well, don't you think one of the purposes of education is to shock students' sensibilities?' When I didn't rise to the occasion, he got bored and hung up.

By the time the story appeared on the front page, any concern about the responsible ways of dealing with sexually explicit images I'd tried to spotlight, as well as any specifics about the context in which such images might be discussed or even the pedagogical goals of discussing them, had clearly fallen prey to word count restrictions. Uninterested in the specifics, the reporter simply made up vivid details. The local controversy was pushed back and my teaching was the lead.

Within a few hours, I received calls from local radio and television outlets eager to have me 'set the record straight'. Talk show listeners rang to say that I was being denounced on the air right now, hoping I'd respond. A Christian news organisation tried to get me on the air without identifying its agenda. While I was in a meeting, my assistant took a phone call from a Texas talk-radio host who started peppering him with questions before bothering to mention that he was actually going out live. 'Pornography being taught at MIT' was referenced on Paul Harvey's nationally syndicated radio show and denounced by Fox News's *O'Reilly Report*. A year later, I was still receiving interview requests. *Rolling Stone* wanted to feature me as teaching one of the ten sexiest courses on American college campuses. As this story made the rounds, it got less and less accurate. I went from 'teaching about pornography' to 'teaching a whole class on pornography' to 'advocating that students consume or produce pornography.'

Such a story justifies showing slightly blurred or carefully cropped porn images on television or in print, or talking about the 'dirty deed' on radio; so it is well suited to a culture that loves to titillate us, but not to analyse or talk honestly about pornography. And the story was fed by a strange coalition of media effects researchers, anti-porn feminists, conservative Christians, or simply old-style humanists upset by the displacement of the Western canon. In the words of one so-called expert on sex addiction, '[Teaching a course on pornography] is like giving a course on cocaine. All you are doing is putting people at risk.'[1] Describing porn classes as 'sick', another media effects researcher, Mary Ann Layden, suggested that teaching pornography was the best way to ensure a dramatic increase in sexual violence.[2] While anti-porn activists have shown students sexually explicit slideshows for several decades, they now argued that any exposure to such images, no matter how they were framed by the instructor, carried a high risk of contributing to rape, sexual abuse and addiction. Ironically, of course, for most of the 19th century, the dominant discourse on erotica assumed that such materials were only appropriate for scholarly examination, since they carried risk for the general population if consumed outside an informed context. With the democratisation of higher education, this anxiety about public access to porn now extends to scholarly research.

I shouldn't complain. My university administration backed me up, all down the line. The article had put a big red bullseye on my chest with a quote explaining that I had never received any complaints about teaching pornography. In the end, though, no one took the predicted potshots. The university president got one angry letter and I received one phone call from an alumnus who worked in the adult entertainment industry and wanted to know how he could help. Many other educators have had their reputations destroyed, lost their jobs, and faced legal sanctions for teaching or researching porn. I was damned lucky.

This isn't to say you shouldn't teach porn. There are many compelling intellectual and professional reasons to do so. But you should be more careful than usual in making pedagogical decisions around this topic. This essay is intended to offer a pragmatic introduction to some of the things you should consider.

Why teach pornography?

Think long and hard about this question. You had better have a good answer, preferably several good answers, since you may need, at some point, to pass them along to students, parents, department chairs, administrators, regents, activists and the news media. Most of these groups are prepared to hear a rational, well-considered justification, but most need convincing. Your students are going to be hit with a lot of questions from their friends and parents and they need to be armed with explanations. One of my favourite stories involves a soft-spoken, fairly conservative young woman who was surprised by her engagement with the work of Candida Royale. She tried to explain to her friends, only to be assured that she couldn't have been watching pornography; if she liked it, it had to be erotica. She insisted that she liked at least some pornography and questioned the ways that these categories got used to classify people and their tastes.

Here are some of my reasons for teaching porn:

1. The public policy debate about pornography is a central issue in media studies. Engaging students with this topic forces them to reflect on the potential social implications of the topics explored elsewhere in your curriculum.
2. Legal and political discourse about pornography often makes somewhat simplistic and ill-informed assumptions about media's influence; media scholars can complicate such assumptions

by bringing their theoretical, historical and critical perspectives to the table.

3. Pornography has been a driving force behind the technological development and deployment of almost every media – print, photography, cinema, video and digital media alike. The attempts to regulate or to promote pornography have certainly shaped contemporary digital culture, impacting everything from the Communications Decency Act and the rise of net filters to the rise of grassroots cultural production. Each new media has, in turn, changed what porn is and how it relates to its consumers.
4. Pornography has emerged as a key area for feminist scholarship and theory. Consuming pornography is one of the central means by which we learn how our society thinks about gender and sexuality. Talking about pornography allows students to broach more difficult questions about sexuality, which they are more apt to deal with from one level removed – through the analysis of images and narratives – than to confront directly.
5. Pornography is an enormous economic force, a media industry larger and more far-reaching than any other sector of commercial culture. To teach media industries without talking about pornography is to give a pretty distorted picture of where the money is.
6. Pornography poses powerful questions about the relationship between form, content and ideology. Examining the very different ways pornographers represent the same basic acts and create different structures of meaning and affect sheds light on how film style operates more generally.
7. The consumption of pornography poses important questions about the nature of fantasy, which can shed light more broadly on the emotional investments people make in popular representations of all kinds. We know far less about the audiences for pornography than probably any other genre of popular entertainment. What investments do people make in erotic images? What place do they play in their lives? What kinds of fan communities or grassroots subcultures have emerged around pornography? Some anti-porn activists argue that the play with interpretation, which surrounds all other media products, shuts down once we turn our attention to pornography, since intellectual activity is over-

whelmed by physiological desire. People mastur-bate to porn, enough said. Even the still limited body of ethnographic work on porn consumption demonstrates an enormous range of interpret-ations of and relationships with sexually explicit images.

8. Even if we decided not to teach pornography, it is increasingly difficult to know where we draw the line, as sexually explicit themes, images, even sty-listic borrowings from pornography, influence mainstream media and as many mainstream works are placed on trial for possible porno-graphic implications. We need to teach students to be reflective about how these categories oper-ate to police taste and to impose ideological con-straints on what ideas can circulate within our culture.

Even if you saw pornography in purely negative terms, these are questions which we would need to address. So, it is surprising that when people read the *Globe* story, almost everyone jumped to the conclu-sion that pornography was being promoted, not cri-tiqued. As Foucault notes, our culture talks obsessively about sex, but who gets to talk and what gets said is shaped by discursive power.

Having said that, one needs to realistically appraise one's own situation. The risks of teaching porn look very different if one is a graduate student or faculty, tenured or untenured, teaching at a con-servative state institution or religious school or at a more progressive liberal arts college, male or female, straight or queer, and so forth. You need soberly to weigh the risks and benefits of teaching such materials. Do your homework. Don't be naive and assume that academic freedom protects you from any and all consequences of your choices in the class-room. It doesn't. Be aware of how your school has dealt with controversies about explicit images in the past and whether there are any university, local or state policies that could impact your decision.

Personally, I think it is irresponsible to discuss pornography in the abstract, in the absence of con-crete images. Without specifics, the debate becomes too easy. Porn opponents can imagine what they want to see; free speech advocates can claim what's on the screen doesn't matter. Both sides project onto pornography their utopian desires or dystopian dreads about sexuality, power, gender, desire and

social justice. Moreover, pornography is many differ-ent things – not even a single genre really – in a society where people label any work that deals with sexuality as pornography. Many different people pro-duce and consume erotic images for many different reasons. So, my goal is to get students to look at, think about, and form their own opinions about specific images, texts and film segments.

Having said this, there are plenty of circum-stances where the showing of sexually explicit images would be inappropriate or counterproductive. A con-troversy erupted several years ago at MIT involving a computer science professor who wanted to get stu-dents to more fully appreciate the importance of internet filters. Before the class started, as the stu-dents gathered, the professor projected shocking and controversial images drawn from various websites. No explanation was given. Quickly, students in the unsupervised classroom started making raunchy and sexist jokes. Even when the class started, there was no attempt to analyse the images themselves; the instructor simply assumed they were bad and dis-cussed the technical challenges of blocking access to them. There were several problems with the instruc-tor's approach. Did the goal of discussing the design and deployment of internet filters provide sufficient justification for projecting images deliberately chosen to offend students? Did the professor bear some responsibility for the climate and context within which those images were consumed? So, as you think about teaching sexually explicit materials, question your own motives. You shouldn't do it if the goal is simply to shock and titillate your students, to 'wake them up', or to demonstrate your own open-minded-ness. Have clear goals and use them to determine what images to show.

A second important question to consider is whether you want to introduce a separate class on pornography or include a unit on pornography in an existing subject. Teaching a separate class allows you to deal with a complex topic with more depth and nuance; the students will have made a conscious decision to study pornography; you can deal with a broader range of topics and issues and gradually come to understand pornography as a genre as com-plex as any other kind of popular fiction. A short unit almost always has to work through the basic debates for and against obscenity law before it examines the materials themselves. The debate has become so polarised that students have a certain amount of baggage they have to resolve before they can think about the topic from any angle other than 'Is porn good or bad for society?' The disadvantage of a separate class is that it continues to ghettoise pornography, pretending that we can draw sharp lines between which works are pornographic and which are merely sexually explicit; you are also teaching the subject only to those students who have worked through some of their basic assumptions, not to a broader cross-section of the student body. Personally, I have opted to integrate one-day, two-day and two-week units on porn into existing classes: in my graduate seminar on media theory and my advanced undergraduate seminars on masculinity, film analysis, and gender, sexuality and popular culture.

I do not teach porn in general enrolment introductory or freshman level subjects. MIT has a long history of accepting extremely accomplished sixteen- and seventeen-year-olds and there are real legal issues about showing pornography to minors, even in an academic setting. To teach pornography in a freshman subject might require me to card all of my students and kick some of them out. But, more importantly, the kind of serious-minded examination of erotic images I want to foster may best be achieved once all of the students have reached a certain level of social, emotional and intellectual maturity. There are many eighteen-year-olds who are more than ready for such discussions, but there are plenty who are not.

This brings us to the issue of content warnings. Some universities mandate that faculty warn students about any potentially offensive content. Well, no, actually, they don't. The issue of content warnings first surfaced in the midst of debates about how universities and colleges would deal with homoerotic content. In the most oft-cited case, a graduate student had shown an art movie, which included explicit representations of gay sex, as part of a course on composition. The Iowa Board of Regents was outraged over this choice and crafted a policy requiring faculty to issue warnings whenever they were going to show works which dealt explicitly with gay themes and content. Some school systems or individual institutions have extended these warning policies to include all sexually explicit works. Yet, however neutrally crafted, these policies are framed with specific ideological assumptions in mind. No one requires you to warn students that the Disney movie you are about to show contains sexist, racist and homophobic content. At many universities, the decision about whether or not to 'warn' students is left to the individual instructor. Some instructors fear that they may be subject to sexual harassment charges if students complain about being forced to watch explicit films without a clear awareness of what to expect. Some state laws hold exhibitors responsible for ensuring that people cannot stumble into explicit images without conscious consent.

In my course on gender, sexuality and popular culture I offer a general warning at the start of the term rather than listing all of the potentially controversial elements in each work. Warnings place the responsibility on the student to make an informed decision whether or not they want to take the course. Other instructors feel, however, that content warnings intensify the stigma surrounding sexually explicit materials; for that reason, they are no more apt to issue warnings when dealing with pornography than with any other genre.

I see some difference between content warnings in a course on pornography and in a unit on pornography. Any student who signs up to take a course on pornography has a pretty good idea of what to expect, though some schools may still require such students to sign consent forms. A media theory class or even a gender, sexuality and popular culture class attracts students with a broader array of goals and expectations. In such contexts, I make sure that they specifically consent to participating in the unit dealing with pornographic materials. No student is required to attend class discussions that focus on pornography – though, in practice, absences are often at a record low. No grade is based on students' response to the material – though students may choose to write about porn within a more broadly defined assignment. The material is specified on the syllabus well in advance. I put signs on the doors so that no one can walk into the room unaware. At the same time, I make it clear that anyone can leave at any time. In fact, no student has ever chosen to leave. Some have fallen asleep, though.

Students come with differing sexual experiences, degrees of previous exposure, attitudes towards sexuality, moral assumptions, and so forth. They may also have conflicting feelings about their own bodies and sexualities that emerge through confronting such images in the classroom. How the instructor shapes the emotional climate of the classroom can have enormous impact on what they get out of discussing porn. Make clear that mutual respect is required at all times. Students may sometimes be overtly hurtful towards those whose sexuality violates their own norms or who come across as naive and inexperienced. Students need to know that even if certain images seem to be exotic or unfamiliar they may well be part of other students' experiences and even if they find certain images distasteful, others may find them desirable or beautiful.

The tone adopted by an instructor can go a long way in defining the quality of the discussion. If the instructor seems uncomfortable with certain topics or with certain forms of sexual expression, students read that discomfort loud and clear. At the same time, if the faculty member is too flamboyant or confrontational, they can silence students or become the focus of their reactions. When the first clip is shown, I lecture through it. This gives them a chance to laugh – at me – for the absurdity of babbling about camerawork while watching someone receive a blowjob. There's almost always some initial uncomfortable laughter that has to be worked through before you can get serious on this topic. We show short segments and discuss them, breaking up the flow of content. I tend to use clinical language in discussing organs or sexual acts, though it can sometimes be effective to make ironic and exaggerated use of the metaphors for the body ('his manhood', for example) which run through pornography, if it gets students to reflect on the assumptions behind that language. I do not leave the room when we are projecting sexually explicit materials to the class.

The issue of whether or not to allow students to check out tapes is vexing. For starters, there is some limited legal protection for projecting images in the classroom; there is much less protection for circulating tapes which can and will be consumed outside of such a well-defined educational context. Once you let the tape out of your control, you can't determine how it is going to be used, yet you may be legally accountable for its circulation. On the other hand, some students are going to feel much more comfortable encountering these images in the privacy of their own rooms. You may also be discouraging close reading practices if you do not allow students to stop and start the video, and make notes in preparation for their papers and assignments.

Similar arguments surround the question of whether students should be encouraged to seek out pornography on their own for use in assignments. Some instructors have argued that getting students to go out and purchase porn forces them to be conscious of the contexts in which it circulates. It also may force students to engage in a more direct way with the emotional stakes and social stigma that surround consuming sexually explicit material. On the other hand, others have argued that there is an ethical difference between encouraging students to study porn in a classroom space and encouraging them to become porn consumers. And sometimes it isn't a good idea to force people to confront things when they don't feel ready to do so. This is especially important when we consider the gendering of the spaces where pornography is sold and consumed.

In many ways, you are damned if you do or damned if you don't, since ultimately most of your critics don't want students to have access to this stuff one way or another. If you distribute it yourself, you are subject to criticism. If you send them out to buy it, you will get slapped about for that. Pick the approach you think you can live with and be ready to justify it if you come under scrutiny.

Anticipate that students are going to have even more difficulty than usual making distinctions between evaluative and analytic arguments. Almost all discussions eventually get drawn back to the question of whether or not pornography is harmful and whether or not it should be legally accessible. Students are also apt to offer unsolicited value judgments about whether or not certain forms of sexuality are 'disgusting' or 'perverted'. Yet, often, the instructor's goals are not to evaluate pornography but to understand more fully how it operates, what images it circulates, what stories it tells, what attitudes it communicates, and what forms of sexuality it embraces or excludes.

I have found the best way to get students to look at what's actually on the screen is to adopt a more comparative approach. For example, one can present two clips with radically different visual styles and ideological framings and encourage students to compare and contrast them. What might seem transparent when examining a single clip in isolation seems highly constructed when reading two clips side by side. Similarly, discussing the very different ways that straight and gay porn deal with the male body for example, or the differences between the ways that female–female sex is depicted in straight male-target porn and lesbian porn can push discussions into a more productive direction. The web now creates a great opportunity to safely visit a range of different spaces where erotic expression circulates and thus get a sense of the different meanings that get attached to these images through their use. For example, you might check out the hip young professionals who frequent a site like www.nerve.com, which consciously seeks to blur the boundaries between pornography and avant-garde art, or monitor the more down-to-earth atmosphere that surrounds the production and circulation of amateur nude portraits at voy.voyeurweb.com, where the models often comment that they don't give a damn whether anyone gets off looking at their images as long as they make them feel good about themselves, or visit a gay chatroom to get a sense of the collaborative production of erotic fantasies, or investigate a site which promises to help women learn to express their own erotic fantasies through words and images as part of feminist self-actualisation, or read slash fan fiction dealing with same-sex relationships between television fandom, or . . .

One of my goals in selecting materials is to shake up the students' preconceptions about what constitutes pornography, who it appeals to and why people consume it. For example, students are intrigued to discover the large number of male–male erotic situations which surface in a straight porn magazine like *Letters to Penthouse*, forcing them to reconsider whether straight culture really defines itself in opposition to homosexuality or has found new ways to make gay sex safe for heterosexuals. Where film is concerned, I make it a point to create some baseline for understanding the norms of the porn industry as well as showing some alternatives which operate on the fringes. One way to create a baseline would be to show works that have been highly successful commercially or won industry-wide recognition. There are an infinite number of ways of selecting tapes, stories, images or websites to show, but the key is to make it a conscious decision, especially since you want students to be examining and reflecting on these images once you get them into the classroom. Don't just run out to the local video shop the night before class and grab an armload of tapes. You wouldn't do that teaching any other media studies

content, but you would be surprised how many people tell me they choose the porn for their class in exactly this fashion.

In every circumstance, providing the students with adequate information about the contexts of the work's production, distribution and reception is important. Anti-porn activists often exhibit images produced over several decades in radically different contexts side by side, trying to collapse the differences between them, and trying to spread the stigma surrounding the most outrageous images across the whole. When we teach pornography, we have an obligation to be more historically and institutionally precise. To consider, for example, what control the performers have over what they do in the film, and how the film circulates; what goals the producers had in making the film; what kinds of audiences consume these works and what place they play in their everyday lives; and what censorship or regulation policies shaped the work's production and distribution.

Students often have more difficulty than usual framing paper topics about pornography. Their culture may not have taught them many different ways of thinking about or talking about such images. They may know how to deal with them in a dorm room or fraternity house; they may know what they think you want to say about how bad porn is because they may have had previous exposure to the anti-porn discourse in its many different inflections. You want to make sure that you couple the pornographic texts you are examining with secondary materials, which give students models for different ways of talking about and reflecting upon pornography. You've probably figured that out already since you are reading this book, but it is even more important than usual to give students good examples of criticism and analysis in dealing with porn. At the same time, you want to frame your assignment in such a way as to avoid students turning in confessional pieces about their own sexual awakenings or more to the point, avoid having students feeling like you want to invade their privacy. You probably need to give explicit signals that this is not what you want to see. Some teachers may feel more comfortable in the therapeutic role than I do and may have other perspectives. In that case, you had best give very clear signals about the degree of confidentiality you can offer students who choose to share some of their experiences with you.

You can act responsibly, make intelligent decisions, create a comfortable classroom climate, develop a thoughtful pedagogical rationale and avoid legal pitfalls, and still find yourself in the midst of a media circus. I know. I've been there. So, what to do when the shit hits the fan? First, shore up your support with those in a position of authority over you – assuming, of course, that they are not the source of the problem to begin with. When I first started teaching porn, I went to my department chair, told him what I was planning to do and why, and asked him what, if any, his concerns would be. When the *Boston Globe* story hit, I briefed my dean on what was happening, clarifying false claims in the article, and providing the rationale behind my classroom choices. And I gave the university president and news office the resources they would need to respond, since I didn't want to see them get blindsided. As the story broke, the news office gave me some valuable advice – feed a story, starve a scandal. In this case, there was no way I was going to be able to control how the story played itself out. I could send a letter to the editor but they could shorten it. I could talk to television or newspapers but they would choose which quotes to run. I could go on a live broadcast but they would decide when to cut me off. So, the best thing to do, hard as it may sound, was to hold my tongue. This doesn't mean simply not seeking out publicity. Don't answer the phone if reporters call. If you talk with them directly, they can say that you declined to comment. If you don't answer, they have to say that they were unable to reach you for comment. In most cases, the news media will soon lose interest in the story, especially if they don't have a face to attach to it.

In some cases, though, ignoring the problem won't make it go away. This is especially true when the university itself seems to be investigating you or threatening punitive actions. In those cases, run, don't walk, to a lawyer's office. You don't want to be defending yourself before an internal investigation without knowing what your legal options are and what the consequences may be of ill-informed comments and actions.

In the end, I am not embarrassed that it's been reported that I teach sexually explicit images in my class. I am proud that I am able to create a space where those images can be dealt with responsibly and without an environment of moral panic, when it is clear that so much of our culture simply can't talk about pornography at all. But I do not seek publicity about this aspect of my teaching. Creating a climate where every student feels free to air his or her perspectives requires that the discussion remain in the classroom and not be trolled through early morning shock-jock shows.

So you still want to teach porn? Good for you. Go in with your mind open. Make responsible and ethical decisions. Be ready to provide an intellectual rationale for your decisions. And watch your back.

NOTES

1. <www.boundless.org/2001/features/a0000S18.html>.
2. Ibid.

1   For a Pornoscape

Paul Willemen

The link between sex and knowledge has been noted many times, from Freud's insight that curiosity necessarily has a sexual dimension to Sartre's discussion of knowledge as a kind of penetrative possession and Foucault's discussion of the 'will to knowledge' as a driving force in the history of sexuality.[1] In fact, the Judeo-Christian cultural template elaborated some thousands of years ago, since when it has mutated into a technology of governance, confirmed the link by way of the phrase 'carnal knowledge'. The control or management of sexual knowing directly engages not only with questions of lineage and social reproduction in the generational sense, but also and perhaps even mainly with the deployment of the full range of the human sensorium in our perception and apprehension of the 'other'. At this point, one could ask for definitions of sex and knowledge and thus make the ensuing discourse veer off into philosophy. Instead, I will merely note the connection between sex and making sense by way of sensory perception, defining that connection, however the terms are specified, as a mode of cognition based on but not reducible to sensory perception. The idea is that perception necessarily involves not only the senses, but also the linguistic dimension of making sense, that is to say: thought (inner speech). The stringent, often sinister taboos that are imposed on the one necessarily implicate the other: a taboo on the representation of sex as a sensory mode of 'knowing' also necessarily involves a taboo on ways of knowing intellectually: the regulation of the one is, at the same time, the regulation of the other.

The linkage between sex and cognition marks the site of what Western culture designates as the paramount instance of a kind of knowing that mobilises the full range of the human sensorium. However, this cognitive urge cannot be associated simply with the desire to see. It insists in and mobilises all our senses. Its privileged association with the look is, precisely, a historical process requiring explanation. This association cannot simply be referred back to an allegedly universal and ahistorical, perennial 'link' between sex and cognition identified by psychoanalysis in terms of sexual curiosity. Curiosity may well have a sexual dimension, but it must not be reduced to it; moreover, the exercise of curiosity, of the desire to know, involves all the senses, and its privileged association with the visual is the product of some concerted, long-term ideological 'work' performed under the aegis of a host of institutions involved in the separation of the senses from the 17th century onwards.[2] Given Foucault's opposition to the notion of the spectacle and given his subordination of vision to the 'will to knowledge', it may seem an irony that it is one of Foucault's immense contributions to cultural history that his work helped to initiate the study of the history of looking.[3] So, what is of interest in the taboos on sex and cognition is that, firstly, they are linked, and, secondly, that each of them nevertheless has an autonomous history of being 'regulated' by different institutional networks.

Fortunately, no taboo was ever capable of erasing what it sought to obliterate, and this is true of both sex and cognition. On the contrary, to impose a taboo on something offers a sure-fire guarantee that whatever is thus put under erasure, is sustained as an object of desire. The pursuit of that desire in the face of the innumerable obstacles put in its way is what gives both sexuality and efforts to 'know' their specific histories.

One way in which the desire for sensual thinking, as Eisenstein once put it, persists, is in what Lévi-Strauss called 'savage thinking', that is to say, bricolage-thinking with objects rather than in terms of abstract syllogisms.[4] This kind of cognitive activity has persisted in spite of the history, chronicled by

Foucault, of the way societies organise and reorganise the human sensorium. The negative aspect of this is glaringly obvious in the continuing popularity of magical thinking (horoscopes, astrology, and so on); its positive dimension found space to operate under the heading of aesthetics, provided we do not accept to limit that label to the Romantic reformulation which sought to detach it from other forms of making sense.[5] One of the best contemporary cultural critics and historians, Susan Buck-Morss, has argued repeatedly – most recently in her book *Dreamworld and Catastrophe: The Passing of Mass Utopia in the East and West* – that aesthetics refer to sensory perception and that

> Under conditions of modern technology, the aesthetic system undergoes a dialectical reversal. The human sensorium changes from a mode of being 'in touch' with reality into a means of blocking out reality. Aesthetics – sensory perception – becomes *an*aesthetics, a numbing of the senses' cognitive capacity that destroys the human organism's power to respond politically even when self-preservation is at stake. Someone who is 'past experiencing,' writes Benjamin, is 'no longer capable of telling . . . proven friend . . . from mortal enemy.'[6]

The linkage between sensory perception and cognition, that is to say, understanding, which Buck-Morss locates in aesthetics means that the reversal into anaesthesia is concerned not so much with a taboo on the senses, but with the installation of a taboo on understanding, on 'knowing'. This is not simply a matter of putting people 'past experiencing', it is also and probably mainly a matter of separating off the sensory from the intellectual, putting a taboo on the latter while redefining the former in strictly quantitative terms. As Jonathan Crary observed towards the end of his epoch-making *Techniques of the Observer*:

> If vision previously had been conceived as an experience of *qualities* (as in Goethe's optics), it is now [in the mid- to-late-19th century] a question of differences in quantities, of sensory experience that is stronger or weaker. But this new valuation of perception, this obliteration of the qualitative in sensation through its arithmetical homogenization, is a crucial part of modernization.[7]

Crary also went on to note, by way of a quote from Georges Bataille, that the common denominator promoted in the shift from the qualitative to the quantitative is money:

> The common denominator, the foundation of social homogeneity and of the activity arising from it, is money, namely the calculable equivalent of the different products of collective activity. Money serves to measure all work and makes man a function of measurable products. . . . Each man is worth what he produces; in other words he stops being an existence for itself: he is no more than a function, arranged within measurable limits, of collective production.[8]

Consequently, the subsequent invocation of anaesthesia in this essay always must be understood in context of a numbing of the senses conditional on a prior separation between the sensory and the intellectual in the context of the capitalist reformatting of human subjects. Seen in that light, it becomes clear that the regulators of representations of sex are not really bothered about sex at all: it is a cover, or, if you prefer, a metaphor for their concern to control ways of understanding[9] in a society that has pursued the separation of the senses. It may be worth noting at this point that my negative description of this separation most definitely does not imply a positive valuation of the way *premodern* social arrangements conceived of the unity of the cognitive and the sensory. The issue really is *not* whether to bemoan or welcome capitalism's displacement of religiously defined modes of perception. On the contrary, the issue is how at any given time, for instance today, a mode of sensory thinking (and of representational practices inviting it) may be conceivable which is conducive to a better, more complex apprehension of the dynamics governing the situation in which we live, unhindered, as much as possible, by either religious or capitalist power devices such as the separation of the sensory from the intellectual.

The two taboos, one on representations of sex and the other on understanding social dynamics, are thus not of the same order, the latter determining the former in spite of (and fairly successful because of) appearances to the contrary.[10] Nor are their histories always so directly linked as psychoanalysis or Foucault would suggest. Each has its own history of shifting – though, it seems, always overlapping –

definitions and fields of application. For instance, the taboo on understanding was quite different under religious-feudal regimes from its imposition and enforcement in the context of the development of industrial capitalism. Nevertheless, the history of both issues demonstrates the kind of consistent linkage that makes it impossible (or: *should* make it impossible) to consider either taboo in isolation. A case in point, to which this essay will return later on, is the seventeenth- and eighteenth-century Western European usage of terms such as 'libertinism' and 'the philosophical novel'.

The taboo on intelligence in contemporary media discourses is as rigorously enforced as the prohibition on representations of the sex act. It is no coincidence that the most intense period of intellectual questioning and analytical-theoretical endeavours in recent history, the decade between, roughly, 1965 and 1975, also witnessed an equally intense concern with the regulation of sexuality along with a concern with the regulation of its representations. Representations of either sexuality or intellectuality are permitted on a mainstream communication platform only on condition that they be distorted into more or less grotesque parodies: from the panting, furniture-destroying bonking in television and film dramas to the display of intellectuality orchestrated, for instance, on British television or on Radio Four by the presenter and author Melvyn Bragg. And even that parody, regularly featuring the *fine fleur* of the Oxbridge establishment, was deemed too explicitly hardcore by the broadcasting authorities. The programme's time was curtailed and its strategic scheduling slot was changed to make way for an even more grotesque (read: more desirable from an authoritarian point of view) simulation presided over by the broadcaster Jeremy Paxman. Besides, when was the last time that you saw a film or a television drama positively valuing intellectuality as intensely pleasurable?[11] There are countless dramas celebrating adrenalin rushes generated by a wide variety of stimuli and practices, but almost never those generating the sensory pleasures of understanding so routinely inscribed in comic strips by way of the lightbulb in a thought-balloon above a figure's head. Instead, it is a safe bet that when a character is signalled to be an 'intellectual', s/he will soon turn out to be a psychopath or seriously impaired as a human being in some other way. The only fictional genre dedicated to the staging

of intellectuality, the detective story, bears the scars of this taboo on understanding particularly prominently: the intellectual must be flanked by a specimen of averagely dim-witted humanity who functions not only to produce the reader-viewer's realisation that the detective is intelligent (otherwise we could not possibly be expected to grasp this fact), but is also the repository of all the positive, decent human values which must, of course, be lacking in the unfortunates afflicted and driven by a desire to understand. The present British and American educational policies seeking to devalue understanding and to replace it by training in increasingly mechanistically conceived protocols of information processing are just one more example of the way the taboo on intellectuality is enforced. The pervasive modularisation of university courses is a case in point. Our media's 'bias against understanding', as one abortive campaign by some journalists a few decades ago called it, is another.

To connect the taboo on understanding with the prohibition of representations of sex may appear odd in the light of the pervasive obligation to speak of sex chronicled in, for instance, Stephen Heath's remarkable book *The Sexual Fix*.[12] However, what Heath shows is that the duty imposed on all of us to saturate the public sphere with sex-talk, to confess or profess 'all' in texts generated in any medium, also requires us to speak of sex in a strictly controlled, regulated manner in which the cognitive dimension of sexual interactions is silenced and replaced by an obligation to consume and to perform according to specific protocols. Sex has been turned into the antidote of thought and, as such, the guarantor of 'authentic' experience. The cognitive dimension of representing sensory perception is thus put under a taboo, reducing the public discourse about sexual interaction to one of three permitted modalities: firstly, a medicalised discourse monopolising the cognitive dimension of sexual practices and functions; secondly, to block the intellectual dimension (that is to say, sex as a practice to think with) by seeking to impose and police moral codes which a particular interest group devised in order to retain or achieve social power. A classic example of this happened during a seminar on pornography at London's National Film Theatre following the publication of Roma Gibson and Pamela Church Gibson's book *Dirty Looks*.[13] When the participants appeared to agree that the aim of the seminar was to try and understand pornography as a fictional genre alongside war films, melodrama, Westerns and so forth, the chief censor in Britain shamelessly declared that 'Pornography must not be understood, it must be censored'.[14] Journalistic discourses about sex fall overwhelmingly into these two categories. The extreme case of such a discourse is the political-terrorist use of verbal and visual representations of rape deployed, for instance, in the Yugoslavian civil war. The third available mode to narrativise sex is to drain descriptive accounts of sexual activity from any cognitive dimension whatsoever in order to present it as pure sensation, as the very antithesis of knowing. Here we find the bulk of representations in both mainstream and pornographic cinema and video. In a roundabout way, the anaesthetic dimension of pornography and its connection with the prevention of understanding is perfectly well known in the public sphere, where it takes the form of complaints about 'numbing' the senses through banalisation. What is mostly left unspecified is precisely what not-numbed senses, a non-banalised sensorium, might be able to convey to us. Perhaps the big taboo here is that sexual activity presents the danger of learning that the widely propagated models of identity, of what individual characters should be like, are totally bogus. Sex at least offers the possibility of realising in a thoroughly untheorised, bricolage mode of 'savage' thought and in an inescapably sensory manner, that individuals are never 'whole', in 'one piece', consistent or even 'integrated', and most certainly not 'unique', not even or precisely not in what we are taught to regard as the most intimate core of our being. The practice of sexuality can teach us, quite easily, that there is no such essential core to begin with. One of the dangers of sex which its representations are supposed to anaesthetise us against may well be that sex is extremely good 'to think with'.

Slavoj Žižek made some telling remarks in this respect. While discussing commodity fetishism, he noted that contemporary forms of fetishism are double:

> Not only are 'relations between people' reified in 'relations between things' (so that critical analysis must penetrate the reified surface and discern beneath it the 'relations between people' which actually animate it – an even trickier 'fetishist reification' is at

work when we (mis)perceive the situation as simply involving 'relations between people', and fail to take into account the invisible symbolic structure which regulates these relations.[15]

The feared cognitive dimension to be kept at bay bears precisely on this need to take into account the workings of this 'invisible symbolic structure' which regulates not only the relations between people, but also the ways in which we can understand these relations: our ways of making sense. The double taboo on sex and understanding, the latter underpinning and determining the former, can be summed up in the widely disseminated injunction to 'stop making sense'. The corollary of this injunction, rarely articulated, is also double: firstly, it means that one should detach the making of sense from sensory experience so that the latter may be made available for commercial exploitation in its own right, and, secondly, it enjoins us to accept and believe in the sense that is made for us. And culture is the realm where different power blocs compete with each other to become the dominant sense-makers. The rest of us are supposed to consume regimes of belief doled out as suitably pre-packaged lumps of culture by a variety of cultural retailers. To quote Žižek again:

> The way one should answer the conservative platitude according to which every honest man has a profound need to believe in something is to say that every honest man has a profound need to find another subject who will believe in his place.[16]

This is rather like television's recourse to canned laughter, relieving viewers of the onerous task of having to 'get' the joke' – mainly because, in an overwhelming majority of cases, there is no joke to get, leaving only the nakedly authoritarian command: laugh here! Pornography pioneered this kind of authoritarian delegation by way of the proposition that 'every honest man has a profound need to find another subject who will believe in his place': a surrogate represented by the male porn performer's ejaculation as the climax of a porn sequence. In perhaps more economic language: porn films convey the need for us, the bourgeois subjects, to find people who will spend in our place.

This process of substitution underpins the change in pornography since approximately 1972.

Prior to that date (as always: with some exceptions) pornography functioned as advertising. The films were shown in brothels or in other situations where prostitutes were made available at the same time. In that context, the real money was made by clients purchasing drinks and, more significantly, one or more bodies with which to satisfy the desires aroused by way of the films or the images. The beauty of the advertising films was that the clients could be asked to pay for that as well. In that respect, porn films pioneered the economics of pop video: the consumer is asked to pay the entrepreneur directly for persuading him/her to purchase a particular commodity, mostly in addition to the entrepreneur's 'recovery' of advertising costs by way of the commodity's price. It is only with the development of capitalism and what Alexander Kluge and Oskar Negt called 'the division of labour between the various receptive faculties of human beings',[17] that the 'pleasure of watching' with the concomitant delegation of enjoyment to the represented 'other' became available as a separately exploitable 'sense' activity. Which is why pornographic cinema was, from the start of cinema's history, both its core and its limit (I forget which particular French director or critic in the 60s stated that cinema was 'watching beautiful women doing beautiful things'). Today, again, pornography helps to 'pioneer' the sought after (by transnational corporations) change in the regulation and organisation of the senses designed to transform people into suitable labour power for what the British government keeps referring to as 'the knowledge industries', that is to say, the working procedures and the cultural processes required by the new global division of labour which assigns the management of information processing technology to the 'advanced' capitalist centres.

The linkage between sex and understanding was also made by Martine Boyer's intelligent though somewhat homophobic book *L'Écran de l'amour*,[18] especially when she described the emergence of the intermediate cinematic genre, the erotic film, as the mainstream industry's response to both the breakthrough of pornographic cinema in the United States, with the release of Gerard Damiano's *Deep Throat* (1972), in some parts of Europe in the 1972–5[19] period and the legal measures taken to re-repress it. The beacon film for the genre, the domesticated version of commercial pornography, was Just Jaeckin's adaptation of Emmanuelle

Arsan's best-seller, *Emmanuelle* (France, 1974), which played continuously for ten years in cinemas on Paris's Champs Élysées and which was distributed in the United States by Columbia. Boyer wrote:

> *Emmanuelle* was perceived . . . as a kind of filmed magazine, that is to say, as an animated tourist brochure used as scaffolding for the building of intimate reveries [according to the rules of] a simple ideology and a complicated psychology. It may well be that a few decades from now [Boyer wrote her book as a university dissertation in 1985] our grandchildren will find it difficult to understand works that are so thin yet so complex. . . . The star-heroine is a woman of today, *with it*, liberated. She is available for love at any time. Better yet: a communicative languor inhabits her. Strictly speaking, this is not about the expression of a person's sensuality, . . . but a kind of obligatory initiatic journey for women of Europe's lower and middle bourgeoisie at the close of the seventies. It has been said that these films are 'aseptic' and that their female stars appear as if covered in cellophane, well laundered and ironed. . . . It is the philosophy of the pill responsibly managed by a woman who is aware of her value and her charms. In return, the woman has to consider herself as a 'good object' (of consumption) and to offer herself as such (equal to men, equal to her 'sisters'). The world in which she moves ignores property relations along with physical or social inequalities. Of course, there are different cultures, different races, different classes, but, thank God, that's a blessing, otherwise she would be bored to death when she travels to the ends of the world. People's sexual pleasure is the only permissible difference, the only equality, the unique universal. There is no sexual difference. Sex does becomes the ideal medium to get to *know the world*. 'Before', she did not know it. 'After', she knows. And in between, she regales the viewer with her expert simulations of pleasure.'[20]

Boyer then goes on to link this representation of knowledge with the stylistic features of the film, stressing its emphasis on wealth and luxury as formulated in the idioms of advertising. In this respect, *Emmanuelle* is the properly Christian response, framed by an equally proper acknowledgment of the terms soon to be officially imposed (via Reagan and Thatcher) by triumphant capital that we should disarticulate (in philosophical terms: deconstruct) human beings and commodify the component bits (pleasures, emotions, gestures, body parts) to make them more amenable to privatisation: making the private marketable by, paradoxically, abolishing it in all but name. The Christianity of the strategy is made clear by Žižek in his challenging *Did Somebody Say Totalitarianism?*[21] In the context of an extended discussion of the crucifixion demonstrating that Christian religion is based on the notion that 'there is no longer any transcendent God with whom to communicate'[22] Žižek notes that:

> The properly dialectical paradox of paganism is that it legitimizes social hierarchy (everyone/everything in his/her/its own place) by reference to a notion of the universe in which all differences are ultimately rendered worthless, in which every determinate being ultimately disintegrates into the primordial Abyss out of which it emerged (dust to dust). In a symmetrical contrast, Christianity predicates equality and direct access to universality precisely through asserting the most radical Difference/Rupture. . . . sins can not only be pardoned, but also retroactively erased with no traces left: a New Beginning is possible.[23]

Emmanuelle offers the tale of an initiation into knowledge through a confrontation with the 'pagan' Orient as typified by a tourist version of Bangkok, and it does so in the mode of a science-fiction discourse presenting not only a Christian 'new beginning', but also the imminent triumph of the global market. The film locates the break point for this new beginning in terms of a new libidinal democracy: the democratisation of pleasure as a commodity exemplified by what is taken as the *sine qua non* of pleasure, sex. It is up to the form of the film to convey what its (science-) fiction discourse sweeps under the carpet: the absurdity of equating pervasive commodification and the imposition of the market as somehow compatible with a democratic economics. In Boyer's words, *Emmanuelle* surfs on the belief that cinema

> has the power to convey a sense of wealth by way of even the most miserable contents: a hut, some rush matting and three desiccated twigs become a luxurious paradise as soon as they are lit as a site suitable to receive the pleasure of a civilised personage.[24]

In other words, the film admits, not in its narrative logic but in the forms of its *mise en scène*, where economic factors do impose themselves – cinema is, after all, an industry – that the democracy of pleasure is reserved for those who can afford it, a fact since then abundantly demonstrated by further developments of a technologised pleasure-market represented most visibly by the internet in a world where the average distance between a person and the nearest telephone is about two kilometres. Those who cannot afford it have to be content with representations (advertising-fiction) that enable them to delegate pleasure and to enjoy 'by proxy' an economic and ideological circuit made possible by the 'separation' of the senses.

It is in the genre of pornography that the taboo on understanding outlined in Žižek's notion of double fetishism is directly and inextricably intertwined with the drive towards anaesthesia required by the development of capitalism as discussed by Susan Buck-Morss. It is this which gives any call for a 'quality' pornographic cinema such a utopian ring. Taking up some of the themes put on the agenda by Boyer, the novelist and publisher Régine Desforges introduced a special issue of *CinémAction* on pornographic cinema (no. 59, 1991) with the plea for the 'reinvention' of porn cinema:

> What I reproach porn cinema for is that it contents itself with showing actors fucking with different partners in different positions. By refusing fiction, it is incapable of renewing itself. At the start, you are emotionally affected by the pornographic images, but then, because there is no dramatic progression and no way of identifying, interest wanes. . . . In order to elicit the viewers' interest anew, porn cinema absolutely must get away from banality. If there were quality hardcore films, the public would follow. It is the general mediocrity of hardcore films that prevented them from gaining real status. In order to attract the public, porn cinema has to reinvent itself.[25]

Arguably, Catherine Breillat's *Romance* (1999) tried to reinvent the genre by refusing the obligatory separation of the sensory from understanding, of aesthetics from cognition, that is to say, by refusing anaesthesia.

The film has many shortcomings: the heroine's male lover is a caricature while the rest of the characters are enacted according to the rules of psychological realism, which makes it particularly easy for male viewers to refuse to recognise themselves in the oppressively phobic relation to sexuality which the boy/man is supposed to represent, not to mention the incompetent bondage scene performed by, of all the professions that could have been attributed to the S/M enthusiast, a teacher. On the other hand, it is plausible to read these deficiencies as parapraxes betraying that the film, although ostensibly adhering to the conventions of psychological realism, is in fact a piece of utopian science fiction demanding to be read as a 'what if . . . ?' narrative. What if Western societies and their cultural industries had evolved enough to be able to represent sexual relations between people in such a way that 'the invisible symbolic structure which regulates these relations', in Žižek's phrase, could be brought to the fore? Obviously, this requires that one imagine a society in which the current power relations do not operate, a society with an entirely different history that would have yielded a different symbolic structure: a social order in which the two taboos did not operate and which, therefore, did not impose that fictional representations of sexuality be separated off into a separate fictional 'genre' into which can be dumped all the images and sounds barred from 'legitimate' fictional narratives. In effect, the most positive thing about Breillat's science-fiction movie is that it asks us to imagine a world without pornography. The notion of a quality pornography that would refuse to separate off the representations of interacting genitalia from the narration of subjects-in-history is a contradiction in terms since under such conditions, pornography would not exist as a distinct narrative genre.

Nevertheless, it is the science-fictional aspect of *Romance* which is capable of reminding us of another possible history, one that could have become 'ours' if only . . . the French Revolution had generated different results and the Old Corruption (the *ancien régime*) had not intervened to prevent the politically articulated desire for Enlightenment from flowering. With the result that the Enlightenment still remains to be achieved, as Habermas never tired of pointing out in the face of the recent neo-obscurantist wave of attacks on the very wish for even the most minimal implementation of the Enlightenment programme.

In an excellent review of re-published French eighteenth-century pornographic novels in *The New York Review of Books*,[26] drawing extensively on Lynn Hunt's ground-breaking *The Invention of Pornography*, Robert Darnton points out that the eighteenth-century publishers and booksellers used the term 'philosophical books' to designate illegal merchandise, whether it was irreligious, seditious or obscene, and that libertinism, as far back as the 17th century, meant 'free thinking'.

By 1750, libertinism had become a matter of the body and the mind, of pornography and philosophy. Readers could recognise a sex book when they saw one, but they expected sex to serve as a vehicle for attacks on the Church, the Crown, and all sorts of social abuses.

Acknowledging that the prototypes of *Emmanuelle* were canonised in a series of first-person narrations attributed to female characters by the male authors in the 18th century and that such female voices 'express men's fantasies, not the long-lost voice of early modern feminism', the representation of 'the female voluptuary who accepts her subjection in order to give full rein to her lasciviousness' nevertheless did constitute 'a challenge to the subordination of women under the Old Regime. Above all, they challenged the authority of the Church, which did more than any other institution to keep women in their place.'[27] Darnton comments that in the philosophical-pornographic novels of the time, 'sex helped readers to think about equality in a deeply inegalitarian society', an egalitarianism mirrored in the minimalisation of sexual difference itself. Darnton is also the one who first noted the relevance of Lévi-Strauss's discussion of bricolage thinking, entitling his review 'Sex for Thought'. Darnton and Hunt both emphasise that pornography has a history. My take on that history of the 'invention of pornography' is one of containing and marginalising the Enlightenment challenge to the Absolutist State propped up and legitimated by the military-religious complex, a nexus eventually replaced by the military-industrial complex used by the bourgeoisie to gain ever more power, until capitalism finally triumphed over the Old Corruption and consolidated under United States' hegemony in the 1950s.

It is in the mid-19th century, with the emergence and first defeats of the working class, narrativised as the emergence of industrial modernity and of the 'mass' as opposed to the French Revolution's 'citizens', that the censorial taboos descended on pornography as state librarians created special sections in

public libraries to prevent 'the masses' from encountering seditious books likely to 'corrupt' the ordinary
reader. This was also, and not by coincidence, the
period when realism was promoted as the new style
in painting (Courbet) and, shortly thereafter, in
literature. Cited by Darnton and Hunt, the pornography scholar Jean Marie Goulemot[28] noted the
paradox: eighteenth-century pornography came closest to realising the programme realism set itself, a
century later, aiming to create a reality effect powerful enough to obliterate the distinction between
literature and life. No wonder that its Enlightenment
potential caused pornographic discourse to be both
forbidden by those representing or nostalgic for the
Old Corruption while the more radical wings of the
New Corruption, the bourgeois entrepreneurs for
whom profit is the basis of social power, with religion
accorded a helpful but subsidiary role, exploited it for
anaesthetic purposes. Both the rising bourgeoisie and
the *ancien régime* agreed, each in terms of their own
agenda, to put a *Denkverbot* (in the way that in the
1970s a *Berufsverbot*, a taboo on employment in the
public sector, was imposed on the militant Left) on
representations of sex, quarantining them from the
public sphere. This is the very *Denkverbot* still pro-
claimed in the 80s by the British film censor at
public seminars addressing pornography as a discursive genre.

One of the drawbacks of approaching pornography in the framework of a history of ideas is that
these ideas keep being replayed *ad infinitum*. The
'make love not war' slogan so popular in the 60s celebrates the seventeenth-century expectation that sex
will 'serve as a vehicle for attacks on the Church, the
Crown, and all sorts of social abuses'; *Emmanuelle*, in
addition to presenting yet another version of the
'myth of the female voluptuary' inhabits the tem-
plates of early Christianity as well as those of mone-
tarist economics and Margaret Thatcher's belief that
there is no society, only individuals pursuing their
own gratification. The American radical cultural
critic and teacher David James wants to have it both
ways, claiming, on the one hand, that:

> In the early 80s certain extremely marginal forms of
> punk and pornography did in fact sustain opposition
> to the aesthetics of the hegemony and to commodity
> culture. Marking a survival of 60s utopianism, these
> forms of erotic and music video . . . constituted a sur-

vival of the project of the classic avant garde – the
turn of cultural practice against the status of art in
bourgeois society as defined by the concept of autonomy and against the distribution apparatus bourgeois
art depends on.[29]

At the same time, James celebrates the 'realism' of
these videos as the 'documentation' of 'illicit sexual
practices' in the 'quasi-verité films' of Jack Smith,
Stan Brakhage and Carolee Schneemann, a tendency
which he extends into the home-video tapes made by
people who exchange these products as a means of
getting 'in touch' with each other. He concludes,
although earlier bemoaning the shift from film to
video, that now 'nothing prevents us from shedding
corporate aesthetics by becoming producers rather
than consumers of television except residual preju-
dices of commodity art production and the internal-
ization of industrial production values'.[30]

James forgets Benjamin's warning that 'because
the lust for profit of the ruling class sought satisfaction through it, technology betrayed man and turned
the bridal bed into a bloodbath'.[31] He also forgets the
politics inherent in the putting into place of realist
aesthetics: radical, yes, but on behalf of a bourgeoisie
keen to emancipate itself from feudal-absolutist,
divinely ordained hierarchical status divisions.
Finally, James also tactfully omits any consideration
of the fact that his two chosen examples, porn and
pop video, are both examples of the way advertising
discourses can be 'autonomised' and presented, that
is to say, marketed, as a way of advertising not simply
one single product, but to impose consumerism as a
lifestyle. Pornography and subsequently music video
reversed the hierarchies that structured the conventional advertising texts: instead of mobilising bundles
of connotations to sell a product, products are
mobilised to sell packages of connotations, in this
case, consumerism.

Indeed, my own lament for the disappearance of
the cognitive dimension in representations of sex
(mercifully the one and only thought which puts me
into the company of the likes of Catharine MacKinnon) functions as a kind of retroactive science fiction:
what if the 'philosophical' and libertinist ideas of the
French Revolution had been able to resist and prevent not only a return *en force* of the Old Corruption
in the form of religion, but also the market ideologies
that have gained the upper hand since then? What if

the Enlightenment had not been aborted by the political requirements of the French Revolution itself which installed melodrama in the place where the 'philosophical' narrative should have been? What if the tensions between a modernising bourgeoisie and, to coin a phrase, a feudalising, religiously legitimated aristocracy had not marginalised the radical egalitarianism of pornography in favour of dramas of lineage and social reproduction couched in the very vocabulary of the absolutist regime: the struggle over virtue and the question of the appropriate moral codes required to guarantee the 'proper' transmission of property relations and exercise of power?

These are the elements of a science-fiction discourse that programmes much of the argument, in the form of fantasy scenarios, both for and against pornography today. Unfortunately, perhaps, we are no longer in the 1700s and our distance from that century is not to be measured in terms of formal analyses of the way the same ideas get formulated in different terms.

A different position must be elaborated *vis-à-vis* the representational practices that concentrate on showing sexual activity. However, that needs to be preceded by a different approach to the history of pornography since the 18th century. In the remainder of this essay, I will try, with the concomitant crudities of such a tentative endeavour, to draw attention to only some of the factors involved in such a history. In Deleuze's terminology, we need to reterritorialise pornography, to re-map the economic and cultural forces along with the way politics bridges and always temporarily 'holds' these forces in particular hierarchical relations. In other words, following Lynn Hunt's example, we need to (re-)map the current 'pornoscape'. This will involve revisiting aspects of comments made earlier, but in a different context and in an attempt to outline a different dynamic in the hope of detecting something that the discursive forms of pornographic cinema and video may be able to convey.

In the context of the ebb and flow of the contest for power between absolutism and capitalism (generating different cultural and political 'figurations' in different nation states taking into account 'local' conditions and histories), one of the many 'compromise' formations was the relegation of pornography to the national libraries' 'hell' as both the feudalising and the modernising sectors made common cause against the mythical creature called forth by the bourgeoisie and which could threaten both contenders for power: 'the mass'.

It is worth quoting Susan Buck-Morss on this topic at some length:

> Who are 'the masses'? The word was launched in the modern era as a term of contempt. Its predecessor, the mob, was an unruly crowd occupying public space and threatening to destabilize the public order. The masses, however, unlike the mob, were not just an occasional social formation. With nineteenth-century industrialization and urbanization, processes that drew people together in large aggregates as a matter of course, the masses became a permanent presence in social life. In quotidian rhythms, they flowed through space as a spontaneous accumulation of persons, anonymous, fungible, and rootless. Organized, the masses are a physical force, a lethal weapon, and as such indispensable to sovereign power. In the nineteenth century, nation states produced mass armies through universal conscription. And yet the explosive force of the masses could always turn against the sovereign agent of the state, which means that absolute obedience in the military was institutionally required.
>
> *Mass society* is a twentieth-century phenomenon. How it differs from mass military institutions is an organizational question. Whereas communication in the latter follows hierarchical lines of command, society as a mass is addressed directly. Modern media technologies are indispensable here, not only for the manipulation of the masses but for mass solidarity in a positive sense. Speed is the decisive factor in media effectiveness. . . . When the voice was transformed into electrical surges transmitted through wire grids rather than the open air, the extension of the aural sense became limitless, as did the visual sense through photographic reproduction. Mass society was synonymous with this infinity of sense perception, achieved through the technological prostheses of the human sensory apparatus.[32]

It is the anaesthetising exploitation of the human sensory apparatus by way of these prostheses, always taking care to avoid or minimise the 'danger' inherent in people's tendency to 'think with objects', which is addressed by pornography along with the majority of other industrialised cultural productions. Let us accept the proposition that it is the radical, free market sector of the bourgeoisie – always an annoying but necessary element in capitalism's operations – which is the main social group that presides over the porn industry. Benefiting from the critical attacks on establishment institutions and powerbrokers during the 60s and propelled by the modernising impetus of May 68 which ended up installing a society fit for the reign of lifestyle advertisers (as Régis Debray pointed out to the consternation of the 'ex-militants' in 1979)[33] this radical bourgeois sector came to prominence in the 70s, along with electronics and arms companies, generating the brief boom in 'legitimate' pornography in print as well as in cinema, and taking a notch further the demands for 'modernisation' evident in the 60s' exploitation cinema: peplums, sexploitational thrillers and comedies which nevertheless were inconvenienced by the need to pay lip-service to the moral codes of the Old Corruption. When the time came to take the power-relay from the immediate postwar ruling cliques who had supervised the defusing of the radical democratic aspirations generated by the war, a number of residual (because necessary only for this defusing work) humanist commitments could safely be junked: education for personal civic responsibility could begin to be replaced by training as required by the IT and other cultural sectors; the positive valuation of individuation, so necessary to secure the masses' support in the fight against absolutism, could now be rolled back and reserved for an ever more restricted sector of the managerial elite, while the rest of us drown in hymns to the delights of communal identities. Simultaneously, the regime of cultural regulation – that is to say, the institutional network where decisions were elaborated on the correct dosage of the anaesthetic to be administered and to which regions of the body-cultural it should be applied – shifted from a reliance on journalism, cinema and radio to an almost exclusive reliance on television which, in turn, 'regulated' the remains of the film industries.

Henceforth, cinema would be increasingly governed by the need to sell to television, to squeeze profits from television spin-offs or to rely on televisual marketing, a development anticipated (hence its radical aura) by postwar film-makers such as Roberto Rossellini, who made television before television became a 'mass' medium, and by the techno-fetishistic sub-groups in the visual arts who turned increasingly to video before, with equally opportunistic enthusiasm, embracing computers, all the better to install advertising at the pinnacle of the newly formatted cultural constellation. The result of this further twist in the marketisation of culture, initiated in earnest about a century earlier, was the further transformation of cultural production into an apprenticeship for consumer culture in which all 'art' aspired to the status of advertising and 'entertainment' merely borrowed advertising techniques to pursue its anaesthetising mission (turn up the soundtrack, prevent thought at all costs, accentuate the visceral).

Within the cloistered domain of pornography, these developments not only found their echo, they were often anticipated. Taking the division of the world into specialised rubrics pioneered by newspapers one step further, television started cataloguing its niche markets and tailoring its productions to ever more restrictively defined 'interest groups' (targeted, local anaesthesia administered alongside the more general anaesthetics of the soaps, news programmes and so on). Pornography followed suit as it switched from the big screen (too collectively visible for political comfort) to the more tolerable (and profitable) privatised video markets in the early 80s. Indeed, it was pornography that spearheaded the sale of video recorders/players and camcorders.[34]

By the early 80s, pornography had developed the kind of shopping-mall approach to narrative which television adopted with programmes such as *Hill Street Blues* (1981-7): a meandering narrative designed to make the largest number of people (units to be sold to advertisers) pass by a series of display windows for different wares (some action windows, some melodrama windows, some romance shops, some thriller shops, some comedy stores and so on), hoping to attract and at least partially satisfy multiple niche-clients with one consumption 'experience'. As always in such developments, the products were, at first, still sold according to a sales pitch rehearsed and honed in relation to the sale of a previous, now outdated product line: the integrated narrative stitched together by the device of a 'coherent' and consistent 'character personality' to which a star performer could be pinned continued to serve as a way of selling compilation tapes which eventually got up to date and were marketed as specialist menus catering for specific tastes and needs. In pornography, the often noted near-absence of a coherent narrative scenario had shown that the demand for such a scenario and an emphasis on psychological verisimilitude were part of the very same dissimulation of 'philosophical Enlightenment' narratives internalised with the development of the conventions of literary realism. The avant-garde and its reactionary twin, modernism, had both dispensed with that particular compromise formation long ago as they sought to forge discourses appropriate for a democratising Enlightenment (in the case of the avant-garde) or for a neo-obscurantism capable of salvaging as much as possible from the Old Corruption's wreckage (in the case of modernism as formulated by, for instance, Clement Greenberg). When ditching its vestigial attachment to the character-based story format, pornography did not resort to the old, allegedly spiritual, values of pre-modernity, but rushed ahead and unapologetically embraced the values of the radical bourgeoisie: it turned itself into advertising and helped to specify a culinary, menu-dominated approach to niche marketing.

In pornography, the transition, first to the 'character-based' narrative from 1972 onwards and quickly followed, with the development of video in the early 80s, by a shift towards a kind of narrative fragmentation[35] more geared to niche markets, can best be traced by way of the tensions inherent in the notion of the 'star' performer. In the 70s, the porn cinema industry sought a greater slice of the film industry's profits by integrating itself into the mainstream distribution and exhibition institutions. The porn industry tried to set up, quite successfully, a kind of star system that would be capable of providing the type of 'personal coherence' delivered by 'characters' in realist fiction. The stars that emerged included Linda Lovelace, Serena, Annette Haven, Ginger Lynn, Traci Lords and others. Revealingly, this strategy to achieve closer proximity to the dominant forms of cinematic (and, by then, televisual) narrative mirrored developments in the 'mainstream' cinema as well as emphasising its divergences from it. A few years ago, Serge Daney wrote:

> Today, the advertising aesthetic seems to have triumphed in utter seriousness. Ten years ago it would have been a paradox to say that Le Grand Bleu [Luc Besson, 1988] and L'Ours [Jean-Jacques Annaud, 1988] were finally nothing more than advertising (I

remember having said that about the first Lelouch films). Now the order of the day is no longer the 'contamination' of cinema by advertising (the question was resolved by Diva [Jean-Jacques Beineix, 1980]. Instead, the dominant form of cinema (the kind that 'works') has reached a post-advertising stage. Cinema now inherits prefabricated shots, ready-to-use clichés, in short – immobile images.[36]

It is worth noting, first of all, that the first Lelouch films Daney has in mind date back to the 60s and include a (censored) soft-core documentary called La Femme spectacle (1964) in the tradition best exemplified at the time by the 'variety' and 'curiosity cabinet' films launched in the late 50s in Italy with Walter Kapps's Paris clandestin (1957) and Alessandro Blasetti's Europea di notte (1959) followed by Romollo Marcellini's Le Orientali (1959) and Luigi Vanzi's Mondo di notte (1960). The genre peaked in 1961 with Giacomo Jacopetti's Mondo cane and eventually petered out around 1973–4 with Jacopetti's Mondo candido (1974), after which the relay baton was taken by the likes of Emmanuelle, clearly showing the pedigree of the genre as it crosses over from the cabaret-loop format advertising individual 'turns' to the 'character-based' story format advertising 'lifestyle'.

Daney's comment shows that the genre then developed further into the sale of a designer 'look' in which the whole film takes on the glossy sheen of objects displayed in shop windows. The narrative in such films displays a peculiar, paradoxical temporality of 'immobile movement': a parade or serial display of consumer goods, as in malls or shopping centres, but strewn along a loosely outlined narrative pathway tailor-made for the purpose. Pornography mimicked this process in its peculiar musical-type of narrative structure in which 'numbers' (choreographed performances) are linked by way of segments of narrative 'filler'. This is the function performed by the star-oriented compilation films which emerged from, roughly, 1986 onwards.

The contradictory tensions in such a process are elucidated by Laurence O'Toole who noted that whereas the porn features of the early 70s (his favourite example is Damiano's The Devil in Miss Jones, 1972) were about conveying the experience of sexual excitement (an echo of the character-based psychological realism attributed to mainstream industrial cinema), by the 90s this had changed from 'Porn being about "real" people having hot sex to body-sculpted, silicone-enhanced superhumans "performing" hot sex'.[37] He also notes how the actors' bodies changed, how the hair became more 'glammed up', the musculature more athletic, the women performers' pubic hair was now more often removed for greater smoothness and enhanced visibility, how in the 90s the male performers were shown as already erect and ready for action rather than the 70s tendency to include the spectacle of male arousal, and so forth. O'Toole also noted how the 'reverse cowgirl' and 'reverse anal cowgirl' positions (a woman straddling a man turning her back to him) became far more prevalent, with the peculiar effect of enhancing both the dimension of the performance and the aspect of non-narrative realist documentary at the same time as the 'performance' begins to acquire overtones of 'performance art' and the film or video turns into a documenting of the performance. What such films achieve (again: generally in advance of television) is the new genre of the 'performed documentary', whereas the older forms of pornography were more straightforwardly in the 'cinema direct' idiom or in the mainstream, 'realist', 'classical narrative' idiom, even though their narrative structure was more closely linked to that of the musical with which it shared a memory of the cabaret and the circus. The performed documentary subsequently became a staple of television channels by way of the so-called docusoaps or 'reality soaps' culminating, for the time being, in the Dutch-pioneered *Big Brother* programme format in 1999.

In pornographic films the star and the character are often collapsed into each other, promising as much three-dimensionality to the characters as psychological realism ever dreamt of while at the same time stressing the 'constructed', that is to say, performed dimension of this quasi-documentary strategy. So, while pornography started promoting the shopping mall as a narrative model at exactly the same time as mainstream television did via *Hill Street Blues*, it did so by integrating the cabaret-variety-loop films into the semblance of a coherent, unified narrative space banking on the sense of continuity provided by the star as the subject of a quasi-biography. In fact, the narrative format of these films, as demonstrated by the *Deep Inside*, *Erotic Starlets* and *Flesh in Ecstasy* series,[38] recalls, as did develop-

ments in architecture as well as in computer games, premodern, indeed medieval discursive forms. In pornography's case, the model was the 'lives of the saints' narrative genre in which a succession of exemplary acts is strung together to the greater glory of the institution which presides over and benefits from such quasi-biographies. In porn, this consists of exemplary scenes culled from the star's professional life to the greater glory of the industry which thus manages to parade a gallery of 'extraordinary' characters with exemplary conduct. Without pushing the analogy unduly, one could say that the *Deep Inside* films and similar series also narrate the lives of martyrs to a Great Cause: the industrialisation of culture and the triumph of capitalism in the West. In other words, the *Deep Inside* films are to industrial culture what the lives of the saints were to pre-modern culture in Europe. These barely unified narratives are stitched into complex intertextual fields (the star's filmography, his/her lookalikes, her specific trademark differences from other star performers, and so on) while reducing the narrative waste represented by the 'bits' in between the sex which even a pretence of secondary elaboration – a script – necessarily entails. The main distinction between the *Deep Inside*-type of films and other compilations (at times also using the *Deep Inside* gimmick, such as Ed Powers's series of *Deep Inside Dirty Debutantes* tapes; number 1 is dated 1992, number 33 was released in 1999) is precisely this residual attempt to find a kind of character coherence that might confirm 'star status' or 'exemplary character' status rather than the collection of compilations focused on specialised positions or activities. These are the, in Daney's phrase, 'post-advertising' films fully conforming to the 'new' strategy of consumer fragmentation and niche marketing. In fact, these films – and this kind of marketing – merely represent a further step along the route of the 'specialisation of the senses' which follows from the ever more differentiated divisions of labour and 'disciplinary' subdivisions in academia. Academically speaking, this development in porn video parallels – and is synchronous with – the proliferation of disciplinary divisions and subdivisions in academia in which every identity group (or fragment of an identity group) and every body part or artistic 'medium' is 'recognised' in departmental structures as a separate objects of special attention and knowledge. Compilation series such *Anal Vision*, *Tail Taggers*, *Gang*

Bang Diaries, Bucky Beavers, Colossal Combos, Black Fuckers, Butt Fuckers, First Time Lesbians, Double D Amateurs, Hirsutism nos 1–10, Hispanic Orgies and so on, have almost completely jettisoned any vestigial 'secondary elaboration' and offer straightforward, specialised menus, relating to the mainstream rather like Sock Shop or Knickerbox shops relate to Harrods. The other main type of compilation tape (except for the continuation of the pre-narrative loop collections) is exemplified by 'docusoap' television formats before these became routinely established in the main broadcast schedules. *Dirty Debutantes* and its off-shoots, *Dirty Dave's American Amateurs, Dirty Doc's Housecalls, Mr Peeper's Amateur Home Videos* etc., are the precursors of both *You've Been Framed* (the British version of home video clips linked by an inane compere who tells the viewer that this stuff must be considered 'funny') and the *Big Brother* programme template.

In this respect, it is clear that pornographic cinema and video closely follow – perhaps more often precede and pioneer – the adaptation of industrial culture to the requirements of a consumer culture that itself is geared to the quick turnover rhythms of finance capital rather than the slower, long-term investment patterns suited to industrial capital. In pornography, the trends identified by Daney are writ large.

In pornography, as in the *Big Brother* programmes, the distinction between amateur and professional performers is blurred as porn performers use their own names (often pseudonyms, nicknames or first names only, again significantly overlapping with the designation of the performers in 'reality soaps' in the press) in the quasi-fictions, giving a documentary gloss as well as a dimension of 'character coherence' to the otherwise totally 'performed' image. A second set of tensions surrounds the image of the male performers in heterosexual pornography. The genre itself derives a kind of continuity and coherence from the fact that the male performers tend to be recruited from a very small pool of players. In many ways, and in spite of the prominence given to the female performers in the marketing of pornography, it is the men's performance that frames the narrative drama. Not only is it their ejaculations (the 'money shot') which punctuate the narrative rhythm as much as the edits, it is their phallic endurance which is the defining dimension of the porn narrative, just as physical endurance is in sports programmes. The women are the raw material required for this demonstration. They, therefore, are infinitely substitutable and the turnover of women is correspondingly fast, much faster than that of the male performers whose presence in film after film thus provides an insight into the conditions of the genre's production (the few dozen men involved in the French and American porn cinemas have filmographies of well over 300 films each). In the industrial production of porn films, the men figure as 'plant' along with other bits of machinery necessary to keep the factory going. The women function more like the different kinds of meat processed and canned for sale in the supermarkets.

In both cases, however, what emerges is a thoroughly industrialised concept of a newly formatted body. It is a body divided into and reduced to its components, those components being further reduced to their specific, specialised capacities (as noted by Boyer earlier in her characterisation of a John Holmes reduced to an admittedly sizeable penis). Gertrud Koch pinpointed this development when she remarked in 1989 that:

> The newer pornographic films demonstrate significant advances, especially in the area of gymnastic-artistic formations. Technique has evolved ... to orgies of group sex that demonstrate athletic control of the body along with simultaneous sexual feats ... Now we have high performance professionals who, in the manner of Taylorization, contribute specialized physical skills to the completion of the final product. Meanwhile, maintenance crews with spare parts stand ready to take care of breakdowns. ... Pornographic cinema emerges at the end of a developmental process in a society of specialization and differentiation.[39]

To sum up, pornography evolved by way of an anti-Enlightenment attack on the eighteenth-century philosophical novel which sought to drain its cognitive dimensions. The kind of narrative that resulted from this onslaught was then further quarantined in 'library hell' in the middle of the 19th century, whence it emerged in the service of anaesthetising cultural strategies. The cinematic version of pornography turned the screw further and pioneered the merger between cultural discourse and advertising while staging a reformatting of the body. Its advertising dimension anticipated the reformatting of the body in action cinema or, at least, accompanied the fantasies that animated action films such as Paul Verhoeven's *Robocop* (1987): the dream of a thoroughly Taylorised body, the separate bits of which can be mined for their seemingly inexhaustible energy-generating capacities. Contemporary pornographic video, more than any other audiovisual form of representation, stages the triumph of Henry Ford's conception of the working body. Susan Buck-Morss, illustrating her remark with a picture taken from Jules Amar's *The Physiology of Industrial Organization* (1918), noted that in his autobiography published in 1923, Ford proudly wrote that

> the production of the Model T required 7,882 distinct work operations, but only 12% of these tasks – only 949 operations – required 'strong, able-bodied, and practically physically perfect men.' Of the remainder – and this is clearly what he sees as the major achievement of his method of production – 'we found that 670 could be filled by legless men, 2,637 by one-legged men, two by armless men, 715 by one-armed men and ten by blind men.'[40]

Presumably all operations could be carried out by 'stupid men' since intelligence is not mentioned as a potentially exploitable quality.

In conclusion, the developments and connections to which I have attempted to draw attention suggest that the current pornoscape in the Euro-American, cultural-economic space does allow us to detect a number of features which contribute to the diagnostic identification of what Raymond Williams called an emergent cultural form. Looked at over the longer term, it is clear that the genre's current forms have acquired their characteristic shapes as a result of a number of pressures. The main determining pressure was the suppression of its cognitive capabilities, that is to say, the suppression of representations of sex as tools for thought. This is the primary pressure which instituted pornography as a separate genre cut off from the rest of the literary landscape. Its anti-authoritarian and anti-religious dimensions were deemed too dangerous at the time of the anti-democratic and obscurantist backlash of the mid-19th century. In addition, the emergence of 'the mass' onto the political and cultural scenes, requiring new and better cultural as well as political management

techniques, further strengthened the case for condemning representations of sex and removing them from the public sphere (incidentally helping to turn pornography into a collector's and connoisseur's item for 'the great and the good'). In this respect, pornography was caught in the very same cultural-political dynamic besetting the reformatting of culture as a whole at that time. Consequently, the disputes between power blocs over the landscaping of the cultural terrain also affected the boundaries drawn around pornography as a 'zone of exclusion', for instance, in debates around realism or in the controversies about whether a particular work was/is art or pornography, the outcome of such disputes betraying which sector of the ruling coalition had the power to decide which representations were to be available to which sectors of society.[41]

The second main consideration is that the struggles around the drawing of boundaries were also caught in a more radical sector of the bourgeoisie's agenda which saw potential profits in the industrial production of a suitably anaesthetised (that is to say, anti-intellectual) version of pornography and sought to make it available for consumption as a discrete, autonomised sensory stimulus contributing to the overall propagation of a *Denkverbot*. In this respect, pornographic productions reconnected with the older but now more prominent discursive genre within which sex stories and images had functioned historically: advertising. The combination of advertising modes of address with the autonomisation of sexual consumption in the context of the industrialisation of culture generated a kind of pornography that was characterised by its proximity to shopping catalogues and shop windows, that is to say, pornography evolved in a manner similar to developments in the retail trade bolstered by the professionalisation of advertising around the turn of the century. With the brief crisis in bourgeois restructuring following from the final political triumph of capitalism after the global wars (1968 and all that), pornography again played a prominent part in struggles to reformat the cultural landscape. In the subsequent digitalisation of cultural production, most evident in the transition from cinema and print via video to computer screens as distribution platforms, pornography, along with other cultural forms but more so, turned the anti-intellectual screw even more tightly in an effort to break down cultural production into specific menu items to be marketed to narrowly defined 'lifestyle' niches (also known as 'subcultures' which obey 'the market' and dutifully signal their adherence to groupings on the basis of 'consumer choice'). At the same time, this kind of pornography, best characterised by compilation tapes and specialised websites, also betrays the coming to prominence within so-called popular culture of the kind of society which the leading sectors of the current ruling power coalition would like to bring about. This is the emergent cultural dimension detectable most directly within action movies and pornography: the further development of Henry Ford's vision of a future labour force. According to this still imagined, fantasised future, the intellectual neutralisation of the (growing number of) people who are to be used as labour power is to be accompanied by the disarticulation of 'bodies' into their constituent – and replaceable – components, that is to say, a fantasy of a thorough industrialisation of the body so that industry may be able to cost the labour power value of specific body parts rather than of 'whole' workers who need to be 'sustained' as people for them to be able to function as sources of energy. This is the fantasy which is making itself felt in the very shapes and contours of what industrial cultural production presents as 'popular' narratives.

What then would a defensible pornography be in the current pornoscape? The position to be defended, given that 'quality' pornography is a utopian fantasy that relies on nineteenth-century cultural notions of realism, psychological verisimilitude and character-based narratives, is a demand to restore to the genre its cognitive capacities. This is not a demand to be addressed to the producers of pornographic film and video, but to its consumers: they (we) are the ones who have to make the effort to read the pornoscape for what it is able to say about the dynamics underpinning and driving contemporary societies. We are the ones who have to rediscover the critical, anti-authoritarian (anti-advertising) dimension in representations of, among other things, sex. The kind of representations that may assist us in this task would then be the kind of sound–image combinations which go counter to the prevailing anaesthetic trends and re-emphasise the complexities of 'knowing' the other. In other words, representations that refuse the drift into virtuality. To quote Žižek one last time:

The true horror of cyberspace is not that we are interacting with virtual entities as if they were human – treating virtual nonpersons as real persons, but, rather, the opposite: in our very interaction with 'real' persons, who are more and more accessible through their stand-ins in cyberspace, we are treating 'real' persons as virtual entities that can be harassed or slaughtered with impunity, since we interact with them only in Virtual Reality.[42]

In brief, the pornographic cinema to be valued is the kind that seeks to recover, without necessarily sacrificing to the demand for character-based narratives, the indexical dimension of images. Perhaps ironically, this is the kind of cinema advocated by Bazin and Kracauer, but shorn of its (now outdated) realist legitimising rhetoric, a cinema that can help the 'agitated viewer', as Kracauer puts it, to transform him/herself into a deliberate, conscious and 'thinking' observer enjoying the pleasures of cognition stimulated and made available by sensory perception. Films that invite such an aesthetic engagement would wear their layer of secondary elaboration lightly, such as 'coherent' scripts or other alibis for indulging in intense, intellectually informed visual and auditory perception. That would be, in the present circumstances in advanced capitalist societies, an antidote to anaesthesia. Of course, the problem with such a prescription can be summed up by way of a question that is difficult but not impossible to answer: How can you tell?

NOTES

1. See Michel Foucault, *The History of Sexuality*, trans. Robert Hurley (New York: Vintage Books, 1980), p. 48, and the statement by Gertrud Koch that 'By means of voyeurism's cognitive urge, the discourse of power is begun', in her challenging essay on pornography, 'The Body's Shadow Realm', trans. Jan-Christopher Horak and Joyce Rheuban, *October* no. 50, pp. 3–29, 1989, reprinted in this volume, pp. 148–63.

2. Arguably since the Renaissance and its elaboration of perspective in the context of the Italian city states' bankers and merchants' attempts to individuate bodies by way of geometrical optics.

3. See, for instance, Martin Jay's *Downcast Eyes: The Denigration of Vision in Twentieth-Century Thought* (Berkeley: University of California Press, 1993);

Teresa Brennan and Martin Jay (eds), *Vision in Context: Historical and Contemporary Perspectives on Sight* (New York: Routledge, 1996); Jonathan Crary, *Techniques of the Observer: On Vision and Modernity in the Nineteenth Century* (Cambridge, MA.: MIT Press, 1990); Susan Buck-Morss, *The Dialectics of Seeing: Walter Benjamin and the Arcades Project* (Cambridge, MA: MIT Press, 1989); Paul Willemen, 'Regimes of Subjectivity and Looking', *The UTS Review* vol. 1 no. 2, 1995; Hal Foster (ed.), *Vision and Visuality* (Seattle, WA: Bay Press, 1988).

4. This thought adapts some propositions put forward by Claude Lévi-Strauss in *The Savage Mind* (London: Weidenfeld and Nicolson, 1966 [1962]), pp. 16–17 and 35–6.

5. My implied argument, in brief, is that the problem of value in aesthetics is to be understood in terms rather similar to the way the United States/Nations has engineered geopolitical compromises by splitting countries. The compromise split between high and low cultures allows the Old Corruption, the 'nobility' and its religious enforcers, to hang on to its pretence of spiritual superiority and refinement while the other half, low culture, provides the bourgeoisie with a terrain in which it can pursue profit. Having to put up with the contempt of those who regard themselves as closer to the higher things in life is a small price to pay. Money heals narcissistic wounds very quickly. The quibbles between the two sets of participants in this 'great divide' splitting the cultural terrain occupy most of what today passes for aesthetic theory.

6. Susan Buck-Morss, *Dreamworld and Catastrophe: The Passing of Mass Utopia in the East and West* (Cambridge, MA: MIT Press, 2000), p. 104.

7. Jonathan Crary, *Techniques of the Observer*, p. 147.

8. Ibid. With due apologies for Bataille's unfortunate and no doubt unintended implication that, somehow, women might escape such a measuring of their worth. Confirmation that both genders are thus measured today can be found daily in insurance claims and legal judgments regarding compensation for loss of limbs or other physical injuries which ignore questions of quality in favour of the limb or body part's value in wage calculations.

9. This is confirmed by the older, pre-modern not to say prehistoric integration of representations of sex in the religious modelling of the world.

10. That the control of representations of sex is one of the important ways of controlling intellectuality is also

borne out by the fact that the dominant way of exerting such controls is *not* by way of manipulation but by the withholding of 'tools to think with', a preventative practice also called 'education in the humanities'.

11. Melvyn Bragg does manage to convey this sense of pleasure, but only in context of displays of third-rate intellectuality.

12. Stephen Heath, *The Sexual Fix* (London: Macmillan 1982).

13. Pamela Church Gibson and Roma Gibson, *Dirty Looks* (London: BFI, 1993).

14. Happily, that censor soon after lost his job. Unhappily, he lost it for being 'too liberal' in the eyes of the government. For more detail, see Laurence O'Toole, *Pornocopia: Porn, Sex, Technology and Desire* (London: Serpent's Tail, 1998), pp. 364–5.

15. Slavoj Žižek, *The Plague of Fantasies* (London: Verso, 1997), p. 101.

16. Ibid., p. 106.

17. Quoted in Koch, 'The Body's Shadow Realm', p. 14.

18. Martine Boyer, *L'Écran de l'amour: Cinéma, érotisme et pornographie 1960–1980* (Paris: Plon, 1990).

19. The French pornographic cinema followed soon after *Deep Throat*, although in a rather peculiar manner. The first commercial porn films in France appear on the mainstream screen in Marseilles in 1973. These were mostly Italian 'bis' [*giallo*] films into which some pornographic scenes had been inserted. One film at the Cannes market of 1970, Peter Rush aka Filippo Walter Maria Ratti's *La Notte dei dannati* (released in 1971) had one single hard-core shot, but that shot had been taken from an entirely different film. For some years, European pornographic cinema would consist of 'carrier films' lasting one hour or so which were presented to the mainstream trade along with a menu of possible inserts varying in degrees of 'explicitness', so that distributors could make the selection of inserts that would comply with their local–national censorship laws.

   In 1974, about 13 per cent of tickets sold in France were for porn films. In 1975, J. F. Davy's *Exhibition* (launching Claudine Beccarie) was top of the box office, but that was also the year that pornography was driven from the mainstream screens by punitive tax legislation and a prohibition on advertising. In 1978–80, porn films become shorter, and by 1980, some porn cinemas used video projection. 1975 also saw the first and last Paris International Porn Film Festival, with its 'Golden Willies' awards (*zizis d'or*) of imports. The winner was Frédéric Lansac's *Le sexe qui parle*.

20. Boyer, *L'Écran de l'amour*, pp. 132–5.

21. Slavoj Žižek, *Did Somebody Say Totalitarianism? Five Interventions in the (Mis)use of a Notion* (London: Verso, 2001), pp. 53–4.

22. Ibid., p. 51.

23. Ibid., pp. 51–4.

24. Boyer, *L'Écran de l'amour*, pp. 132–5.

25. *CinémAction*, no. 59, 1991, p. 9.

26. Robert Darnton, *New York Review of Books*, 22 December 1994, pp. 65–74; Lynn Hunt, *The Invention of Pornography: Obscenity and the Origins of Modernity, 1500–1800* (New York: Zone Books, 1993).

27. Ibid., pp. 65–74.

28. Jean Marie Goulemot, *Ces livres qu'on lit d'une main: Lecture et lecteurs de livres pornographiques au XVIIIe siècle* (Paris: Alinea, 1991), pp. 134 and 153–5.

29. David James, 'Hardcore: Cultural Resistance in the Postmodern', *Film Quarterly*, vol. 42 no. 2, Winter 1988–9, pp. 31–9; reprinted in Brian Henderson and Ann Martin (eds), *Film Quarterly: Forty Years – A Selection* (Berkeley: University of California Press, 1999), pp. 225–38.

30. Ibid., pp. 31–9.

31. Quoted in Buck-Morss, *Dreamworld and Catastrophe*, p. 103.

32. Ibid., pp. 134 and 137.

33. Régis Debray, 'A Modest Contribution to the Rites and Ceremonies of the Tenth Anniversary', *New Left Review*, no. 115, May–June 1979, pp. 45–65. Especially with hindsight, Debray's diagnosis in 1979 was uncannily accurate, noting, for instance, how 'Classical humanism passed the torch to MIT systems analysis, the *école normale* graduates in the ministerial offices to brains-trusts of trained administrators. Subversion played a part in the passage from the old to the new, but all it destroyed was the relations linking management techniques to methods of domination within liberal society. We have moved on from a shy technocracy (hidden behind patriarchal charisma) to a triumphant technocracy; in other words from flagrant authoritarianism (but only a façade) to shy authoritarianism (more diffuse and more real). The baton has been passed on successfully' (pp. 50–1), and, in relation to the hype later known as postmodernism: 'In the developed capitalist system, crisis is a normal state, the sign of good health, the mainspring of its advances. . . . The revolutionary kernel of the message of May: the revolution is no longer needed. Henceforth, things will sort themselves out unaided, on the social level, either pre- or post-politics (open to choice); that is, without direction, planning or conscious will' (p. 55). In Ukania, late as usual, Tony Blair finally got hold of the baton in the early 90s, supported, significantly, by ex-lefties who appealed to the lessons of '68 as they joined demos or associated themselves with other political public relations groups. Of course, this assessment of '68 does not preclude the realisation that *some* aspects of that period's cultural ferment pursued a democratising agenda taking advantage of the instability involved in any transitional 'crisis'. The problem is to distinguish within inevitably complex and contradictory actions and statements those which accelerate change in the democratic as opposed to the bourgeois modernisation vectors of social change.

34. In this context, it may be useful to speculate on the forces that establish the dividing lines between the public and the private. It would appear to be the case that the private is controlled and regulated via the public sphere. The private is licensed by the public sphere and the fluctuations in the division between the public and the private will vary according to an authority's assessment of whether an individual (suitably qualified by class attributes) may be 'trusted' to use culture in the manner prescribed by authority. When mismatches threaten, the public authorities intervene to re-draw the borderlines. This is the terrain where the radical bourgeoisie which seeks to profit from potential customers comes into conflict with the politically hegemonic bourgeoisie (the sector which elaborates and enforces the necessary compromises between class forces to guarantee the reproduction of a social order conducive to the long-term maintenance of capitalist relations of production). Consequently, this is also the area where anti-capitalist forces may find common ground with the radical *laissez-faire* wing of the bourgeoisie. Obviously, this has implications for the cultural politics involved in arguments about pornography.

35. A development paralleled in the change from the cinematic musical to the pop promo video. For a discussion of the analogy between pornography and musicals, see Paul Willemen, *Looks and Frictions* (London: BFI, 1994), pp. 122–3.

36. Serge Daney, 'From Movies to Moving', *La recherche photographique*, no. 7, 1989, trans. Brian Holmes, reprinted in *documentadocuments*, 1995, p. 78.

37. Laurence O'Toole, *Pornocopia*, p. 81.

38. The *Deep Inside* films were pioneered by Annie Sprinkle with *Deep Inside Annie Sprinkle* in 1981, followed by *Way Up Deep Inside Hedvig Hillstrom* (aka *All About Hedy Hill*) also in 1981. Then after some years, the genre began to take off in a more standardised format with *Deep Inside Ginger Lynn, Deep Inside Vanessa Del Rio* and *Deep Inside Traci Lords* in 1986. A few more such films followed before producer Jack Stephen launched his series in 1991. A boom of *Deep Inside* films followed in the early 90s.

The *Erotic Starlets* series was Jack Stephen's first CDI Home Video anthology venture dedicated to 'star' performers starting in 1986 with a compilation of Stacey Donovan's fuck scenes, followed by compilations featuring Bunny Blue, Desiree Lane and many others. In 1991, Stephen picked up the *Deep Inside* gimmick and launched another series of compilation tapes featuring the actress mentioned in the film's title, often, as with re-issued CDs, containing some 'extra' material (off-cuts, unreleased scenes, some interview inserts).

The *Flesh in Ecstasy* series started in 1987 by Gourmet Video with a compilation of Blondie Bee's films, followed by similarly titled anthologies dedicated to Samantha Strong, Purple Passion, Jeanna Fine and many others.

39. Koch, 'The Body's Shadow Realm', p. 18.

40. Buck-Morss, *Dreamworld and Catastrophe*, p. 103.

41. As I am finishing this essay, just after an attempt by some political and police authorities to destroy a book by Robert Mapplethorpe has been averted, the police, again acting on behalf of a bid for power by lower-middle-class cultural and moral values (such as racism, xenophobia, fear of sexuality and especially of the paedophile tendencies lurking within the advocacy of 'family values') have threatened to raid an art gallery to remove some of Tierney Gearon's photographs and to impound the catalogue of the exhibition. The police threat also confirms that the populist 'hunt' for 'perversion' only succeeds in maintaining the dangerously perverted in positions of power: those who feel themselves overwhelmingly driven to commit sex crimes and engage in public campaigns to erect the defences they feel they need, are entrusted with the power to regulate representations.

42. Žižek, *Did Somebody Say Totalitarianism?*, p. 136.

2 Generic Overspill: *A Dirty Western*

Edward Buscombe

Within the ultra-low budgets on which pornographic films are made, there never seems to be money for a decent script, though perhaps if there were it would be wasted on performers who can act only below the waist. Narrative tension and character motivation, the things which preoccupy Hollywood script conferences and require endless rewrites to get right, are mostly in short supply. Instead, porn films lurch from one sex scene to another, often all but dispensing with plot, offering their own particular version of 'the cinema of attractions'.

But audiences obstinately seem to require a story of sorts, all the same. One way of supplying at least a modicum of narrative structure is to steal it from elsewhere, and so porn films have habitually been parasitic on other genres, giving us pornographic thrillers, horror, science fiction, even musicals, and, of course, Westerns. So, *The Opening of Misty Beethoven* (1976) borrows the plot of *My Fair Lady* (1964), the porno *Bonnie and Clyde* (1993) is a straight steal from Arthur Penn's 1967 film, and *Sex World* (1978) remakes Michael Crichton's *Westworld* (1973), a hybrid of Western and science-fiction film. Recent examples in this mode include *Erotic Witch Project* (2000) and *Playmate of the Apes* (2002). Sometimes only the title is lifted, such as the bondage title *101 Dominations* (2000), a punning reference to the 1961 Disney cartoon feature *101 Dalmatians* which doubtless had Walt spinning in his grave.

The Western genre offers plenty of scope for this sort of thing, along the lines of *Hard on the Trail* (1971), the solitary hard-core Western recorded in Phil Hardy's authoritative reference book ('sultry action along the trail').[1] A more recent example, showing the minds of pornographers run along fixed tracks, is *The Quick and the Hard* (1999), alluding to Sam Raimi's *The Quick and the Dead* (1995). Nor is it only the titles that encourage a porno twist. The iconography of the Western readily lends itself to

being fetishised. Leather chaps and belts call attention to the male genital area, and guns, of course, speak for themselves; remember Kirk Douglas giving a gunplay lesson in *Man without a Star* (1955): 'Take it out quick and put it away slow.' Western verbal clichés too are tailor-made for a porno twist, as in the sleeve copy for *Every Which Way She Can* (1981):

> The Wild West was never wilder. These hot and sensual cowgirls set saddles ablaze as they repeatedly head 'em up and move 'em out. It's lots of good times on the range and everywhere else! A movie that will start your spurs spinning and keep you lusting for more and more . . .

Or this from *Desperado* (1994): 'These gals could turn a tinhorn into a longhorn with the wink of an eye, a flash of a thigh and if that's too subtle [sic], a barnyard blowjob always did the trick.'

A Dirty Western (1973) does not have a particularly ingenious title, but it begins in true generic fashion with a shot of riders in a landscape. An animated credit sequence has shown us a prison breakout, and we then see three convicts in striped uniforms riding hard. Meanwhile back at the ranch the man of the household has to go off on a cattle drive, leaving his wife behind with their daughters, one of whom is about to be married. He pauses only to have sex with his wife. She fellates him, then, in the approved porno manner, delivers his ejaculate in a manner visible to the spectator. A moment later he is erect again; cowboys are *extremely* virile.

He leaves, the convicts arrive. The leader, wearing an eyepatch (i.e. he's a very bad guy), orders the wife to undress. She protests but he is adamant. 'After seven years in jail, if I want to see tits I will!' He then has sex with her on the kitchen table. The two other convicts are about to do the same with the young girls when the mother offers herself instead,

Bareback Rider, 1974 by Douglas Kent Hall

and the two of them fuck her together. Leaving the mother tied up, the convicts ride off with the three young girls as hostages. At a water hole they all pause to have sex, with the girls performing the difficult feat of underwater fellatio, then they ride some more before stopping in a cave. One girl says to the others to give the men as much sex as they want in order to exhaust them and make escape easier. Various sex acts ensue, without any obvious physical coercion. The pursuing posse approaches. The ballad which has intermittently been heard on the soundtrack bursts out again: 'Someone's going to die today, With their lives they're going to pay.' One of the girls grabs a gun and together they despatch all three convicts just before the mother arrives with the posse. Justice has been done.

Rape, or the threat of it, is a staple of Western narrative. It is at the heart of John Ford's magisterial *The Searchers* (1956), in which their white relatives assume that the Edwards girls captured by Comanches will be raped. In Anthony Mann's *Man of the West* (1958) Julie London is first forced to strip, then later raped. It's the motor which drives the plot

in *Rancho Notorious* (1952) and *The Last Train from Gun Hill* (1959). Around 1970 rape becomes more prominent in the Western and, with the relaxation of censorship, can be portrayed more graphically, for example in *Two Mules for Sister Sara* (1969), *Soldier Blue* (1970), *Little Big Man* (1970), *The Hunting Party* (1971) and *Hannie Caulder* (1971). Clint Eastwood performs a casual rape in *High Plains Drifter* (1972). Sam Peckinpah's *Straw Dogs* (1971) may be a Western only in spirit, but includes a rape so explicit the British censor has only recently allowed the release of the film on video.

Rape in these films of the early 70s is brutal, disturbing, unpleasant, though for the male audience a frisson of sexual excitement may be intended. By contrast, *A Dirty Western* lacks the sense of menace that the rape situation seems to require. It has a curiously lethargic air, even for a pornographic movie, where narrative tension is the exception. I don't mean that what the convicts perform on the women isn't really rape. Though they exercise minimal force (the wife gets slapped once), they are armed and thus the possibility of violence is there. But compared to the

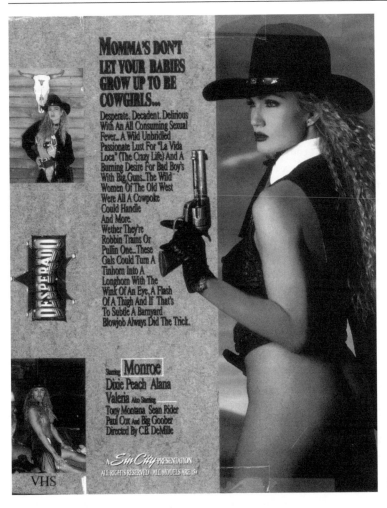

Video cover for *Desperado* (1994)

Lee J. Cob, Gary Cooper and Julie London in *Man of the West* (1958)

Robert Culp and Raquel Welch in *Hannie Caulder* (1971)

mainstream Westerns of the period, both the threat and the execution lack conviction. The response of the women is somewhat ambiguous. The noise the wife makes when being raped by the first convict is the same sort of 'oh, oh' that she makes earlier when being fucked by her husband. During all the sex with the convicts the background music is the kind of syrupy lyrical stuff that accompanied mainstream consensual sex scenes in the early 70s; it doesn't communicate danger. When the young girls have sex with the convicts they don't struggle. Indeed, the convicts perform cunnilingus on them and bring them to orgasm, not an act, perhaps, associated with violent rape.

For all I know there may be porn films featuring violent rape scenarios, but I haven't seen any. Nor is it a feature of the classics of film pornography contemporaneous with *A Dirty Western* such as *The Devil in Miss Jones* (1972), *Behind the Green Door* (1972) and *Deep Throat* (1972), which feature women who are willing, indeed enthusiastic, as they are in such pornographic literary classics as *Fanny Hill* and *The Story of O*.

Why then *is A Dirty Western* based on a rape scenario, if such scenes are not central to the pornographic genre? Tentatively it might be suggested that since at the time it was made rape featured strongly in Western plots, then if one was going to borrow from the genre, one might as well employ such plot motifs as were current. But something seems to have happened in adapting the rape scenario from one genre to another. This may be related to the fact that cross-genre films, such as Western pornos, always appear to be more centrally located in one genre than another. Thus the musical Western *The Harvey Girls* (1946) is more a musical than a Western (because it's essentially a boy meets girl story). *Westworld* is more a science-fiction film than a Western (because it's essentially about technology getting out of control).

And *A Dirty Western* is more a porn film than a Western, because it's essentially about fucking for fun. So although the plot is based on rape the film cannot summon up any conviction in its portrayal. Its heart is not in the scenario it has borrowed. All the time, you feel, it's on the verge of jettisoning the rape plot and just getting on with the sex action, in which, untypically in a Western but typically in a porn film, the women would enjoy themselves as much as the men, if not more so. Perhaps this argues for a certain incompatibility between the two genres, at least in the early 70s. The Western has so much more invested in extreme notions of masculinity, and thus rape may be a logical outcome of the genre's view of men's relationship to women. In the porno film it's not.

Further research might prove this tentative conclusion unreliable, but the evidence is not easy to assemble. Porno films don't stay in circulation very long, and there are few new titles in the Western/porno category. Just as the Western itself has fallen out of favour in Hollywood, so the Western porno is now a rarity, surviving mainly in the gay sub-genre with titles such as *The Hung Riders* (1994), referring to *The Long Riders* (1980), or *How the West Was Hung* (1999), harking back to *How the West Was Won* (1962). A recent trawl didn't throw up much else apart from a curiosity such as *Snakedance* (2001), a kind of New Age 'lyrical' porno film in which 'Native Americans' demonstrate how as well as being in harmony with the environment they invented advanced sexual practices such as wife-swapping and 69. It's about as far from the macho world of the Western proper as you could get.

NOTE

1. Phil Hardy, *The Western* (*The Aurum Film Encyclopedia*), (London: Aurum, 1991).

3 Machines That Make the Body Do Things

Jane Gaines

I'm calling this 'machines that make the body do things' as a way of directly confronting an apparent cultural confluence. This is the confluence between the charges made *against* moving image machines and the claims made *for* them, a development that has 'snuck up on us', so to speak. What is interesting to me is the way in which these charges and claims appear to be based on the same assumption: that these machines produce bodily movement. Particularly in relation to the question of sexual practice, we are familiar with the conservative cultural forces that fear what the pornographic moving image can do to bodies. Likewise, we are thoroughly familiar with the underlying premise of the international pornography industry, the universally assumed premise that machine-made images 'make' people do sexual things to themselves as well as to or with others. Although at political odds (and adhering to different ontologies), the conservative porn-watchers and the porn industry are paradoxically in agreement: these images can and do 'move' bodies in mysterious ways. In the following I want to think about the question of machines moving bodies in relation first to feminist film theory as it impinges on documentary studies and second in relation to old versus new technologies. Halfway through, I want to ask what, if anything, the umbrella of the postmodern contributes to these questions.

Now let me turn to the realm of critical theory, at once oblivious of the literal-minded behaviourism of the public discourse around sexualised images and oddly attuned to it. Although my concern here finally is with neither the anti-sex Right nor the pornography industry, I want us to consider an important shift in film theory circles against the backdrop of the public discourse. These are circles clearly informed by pro-sex feminism, a movement that has historically been very wary of making any argument that could play into the hands of conservatives.[1] What I find remarkable is the way that the rhetoric of our own theory has evolved from an earlier cautious position (perhaps aware of public debates) in which images had no direct measurable 'effect' on the body to the contemporary position of the area of research we have come to call 'porn studies' in which machines do *do* things.[2] Here, although the question of 'effects' is sidestepped, the assumption is that *machines do make bodies*. Suddenly it has become important to theorise the machine as 'moving' the body, following Richard Dyer's early assertion.[3] What has happened? Earlier film studies, intent on distancing itself from empiricism and interested in replacing any lingering behaviourism with the notion of ideology, was a field that might not have been comfortable asserting that the motion picture machine makes, moves, or manipulates bodies in any way. Indeed, the Althusserian notion of 'positioning' that evolved from the 70s, the furthest thing from behaviourism, was intended to go far beyond notions of manipulation.[4] We have, however, stepped away somewhat from this conceptualisation. But now that we have reacted against the totality of ideological 'positioning', a formulation that seemed unable to allow for either political resistance or unpredictable physical bodies, where exactly are we in relation to this theorisation? Is an interest in machine-made bodies just another way of talking about ideological 'positioning' or is it a part of the reaction against the stubbornness of the 'positioned' subject? What are the advantages, if any, to now arguing that motion pictures *move* bodies? Is this a compromise theorisation, halfway between 'positioning' and 'manipulating'? Or is this an entirely different theorisation that is taking us in another direction? I will do little more than suggest that we are at an interesting juncture since in the following I raise far more questions than I am accustomed to answering in a single essay.

Perhaps it began with the use of Foucault in feminist film theory.[5] Here we cannot overestimate the importance of Linda Williams's utilisation of Michel Foucault's concept of 'implantation of perversions' in her ground-breaking feminist analysis of the pornographic moving image, *Hard Core*.[6] Her thesis, to review, is that perversions such as fetishism were cinematically 'implanted', that is, established through and by means of the mechanical devices that played and replayed erotic movements beginning certainly as early as Edward Muybridge's still image precursors of motion pictures. And here I am taking the quotations marks off the word *perversions* on the assumption that my readers understand that in this critical context such a charged concept (the definition of which continues to be in dispute in the larger culture) is in what might be called 'invisible quotes'. In arguing that such perversions were 'implanted' by machine(s), Williams, in *Hard Core*, challenges a basic assumption of feminist film theory, an assumption with its origins in the work of Christian Metz as well as Laura Mulvey.[7] This basic premise might be thus summarised: since the motion picture apparatus 'plays to' key perversions (voyeurism and fetishism), these perversions must somehow pre-exist that apparatus.[8] Going further beyond this idea that the machine finds desires and fascinations ready-made, that it has no part in *producing* them but rather only *encourages* pre-existing desire, Williams asserts that 'the machine would produce a new kind of body'.[9] It is not that the machine unproblematically manufactures perversions. From the top down it produces *the body* guaranteed to 'have' these particular perversions. And, think of it, how would it be possible to produce the perversions without at the same time producing the body to go with them? To produce what might be called the 'perverted' body?

In the more recent 'Corporealized Observers', Williams goes further, arguing that 'the body moves and is in turn moved by the machine', suggesting that there is a circularity to the process, the moving body working the machine that is causing it to be moved.[10] The motion picture *does*, then, produce bodily consequences. As she says, 'image-machinery will produce its effects'. Here it is. The bold feminist admission of what anti-porn groups have feared the most: machines making the body do all manner of perverse things. Citing the history of technologies of visuality over the last two centuries, Williams concurs with Jonathan Crary who sees a development of those machines that (in a kind of post-structuralist

move) increasingly produce the body that they assume.[11] The culmination of these developments, I would argue, is the attempt to destroy a hard and fast boundary – the division between the world of representations and the world that is *not just representations* (my term that temporarily gets us around the problem of the ostensible 'reality' of the world). Speaking about this boundary-crossing as the 'dissolution of (the) separation between spectator and scene', Williams seems to be thinking about a 'making' of the body that wants no screen/body divide. This 'making' I see manifested in the desire of every porn spectator to obliterate the distance between (him)self and the screen (and here I do mean 'him').[12] And it is this attempt to obliterate the difference, to reach out and touch the image, to 'come' simultaneously with the porn actors and actresses who seek this obliteration with invitations to 'come all over me', that characterises moving image pornography, that helps to define its generic particularity. Here it is that the ontology of documentary is so relevant. Pornography asks for the impossible from the spectator. It asks that that he both *treat* the representation as a representation and that he (again he) *not* treat the representation as a representation. Why else does the female porn star ask the viewer *not* to 'come all over my image' but to 'come all over *me*'? Pornography requires the breach of real world/fantasy world separation, asking its viewer to 'really' come.[13] It also asks its viewers to produce the ultimate sign that something 'really' happened. Thus it is that pornography represents a limit case in the theorisation of representation. In its direct address to the viewer it seeks to produce an immediate, involuntary response to that representation. The 'image-machinery' strives to produce the bodily.

Both Linda Williams and Richard Dyer before her have suggested that bodily response to theatrical drama is a generic question. Williams, in her important article on 'body genres' asserts that horror, melodrama and porn make the body scream, cry and come.[14] And Dyer in an earlier *Jump Cut* article compares pornography to 'weepies, thrillers and low comedy', genres 'realized in/through the body', and hence their low status.[15] But of these genres, it is pornography that dramatically illustrates the potential of the cinematic machine to 'make the body do things' as well as to 'make the body', the difference between which is the topic of this essay. Pornography, given this fence-sitting position, thus also challenges us to think through the philosophical problem of representation and its realities, representation, actually *sandwiched* by two realities – the reality of the spectator and the reality of the pro-filmic event. And in relation to these two realms, realms that have been the object of study of the emerging field of documentary film studies, hard-core pornography offers some new theoretical challenges.[16] Questions of realism are tied up with particular pulpabilities. Hard core, as Williams would tell us, is concerned about two 'reallys', or rather, two cases of 'really' coming. First, it is concerned with the pro-filmic male actor who must not 'act' but who must 'really' come, displaying the 'truth' of sexuality in his ejaculative display (the 'money shot'), and second the ideal (male) spectator who it is assumed will 'really' come along with and because of the image.[17] Our critical questioning of all forms of heterosexual presumption kicks in here. Williams and other feminists have also trained us to ask about the female in pornographic discourse. Thus we must ask about the female porn star in relation to this all-important 'really'. How do we know when and if the female porn star 'really' comes? And the female spectator? What about her? All we can say about the female spectator is 'who knows?' It would seem, even given the new possibilities opened up in 'porn studies', that we have reached a stalemate in relation to this problematic. One of the reasons for this stalemate, I suspect, is the very inequivalency of the gendered production of the sign of the real. Even given the new lesbian discovery of the spectacularised female ejaculation (on top of the *assertion* that the machine moves the body), we still do not know whether or not the machine makes the preponderance of *female* spectators do anything.[18] We do not know if the machine does anything at all to or for women (whichever preposition you prefer here). Let us put the question of heterosexual or lesbian content on hold here and look at the issue of the female spectator and the machine from another angle.

THE ELECTROMECHANICAL VIBRATOR

In order to get some distance on this issue I want to turn to another set of questions. These are questions that arise in the consideration of an entirely different machine, a device that has a proven record, a mechanism that is the epitome of the machine that 'makes the body do things'. The machine I want to consider is the electromechanical vibrator. Rachel Maines, in her recent, much acclaimed, *The Technology of Orgasm*, is motivated in her research by the same issues that spurred feminists to study the representation of female pleasure in pornography.[19] In this technological history we find a striking parallel. We find the turn of the century medical establishment studying the same phenomenon that the pornographic film industry (according to Williams) has been intent on probing: the female orgasm. Yet there is an important difference in the approaches taken by Williams and Maines. Whereas Williams sees hard core as bent on making visible the invisible – the female sexual response that happens 'out of sight', probed by a fascinated camera – Maines investigates the history of the pathologisation of female sexual desire. Most important for feminists, however, is the resonance between these studies which go hand in hand as feminist exposés of the long history of male refusal to understand female sexual response. Most dramatic in Maines's account of this particular male myopia is the history of the medical treatment for hysteria, the physician's manual manipulation of the clitoris of the sufferer to the point where she experienced what was called the 'hysterical paroxysm', in other words, an orgasm. An orgasm in the physician's office no less. And this was apparently not a one-time occurrence, as Maines tells us. Women, and particularly those who could not secure the desired results through sexual intercourse (single women, widows, nuns), returned to their physicians on a periodic basis for treatment. Physicians, understanding this to be a lucrative practice, obliged (or recommended midwives). Some doctors, however, complained of the inordinate amount of time it could take to receive results (up to an hour) and specific skill was needed to achieve any results at all. Thus it was not surprising that physicians would welcome electromechanical solutions to the problem of producing orgasms in their female patients.

The trend in the mechanisation of the physician's task was not unopposed, and at least one important American physician would write on the treatment of hysterical women that machinery of this kind might be 'poor substitutes for the hand of the masseur'.[20] But the benefits of mechanising the treatment for hysteria outweighed the drawbacks. The machine was found to be superior to the hand, particularly as it tirelessly produced such sustained vibration. In 1917, one physician would assert that 'No human hand is capable of cummunicating [sic] to the tissues such rapid, steady and prolonged vibrations, and certain kneading and percussion movements, as the vibrator'.[21] Of all of the virtues of the vibrator extolled in the early literature, that of efficiency is most consistently stressed, and it is clear from existing evidence that most physicians found the hand stimulation of hysterical women to be tedious and not cost-effective in terms of their time. (Accounts of those physicians who found personal or physical gratification in the practice seem to be missing from the record.) By the 1910s, however, women were taking the method of electromechanical relief of sexual tension into their own hands, so to speak, and the number of companies supplying machines (usually by mail) rose to a high of twenty in the US. The Swedish Vibrator Company of Chicago, in an ad seeking sales agents, described their product as 'a machine that gives 30,000 thrilling invigorating, penetrating, revitalizing vibrations per minute'.[22] Sears, Roebuck and Company, which has long been a discreet source of vibrators, advertised three models in their *Electrical Goods* catalogue in 1918, and although vibrators were classified with small household appliances such as toasters and irons, the top-of-the-line Star vibrators were advertised as 'Such Delightful Companions'.[23] The phrasing of this recommendation would lead us to believe that women were having sex with machines, not that they were finding sexual relief with the aid of machines. But the medical motive was predominant up until the 60s. Not until then did the vibrator finally find acceptance as a sex toy. Before the 60s, this medical motive went a long way towards justifying satisfying results. It would not be surprising, then, to find a strangely mixed set of claims in advertising for the vibrator. One such ad in 1910 claimed that the device could get to the sources of disease by sending 'the rich, red blood leaping and coursing through your veins and arteries' which 'makes you fairly tingle with the joy of living'.[24] Thus with every promotional ploy there might be a hint of benefits over and above health, hints such as the reference to the unmistakable 'tingling' felt in various parts of the body.

Hard core, as Williams defines it, is entertainment that presents 'maximum visibility' of the 'thing',

evidence of the involuntary convulsion that is the sign of sexuality. It is the 'truth' of the body revealed to the camera.[25] It is also supposed that this camera 'truth' has particular value given that female sexual expression is so elusive and, in Williams's analysis, pornography's aim is to probe this mystery, the very sign of which is the involuntary convulsion. But if pornography (through its various machine manifestations) is obsessed with what it cannot know or guarantee, is ever in search of the Foucauldian 'knowledge-pleasure', attempting thousands of scenarios, angles, positions and partnerings in its tireless search, the electromechanical vibrator makes its obsession seem all for naught. The vibrator steps into the history of sexual technologies and produces the desired results automatically and efficiently. The straightforward use of the vibrator is nothing more nor less than the voluntary production of the involuntary. Perhaps even more importantly, however, the early vibrator produces these results *without penetration*, telling us that women's pleasure organs are located on the outside, not the inside. This is the crucial fact that centuries of physicians and husbands as well as most pornographic films and tapes still refuse to believe, a point I will return to in a moment. Rachel Maines confirms other feminist suspicions. Like feminist scholars studying pornography she finds in her research on the vibrator a familiar paradigm: the privileging of penetration. However, as her historical study so adroitly shows, this privileging produced a fortuitous advantage for the sex toy. Since the vibrator was not originally designed to penetrate, it was not perceived as the rival of the penis.

In the history of Western sexuality, then, the vibrator enters as a deeply subversive machine, negating some of the basic premises of heterosexual pornography. These are the premises that Williams, in *Hard Core*, finds dedicated to the principle that male and female sexuality are basically the *same*.[26] While traditional pornography doggedly insists on *same* desires for *same* practices, *same* orgasms and *same* enthusiasm for penetration, the vibrator, used predominantly by women (with some gay men as exceptions) disproves the rule of sameness. Its historical evolution irrefutably demonstrates that it was designed for anatomical women and prescribed exclusively for them, even though in recent years it has become associated with heterosexual sex play, a development largely responsible for the eclipse of its exclusive use by women. Still, even given heterosexual partnering practices, the vibrator remains the woman's device. Clearly we should also ask about women together as well as women alone at this point. And here, the lesbian use of vibrators is another important story. Not surprisingly, however, Rachel Maines's historical research doesn't turn up evidence to fill out the historical record. Whatever its limitations, this history of the vibrator still reinforces the strongest, most politically potent point that Williams makes in *Hard Core*. This point is that *pornography's proliferation of perversions can be understood as subversive insofar as the prevalence of pornography has also meant a proliferation of sexual contradictions.*[27] The most glaring of these contradictions, she says, is that the genre that holds out promise of women's pleasure and in the end offers not women's pleasure but the spectacularised male ejaculation instead. Now we must add to this a twist. The historical contradiction has also produced for some women a secret weapon. What many women know, it would appear, is that the exterior vibrator secretly produces pleasure that rivals (and even exceeds) the pleasure produced by penetration. The vibrator is the off-stage instrument that makes up for the fact that pornography has failed to understand (and more importantly produce) women's pleasure. The vibrator is able to produce what the 'spectacularised ejaculating penis' *cannot* since, unlike much of pornography which is obsessed with the relocation of the clitoris, the vibrator is designed for use on the clitoris *in its actual location* (it is not, for instance, designed to be used in the throat).[28] The 'money shot', the apparent victory of the visual over the tactile, is thus a temporary triumph.[29] For women, it is the vibrator that produces the orgasmic 'pay off'. For the sake of clarity, I should say that here I am making a distinction between orgasms produced on and off screen, in the world of representation, and in the world that is *not just representations*. (Although it is not my subject here I want to acknowledge the representation of the vibrator in the context of pornographic narratives found on screen as early as the 1920s in a film called *Widow's Delight* in which a matron rejects the kiss of a suitor in favour of her vibrator.)[30]

My reader may be somewhat confused by what seems to be the apples and oranges comparison I am making here. That reader may argue that we are talking about two very different types of machinery that if they can be said to 'produce' do so in significantly different ways. In answer to this, I would say that the point is to force the comparison to yield insights.

Moving-image pornography is the machine that gives us the representation of the 'thing' whereas the vibrator is the machine that produces the 'thing itself'.[31] I have thus far been comparing the electromechanical, battery-driven vibrator to the pornographic apparatus with emphasis on the screen, the projection of the camera-produced image on the theatrical screen or displayed on a video monitor screen. However, a much more interesting comparison might be between the hand-operated vibrator and the hand-held, lightweight videotape camera.[32]

Thus let me return to my original concerns having to do with the implications of arguing that the machine produces the body. What is the gain for us in the argument that the machine produces the body? Although I am not yet prepared to answer this question, I am prepared to make two points. First, we need to make a distinction between the argument that the machine 'makes the body do things' and the argument that the machine 'makes the body'. While 'making the body do things' can result in the production of a particular body, a body constructed by the things that it is made to do, a body made or produced as (perversely) sexual because it does these things over and over again, we also have to consider that a body *made* the machine and that bodies perform *for* the machine. This top to bottom reconceptualisation brings us closer to the Foucauldian concept of 'implantation' which seems to imply the deep rootedness of the culture of mechanised sexuality. Still, I worry that the formulation of the machine as 'making the body' do this and that always hearkens back to the behaviourism of effects studies, even as the concept becomes attached to constructivism.

For ultimately I would conjecture that the concept of the machine producing the body has its deepest affiliation with constructivism, that particular constructivism that empowered feminism with the argument that our biological bodies are *not* our destiny, since those bodies are constructed. However, this social-construction-of-everything approach to the world has recently been re-evaluated by Judith Butler who, to the chagrin of some feminists, asks what is left over after the cultural (gender) has imposed itself on the biological (sex).[33] My example of the location of the clitoris would seem to elucidate Butler's point. There *are* some aspects of life that still almost elude social construction, and while the social history of the vibrator dramatically demonstrates the way that female sexual needs were constructed as they were pathologised, the physiology of orgasm itself (as well as the location of the clitoris) still stubbornly insists that it pre-exists our cultural attempts to make sense of it. So is the constructivist argument the argument that we always want to make? Do we need to admit exceptions to the rule of constructivism only to leave the door open to biologism? Is a constructivist argument a gain if such an argument makes it difficult if not impossible to consider what could conceivably *not* be made by the machine?

An easier feminist advantage to claim for the argument that the machine 'makes the body' is the reinforcement of the analogy between machine and body. This is basic Foucault, reiterated by Linda Williams, whose work assumes that 'sexual activities have an element of the mechanical, of the body as machine'.[34] And as we turn back to our comparison between the cinematic apparatus (conveying pornography) and the vibrator as producers of orgasms, we have to note that the two have in common a certain *efficient* approach to the production of pleasure. More obvious in the vibrator (the machine that replaced the tired hand), this efficient approach to sexuality, however, has been recently criticised by feminists. Rachel Maines quotes one such outraged feminist:

> Has the vibrator, once considered a therapeutic device, become a sort of microwave oven of the bedroom – a fast, efficient means of getting sexual pleasure? Is the most efficient orgasm the best orgasm? Is the bedroom really the place for a time-saving device? If so, what are we saving all this time for?[35]

This feminist would seem to be objecting to a perceived mechanisation of sexual pleasure, an argument that seems consistent with mainstream feminism's idealisation of romantic erotics. Here, however, I would argue that we must not forget to weigh the efficient, vibrator-produced orgasm against no orgasm at all. After all, what is more or less time when compared with more or less pleasure? However, the issue of efficiency may be moot here. The question of efficiency still needs to be applied to mass-marketed sexual fantasies, a question not addressed sufficiently by 'porn studies'. But the question of the analogy between the body and the machine raises even more difficult questions, questions that I want to list: Insofar as the videotape machine facilitates 'getting off', does it get men, women or both 'off' more efficiently? More efficiently than what? Human hands? Tongues? More efficiently than private fantasies and traditional sexual intercourse?

INTERNET PORNOGRAPHY

As I have said, the pornographic viewing machine and the mechanical vibrator have only been brought together here to force some questions about the way machines can be said to construct bodies. My main concern has been the gender differential in sexual pleasure. But the question raised by discussions of mechanisation and pleasure leads to a much larger philosophical concern hinted at in the formulation of the question as one of how the viewing machine *makes the body*. Here I want to get at the question from yet another direction. Instead of looking back to the history of a particular pleasure instrument (and the assumptions surrounding its use), I want to look forward to consider how the advent of a new delivery system and mode of viewing sexualised images situates the body. But rather than an actual leap into the fray the following is intended as a kind of preface to a consideration in which I suggest that there might be implications for feminist 'porn studies'.

For the internet is the penultimate realisation of Linda Williams's 'pornotopia'. To preview some of its claims: 'Over 50 Hidden Cameras in School Dorms!' '20 Live Sex Asian Showrooms, 24 Hours a Day', 'Fast Streaming Sex', 'Live Explicit Action Plus Live Chat Rooms', 'Nasty Penetration – Sex Is at Your Fingertips'. No longer relegated to shelves at the back of the video store and tiny stores on urban backstreets, pornographic imagery 'fills' most of the space that constitutes the internet, and while popular wisdom says that it constitutes over 50 per cent some estimates have it as high as 90 per cent of the space.[36] The sheer infinitude and availability of pornography on the World Wide Web requires media scholars to take serious note and in so doing to significantly rethink our current theorisations of spectatorship as well as the conditions of existence in the current century. I see this as a historical opportunity for theory. If we take constructivism at its word, for instance, electronic representation is not anything other than what we theorise it to be. One *could* say, therefore, that we are currently positioned to theorise it into being. And at this moment there is a great rush to theorise – a gold rush for theory in which every couch theorist will have something to say in hopes of shaping (all the while believing that we are and it is already shaped). This moment is somewhat reminiscent of the moment in the 60s when the ubiquity of everyday television demanded such theorisation. The phenomenon of popular television as it impinged on everyday life seemed to require immediate explanation, and a culture latched onto the instant wisdom of Marshall McLuhan's *Understanding Media*.[37] What is now desired is theory to give order to the chaotic expansion of capital as manifested in global electronic culture. From the point of view of the history of film studies, Anne Friedberg has wisely cautioned about the pitfalls of theorisation, given the current speed of change. As she says in response to the demand for theory: 'And yet it is more than apparent that with the speed of such rapid and radical transformations, our technological environments cannot be conclusively theorized.'[38]

Theories of the postmodern condition, however, may have an edge over any and every theory offered to explain the phenomenon of the World Wide Web. The undisputed advantage that this theorisation has over other approaches is its original grounding in a Marxist account of the expansion of capital which has historically insisted on thinking a complex and comprehensive set of connections between the economy, the subject and the society. If we are to start anywhere in our attempt to describe and critique the infinite netherspace of internet pornography one would think, then, it would be with the notion of the postmodern which takes as its basic assumption that it (postmodern culture) is a readable symptom writ large, a symptom that tells us something important about the 'world space of multinational capital', to refer to Fredric Jameson's object of theory.[39] And it would seem that internet pornography would be perhaps the most symptomatic of all of the manifestations of multinational encroachment, certainly since it has so visibly and irredeemably evidenced cultural production as nothing more than commodity production; certainly since it is something to point to and something to despise, something which

is clearly indicative of something larger somewhere else. I have a few objections to the characterisation of the contemporary consumer landscape as postmodern. I worry that the postmodern diagnosis (for that is what it is) will be thought to suffice as a description of either the general expanse of internet culture or the specific economic and cultural phenomenon of the electronic availability of pornographic images. First, and most easily, I would remark on the way the concept of the postmodern has been easily peeled off from the rest of Jameson's politically informed paradigm. It is, after all, in the form of a despairing diagnosis of a sick society that we often find the postmodern referenced in contemporary cultural criticism. This is to say nothing of the straitjacketing of the concept. I actually think that the theorisation of the postmodern is another of those interesting examples in the history of criticism of a remarkable and breathtakingly brilliant critique that, through use and over time, has subsequently turned into a critical formula.[40] Perhaps the seeds of what I call the doomsdayism of postmodern theory are there in the original, perhaps not. And it is difficult to argue that the forgone conclusions are built into 'The Cultural Logic of Late Capitalism' for all time since it is not in the seminal essay itself so much as in the subsequent attempts to apply the theory that I find the dead-endedness.

My example of how the notion of the postmodern has come to work like a theoretical clamp is drawn from the amazing contemporary work of Vivian Sobchack[41] who offers us a kind of 'before and after' approach to the use of key critical concepts as well as a dialogue with Jameson's essay. It is only because Sobchack is such an astute critic and scholar of electronic culture that it is even possible to work through the realignments in her thinking to productive ends. Perhaps, one could surmise, it is because as a phenomenologist she has insisted on such thorough description that she would think it was important to look at the same technological formation more than once. A radical change in conclusions is not unheard of in cultural criticism, but Sobchack's shift in tone from the mid-80s' 'The Scene of the Screen', to the more recent 'Nostalgia for a Digital Object' is striking enough to describe as a kind of recanting of an earlier position. That earlier position, as I will argue, was written under the sign, so to speak, of questions of the postmodern, and thus paints a bleak picture of electronic space, describing it in terms of those characteristically dismissive phrases and in terms of what it lacks (temporal thickness, bodily investment, historical consciousness). It is superficial and flat, she says. She echoes Jameson's famous 'depthlessness' critique, saying, 'Images on television screens and computer terminals seem neither projected nor deep'.[42] Another cue is taken from Jameson's assessment of the contemporary fate of 'feeling', of the space of the realm in which things are felt. Most significant in terms of our focus, internet pornography, he describes postmodern products as, although not completely lacking in feeling, better understood as 'intensities' which are suddenly 'free-floating and impersonal'.[43] Sobchack, in 'The Scene of the Screen' essay, builds on this theorisation in her location of the body in cyberspace. Quoting as well as echoing but also significantly adding to Jameson, she observes that electronic space does not invite and cannot accommodate inhabitation: 'It denies or prosthetically transforms the spectator's physical human body so that subjectivity and affect free-float or free-fall or free-flow across a horizontal/vertical grid.'[44] Conclusively, the thoroughly disembodying experience of electronic spectatorship signals a 'crisis of the flesh'.[45] In her final analysis, it is disconnection from the body that, more than anything, defines the electronic condition.

Before I take up the question of how to study internet pornography if the delivery system itself is understood as disembodying to begin with, I want to reiterate one more time the problem I find with the postmodern formula. The problem is with the kind of criticism it has encouraged, a function, it should be said, not so much of its status as formula but in relation to a high culture bias in the formulation. There is where the problem lies. The degree to which high culture assumptions are built into the diagnosis (depth over surface, history over instantaneity, genuine feeling over intensity, longevity over temporality, transformation over stimulation, the body over disembodiment) is the degree to which postmodern theory is unable to deal with the popular. And here by popular I mean not only popular films, popular television and popular uses of digital diversions but popular sexual practices. Finally, my quarrel is with the tone as well as the capacity of this analysis to encourage and fertilise new critical work. How will we continue to sustain interest in our conclusions if

our assessment of electronic culture as postmodern culture is always 'prognosis negative'?[46] How are we to grasp, define and explore the newness of electronic culture if the outcome of our research is always the same, confirming the conclusions of the master theorists of the contemporary moment? How are we to order and explain? Vivian Sobchack has in fact answered my long question in her recent work on QuickTime movies. An about-face from the earlier 'The Scene of the Screen', Sobchack finds in the phenomenon of QuickTime movies, electronic culture in what might be called its 'primitive' moment, a time analogous to the moment a century ago when motion pictures were moving by fits and starts. Not only are the internet tiny movies reminiscent of Muybridge, flip books and kinetoscopes, but, says Sobchack, they return us to the curiosities of the 16th and 17th centuries, to reliquaries and 'memory boxes'.[47] They are akin to the charming clutter of the work of Joseph Cornell, boxed and nested and full of surprises and secrets. Most striking, the possibilities of streaming, of the electronic attempt to load movement and to deliver moving images in small boxes (sometimes succeeding, sometimes failing), appear to have influenced Sobchack's analysis. Now electronic space looks significantly different.

The computer is no longer depthless, it is a 'fathomless memory box'.[48] The electronic space that was earlier so flat and superficial is now described in terms of its infinitude, its database potential seen in terms of a labyrinth.[49] Suddenly, computer space seems full of promise, continuous with a historical past (that it remembers) but striving to develop its own capacities for repetition and duplication.[50] And finally, pertinent to the question of the bodily experience of exploring net space, Sobchack finds that rather than deadening the feelings, the miniaturisation of the moving image actually 'intensifies' the experience of viewing.[51] Thus, in the last analysis, it is Sobchack's unprecedented reconsideration that gives me hope that the novelty of internet pornography itself – its form and function – will have its eventual impact on megatheory itself. In this situation, there is also an opportunity to change theoretical directions, to test new paradigms, to challenge tired assumptions, or to return to under-examined areas of investigation.

Immediately I would want to explore a new paradigm that implicates an old one.

High on my list of formulations ripe for reconsideration is the theory of voyeurism, that paradigm of the peephole and the visual aid that seems never to have lost its association with the pathological and its link to a Victorian prudery that never described more than a fraction of the world population. Let us start with the hardware alone. The computer screen is not now and never will be a peephole and the question of requisite voyeuristic distance has been replaced with the question of deceptive proximity of the screen, a screen that offers the perfectly balanced illusion of connection and the reality of disconnection. At least one of the theorists of the new media has called our attention to critical antecedents that add key ingredients to our analysis of spectatorship. Lev Manovich, for instance, has productively recalled for us the origins of the technology of the computer screen in military surveillance, arguing that this new screen, the screen of real time, is constantly changing, corresponding to updated data stored in memory in the case of the computer image. The fact of the constant reproduction (through scanning) of the image means that the real-time image is not exactly an image (in the ways we have traditionally thought of the image).[52] One would think that serious questions about the constitution and the status of the image itself would deflect back onto theories of sexual looking.

Some, insisting on the utility of the voyeurism paradigm, may argue that internet porn viewing is single and secret. It could be argued in response that it is at the same time very mass and simultaneously shared, simultaneously personal and impersonal and even that the public/private distinction is not so useful here since we are strangely open to the world as well as cut off from it in internet spatiality. The question of electronic perception vis-à-vis the computer terminal also leads us to wonder about the postural 'protocol', that bodily equivalent of the conventions that govern the programs that deliver us the bits of information that produce the imagery that we process, that we use in the performance of operations in an imaginary space, to take Alex Galloway's work in a slightly different direction.[53] Basically, we sit looking at a display but what is different about this electronic display (case) (and what differentiates it from television even with its remote controls) is that we are simultaneously looking and touching, 'punching up' or clicking on. We are touching something into nothing. We seem to produce the real-time screen image with our fingertips. And it is this simultaneous looking that touches and touching that looks that suggests the paradigm that I think has so much to offer as it takes us beyond the limits of voyeurism and towards a theory of perception in the electronic age.

Here I appreciate Vivian Sobchack's refinement of the phenomenological conceptualisation of synaesthesia which would seem to have new utility as it explains the sensorial interrelationships that in sum are the technologised experience of bodily consciousness.[54] Synaesthesia would allow the de-emphasis of vision, replacing the dominance of the eye with a vision always informed by all other means of sensory access. The phenomenon anticipates a 'cooperation' and 'commutation' between the senses, a 'metaphoric exchange' and 'translation' from one to the other.[55] Sobchack's concept of the 'cinesthetic' subject offers a theory of sensory receptivity and reciprocity for the electronic age, which offers much more than the much-touted interactivity, I think.

Merleau-Ponty on the metaphors offered by the body, stretching them over the holes, writes: 'Once again, the flesh we are speaking of is not matter. It is the coiling over of the visible upon the seeing body, of the tangible upon the touching body, which is attested in particular when the body sees itself, touches itself seeing . . .'[56] Quoting Malraux who said, 'I hear myself with my throat', he demonstrates the essential reciprocity of the senses, the intersection of appendages.[57] Nothing is divorced. Is this useful to us as we make sense of contemporary touchtone moments, of the radical scrambling that defines our daily experiences? Rather than the old frenzied visible, the start and stop of the projector at the back of the room, the threat of the divorce between image and sound through electrical dysfunction, we live with electronic magic, meaning that we touch screens with our eyes, seeing with our fingers because we are offered it all at our fingertips by means of our fingertips.

TIME FOR A CONFESSION

I never intended to let the subject of vibrators take over this discussion of the theoretical question of moving-picture machines and the bodily realities they do or do not produce. This question, I maintain, is crucial for all aspects of documentary studies, a project that has been dedicated to the analysis of the real-seeming image and the unreal-seeming world. Such an investigation goes a long way towards helping us with the question of the interrelation between machines, and in particular, machines that are thought to 'produce' involuntary reactions, that is, reactions thought to be genuine, to be signs of the real. Let me pose this as a question: How do machines work in concert with other machines to 'sexuate' the body?[58] We must not be satisfied with the idea that one machine produces fantasies and the other machine produces stimulation. For here, I would like to suggest that the vibrator itself (in its contemporary manifestations at least) makes significant contributions to the fantasy. (Why the multitudes of colours and shapes if not for the sake of the enrichment of the fantasy?) And here I am relying on Elizabeth Cowie's productive theorisation of fantasy as the *mise en scène* of desire, the laying out that is not necessarily the having.[59] If the vibrating wand gives rise to fantasy imagery why can't the image machine produce stimulation? Perhaps vibrating sex toys used in concert with pornographic on-screen images are used to synaesthetic ends; perhaps the images are felt and the feelings seen.

But why are we singling out vibrators and videotape players as the only machines that work to 'sexuate' the body? Where do we stop when we consider machines that make the body do things? What about household appliances that produce electric shocks? Machines that produce responses that seem beyond our volition? What about electromechanical technologies that keep the body alive? Why, when media scholars have historically sought to separate moving-picture machines from other such machines would they now want to examine this function of that machine – the moving of the body function?

I never intended to go into such depth in an article that didn't set out to be about sex toys, and therefore the last thing I want to do is an ethnography of the use of vibrators. Instead, I have opted for the much easier task of looking at a few of the machines themselves. An analysis of the contemporary iconography of the vibrator yields important insights about the interrelation between realism and 'irreality', or better, realism and whimsy. My limited research began with a perusal of the website www.Sextoys.com, a site that leads into an unimagined and unimaginable world, particularly for someone who has never set foot in a sex shop. What strikes the feminist scholar immediately is something that should come as no surprise – the predominance of vibrators disguised as penises, so many that one wonders if the desire is for the one or the other, the sensation or the thing. Or is this about the realisation of the fantasy that in Williams actually produces 'the thing itself'? The feminist analyst is again attracted to the plethora of contradictions. These are the contradictions suggested by such models as the Rotating Sexagon – 'truly better than real', the Raw Studs Multi-Speed Big-Veined Life-like 8″ Ivory Vibrator, Vibrating Soft Jelly with special Ridges and Textures, and the Hard Throb – 'The ultimate realistic vibrator'. Why, I wonder, go to all this trouble? Why the attempt at realism that flies in the face of reality? Of probability? I ask this, not just in consideration of the bizarre colours and shapes, of the Hot Pink (Clitterific) model but the Glow in the Dark model, the Giant Torpedo Flesh, Lil Banana flesh, Octo-pussy and Pearl Panther models. I ask this about the unlikelihood that something could be skin-like and still have diamond-patterned ridges. But more importantly, I ask this about the manufacture of the simulated penis that is eternally hard, ever hard. Every woman knows that there is no such thing.

On the serious side, in operation here are two distinct and distinctly incompatible aesthetics. There is the hokey Halloween costume aesthetic of fake body parts – silicon penises rather than of green rubber faces as opposed to the attempted realism of flesh tones, enlarged veins, and even a Foreskin Lover in white flesh or black flesh tones (ostensibly for black women). But the ultimate in vibrator Halloween humour is a model called 'Monica Blows' or 'Bill's Choice'. To quote the promotion: 'The cigar that shocked the nation. Authentic vibrating rubber cigar, which is an authentic satirical shot at the authentic absurdity of authentic American politics, wrapped in authentic cellophane.' Includes a 'Certificate of Authenticity'.

I maintain that documentary film theory has something to learn from any study of these preposterous claims to authenticity. That the new process could be simultaneously not real and 'true to life' did not seem to concern either promoters or viewers. The battery-run sex toy that descends from the old steel wand acknowledges the fantasy element in sex with its colours and animal, vegetable and fruit shapes, and simultaneously strives for a realism that it comes nowhere near achieving. An anecdote in support of this observation: In a telephone interview, I asked one of the saleswomen at Dream Dresser, an LA sexual accoutrements store, about the sales of fuschia, lavender, hot pink, green and red vibrators. She said that her customers definitely preferred colours to flesh tones. Of course I asked, 'If women want vivid colours then why the attempt to look like a penis at all?' To which she answered, 'Women consider that it looks realistic therefore it is realistic.' Perhaps the semi-realism of the penis-shaped (green) vibrator also contributes to the apparently necessary illusion that it is the penis that produces satisfaction.

The results of my very informal research also leads me back to Linda Williams's profound insight into the deepest of all of the discrepancies in contemporary pornography – the discrepancy between penetration and the actual location of female sexual pleasure. When I asked her about her bestselling model, my informant at Dream Dresser told me that the most popular model with women in the Los Angeles area in the last three years was *not* the classic vibrating cone designed for clitoral stimulation only. The most popular model was now the double-duty model that produced clitoral stimulation *and* penetration simultaneously. This new model is then the perfect companion to the version of female sexual pleasure portrayed in the majority of contemporary heterosexual porn tapes. Here is now the machine that 'finishes off' the female partner, that contributes to the bodily realisation of the fantasy on the screen, that makes the body do what the image can't exactly do all on its own. The problem with these double-duty vibrators that promise so much reality – the reality of the fantastic 'paroxysm' – however, is that they still stubbornly insist on penetration. These machines almost get it, but not quite. To the assertion that penetration produces the real thing, as feminists we need vehemently to respond, 'Close, but no cigar'.

(An earlier version of this article was delivered as a paper at the Visible Evidence VII Conference at UCLA, Department of Film and Television (August 1999) as well as at the Changing Frames Conference, Department of Film and TV, San Francisco State University (April 2000). This version was significantly influenced by conversations with Vivian Sobchack following the UCLA conference and I am indebted to her for confirming my interest in synaesthesia as an approach to sexualised looking. I want to thank Susan Mogul for giving me a copy of her feminist vibrator satire, *Take Off* (1974), which deserves an entire article.)

NOTES

1. See my 'Feminist Heterosexuality and Its Politically Incorrect Pleasures', *Critical Inquiry* 21, no. 1 (Winter 1995), pp. 382–410, for some background on the 80s' 'sex wars' and the debates within feminism that fill out this important moment.

2. For an overview (however popularised) of the subfield of feminist film criticism see M. G. Lord, 'Pornutopia: How Feminist Scholars Learned to Love Dirty Pictures', *Lingua Franca* April/May (1997), pp. 40–7. See Laura Kipnis, *Bound and Gagged: Pornography and the Politics of Fantasy in America* (Durham, NC: Duke University Press, 1999); Cindy Patton, 'Hegemony and Orgasm – or the Instability of Heterosexual Pornography', *Screen* 30, nos 1 and 2 (Spring 1989), pp. 100–13; Constance Penley, *NASA/Trek: Popular Science and Sex in America* (New York, NY: Verso, 1997); and works by Linda Williams.

3. Richard Dyer, 'Male Gay Porn: Coming to Terms', *Jump Cut: A Review of Contemporary Media* 30 (March, 1985), pp. 27–9.

4. Louis Althusser, 'Ideology and Ideological State Apparatuses (Notes towards an Investigation)' in *Lenin and Philosophy and Other Essays*, trans. Ben Brewster (London: New Left Books, 1971).

5. Michel Foucault, *The History of Sexuality*, Vol. I, Robert Hurley (trans.) (New York: Pantheon Books, 1978).

6. Linda Williams, *Hard Core: Power, Pleasure, and the 'Frenzy of the Visible'* (Berkeley: University of California Press, 1989). Actually, it was at a conference in Milwaukee in the late 70s that Williams first delivered the paper that introduced this concept into feminist film theory. It was later published as 'Film Body: An Implantation of Perversions', *Ciné-tracts*, no. 12 (Winter 1981), pp. 19–35, and reprinted in Philip Rosen (ed.), *Narrative, Apparatus, Ideology* (New York: Columbia University Press, 1986), and it became the basis of Chapter 2, 'Prehistory: The "Frenzy of the Visible" ' in *Hard Core*. Although Foucault's concept has been available to film scholars working on the pornographic image (most outside

France) for several decades and certainly through the Althusserian moment in the mid- to late 70s, the relation between 'implantation' and 'positioning' was never exactly probed.

7. Christian Metz, 'The Imaginary Signifier', *Screen* vol. 16 no. 2 (1975), pp. 14–76; Laura Mulvey, 'Visual Pleasure and Narrative Cinema', *Screen* vol. 16 no. 3 (1975), pp. 6–18.

8. Williams, *Hard Core,* pp. 45–6.

9. Ibid., p. 45.

10. Linda Williams, 'Corporealized Observers: Visual Pornographies and the 'Carnal Density of Vision" ', in Patrice Petro (ed.), *Fugitive Images: From Photography to Video* (Bloomington: Indiana University Press, 1995), p. 20.

11. The degree to which Williams has been influenced by Jonathan Crary's Foucauldian approach and his theorisation of the 'corporealization of vision' is clear in her introduction to her edited collection, *Viewing Positions: Ways of Seeing Film* (New Brunswick, NJ: Rutgers Unversity Press, 1994), pp. 6–7. His 'Modernizing Vision', reprinted there, is essentially an overview of the argument in the earlier *Techniques of the Observer: On Vision and Modernity in the Nineteenth Century* (Cambridge, MA: MIT Press, 1990). It would be interesting to consider the degree to which Crary's argument (which challenges to some degree some of the crucial assertions of 70s' film theory) has modified important paradigms within the field.

12. Williams, 'Corporealized Observers', p. 37.

13. Only after completing this essay did I read John Champagne's discussion of gay pornography, *The Ethics of Marginality: A New Approach to Gay Studies* (Minneapolis: University of Minnesota Press, 1995), which is extremely important for the ways in which it helps us to think through the differences between heterosexual and gay pornography. I realise that I have not touched upon these questions at all here. However, something that Champagne says about the discrepancies between 'really' coming and the assumptions of moving image pornography that you will come 'with the image' are relevant to my argument. 'Anyone,' he says, 'who has attempted to "get off" on pornography realizes that it is rare that one can manage to achieve orgasm at the moment of maximum arousal, because, unless one is watching on a video player with an extremely high-resolution pause feature, the image necessarily changes.' (p. 48)

14. Linda Williams, 'Film Bodies: Gender, Genre, and Excess', *Film Quarterly* vol. 44 no. 4 (Summer 1991).

15. Dyer, 'Male Gay Porn: Coming to Terms', p. 27.

16. See, for an update on these interests, Jane M. Gaines and Michael Renov (eds), 'Introduction: The Real Returns', in *Collecting Visible Evidence* (Minneapolis: University of Minnesota Press, 1999).

17. Williams, *Hard Core*, pp. 33, 49–50.

18. See Chris Straayer, *Deviant Eyes, Deviant Bodies: Sexual Re-orientations in Film and Video* (New York: Columbia University Press, 1996), pp. 244–9.

19. Rachel P. Maines, *The Technology of Orgasm: 'Hysteria,' the Vibrator, and Women's Sexual Satisfaction* (Baltimore, MD and London: Johns Hopkins University Press, 1999).

20. Ibid., p. 71.

21. Ibid., p. 97.

22. Ibid., p. 103.

23. Ibid., p. 104.

24. Ibid., p. 107.

25. Williams, *Hard Core*, pp. 49–50.

26. Ibid., p. 50.

27. Ibid., p. 91.

28. Ibid., pp. 112–14.

29. Ibid,. p. 101.

30. Maines, *The Technology of Orgasm*, p. 108.

31. Williams, *Hard Core*, p. 72, talks about how hard core promises to 'present evidence of the "thing" itself,' the 'thing' being an involuntary convulsion.

32. Elsewhere, I have compared the 'wobbliescope' aesthetic of the *cinéma vérité* camera to the penis: Jane Gaines, 'Lonely Boy and the *Vérité* of Sexuality', *Canadian Journal of Film Studies*, vol. 8 no. 1 (Autumn 1999), pp. 102–18. However, particularly in the hands of a woman, the *vérité* camera can have a much more remarkable prosthetic function. My best example from the contemporary period would be the camerawork of television star (*Baywatch*) Pamela Anderson Lee in the best-selling *Pam and Tommy Lee: Hardcore and Uncensored*. Originally produced for the internet market, the tape is ostensibly the uncut honeymoon footage shot by Lee and her then-husband, rock star Tommy Lee. The story that the tapes were stolen from a locked safe in their home contributed to the pornographic 'truth value' of these home movies. Later, the couple's legal battles with IEP (Internet Entertainment Provider) contributed to the illusion that the tapes were illicit, although it appears that Pam and Tommy had actually given IEP

the rights to internet exhibition although not videotape sales. Chuck Kleinhans, in 'Sex and Documentary: The Pamela Anderson/Tommy Lee Tape', paper presented at Visible Evidence VIII, University of Utrecht, Amsterdam, August, 2000, fills us in on the outcome of the court case which the couple lost. (They had commented on the case while on the Howard Stern radio show as Stern commented on it as he viewed it.) Importantly, Kleinhans argues that it is the 'small handheld video camera' that produces the sex scenes as 'up close and personal' and therefore pornographic.

33. Judith Butler, *Bodies That Matter: On the Discursive Limits of 'Sex'* (New York: Routledge, 1993), p. 5.

34. Williams, 'Corporealized Observers', p. 19.

35. Maines, *The Technology of Orgasm*, p. 110.

36. In conversation with John Perkinson, owner, Thee View (Wilmington, North Carolina), Durham, North Carolina, 28 February 2001.

37. Marshall McLuhan, *Understanding Media* (New York: McGraw Hill, 1964).

38. Anne Friedberg, 'The End of Cinema: Multimedia and Technological Change', in Christine Gledhill and Linda Williams (eds), *Reinventing Film Studies* (New York: Oxford University Press, 2000), p. 450.

39. Fredric Jameson, *Postmodernism, or the Cultural Logic of Late Capitalism* (Durham, NC: Duke University Press, 1991), p. 54.

40. Another example is the remarkable formulation of patriarchial cinema found in Laura Mulvey, 'Visual Pleasure and Narrative Cinema', pp. 6–18. Music theorists have proposed the concept of synaesthesia to explain how the connotations from one sign system can be exchanged for those in another, explaining how it is that the music track and the image track can so easily carry the same meanings when brought together in the motion picture.

41. Vivian Sobchack, *The Address of the Eye: A Phenomenology of Film Experience* (Princeton, NJ: Princeton University Press, 1992); 'The Scene of the Screen: Envisioning Cinematic and Electronic "Presence"', in John Thornton Caldwell (ed.), *Electronic Media and Technoculture* (New Brunswick, NJ: Rutgers University Press, 2000); 'Nostalgia for a Digital Object: Regrets on the Quickening of QuickTime', unpublished paper, 1999; and 'What My Fingers Knew: The Cinesthetic Subject, or Vision in the Flesh', unpublished paper, talk delivered at Duke University, September 2001.

42. Sobchack, 'The Scene of the Screen', p. 151.

43. Jameson, *Postmodernism*, p. 16.

44. Sobchack, 'The Scene of the Screen', p. 152

45. Ibid., p.153.

46. If we look closely, Jameson's thinking is not necessarily as pessimistic as that of others who advance the postmodern diagnosis. To give an interesting example of how he holds out hope: 'As for that reality itself, however – the as yet untheorized original space of some new 'world system' of multinational or late capitalism, a space whose negative or baleful aspects are only too obvious – the dialectic requires us to hold equally to a positive or 'progressive' evaluation of its emergence, as Marx did for the world market as the horizon of national economies, or as Lenin did for the older imperialist global network' (*Postmodernism*, p. 50).

I have situated Jameson in relation to the cultural studies methodology that looks at the progressive-reactionary doubleness of the popular and the origins of this theorisation in the Frankfurt School in my 'Dream/Factory', in Christine Gledhill and Linda Williams, *Reinventing Film Studies*. 'Prognosis negative' is a reference to the Bette Davis role in *Dark Victory* (1939).

47. Sobchack, 'Nostalgia for a Digital Object', p. 10.

48. Ibid., p. 5.

49. Ibid., p. 8.

50. Ibid., p. 20. My own interest is in the indefatigable repetition of internet pornography, taken to the degree where it is possible to see that, as in Deleuze, 'In every respect, repetition is a transgression.' See Gilles Deleuze, *Difference and Repetition*, trans. Paul Patton (New York: Columbia University Press, 1994), p. 3.

51. Sobchack, 'Nostalgia for a Digital Object', p. 15.

52. Lev Manovich, 'Towards an Archaeology of the Computer Screen', in Thomas Elsaesser and Kay Hoffman (eds), *Cinema Futures: Cain, Abel or Cable?: The Screen Arts in the Digital Age* (Amsterdam: Amsterdam University Press, 1998), p. 31.

53. Alex Galloway, 'Protocol, or, How Control Exists after Decentralization', PhD dissertation, in progress.

54. My first encounter with the possibilities of synaesthesia as a productive starting point for understanding the reception of film and television was in Andrew Goodwin's important book on music video. Although synaesthesia has its wider usage as medical terminology as applied to clinical cases of

neurological disorder, music theorists have utilised the concept to explain how the connotations from one sign system can be exchanged for those in another, explaining how it is that the music track and the image track can so easily carry the same meanings when brought together. See Andrew Goodwin, *Dancing in the Distraction Factory: Music Television and Popular Culture* (Minneapolis: University of Minnesota Press, 1992), p. 50.

55. Sobchack, *The Address of the Eye*, p. 76.

56. Maurice Merleau-Ponty, *The Visible and the Invisible* (Evanston, IL: Northwestern University Press, 1968), p. 146.

57. Ibid., p. 144.

58. The term is from Kendall Thomas who argues that sexuality is always 'racialised' and race is always 'sexuated'. See Kendall Thomas, ' "Ain't Nothin' Like the Real Thing": Black Masculinity, Gay Sexuality, and the Jargon of Authenticity', in Wahneema Lubiano (ed.), *The House That Race Built* (New York: Random House, 1998), p. 130.

59. Elizabeth Cowie, *Women and Representation: Cinema and Psychoanalysis* (Minneapolis: University of Minnesota Press, 1997), p. 133.

4   There's No Place Like Home: Further Developments on the Domestic Front

Jane Juffer

I despise this stuff – some of it is really raunchy. But the fact is that an awful lot of people here in Utah County are paying to look at porn. What that says to me is that we're normal.

Attorney Randy Spencer, upon successfully defending a Provo, Utah, video store owner from charges of selling obscene material in one of the most conservative areas in the US.[1]

If the people who make and sell pornography are this 'normal' – and varied – might not the audience be, too? It can't be merely the uneducated and unemployed who shell out the $10 billion. And it isn't. Porn moguls describe a market as diverse as America.

New York Times Magazine reporter Frank Rich, upon completing an investigation into the porn industry.[2]

Pornography consumption, it would seem, is becoming a 'normal' practice in the US, an accepted part of home entertainment, a domestic technology.

This normalisation depends in part on porn's circulation via new media technologies such as satellite television, DVDs and the internet, all of which rely on the home as a primary site of consumption. And porn's imbrication with domestic sites is intimately connected to its integration in the global economy; porn in the US is at least a $10 billion business engaged in by some of the biggest and most 'reputable' companies. General Motors, the world's largest company, makes more money on graphic sex films through its DirecTV subsidiary every year than Larry Flynt makes on his *Hustler* empire. AT&T Corp., the nation's biggest communications company, offers a hard-core sex channel called the Hot Network through its broadband cable service and owns a company that sells sex videos to nearly a million hotel rooms. Time Warner, EchoStar Communica-

tions, Marriott International, Hilton, OnCommand and Rupert Murdoch's News Corp. all have significant stakes in the porn industry.[3]

Increasingly, corporations legitimate porn through the philosophy that undergirds the free market: the self-regulated individual defined by consumer choice. Like any commodity, porn is a choice, which, if made responsibly, need not indicate moral depravity nor require governmental regulation. A spokesperson for AT&T Broadband defends the company's involvement in porn: 'We call it choice and control. Basically, you use your remote to block out any programming you don't want. But if you want it, we offer a wide range of programming that is available in the market we're in'.[4] And a representative for EchoStar, which sells adult pay-per-view through its DishNetwork satellite division, says 'we have something for everybody, from Irish hurling to cricket. Adult is there if you want it.'[5]

Who benefits from the normalisation of porn viewing practices within the space of the home? Who represents the consumer norm, and to what degree has the proliferation of porn within the routines of everyday life relied on a normalisation of sex itself to fit an industry image of the self-regulating individual? At the risk of generalising, it seems accurate to say that most porn now available on television through cable and satellite assumes a heterosexual, coupled audience, and that it remains informed by the history of catering mainly to men, although this has definitely been cut through with a desire to appeal to the female partner as well. Gay and lesbian porn is not a featured part of the television menu; interestingly, the *New York Times Magazine* reporter quoted above, shortly after noting the diversity of porn consumers, unreflexively comments that gay male porn is still a 'niche market' that 'hasn't cracked the national mass market of TV'. The hard-core video and DVD market, as distinct from less explicit cable and satellite fare, is in fact more diverse, catering to all kinds of desires, but even that aspect of the industry is seeking a 'cleaner image'. Anticipating a crackdown on porn by conservative US Attorney General John Ashcroft, some of the major porn outlets issued guidelines to producers and directors in early 2001 that encourage a ban on certain practices in hard-core porn, including male/male penetration, bisexual encounters, and the nearly standard facial money shot, in which the male performer ejaculates on the face of the female performer.[6]

In some ways, then, the mainstreaming of porn is predicated on the very norms many feminists have argued against: heterosexual, middle-class, fairly conventional sex. Yet we can't simply dismiss the fact that many porn texts that explicitly represent women's sexual pleasures are now widely available in the home, on television, and that one doesn't even need to risk the embarrassment of being seen renting a porn video at the local store in order to receive instructions in the art of cunnilingus. As Linda Williams noted in her 1989 *Hard Core*, porn is one of the few genres that doesn't punish women for being sexual, and with the recognition of women's consumer power, the focus on female pleasure has generally intensified.[7] Hence, while criticising the norms that marginalise some sexual practices, we should also be wary of judging desires and in the process establishing a standard of transgressive sex against which all other forms of sex are castigated as vanilla, straight, co-opted. The normalisation of porn presents some interesting possibilities for the rearticulation of such family values as marriage and asexual mothering, for example. And it's sometimes hard to distinguish between practices that porn producers follow in order to avoid regulatory ire and practices that appeal to some women who have avoided porn because they perceive it to be a masculine genre that demeans women. The Hot Network, for example, says that it will not show violence, non-consensual sex, drug use, forced bondage, and sex with minors.

The challenge, thus, in the face of this complex conjuncture of events shaping pornography and the home is to acknowledge the possibilities of the 'mainstreaming' of porn yet also reject the corporate notion of the home as a site of individual, private choices. Rather, we must see the home as connected to other sites, asking how women's mobility between the home, work, errands and leisure shapes the pos-

sibilities for porn consumption. This move is especially critical now because women arrive at this moment of 'household choice' without having passed through a period in which public spaces catered to women as porn consumers. Public sites of access and representation, such as bookstores, theatres and video stores, help determine whether women feel comfortable consuming sexually explicit texts precisely because these sites (could) provide public legitimation of women's sexual desires. Hence, whether women feel comfortable watching porn on pay-per-view will in some ways be determined by broader notions of whether it's considered acceptable for women to consume porn. And it's partially because of the historical articulation of porn to men that we must refuse the idea that the normalisation of some porn will automatically produce equal access for women. Attention must be paid to the various marketing distinctions that distance some sexually explicit materials from porn – categories such as women's erotica, sex stores for women, and cable/video erotica for women. Although some feminists have critiqued the erotica/porn distinction as one engaged in the essentialisation of desire, I argue that the categories serve mainly to increase access in a manner not always tied to content; texts sold under the rubric 'erotica' may be just as explicit as some pornography yet appear more 'women-friendly' because they are 'not pornography'.

Understanding household consumption requires a shift in the terms of the porn debates, which have been mainly defined by standards of liberation and oppression, as I will discuss below. I'm interested in porn consumption as a mundane practice determined within the routines of everyday life; I propose a politics of access and mobility, which requires one to consider how porn is shaped by government and industry policy, at particular sites – issues largely ignored in the polemics of the anti-porn/pro-sex debates. In focusing on the mundane, I mean not to negate or disregard the excesses of the erotic but rather to inquire into how the conditions of everyday life shape the times and places where and when erotic practices can occur. This emphasis shifts the study of porn from the reading of sexual fantasies and the judgment of correct desires to what Foucault calls the 'practices of freedom':

Isn't the problem rather that of defining the practices of freedom by which one could define what is sexual pleasure and erotic, amorous and passionate relationships with others? The ethical problem of the definition of practices of freedom, it seems to me, is much more important than the rather repetitive affirmation that sexuality or desire must be liberated.[8]

Accordingly, I am interested not in what women experience when they consume porn but rather in the routes/paths they have to travel in order to find the time and space for consumption. I consider three sites in their relation to the home – women-friendly sex stores (and their catalogues and internet sites), Borders and Barnes and Noble bookstores, and Blockbuster video stores. All represent, in different ways, the mainstreaming of porn for women – the potential transformation of the domestic sphere into one of sexual pleasure. These three sites are, to varying degrees, sites where sex is commodified, but not in an always predictable fashion. Furthermore, they are sites that intersect with many women's everyday lives; in other words, they are convenient, an important criteria to consider in the pursuit of practices of freedom. However, access across groups of women is still uneven, dependent on things such as income and legal status; the regulation of women's identity in the home via government policy has been and continues to be, for some women, an important factor in gauging women's practices of sexual freedom.

THE PORNOGRAPHY DEBATES
Debates on sex and sexuality, often focalised through pornography, dominated feminism for much of the 80s and into the 90s, and while many useful issues were raised, very little of the discussion on porn focused on women's *access* to sexually explicit texts within the space of the home. Too often, the debates were polarised around an oppression/liberation binary, with anti-porn feminists arguing that women are always already porn's victims, and 'pro-sexuality feminists' arguing, although much more complexly, that porn is open to multiple interpretations, and that women can appropriate pornographic texts, producing subversive readings that indicate sexual agency. Pro-sexuality feminists also celebrated artists like Annie Sprinkle, a transgressive poster child for the 90s, who defied the notion that women's sexuality should be contained to the private sphere. Without dismissing the importance of work on

transgressive sex, I argue that we need a more structured theory of agency, one that sees the home as an important rather than a co-opted or bourgeois site; we must not cede the territory of the home to politicians or CEOs nor dismiss texts that try to fit within conceptions of domesticity just because they do not correspond to academic assumptions about what constitutes a transgressive text. Women are best served when we focus on access to a wide variety of texts within the routines of everyday life, even if some of those texts seem quite limited in their challenge to dominant norms shaping sex and gender. What we need, then, is a theory of agency predicated not on transcendence of material conditions in pursuit of liberation, but rather one of structured mobility between various sites. As Lawrence Grossberg argues, agency is constituted by 'relations of participation and access, the possibilities of moving into particular sites of activity and power, and of belonging to them in such a way as to be able to actually enact their powers'.[9] How, then, are women able to move into positions of the production and consumption of porn? None of the positions that have dominated the porn debates have adequately explored porn access through a structured definition of agency, as I go on to discuss.

THERE'S NO PLACE LIKE HOME
Much government discourse in the 20th century tried to establish pornography as a threat to the home in order to fix women in their proper roles as wives and mothers in need of patriarchal protection. This tendency has in some ways been exacerbated with the growth of new technologies, which has produced a nostalgic anxiety for a more settled time, when public and private spaces could be more easily delineated. The attempts to fix the meaning of home along some traditional notion of family suggest a conservative defensiveness and insecurity, what Doreen Massey calls 'a desire for fixity and security of identity in the middle of all the movement and change' – a desire that is fulfilled by 'delving into the past' in a search to give home 'an unproblematical identity constructed out of an introverted, inward-looking history based on delving into the past for internalized origins'.[10] If agency, as I describe above, is a question of movement into positions of access, government legislation and discourse on porn have historically tried to ensure women's victim status in

order to limit their mobility outside the home and thus their access to porn; they also have defined women's tasks within the home so as not to acknowledge the intersections of non-procreative sexuality and other domestic roles.

Legal decisions in both Great Britain and the US from the mid-19th century until the 1960s often relied on the standard of the 'little girl' who needed protection from porn's public presences. The 50s marked the gradual awareness of the need to recognise women's particular pleasures, facilitated in part by the Kinsey report of 1953, which stressed the importance of the clitoral orgasm and suggested that women weren't fulfilled through traditional intercourse. In the 60s, legal decisions that restricted the category of 'the obscene', the women's and gay rights' movements, the birth control pill, and the growth of the porn industry all contributed to an environment in which women were acknowledged as sexual beings and, by the early 70s, as consumers of porn. Porn's increasing public presences and legitimation had the potential to redefine domestic relations; as Linda Williams notes, there was a moment in the 70s when pornography became a household word and a government commission (the Lockhart report, 1973) actually endorsed the consumption of porn as a 'healthy' practice.

It was a relatively brief moment, however, and in some areas of the country, the proliferation of porn only increased attempts to restrict its dissemination. Many cities deployed zoning regulations that limited porn to certain areas that were far removed from 'family' zones that had homes, churches and schools. And during the 80s, a new presidential-appointed investigation into porn, popularly known as the Meese Commission, returned to the standard of woman-as-little-girl in need of protection from porn's pervasiveness. In the attempt to quash porn's public presences, the conservative commission found a group of strange bedfellows in anti-porn feminists Andrea Dworkin and Catharine MacKinnon. Yet the rhetoric of the porn in public threat was belied by the commission's continual infantilising of women, which revealed that the commission was equally if not more concerned with using porn as a way to restore patriarchal relations in *both* public and private. For example, the commission argued that the porn industry exploited young women: 'perhaps the single most common feature of models is their rela-

tive, and in the vast majority of cases, absolute youth.'[11] The commission then used this concern to homogenise all women as victims. After hearing anecdotal evidence from selected porn performers, the commission conflated their lives with the lives of all women:

> the evidence before us suggests that a substantial minority of women will at some time in their lives be asked to pose for or perform in sexually explicit materials . . . if our society's appetite for sexually explicit materials continues to grow, or even if it remains at current levels, the decision whether to have sex in front of a camera will confront thousands of Americans.[12]

Women – many of whom are either porn performers or potential performers – thus need the protection of the state, justifying regulation that is purportedly about cleaning up the public sphere but actually works to legitimate traditional gendered relations premised on women's sexual purity.

With the explosion of the video market in the 80s and the subsequent growth of new technologies in the home, regulation has had to shift correspondingly. Conservatives have found themselves in an awkward position: how to regulate the home, the site of so-called privacy; when pornography enters via cable wires, satellite dishes and the internet, who should be held responsible? This has led to an intensification of rhetoric focusing on pornography's threat to children on the internet, which also reinforces the role of mothers as guardians of the domestic sphere. Consider, for example, the historical shift between the Meese Commission's focus on women as victims and the 1995 debates on the Communications Decency Act of the Telecommunications Act. In debates leading to passage of the CDA,[13] the regulatory rhetoric was no longer women as porn victims but rather mothers as moral guardians of a home under siege by internet porn. Although there is an overlap between the categories 'victim' and 'moral guardian', the new fear about the internet focused on children. This fear was fuelled by an infamous Carnegie–Mellon study – later largely discredited – released in spring 1995 that purported to document the widespread use of internet porn; the cover of *Newsweek* featured a terrified child, with the headline 'Cyberporn: A New Study Shows How Pervasive and Wild It Really Is. Can we protect our kids – and free speech?' Senator James Exon, the primary sponsor of the CDA, was one of several who recounted during congressional debate anecdotes about mothers horrified by the discovery of how easily their children could find internet porn, and reasserting their desire to police computer technology for the benefit of the entire household.

New technologies of porn have produced similarly contradictory regulatory impulses in Britain. In November 2000, for example, the president of the British Board of Film Censors, Andreas Whittam-Smith, issued a press release calling for an increase in the number of licensed sex shops in Britain. Apparently, Whittam-Smith was convinced that the closure of sex shops in Britain (there are now only 65, compared to about 400 in 1982), had contributed to growing demand for hard-core porn via the internet and satellite television. Clearly, Whittam-Smith believes that porn is easier to regulate when it's out in public. At the same time, ironically, Home Secretary Jack Straw announced that the government was 'contemplating a new criminal offence for failure to take reasonable care to prevent a child from watching a "Restricted 18" classification film'.[14]

Indeed, despite the growing recognition of porn as a profitable, mainstream business, there will always be a conservative political component that tries to reestablish a binary between the home and porn. Furthermore, government policy has never ceased to regulate groups of women whose sexuality is suspect because of their economic dependency. For example, at roughly the same time that the US Congress was debating porn on the internet, valorising middle-class mothers as moral guardians, it was pushing through the so-called 1996 Personal Responsibility Act, which demonised low-income mothers as threats to the moral fabric of the nation. The PRA, which abolished the nation's sixty-year commitment to helping poor families via the Aid to Families with Dependent Children programme, gained support in part because of the representation of welfare mothers as unable to control their sexuality and content to rely on the state for support rather than find a husband (any husband, it would seem) to support them.[15]

So-called reforms in immigration policy are often fuelled by a rhetoric similar to welfare propaganda: undocumented women, especially from Latin America, are said to come to the US by the hordes to have their babies be born as citizens and then take advantage of social services. As with welfare reform, immigration 'reform' unfairly penalises immigrant women based on the myth that they can't control their sexuality and hence won't be able to become 'self sufficient'.[16] Welfare reform is linked to immigration policy in an insidious manner, leaving the most vulnerable of women – single immigrant mothers, many of whom are undocumented, without recourse to public assistance for their children: almost half of the projected $54 billion savings in welfare cuts was achieved by restrictions on immigrants.

The combined effect of immigration and welfare policy is to sanction as good mothers middle- and upper-class women who are either part of a nuclear family or who prove their worth through economic self-sufficiency and moral respectability; indeed, in this discourse, it is impossible to be morally respectable without being economically self-sufficient. Working-class and immigrant mothers find it much more difficult to join this class; they are assumed to be unworthy because of the inability to control their sexuality and their subsequent dependency on the state. Access to and consumption of sexually explicit materials within the routines of everyday life seems remote for women in these economic conditions; the stigma associated with sexuality that is not a choice also reinforces the binary through which other women frame their consumption of erotica/porn as another aspect of self-sufficiency, a route to 'healthier' personhood.

THE ANTI-PORN FEMINISTS

In many respects, the anti-porn feminists have produced a victim discourse similar to the government discourse, often in collusion. As critics have noted, MacKinnon, Dworkin and other anti-porn feminists are committed to an ahistorical politics of victimiser and victimised, in which men and women are fated to play out the roles to which porn has the sole power to confine them. Their position is not only ahistorical but also placeless: porn exists everywhere, and everywhere manifests itself in the same manner; from cyberspace to Bosnia, women and children everywhere are destined to be its victims, without ever achieving access to positions that might help them reconfigure porn's meanings and uses. The Meese Commission and other similar bodies used the porn-is-pervasive argument to justify the need to draw boundaries around a threatened home; the anti-porn feminists claim that porn is pervasive in order to justify their claim that porn knows no boundaries and thus neither should their legal attempts to declare a huge category of texts to be violations of women's civil rights.

In this tradition, the different media technologies through which porn travels are irrelevant. As Mac-Kinnon says about the Carnegie–Mellon internet porn study: 'like pornography everywhere else, before and after it becomes images in cyberspace, it is women's lives.'[17] Furthermore, porn consumers have no power to interpret texts differently; the production of porn, which is always assumed to exploit women (no mention is ever made of male porn performers), is conflated with the consumption of porn, in one seamless, oppressive effect.

Questions of agency defined in terms of access, mobility and the capacity to move into positions of power so as to be able to produce, distribute or gain access to pornography of choice are rendered moot because pornography is already everywhere, always available to everyone – this argument actually limits access. Not surprisingly, one effect of their legal efforts has been the confiscation of gay and lesbian porn, including one of Andrea Dworkin's own lesbian novels, which was seized in Toronto after Canada passed anti-porn legislation modelled on the Dworkin–MacKinnon ordinance that was ruled unconstitutional.

PORN AND TRANSGRESSION

If the above positions deny women any agency in relation to porn, pro-sexuality feminists have perhaps overcompensated in their articulations of porn's ambiguities and in their reluctance to situate porn or women in relation to porn because the governmental and anti-porn positions have been so confident about porn's effects. As Ann Snitow writes, 'Since one of the faultlines of anti-pornography theory is its misplaced concreteness, I can't be correspondingly specific about how I would go about working to alter the often limited, rapacious or dreary sexual culture in which women – and also men – now live.'[18] In place of 'concrete analysis,' pro-sexuality feminists have often invoked the pleasures of transgressive readings, a strategy characterised in the collection *Caught Looking* from which Snitow's essay comes. This collection reprints a wide variety of porno-graphic images without direct commentary, inviting readers to take pleasure in their own interpretations. Although I certainly don't want to deny this realm of individual pleasure, I also want to argue that asserting it alone does not do much towards transforming the conditions that shape the possibilities for consumption. In other words, it counters the victim status posited by anti-porn feminists and conservatives by asserting an agency that is based on the powers of the individual; furthermore, the agency is usually connected to a kind of transgression – either the transgressive text or the act of transgressing mainstream texts. In this context, agent status is guaranteed if the agent's identity is defined in terms of her ability to evade confinement to any place, able to freely transgress boundaries of public and private.

Certainly, not all pro-sexuality feminists have pursued transgression; Linda Williams's *Hard Core*, for example, addresses the historical conditions of the development of the genre of hard-core porn – although she relies mainly on textual analysis and rarely mentions sites of porn production or consumption. Aspects of Laura Kipnis's 1996 *Bound and Gagged* are site-specific – but she constantly returns to the psychological value of transgression. Pornography is worthy of study because of its ability to reveal the insecurities of our collective national psyche: 'Pornography provides a realm of transgression that is, in effect, a counteraesthetics to dominant norms for bodies, sexualities, and desire itself.'[19] In three volumes of pro-sexuality essays on porn published in the early 90s – when publishing on feminism and porn peaked – only a handful of the forty-three total essays even mention the proliferation of erotic texts, both print and video, aimed at women produced in the previous twenty years, tending instead towards essays on the transgressive work of artists such as Robert Mapplethorpe and Annie Sprinkle.[20] On the latter, Chris Straayer argues that in Sprinkle's performances, 'pornography's naturalist philosophy spreads outward, merging private and public realms, simultaneously intensifying and diffusing the pornographic sensibility'.[21] Here, pornography *erases* space – the transgressive text qualifies as such because it disrespects boundaries that have confined female sexuality. Such a celebration of transgression ignores the importance of locating porn, resulting in a largely placeless model of agency that does not challenge conservative attempts to inhibit access through freezing women in the home, nor corporate invocations of the self-regulating home.

It's critical to analyse both public and private spaces, in their relation to each other. The intense privatisation of porn within the space of the home necessitates a rejection of the idea that the home is indeed private; we must theorise women's ability to travel outside the home to sites of pleasure and work in order to understand the possibilities of porn consumption within the home. Access is still a matter of identity; women's access to porn is different from men's, and poor people's access is different from middle-class people's, etc. Yet this identity is not essential but rather a product of movement between places. As Grossberg puts it, 'identities exist in the structural possibilities of mobility and stability'.[22] In this view, 'space is no longer the empty gaps between places – it has a dimensionality of its own that is constituted by the trajectories that move across it'.[23] Women's identity in relation to porn and the home is formed through their paths between sites of work, leisure and home, and within the home, by their movement from room to room, engaged in cleaning, cooking, childcare and leisure activities. Among these sites of leisure both inside and outside the home are sources of sexually explicit texts and toys, including catalogues, internet sites, bookstores, and video stores. These sites are inevitably part of the marketplace and 'normalisation', but they also contradict the assumption that sites of easy access offer only predictable representations of sex.

VIBRATORS AS DOMESTIC APPLIANCE

Vibrators have held a vexed position as a domestic/sexual technology. Since their first use in the US in the late 1800s, vibrators have been applauded for their efficiency within household economies. Doctors considered massage a valid treatment for hysteria[24] and found that vibrators made house calls more expedient. By the early 1900s, vibrators were advertised quite widely as home appliances that could improve health, induce relaxation and polish the furniture! One 1906 invention 'could be used on the face, head, and body'; and, 'in its larger or heavier forms for rubbing down and polishing all kinds of woodwork, furniture, &c., that are given a rubbed or polished finish'.[25] Sears, Roebuck's *Electrical Goods*

catalogue for 1918 advertised, under the headline 'Aids that Every Woman Appreciates', a 'vibrator attachment for a home motor that also drove attachments for churning, mixing, beating, grinding, buffing, and operating a fan'.[26] This shift from the medicalisation of the vibrator to its status as household appliance corresponded with the shift from women as sickly creatures (who could not use their vibrators on their own) to managers of efficient households (who could use vibrators under the auspices of housework); domestic work was professionalised and the field of home economics developed in the early 20th century.

Vibrators did not begin to acquire some mainstream legitimacy as sexual technologies until the 1960s, with the proliferation of information about women's bodies and pleasures (especially clitoral orgasm), ranging across sexology, sex therapy and various strands of feminism. It's important to note here that although the vibrator is popularly imagined as phallic, it comes in different shapes with various attachments and serves different stimulatory purposes, certainly not just penetration. However, the phallic associations of the vibrator caused much anxiety in both heterosexual and lesbian communities, the former because the vibrator promised women self-sufficiency and the latter because the vibrator suggested a kind of false consciousness, a desire to be penetrated. Noted sex therapist Helen Kaplan said in a 1976 article, 'In therapy we suggest the vibrator as a last resort, and if your partner objects, you should not use it.'[27] Mainstream women's magazines worried about the vibrator as a potentially addictive machine, raising the spectre of dirty homes and neglected children; writer Claire Safran warns in *Redbook*, 'Reports are that over the course of an hour or so a woman can have as many as 50 consecutive orgasms using the machine.'[28] Even by 1980, in an *Esquire* article documenting the decade-long growth in vibrator sales, writer Mimi Swartz inquires, 'Has the vibrator become a sort of microwave oven of the bedroom, a fast, efficient means of getting sexual pleasure? Is the most efficient orgasm the best orgasm? Is the bedroom really the place for a time-saving device?'[29] Furthermore, some critics lamented the commodification of natural sex through a machine; anthropologist Margaret Mead, quoted in Safran's *Redbook* article, said, 'Americans seem to prefer having machines to do everything. We have invited mechanical gadgets to substitute for what is natural. Machines alienate people from their bodies and from their emotions.'[30]

Fear of vibrator as technology has dissipated over the course of the 80s and 90s – perhaps because, as it turns out, few women have chosen vibrators over partners; concerns about more 'threatening' technologies such as the computer have even abated over the last few years. Perhaps as men and women share access to technologies such as the VCR and computer (in some households, at least), the threat of woman as cyborg declines. However, a significant percentage of women in several sexological studies in the 90s still report guilt about masturbation, suggesting that buying a vibrator in a sex store may not be the easiest thing to do. Furthermore, many women simply don't have access to the women-friendly sex stores that have sprung up in various locations: Good Vibrations in San Francisco and Berkeley, Eve's Garden in New York, the Ann Summers chain in Britain, to name a few.

Many of these stores, however, have on-line sites and mail-order catalogues, and this introduces an important link between the technology of the vibrator and the technology of the computer. Shopping for vibrators and other sex toys as well as getting information about the body and safe sex on the internet represents a virtual link between private and public spheres; it's a kind of sexual mobility that recognises women's more limited physical mobility outside the home (you especially can't go to a porn video store with children) and potentially connects women to a virtual community of support. Women are still positioned as the primary household consumers – continuing the long history of radio and television assumptions about women at home – but this time, the shopping is for their own masturbatory pleasures – for the production of orgasms. Furthermore, many women-friendly sites usually do not play on women's insecurities about beauty and body type, and they don't suggest that vibrator usage should ultimately lead to a better sex life with your partner. Some advertising acknowledges the interplay of everyday routines with sexual pleasure. One Good Vibrations catalogue, for example, is organised around the theme 'A Day of Erotic Pleasure': 'Instead of hitting the snooze button on your alarm clock, why not reach for a vibrator instead? Meet your lunch date for an afternoon quickie or attend your

next staff meeting wearing one of our quietly vibrating toys,' says the opening page. The rest of the catalogue features toys for different times of the day: a butt plug for the long commute, a set of three Black Lace novels to read on the subway, the Auto Arouser vibrator that plugs into the cigarette lighter of a car. And the Orbit is a remote-controlled vibrating egg that 'allows you to tickle your lover's fancy from across a crowded room'.

In some contrast to Good Vibrations, Ann Summers, the British chain of sex stores for women owned by Gold Group International, focuses less on women's mobility and autonomy and more on women's identity at home, as part of a heterosexual couple. Owner Jacqueline Gold has been interviewed saying that vibrators are great sex toys for couples. In her autobiography (interestingly titled *Good Vibrations*), she relates an anecdote about a man who wouldn't let his wife go into one of their shops to buy a vibrator for fear she wouldn't need his services any longer. That's no longer the case, Gold says, 'We find that people are buying them today to have fun with together – not as a replacement.'[31] Gold is featured on the Ann Summers' website in various poses in different rooms of her luxurious home; the company also features a variation on the Tupperware home party, employing women to sell lingerie and toys in the home. Like a more explicit version of the US-based lingerie chain, Victoria's Secret, Ann Summers relies on heteronormative assumptions about the home and sex, even as it expands them to emphasise women's pleasures. For the reasons stated above, I want to avoid judgments here about which texts or toys are more transgressive. However, it's also important to note that Ann Summers and Victoria's Secret achieve mainstream legitimacy for sex toys and lingerie because of their coincidence with heteronormativity, whiteness, and fairly conventional standards of female attractiveness.[32] Precisely because of this intersection with normative standards, both catalogues present interesting possibilities for rearticulations; for example, women who feel comfortable ordering a vibrator from Ann Summers because it seems 'normal' may then use the vibrator in 'non-normative' fashion.

SUPERSTORES AND SEX

In her introduction to the first volume of *Herotica: A Collection of Women's Erotic Fiction*, published by the feminist collective Down There Press in 1988, Susie Bright described the writers as 'pioneers' in 'putting women's sexuality into public consciousness'. She added, 'With any luck, this anthology will find its place not only under the bed but on a few coffee tables and in a few libraries as well.'[33] A feature story on Bright in the January/February issue of *Book* magazine showed how successful Bright has been in using the written word to make women's sexuality public. In a full page colour photo, Bright is seated on a bench on what appears to be any main street in America. Wearing black fishnet hose, red boots and a short skirt, Bright holds a copy of Pat Califia's *Public Sex: The Culture of Radical Sex*, and, peering over her glasses, smiles broadly at the camera. Next to her on the bench, two androgynous people kiss passionately, and peering over Bright's shoulder, engrossed in the book, are three rather average-looking men. The article itself is an advertisement for Bright's new book, *How to Write a Dirty Story*. Following Bright and her eleven-year-old daughter through the routines of their everyday life – the supermarket aisles as Bright picks out melons, their Victorian house, the living room as Bright sits down to knit – the writer makes Bright appear exotic and interesting precisely because she combines the everyday with the erotic, the reputation as 'America's ranking connoisseur of sex, porn, and freedom of physical expression' with being an ordinary mom.[34]

Not too ordinary, though. If it has now become acceptable for a mother in fishnet hose to read *Public Sex* in public and advise the public on how to write a dirty story, then what is needed to still distinguish 'erotica' from 'porn' is what has always made 'women's erotica' distinct from porn – a literary pedigree. In featuring Bright, *Book* magazine, which Barnes and Noble customers receive at home upon subscribing to their Readers' Advantage club, helps produce the distinctiveness of the literary, and by linking sex to the literary, Barnes and Noble both benefits from the explosion of interest in porn and marks a distinction from the 'cruder, less artistic' forms of porn. And although Bright no longer links her work to women's identity, the last twenty years have seen a veritable explosion in identity erotica defined by gender, sexuality, race, ethnicity, even religion, spurred in part by the ongoing *Herotica* series, now edited by Marcy Sheiner, who also edits another series, *Best Women's Erotica*. Even the erotica marketed specifically as

'women's erotica' is wide ranging in its representations of desire, including married straight couples, lesbian couples, group sex and almost everything else one might imagine. The category of 'women's erotica' has become – or perhaps it always was – mainly a marketing category, a means of selling explicit literary texts to women who are attracted to the distancing from porn garnered via both the rubrics 'women' and 'erotica'. This double protection has made literary erotica one of the more explicit and varied genres for women that is also relatively cheap and available at many bookstores.

Barnes and Noble is a study in the contradictions of an aesthetic discourse that maintains a cultural purchase even as it seeks a wide audience. The bookstores with their indoor cafés function as quasi-public sphere coffee houses, increasing access to books even as the company puts independent stores out of business. Barnes and Noble attaches middle-brow cultural capital to the practice of reading – 'great literature,' that is. In the café where 'Starbucks coffee is proudly sold', one sips lattes surrounded by drawings of T. S. Eliot, Virginia Woolf, James Joyce and other canonical cronies (sadly, no Anaïs Nin or Pauline Reage). Discriminating taste in coffee complements literary taste. Large comfortable couches and chairs are scattered throughout the store; unlike the more low-brow B. Dalton stores in shopping malls, the superstores are for people of leisure and hence intellect. 'Canonical' also encompasses the *New York Times* bestseller list; books that make this indicator of literary value are discounted 30 per cent. Literary value is diffused throughout the store; the genre of women's romance novels, for example, is elevated above the status it achieves at the supermarket by virtue of its shared space with 'high culture' novels, history and art books.

The superstores bring this cultural capital into line with community values – counteracting the image of the large chain with local involvement. Both stores regularly sponsor appearances by local authors and artists, reading groups, children's story hours and other events with community tie-ins. They are simultaneously cosmopolitan and local, literary and popular, leisurely and expedient. In terms, then, of women's access to erotica, the superstores represent a safe space: large stores, easily accessible, with events for children, and aesthetic legitimation for any purchase. It is perhaps one of the few places where a mother can purchase a volume of explicit S/M fantasies for between $8 and $12 and the latest book in the Harry Potter series without feeling like a 'bad mom'.

The categorisation of erotica differs between the stores; Barnes and Noble stocks erotica in three sections: literary anthologies, sexuality and gay and lesbian literature; Borders adds to those possibilities a fourth section directly marked 'Erotica', usually next to the literature section. A wide variety of texts is available at both stores, although Borders clearly has the more explicit commitment to stocking erotica and making it easily accessible (however, for some women, going to the 'Erotica' section may be more embarrassing than simply perusing the 'Literary Anthology' section). Anthologies by major publishing houses, such as Bright's *Best American Erotica*, as well as books by independent houses, such as Masquerade Books, Cleis Press, and Carroll and Graf, are available, representing different kinds of fantasies and levels of explicitness. Because of the legal history that has more often granted legitimacy to print ('the literary') than film (more often 'the pornographic'), these mainstream bookstores fear no legal consequences for selling even the most hard-core fantasies.[35] Borders, for example, carries a series titled 'X Rated', published by the 'X Libris' division of Little, Brown, which features explicit covers such as the one on *Private Acts*, of a naked woman, breasts exposed, with hands cuffed behind her back.

These erotic books travel easily, much easier than adult videos – especially in a bag adorned with the face of Virginia Woolf. Many volumes have 'tasteful' covers, suggesting they can be read in subways, left out on coffee tables; indeed, one of the questions on the Black Lace reader survey asks, 'Would you read a Black Lace book in a public place – on a train, for instance?' We can thus connect aesthetic value to spatial mobility, applying Grossberg's definition of agency as mobility between the 'specific places and spaces that define specific forms of agency and empower specific populations'.[36] Literary value facilitates women's mobility between different sites – the bookstore and the home, for example. Returning home with a volume of erotica indicates a certain degree of sexual agency, one defined by everyday routines and yet possibly exceeding them as well.

Although the erotica content is very diverse, we can discern the attempt by book editors, publishers and writers to integrate elements of the everyday into the erotic; this tactic distinguishes erotica from the often more placeless and timeless world of pornography. Women's erotica also picks up on the bodily discourses that legitimated the use of the vibrator with a specific attention to women's orgasms; the clitoris is perhaps the most frequently featured body part – but the body takes form within everyday routines. The challenge, thus, is to eroticise and 'everyday' the body without collapsing the two, making sex too mundane. The British erotic series for women, Black Lace, published by Virgin Publishing and marketed as 'erotic fiction by women for women', illustrates this negotiation between the need to normalise erotica as a genre safe for women within the conditions of everyday life and yet not collapse erotica into the mundane. Surveys at the end of many Black Lace novels address this negotiation; a series of questions inquires into the kinds of female and male protagonists readers find appealing ('do you like a female protagonist who is dominant, submissive, naïve, kinky,' etc?). Female protagonists combine sex with careers; a recurrent theme is the successful career woman who searches for a space to express her masochistic desires. The mundane is intertwined with the erotic; in some novels, the intersection becomes quite bold precisely because mothers are not supposed to be erotic. In *Like Mother, Like Daughter* (1999), fifty-year-old Liz seduces her daughter's boyfriend and other twenty-something men, discovering that middle age can bring new forms of sexual pleasure. Her daughter, Rachel, is initially chagrined: 'Mothers and sex don't mix, do they?' she asks her boyfriend upon suspecting he finds her mother attractive.[37] Eventually, however, Rachel comes around to seeing things her mother's way, and the family (including the husband/father) is happily united around their various sexual practices, rearticulating 'family values' in a final, orgiastic scene.

THE FAMILY VIDEO STORE

If Barnes and Noble and Borders are family-friendly sites that nevertheless lend themselves to erotic accessibility for women, to what degree can we say the same about Blockbuster, the world's largest video retailer and the most insistent on its family values? Since its inception, Blockbuster has refused to carry X- or NC-17-rated videos; recently, however, in the face of technologies such as DVD and satellite threatening the video market, Blockbuster has had to consider new strategies, including the incorporation of more sexually explicit fare. That's why Blockbuster becomes an important site to consider: a place that has from its inception defined leisure activity for women as one of clearly delineated family values has expanded that definition to include the possibility of sexual pleasure and children's activities coinciding at one site, representing both expanded access for women and public legitimation of their desires.

Blockbuster's policy of not renting X-rated videos actually began before the well-known entrepreneur Wayne Huizenga bought into the company and started eating up independent stores throughout the country. Blockbuster began as a small Dallas chain in 1985, a time when video stores were booming as the VCR became a household appliance (video retail stores grew from 7,000 outlets in 1983 to 19,000 by 1986).[38] Many video stores garnered a significant portion of income from porn rentals; Blockbuster decided to distinguish itself through a family values theme. Blockbuster continued the theme in 1987 when Huizenga bought into it and then quickly became its chairman; at the 1988 Video Software Dealers Association convention in Las Vegas, Blockbuster marketing executive Tom Gruber showed video clips of Blockbuster's bright, well-lit interior, contrasting it to outlets represented as dark and dingy, suggesting porn outlets. Blockbuster also emphasised its 'kids' first' theme and named itself 'America's Family Video Store'. These were the Reagan–Bush years, and the Meese Commission had just prompted a crackdown on porn. In 1988, Blockbuster implemented a 'youth-restricted viewing programme' that went one step beyond the no-X policy, 'reviewing and restricting the rental of videos deemed inappropriate to children under age 17'. Then, in 1991, Blockbuster announced it would not carry NC-17-rated videos; the new rating was initiated by the Motion Picture Association to allow more flexibility for 'artistic films'.

The consolidation of family values policies happened during incredible growth years for the company. When Huizenga bought into Blockbuster, it was a $7 million chain of nineteen stores; by 1994, when Huizenga sold it to Viacom, it was a $4 billion enterprise with more than 3,700 stores in eleven countries and fifty million card-carrying customers. But in 1994, Huizenga thought he saw the writing

on the wall – that Blockbuster wouldn't be able to keep up with new technologies – and he turned out to be right. Video rentals have levelled off in the face of cable, satellite television and the internet. In fact, Blockbuster struggled so much in the mid-90s that its new parent company, Viacom, was reportedly close to spinning it off. Since 1998, however, Blockbuster has recovered through a number of strategies that have re-consolidated its hold on the market; for example, the company has itself expanded into new technologies, now offering DVDs and DirecTV satellite systems.[39]

Blockbuster has also begun stocking more sexually explicit videos, although it still will not carry NC-17- and X-rated films, a policy that has helped stymie the production of NC-17 films, given the fact that success at Blockbuster is one of the primary determinants of studio production profits.[40] Ironically, then, Blockbuster has managed to eviscerate the NC-17 rating system while simultaneously maintaining the moral high ground even as it profits from the more palatable genres of erotic thrillers, cable erotic series turned into videos, and now, through its collaboration with DirecTV, more explicit porn offered on pay-per-view.

My point is not to revert to judgment and dismiss the erotic videos Blockbuster carries as simply co-opted because they are less daring/explicit. Rather, the point is to examine what can be represented about women and sex at public sites in order to expand the possibilities for what can be practised at home. Given this objective, it must be acknowledged that Blockbuster holds considerable potential to multiply the practices of sexual freedom. For example, Blockbuster's continued self-representation as family-friendly makes it an innocuous and easy site for mothers with little time away from children. Furthermore, there's no stigma attached to going into a 'porn section' because there is none: the sex videos are scattered through new releases and drama – which also makes them somewhat more difficult but not too hard to find.

The question, though, is how the video box covers and video content represent women and sex, and here we can say that Blockbuster's propensity to carry videos made for the heterosexual couples' market returns to a more traditional conception of how sex fits in the household economy, in contrast to the kinds of pleasures encouraged, for example, in catalogues for sex toys and literary erotica. The greater historical burden on visual representation to be less explicit in order to avoid regulation functions, whether intentionally or not, to reinforce the myth that women's pleasures are fulfilled through heterosexual intercourse; attention to the clitoris that dominates women's literary erotica and sex toy catalogues is replaced by breast shots and simulated sex in the missionary position, the obligatory moaning and facial expressions indicating the woman's pleasure. The problem is not heterosexual sex in itself but rather that its representation in these videos elides the representation of women's pleasures.

Furthermore, many of the erotic videos for rent have first appeared on premium cable channels; Cinemax and Showtime in particular have found a profitable niche market in late-night couples' programming that is explicit but not hard core. For example, the made-for-cable Showtime series *Red Shoe Diaries* frames women's desires in terms of a male narrator's attempts to understand women. Blockbuster carries many copies of the cable series, usually three episodes per tape. Former *X-Files* star David Duchovny is the series' narrator; he is desperately seeking answers to his own lost love by running an ad in the newspaper that solicits erotic diary entries:

> Women. Do you keep a diary? Have you been betrayed? Have you betrayed another? Man, 35, wounded and alone, recovering from the loss of a once-in-a-lifetime love. Looking for reasons why. Willing to pay top dollar for your experiences. Please send diary to Red Shoes.

In a nostalgic rejection of such modern-day technologies as the internet, Duchovny receives the hand-written entries at various post-office boxes, accompanied by his loyal dog Stella. He reads a few lines of the letter; the scene then shifts to the enactment of the sexual predicament, told in the woman's voice, as she struggles with how to negotiate love and sex within some kind of everyday context, not unlike the *Black Lace* series. The episodes always contain a steamy sex scene, although rarely is it very explicit. At the end of each episode, Duchovny returns us to the position of voyeur/moral exemplar, commenting cryptically on the dilemma, offering a version of 'what does woman want?' Hence, although the series

stresses women's sexual agency in that she is always the protagonist, it does so within the framework of male narration and desire. Although this positioning does not determine consumption, it represents in a public site a fairly traditional articulation of sex and romance.

CONCLUSION: REVISITING TRANSGRESSION

I want in conclusion to consider briefly the ways in which domestication may sometimes constitute transgression. By transgression, however, I mean something quite different from the valorisation of individuals' subversive abilities to appropriate texts. Rather, I want to recall the Latin roots of the word – *trans*, meaning, literally, 'across', and *gradi*, meaning, 'to step'. Transgression then in its literal sense means to 'go beyond the bounds or limits prescribed by (a law, command, etc.)'. This going beyond requires that we recognise the material factors that restrict movement before we can devise the means for the reconfiguration that will free one to 'go beyond' the boundaries established by government regulation and other factors inhibiting women's access to porn. Material transgression is necessary for the domestication of porn – it indicates the ability of women to literally enter into the means of production, to step across the threshold of an adult video store, to access an online sex toy shop, to buy a volume of literary erotica. In the pursuit of widespread access for all women, however, we cannot lose sight of the fact that such an expansion will not involve doing away with some of the (less transgressive) texts as women's desires 'evolve' into some uniform standard of radical sexual practice. Nor should that be the goal of a feminist politics of pornography.

NOTES

1. Quoted in an article by Timothy Egan, 'Wall Street Meets Pornography', *New York Times* online, <www.nytimes.com/2000/technology/23PORN.html>, 20 October 2000.
2. Frank Rich, 'Naked Capitalists', *New York Times Magazine*, 20 May 2000.
3. See Egan 'Wall Street Meets Pornography', for a further enumeration of corporations and porn.
4. Ibid.
5. Ibid.
6. See Mark Cromer's article in *The Nation*, 'Porn's Compassionate Conservatism', 26 February 2001.

7. Linda Williams, *Hard Core: Power, Pleasure, and the 'Frenzy of the Visible'* (Berkeley: University of California Press, 1989).

8. Michel Foucault, 'The Ethics of the Concern of the Self as a Practice of Freedom', in Paul Rabinow (ed.), *Michel Foucault: Ethics, Subjectivity, and Truth* (New York: The New Press, 1984), p. 283.

9. Lawrence Grossberg, 'Identity and Cultural Studies: Is That All There Is?', in Stuart Hall and Paul DuGay (eds), *Questions of Cultural Identity* (London: Sage, 1996), p. 99.

10. Doreen Massey, *Space, Place, and Gender* (Minneapolis: University of Minnesota Press, 1994), pp. 151–2.

11. US Commission on Obscenity and Pornography, *Report of the Commission on Obscenity and Pornography* (Washington, DC: Government Printing Office, 1970), p. 229.

12. Ibid., pp. 839–40.

13. The Supreme Court later ruled that the CDA was so broad as to be unconstitutional; it ruled that speech on the internet should be accorded the same First Amendment rights as books and newspapers.

14. I draw for this information on Phil Hubbard, 'Panic on the Streets of London: Obscenity, Morality, and Visibility', unpublished manuscript.

15. Under the provisions of the PRA, state governments receive block grants to distribute as they choose, with five-year limitations on aid.

16. For example, the 1986 Immigration Reform and Control Act offered amnesty to undocumented people who had been in the country since 1982. However, it included a provision that denied amnesty to anyone 'likely to become a public charge' and included a five-year ban on welfare and food stamps for anyone who did qualify for amnesty. Hence, if women had ever received welfare, they wouldn't qualify for amnesty; and if one wanted to apply for amnesty, she was then disqualified from applying for welfare for the next five years. Under this policy, women remain in exploitative conditions because they're undocumented, retaining a low-wage employment force for factories, domestic, agricultural and sex work. The assumption is that immigrant and poor women have fewer rights as mothers to care for their children because they carry more 'value' in terms of their labour capacity.

17. Catharine MacKinnon, 'Vindication and Resistance: A Response to the Carnegie-Mellon Study of Pornography in Cyberspace', *Georgetown Law Journal* 83 (1995), pp. 1,957–67.

18. Ann Snitow, 'Retrenchment vs. Transformation: Politics of the Anti-Pornography Movement,' in Kate Ellis *et al.* (eds), *Caught Looking: Feminism, Pornography, and Censorship* (New York: Caught Looking, 1986), p. 17.

19. Laura Kipnis, *Bound and Gagged: Pornography and the Politics of Fantasy in America* (New York: Grove Press, 1996), p. 166.

20. I'm referring to Lynne Segal and Mary McIntosh (eds), *Sex Exposed: Sexuality and the Pornography Debates* (New Brunswick, NJ: Rutgers University Press, 1993); Alison Assiter and Avedon Carol (eds), *Bad Girls and Dirty Pictures: The Challenge to Reclaim Feminism* (London: Pluto Press, 1993); and the first edition of this collection, Pamela Church Gibson and Roma Gibson (eds), *Dirty Looks: Women, Pornography, Power* (London: BFI, 1993).

21. Chris Straayer, 'The Seduction of Boundaries: Feminist Fluidity in Annie Sprinkle's Art/Education/Sex,' in this volume, pp. 224–36.

22. Lawrence Grossberg, 'Where is the "American" in American Cultural Studies', in Lawrence Grossberg (ed.), *Bringing It All Back Home: Essays on Cultural Studies* (Durham, NC: Duke University Press), p. 290.

23. Ibid., p. 291.

24. See Rachel Maines, *The Technology of Orgasm: 'Hysteria', the Vibrator, and Women's Sexual Satisfaction* (Baltimore, MD: Johns Hopkins University Press, 1999). In this history of vibrators, Maines notes that 'massage to orgasm of female patients was a staple of medical practice among some . . . Western physicians from the time of Hippocrates until the 1920s' (p. 3).

25. Mimi Swartz, 'For the Woman Who Has Almost Everything', *Esquire*, July 1980, p. 58.

26. Maines, *The Technology of Orgasm*, pp. 19–20.

27. Quoted in an article on vibrators by Claire Safran, 'Plain Talk about the New Approach to Sexual Pleasure', *Redbook*, March 1976, pp. 86–7.

28. Ibid., p. 86.

29. Swartz, 'For the Woman Who Has Almost Everything', p. 63.

30. Safran, 'Plain Talk about the New Approach to Sexual Pleasure', p. 81.

31. Jacqueline Gold, *Good Vibrations*. Information on Jacqueline Gold's autobiography and the company can be found at <www.jacquelinegold.com>.

32. Both companies feature models of colour, but the majority of models are Anglo; all the models are slender and young.

33. Susie Bright (ed.), *Herotica: A Collection of Women's Erotic Fiction* (San Francisco, CA: Down There Press, 1988), p. 5.

34. James Sullivan, 'The Bright Stuff', *Book* (January/February 2002), pp. 52–3.

35. The exception to legal challenges is anything that might be seen as child pornography.

36. Grossberg, 'Identity and Cultural Studies', p. 102.

37. Georgina Brown, *Like Mother, Like Daughter* (London: Black Lace, 1999), p. 150.

38. Information on Blockbuster comes from Gail De George, *The Making of a Blockbuster: How Wayne Huizenga Built a Sports and Entertainment Empire from Trash, Grit, and Videotape* (New York: John Wiley & Sons, 1996).

39. Most significantly, it has signed a series of revenue-sharing deals with the major Hollywood studios; basically, Blockbuster gives studios a share of its rental revenue in exchange for low prices on movie titles, enabling the company to buy more copies of hit videos upon their release. Independent retailers filed a class-action, anti-trust suit against Blockbuster, claiming that revenue-sharing drove them out of business. However, a federal judge denied their request for class-action status. According to the National Association of Video Distributors, 4,500 small retailers have closed since 1998.

40. For a brief discussion of Blockbuster's decision to stock more sexually explicit videos, see Jon Lewis, *Hollywood v. Hard Core: How the Struggle over Censorship Saved the Modern Film Industry* (New York: New York University Press), p. 292.

5   Only the Literal: The Contradictions of Anti-Pornography Feminism

Lynne Segal

Pornography makes the world a pornographic place establishing what women are said to exist as, are seen as, are treated as, constructing the social reality of what a women is and can be . . . Stopping pornography . . . is women's only chance to gain, in or out of court, a voice that cannot be used against us.
(Catharine MacKinnon)[1]

Pornography charts a domain of unrealizable positions that hold sway over the social reality of gender positions, but do not . . . constitute that reality; indeed it is their failure to constitute it that gives the pornographic image the phantasmatic power it has . . . My call . . . is for a feminist reading of pornography that resists the literalization of this imaginary scene, one which reads it for the incommensurabilities between gender norms and practices that it seems compelled to repeat without resolution. (Judith Butler)[2]

The 'sex wars' within feminism have lasted a very long time; as Lisa Duggan and Nan Hunter chronicle in their coverage of the continuing combat.[3] Thought to have peaked when the prestigious Barnard Conference 'Towards a Politics of Sexuality' was aggressively picketed by rival feminists from the 'Coalition for a Feminist Sexuality Against Sado-masochism', in New York in 1982, the cannons are still firing .[4] 'Pornography' remains the issue which I am most regularly asked to address, most recently, reluctantly agreeing to present my 'maiden' address to the Women and Psychology Conference on just that topic – the theme of the day.[5] Ironically, more textually than visually literate, I have never especially been drawn to analysing 'pornography', and certainly not for years on end. But then, for better or, more usually, for worse, the debate over pornography eternally returns: especially since powerful feminist voices have for some time now been feeding new lines to old forces of moral conservatism. From the

close of the 1970s, it has been impossible to write about sexuality or sexual politics (as a feminist) without being hi-jacked by, and forced to take a stand upon, the issue of pornography.

Hence my own entrapment in a maddeningly deadlocked debate where my side, although, ironically, called the 'pro-sex brigade', has the least titillating lines and is forced to address an agenda not of our own making. The deadlock is hard to shift because the dispute, although superficially about evidence that pornography is harmful, is at bedrock about competing feminist foundations: the place given to men and their sexuality as the root of women's oppression, as against the rejection of any such single origination. The debate is particularly dull for the 'anti-anti-pornography' feminist position, because it has to argue the unexciting case of 'sweet reason': to insist on complexity, and reject any single analysis or unitary viewpoint.[6] This is a world apart from the fire and brimstone of anti-pornography feminism, whose leading theoretician, Catharine MacKinnon, and maestro of rhetoric, Andrea Dworkin, hit us with their pounding, rhythmic, repetitive prose, and their exceptionally sadistic sexual imagery, to produce a type of passion seemingly all their own; although actually evocative of the moral rhetoric familiar in puritan barnstorming through the ages. The one thing which pornographers and anti-pornographers have in common is the desire to arouse and shock: 'Imagine', MacKinnon opens her latest book to command:

> You grow up with your father holding you down and covering your mouth so another man can make a horrible searing pain between your legs. When you are older, your husband ties you to the bed and drips hot wax on your nipples and brings in other men to watch and makes you smile through it. Your doctor will not give you the drugs he has addicted you to unless you suck his penis.[7]

There is a precedent. Surveying the popular consumption of denunciatory literature on the harmful effects of masturbation a century ago, Porter and Hall conclude that it probably served the obverse function of its surface message: anti-masturbation texts became themselves a source of masturbatory stimulation.[8] This possible twist in the uses and abuses to which texts and images may be put, however, is largely absent from the current debate.

DEFINITIVE AMBIGUITIES

Whatever the rhetorical interplay between pornography and anti-pornography, it seems hard to deny that the genre is notoriously difficult to define: its meanings shift; its productions diversify. Walter Kendrick's witty history of sex and censorship illustrates this well, as the many obscenity trials of the 20th century slowly uncoupled the 'pornographic' from anything 'experts' could affirm to be of 'scientific' or 'literary' value: 'pornography' officially became words or images designed primarily for sexual arousal, without redeeming social importance.[9] In more detail, Linda Williams has mapped the continuous and continuing changes in pornographic productions, as new sexual questions and anxieties come into play.[10] In the early Stag Films of the 1920s, for example, the question of women's sexual pleasure was never an issue, as men gazed at the forbidden display of female genitals (in screenings from which women were strictly excluded). In contrast, the full-length porn movies of the 1980s purport to represent both men and women as sexual subjects, and the issue of satisfying women's (supposedly insatiable) desire drives the plot forward. Misogyny unquestionably pervades much of the genre, although the recent emergence of self-consciously pro-women pornographic productions now attempt to represent female sexual agency always, only, as 'positive', hoping to subvert or resignify its traditional codings. The latter would include Candida Royalle's 'Femme Productions', Annie Sprinkle's 'Post-Porn Performances', Scarlot Harlot's 'postmodern prostitute art', and numerous other lesbian and straight creations designed primarily for arousing women. These all routinely encounter the censor's firm hand, both in the US and, when imported, here in the UK.[11]

Williams herself, and many in her wake, argue that the greatest change in recent decades is that the 'pornographic marketplace is now almost as eager to address women as desiring consumers as it once was to package them merely as objects of consumption'.[12] This has resulted in more women using certain types of pornography: in the US 40 per cent of 'adult videos' are said to be purchased by women, according to an often quoted figure from *Time* magazine,[13] while the admittedly far from disinterested *Adult Video News* survey reported 63 per cent of all pornography tapes being rented by couples, or women.[14] Today it would seem truer than ever that the borders of the 'pornographic' shift and blur into other genres (the uncontrolled, non-commercial productions of nerds on the internet creating endless new possibilities, and problems). Meanwhile, much of what anti-pornography feminists refer to as classic instances of 'pornography' are taken from the Slasher and Horror movie genre, with its own distinct history and ways of reading imagery and text.[15]

Yet it still remains predominantly men who produce most of the sexual images of women: continually repositioned, passively, as object, icon and fetish of male desire – whether in pornography, cinema or elsewhere. In the stock top-shelf wank-mags, it is men's sexual desires and needs which are catered for, fuelling the prevailing pornographic narrative, with its own conventional code words and images. (Attempts to produce somewhat similar porn mags for women have so far met with little commercial success.) Here, as nowhere else in most men's lives, infantile grandiosity is fully catered for: men are inexhaustibly desiring, tumescent and irresistible; women insatiably available. Whether we respond with derision, sympathy, horror or indifference to what this suggests about men's ruling sexual trepidations will influence the stand we take on pornography.

Sexually explicit material, when not enshrining its belief in the only 'legitimate' place and purpose of sex (in marriage, for procreation), has always been labelled 'obscene' or 'pornographic' by moral conservatives. In contrast, liberals want to keep public surveillance and censorship of sexual material to a minimum (when consumed privately and willingly). The tricky matter of definitions does not trouble moral conservatives who, in the famous words of Judge Potter Stewart, 'know it when [they] see it'.[16] Liberals are much less certain about when they see it and have successfully called upon the law to limit its meanings. Some contemporary feminists have been just as suspicious of fixing the meanings of 'pornography', aware that their own texts and images have often been officially declared 'pornographic', and subject to censorship. (Recently in Britain the Advertising Standards Authority was moved to caution the Royal Shakespeare Company for distributing a self-portrait of a naked, hugely pregnant woman with bandaged head, by feminist photographer Clare Park, following complaints that the photo was 'crude and offensive, suggesting violence towards women and degrading pregnancy'.) Other feminists now turn to the law to expand the meaning of 'pornography', and close down its production. They are responsible for the new public discourse on images which 'degrade' and 'dehumanize' apparent in the previous complaint (holding them responsible for violence towards women): one appropriated to conservative rhetoric, restoring its strength.

FEMINIST REAPPRAISALS

Sexuality was always accorded a central place in the analysis and politics of women's liberation. Feminists initially sought to celebrate female sexuality: liberating it from male-centred discourses and sexist practices to uncover women's own 'autonomous' sexuality. (Foucauldian insights had not yet been assimilated by feminists, to undermine faith in our own 'essentializing' inner messages and counter-truths: though in fact some women even then, I recall, were always a little wary of generalizing about sexual experience).[17] However, early feminist ideas linking women's liberation to greater sexual confidence soon fizzled out – at least within heterosexual encounters (though it quickly found a home in mainstream women's publications, like *Cosmopolitan*). The pressure of challenging the ubiquitous milieu of men's power over women was always going to overshadow any beneficial effects of women's individual pursuit of pleasure. (Which was never, in itself, a good reason to abandon it.)

In *Straight Sex*[18] I traced the interconnecting strands leading towards the growth of a more pessimistic, sexual conservatism within feminist thinking from the close of the 1970s: the theoretical deficiencies of feminist borrowings from a behaviouristic sexology; the symbolic centrality of the hierarchical binaries roping gender to sexuality; the tenacity of men's power in relation to women, and their endemic abuse of it, especially in sexual matters;

a more conservative political climate. Forceful feminist writing was soon reinscribing old patriarchal 'truths' centred on the polarizing of male and female sexuality – his: predatory, genital, exploitative and dominating; hers: gentle, diffuse, nurturing and egalitarian.[19]

Coupled with shifts in feminist sexual politics and theory, pornography became *the* feminist issue of the 1980s, at least for its best-known (North American) white spokeswomen. This was the first of several theoretical reappraisals insisting that sexuality was the overriding source of men's oppression of women. Catharine MacKinnon later summarized this contentious rewriting: 'feminism is a theory of how the erotization of dominance and submission creates gender, creates woman and man in the social form in which we know them'.[20] The second transformation cited 'pornography' as the cause of men's sexual practices, now defined within a continuum of male violence. Male 'sexuality' was irrevocably fused to 'domination', redefined as an urge to power.

Some feminists saw these moves, as I did, as part of a reaction to more conservative times, and the setbacks faced by feminist activism, especially in the US (where anti-pornography feminism arose at the close of the 1970s). Pornography, Ann Snitow suggests, became a metaphor for women's defeat, now that feminists in general were less confidently on the offensive. Isolating sexuality and men's violence from other issues of women's inequality was not only a defensive tactic for women, but one in perfect harmony with the rising tide of conservative backlash against radical politics generally.[21] The Right has always liked to demonize sexuality, and have us see it as the source of all our ills, ensuring that they would move swiftly into alliance with anti-pornography feminism. However vigorously we hear it denied, Dworkin and MacKinnon's alliance with the Moral Right is now well documented.[22]

The strength of the new feminist discourses against pornography (once MacKinnon added her legal arguments to Andrea Dworkin's indictment of pornography as men's literal domination and torture of women) was to declare it a violation of women's civil rights.[23] It serves to convince men that women are inferior, and hence do not deserve equal rights. Pornography should not be seen as merely a form of representation – sexist and offensive images or words – but should be seen as *literally* harming women and creating gender inequality. It causes men to injure and violate women both in its creation – a claim passionately and repeatedly attacked by sex workers themselves[24] – and in its consumption: teaching men to injure and debase women through linking their sexual arousal to degrading images of women. In the last few years, anti-pornography feminists have further strengthened their position by uniting the new forces fighting 'Hate Speech' in the US (Matsuda *et al.*, 1993).[25] Pornography should not be protected in the name of 'free-speech' (the 1st Amendment of the US constitution), but criminalized as against equality (the 14th Amendment): 'The law of equality and the law of freedom of speech are on a collision course in this country', MacKinnon declares.[26]

Feminist anti-pornography arguments are seductive because most mainstream pornography obviously embodies the most outrageously sexist (often also racist) imagery. That is its function: to position women as – and only as – passive, commoditized, objects for men's sexual arousal. It does disturb many women (and many men as well). Moreover, feminist goals never have, nor ever could be, simply reduced to liberal goals: concerned only with the issue of censorship, rather than with who has access to the media, and the content and effects of media messages. Cultural production has always been seen as a site for the struggle and intervention of silenced voices (like the feminist graffiti artists, aggressively subverting and humorously reinscribing many a billboard: 'If this car were a woman, she'd run you down', etc.[27] Pornography's standard servicing of men's narcissistic fantasies of female sexual availability was always an injurious affront to feminist attempts to eliminate sexual harassment, rape and violence against women. All the more so in societies like our own which have proved unable, and until recently unwilling, to offer women protection from widespread sexual harassment, abuse and violence.[28] It seems to offer, at the very least, a convenient scapegoat for rage against such abuses. Convenient, but also hazardous, when not directly menacing.

For if the force driving anti-pornography feminism is the belief that it is commercial pornography which lies behind the subordination and abuse of women in society, we are allowing ourselves to be seriously deluded. First of all, anti-pornography feminism has systematically misrepresented the content of mainstream pornography as 'violence'.[29] Secondly,

it has consistently misrepresented studies of effects of pornography, falsely claiming that psychological and sociological surveys offer consistent and conclusive proof that pornographic images cause sex crimes ('not even courts equivocate over its carnage anymore'.[30] Thirdly, it disavows all knowledge of the nature of fantasy and all recent theories of representation: where meaning is seen as never fixed in advance, but determined by its broader discursive context as well as its specific interpretive audience. Finally, and most fundamentally of all, however, anti-pornography feminism fails to address the elementary point that the role of commercial pornography in depicting a crude, imperious and promiscuous male sexuality, alongside female receptivity and vulnerability, is *completely* overshadowed by, and entirely *dependent* upon, the official discourses and imagery of science, medicine, religion and mainstream cultural productions (high or low), prevalent all around us.

PORNOGRAPHIC IMAGERY AND GENDER DISCOURSES

The offensive codings of the sexually explicit significations of commercial pornography mimic, even as they sometimes function to unsettle, the ways in which women are subordinated in the heartlands of the most authoritative and revered (even scared) discourses of our culture. Illustrations could be drawn from a whole range of genres, where the subordinating binaries of gender specification are always already in place. Popular biological texts, such as Donald Symons's *The Evolution of Human Sexuality*, for example, summarize human female sexuality as 'continuously copulable', human male sexuality as perpetually ready to copulate: 'women inspire male sexual desire simply by existing'.[31] This is not pornography, but 'science'; in fact, with the flowering of the oldest repetitions of social Darwinism in the current conceits of 'new evolutionary theory', it is once again becoming the most accessible scientific discourse around. Naively, Symons even draws our attention to the connection between his biological rendering of men's ever-ready sexual desire (accompanying women's ever-available sexual condition) and men's pornographic fantasies, as scientifically explaining rather than emotively expressing one staple of pornographic fantasy: men's basic biological drive for 'easy, anonymous, impersonal, unencumbered sex with an endless succession of lustful, beautiful, orgasmic women'.[32]

Meanwhile, as sex therapists are all too well aware, outside the sexist metaphors and phallic hubris of scientific discourse (or their pornographic mirrorings), the homonoid penis is anything but permanently erect, anything but endlessly ready for unencumbered sex, anything but triggered by the nearest passing female: even when she happens to be his wife, mistress or lover – willing and eager for sex.[33] This is the critical force behind Judith Butler's recent analysis of pornography, suggesting that it depicts just those 'unrealizable positions' that always already predetermine our social expectations of gender positions. But far from pornography itself constructing the social reality, it serves rather to mock the impossible distance between gender norms and practices 'that it seems compelled to repeat without resolution'.[34]

Nobody needs pornography to remind them of the hierarchical 'truths' of sexual difference; some, indeed, turn to it escape them, identifying with who-knows-what position of domination or subjection as they gaze upon its products. It is dominant ideology itself, with its obsessive disdain for what it regards as the gross material body and its functions – of secretions, odours and open orifices; perspiration, pulpy flesh and fluctuating organs – which works to produce the quite inevitable pull of the tauntingly illicit. As Peter Stallybrass and Allon White suggest, the bourgeois subject 'continuously defined and redefined itself through the exclusion of what is marked out as low – as dirty, repulsive, noisy, contaminating'.[35] The pornographic is what high culture wants to banish and abject, it is thus necessarily about excess and extremity. 'Even if there were no pornography', as Richard Goldstein writes, 'there would be pornography. We would still be left with the content of our fantasies, and our fantasies would still be laced with those images of "submission and display" by which anti-porn activists define pornography'.[36] This is why men themselves (especially middle-class men in closest contact with feminism) have rallied to the anti-pornography cause, and only a tiny minority of men – usually gay men – have publicly explained or defended their own use of pornography: 'Everyone knew porn wasn't right', one of the few straight men to write of his 'passive' and 'often guilty' consumption of pornography admits: 'Its double standard was too obvious; women didn't traffic in sexually explicit images of men'.[37] Indeed a large part of the appeal of the most popular pornographic magazines, like *Hustler*, to their overwhelmingly working-class male audience, is their deliberate incitement of a class resentment of high culture and bourgeois women.[38]

Pornography is thus only one of a multiplicity (the least esteemed, least convincing, often almost contradictory) of phallocentric and misogynistic discourses fashioning our images of gender and sexuality. Those who are most eager to reiterate its unique offensiveness face the problem that surveys of what is packaged as pornography show that violent imagery is rare, rather than definitive, of the genre. Moreover, men are more likely than women to be depicted as 'submissive' in the S/M or bondage imagery available.[39] This means, of course, that were there any truth in our direct mimicry of the pornographic, feminists should be out fly-posting this centuries-old dominatrix pornography, not trying to eliminate it. Again, at odds with its supposed 'addictive' nature, the violent imagery which does appear in pornography has been consistently found to be decreasing rather than increasing since 1977.[40] A host of empirical enquiries, from The Netherlands, Sweden, Denmark or the US, have all failed to find any consistent correlation between the availability of pornography and sex crimes against women, many indeed have found negative correlations (not that this tells us anything about causality).[41] Overall, the main finding from the avalanche of correlational studies carried out over the past 20 years is their inconsistency, both with each other, and with the claims of anti-pornography texts.

Nevertheless, it is anti-pornography campaigners, and not their critics, who have had most success in shifting the legal debate in favour of censorship throughout the 1990s and they have greatly boosted their appeal by joining forces with others campaigning against the far less contentious injuries of 'Hate Speech', now flourishing in the US. In her collection on 'Hate Speech', Mari Matsuda describes how 'Racist hate messages, threats, slurs, epithets, and disparagement all hit the gut of those in the target group'. They function as a type of verbal harassment not only subordinating the person addressed, but undermining their capacity to work, study or even exist in the public sphere: ' the victim becomes a stateless person'.[42] Similarly, MacKinnon argues that pornography is not an expression, representation or symbol, rather it is itself an injurious act. Here she misapplies the philosopher J. L. Austin's distinction between perlocutionary speech acts, where a person saying something (such as 'John smuggled heroin from Bangkok'), and its possible consequences, are distinct, and illocutionary speech acts, where the conventions surrounding a particular person's speech act has immediate binding effect (such as when a judge passing sentence on John, in court, uses the utterance 'I sentence you to 25 years').[43] Pornography is action, MacKinnon argues, because it generates penile arousal to degrading images of women, and this in turn establishes how women are seen, treated, and able to exist in the world. (Even were we to agree that there is a connection between the 'erections and ejaculations' accompanying pornographic 'speech acts' and the subordination of women, that subordination would be a 'consequence' of pornographic perlocutionary 'speech', not an illocutionary 'enactment' of it.) In any case, MacKinnon concludes, with pornography now defined as action rather than speech, it no longer qualifies for any special protection.

It is over a decade since MacKinnon and Dworkin first drafted their Model Ordinance, arguing that women can only assert their civil rights and become fully human once they win the battle against pornography. The Ordinance classifies pornography as sex discrimination ('the graphic sexually explicit subordination of women through pictures or words') and urges those who have suffered 'harm' from it to seek damages through the courts from its makers, sellers and distributors – public or private.[44] After initial success in Minneapolis, the Ordinance was eventually defeated in various states of the US following prolonged legal battles, but in Canada anti-pornography feminists (assisted by MacKinnon) have been victorious, with the adoption of a modified version of the Ordinance in the *Butler* Supreme Court decision in 1992. The most significant aspect of this decision was its acceptance of a clear link between 'obscenity', defined as 'undue exploitation of sex', and harm to women.[45] There are ongoing campaigns for the implementation of the Ordinance in Britain, spear-headed by Catherine Itzin.[46]

Other feminists, who have – often reluctantly – felt compelled to fight the Ordinance, in and outside the courts, argue that the relentless pursuit of such legislative change is pernicious: relying upon vague and ambiguous terms which are certain to backfire against the sexually powerless it supposedly protects.

Today, MacKinnon rejoices that Canadian law 'is less worried about the misfiring of restrictions against the powerless and more concerned about having nothing to fire against abuses of power by the powerful'. This is not, she adds: 'big bad state power jumping on poor powerless individual citizens. What it did was make space for the unequal to find voice'.[47] What it did, according to those who have been monitoring the law's effects, is quite the reverse. Since the *Butler* decision, straight mainstream pornography is flourishing, but any representations of alternative sexualities are facing increasingly intense censorship, as Brenda Cossman and Shannon Bell document. Almost immediately, following the ruling, the gay and lesbian Glad Day Bookshop and Little Sister's Art and Book Emporium, both faced harassment (the former brought to trial and convicted for selling the lesbian magazine *Bad Attitude*). Books by Genet, Duras, even Noel Coward's biography, as well as *Quim*, *Bad Attitude*, and the gay newspaper *The Advocate*, have all been seized, while Toronto's cultural funding for lesbian and gay artists has been largely withdrawn, along with that for the annual gay and lesbian film festival.[48] The misappropriation of this new Canadian law, not against most men's cosily familiar sexist pornography, but against the more unsettling productions of women and gay men which might work to subvert them, has been the precise and predictable outcome.[49]

In the area of race, similar – not unpredictable – reversals occur in relation to whose speech remains protected (as before), and whose speech gets censored. Thus it is the performances of black rap groups, 2 Live Crew and Salt 'n' Pepa which have recently been targeted for censorship in US courts, fortifying hegemonic conservative racism: 'rap is the special contribution of blacks to American cultural degeneration', the conservative critic Stephen Macedo affirms.[50] As Judith Butler explores in her latest book, *Excitable Speech*, once there is an overriding importance attached to individual speech utterances at the expense of collective action against underlying structures of sexism or racism, we get what she criticizes (perhaps to the surprise of some of her supporters and critics alike) as 'the "linguistification" of the political field': 'the dignity of women is understood to be under attack not by the weakening of rights to reproductive freedom and widespread loss of public assistance, but primarily by African-

American men who sing'.[51] Meanwhile, black cultural theorist Henry Louis Gates, Jr has written of the dangers of allowing courts to decide what is 'injurious' speech, suggesting that the black rap being censored should be recognized as providing works of literary and cultural value in the context of indigenous significations in African-American folk art.[52] 'Paradoxically and poignantly', Butler concludes, 'when the courts become the ones who are invested with the power to regulate expressions, new occasions for discrimination are produced in which the courts discount African-American cultural production as well as lesbian and gay self-representation as such through the arbitrary and tactical use of obscenity law'.[53]

INSCRIBING PSYCHOLOGICAL REDUCTIONISM

Part of the success of the anti-pornography movement over the past 15 years has been its ability to mobilize scientific research in support of its arguments, rather than the anecdotal narratives of harm it had previously relied upon. It is possible to connect the image of human beings in anti-pornography rhetoric with that which still dominates theorizing and research in psychology. In a recent essay, the Canadian researcher Thelma McCormack highlights the similarities, commenting upon the experimental studies of leading pornography researchers, Donnerstein and Malamuth: 'The subjects in these experiments, almost always men, are excited by the sexual stimulus and respond on cue. There is no notion of vicarious experience, no concept of catharsis in what is a very rigorous positivist design'.[54] As McCormack argues, the parallel between this type of reductive psychological research and the arguments of anti-pornography feminists is more than accidental.

More graphically, Mandy Merck explores MacKinnon's frequent deployment of the figure of the dog in her canine-conditioning model of pornography's effects, in a way which 'imbricates masculinity with bestiality via the discourses of behavioural psychology'.[55] Such discourses allow MacKinnon to collapse diverse texts and images into concrete acts and deeds, avoiding all need for reference to context, meaning or interpretation. 'Pornography works as a behavioural conditioner, reinforcer and stimulus', MacKinnon announces, 'like saying "kill" to a trained guard dog — and also like the training process

itself'.[56] In her latest bestseller, *Only Words*, MacKinnon explains that men react to pornography with penile erection, whether they wish to or not:

> In human society, where no one does not live [sic!], the physical response to pornography is nearly a universal conditioned male reaction, whether they like or agree with what the materials say or not. There is a lot wider variation in men's conscious attitudes towards pornography than there is in their sexual responses to it.[57]

Of course, were this to be true, it would tell us nothing at all about what actions men might choose to take, if any, in relation to women. A bulge in the trousers is not in itself threatening, unless it happens to contain a gun, as a strong woman (once jailed for her own supposedly 'pornographic' stage performances) liked to mock. This does not trouble MacKinnon, since she seems to think human consciousness and intentionality of no great consequence for human action. Moreover, MacKinnon's man-as-dog does not just salivate (penilely) at the sight of female flesh but, more mysteriously for a conditioned reflex, must have ever 'stronger' triggers: 'Explicit sex, after a while, puts men to sleep. It takes increasingly explicit violation, meaning violence, to wake them up, erotically speaking . . . more and more violence has become necessary to keep the progressively desensitized consumer aroused to the illusion that sex is (and he is) daring and dangerous'.[58] (If you were hoping MacKinnon might provide just a hint or gesture towards evidence here, or anywhere else, you will be disappointed.)

Once again, however, the discourses and practices of many psychologists dovetail with MacKinnon's fanciful meditations. They are perfectly in harmony with the method and outcome of much psychological research on pornography which chooses, as its 'incontestably objective measures' of the effects of the genre on men's actions, responses of a wholly different order. Thus Eysenck and Nias, in the influential *Sex, Violence and the Media* (1978), draw their conclusions about the genre from measuring penile expansion (via a penile plethysmograph) as a response to depictions of sex acts — a response which, as others have noted, is as likely as not to be connected to the oddity of wearing the equipment in the first place. At the same time as warning their readers of the dangerous effects of pornography, however,

Eysenck and Nias themselves take pains to reiterate the dominant message of straight pornography: drawing attention to men's sexual prowess. But whereas their discourse comes with the powerful cultural authority of 'scientific truth', the latter comes defined as officially 'worthless', the literally superficial. Thus Eysenck and Nias are quick to assure what they call 'women's lib' that 'high libido' is correlated with 'masculinity' (assuming feminists will dispute this). One might expect them to be a little disappointed that they actually found 'considerable overlap' in reported rates of male and female arousal to their images of sex acts, but instead they cheerfully dismiss this by questioning the 'typicality' of the women who volunteer for their research; although not, of course, the men.[59] Objective measurements hold no threat for those who know how to read them.

Donnerstein et al.'s[60] subsequent meticulous laboratory records of the 'effects' of pornography also tell us who knows what – as they will later admit – about men's likely sexual conduct, when what they typically choose to measure is young male students' obedient delivery of electric shocks for memory failures following exposure to different types of sexually explicit stimuli. What is not known about these studies is that they are best seen as measurements of the effects of arousal on performance, since any other form of arousal – from the viewing of an eye operation to delays in a traffic jam before arrival – can be substituted for what is supposedly being measured – the viewing of pornography – with much the same effects, or lack of them, on shock delivery.[61] When experimenters do actually test directly for increases in self-reported calloused attitudes towards women following exposure to pornography, they find that interpretive context is important – debriefing subjects about sexual violence and its effects, after viewing the most 'violent' and 'degrading' pornography, led to the immediate and continued lowering of 'callousness' response scores. These authors later admit that there is a problem in generalizing their results to what they call behaviour in 'real life'.[62]

THE CUNNING OF PORNOGRAPHY

The most frustrating feature of both anti-pornography feminism and psychological research on pornography alike is that they lead us away from rather than towards any understanding of the issues we are supposedly addressing. The basis of the cosy alliance between mainstream psychological research and anti-pornography feminism is the literalist theory of language and representation they share. Rather than insight into the construction of meanings, what we get from positivistic psychology is the complete evacuation of any attempt to grapple with the dynamics of pornographic production and consumption – fantasy, projection, identification or representation – and the encouragement of modes of analysis that work to reduce, systematize and close off debate. What we get from MacKinnon and Dworkin, both experts at the art of arousal and manipulation, is the discursive mirroring of the most disturbing codes and conventions of pornography itself.

Some have begun to analyse the rhetorical structure of MacKinnon's work in order to understand its remarkable power and influence. On the one hand, no less an authority than Richard Rorty declares MacKinnon a new prophet of our age (his words enthusiastically endorse the dust jacket of Only Words); on the other hand, anti-pornography is the best-funded feminist campaign in history. As feminist philosopher Wendy Brown has recently argued, the theory of gender in anti-pornography feminism 'mirrors the straight male pornography it means to criticize': in MacKinnon and Dworkin's rhetoric women are always and only their sexuality; women exist in an 'always already sexually violated condition', the social construction of 'femininity' has no flexibility or complexity; there are no ways women can overturn this construction – lesbian sexuality, here, can no more escape the eroticization of dominance and submission than straight women who try to embrace sexual autonomy.[63] In this way, Brown concludes (inflecting Baudrillard on Marx) 'MacKinnon assists in the cunning of pornography', declaring women's emancipatory struggles deluded and impossible: 'MacKinnon formulates as the deep, universal, and transhistorical structure of gender what is really a hyperpornographic expression'.[64]

Moreover, MacKinnon does this strange work on behalf of traditional patriarchy, just when, on all fronts, old gender regimes are most under attack (again, one function of mainstream pornography itself). And finally, the quality, style and thrust of MacKinnon's prose bears all the hallmarks of pornography, its single repetitive point of women as passive victims 'incessantly reiterated, reworked, driven, and thrust at its audience' (like that of Dworkin, who was there before her, or John Stoltenberg, Jeffrey Masson and other male sympathizers, in their wake).[65] Another feminist philosopher, Drucilla Cornell, has suggested MacKinnon 'fucks her audiences'.[66] More politely, Brown concludes that MacKinnon suspends us 'in a complex pornographic experience in which [she] is both purveyor and object of desire and her analysis is proffered as substitute for the sex she abuses us for wanting'.[67] In this way, MacKinnon seduces her audiences with easy identifications: the pleasures of the familiar repackaged as radical, the comforts of conservatism, and the dismissal of past feminist victories and any serious possibilities for change. A winning ticket, in these times, if ever there was one.

RETHINKINGS AND RESIGNIFICATIONS

In the face of this orchestrated arousal of libidinal despair, what can those of us say who want to talk about the complex nuances of 'pornography'? In true behaviourist spirit, MacKinnon repudiates any psychological perspectives which try to shed light on the complexities of psychic life or the nature of fantasy. In particular, she has only the harshest criticism of Freud, who devised 'the theory of the unconscious', and 'invented fantasy', simply to hide the reality of men's continual sexual violation of women. 'I think feminism is developing a non-Freudian theory of sexuality', she argues, one which recognizes that 'sexual liberation' (a notion she curiously believes 'derives from Freud') is a 'male rationalization for forcing sex on women'.[68] It is the light psychoanalytic reflection might shed on the 'pornographic' psychic life of women and men alike (most of whom are not 'forcing sex on women') which threatens MacKinnon's literality. Certainly, the diversity of pornographic material seems but a pale reflection of the often troubling excesses of our actual dreams and fantasies, as Richard Goldstein comments:

> Readers of The New York Times were shocked (or perhaps consoled) to learn last year that men and women, straight and gay, frequently fantasize about forced sexual encounters. According to that study, coercian ranks with group sex and anonymity in the basic repertoire of sexual reverie. Among lesbians surveyed, rape was the most frequent sexual fantasy. Dreams of romantic interludes ranked far behind fantasies of rape and promiscuity.[69]

Psychoanalytical readings suggest a way of understanding the bizarrely 'pornographic' nature of our fantasy life: where excitement and danger, pleasure and pain, adoration and disgust, power and powerlessness, male and female, even life and death, smoothly fuse and separate out again without damage or distress – except perhaps to our internal psychic censors troubled by incompatibilities, not with 'real life', but with internalized moral values. Moreover, in readings true to the complexity of Freud's own thinking on the topic, fantasy is not thought to be reducible to wishful thinking or daydreaming about some concretely desired experience. There is simply no straightforward connection between the dynamics of desire in fantasy and the satisfactions sought in material reality. Fantasy is its own object, in the sense that it allows for multiple identifications across different people and positions, or for any other indulgence of the logically impossible. As Laplanche and Pontalis clarify for those trying to understand psychoanalytic thought:

> Fantasy is not the object of desire, but its setting. In fantasy the subject . . . cannot be assigned any fixed place . . . As a result, the subject, although always present in the fantasy, may be so in a desubjectivised form, that is to say, in the very syntax of the sequence in question.[70]

Here too, men's fetishistic need for visual proof of phallic potency, alongside their craving for visual evidence of female desire, should be seen in relation to men's specific fears of impotence, feeding off infantile 'castration' anxiety and the threat women pose to their sense of manhood: through pornography real women can be avoided, male anxiety soothed, delusions of phallic prowess indulged. The more complex pleasures of bisexuality and the capacity for identification with the 'opposite' sex, as well as the enjoyment of passivity, the eroticization of penetration and pain, are all readily available psychoanalytic explanations of men's (and also women's) use of pornography.

Hence the serious danger of basing one's politics about pornography on assumptions of fixed identifications and aspirations. From this perspective, MacKinnon could hardly be more misleading in declaring 'fantasy' a simple expression of ideology.[71] Given the well known incidence of fantasies of powerlessness from leading patriarchs, fantasies of being sexually dominated by black men (or women) enjoyed by white racists, and of rape fantasies by feminists, it should be clear that there is a rather dramatic *disjunction* between beliefs in one's own right to rule and fantasies of domination. Such fantasies do not express wavering convictions of social superiority, but rather have the autonomy and complexity of psychic existence. (This is why the vast literature on flagellation consumed by Victorian gentry, usually portraying male 'victims', sadly did nothing to dent their confident control of empire, industry and household.) We are all, especially feminists, entitled to a lowering of ignorance about the nature and force of fantasy, and hence to the lowering of personal anxiety about the sources of sexual excitement. Pornographic fantasy has no straightforward connection with what would be presumed to be its 'real-life' enactment, unless it is a *stylized* 'enactment' (as in consensual S/M) under the fantasizer's own control.

It is also relevant here that those who are socially powerful have not always exploited the relatively powerless (in all ways, including sexual), but projected the troubling, 'dirty' aspects of sex onto them. This is why it is not only women's bodies, but black and working-class bodies, which are mythically invested with sexuality in dominant Western discourse and iconography. It is the dynamic interplay between power and desire, attraction and repulsion, acceptance and disavowal, which eroticizes those *already* seen as inferior (and thereby gives them in fantasy a threatening power). It is not, as some feminists believe, the eroticizing of an object which creates it as inferior, but rather the other way around: assumed inferiority creates an erotic aura. (MacKinnon writes of pornography as sex for 'those who want to wallow in filth without getting their hands dirty' or 'violate the pure and only get their hands wet'.[72] Nevertheless, the sexualization of 'inferior' bodies does become a signification of difference, and a measure of the superiority of those who disown and distance themselves from such bodies. This is why any naked, eroticized display of the white male body remains so taboo outside pornography and, even there, will serve to threaten other white men: hence the subversive potential of such display.

Psychoanalytic reasoning suggests that infantile fears and desires, cross-sex identification (present in men's enjoyment of the ubiquitous lesbian number in pornography) and homosexual attachment (present in men's pleasure in watching other penises in action), all inform the content of pornography and men's and women's responses to it. But psychoanalysis has always had less of a purchase on the convoluted but nevertheless inevitable grounding of psychic experience in wider cultural meanings. Men's dread of 'femininity' and need for phallic reassurance is finally only comprehensible in the context of women's social subordination and the definitive ties of 'masculinity' to power and authority. Yet whatever men's social power (increasingly under threat for some men), their actual sexual potency has always been precarious. Rather than endorsing the myths carried by some of the most readily available pornography, and much else besides, we need to insist upon the precariousness of bodily masculinity and the possibilities for women's sexual empowerment. This returns us again to the incommensurabilities between gender norms and gender practices, especially marked in the sexual lives of men.

Instead of insisting upon the literal truths of pornography, other feminists (often combining psychoanalytical and deconstructive methods) have seen sexual representation as a site of political and discursive struggle – including struggle around just those sex acts which some find self-evidently 'degrading' and 'dehumanizing'. The theoretical inspiration behind Butler's recent foray into this area is precisely the suggestion that discourses do *not* fix meaning once and for all, which is why lesbians and gays have fought back as 'queer', just as certain racial signifiers have been reclaimed: to be hailed as 'black' was once the height of humiliating injury. Similarly, sex radicals – especially as sex workers – are only all too well aware of the hatred of women in the speech that labels them 'whore', 'cunt' or 'dyke', alongside the sufferings and exploitation of many sex workers, but some increasingly fight to turn around the intended injury and victimization, and fight for the rights of sex workers.[73] 'One is not simply fixed by the name that one is called', as Butler writes, 'the injurious address may appear to fix or paralyse the one it hails, but it may also produce an unexpected and enabling response'.[74]

From this perspective, if we want to keep any creative space open for ourselves as sexual agents (rather than encouraging fantasies of female victimization) the very last thing we want to do is remorselessly censor certain words and images: trying to fix their meanings, independently from seeking to understand their representational and social context, or complex psychic investments. This smacks of the very worst alliances between an unthinking psychology and a political culture of denial: premised on not wanting to understand or even acknowledge the underlying causes, or effects, of pervasive injustices, but seeking instead to locate familiar scapegoats. We see its nadir in the media with the blaming of video-nasties for the shocking murder of the toddler James Bulger in Liverpool in 1993 (and the frightening clamour for vengeance), extinguishing any attempt at understanding the sad, impoverished, painful lives of the two ten-year-old children responsible for the murder.

Reprinted by permission of Sage Publications Ltd. Segal, Lynne, 'Only the Literal: the Contradictions of Anti-Pornography Feminism' in *Sexualities*, vol. 1 no. 1, 1998, pp. 42–62 (© Sage Publications Ltd, 1998).

NOTES

This article is a version of a talk delivered at the Psychology of Women Conference, June 1996.

1. Catharine MacKinnon, *Feminism Unmodified: Discourse on Life and Law* (London: Harvard University Press, 1987), p. 68.
2. Judith Butler, *Excitable Speech: A Politics of the Performative* (London: Routledge, 1997), pp. 68–9.
3. Lisa Duggan and Nan Hunter, *Sex Wars: Sexual Dissent and Political Culture* (London: Routledge, 1995).
4. Carole S. Vance (ed.), *Pleasure and Danger: Exploring Female Sexuality* (London: Routledge & Kegan Paul, 1984).
5. This article is a version of a talk delivered at the Psychology of Women Conference, June 1996.
6. Duggan and Hunter, *Sex Wars*, p. 1.
7. Catharine MacKinnon, *Only Words* (London: Harvard University Press, 1993), p. 1.
8. Roy Porter and Lesley Hall, *The Facts of Life: The Creation of Sexual Knowledge in Britain, 1650–1950* (New Haven, CT: Yale University Press, 1995), p. 104.
9. Walter Kendrick, *The Secret Museum: Pornography in Modern Culture* (New York: Viking, 1987).
10. Linda Williams, *Hard Core: Power, Pleasure and the 'Frenzy of the Visible'* (London: Pandora, 1990).
11. Shannon Bell, *Reading, Writing and Rewriting the Prostitute Body* (Bloomington: Indiana University Press, 1994).
12. Williams, *Hard Core*, p. 230.
13. *Time*, 30 March 1987, cited in Dany Lacombe, *Pornography and the Law in the Age of Feminism* (Toronto: University of Toronto Press, 1994), p. 176.
14. *Adult Video News*, cited in Bill Thompson, *Soft Core* (London: Cassell, 1994), p. 239.
15. Carol Clover, *Men, Women and Chainsaws: Gender in the Modern Horror Film* (London: BFI, 1992).
16. Cited in Williams, *Hard Core*, p. 5.
17. Lynne Segal, *Straight Sex: The Politics of Pleasure* (London: Virago, 1994).
18. Ibid.
19. Robyn Morgan, *Going Too Far* (New York: Vintage Books, 1978), p. 181.
20. MacKinnon, *Feminism Unmodified*, p. 149.
21. Ann Snitow, 'Retrenchment vs Transformation: The Politics of the Antipornography Movement', in Kate Ellis (ed.), *Caught Looking: Feminism, Pornography and Censorship* (New York: Caught Looking Inc., 1986).
22. Duggan and Hunter, *Sex Wars*.
23. Andrea Dworkin, *Pornography: Men Possessing Women* (London: The Women's Press, 1981); MacKinnon, *Feminism Unmodified*.
24. Frances Delacoste and Priscilla Alexander (eds), *Sex Work: Writings by Women in the Sex Industry* (London: Virago, 1988).
25. Mari Matsuda, *et al.* (eds), *Words That Wound: Critical Race Theory, Assaultive Speech, and the First Amendment* (Boulder, CO: Westview Press, 1993).
26. MacKinnon, *Only Words*, p. 71.
27. See Jill Posener, *Louder Than Words* (New York: Pandora, 1986).
28. Sue Lees, *Carnal Knowledge: Rape on Trial* (Harmondsworth: Penguin, 1996).
29. Thompson, *Soft Core*.
30. MacKinnon, *Only Words*, p. 37.
31. Donald Symons, *The Evolution of Human Sexuality* (Oxford: Oxford University Press, 1979), p. 284.
32. Ibid.
33. Leonore Tiefer, *Sex Is Not a Natural Act* (New York: Westview Press, 1995).
34. Butler, *Excitable Speech*, p. 69.
35. Peter Stallybrass and Allon White, *The Politics and Poetics of Transgression* (London: Methuen, 1986), p. 12.

36. Richard Goldstein, 'Pornography and Its Discontents', in Michael Kimmel (ed.), *Men Confront Pornography* (New York: Crown, 1989), p. 71.

37. Peter Weiss, 'Forbidden Pleasures', in Kimmel (ed.), *Men Confront Pornography*, p. 78.

38. Laura Kipnis, *Ecstasy Unlimited: On Sex, Capital, Gender, and Aesthetics* (Minneapolis: University of Minnesota Press, 1993).

39. Anne McClintock, 'Sex Workers and Sex Work: Introduction', *Social Text* 37, 1993, p. 6.

40. J. Scott and S. Guvelier, 'Sexual Violence in *Playboy* Magazine: A Longitudinal Content Analysis', *Journal of Sex Research* no. 23, 1987, pp. 241–50; Donald Howitt and Graham Cumberbatch, *Pornography: Impact and Influences* (London: Home Office Research Planning Unit, 1990); and Thompson, *Soft Core*.

41. Michael Goldstein and Harold Kant, *Pornography and Sexual Deviance* (Berkeley: University of California Press, 1973); Larry Baron, 'Pornography and Gender Equality: An Empirical Analysis', *Journal of Sex Research*, vol. 27 no. 3, 1990, pp. 363–80; and B. Kutchinsky, 'Pornography and Rape: Theory and Practice? Evidence from Crime Data in Four Countries Where Pornography Is Easily Available', *International Journal of Law and Psychiatry* vol. 13 no. 4, 1990, pp. 409–27.

42. Mari Matsuda, *et al.*, *Words that Wound*, pp. 23 and 25.

43. Butler, *Excitable Speech*, p. 17.

44. MacKinnon, *Feminism Unmodified*, p. 176.

45. Lacombe, *Pornography and the Law in the Age of Feminism*, pp. 133–6.

46. Catherine Itzin, *Pornography: Women, Violence and Civil Liberties* (Oxford: Oxford University Press, 1992).

47. MacKinnon, *Only Words*, p. 103.

48. Brenda Cossman, *et al.*, *Bad Attitude/s on Trial: Pornography, Feminism and the Butler Decision* (Toronto: University of Toronto Press, 1996), pp. 2–4.

49. Lacombe, *Pornography and the Law in the Age of Feminism*.

50. Stephen Macedo (ed.), *Reassessing the Sixties: Debating the Political and Cultural Legacy* (New York: W.W. Norton, 1997), p. 29.

51. Butler, *Excitable Speech*, pp. 74 and 23.

52. Henry Louis Gates, Jr, 'An Album Is Judged Obscene; Rap, Slick, Violent, Nasty and, Maybe Helpful', *New York Times*, 17 June 1990.

53. Butler, *Excitable Speech*, p. 7.

54. Thelma McCormack, 'If Pornography Is the Theory, Is Inequality the Practice?', paper presented to the Senate Chamber of York University, Toronto, Canada, for discussion on 'The Limits of Freedom and Tolerance', 20 October 1993, p. 14.

55. Mandy Merck, 'MacKinnon's Dog: Anti-porn's Canine Conditioning', in Nancy Hewitt, Jean O'Barr and Nancy Rosebaugh (eds), *Talking Gender* (Chapel Hill: North Carolina Press, 1996), p. 76.

56. MacKinnon cited in Merck, 'MacKinnon's Dog', p. 67.

57. MacKinnon, *Only Words*, p. 37.

58. MacKinnon, *Feminism Unmodified*, p. 151.

59. H. J. Eysenck and H. Nias, *Sex, Violence and the Media* (London: Paladin, 1978), p. 236.

60. Edward Donnerstein, Daniel Linz and Steven Penrod, *The Question of Pornography* (New York: Free Press, 1987).

61. Thompson, *Soft Core*, p. 118.

62. Augustine Brannigan and Sheldon Goldenberg, 'The Study of Aggressive Pornography: The Vicissitudes of Relevance', *Critical Studies in Mass Communication*, vol. 4 no. 3, 1987, pp. 185–96; Donnerstein *et al.*, *The Question of Pornography*, p. 178.

63. Wendy Brown, *States of Injury: Power and Freedom in Late Modernity* (Princeton, NJ: Princeton University Press, 1995), p. 88.

64. Ibid., p. 87.

65. Jeffrey M. Masson, 'Incest, Pornography and the Problem of Fantasy', in Kimmel, *Men Confront Pornography*; John Stoltenberg, 'Pornography and Freedom', in Kimmel, *Men Confront Pornography*.

66. Drucilla Cornell, *Beyond Accommodation* (London: Routledge, 1991), p. 119.

67. Brown, *States of Injury*, p. 91.

68. MacKinnon, *Feminism Unmodified*, pp. 51 and 143.

69. Goldstein, 'Pornography and Its Discontents', p. 71.

70. Jean Laplanche and Jean-Bertrand Pontalis, 'Fantasy and the Origins of Sexuality', in Victor Burgin (ed.), *Formations of Fantasy* (London: Methuen, 1986), p. 26.

71. MacKinnon, *Feminism Unmodified*, p. 149.

72. MacKinnon, *Only Words*, p. 25.

73. Kipnis, *Ecstasy Unlimited*; Bell, *Reading, Writing and Rewriting the Prostitute Body*.

74. Butler, *Excitable Speech*, p. 2.

6   Virtual Child Porn: The Law and the Semiotics of the Image[1]

Chuck Kleinhans

In April 2002, the US Supreme Court delivered its judgment of a case involving 'virtual child pornography' (*Ashcroft v. Free Speech Coalition*).[2] My concern here is to discuss the underlying issues of this case and elaborate some of its implications and closely related issues. I believe there is a considerable gap between the development of visual semiotic analysis and visual culture studies on the one hand and on the other hand, the juridical and political fields of policy, law and enforcement. It is a somewhat familiar gesture to critique established agencies for not understanding visual culture. But examining these issues also reveals some of the signifying absences in contemporary media studies. That is, problems with 'our' theories are revealed when set against the pragmatics of the existing social world. In turn, the political world shapes the very possibility and nature of any research and knowledge in this area.

We live in a time of contested understandings of childhood. The world of images depicting children operates within a dialectic of expansion and control. As the commercial imperative of contemporary capitalism works to expand consumption, it has increased marketing and advertising to and for children. In the process, it continuously expands the sexualisation of children's images. In response to proliferating erotic images of children, other forces at many social levels attempt to control and contain child sexuality, especially in image culture. The focal point for this conflict has become sexualised *images* of children, including child pornography.

The way in which this conflict around images of children has developed can be seen in some advertising milestones. Selling relatively expensive designer jeans, in the early 80s Calvin Klein widely used an image of fifteen-year-old Brooke Shields with the caption, 'nothing comes between me and my Calvins', a double entendre that conveyed brand loyalty and not wearing underwear. Mildly controversial owing to its acknowledgment of teen sensuality, the ad was remarkably successful; and Klein's advertising has continued the trajectory.[3] In the late 80s, an ad for cologne, Obsession for Men, featured model Kate Moss, notably young, shot topless from the waist up, but also with marked cleavage as she held her arm over her breasts. Later, in 1994 a huge controversy erupted over a series of print ads and television commercials for Calvin Klein jeans that seemed to many protesters as encoded with the signifiers of child pornography. Although quickly withdrawn, the ads nevertheless stimulated a 30 per cent increase in the jeans' sales, conforming to the ad world's logic that teens find transgression appealing. A few years later, the fallout from the 1994 controversy seemed to linger when protests erupted over Calvin Klein ads for children's underwear. More recently, Abercrombie for Kids was criticised for selling thong underwear for girls as young as seven. The company responded that they were intended for ten-year-olds, an age at which, according to the company, girls are style conscious and want underwear that does not produce a visible panty line.[4]

Although sexuality is always a sensitive social and political issue, over the past thirty years, discourse around sexuality at many social levels has focused more and more on visual representations. And although images often evoke protest and legal/political efforts at restraint, in an unremarked way, verbal descriptions of sex have become more and more common and frank in the mass media. For example, Special Prosecutor Kenneth Starr's report which led to the Clinton impeachment events was published in full in local newspapers and was easily available online. It included explicit descriptions of the Clinton–Lewinsky sexual activities which were also discussed on television news and on TV and radio talk shows. Almost every literate child in the US at that time was aware of the details of oral sex, cigars as sex toys, ejaculation stains on clothing, and so forth. A measure of the current climate: a recent Home Box Office cable network documentary produced for their Family channel. *Middle School Confessions* (2002) interviews eleven- to fourteen-year-olds; and we hear and see a twelve-year-old girl and her female friends who discuss giving boyfriends manual and oral sex. While this level of frankness is commonly available in verbal form, elsewhere, in response to Calvin Klein ads, a national campaign attacks photos of children innocuously posed in ordinary underwear with critics claiming to be able to read signifiers of a little boy's penis in the image. Increased surveillance produces more suspicious readings. The famous Coppertone suntan lotion image of a little girl having her swim pants pulled down by a playful pup to reveal her tanline and buttocks was used for fifty years within the common understanding of it as 'innocent'. Today the same image carries the connotation of 'smutty'.

BACKGROUND

To give a little background: some particular characteristics of the US political and social scene shape the discourse about child pornography. The US is remarkably more religious than other advanced capitalist countries. The combination of Puritan origins, the continuous arrival of new religious immigrants, conservative Irish domination of the Roman Catholic Church, and a widespread Protestant fundamentalism which has gained organised political power in the past thirty years, all produce a substantial backdrop to legal action and social policy. At the same time, most municipal judges in the US are elected, not appointed, and judicial appointment has been increasingly directed by conservative political manoeuvres, especially in appointments to federal courts.

One consequence of the rise of second wave feminism in the late 60s was increased awareness of and organising around sexual assault, including assault on children. While progressive social forces brought forward issues formerly shrouded in shame and privacy, the Right capitalised on fears to make arguments for increased surveillance and regulation. Logically inconsistent but emotionally powerful arguments invoke the need to protect children's 'innocence', at the same time that conservatives demand severe punishment of children who break the law. With the

definition of 'youth' and 'child' highly contested for the past three decades, there have been attempts to define the human foetus as a person with rights, enactment of laws binding judges to severe penalties in criminal sentencing of minors, and an increasing trend to define children as adults in drug, assault and murder cases. Concurrently, eighteen years is the federal demarcation of adulthood, and new laws try to forbid minors access to contraception and abortion without consent of both parents (even when one is absent, not involved, negligent, etc.).[5]

At the same time, commercial culture has increasingly expanded into marketing for and to children,[6] most obviously in selling clothing fashions as sexy. And children and youth have more access to information and entertainment previously marked off as 'adult'. Fearful of a capitalist mass culture which seems to be increasingly encroaching on the space of the family, many parents respond with anxieties about protecting children from the internet, media and sexual threats. This works out within a nervous dialectic in which children are held to be 'naturally' innocent yet simultaneously implicated in dangerous sexuality. Rather than seeing children as humans going through a complex and contradictory maturation process, they are often posited as pure, yet easily corrupted by exposure to image material.

Since the beginning of the Reagan administration in 1981, moral panics centring on sexual predation of children and youth increased in number and intensity. These have ranged from sensational news stories about victimisation in child daycare centres (later shown to be pure fiction) to images of missing children on milk cartons (in fact almost all such children are runaways, throwaways, or those illegally taken by a parent in a custody battle). In popular culture representations, child abduction and sexual assault narratives have become a common recurring theme in television police procedural dramas.[7]

THE STATE INTERVENES

Following a landmark Supreme Court decision on child pornography *(New York v. Ferber*, 1982), Congress passed a major change to US law, the Child Protection Act of 1984, which removed the Miller obscenity standards from child images and raised the age of majority to eighteen.[8] It eliminated the previous restriction to commercial trafficking (and thus allowed prosecution for non-commercial transactions), restricted concerns to visual depiction, and substituted the broader term 'lascivious' for the previously used 'lewd'. Under the new law, interpretation of the image was determined by a variety of factors. Not all these elements were necessary, the clustering was important: the image's focal point was the pubic area; the setting was sexually suggestive; the pose unnatural; the attire inappropriate for the age of the child; the child could be fully clothed, or partially clothed, or nude; the model displays sexual coyness or willingness; and the image is designed to elicit a sexual response. Therefore the legislation shifted attention from the child porn image as a document of an event (realism) to questions of intent (communication) and the viewer's act of reading the image (reception, interpretation).

The theory underlying the Child Protection Act could be called a rightwing post-structuralism. Fears of sex lead to surveillance and control. The Act changes the agenda from catching child molesters and helping victims to the surveillance of images. As a result, the visual representation of the sexualised child becomes the central point of cultural contention. At the same time, the culture holds to an extreme denial of child sexuality. This denial is largely structured along the lines of class and education, that is differentiated by taste, not objective criteria. Thus high cultural capital readers could look at the kind of child modelling contests made famous by the murder of JonBenet Ramsey as 'white trash' events marked by highly artificial hair style, make-up, clothing and performance, but the same readers might be oblivious to the sexual subtexts of female child figure skating contests, gymnastic performance and ballet.[9]

In 1996, Congress passed the Communications Decency Act (CDA) attempting to control what was seen as a menacing availability of pornography to children using the internet. That Act makes it a crime to have adult material on-line where children can find it. The provisions of the law were immediately challenged and were never put into effect because the Supreme Court found it too sweeping and believed it interfered with legally protected free speech. In 1996, Congress also passed the Child Pornography Protection Act (CPPA) which is what I'm focusing on here. After the CDA was rejected, Congress passed the Child Online Protection Act (COPA, 1998), which required commercial websites to collect a proof of age (typically a credit card number) before allowing access to material deemed 'harmful to minors'. In May 2002, the Supreme Court returned to the lower courts COPA matters involving the issue of community standards in relation to internet pornography.[10] A further law, the Children's Internet Protection Act (CIPA), required public libraries to filter internet access to material deemed harmful to minors. It is under appeal to the Supreme Court. Congressional committees have generated new legislation, endorsed by Bush's Attorney General John Ashcroft, who entered office with a determined position to attack pornography.[11] Doubtless this will be an ongoing matter of contention and concern among the three branches of government, as well as among specific organisations and social and political movements.

This area of debate around pornography has traditionally been the domain of free speech advocates, on the one hand, and politically and religiously conservative censorship forces, on the other. In the 80s feminists joined the debate (on both sides), and the art world and cultural analysts were drawn into the discussion. This type of cultural contention erupted into the 'sex wars' phenomenon and was mixed with 80s' social activism, such as the AIDS movement.[12] More recently the discussion has expanded to include concerns about new technologies, media representations of violence, changing definitions of childhood, concerns about child molestation (and abduction, assault and murder), the globalisation of the internet and other communication businesses, and a fuller analysis of visual culture accounting for factual documentation and representation.

In the past, the mere fact of a photograph (or movie or video or other reproductive technology) of a child engaged in sexual activity was evidence of a crime in the eyes of the law. The image was proof (*New York v. Ferber*, 1982).[13] However, the current state of image art allows virtual images of children engaged in sexual acts so that those images can be created without the actual participation of children. In the last six or seven years, for example, the most familiar or commonly available images of this kind on the internet were still images of teen pop music star Britney Spears, both nude and engaged in sexual behaviour.[14] Such images are manufactured by combining authorised publicity, modelling and photojournalism images of the star's face with the bodies of other, presumably adult, women. These recombinant images, relatively easily manufactured with Photoshop and other digital image manipulation programs, can be easily published on the web, where they circulate quickly and widely.[15] Another possibility is to use purely computer-generated image (CGI) technology for both still and moving images. The feature-length dramatic action film *Final Fantasy: The Spirits Within* (Hironobu Shakaguci, 2001) is generally acknowledged as a breakthrough in producing photo-realistic depictions.[16] Doubtless the technology will only improve and become less expensive and more widely available. Thus in the near term we can expect totally artificially generated photo-realistic CGI images of children in both still and moving image media.

Computer-constructed or -modified images can produce 'plausible' photo-realistic images which do not document what they purport to show. Previous US laws interpreted pornographic drawings as different from photographic images and not actionable as child pornography. For example, Japanese *anime* and *manga*-style images of child sexuality are easily found on the internet, as are cartoon images of *The Simpsons* children engaged in sexual activities. Technically, simple photographic nudity of children is not presently actionable. But in fact, enforcement and prosecution vary. In most jurisdictions photo processors are required to report to local police any images they receive of nude children or any clothed children posed in sexually suggestive ways – obviously a subjective judgment. Then police and prosecutors make a further judgment call. As a result some parents who have taken pictures of the kids in the bathtub are investigated, interrogated and arrested for child pornography. In the worst cases, the children are taken by government agents (and placed in foster care or juvenile detention) until the matter can be settled.[17] I want to acknowledge that this happens, but also point out that pictures of children, for example, in nudist/naturist publications and websites (often posed among adults) are technically legal.

The history of documentary photography includes images of naked children, such as the famous image of a naked young Vietnamese girl running towards the camera after a napalm attack. And art photography includes figure studies such as Edward Weston's nude images of his pre-pubescent son, Neil. However, in the past twenty years, some professional photographers have run afoul of the law and critics, most famously Sally Mann for pictures of her children, and Robert Mapplethorpe and Jock Sturges for pictures of minors taken with the parents' permission.[18] In 1994, a controversial Supreme Court case, *Knox v. United States*, redefined photographic child pornography. It shifted the basis from using the photo as evidence from a crime scene to judging a photo as a representation.[19] In this scheme, it did not matter if a real child had been harmed, and clothed children could be interpreted as lasciviously or indecently displayed. Once again, the point is that the law increasingly allows for cases to be decided on the basis of sexual image interpretation, while defining 'sexually suggestive' is always a subjective judgment call. You can easily find within contemporary US culture many examples of this kind of overlapping confusion: kids in underwear or swimsuit ads may be censored, while kids dressed in sexy adult garb and dancing suggestively can be found in child modelling contests, child model websites and some children's entertainment, e.g. the Venezuelan TV show, *El Club de los Tigritos*, broadcast in the US on Spanish language networks.

During the mid-90s an expanded internet, boosted by computer sales, allowed for a more widespread distribution of photos of (ostensibly) Russian and Ukrainian (and for a while Romanian) female children ranging from about six years old to post-pubescent teens. These occurred on many 'Lolita' sites. Increased policing somewhat reduced these images' availability, but some Lolita sites remain active. Generally the photos mimic 'artistic' posing conventions ranging from discreet to genital display, but not (to my knowledge) sexual activity.[20] Samples of such photos are displayed on the initial pages of websites that feature such material.[21] Presumably, more revealing images are available after a credit card payment establishes membership. Since 'Lolita' has become a popular search term, almost all pay porn sites with images of young women use the term, although if based in the US, the site probably has eighteen-year-old models. Lolita images had some previous presence on the no-fee adult sections of US web services such as MSN, Yahoo and Lycos, and others which disappeared with the end of the dotcom bubble, but such under-age images are now forbidden by the web hosts.[22]

VIRTUAL AND PERFORMED IMAGES OF THE SEXUAL CHILD: THE SUPREME COURT DECIDES

The decision the Supreme Court faced in *Ashcroft v. Free Speech Coalition* was to judge if recombinant photo-realistic images and CGIs are granted 'free speech' protections or if they fall into another category. Similarly, photo images of models who *appear* to be under-age were considered by the court. Such images range from the implausible to the borderline: e.g., a well-known adult performer dressed up in juvenile-signifying clothing, with a lollipop, teddy bear, hair in pigtails at one extreme, to slim, petite, small-breasted, youthful-looking females and boyish male models at the other. At present such images appear widely in print and on the internet within an editorial framework that states that the young women (in particular) have just turned eighteen. For example, the *Hustler* franchise run by Larry Flynt has a successful video/DVD and magazine series, 'Barely Legal', in which the captions, text copy and voice narration indicate explicitly that the actors have just turned eighteen. A gonzo video competitor even has the model display her driver's licence in a close-up to verify her legal age before the action begins.[23] In the 70s, US hard-core theatrical porn films often presented dramatic fictional stories of minors engaged in sex with each other and with adults.[24] Particularly in the Reagan era, such images were targeted for prosecution, so they were withdrawn. They have reappeared erratically in the 90s: for example Max Hardcore's short-lived *Cherry Poppers* series with adults performing both pre-teen and teen roles.

On 16 April 2002, the Supreme Court gave its verdict in *Ashcroft v. Free Speech Coalition*, challenging a provision of the 1996 Child Pornography Prevention Act. By a split decision, the majority affirmed that visual child pornography remains centrally defined by the fact that it is the recording of a crime and that its production creates victims. With virtual images, the 6–3 majority reasoned, these two elements are not present. In another aspect the court decided 7–2 that the government could not criminalise presenting adults as children, which the CPPA had included. For the CPPA, 'appears to be' was actionable, as was any advertising or merchandising that promised under-age sexual depictions, even if these were not in the image. In her opinion, Justice

O'Connor found that 'appears to be' in the CPPA covered two categories of speech: pornographic images of adults that look like children ('youthful-adult pornography') and pornographic images of children created wholly on a computer without using any actual children ('virtual-child pornography'). She found the ban on the former too broad and therefore unacceptable, but she did not agree that the ban on virtual-child pornography was unacceptable. The conservative minority found the CPPA reasonable and constitutional.[25]

Part of the problem here is that legal definitions of 'child' are neither simple nor consistent. In the US the age of consent for legal sexual activities ranges from fourteen (Iowa, Missouri) to eighteen; the age for operating a motor vehicle is sixteen, the age for voting is eighteen and the age for drinking alcohol is twenty-one. For pornographic images, the model must be eighteen for the image to be legal. In a famous case from the 80s, it was found that Traci Lords had made about 200 pornographic films between ages fifteen and eighteen, even operating her own production company. When it was discovered she was under-age, all of those images, films and videos became child pornography, and possession of them illegal.[26]

Some analysts want to distinguish pre-adolescent children from adolescent children in setting up the terms of this discussion. (I have heard such distinctions recently in news reports and commentary regarding the current US scandal of Roman Catholic priests found to be paedophiles.) But defining borders, particularly in visual terms, is a very tricky business. Because human beings go through stages of development – both physical and emotional – and because there is no perfect correlation of visual markers to chronological age, the norms to distinguish pre-pubescent, pubescent, adolescent, and adult by secondary sexual characteristics are problematic. For example, any appeal to physical development is confounded by considerable variation in breast or penis size. The appearance and amount of pubic hair varies with individuals, and it cannot visually be relied on since it can be removed.[27] Further, the average onset of puberty in the US has tended to be earlier than in the past: currently the norm for African-American females is nine, and for white females eleven. Obviously the basis for any law distinguishing pre-adolescent and adolescent rests on an expectation and determination of emotional as well as physical maturity, ability to make decisions with informed consent, and status as a dependant minor.

In delivering the majority opinion on the CPPA, Justice Kennedy wrote the following referring explicitly to films:

The CPPA prohibits speech despite its serious literary, artistic, political, or scientific value. The statute proscribes the visual depiction of an idea – that of teenagers engaging in sexual activity – that is a fact of modern society and has been a theme in art and literature throughout the ages. Under the CPPA, images are prohibited so long as the persons appear to be under 18 years of age. 18 U.S.C. Sec. 2256(1). This is higher than the legal age for marriage in many States, as well as the age at which persons may consent to sexual relations. See Sec. 2243(a) (age of consent in the federal maritime and territorial jurisdiction is 16); *U.S. National Survey of State Laws* 384 – 388 (R. Leiter ed., 3d ed. 1999) (48 States permit 16-year-olds to marry with parental consent); W. Eskridge & N. Hunter, *Sexuality, Gender, and the Law* 1021 – 1022 (1997) (in 39 States and the District of Columbia, the age of consent is 16 or younger). It is, of course, undeniable that some youths engage in sexual activity before the legal age, either on their own inclination or because they are victims of sexual abuse.

Both themes – teenage sexual activity and the sexual abuse of children – have inspired countless literary works. William Shakespeare created the most famous pair of teenage lovers, one of whom is just 13 years of age. See *Romeo and Juliet*, act I, sc. 2, l. 9 ('She hath not seen the change of fourteen years'). In the drama, Shakespeare portrays the relationship as something splendid and innocent, but not juvenile. The work has inspired no less than 40 motion pictures, some of which suggest that the teenagers consummated their relationship, for example, *Romeo and Juliet* (B. Luhrmann director, 1996). Shakespeare may not have written sexually explicit scenes for the Elizabethan audience, but were modern directors to adopt a less conventional approach, that fact alone would not compel the conclusion that the work was obscene.

Contemporary movies pursue similar themes. Last year's Academy Awards featured the movie *Traffic*, which was nominated for Best Picture. See 'Predictable and Less So, the Academy Award Contenders,' *N.Y. Times*, Feb. 14, 2001, p. E11. The film portrays a teenager, identified as a 16-year-old, who becomes addicted to drugs. The viewer sees the degradation of her addiction,

which in the end leads her to a filthy room to trade sex for drugs.[28] The year before, *American Beauty* won the Academy Award for Best Picture. See ' "American Beauty" Tops the Oscars,' *N.Y. Times*, Mar. 27, 2000, p. E1. In the course of the movie, a teenage girl engages in sexual relations with her teenage boyfriend, and another yields herself to the gratification of a middle-aged man. The film also contains a scene where, although the movie audience understands the act is not taking place, one character believes he is watching a teenage boy performing a sexual act on an older man.[29]

While Justice Kennedy recalls the film depicting 'a teenage girl . . . yields herself to the gratification of a middle-aged man', I presume that those of us in media studies recognise this as a *fabula*, to use David Bordwell's recirculation of the Russian Formalist concept.[30] That is, Justice Kennedy constructs this event in his memorial experience/interpretation of the film. If we were using a properly Bordwellian analysis of the film's narration, we would say that one scene shows the *desire* of the middle-aged man (Lester, the Kevin Spacey character) for his daughter's girlfriend, but not the action. The fantasy, not the actual behaviour is depicted in the 'rose petal' sequence where Lester, at night lying in bed, fantasises Angela (Mena Suvari) the young woman (who is at least sixteen since she can drive) nude in a bed of rose petals, some of which strategically cover her breasts and genital area. In a second sequence, at the end of the film, Angela flirts with Lester and entices him into sex which goes as far as touching (but not passionate embrace or kissing) and slowly undressing. She is reclining, he undresses her, opening her blouse to display her breasts. He is lightly kissing one breast when she reveals that (unexpectedly, given her previous verbal sexual bravado) this is her first time. The revelation stops Lester, and the scene cuts to one with food as a substitute pleasure as she (clothed) finishes a sandwich he prepared for her.

Clearly, at this point we have something to say to seven Supreme Court justices (and their law clerks) in terms of visual analysis: 'a teenage girl . . . yields herself to the gratification of a middle-aged man'. The cinematic narrative problem (for the filmmakers) here is precisely defending Lester from the charge of child sexual assault. The script accomplishes this in several ways, including the film's narration to this point. In the above sequence Lester is clearly presented in his 'new' liminal blissed-out state of mind (he has just been working out, smoking marijuana, and had his ex-Marine neighbour come on to him, whose advances he gently declines). Rather than his being an aggressor, the dramatic narration emphasises that the girl is initiating the action – thus she hardly 'yields' – and Lester is hardly gratified in a carnal sense.[31] Indeed, Lester's decision establishes his final transcendence over the middle-class suburban American life which the film satirises. It also, unmistakably in its historical moment, replays the national drama of the Clinton–Lewinsky affair with the young woman as the initiator.

The instigating action for Lester's change at the beginning of the film is his attraction to Angela (the blonde angel). He makes the decisive move of quitting his meaningless job and then reverting to an adolescent boy's fantasy life of working out, driving a sporty car and (ridiculously) working for minimum wages in a fast food restaurant though he doesn't need the money. Throughout, as the signifier of his basic goodness, he sadly regrets his daughter's life and his inability to communicate with her. As he transcends his initial sexual fantasy, he gains a new state of understanding and acceptance; within the moral economy of the film, achieving this condition is punished by death. Certainly *American Beauty* is fairly superficial as social criticism, using easy stereotypes, as compared with a film like *Happiness* (Todd Solondz, 1998), which presents a much more acid critique of US society and values by both ironically and sympathetically depicting a child molester, a murderer, and marginal sexual practices.

THE RESEARCH PROBLEM

Defining child pornography is a first step for further analysis. But any definition is difficult because of different and competing discourses that contain ideologies about childhood, sexuality and the nature of visual documentation and representation. Obviously the 'old' legal definition of child pornography (*New York v. Ferber*, 1982), that it documented a crime of sexual assault, was rather simple; it pointed first to the felony of sex with a minor. In that sense the primary crime was the sexual activity and the visual record was of secondary importance. However, possession and circulation of the visual recording was also a criminal issue. But many explicitly sexual images exist without factual information about the

people depicted. For example, what constitutes the visual depiction of a *child*, since the photographic record itself is often quite unreliable in terms of definitively revealing age and thus legal status? Is simple nudity criminal? Is sexual suggestiveness criminal, and if so what constitutes suggestiveness?

It is difficult to examine these questions analytically because they exist within a complex set of overlapping and contradictory discourses including the legal/juridical, the cultural, the political, the aesthetic and the communicative. In the current situation of digital imagery and global internet circulation of images, quantitative changes have produced a qualitatively different situation and it can be fairly agreed on by all concerned that we've arrived at a new stage.[32] Technological change now does put into the hands of anyone who can afford it and has access to children, the ability to take and circulate images of children engaged in sexual activity. Today, forty-plus years beyond the Polaroid camera, and twenty-plus years into consumer video camcorders, and six years into consumer-format digital still cameras, the idea of hard-core paedophiles taking their rolls of film to the one-hour photo processor in their neighbourhood seems truly bizarre. But regrettably, as we've seen repeatedly in an era and aura of moral panic, innocent parents taking pictures of their children can be falsely accused.

Politically, we've seen a drastic expansion in the surveillance and policing of children and images of children. Thus the concern for 'protection' of the 'innocent' has the unintended consequence of focusing much more attention on children and representations of them, and in particular of looking for traces of sexual behaviour or intentions. Ironically, at the same time that legal and social surveillance of children's sexuality has increased, as a research question, the status of child sexuality has been vastly restricted since the Reagan era. Due to administrative and legislative pressures, it has been virtually impossible to get any funding for clinical or survey research.[33] As with increasing restrictions on sex education, asking a child about sexual activity is forbidden.[34] With child pornography, since no one is allowed to have it or study it, the only source of information we have about what it is comes either from police and prosecutors, felon paedophiles or child participants. There is no 'outside' reference, as is the case in illegal drug use, where medicine produces knowledge outside the legal system and the culture of users.[35]

By default, the best critical intellectual analysis of children and sexual images develops within cultural studies, broadly construed. James R. Kincaid's *Child-Loving: The Erotic Child and Victorian Culture* provides essential historical background, and his subsequent *Erotic Innocence: The Culture of Child Molesting* surveys recent events in the cultural landscape.[36] From a perspective in art history and criticism, Anne Higonnet's *Pictures of Innocence: The History and Crisis of Ideal Childhood* supplies an extensive analysis of images of children, including controversies around sexualised photos.[37] And concentrating on child pornography within the framework of critical legal studies, Amy Adler examines the issues from a Foucauldian perspective in her essential article, 'The Perverse Law of Child Pornography'.[38] Yet all these studies are limited due to restricted or non-existent data.

The contrast between two recent books underlines the issues. In a carefully investigated and reasoned study of children and sexual information in the US today, *Harmful to Minors: The Perils of Protecting Children from Sex*,[39] Judith Levine argues that by and large concerns about 'child pornography' are a smoke-screen for a repressive agenda fuelled by the Christian fundamentalist Right and enacted for political reasons to keep children ignorant of sexuality and their choices about it. She begins her book with a discussion of official censorship and then continues with a discussion of the contemporary moral panic over abduction, paedophilia and child incest. Levine finds that despite media sensationalism and panic peddling, the most reliable reports indicate that for the past thirty years, there has been very little child pornography available.

> Aficionados and vice cops concede that practically all the sexually explicit images of children circulating cybernetically are the same stack of yellowing pages found at the back of those X-rated shops [in 70s' raids on Times Square], only digitized. These pictures tend to be twenty to fifty years old, made overseas, badly reproduced, and for the most part pretty chaste. That may be why federal agents almost never show journalists the contraband.[40]

Allowed to see downloaded files by the US Customs Service, Levine found three of fifty to be mildly pornographic. She cites experts who claim that most on-line child pornography sites are actually police-run traps. She argues that federal and local police officials have used vastly expanded definitions of pornography and techniques of entrapment to justify their expensive policing of internet porn. Making a similar point in *Bound and Gagged* Laura Kipnis provides a detailed case study of such police entrapment on-line which seemed to result in a conviction only on the basis of fantasy that was fed and fuelled by police enticement.[41]

In contrast, Philip Jenkins's book *Beyond Tolerance: Child Pornography on the Internet* indicates a considerably larger and more substantial pornographic activity. Jenkins began this work after writing *Moral Panic: Changing Concepts of the Child Molester in Modern America*, a historical and social constructionist analysis of child sex abuse.[42] He turned to the internet with a particular emphasis not on commercial or amateur websites, but on bulletin boards with restrictions on admission or private areas for exchange of text and image material. There he found an extensive circulation of image material. His research was done by investigating with his computer browser disabled so he could not actually see the image material, and thus it is based on the written discourse on the sites, not the pictures.[43] In his book Jenkins carefully outlines the legal circumstances for his investigation. Subsequently he has written on the methodological and epistemological research problems restricting scholarly analysis, and effective policing of child abuse.[44]

There is a grey area here in terms of public and social discussion of the issues of both child sexuality and child pornography, which are very separate issues. Society provides overwhelming support for the proposition that photo/video images of prepubescent children engaged in sexual activities with adults are clearly the documentation of criminal sexual assault on a child and the crime is in the assault itself; the image is an ancillary artifact and should be censored. Yet the agenda of most anti-porn activism is much larger, as made clear by efforts to shift the line on 'appears to be' or 'youthful-adult'. Obviously fantasy is a tricky thing to regulate unless one takes a rigid stand against any kind of imaginative dissembling. For example, some adults want to engage in role-playing activities with other adults, but does an adult–child role-playing site cross the line? That is, does the very pretence of 'Daddy/Daughter' sexual play among adults stand for something so dangerous that speech about it must be forbidden? The Supreme Court decision in *Ashcroft v. Free Speech Coalition* would seem to allow image material. Yet, as Laura Kipnis points out in a case study of police entrapment, the verbal imagining of illegal sexual activity can result in prosecution and guilty conviction.[45] Similarly, Jenkins provides information on a case where a man placed on probation for having pornographic images of children subsequently was found to have self-authored fictional narrations of child sexual abuse (not image material), which upon discovery landed him in jail.[46]

CELEBRITY CASES

Much of the public awareness of child pornography circulates through the press's attention to high-profile child abduction and murder cases when it is revealed that the culprit possessed illegal images. But beyond direct criminal cases, celebrity cases also gain considerable attention. In the early 90s popular rising star Rob Lowe had his career derailed for a while when videotapes of him engaged in sex with a fourteen-year-old girl appeared and were widely pirated, though he was never charged; he ended up in the late 90s a major actor on the prime-time TV series *The West Wing*. In a similar case, popular African-American singer R. Kelly, known for both his gospel roots and his sexually provocative hits, was charged with twenty-one counts of child pornography in Chicago in June 2002 when pirate copies of a videotape of Kelly having sex with a minor circulated widely in the city's black neighbourhoods.

Several high-profile celebrity cases at the time of writing (May 2003) dramatise the issues. Rock musician Peter Townshend (of The Who) was issued a formal warning by Scotland Yard for viewing child pornography on the internet, and his name will appear on Britain's sex-offender register.[47] Actor Paul Reubens (Pee Wee Herman) faces prosecution on possession of child pornography for images he collected from 50s' and 60s' male physique magazines. Richard Goldstein explains in the *Village Voice*:

> During the '50s and '60s, no one was concerned that some models were underage, since they were not shown having sex or even engaging in what tea-room graffiti of that era called 'showing hard.' Today these same

images would qualify as child porn under a standard that has expanded so that it now includes not just hardcore images but photos of anyone under 18 displaying 'sexual coyness' or a 'lascivious' intent.[48]

He concludes:

> [T]he fixation on erotic images as opposed to criminal behavior may have unintended consequences. . . . An image that once seemed tender, since its sexual meaning was repressed, is now terrifying because it reads as explicitly erotic. The process of sensitizing us to child porn also forces us to eroticize children. Whether we intend to or not, we begin to see the world from a pedophile's perspective.[49]

POLICING CHILD PORNOGRAPHY

Amy Adler argues convincingly that the law on child pornography produces a heightened regard for the sexualised child:

> the burgeoning law of child pornography may invite its own violation through a dialectic of taboo and transgression. . . . The law may unwittingly perpetuate and escalate the sexual representation of children that it seeks to constrain. In this view, the legal tool that we designed to liberate children from sexual abuse threatens us all, by constructing a world in which we are enthralled – anguished, enticed, bombarded – by the spectacle of the sexual child.[50]

But it also directs attention and resources to visual culture rather than criminal assault.

The efficacy of intervening for child victims by pursuing images needs to be examined critically. Several vigilante websites which ostensibly act to find internet child pornography and alert police are functionally gateway resources for paedophilic information. One such site reproduces partial images (waist up) it claims are examples of porn images (reproducing the face of the boy victim) and a digitally obscured image of an adult/child sex act.[51]

The police questionably use extensive and expensive resources to pursue child pornography rather than child abusers. For example, a Texas couple was arrested, prosecuted and jailed for operating what police described as a vast internet child pornography operation. The couple offered a credit card verification service for 250,000 customers that allowed entry to about 5,000 porn sites. Two of those 5,000 were found to carry child pornography.[52] The FBI then took over the site and ran it for two years offering the quarter-million subscribers child porn videos, CD-ROMs and magazines. From the small number who responded, 100 arrests were made. The press version claimed the FBI broke up a child porn ring of 250,000. The names of foreign respondents were turned over to their national police which resulted in additional arrests. Another famous case, 'Operation Candyman', prominently announced to the press by Ashcroft and the FBI a month before the *Ashcroft v. Free Speech Coalition* decision, targeted members of an on-line bulletin board group.[53] However, later reports questioned the process and effectiveness of the operation, and some initial search warrants were found to use 'reckless disregard' for the truth.[54]

The emphasis on images can make good publicity for the police and result in high-profile convictions. But if these are based on people who are only circulating images and not the original producers, the arrests do not intervene to stop the instigating abuse. Nor do these kinds of prosecutions affect child sexual abuse. That real abuse is most often not recorded and circulated in image media but is marked on the body and mind of the child victims. In terms of priorities, if the police, prosecutors, judges and legislators concentrate on images, that still leaves abused children defenceless.

Obviously in contemporary society visual culture is acutely political.

A government that increasingly uses media image, rhetorical motions, and political spin to affect public opinion will find spectres of child pornography a useful tool. While I was completing this article, the Bush administration passed and signed a massive tax-cut programme targeting the wealthiest strata of the population. Last-minute manoeuvres eliminated a proposed increase in tax deductions for children for the working poor: families making $10,000 to $26,000 a year. The individual states face major economic crises and are cutting welfare, public housing, health services, and child and family services. And we know that family violence increases with economic decline. Analysts of media culture – from the Right, Left and Centre; activists and academics; professionals and lay people – need to reflect on what is the most important area for intervention. In the present moment of increasing unemployment and

rapidly declining social services, we face hard choices. We need to not only think about images; we need to intervene for the children at risk and in danger.

NOTES

1. First given as a paper at the Society for Cinema Studies conference, Denver, May 2002. A somewhat different version of this essay will appear in the *Journal of Visual Culture.*

2. Available at the Library of Congress website, <www.loc.gov>. A useful summary of recent law on internet pornography and children: Jason Krause, 'Can Anyone Stop Internet Porn?', *American Bar Association Journal*, September 2002, pp. 56–61. An extensive background survey which I draw on throughout this article is Eva J. Klein, Heather J. Davies and Molly A. Hicks, *Child Pornography: The Criminal-Justice-System Response* (Alexandria, VA: National Center for Missing and Exploited Children, 2001); downloadable copy at <www.missingkids.org>. The publication is an extended survey by the American Bar Association Center on Children and the Law.

3. The key ads are reproduced on several websites. See Barbara Welch Breder and Karla Tonella, 'Calvin Klein' (1997), <www.uiowa.edu/~commstud/ advertising/cklein/ckhome.htm>; 'Calvin Klein: Case Study Assignment' (n.d.), Media Awareness Network, <www.media-awareness.ca/english/ resources/educational/handouts/ethics/ck_case_study _assignment.cfm>; 'Brandon' (n.d.), The Commercial Closet, <www.commercialcloset.org/cgi-bin/iowa/ portrayals.html?record=2>; 'Unofficial Calvin Klein Ads Archive' (n.d.), <www.dolphin.upenn.edu/ ~davidtoc/calvin.html>; Linnea Smith (n.d.), 'Calvin Klein', <www.talkintrash.com/adv/CK>.

4. Abercrombie for Kids was earlier criticised for using male and female nude teen models in one edition of their clothing catalogue. The objection to thongs was directly aimed at the merchandise available in mall stores and by catalogue, not ads, since the only images were of the product itself. See Vikki Ortiz, 'Parents Say Kid's Thong Is Just Plain Wrong', *Journal Sentinel Online* (Milwaukee), 17 May 2002, <www.jsonline.com/news/gen/may02/43941.asp>.

5. Age of consent for sexual activity and marriage varies from state to state. The District of Columbia and thirty-nine states recognise sixteen as the age of consent for sexual activity. However, they must be eighteen to be photographed having sex. US teens can

drive unsupervised at sixteen, vote, enlist in the armed forces, and obtain a credit card at eighteen, but cannot legally drink alcohol until twenty-one. The definition of legal and practical adulthood and maturity involves shifting borderlines.

6. For a broad perspective on the issues see Seiter, and Jyotsna Kapur, 'Out of Control: Television and the Transformation of Childhood in Late Capitalism', in Marsha Kinder (ed.), *Kid's Media Culture* (Durham, NC: Duke University Press, 1999), pp. 122–36.

7. For example, the 2002–3 season of broadcast network shows, *Law and Order: Special Victims Unit* and *Without a Trace,* have used these storylines.

8. The landmark 1972 Supreme Court ruling in *Miller v. California* established the principle of communities setting their own standards for obscenity. Thus San Francisco could have very liberal standards while small towns in the Deep South could be extremely conservative.

9. The Ramseys were an upper-class family economically; the mother participated in beauty queen contests while a young woman in the South and passed the contest culture on to her daughter at an early age.

10. While the Miller local standards plan was functional in an era when distribution issues focused on the local bookstore and movie theatre, changing technologies of distribution and exhibition such as videotape, DVD, cable, satellite and the internet changed local availability. As a result regulators have turned increasingly to age as the key national barrier to child access.

11. As a senator, Ashcroft was a leader in promoting religious conservative positions, and his appointment was seen as the major recognition of Christian fundamentalist politics in Bush's cabinet appointments. The 11 September 2001 attacks drastically changed priorities, and the Attorney General's office has not prioritised pornography issues. Ashcroft signalled his understanding of art when he had curtains placed over an art deco statue, *The Spirit of Justice,* with an exposed breast in the lobby of the Justice Department. See 'Curtains for Semi-nude Justice Statue', BBC News, 29 January 2002, <www.news.bbc.co.uk/1/hi/world/americas/17788845.stm>.

12. A thorough account from the feminist anti-censorship position is Lisa Duggan and Nan D. Hunter, *Sex Wars: Sexual Dissent and Political Culture* (New York: Routledge, 1995). A recent anthology recapitulates and updates the feminist anti-pornography position (while being grossly misleading in its claim to be fair and balanced): Drucilla Cornell (ed.), *Feminism and Pornography* (Oxford: Oxford University Press, 2000).

13. *Ferber* was the first decision that specifically addressed child pornography as a special category. Previously the matter was handled under general obscenity law. In 1984 Congress enacted legislation to deny any free speech protection for images of children and raised the age of adulthood from sixteen to eighteen.

14. Spears turned eighteen on 2 December 1999, at which time she had a well-established career and image (including schoolgirl-style clothing), including a frequently noted and commented-on breast enlargement. Many of the initial fake images concentrated on showing her topless.

15. Additional issues are the legal implications of privacy and publicity for celebrities, and image ownership. For a full discussion see Jane Gaines, *Contested Culture: The Image, the Voice and the Law,* (Chapel Hill: University of North Carolina Press, 1991). I discuss a pirate video distributed on the internet in Chuck Kleinhans, 'Pamela Anderson on the Slippery Slope', in Jon Lewis (ed.), *The End of Cinema as We Know It: American Film in the 1990s* (New York: New York University Press, 2001), pp. 287–99.

16. Based on a popular videogame, the sci-fi adventure features characters who generally maintain a military bearing, thus making CGI limits on body language and facial expression less of a concern.

17. In these circumstances some parents have felt coerced into 'confession' of some wrong-doing (against their actual behaviour) because their children were held hostage by the legal system. See Judith Levine, *Harmful to Minors: The Perils of Protecting Children from Sex* (Minneapolis: University of Minnesota Press, 2002).

18. These cases and others are well analysed in Anne Higonnet, *Pictures of Innocence: The History and Crisis of Ideal Childhood* (New York: Thames and Hudson, 1998).

19. Detailed in Higonnet, *Pictures of Innocence*, pp. 182–5.

20. Robert Grove and Blaise Zerenga, 'The Lolita Problem', *Red Herring*, January 2002, pp. 47–53. (Given the nature of the internet, these sites may not actually be located on computer servers in Russia and the Ukraine.)

21. These commercial sites seem particularly volatile, though it is unclear to me if this is because of business changes or legal matters. At the time of writing, the site ukranian-angels.com contained such images, although it had changed its name to 'gentle angels' on the first page.

22. Some anti–child porn organisations describe conducting their own investigations and alerting web administrators and police agencies of violations. However, since computers download images from remote servers, to actually view such material the vigilante viewers break the law against possession. Even when subsequently removed to the 'trash', the file remains until overwritten because technically only the directions to the file are erased and thus can be revealed by high-tech forensic investigation. At present, alerting police to illegal images on the internet is not a legal defence; a reporter who did so was arrested for possession of the images he found during an investigation. Various porn sites frequently offer software that promises to erase all traces, as well as encryption programs that give increased security for files.

23. *Bring'um Young* (d. Jon Dough) series, c. 2001.

24. For example: *Debbie Does Dallas, Oriental Babysitter, Little Girls Blue (I and II)*, and *First Time at Cherry High* (later re-titled and re-released as *First Time at Cherry U*).

25. O'Connor apparently meant to address CGI, but did not address recombinant pornography using real children (but taken from non-pornographic behaviour) combined with images of adult genital activity.

26. However, some of her film work from that period is available in France and the Netherlands (both of which use a different age of majority for sexual images), and still images occasionally appear on the internet.

27. In paediatrics the standard scale for determining maturation is the Tanner staging scale which relies on breast development in girls and genital development in boys and pubic hair growth in both. Tanner and a colleague have gone on record that the scale is not reliable for determining a child's age from image materials in court proceedings: Arlan L. Rosenbloom and James Tanner, 'Misuse of Tanner Scale' (letter), *Pediatrics*, vol. 102 no. 6, 1998, p. 1494.

28. It's a sign of the times that the Supreme Court equates artistic merit and seriousness of purpose with winning the Academy Award. A sceptic can easily argue that the sex scene in *Traffic* serves largely to recreate for the contemporary white American audience the same knee-jerk racism as D. W. Griffith's *The Birth of a Nation*. Both depict black men having sex with white women as horrifying.

29. US Supreme Court, *Ashcroft v. Free Speech Coalition*.

30. David Bordwell, *Narration in the Fictional Film* (Madison: University of Wisconsin Press, 1984).

31. Obviously one can still object to the film's presentation of the fantasy and defence of Lester. For such a reading, see Kathleen Karlyn, 'Too Close for Comfort: *American Beauty* and the Incest Motif', paper presented at the Society for Cinema Studies, Denver, May 2002.

32. As has been widely noted, the internet creates a global community. The 1972 Miller decision allowed that different places could regulate pornography in different ways. Functionally this meant that local prosecutors made decisions about what was acceptable and not, and police then followed these guidelines. As businesses adapted to the local conditions, different locales might allow different materials to be sold. For example in the early 80s, postal inspectors used Tennessee, with very strict laws and interpretations, to take action against national mail-order pornography. The businesses shifted to United Parcel Service and similar delivery services to avoid the problem. But the internet negates this standard, since it is available nationally and internationally. In a case decided in May 2002, the Supreme Court returned a case dealing with this issue to the Appeals Court. The justices were quite diverse in their reasoning, with the most conservative members indicating that they would make the most conservative locality the national norm, and the more liberal members finding this unreasonable. So the issue will doubtless return at a future time

33. In sharp contrast, studies of children and violence, especially effects of representations of violence on children in the media, are extensively funded and subsequently used in policy formation, national and local legislation, advice to parents and teachers, and so forth.

34. Conservative political and religious objections tend to reveal a fear that such research would demonstrate various sexual activities are 'normal' and therefore would undermine the conservative position, much as conservatives hold the Kinsey studies as a major cause of postwar liberalisation in thought and behaviour about sexuality.

35. Some argue for an academic exception for research purposes. See Clay Calvert, 'Opening up an Academic Privilege and Shutting down Child Modeling Sites: Revising Child Pornography Laws in the United States', *Dickenson Law Review*, 2002, pp. 253–85.

36. James R. Kincaid, *Child-Loving: The Erotic Child and Victorian Culture* (New York: Routledge, 1992) and *Erotic Innocence: The Culture of Child Molesting* (Durham, NC: Duke University Press, 1998).

37. Anne Higonnet, *Pictures of Innocence: The History and Crisis of Ideal Childhood* (New York: Thames and Hudson, 1998).

38. Amy Adler, 'The Perverse Law of Child Pornography', *Columbia Law Review*, 101, March 2001, pp. 209–73.

39. Judith Levine, *Harmful to Minors: The Perils of Protecting Children from Sex* (Minneapolis: University of Minnesota Press, 2002). Levine is an investigative journalist who argues strongly in the second half of the book for liberal reform of sex education. Levine's book was severely attacked by the extreme Right before publication. The University of Minnesota Press has a discussion of the controversy and links to major documents (University of Minnesota Press, 'Harmful to Minors', <www.upress.umn.edu/books/L/levine_harmful.html.2002>. A good complement to Levine is Marjorie Heins, *Not in front of the Children: 'Indecency'. Censorship, and the Innocence of Youth* (New York: Hill and Wang, 2001), which has a more historical range in addressing the question from a civil liberties' perspective.

40. Levine, *Harmful to Minors*, p. 36.

41. Laura Kipnis, *Bound and Gagged: Pornography and the Politics of Fantasy in America* (New York: Grove Press, 1996).

42. Philip Jenkins, *Beyond Tolerance: Child Pornography on the Internet* (New Haven, CT: Yale University Press, 2001); *Moral Panic: Changing Concepts of the Child Molester in Modern America* (New Haven, CT: Yale University Press, 1998).

43. In this aspect it is similar to Roland Barthes' *The Fashion System* (New York: Hill and Wang, 1983), an analysis of the structure of the fashion industry, based on an analysis of the captions, not the pictures, in *haute couture* journalism such as *Vogue, Elle*, etc.

44. See Philip Jenkins, 'Stranger Than Fiction', 2001 in *Nerve.com.*, <www.nerve.com/opinions/JenkinsP/strangerThanFiction>; 'Bringing the Loathsome to Light', *Chronicle of Higher Education*, 1 March 2002,

p. B16; and 'Online: Second sight: Cut child porn link to abusers', *Guardian*, 23 January 2003.

45. Kipnis, *Bound and Gagged*, pp. 3–63.

46. Jenkins, 'Stranger Than Fiction'.

47. Missy Schwartz, 'Monitor', *Entertainment Weekly*, 23 May 2003, p. 22.

48. Richard Goldstein, 'Persecuting Pee-Wee: A Child-Porn Case That Threatens Us All?', *Village Voice*, 15–21 January 2003, <www.villagevoice.com/issues/0303/goldstein.php> (accessed 31 October 2003).

49. Ibid.

50. Adler, 'The Perverse Law of Child Pornography', p. 209.

51. It is almost impossible to determine the authenticity of such claims, unless one has police powers. Assuming these sites are sincere – and the images authentic – some show no compulsion about reproducing the face of under-age victims. This disregard for victim rights and privacy is so blatant, that one can easily wonder if it is simply a cleverly disguised paedophile site which uses 'exposing paedophiles' as a ruse. See *Better a Millstone*, <www.shadow-net.com> (accessed 7 December 2002).

52. In court the couple claimed ignorance of the contents of the 5,000 various sites and said that they were simply providing a clearance service. These claims were not accepted as defences. However, section 230 of the Communications Decency Act, which was not challenged (although the Act was found unconstitutional on other grounds by the Supreme Court), provided that interactive computer services could not be considered publishers and held liable for content (Edward A. Cavanzos, ' "Safe Harbor" Provision Protects Providers', *Texas Lawyer*, vol. 17 no. 33, p. 23, 22 October 2001). Using the CDA rule, in a Florida Supreme Court decision on an American Online case, internet service providers are not held liable for civil damages for pornographic content they may carry on bulletin boards (Susan R. Miller, 'AOL Not Liable for Porn, Florida Justices Rule', *law.com/Miami Daily Business Review*, <www.law.com>, 2001; 'Mother of Child Porn Victim Asks High Court to Review ISP Immunity', *Computer & Online Industry Litigation Reporter*, vol. 19 no. 2, 7, 11 September 2001).

53. 'FBI news release on Operation Candyman', CNN.com (18 March 2002),

<www.cnn.com/2002/US/03/18/operation.candy
man.release/index.html>.

54. S. Silberman, 'The United States of America v. Adam
    Vaughn', *Wired*, vol. 10 no.10 (2002),
    <www.wired.com/wired/archive/10.10/kidporn.html>;
    Kathee Brewer, 'Judges Throw out FBI Evidence in
    Candyman Cases', AVN Media Network (2003),
    <www.avonline.com/issues.200303/newswarchive/
    030703_lead.shtml>.

7   Defycategory.com, or the Place of Categories in Intermedia

Amy Villarejo

Sexual exhibition on the internet, particularly in the form of webcams (offering continuous digital displays of everyday life on the World Wide Web), arouses less pleasure than speculation and concerned hand-wringing among academics. The two dominant rhetorics wielded by many scholars emerge cogently in a *Chronicle of Higher Education* commentary, in an editorial section actually entitled 'Deconstruct This'. The first celebrates webcam display as 'a new kind of gathering', a participatory endeavour that sparks reflection on technology and that validates the elegance and beauty potentially to be found in our own daily lives. Becoming our own observers, we see ourselves anew, and, boy, are we fabulous! At the other end of the spectrum, a scholar of communications law worries in exemplary fashion about what he calls 'exhibitionism in the service of voyeurism', whereby others voluntarily sacrifice the precious right to privacy for our pleasure in watching. From his perspective,

> This raises the question: Why are we so infatuated with others' lives, when perhaps we should be more concerned with our own lives, our own interaction with people in our own community? We develop a false sense of intimacy with these individuals, and it's troubling to think that we vicariously live our lives through their lives. It's obligation free.[1]

On the one hand, then, webcam display fosters community, connection and reflection; on the other hand, webcams forestall action, displace interaction and let us off the ethical hook. What, I wonder, would these scholars make of Timo and his site, the contradictory, swirling and defiant world of defycategory.com?

This chapter first describes that website as its object of inquiry, then follows with the work of demystification, arguing perhaps rather predictably that neither the celebratory nor the guilt-laden logic of scholarly commentary captures the structural mobility and textual density of digital display, sexual or otherwise. Such categorical celebrations and refusals, in other words, reify the elusive objects, websites, under scrutiny and cloud critical understanding of their grounds of meaning-making. Countering a sort of techno-determinism, I argue against lumping a variety of forms of self-disclosure under a single rubric of sexual cyber-exhibitionism. Beyond this initial gesture of debunking, however, the central contribution I seek to make has to do more with the 'otherwise' in 'sexual, or otherwise', that is to say, the sense in which twenty-four-hour webcam sites such as Timo's defycategory.com are neither wholly devoted to what we might call the visibly sexual (that is, the visual vocabulary of telos and fulfilment central to pornographic storytelling, the display of penises or anuses, or the payoff of nudity and penetration much-awaited by many visitors), nor are they at the same time devoid of connections to that domain or to sexual dissidence. Instead, defying categories, they might be understood pedagogically as lessons in undoing dog-eared and pious invocations of sexuality, pointing us both backwards and forwards towards surprising connections: in this regard, as I will explain, I see defycategory as having as much in common with Andy Warhol and his legacy than with 'webcams' understood as entirely new technologies breaking with the old.

To be more specific, this essay traces my own engagement with Timo's site as I taught it in a survey course at Cornell University in the state of New York, a course burdened with the lengthy title, 'History and Theory of Documentary and Experimental Film'. Pursuing as best we could the possibilities of that delicious matrix called 'camp' outlined initially by Susan Sontag, my students and I sought to position defycategory.com in a lineage begun with Andy Warhol (we screened 'his' film *Camp*) and embodied further in the subsequent works of George Kuchar, Jack Smith and Kenneth Anger (*Hold Me While I'm Naked* [1966], *Flaming Creatures* [1963] and both *Fireworks* [1947] and *Scorpio Rising* [1963], respectively). This chapter, then, speaks to others who teach media in hopes of making that lineage reverberate in 'studying' a website. In what follows, I try to make visible the various difficulties posed by teaching websites in the classroom, but I am also concerned, if here more obliquely, with the 'place' of sexuality in the presentation of the American avant-garde, the New York underground, the legacy of experimental cinema and the history of cinema more generally. Pedagogy does not represent to me the pinnacle of 'practice' (as it is frequently opposed by instrumentalists to 'theory') or of *engagé* scholarship; instead, I use the classroom in this chapter as an opening into questions regarding sexual rhetoric frequently banished by the scholarly apparatus: how do we speak to ourselves and our students about pleasure? How do we hear the language of pain?

THE SITE

Defycategory.com is a personal site, in the sense that we might speak of the personal film. Enunciated entirely from the worldview of its proprietor and webmaster, Timo, the site combines text, photo galleries and links with its webcam display; each of its components reveals facets of Timo's life (his family, his friends, his apartments, his decorating, his jobs, his cats, his sexual life). The site has also spilled beyond the contours of the internet: it has been the subject of magazine articles, as well as of a German television programme devoted to several American webcams, *Ein Expeditionsberich von Tilman Jens*.

'You are here to pay attention to me.' Timo's credo, irresistible to the press, lays bare the essence of his site as well as the fraudulence, or at least irrelevance, of distinctions between observers' genuine contact and distracted attention. There is but one ego at issue in Timo's world. As one article puts it: '[H]e invites you to watch his life unfold one picture at a time, even to capture images for your future enjoyment, "knowing that you were there".'[2] As with the experience of watching live television, 'having been there' *is* the retrospective guarantee of contact, and that contact is organised wholly around the person of Timo.[3]

Like Warhol, Timo depends on brevity to pack a punch. In a section of defycategory.com devoted to

words, Timo collects his wisdom under a set of keywords upon which one can click to reveal aphorisms or short narratives. The words include shit, faggot, drag, smoking, pain, melodrama, need, nice, love and clean, among others. Under the word 'dollar', one reads this certainty regarding value (a rule I, for one, attempt to live by): 'Never pay more than a dollar for anything, otherwise you just don't get as much.' Responding to a reporter's inquiry regarding the regulation of adult sexual material on the internet, particularly to protect children, Timo snaps, 'Fuck children. The Internet is not a babysitter'.[4] At times more arch than droll, Timo's wit repels as much as it attracts. It also conceals.

Words are not, however, as central to the site as are images, and the webcam is not the only vehicle for image display. Links to current choices in music, or to his eBay items for sale, or to other favourite sites, supplement the majority of the images having to do with the fullness and richness that is Timo's life. Again, Timo: 'If you look at my site carefully and still come away with the notion that my cock is the best thing about me, I find that insulting.'[5] In addition to the webcam, Timo's Java galleries rotate snapshots of Timo's everyday: trips to visit family and friends in upstate New York (I myself have been on display in this capacity), a particularly fetching arrangement of new curtains, as well as loads of men (friends, lovers, acquaintances, would-be lovers) in and around the two gay communities in which Timo has circulated, in Rehoboth Beach, Delaware, and Washington, DC Past achievements of Timo's may be archived in these galleries, such as the Mexican upside-down room he fashioned in the DC apartment he vacated for permanent residence at the beach: an entire 'Mexican-themed' room suspended, upside-down, from the ceiling of his kitchen.

No wonder his fans range from housewives in Columbus devoted to his decorating tips to a surprising number from the island of Tonga! To help me with this chapter, Timo supplied me with a 'Site Activity Analysis' of a week's traffic at the end of the year 2000. Such a document I had never seen; the amount of information one can glean from it, depending upon one's purposes, is simply astonishing. In a single week, for example, *excluding* hits on the webcam accessed directly, defycategory.com had 65,727 hits. Averaging things out, it seems as though the site receives about 6,000 visitors per day, and each session lasts on average a bit over two minutes. Some sessions lasted as long as thirty-one to forty-five minutes, and a few exceeded an hour. A webmaster needs, of course, to learn how visitors accessed the site, at which 'entry point' pages, show operating systems (by type and by brand), through which referring domains or search engines or URLs and the like. While these sites might be understood to be entrepreneurial ventures, they beckon, as these data suggest, towards immensely complicated relationships with economy and technology (also with regulation and piracy) irreducible to that designation. Ill-equipped to digest those details (though prompted to learn more), I found myself more drawn to the sheer numbers and to speculative nonsense regarding the geographic breakdown of the site's traffic (2,760 sessions from Virginia, 848 from California, 58 from Germany and 22 from . . . Tonga).

Whatever the various breakdowns might disclose to a different and better disciplined eye, a few working propositions did suggest themselves to me regarding the assumptions we make when we speak of 'webcams' or sexual display on the net using Timo's site as exemplary (and it *is* exemplary in the sense that it is one of the most heavily trafficked such sites up and running as of this writing):

1. Webcams are not all equal. Some pop on the scene for 'one-time-only' events (a particular sexual encounter, a live birth), some reveal only a portion of their subject's activities, and some, like Timo's, operate '24/7,' twenty-four hours a day, seven days a week. Some emanate from Gothic couples towards their compatriots, some from fat women towards their admirers. Some display gay men's sexual lives. Most do not.

2. Webcams are embedded in structured sites such as Timo's, sites devoted to a number of projects in addition to, or supplementary to, or perhaps even ancillary to the display of everyday life webcams offer. How those structures and components might be understood textually in relation to webcam display is one necessary question. But the structures and effects of such complex sites are largely hidden from those of us who neither engineer nor engage closely with them. Timo receives over 300 pieces of mail each day from his admirers, none of which is available to those who

bemoan a lack of community. Likewise, few commentators who provide media soundbites even mention the architecture of these sites, ranging from their additional textual materials (words, photo galleries, links, etc.) to their literal infra-structures requiring massive bandwidth and commensurate ingenuity.

3. Webcams have precedents *and* pose new questions. Well-rehearsed oppositions between the public and the private, the genuine and the ersatz, the seer and the seen: these seem to circumscribe debate about display on the web and through webcams in particular. From my limited exposure to Timo's site and the task of teaching it, I found that some other 'old' ideas, such as camp, were more helpful in managing the questions the site provokes, and I found that some 'new' possibilities emerged from that discussion.

TEACHING TIMO

I return to the course in which I decided to try to teach this site, as much to 'incorporate new media', as our administrative memos seemed to encourage, as to illustrate to my students that the ideas and practices of the underground were not banished to some distant past (as the 60s for them represents) but are alive and relatively well. The course covers the global history of documentary film through 1945 (from the Lumières' *actualités* to propaganda films of World War II) and the entire history of experimental cinema (movements of the avant-garde, structural film, pure film and the underground, as well as hybrid forms such as the personal documentary). Unlike many survey courses, it combines the study of documentary film with experimental film in order to produce connections between these usually isolated domains, such as one might encourage in examining French film of the 20s. But like many survey courses, its scope is vast, and it therefore requires constant vigilance to keep these connections alive rather than settle in the routine of a Cook's tour: if it's Tuesday, it must be Grierson. The reasons for invoking this context are not to muse upon the ways in which a digital 'text' such as defycategory.com can interrupt or complement the layout of such a survey course, but to acknowledge that even as I chart the syllabus, such interruptions are *already* in 'place'. The students whom I teach, in other words, have already been transformed by hypertextual thinking, by digital modes of linking and surfing. They incorporate screen grabs into their weekly papers with seemingly zero technological effort; they frequently correct Erik Barnouw and David James (our 'textbook' interlocutors) with little factoids they've unearthed on some Vertov site or other, and they make constant reference to other vaguely noted worlds in which they've encountered Dada, or montage, or Walter Benjamin. Some of them are web designers; they make substantial amounts of money doing for the faculty what we do not know how to do. They are comfortable with speed and surface, with trial and error. They are, in most ways, my digital mentors, and they are, more importantly, a steady reminder that the structures we conjure are met by others.

The second half of the semester is devoted to postwar experimental film, and in my syllabus I build two weeks of that work around the idea of camp, not as a self-evident cornerstone in monumental film history but as a problematic that seeks to do at least two important things. First, it renders the sexual politics of the late 50s through the 70s central to our study, against those formal or mythic studies of the avant-garde that read erect penises as the fetish objects they seek to mock (as in Anger's *Fireworks*). Second, camp makes visible a set of relationships between those works that think of themselves as belonging to the avant-garde or have been consigned there and both mass and popular culture (relationships that, by the way, also deepen those between experimental and documentary film). By way of definition, I follow Matthew Tinkcom in understanding camp as an 'alibi for gay labour', a set of discursive gambits that mark cultural production as wrought by homosexual hands even while that mark is strenuously concealed.[6] While it is possible, as many have done, to contain camp in the pre-Stonewall years, many also further insist upon its historically contingent and specific status as a strategy through which urban, mostly white, gay men in the 40s and 50s manufactured the codes of a community. Restricting camp to *those* years and *that* small subculture simultaneously banishes it as retrogressive, pre-liberatory, mired in the murk of shame and the torment of the closet associated with gay and lesbian life 'before' liberation and the language of 'coming out', pride and that internationally banal symbol of gay liberation, the rainbow flag. If there is any reason for arguing

that camp is not *contained* firmly in the past but *rooted* there, it is to insist upon the mutability, the instability of the borderline between shame and pride that is overwhelmingly evident in the cultural production of the mid-century, if not commensurately reflected in the progressivist histories about the period.[7] It is likewise to open camp, as others have done, to a more generalised abstraction whereby camp makes similarly unstable the very mechanisms of valuation. It is one, and only one, lever that works the relations between exaltation and degradation, between art and trash, between reverence and drivel. But there is a further twist: if camp is playful in its production of abstractions and wily in its capacity for destabilisation, camp is, in temporal terms, coy. Like the in-joke, with camp the question, 'Do you get it?' is usually answered in advance, a fact that poses a certain challenge to teaching.

How to teach Kenneth Anger, the Kuchar brothers, Jack Smith, Andy Warhol and Timo, I wonder, if *not* however to insist upon the challenges they pose formally, ideologically, politically and sexually, all together, all at once? Camp would seem to be central to their own preoccupations, as well as to some critical discussions of their work, and it would thus seem reasonable to use camp as one classroom lens for working with Warhol's film *Camp*, Anger's *Fireworks* and *Scorpio Rising*, George Kuchar's *Hold Me While I'm Naked*, and Timo's site. In answer to the question put to my students regarding these projects, 'Do you get it?', my students respond with a thunderous NO. It seems that my mentors in things digital are, I find, dismally under-educated in sexual politics. In fact, so scarce has been any discussion of sexuality in their classrooms that it meets with something that looks like resistance. Not one of my students miraculously has yet, for example, resisted learning about internationalism or the radical Left in order to make sense of *The Spanish Earth* (1937) or *Native Land* (1942), yet the history of Stonewall and gay liberation (infrequently brought into the critical conversation regarding the films I have mentioned) easily offers itself to my students as 'extraneous' or 'irrelevant'. Similarly, and even more surprisingly to me, I have yet to hear a single student bemoan the three full class sessions devoted to the Empire Marketing Board/General Post Office/Crown Unit films: somehow they are able to simulate utter absorption in the mechanisms of mail delivery, yet the moment when a young Kenneth Anger pulls his fetish-phallus out from under the sheets in *Fireworks* barely solicits a giggle during the first screening!

It is worth distinguishing between, for example, the ostensibly private consumption of sexually explicit materials on the web or elsewhere and the comparatively public and shared responses to these materials in the classroom (under the eyes and ears of the professor), just as it is worth remarking that my students, of course, have varied and developing erotic lives and imaginaries. It would not be sufficient, then, to allege that homophobia alone dictates their cool responses to Anger or to the eerie creature-scapes of Jack Smith, and neither would it be productive to suggest that they are too distant from the moment or place of *Fireworks*' enunciation to relish its energy; the film is, after all, a low-budget adolescent experiment shot much as college student films are (clandestinely, cheaply, quickly). Anger's joke, in other words, does not quite rely upon shared homosexual desire (or upon its postwar determinations) but instead upon its *possibility* emerging from a normative scene: a seventeen-year-old boy's masturbatory fantasies, a middle-class household, an annual Christmas ritual. It is camp, specifically, that operates the distance between the place of the normative, the surface of the already-known, and the wink that acknowledges gay labour that has been effaced in the production of that glamorous and alluring surface. And it is camp that makes possible a swerve in the understanding of the avant-garde as a series of 'personal statements' to a set of industrial criticisms or parabases, indictments through citation of the poverty of social 'reality'.

This swerve makes possible a number of positions for students, scholars, makers and teachers that are crucial for understanding not film form but our relation to it: in inquiring after, as my student Robert Schauffelberger puts it, 'the ingredients of that which normally fascinates it', the gifts of irreverence, humour and appreciation of our situatedness within mass and popular culture beget a deeper understanding of the contradictory valences of cultural production, both 'underground' and mainstream. Irreverence borne of a saturated knowledge of mass and popular culture also can provide a ground for students to encounter dissident sexualities and formulations of pleasure and pain. Another student, Nick Phillips, interrogates the structural irony of camp through this

proximity to the codes of industrial production in Warhol's film, in which

> a diverse group of underground oddballs lounge around in a large, barren room, obviously aware of the camera yet unconcerned with making comprehensible for the viewer their conversation. As the film progresses, the various assembled characters put on semi-performances, ostensibly for the viewer yet not available to the viewer in any coherent or fully realized way. . . . The performances of *Camp*, composed as they are of in-jokes, bizarre dances (Swan's opening dance in Roman Gladiator garb) or defiant anti-performances, offer a kind of pathetic mimicry of mainstream movies, exposing what lies implicit in Hollywood's conception of glamour and the creation of celebrity. While Hollywood glamour is completely seamless, concealing to the utmost its modes of production, *Camp* lays bare the fact that it *is* a production . . . In this way, *Camp* enacts a kind of double critique of Hollywood cinema and of itself, exposing the fakeness of Hollywood while embracing the fakeness as a badge of pride.

That this passage understands the 'underground oddballs' as wielding critique is both a necessary corrective to continuist social histories that elide the critical functions of camp by placing it in the comfortable distance of the past and also an invitation to think the consequences of metonymy, the substitution of a film title, *Camp*, for the incipient theoretical conception, camp. Insofar as camp-the-quasi-concept is tied to wit, to the in-joke, to verbal dexterity and therefore to a certain definitional enterprise, camp lives on in Timo's site, to which I now want to return, through the force of this lineage.

CAMP TIMO

The webcam display in defycategory.com, as I have suggested, is but one element of the site. Timo is not simply or only or merely or plainly queer-for-all but is also profoundly committed to the manufacture of stardom through the discourses of camp, revealing the dependence of glamour and various other practices of popular culture upon gay labour. In the remainder of this chapter, I emphasise the various dimensions of gayness that are occluded by the generalised discussions of webcam display with which I opened. In situating Timo's site within a lineage of gay film-making understood through the rubric of camp, however, I want to place equal emphasis on at least two realities of gay cybersex I take as axiomatic: (1) virtual sex is safe sex; and (2) gay sexuality is policed, regulated, harassed and condemned as virulently in cyberspace as it is on the street. For these two reasons, with all sorts of qualifications possible, my tone remains affirmative in consort with Timo's (with whose voice I end in a long citation).

As with Anger or Warhol, Timo undertakes the realignment of a worldview, a double-movement of critique whereby our investments in 'what normally fascinates us', in the surface or gleam of the familiar, are subject to autopsy, and we are simultaneously given a relentlessly close look at something else. Because Timo's gaze falls upon an extremely large orbit (indeed, his graphic tastes tend towards the astronomical), I have selected a few arenas by way of example, and I encourage readers to log on for further amplification.

DECORATING: As all gay men (and likely many others) have long known, a small army of queens has long fed Martha Stewart her decorating ideas. Timo ought to have been at the command of that battalion, for his own inventions (beyond the aforementioned Mexican upside-down room) surpass those of the titular queen of the home. He makes easy mention in correspondence: 'Drapery projects await me . . . with several thousand pine cones in reserve already for the valences.' Staples of decorating culture converge in Timo's world, a kind of litany of modern queer taste: Barkcloth, McCoy, faux surfaces, Eames, Fiesta . . . Many of them not habitual Martha-watchers, my students nonetheless made quick connections between the labours of home and the labours of the set, rendering visible to them the work of set designers, hairdressers, make-up artists and others whose traces camp reveals in the shiny surfaces of mass cultural products. At the same time, Timo's excessive projects, like Martha's, disclose the ways in which camp tweaks value in unexpected directions: massive investment (several *thousand* pine cones?) yields a sort of social status akin to having out-Jonesed the Joneses.

CRITIQUE OF BOURGEOIS CULTURE: And yet, in the world of defycategory.com, bourgeois gay life comes under powerful scrutiny, though not without contradictory effects. The community of Rehoboth Beach, a resort town shared by upper-middle-class gay men and straight people from the metropolitan Washington, DC, area, provides Timo with endless material for self-positioning. On the one hand, the resort life obviously beckons, providing models of leisure (lounging in Tiki-style bars, setting up umbrellas on the beach), a resort ethos of life divorced from the hectic pace of the city, and a current of consumption or a parade of commodities alluring in their surfaces. On the other hand, as a year-round resident in a beach town and a worker in the service industries that sustain bourgeois leisure, Timo resists defiantly the categories and ideological traps of his compatriots, taunting his neighbours with pink flamingos or deliberately seeking to set his taste apart from his fellow townsfolk. In such circumstances, decorating is not an activity but a sword, wielded at an uncomprehending but likely offended throng of lawyers, toting Italian stainless steel ice-cream makers from their SUVs.

MELODRAMA: In defiant protests such as these, one glimpses elements of melodrama, but not, I think, those elements one might usually suspect. Contrary to the frequent habit of identifying melodrama with excess or hyperbole, in Timo's self-fashioning I see his attempt to express the inexpressible, straining to articulate that vast and inchoate reserve of anguish that wit conceals. I am not suggesting that he accepts uncritically the terms of melodrama; to the contrary, he has elaborated his own powerful critique of its conventions and its traps. What I am suggesting is that melodrama is a powerful conception for understanding how Timo's site orchestrates contradictory elements: pathos, individualism, cliché, wit, intensely felt emotion, drama, *mise en scène*, stardom and the everyday. My students were particularly drawn to Timo's story, under the word 'faggot', described by one, Carrie Hoffman, as a saga of 'growing up persecuted by his classmates for being both gay and smart'.

Others have been drawn to that story, too, and with it I close. A young fan's letter is representative:

Thank you for this site. I am a 17 year old gay male that has been so utterly confused for the past two years. I like you defy the category, so not only have I not been able to fit into my high school atmosphere, but I haven't ever felt like I fit into the gay community. Your words page is spectacular! The entire piece you wrote under 'faggot' was exactly what my life has been. I have been greatly hurt by my experiences but have turned out stronger, more confident and wiser. But [what] I loved best was that being gay is not all that you are. Or what you have. You, like myself, obviously have so much more to offer, and are so much more than just gay. Intelligence, humor, and happiness is [sic] what both you have chosen to shape your life, and I couldn't agree with you more. Thank you for being such an incredible role model for a gay teen. It is greatly appreciated.

Here is that entry under 'faggot'. I close with this lengthy citation of Timo's own voice because I find it a dazzling and powerful challenge.

I was in the third grade when I learned the word faggot. I heard it on the bus. It was directed at me. I soon came to realize that until I left my home town of adulterous wife-beating drunks, there would be no escape from any association with that word on a daily basis.

I suppose that the constant derision and name-calling has scarred me indelibly forever. I suppose also that I was lucky to escape with my life . . . not to have been beaten senseless by a horde of drunken rubes or even taking my life by my own hand. Unlike some others, I survived the beatings and the taunts. I endured the destruction of my physical property. I was able to overlook the limitations imposed upon me by others as a result of my sexuality. Furthermore, I annihilated my classmates with my superior grades and class participation . . . which resulted in even further humiliation and hatred. Being very smart I did make one very poignant observation: fingering the perpetrators only made things worse. So I am left wondering about the upright conservative family values of the assholes in my home town. How is it that they are able to look themselves in the eye and identify one another as loving Christians? I grew up in a VERY white-bread community . . . no blacks . . . one Jew . . . one homosexual, ME, or so I was led to believe. In the ten years from third grade until I graduated from high school I endured countless physical attacks, sucker punches, tripping, pushing, shoving, numerous insults, flagrant hatred and undeniable discrimination . . . and not one person ever came to my defense . . . not one teacher or a bus driver, nor the school nurse, not a principal or a vice principal, nor the gym teacher nor the guidance counselor, nor a lunch room monitor, not even my parents or my grandparents . . . not one single person ever raised a hand to stop my persecution. In a ten-year span of time I find it unlikely that all of these people had no idea what was going on. In such a small town as mine the likelihood of these attacks going unnoticed is slim to none. I was the church organist from the age of twelve and directed the choir . . . but still my exemplary participation in community life at this early age simply was not enough to spare me the humiliation and taunts of my peers. It appears then that it is perfectly acceptable to use a faggot for what he is worth . . . but simply not worth defending him while he is being shit on.

What does all this mean . . . ? It means that the predominant sentiment in late 20th century America is this: faggots only get what they deserve. And to think that people actually wonder why at times I am such a short-fused bitch.

NOTES

1. 'All Me, All the Time,' in the *Chronicle of Higher Education*, 15 December 2000, p. B4.
2. Michael Kealy, 'Cyber Strip Tease', *Fab National* 12 (1998), p. 44.
3. See Jane Feuer, 'The Concept of Live Television: Ontology as Ideology', in E. Ann Kaplan (ed.), *Regarding Television: Critical Approaches – An Anthology* (Los Angeles, CA: The American Film Institute, 1983), pp. 12–21.
4. Ibid.
5. Ibid.
6. See Matthew Tinkcom, *Working Like a Homosexual: Camp and Question of Value* (Durham, NC: Duke University Press, 2002).
7. I have elaborated this argument further in 'Forbidden Love: Pulp as Lesbian History', in Ellis Hanson (ed.), *Out Takes* (Durham, NC: Duke University Press, 1999), pp. 316–45.

8 Cybersex

Stacy Gillis

People in virtual communities do just about everything people do in real life, but we leave our bodies behind.

Howard Rheingold[1]

What, ontologically speaking, is the body? What is its 'stuff,' its matter? What of its form? Is that given or produced?

Elisabeth Grosz[2]

I begin with a confession. I am a cybersex addict. I have been to the Cybersex Addiction Help site and I have taken their self-diagnosing quiz.[3] 'Sexual Addiction may be a concern' for me as: a) I frequently become irritable when asked to get off the computer; and, b) my family and friends are concerned about the amount of time I spend on-line. The Cybersex Addiction Help site offers me several options to deal with my addiction. However – and this is where I find myself in difficulties – I am also a *cybersex virgin*. Indeed, this should be apparent from my terminology. If I really knew what I was doing, I would not be calling it cybersex. To have cybersex – and this is no OED definition – is 'to cyber'. But it is not for lack of trying that I am a cybersex virgin. I have spent time and money looking for cybersex. Huddled in front of the computer screen, I type *sex* into a search engine. The results are around 150,000,000 pages. This seems a few too many to trawl through even for an experienced websurfer. So I type in *cybersex*. The results are 600,000 pages, which is a bit more manageable. As I begin to wade through them, mouse clicking merrily in anticipation, I fondly suppose that I am engaged in cyber-foreplay.

But I am foiled again. These hits can be roughly split into two groups. One group consists of visual pornography. Pornography is the great industry of the internet,[4] quickly colonising this form of technology as so many others. Sadie Plant has noted the masculine sexualisation of technology, both in terms of hardware development and semiotics:

> This phallic quest has always played a major role in the development and popularization of visual techniques. Photography, cinema and video have all been grabbed by pornographers, and long before the development of simulating stimulating data suits, sex with computers was well advanced. Sex has found its way into all the digital media . . . and both hardwares and softwares are sexualized. Much of this activity is clearly designed to reproduce and amplify the most clichéd associations with straight male sex. Disks are sucked into the dark recesses of welcoming vaginal slits, console cowboys jack into cyberspace, and virtual sex has been defined as 'teledildonics.' Here are more simulations of the feminine, digital dreamgirls who cannot answer back, pixeled puppets with no strings attached, fantasy figures who do as they are told.[5]

The semiotics of sexual engagement are at the core of the way in which we understand and describe technology, whether software or hardware. Pornography, however, in its web incarnation is largely pictorial, infinite bodies displayed in a variety of poses and positions with a long representational heritage. There is no sex here, no bodily exchange of fluids, only masturbation or the promise thereof. Rightwing pundits were self-indulgently smug when it became apparent that the web – as had been warned – was indeed home to millions of sites devoted to 'sex'. The plethora of visuals that pop up in innocent surfing or the lascivious advertisements which appear in email inboxes are testament to the ability of the sex industry to deploy new technologies as quickly and as profitably as possible. However, at the risk of valorising a traditional kind of body-contact – which is the last thing the web is doing – what the majority of websites host is pornography, not sex. While pornography websites have consolidated the largely masculine model which links masturbation with visuality, cybersex is misnamed if grouped under the same heading. To label these sites as cybersex constitutes a misreading of the act of cybersex. Cybersex is a synchronous sexual exchange – an exchange not possible within the stasis of these pornography sites.

The other group of hits, like the Cybersex Addiction Help site, warns of the dangers of cybersex. The labelling of cybersex as an addiction positions it as a vice, similar to pornography. In August 2002, the BBC reported that

> [a]n estimated 15% of internet users have visited sex chat rooms or pornographic sites, according to the latest research. And almost 9% of people who use the Internet for sex spend more than 11 hours per week looking for erotic content.[6]

The conflation of cybersex and on-line pictorial pornography enables the identification of cybersex as a dangerous preoccupation that disrupts and threatens 'real-time' relationships. The National Council on Sexual Addiction and Compulsivity estimated that, in 2000, there were over two million sexually addicted internet users, both in and out of recovery, in America.[7] The Cybersex Addiction Help site which assures me that I am a cybersex addict locates the blame for an individual's relationship with a computer and/or the internet in the technology: 'Alone with only the computer for company, cybersex participants are in fact isolated from real human contact. Cybersex objectifies the participants. They are often reduced to body parts.'[8] This reductionist account of technology also ignores, among other things, the mediation of technology in most human interactions. Slavoj Žižek argues that 'cyberspace merely radicalises the gap constitutive of the symbolic order: (symbolic) reality always already was "virtual"; that is to say, *every access to (social) reality has to be supported by an implicit phantasmic hypertext*'.[9] The definition provided by the Cybersex Addiction Help site – and by medical discourse – neither relates textual exchange to sexual exchange nor separates cybersex from 'sex with machinery'. The reduction to 'body parts' which the Cybersex Addiction Help site identifies does not entertain the possibility of a subject, let alone a body, being contributed by the 'addict'.

I do not want either of these – neither pornography nor admonition will help me with my addiction.

What I want to do is to experience the exchange of bodily fluids that marks out the domain of physical sexual experience between bodies. There are sites that describe sexual exchanges but these are records not interactions. What I want is to experience the connection achieved between two bodies via an exchange of text. To be more precise, I want to know if a connection between two bodies can be made in this way, and how. Has the body moved beyond its physicality in our technoculture?[10] Arthur and Marilouise Kroker speak of a 'body fear' when they point out that '[i]n technological society, the body has achieved a purely rhetorical existence: its reality is that of refuse expelled as surplus – matter no longer necessary for the autonomous functioning of the technoscape'.[11] And now my final confession – I am not interested in having cybersex. Rather, I wish to watch/read others doing it in order to explore the interaction of words and the configurations of on-line bodies.

What is cybersex? Does it constitute 'contact'? Where is the body in cybersex? The possibilities of cybersex should be endless as ever-quickening technological obsolescence provides new fora for sexual engagement. The internet, the World Wide Web, chatrooms, CD-ROMs, mobile phone networks, virtual reality, interactive digital entertainment, biomedical technologies, artificial life, digital imaging and so forth are transformative paradigms in our technoculture. And this technoculture is partly predicated upon an erotics of technology.[12]

> Our love affair with computers, computer graphics, and computer networks runs deeper than aesthetic fascination and deeper than the play of sense. We are searching for a home for the mind and the heart. Our fascination with computers is more erotic than sensuous, more deeply spiritual than utilitarian.[13]

With the range of technological options, it should follow that there are a host of different ways in which to have cybersex. Indeed, Sherry Turkle notes that cybersex is at the heart of much on-line exchange: 'In cyberspace, this activity is not only common but, for many people, it is the counterpiece of their on-line experience'.[14] Certainly, images of cybersex in science fiction bear testimony to fantastic projections of pleasure and technology, although often negatively imagined. William Gibson's *Neuromancer* introduced neural simstim, a direct plug-in of (largely) sexual pleasure.[15] In Woody Allen's *Sleeper* (1973), the orgasmatron is a virtual sex booth. In *Minority Report* (2002), John Anderton visits a techno-punk who runs a business in which body-encasing sleeping-bags can simulate any experience, including sexual intercourse. Cyberspace is presented as a space that can satisfy every desire, particularly the desire to escape 'the meat' of the body.[16] William Burroughs makes clear the sexual potential of technology: 'You can lay Cleopatra, Helen of Troy, Isis, Madame Pompadour, or Aphrodite. You can get fucked by Pan, Jesus Christ, Apollo, or the Devil himself. Anything you like likes you when you press the buttons.'[17] Indeed, it is hardly surprising that cybersex has a home in science fiction and cyberpunk as the key terms of this argument – cybersex and embodiment – are contained within the new bodies of science fiction. 'Science fiction, a genre specific to the era of rapid technological development, frequently envisages a new, revised body as a direct outcome of the advance of science.'[18] Cyberpunk and theorists of the cyber endorse an ideological fantasy of bodies mixing in virtual space. But 'virtual' is all too easily interpreted as a simulation of RL ('Real Life'). However, the reality of cybersex does not have much in common with these technological fantasies. Cybersex is textual sex – a textual jouissance. Desire may enable these cyberpunked technologies to provide an alternative to the mind/body duality, but cybersex itself remains immured in the confines of text and the scrolling screen.

Although the cybersex addiction sites consider every form of visual and textual pornography on the Web to be cybersex,[19] this argument is concerned with synchronous textual/sexual exchange. Although in use prior to this point, these textual exchanges became common in the Multi-User Domains (MUDs) of the late 70s. The rooms, objects and characters that populated these chatrooms were merely different sub-programs which could interact according to rules roughly corresponding to the physical laws of reality. One could create characters, decorate rooms and construct objects almost at will. The key is that these worlds were created textually rather than visually. What the participants saw was a slowly moving script consisting of dialogue and stage directions creeping up the computer screen. What one 'saw', one read; what one 'did', one wrote. This

was a reality populated by descriptions that may not have had any correlation with the physical body typing the descriptors.[20]

> A player of a MUD system is not a transparent medium, providing nothing but a link between external and internal cultural patterns, between actual and virtual realities. The player is the most problematic of virtual entities, for her or his virtual manifestation has no constant identity. MUD characters … may evolve, mutate, morph over time and at the whim of their creator. All of these phenomena place gender, sexuality, identity and corporeality beyond the plane of certainty.[21]

This scrolling text read much like a multiple-authored novel with multiple protagonists. The result is a textual simulation of 'reality' as well as a record of the virtual reality. It was in this textual simulation that cybersex (occasionally referred to as MUDsex) appeared. By the early 90s, MUDs had evolved into Multi-User Simulation Environments (MUSEs), Massively Multiplayer Online RolePlaying Games (MMORPGs) and Multi-User Shared Hallucinations (MUSHs). On-line environments now uniformly possess a pictorial element, but the interaction between characters remains textual, with the dialogue and directions located at the bottom of the screen. Cybersex does occur in these on-line games but it is now more often found in internet chatrooms.[22] These chatrooms operate (similar to the MUDs) via non-pictorial, text-scrolling communication. Despite technological innovation, cybersex remains, essentially, the joy of text.[23]

Unlike erotica, which is asynchronic, the text of cybersex is synchronous, bringing its perils and its pleasures:

> Sharing time brings a sense of presence to the virtual interaction of the participants which is undoubtedly one of the main appeals. Real-time also has its costs – on the one hand (pun intended) the keyboard requires constant attention in order to be an active participant, and a constant negotiation with one's partner(s) is required.[24]

The required negotiation with the constantly-talking and constantly-being-described body in cybersex positions it as outside pornographic solipsism. The possible confusions implicit in a cybersexual encounter are revealed in the following extract:

GREGORY: reach out your hand, sweetheart.
Laurie: I would have to take it in my mouth and suck it until you came, so i could swallow it.
GREGORY: god, i'm really going fast. touching the computer screen. Laurie, that would be super, closing my eyes, dreaming.
. . .
Laurie: want to try anal?
GREGORY: Laurie, my speciality. do you get off on it?
Laurie: still pretty new at it. I need to be broken in. Maybe you could help. Let's lube up and go in!
. . .
GREGORY: lube important. lots of touching, kissing. get really relaxed, really trust me. talk to Laurie, quiet voice, loving voice.
Laurie: oh god!
Laurie: Have you done it a lot? pretty good at it?
GREGORY: lot of rubbing with penis, about to break out of its skin. real relaxed. lubing up (K-Y, breakfast of champions).
GREGORY: Iive [sic] done it a fair amount. You have to be real relaxed. Go in very slowly.
Laurie: yes I know.
Laurie: Pedro tried and tried and never could get his dick in there.
GREGORY: have both hands on your clit, massaging it. that's the problem with the huge dick. it won't fit, Laurie.
Laurie: you could force it.
Laurie: slowly force it in. would be so tight very tight fit.
Laurie: tighter than virgin pussy.
GREGORY: get the head in with circular motion, and don't put the entire penis in there, or Laurie will lie on her stomach for three days. it's real tight, but the relaxation is the key.
GREGORY: I did it wrong one time, and she got hurt (not badly hurt), but i felt like ten species of jerk, slowly, and if she says 'stop,' stop!
Laurie: are you behind me or on top of me with my legs up real high?[25]

What does a physical record do to the act of sex? Reading this cybersexual encounter – the act-as-it-was-recorded – positions the reader as a consumer of pornography, of erotica. The slippage between the immediate act and its recorded history is encapsulated in the scrolling text. The post-encounter viewers can choose to move through the encounter in a number of ways whereas the participants' desire would have been tantalised by the time waiting for the next chunk of text to appear on the screen. This desire would have extended beyond Laurie and GREGORY. Cybersex can take place in public chatrooms – with other members 'watching' and/or providing encouragement – or in private passworded areas of the chatrooms.[26] When this exchange took place in an open chatroom the other inhabitants viewers/readers participated through reading, similar to Laurie and GREGORY's participation.

In these situations, the constant negotiation via text allows for a slippage of meaning, and the tricky negotiations of the e-body are foregrounded. At the same time as one is being told what one is doing, one could be typing in a different action, thereby multiplying the body. The mixture of apparent real-time action and the description of what might happen also complicates the issue. GREGORY says that he is 'going really fast' and 'touching the computer screen'. What is touching the computer screen – his face, his hand and/or his penis? The conflation of the screen of his computer with the body of Laurie cuts to the heart of the issue of embodiment in cybersex. Where are the bodies in this sexual exchange? And the crucial point is the question which Laurie finally has to ask: 'are you behind me or on top of me with my legs up real high?' Laurie may know where she wants her body to be and where she thinks it is, but she is unsure of where GREGORY's is. Not being able to read the codes, Laurie is paradoxically both inside the sex act and outside of it. Having to describe what one is doing removes one from the certainty associated with sex. Moreover, in this intimacy wrought by reading and writing, there is another layer, one which could be labelled voyeurism as Laurie and GREGORY are both doing as well as watching/reading. While the telling of fantasies is included, the main thrust of communication is in the present active tense of doing and feeling. While the reader/viewer of the act-as-it-happens is participating in a voyeuristic sexual relationship with the participants, the reader/viewer of the act-as-it-was-recorded, is experiencing pornography. It is only the record which is pornographic.

Although the etymology of pornography as 'harlot' and 'writing' suggests a similarity between pornography and text, Beverly Kaite points out that the 'pornographic body knows no textual limitations'.[27] But as we have seen with Laurie and GREGORY, the exchange of looks which circulates within libidinal economies is not possible in cybersex. Moreover, the penetrative gaze of pornography is absent from cybersex. Elizabeth Reid argues that

> [v]irtual sex is the least and the most expressive of virtual interactions. In its description of purely would-be physical interaction, it is the least overtly cultural of interactions. It draws most heavily on external cultural factors in its dramaturgical nature, and it is without doubt among the dramatically affective of virtual happenings. Real desire and arousal are evolved among participants, a reaction hugely dependent upon each person's external cultural experience.[28]

Cybersex differs from pornography in two crucial aspects: it is not an asexual discourse nor is it a fantasy of practice. It is a sexual practice. So what exactly *is* the difference between sex and cybersex? Both are a real-time engagement of experience between two or more individuals. Distance is the obvious factor. At one end, one hand on a body and the other on a keyboard; miles of wires and connectors and dial-up procedures; on the other end, one hand on a keyboard and one hand on a body. In cybersex, not only are the participants' physical bodies and biological sex unknowable but there is an uncertainty in how one's partner is participating – does the action on the computer screen extend beyond typing? Cybersex is a sexual act conducted semiotically, albeit one in which signified and signifier are always potentially disengaged and, crucially, in one of the situations which is normally perceived as outside the territory of the metonymic gap.

The comparison of cybersex with phone sex is a fruitful one, and Allucquère Rosanne Stone provides a useful account of the 'tokens' used in phone sex:

> Phone sex is the process of constructing desire through a single mode of communication, the human voice.... In phone sex, once the signifiers begin to 'float' loose from their moorings in a particularized physical experience, the most powerful attractor becomes the client's idealized fantasy.... In enacting such fantasies, par-

ticipants draw on a repertoire of cultural codes to construct a scenario that compresses large amounts of information into a very small space. The provider verbally codes for gesture, appearance, and proclivity, and expresses them as a verbal token, sometimes compressing the token into a single word.... The client uncompresses the token and constructs a dense, complex, interactional image.[29]

In phone sex, the absence that enables the desire is given particularisation by the token. Similarly, in cybersex, the material and the visual are doubly conflated as the tokens of desire are both action and transcript, doing and reading. The interaction is in both the act of reading and unpacking the token, as well as in writing and the mingling of words and phrases on the screen. In cybersex, the levels of coding that can be imbued in a voice are lost and the *particularisation* becomes paramount, rather than the token. This particularisation is achieved wholly through the strokes of the computer keyboard and the microchip.

The loss or absence which is implicit in compressing a token into a single word is increased not only by the loss of the voice but also by the loss of physical marking. Katherine Hayles has commented on the implications of creating text through typing:

> Interacting with electronic images rather than with a materially resistant text, I absorb through my fingers as well as my mind a model of signification in which no simple one-to-one correspondence exists between signifier and signified. I know kinaesthetically as well as conceptually that the text can be manipulated in ways that would be impossible if it existed as a material object rather than a visual display.[30]

The *potentiality* of meaning lost through the homogenising computer keyboard dematerialises the body sitting at that keyboard. The immediate manoeuvring of the text and its foregrounding as a visual display, rather than a material object, bear direct relevance to the position of the body in cybersex. The body, like the text, can be manipulated in ways that would not be possible if it was a material object rather than a textual display. And so the technology that allows synchronous communication is posing an old problem in a new way. What is the body? Cybersexual sensibilities are mobilised around an imaginary physical body, enabling overly simplistic readings which rely on that cyberpunk fantasy of bodies mixing in virtual space. 'The phenomenological experience of cyberspace depends upon and in fact requires the wilful repression of the material body'.[31] The Cartesian mind/body duality is supposedly erased in cyberspace; the *res cognitans* (thinking mind) and *res extensa* (the physical object) are no longer in opposition to one another. But cybersex brings into question the supposed splitting of mind and body in cyberspace. What form of bodies, what form of minds are interacting in cybersex?

While the reconfiguration of the body via technology is not a recent development, the cybernetic-enabled mind-as-not-body fantasy of information as the antithesis of the corporeal results in the body losing its corporeality in fantasies of cyberspace. The danger of such a model is the seduction of the physical/virtual binary. This can be too easily used to imagine the body in cyberspace, allowing a body/mind distinction. This latter binary allows an understanding of cyberspace as an *alternative to* the physical world rather than an *extension of* it. The Cartesian dualism of mind and body is still entirely too seductive in the post-Enlightenment. Stone points out that cyberspace problematises the question of agency within this dualism. It 'pose[s] new problems: not simply problems of accountability (i.e., who did it) but of *warrantability* (i.e., did a body/subject do it). The issue of warrantability – that is, is there a physical body involved in this interaction *anywhere*? – is one such'.[32] Thus the metaphysics of presence allows for an on-line (or e-)agency which possesses the qualities of the body but which is a body *emptied* of meaning.

Kenosis is the self-renunciation of divine nature, exemplified by Christ in his human incarnation. It literally means an emptying out. If the text of cybersex is a re-drawing of the body, via the keyboard, on the screen then one can argue that the body undergoes kenosis. It is emptied of its physical and sensory meanings of sitting at a keyboard, staring at a screen. If the attributive body of performative actions, behaviours and utterances has no place in cyberspace, it is hazardous to suggest that this means there are no bodies in cyberspace. Hayles has identified embodiment – or rather the 'erasure of embodiment' – as the crux of debates about identity.[33] Challenging the materiality/information separation, she argues that

'[i]n contrast to the body, embodiment is contextual, enmeshed within the specifics of place, time, physiology and culture, which together compose enactment'.[34] Embodiment does not mean the body, and the notion of embodiment allows for an understanding of how bodies can appear on-line. Embodiment results from exchange and differentiation rather than representation or a material corporeality. Thus, the on-line body is striving – albeit never fully successfully because the fingers are always hitting the keys – to move beyond its functions. The phenomenology of that body at the keyboard problematises on-line embodiment. '[I]t should also be noted that such a body experience is one which is not simply co-extensive with a body outline or one's "skin" '.[35] This suggests that we still have a relation to our bodies, even in cyberspace where subjectivities are not defined by corporeality.[36] Ultimately, the body sitting at the keyboard is *always* sitting at the keyboard, although its on-line configuration(s) is kenotically achieved.

I have been wary of using the term cyborg to describe the possibilities of the body in cyberspace. A cyborg is a person whose physical tolerances or capabilities are extended beyond normal human limitations by a machine or other external agency that modifies the body's functioning. The question here is whether normal human limitations are extended by the technological interfaces of cybersex. Does engaging in cybersex make one a cyborg?

> Modern medicine is also full of cyborgs, of couplings between organism and machine, each conceived as coded devices, in an intimacy and with a power that was not generated in the history of sexuality. Cyborg 'sex' restores some of the lovely replicative baroque of ferns and invertebrates (such nice organic prophylactics against heterosexism) . . . the cyborg [is] a fiction mapping our social and bodily reality.[37]

Donna Haraway argues that the only viable bodies in postmodernity are cyborgic bodies that are enabled and sustained by communication networks and other hybrid discourses. The seductive nature of Haraway's cyborg – a term she first used in 1985 to refer to that mixture of biology and technology challenging accepted identities – has meant that the inhabitants (and theorists) of our technocultures are only too happy to refer to themselves as cyborgs. Too often the term 'cyborg' is used without due consideration of what kind of body *is* or *should be* contained therein. Haraway may claim that '[t]he cyborg is our ontology; it gives us our politics',[38] but this is an ontology that is counter-epistemic. The seductiveness of the cyborg metaphor frustrates a way of thinking through, rather than about, embodiment in cyberspace.

If safe sex is sex in which fluids are not permitted to mingle by the use of a prophylactic, then the safest sex is that in which bodies may mingle but fluids are separated not by mere rubber but by distance. It is possible to have sex with someone without flesh touching flesh (through gloves, clothing, condoms, etc.) but the fact that this counts as 'sex' – whereas not being in sight of each other does not – conveys cultural assumptions about the 'body' involved. The bodies entwining in cybersex are partly predicated upon the body fear of the late 20th century. As the materiality of the body is more and more threatened by the danger of disintegration and the threat of permeability, the apparent bodiless promise of cyberspace is all the more seductive. Cybersex allows us to engage in bodily pleasures while escaping from the material confines of our physical body. '[T]he desperate rhetoric of clean bodily fluids signals the existence of the postmodern body as *missing matter* in the cyberspace of a society dominated by its own violent implosion in loss, cancellation, and parasitism'.[39] Cyberspace appeared to promise sex without fear of consequences. The very physicality of AIDS ensures that cybersex is a seductive choice. But, and herein lies the crux of this argument, there is rape in cyberspace. Cyber-rape decisively indicates that cybersex is *not* pornography. Julian Dibbell provides a compelling account of how a rape occurred in a MUD.[40] One character took control of another character and forced the victim's character to carry out sexual acts on his character. The other characters in the room witnessed the rape, many thinking that the victim was the aggressor. The result of the rape was that the members of the MUD had an on-line debate about (a) whether this act of e-violence constituted rape; and (b) what should be done about it. The MUD characters agreed that the on-line self is an extension of the body at the keyboard and that rape was not only a rape against the body but also the self.[41] Cybersex may offer the ostensible haven of safe sex but the configuration of our on-line bodies – embodiment – allows for a social contact. The kenotic embodiment of hypothetical bodies is a model of what is happening at all times in discursive networks.

While e-tech has long been implicitly cited as the precursor of a new flesh, the means by which the internet participates in the evolution of mechanisms materialising a normative body are only now beginning to come into academic light. The leaky nature of cybersex means that cybersex is masturbation, mutual masturbation, erotica, pornography and sex all at the same time (although not in the same place). Cybersex allows for social contact that is the exterior to the disengaged nature of pornography. However, the final word rests with the above-mentioned rightwing pundits. Cybersex is read, and obtains a social existence, as a version of on-line pornography by contemporary medical discourse. However, as Jennifer Wicke has pointed out, '[p]ornography needs to be understood as a genre, indeed a genre of consumption, with many branches, in order to break down the monolith of "pornography" that can only serve to turn it into an allegory'.[42] Cybersex is both informed by pornography and informs it. An understanding of the way in which the body and embodiment are used in cyberspace and cybersex inform, in turn, an understanding of how pornography is consumed. Both cybersex and pornography, however they are defined, are concerned with the erotic. 'Erotic perception is a *cogitatio* which aims at a *cogitatum*; through one body it aims at another body, and takes place in the world, not in a consciousness'.[43] The aiming of a body towards another is an act of sexual desire located within *perception*. It is this perception which allows for the bodies of cybersex. The text of cybersex is a pornographic erotic achieved through cybernatic kenosis. Cyberspace radicalising the 'gap constitutive of the symbolic order'[44] is predicated upon the notion of a kenotic emptying of the body's meaning – the body remains but is simply a process of meaning-making through the flickering of hypertext, a process that produces far more fluid versions of itself.

NOTES

1. Howard Rheingold, *The Virtual Community: Finding Connection in a Computerised World* (London: Secker & Warburg, 1994), p. 3.
2. Elizabeth Grosz, *Volatile Bodies: Towards a Corporeal Feminism* (Bloomington: Indiana University Press, 1994), p. 189.
3. 'Cyber Sex Addiction', Sexual Recovery Institute (2001) <www.cybersexualaddiction.com/Faq.cfm>

accessed 29 November 2002. The Cybersex Addiction Help site does not address the nature of cybersex, making no distinction between cybersex and, for example, paedophilia.

4. The internet is a global communications network connected by fibre-optic cabling. The World Wide Web is that part of the internet used most often. The latter consists of all the resources on the internet that utilise Hypertext Transfer Protocol (http).

5. Sadie Plant, *Zeros and Ones: Digital Women and the New Technoculture* (London: Fourth Estate, 1997), p. 181.

6. 'Net Sex Addiction on the Rise', BBC News, 6 May 2000 <www.news.bbc.co.uk/1/hi/sci/tech/738699.stm> accessed 29 November 2002.

7. The addiction figures vary, largely because of a misunderstanding about the nature of cybersex. Looking at visual on-line pornography constitutes cybersex for many of the anti-cybersex sites, although pornography consumption is an asynchronous non-dynamic activity.

8. 'Cyber Sex Addiction'.

9. Slavoj Žižek, *The Plague of Fantasies* (London: Verso, 1997), p. 143; emphasis in original.

10. Neil Postman, *Technopoly: The Surrender of Culture to Technology* (New York: Alfred A. Knopf, 1992), distinguishes late capitalism as a technopoly, that is, a 'culture [that] seeks its authorization in technology, finds its satisfactions in technology, and takes its orders from technology. This requires the development of a new kind of social order, and of necessity leads to the rapid dissolution of much that is associated with traditional beliefs' (p. 71).

11. Arthur Kroker and Marilouise Kroker, 'Theses on the Disappearing Body in the Hyper-Modern Condition', in Arthur and Marilouise Kroker (eds), *Body Invaders: Sexuality and the Postmodern Condition* (Macmillan: Basingstoke, 1988), p. 21.

12. See Chapter 8, *passim*, in Rheingold, *The Virtual Community*, for an account of how the French Minitel was largely given over to text-sex on the messageries rose, the 'pink' sex-chat services.

13. Michael Heim, 'The Erotic Ontology of Cyberspace', in Michael Benedikt (ed.), *Cyberspace: First Steps* (Cambridge, MA: MIT Press, 1991), p. 61.

14. Sherry Turkle, *Life on the Screen: Identity in the Age of the Internet* (London: Weidenfeld and Nicolson, 1996), p. 223.

15. William Gibson, *Neuromancer* (London: Victor Gollancz, 1984).

16. For more on the interface between human and machine in film, see Claudia Springer, 'The Pleasure of the Interface', *Screen*, vol. 32 no. 2 (1991), pp. 303–23.

17. William Burroughs, *The Adding Machine: Collected Essays* (London: John Calder, 1985), p. 86.

18. Mary Ann Doane. 'Technophilia: Technology, Representation and the Feminine', in Mary Jacobus, Evelyn Fox Keller and Sally Shuttleworth (eds), *Body/Politics: Women and the Discourse of Science* (London: Routledge, 1990), p. 163.

19. The National Council on Sexual Addiction and Compulsivity defines three kinds of cybersex. The first and most common form is the on-line exchange of pornography in snapshot and video formats. This exchange may take place via email, newsgroups or home pages. The second form is synchronous (live) communication such as chatrooms and interactive home pages. Finally, pornographic software and files may be distributed on diskettes or compact disc. See 'Cybersex and Sexual Addiction', National Council on Sexual Addiction and Compulsivity, <www.ncsac.org/cybersex.htm> accessed 29 November 2002. No distinction is made between sex, masturbation, pornography and/or sexual exchange.

20. I am decisively not arguing that cyberspace provides an ideal space for playful 'passing'. A much-discussed example of on-line identity-swapping took place in 1982 on CompuServe. The male psychiatrist Sandford Lewin found that when he signed on with the gender-neutral title of 'Dr', women talked more openly with him. He created disabled, disfigured, bisexual Julie Graham. Trapped by the intimate relationships he/Julie had forged, Lewin eventually tried to kill off Julie to rid himself of the obligation. When his cover was blown, the on-line reaction was one of extreme anger and analogies of rape were made. Lewin's relationship with his on-line personae has been the subject of much interest: '[h]is responses had long since ceased to be a masquerade; with the help of the on-line mode and a certain amount of textual prosthetics, he was in the process of becoming Julie. She no longer simply carried out his wishes at her keyboard, she had her own emergent personality, her own ideas, her own directions'. See Allucquère Rosanne Stone, *The War of Desire and Technology at the Close of the Mechanical Age* (Cambridge, MA: MIT Press, 1995).

21. Elizabeth M. Reid, 'Text-Based Virtual Realities: Identity and the Cyborg Body', in Peter Ludlow (ed.),

High Noon on the Electronic Frontier: Conceptual Issues in Cyberspace (Cambridge, MA: MIT Press, 1996), p. 327.

22. In, for example, Anarchy On-line, it is possible to buy sexy clothing, including lingerie, for one's avatar.

23. This is in contrast to the holoporn in William Gibson's *Count Zero* (London: Victor Gollancz, 1986), which is non-textual but reliant upon spoken directions:

> Towel around his shoulders, dripping water, he followed the narrow hallway to his bedroom, a tiny, edge-shaped space at the very back of the condo. His holoporn unit lit as he stepped in, half a dozen girls grinning, eyeing him with evident delight. They seemed to be standing beyond the walls of the room, in hazy vistas of powder blue space, their white smiles and taut young bodies bright as neon. Two of them edged forward and began to touch themselves.
>
> 'Stop it,' he said.
>
> The projection unit shut itself down at his command; the dreamgirls vanished. The thing had originally belonged to Ling Warren's older brother; the girls' hair and clothes were dated and vaguely ridiculous. You could talk with them and get them to do things with themselves and with each other. (pp. 47–8)

24. Peter Edelman, 'MUDsex' (29 September 1999) <www.tao.ca/~peter/athesis/MUDsex.html> accessed 29 November 2002.

25. 'Transcript of Cybersex in an AOL Chat Room', *Cyborgasms: Cybersex amongst Multiple-Selves and Cyborgs in the Narrow Bandwidth Space of America On-line Chat Rooms* (1996) <www.socio.demon.co.uk/Cybertrans.html> accessed 29 November 2002. Laurie and GREGORY are, of course, possibly pseudonyms. The reader – whether Laurie, GREGORY or us – has no way of knowing if they are the biological sex they are claiming. Cyber-cross-dressing, particularly in this textual form, raises questions about sexed writing. Does a cybersexual encounter elicit a script wherein biological sex is transparent?

26. Branwyn identifies three variations of textual cybersex: real-world (describing and embellishing what you are really doing); pure fantasy (similar to fantasy role-playing games); and, tele-operated compu-sex (one party gives instructions to another party). See Gareth Branwyn, 'Compu-Sex: Erotica for Cybernauts', in David Bell and Barbara Kennedy (eds), *The Cybercultures Reader* (London: Routledge, 2000), pp. 399–400.

27. Beverly Kaite, 'The Pornographic Body Double: Transgression Is the Law', in A. and M. Kroker (eds), *Body Invaders*, p. 150.

28. Reid, 'Text-Based Virtual Realities', p. 340.

29. Stone, *The War of Desire and Technology at the Close of the Mechanical Age*, p. 94.

30. N. Katherine Hayles, *How We Became Posthuman: Virtual Bodies in Cybernetics, Literature, and Informatics* (Chicago, IL: University of Chicago Press, 1999), p. 26.

31. Anne Balsamo, *Technologies of the Gendered Body: Reading Cyborg Women* (Durham, NC: Duke University Press, 1996), p. 123.

32. Stone, *The War of Desire and Technology at the Close of the Mechanical Age*, p. 87; emphasis in original.

33. Hayles, *How We Became Posthuman*, p. xi.

34. Ibid., p. 196.

35. Don Ihde, 'Bodies, Virtual Bodies and Technology', in Donn Welton (ed.), *Body and Flesh: A Philosophical Reader* (Oxford: Blackwell, 1998) p. 351.

36. Even if embodiment is not contained by essentialism, the seduction of the body/mind binary could enable, rather than traduce, the sex/gender binary. See Thomas Foster, '"The Postproduction of the Human Heart": Desire, Identification, and Virtual Embodiment in Feminist Narratives of Cyberspace', in Mary Flanagan and Austin Booth (eds), *Reload: Rethinking Women and Cyberculture* (Cambridge, MA: MIT Press, 2002):

> Should the transformative possibilities of cyberspace be emphasized, or is it necessary at the present moment to emphasize the inescapability of embodiment? Turning the question around, is it possible to capitalize on the opportunity virtual systems represent for reimagining the relation between mind and body, without simply erasing embodiment entirely. (p. 472)

37. Donna Haraway, 'A Cyborg Manifesto: Science, Technology and Socialist Feminism in the Late Twentieth Century', in *Simians, Cyborgs, and Women: The Reinvention of Nature* (New York: Routledge, 1991), p. 150.

38. Ibid.

39. Arthur Kroker and Marilouise Kroker, 'Panic Sex in America', in A. and M. Kroker (eds), *Body Invaders*, p. 11; emphasis in original.

40. Julian Dibbell, 'A Rape in Cyberspace; or How an Evil Clown, a Haitian Trickster Spirit, Two Wizards, and a Cast of Dozens Turned a Database into a

Society Text-Based Virtual Reality: Identity and the Cyborg Body', in Ludlow (ed.), *High Noon on the Electronic Frontier*, pp. 376–95 *passim*.

41. The end result was that the attacker was banned from the MUD. However, it was possible for the IRL person to construct another MUD character and to log on again. For more on this see Turkle, *Life on the Screen*, pp. 250–4.

42. Jennifer Wicke, 'Through a Gaze Darkly: Pornography's Academic Market', in this volume, pp. 175–87.

43. Maurice Merleau-Ponty, 'The Body in Its Sexual Being', in Donn Welton (ed.), *The Body: Classic and Contemporary Readings* (Oxford: Blackwell, 1999), p. 158.

44. Žižek, *The Plague of Fantasies*, p. 143.

9 Idol Thoughts: Orgasm and Self-Reflexivity in Gay Pornography

Richard Dyer

What makes (gay) pornography exciting is the fact that it is pornography.

I do not mean this in the sense that it is exciting because it is taboo. The excitement of porn as forbidden fruit may be construed in terms of seeing what we normally do not (people having sex), what is morally and legally iffy (gay sex) or what is both the latter and, in Britain, not that obtainable (pornography itself). All of these may constitute porn's thrill for many users, but they are not what I have in mind here.

Nor do I mean that the category 'pornography' makes pornography exciting because it defines the terms of its own consumption and is moreover a major player in the business of constructing sexual excitement. Pornography does indeed set up the expectation of sexual excitement: the point of porn is to assist the user in coming to orgasm. However, it is also the case that no other genre can be at once so devastatingly unsatisfactory when it fails to deliver (nothing is more boring than porn that fails to turn you on) and so entirely true to its highly focused promise when it succeeds. In this pragmatic sense, porn cannot make users find exciting that which they do not find so. Yet in a wider sense, pornography does help to define the forms of the exciting and desirable available in a given society at a given time. The history of pornography – the very fact that it has a history, rather than simply being an unvarying constant of human existence – shows that excitement and desire are mutable, constructed, cultural. There can be no doubt at all that porn plays a significant role in this, that it participates in the cultural construction of desire. However, this too is not what directly concerns me here.

When I say that it is the fact that it is porn that makes porn exciting, I mean, for instance, that what makes watching a porn video exciting is the fact that you are watching some people making a porn video,

some performers doing it in front of cameras, and you. In this perception, *Powertool* (1986) is not about a character meeting other characters in a prison cell and having sex; it is about well-known professional sex performers (notably, Jeff Stryker) on a set with cameras and crew around them; it's the thought and evidence (the video) of this that is exciting. Now I readily concede that this is not how everyone finds porn exciting. For many it is the willing suspension of disbelief, the happy entering into the fantasy that *Powertool* is all happening in a prison cell. I shall discuss first how a video can facilitate such a way of relating to what's on screen, and it may indeed be the most usual way. Yet I do not believe that I am alone or even especially unusual in being more turned on by the thought of the cameras, crew and me in attendance. I shall look at this phenomenon in the rest of the article, focusing especially on the videos of the current gay porn star, Ryan Idol. I shall end by considering the apparent paradox of such self-reflexive porn – that it is able to indicate that it is 'only' porn and yet still achieve its orgasmic aim.

Gay porn videos do not necessarily draw attention to their own making. By way of illustration, let me consider one of the more celebrated scenes in gay porn, the subway sequence which forms the last part of *Inch by Inch* (1985).

A subway draws up at a station; a man (Jeff Quinn) enters a carriage of which the only other occupant is another man (Jim Pulver); after some eye contact, they have sex, that is, in the matchlessly rigorous description of *Al's Male Video Guide*, 'suck, fuck, rim, titplay';[1] at the next station, another man (Tom Brock) enters the carriage but the video ends, with a title informing us that 'the non-stop excitement continues . . . in the next Matt Sterling film, coming February 1986'.

This sequence unfolds before us as an event happening somewhere of which we are unobserved observers. In other words, it mobilises the conventions of realism and 'classical cinema'.[2] The first term indicates that what we see we are to treat as something happening in the real world. The second refers to the ways in which a film or video places us in relation to events such that we have access to them from a range of vantage points (the many different shots and the mobile camera that compose a single sequence in such cinema), while not experiencing this range as disruptive or (as it is) impossible; a special feature of this cinema is the way it enables the viewer to take up the position of a character within the events, most obviously through the use of point-of-view shots and the shot/reverse shot pattern. Videos do not really give us unmediated access to reality, nor do viewers think that they do. What I am describing are particular (if commonplace) ways of organising narrative space and time in film and video (between which I make no distinction for the purposes of this discussion).

The realism of the *Inch by Inch* sequence is achieved most securely by the use of location shots taken in a subway. These open the sequence and punctuate the action five times, reminding us of a real life setting that had to really exist in order to be filmable. The interior of the subway carriage could be a set – it looks very clean and the graffiti are too legible and too appropriate ('SUCK', 'REBELS', 'BAD BOYS') to be true – but the accuracy of the seating and fittings, the harsh quality of the lighting and the fact that all four sides of the carriage are seen, suggest either an unusually expensive set or an actual carriage rented for the occasion. The lack of camera or set shake suggests that the lights passing outside are indeed passing rather than being passed, but the care with which this is done is itself naturalistic. The high degree of realism in the setting is complemented by filmic elements associated with realism, such as hand-held camera and rough cutting on action. Further, the sound gives the appearance of having been recorded synchronously with the action, so that the grunts, heavy breathing, gagging, blowing and 'dialogue' ('Suck that cock', 'That feels good' etc.) don't sound like they've been added later, as is more usual with porn videos.

The performances too suggest a realism of genuine excitement. Both performers have erections most of the time (by no means the rule in porn) and their ejaculations, partly through the skill of the editing but also in some longer takes, seem to arise directly from their encounter. This compares favourably with the worked-for quality betrayed in much porn by the sudden cut to an ejaculation evidently uninspired by what the performer was doing in the immediately preceding shot. To such technical realism we may add a quality of performance, a feeling of abandonment and sexual hunger (especially on the part of Jim Pulver), unsmiling but without the grimly skilled air of many porn performances.

The quality of abandon relates to the idea of the real that all the above help to construct. This is a notion that anonymous sex, spontaneous, uncontrolled sex, sex that is 'just' sex, is more real than sex caught up in the sentiments that knowing one's partner mobilises or sex which deploys the arts of sexuality. As John Rowberry puts it, 'The sensibility of wantonness, already considered anti-social behaviour when this video was released, has never been more eloquently presented'.[3]

The rules of classical cinema are used in the sequence with exactly the degree of flexibility that characterises their use in Hollywood. The first, establishing interior shot of the carriage shows both Jeff and Jim and thus their position in relation to one another. Both sit on the same side of the carriage and the camera is positioned behind Jim's seat pointing along the carriage towards Jeff. The first cut is to a medium close-up of Jeff, with the camera pretty much the same angle towards him as in the establishing shot – thus the spatial dislocation is only one of relative closeness and not one of position; it may be said to resemble the activity of the human eye in choosing to focus on one element out of all those before it; in short, we don't notice the cut but go along with its intensification of the situation, allowing us to see the lust in Jeff's eyes.

The next cut is to Jim. The direction of Jeff's gaze in the previous shot, as well as the continuing effect of the first, establishing shot, do not make this sudden change of angle disturbing. Moreover, although the camera is at 45 degrees to Jim, just as it was to Jeff, and although Jim is looking to right off-screen and not at the camera, just as Jeff was looking to his left off-screen, nonetheless we treat the shot of Jim as if it is a shot of what Jeff sees, as a point-of-view shot. I think that this is true despite one further discrepancy, namely that, although Jeff's gaze is clearly directed at Jim's face (and still is in the next shot of him), nonetheless this shot of Jim is a medium shot from a lowish angle, which has the effect of emphasising his torso (exposed beneath an open waistcoat), the undone top button on his jeans and crotch; in other words, Jeff, in the shot on either side of this, is signalled as looking at Jim's face (even, it appears, into his eyes), yet this shot, if taken as a point-of-view shot, has him clearly looking at Jim's body. Yet such literal inaccuracy goes unnoticed, because of the shot's libidinal accuracy – it's not Jim's eyes but his chest and crotch that Jeff wants.

These few shots show how very much the sequence is constructed along the lines of classical cinematic norms, how very flexible these norms are, and in particular how they can be used to convey psychological as much as literal spatial relations. Such handling characterises the whole sequence, which it would be too laborious to describe further. However, the sequence, like much porn, does also push the classical conventions much further than is normal in Hollywood, perhaps to a breaking point.

Linda Williams, in her study of (heterosexual) film/video pornography, *Hard Core: Power, Pleasure and the 'Frenzy of the Visible'*, discussed the way that the genre has been propelled by the urgent desire to see as much as possible of sexuality, by what she calls 'the principle of maximum visibility'.[4] Two aspects of this are particularly relevant here.

One is the lengths to which porn goes to show sexual organs and actions. Williams lists some of the ways that this has operated: 'to privilege close-ups of body parts over other shots; to overlight easily obscured genitals; to select sexual positions that show the most of bodies and organs . . . to create generic conventions, such as the variety of sexual "numbers" or the externally ejaculating penis'.[5] These are what a friend of mine calls 'the plumbing shots' and are presumably what made John Waters remark that porn always looks to him 'like open-heart surgery'. The camera is down on the floor between the legs of one man fucking another, looking up into dangling balls and the penis moving back and forth into the arsehole; or it is somehow hovering overhead as a man moves his mouth back and forth over another's penis; and so on. Such spatial lability goes much further than classical norms, where the camera/viewer may, in effect, jump about the scene but will not see what cannot be seen in normal circumstances (even in actual sex one does not normally see the above, because one is doing them). Very often the editing of

these sequences betrays gaps in spatial and temporal continuity, ignored, and caused, by the 'frenzied' (to use Williams's suggestive term) will to see. The moment of coming is sometimes shot simultaneously from three different camera positions, which are then edited together, sometimes one or more in slow motion. Such temporal manipulation through editing again breaks the coherence of classicism. Devices like this may work because – as in the 'incorrect' shot of Jim described above – they are in tune with the libidinal drive of the video. But they may also draw attention to the process of video-making itself, so that what the viewer is most aware of is the cameraperson down on the floor, the performer's climax shot from several cameras, or the editor poring over the sequence, things that may spoil or may, for some, enhance the excitement of the sequence.

The other aspect of the 'principle of maximum visibility' of interest here, and central to Williams's book, is showing what is not, and possibly cannot be, seen in actual sexual intercourse, most famously the ejaculating penis. Here the difference between straight and gay porn is especially significant. As Williams discusses, much of the 'frenzy' of heterosexual porn is the desire to show and see what cannot be shown and seen, female sexual pleasure, something of no concern to gay (as opposed, of course, to lesbian) porn. Equally, the oddness of showing the man ejaculating outside of his partner's body is less striking in gay porn; withdrawal to display (especially when involving removing a condom, or ignoring the fact that in the fucking shots he is using one) is odd, but much (probably most) actual gay sex in fact involves external ejaculation (and did so even before AIDS).

Yet this insistence on seeing the performers' orgasm is an interesting feature of gay porn too. As in straight porn, it brings the linear narrative drive that structures porn to a clear climax and end (cf. Dyer, 'Coming to terms'),[6] as well as relating to the importance of the visible in male sexuality. Within gay sex, seeing another's orgasm is delightful because it is a sign that the other is excited by one and is even a sort of gift, a giving of a part of oneself. Such feelings are at play in come shots in gay porn. Additionally, one may see come shots as a further dimension of a video's realism. Come shots are rarely, if ever, faked; we really are seeing someone come. This is happening in the story and fictional world of the video, but it's also happening on a set. Its conventionality, its oddness when involving withdrawal, the often disruptive cut that precedes it, all draw attention to it as a performance for camera. This breaks classical norms, but it is the foundation of the excitement of pornography that I want to discuss in the next section.

If gay porn, like straight, runs the risk of disrupting its own illusionism, some of it has been happy to capitalise on this. Most gay porn is like the subway sequence in *Inch by Inch* (though less accomplished in its deployment of codes of realism and classicism), but a significant amount is not. In its history (not much shorter, according to Waugh,[7] than that of the straight stuff), gay film/video porn has consistently been marked by self-reflexivity, by texts that have wanted to draw attention to themselves as porn, that is, as constructed presentations of sex.

This may be at the level of narrative: films about making porn films (*Giants*, 1983; *Screenplay*, 1984; *Busted*, 1991; *Loaded*, 1992); about taking porn photographs (*Flashback*, 1980; *Juice*, 1984; *Bicoastal*, 1985; *Make It Hard*, 1985; *Rap'n about 'ricans*, 1992); about auditioning for porn films (*The Interview*, 1981; *Abuse Thyself*, 1985; *Screen Test*, 1985); about being a live show performer (*Le Beau mec*, 1978; *Performance*, 1981; *Times Square Strip*, 1982; *The Main Attraction*, 1989); about having sex in porn cinemas – just like the patrons (*The Back Row*, 1973; *Passing Strangers*, 1977; *The Dirty Picture Show*, 1979). It may be at the level of cinematic pastiche or intertextual reference (*The Light from the Second Storey Window*, 1973; *Adam and Yves*, 1974; *The Devil and Mr Jones*, 1974; *Five Hard Pieces*, 1977; *Cruisin' 57*, 1979; *Gayracula*, 1983; *Early Erections*, 1989).[8] It may be a display of a star, someone known for being in porn (*Best of the Superstars*, 1981; the *Frank Vickers Trilogy*, 1986–9; *Deep Inside Jon Vincent*, 1990; *Inside Vladimir Correa*, 1991; or more specifically a film about being a porn star, showing him on the job (*Inside Eric Ryan*, 1983; *That Boy*, 1985). There are even successful films that are histories of gay porn (*Good Hot Stuff*, 1975; *Eroticus*, 1983). Where the film does not refer to film porn as such, it may well refer explicitly to the psychic elements necessary for the production of porn: narcissism (e.g. a man making love to his own mirror image [*Le Beau mec*; *Pumping Oil*, 1983]); exhibitionism (e.g. a body-

builder fantasising posing nude [*Private Party*, 1984]); voyeurism (*Le Voyeur*, 1982; *On the Lookout*, 1992); and dreaming and fantasising themselves, two of the commonest motifs in gay porn films, resulting in elaborate narrative structures of flashbacks, inserts, intercutting and stories within stories. All of these elements of content can be supplemented by the form of the film itself. The *Interview* films (1989–) for instance have the subject talking to the off-screen but heard director while stripping, working out and masturbating. *Roger* (1979) cuts back and forth between long shots and close-ups of the action (Roger masturbating), using different shades of red filter, the rhythmic precision of cutting drawing attention to itself and hence to the film's construction of a celebration of its eponymous subject.

I am far from claiming that this tradition of self-reflexivity is characteristic of most gay porn. If the list I have given (itself very far from complete) is impressive, it constitutes but a drop in the ocean of the massive gay film/video porn business. Yet the tradition is there and encompasses many of the most successful titles. The self-reflexive mode would not be so consistently returned to, did it not sell – and it would not sell if it did not turn people on. Moreover, it is not unreasonable to assume that some people (like me) take pleasure in non-self-reflexive porn by imagining the rehearsals, the camera and crew, by focusing on the performers as performers rather than as characters.

I want to examine gay porno self-reflexivity by focusing on the work of one highly successful contemporary porn star. Ryan Idol is a young man who must have blessed his parents and perhaps God that he was born with so appropriate and serviceable a name. Few stars can have got their own name so often into the title of their videos (*Idol Eyes*, 1990; *Idol Worship*, 1992; *Idol Thoughts*, 1993) or had it used as the basis for so many puns in magazine feature spreads ('Ryan Idol, Yours to Worship' [cover *Advocate Men*, July 1990]); 'Idol Worship' and 'Pinnacle' [cover and feature title, *Advocate Men*, March 1993]; 'Richard Gere Was My Idol – So to Speak' [*The Advocate Classifieds*, 18 May 1993]). Ryan seems to have no existence, no image, other than that of being the subject of sexual adulation. What is exciting about him is that he is a porn star.

There is with all movie stars a potential instability in the relationship between their being a star and the characters they play. When the fit is perfect – Joan Crawford as Mildred Pierce, Sylvester Stallone as Rocky Balboa – we do not, except in a camp appreciation, sit there thinking we are seeing a movie star baking pies by the score or becoming World Heavyweight Champion; in so far as the discrepancy worries us at all, we resolve it by seeing the role as expressive of personality qualities in the star – in the case of Joan and Sly, for instance, variations on notions of working-class advancement. There is, in other words, a set of cultural categories to which both role and star image refer, beyond that of simply being a very famous performer in movies. Porn stars – like, to some extent, musical stars – cannot mobilise such reference so easily; they are famous for having sex in videos.

There can be an element of wider social reference in porn stars' images. The extremely successful Catalina company has created an image of the California boy, with no existence other than working and making out. This is an image that seems to offer itself as stripped of social specificity, a sort of pornographic utopia uncontaminated by class, gender or race, although it is of course highly specifically white, young, US and well fed. Residually, gay porn stars are still generally given social traits. Jeff Stryker, for instance, perhaps the biggest contemporary star, is repeatedly associated with working-class iconography, through roles (a mercenary in *Stryker Force*, 1987, a garage mechanic in *The Look*, 1988, a farm boy in *The Switch Is On*, 1987) or accessories in pin-ups (spanners, greasy jeans). This is often reinforced by the idea of him as an innocent who, willingly but almost passively, gets into sexual encounters (as in his gaol videos, *Powertool*, 1986 and *Powerful II*, 1989, or the farm boy in the city narrative of *The Switch Is On*). It would however be hard to say anything even as broadly definite as this with Ryan Idol, even though he played a lifeguard (*Idol Eyes*, 1990), college quarterback (*Score Ten*, 1991) and naval officer (*Idol Worship*, 1992). Even these roles in fact play upon the one clear role that he has, being a porn star.

The sense of his not offering anything but himself as body is suggested by his readiness to play with different body images in his many porn magazine spreads. In *Advocate Men* in July 1990, he has almost bouffant hair with a still boyish face and body. This look is capitalised on in the spread in the November 1991 issue of the short-lived *Dream*, which seemed

to be addressing itself to men and women, straight and gay simultaneously; unusually for an Idol spread, there are no shots with erections, he is posed on black satin sheets and his expression is one of practised but unsullied yearning. Before that (at least in terms of publication, if not actual shoot), in *Mandate*, June 1990, the hair is cut much shorter at the sides, the top more obviously held stiffly in place with spray, he uses a leather jacket as prop, and poses more angularly, which, together with harder directional lighting, makes him look both more muscley and more directly sexual. Something similar is achieved in *Jock*, December 1991, though with more tousled hair and the fullest sense of social reference (a locker-room and football gear, part of the publicity for *Score Ten*). By 1993, however, there was a more radical alteration of the image, and in two, almost simultaneous forms. His hair is long and Keanu Reeves-ishly floppy now and his body less defined. In *Advocate Men*, March 1993, he poses by a pool, more in the 'art' style of a gay photographer like Roy Dean than this magazine's usual house style. In *Mandate*, June 1993, he is sweaty, with grease marks on his body, a much raunchier look, which is picked up in his pictures in *The Advocate Classifieds* for 18 May 1993, which have some residual boxing iconography.

There are continuities in this imagery, but these serve to emphasise him *qua* porn star. The thong tan-line is unchanging, a tanline associated with exotic dancers, that is, sex performers. More significantly, he consistently poses in ways that relate very directly to the viewer. He holds his body open to view, his arms framing rather than concealing it, his posture, especially from the hips, often subtly thrust towards the camera (especially notable in shots lying on his side in *Dream* or seated in *Torso*, December 1991). This sense of very consciously offering the body is reinforced by the fact that he almost invariably looks directly, smilingly, seemingly frankly, into the camera, and has an erection. The only variation in the latter is that it is more often free standing or lightly held in the early photos, more often gripped and pointed in the later ones. There is absolutely no sense here of someone being observed (as if voyeuristically) as they go about their business nor of someone posing reluctantly, embarrassedly, just for the money. That impression is reinforced by interview material: 'I'll do maybe one or two adult films, mostly as an outlet for my exhibitionism',[9] 'Ryan reveals that he likes show-

ing off his big body. "I like doing it and I like watching it," he says.'[10] In *Ryan Idol: A Very Special View*,
1990, scripted by Ryan himself, he talks at length
about the pleasures of posing for photographs and of
being an exotic dancer.

His magazine spreads, a vital component of any
porn star's image, construct him as nothing other
than a porn star, and this is echoed by the information on his life. Porn stars are seldom given an
elaborate biography, but there is usually an implication of something in their lives other than pornography. Though Ryan has not made so many
videos, he has done very many photo spreads and
personal appearances. Interviews with him give the
impression that that is what his life consists of, the
more so since the establishment of the Ryan Idol
International Fan Club (which includes a 'hot line', a
co-star search, a 'Win a Date with Ryan Contest',
and a sales catalogue, including posters, T-shirts, pictures, 'paraphernalia' and cologne; in short, 'We're
offering [the fans] many, many ways to get closer to
Ryan Idol'.[11] *A Very Special View* offers a day in the
life of a porn star, but unlike other such videos featuring, for instance, Vladimir Correa or Jon Vincent,
Ryan's day does not consist of sexual encounters but
a photo shoot, a strip show and doing solos for us.
His career even has its own narrative dynamic, to do
with the gradual extension of what he does on
camera. In all his videos he does solos and in most he
is sucked off; in *Idol Eyes*, the penis in the close-ups
of him fucking Joey Stefano is in fact David Ash-
field's, as subsequent coverage revealed; but in *Score
Ten* he did his own stunt work and, with a fanfare of
publicity, in *Idol Thoughts* he sucks someone else off.
This trajectory, itself following the pattern of many
porn narratives, is part tease, keeping something in
reserve for later in the career, but also part play with
the question of sexual identity – Ryan makes straight
porn videos, was 'open' in early interviews ('I share
my lovemaking equally with women and men',
Dream), though much less equivocally gay more
recently (' "Do you enjoy sucking dick?" "What do
you think? I think it's a turn-on. And I think that
question is pretty much answered in *Idol Thoughts*" ',
The Advocate Classifieds). Such fascination with the
'real' sexual identity of porn stars in gay videos is a
major component of the discourse that surrounds
them, but it also contributes to the sense that with
Ryan sex is performance rather than identity.

His videos further emphasise his existence as
porn star. Only two are actually about him being a
porn star (*A Very Special View* and the footage in *Troy
Saxon Gallery II*, 1991) but the rest all play with the
idea of his having been in the pleasures of looking. In
Idol Eyes he spies on others having sex but is first
really turned on by looking at himself in the mirror,
getting into different outfits in front of it and masturbating at his own image. His voice-over talks
about his learning to get off men through getting off
on himself (a casebook statement of one of the
Freudian aetiologies of homosexuality). Similarly in
A Very Personal View he jacks off looking at himself
in the bathroom mirror, saying in voice-over:
'Nothing wrong with that – I do enjoy being with
myself – sometimes it's much more exciting –
especially when someone . . . might be watching' (a
rider I'll return to). In *Score Ten* he masturbates in
front of a fellow student (as payment for the latter's
having written a paper for him), posed on the bonnet
of a car with the student inside, so that he, Ryan, is
framed and kept distant by the windscreen. *Idol Worship* has him strip off and masturbate in the control
room of the ship he commands, all the while telling
the crew not to look, to keep their eyes on their
instruments, orders which they obey. *Trade Off*
(1992) is about Ryan and Alex Garret as neighbours
spying on each other through their windows. Thus
we have voyeurism (*Idol Eyes*, *Trade Off*), narcis-
sism/self-looking (*Idol Eyes*, *A Very Special View*), display (*Score Ten*), denial of looking (*Idol Worship*), a
series of entertaining plays on what is at the heart of
porn: looking, showing, being looked at.

The most sustained exploration of this is *A Very
Special View*, especially in the opening and closing
solo sequences. In the first, Ryan is discovered by the
camera when he wakes up and masturbates; this is
accompanied by a voice-over in which he says he
does this every morning and how he enjoys it. The
treatment is for the most part classical; we are invited
to imagine that Ryan doesn't know we are there and
has added the commentary later. Yet even here Ryan
teases us with the knowledge that he does know we
are, as it were, there.

The sequence is in two parts, the first on the bed,
the second in the bathroom. At the end of the first,
Ryan is pumping his penis hard and glances at the
camera momentarily and then again on a dissolve to
the bathroom sequence. It is in the latter that Ryan

makes the remark in voice-over quoted above, that it can be more enjoyable to make love to oneself, 'especially if someone might be watching'. Earlier in the sequence he has evoked the possibility of another person being present:

> There's no better way to start the day than to stroke my cock and bring myself to a very satisfying orgasm. Come to think about it, there is one better way and that would be to have someone working on my hard cock as I awake and slowly, slowly getting me off.

This comment runs the risk of reminding the viewer of what is not the case, that he is not in bed with Ryan sucking him off. The later comment alludes to what is the case, that someone is watching him – the camera/us. This immediately precedes his orgasm, so that what is in play as he comes is the fact of looking and being looked at.

When we first see him in the bathroom, he is looking at himself in the mirror, and several other mirrors duplicate his image. He masturbates in the shower, but a close-up towards the end makes it clear that he is still appraising himself in the mirror. When he comes, he looks straight ahead, head on to the camera. But is he looking at the mirror or the camera, at himself or us? Either or both, for our pleasure in him is his pleasure in himself.

The last sequence plays much more strongly on the presence of the camera and Ryan as image. He goes into a friend's bedroom to have a rest. He strips to his briefs and gets on the bed, then turns to the camera, saying 'Do you want to see?', a rhetorical question in a porn video, and takes off his briefs. The sense of him as a performer is emphasised by the mirrors in the room. Not only do they connote display, narcissism and exhibitionism, they are also the means by which we see the cameraman from time to time. Perhaps this is an accident – 'bad' video-making – but with a star like Ryan it is entirely appropriate. What is he but someone being filmed? At two points we see an image of him which the camera draws back to reveal has been a mirror image; any distinction between the real Ryan and the image of Ryan is confounded.

Most remarkable though is Ryan's constant address to the camera. Once he runs the risk of reminding us of other, unavailable possibilities – 'Imagine it any way you want', he says, but of course

should we wish to imagine having sex with him, we have to imagine something other than what we are seeing. But for the rest he talks entirely about the situation we are watching. He speaks of his control over his penis ('I make it do what I want'), an obvious asset in a porn star. He draws attention to the narrative structure of the sequence, its progress towards orgasm, by saying that he is about to come, but won't do it just yet, how he likes to hold off for as long as possible. He even draws attention to the porn viewing situation, by saying twice that he wants the viewer to come with him, something porn viewers generally wish to do. The shouts that accompany his orgasm are punctuated by glances at the camera, still conscious of our intended presence, still reminding us that he is putting on a show for our benefit.

In emphasising self-reflexive gay porn, I not only don't want to give the impression that it is the more common form, but also don't want to suggest that it is superior to less or un-self-reflexive examples. Intellectuals tend to be drawn to the meta-discursive in art; since what they themselves do is a meta-activity, they take special comfort from other things that are meta, like self-reflexive art. Yet it interests me that so viscerally demanding a form as pornography (it must make us come) can be, and so often is, self-reflexive.

According to much twentieth-century critical theory, this ought not to be so. It has long been held that work that draws attention to itself – cultural constructs that make apparent their own constructedness – will have the effect of distancing an audience. A film that draws our attention to its processes of turning us on ought not to turn us on; you shouldn't be able to come to what are merely terms. As Linda Williams puts it, pornography has a problem:

> Sex as spontaneous *event* enacted for its own sake stands in perpetual opposition [in porn films] to sex as an elaborately engineered and choreographed *show* enacted by professional performers for a camera.[12]

Yet, as I have tried to show, in much gay porn, at any rate, the show *is* the event.

This is of a piece with much gay culture. Being meta is rather everyday for queers. Modes like camp, irony, derision, theatricality and flamboyance hold together an awareness of something's style with a readiness to be moved by it – *La Traviata, Now Voy-*

ager and 'Could It Be Magic' (in Barry Manilow's or Take That's version) are no less emotionally compelling for our revelling in the facticity. The elements of parody and pastiche and the deliberate foregrounding of artifice in much gay porn are within this tradition. Episodic films like *Like a Horse* (1984) and *Inch by Inch* move from one obviously constructed fantasy to another – from a jungle encounter to a no-place, abstracted leather sequence to an Arab tent, from a studio rooftop to a studio beach to a studio street – without for a moment undermining their erotic charge. This is characteristic of the way we inhabit discourse. We are constantly aware of the instability of even our own discourses, their hold on the world still so tenuous, so little shored up by a network of reinforcing and affirming discourses, and yet our stake in them is still so momentous. We see their deliberation but still need their power to move and excite; it's thus so easy for us to see porn as both put-on and turn-on.

This, though, is not mainly what is at play in the Idol oeuvre. For here there is no sense of putting on a fantasy, no sense of performing anything other than performance. The idea of sex as performance is generally associated with male heterosexuality, and the element of working hard to achieve a spectacular orgasm is certainly present in much gay porn. Yet performance in the Ryan Idol case means much more display, presentation, artistry, the commitment to entertainment – literally a good show. It is a construction of sexuality as performance, as something you enact rather than express.

Gay men are as romantic and raunchy, as expressive and essentialist, as anyone else. Yet much facilitates a perception of (gay) sex as performance. Owning to one's gay identity – itself so fragile a construct – is perilous: seeing sexuality as performance rather than being is appealing, since it does not implicate that compelling notion, the self. At the same time, dominant culture does little to naturalise our sexuality, making it harder to see gay sex acts as a product of pure need. We are less likely to think of gay sex in terms of biology than of aesthetics.

Paradoxically, there is a kind of realism in pornographic performance that declares its own performativity. What a porn film really is is a record of people actually having sex; it is only ever the narrative circumstances of porn, the apparent pretext for the sex, that is fictional. A video like *A Very Special View* foregrounds itself as a record of a performance, which heightens its realism. It really is what it appears to be.

This realism in turn has the effect of validating the video, and the genre to which it belongs. By stressing that what we are enjoying is not a fantasy, but porn, it validates porn itself. As Simon Watney has argued, the importance of doing this in the age of AIDS could not be greater.[13] And by specifically celebrating masturbation, videos like Ryan's also validate the very response that porn must elicit to survive, that is, masturbation. The most exciting thing of all about porn is that it affirms the delights of that most common, most unadmitted, at once most vanilla and most politically incorrect of sexual acts, masturbation.

Reprinted by permission of Blackwell Publishing from *Critical Quarterly*, vol. 36 no. 1, 1994, pp. 48–62.

NOTES

1. *Al's Male Video Guide* (New York: Midway Publications, 1986), p. 132.
2. For a brief account of 'classical cinema', see the entry in Annette Kuhn and Susannah Radstone (eds), *The Women's International Companion to Film* (London: Virago, 1989). For a more exhaustive account, see David Bordwell, Janet Staiger and Kristin Thompson, *The Classical Hollywood Cinema* (New York: Columbia University Press, 1985).
3. John Rowberry (ed.), *The Adam Film World Guide*, 14(11) (Los Angeles, CA: Knight Publishing Corporation, 1993), p. 93.
4. Linda Williams, *Hard Core: Power, Pleasure and the 'Frenzy of the Visible'* (Berkeley/Los Angeles: University of California Press, 1989), p. 48.
5. Ibid., p. 49.
6. Richard Dyer, 'Coming to Terms' in *Only Entertainment* (London: Routledge, 1992).
7. Tom Waugh, *Hard to Imagine: Gay Male Eroticism in Photography and Film, from its Origins to Stonewall* (New York: Columbia University Press, 1995).
8. These films refer respectively to *A Star Is Born*, Garbo, Cocteau and Brando movies, *The Devil and Miss Jones*, fifties stag movies (and *Five Easy Pieces* of course), *American Graffiti*, *Dracula*, and educational television documentaries.
9. *Advocate Men*, July 1990, p. 48.
10. *Prowl*, June 1991.
11. *The Advocate Classifieds*, 18 May 1993, p. 51.
12. Linda Williams, *Hard Core*, p. 147; Williams's italics.
13. Simon Watney, *Policing Desire: Pornography, AIDS and the Media* (London: Methuen/Comedia, 1987).

10   The 'World' of All-Male Pornography: On the Public Place of Moving-Image Sex in the Era of Pornographic Transnationalism

Rich C. Cante and Angelo Restivo

Despite its oft-presumed critical 'disposability' relative to other sectors of the contemporary mediascape, and despite the now established fact that its reception contexts are much more fluid and unstable than are those of most other moving-image genres, pornography provides crucial ideological sites at which social subjects are situated in relation to the world. This 'world' is always figurative as well as literal, simultaneously needing to be written with a capital and a lower-case first letter, and with and without the quotation marks. This concept is an important one for thinking about pornography not just in the context of transnationalism. From a phenomenological perspective all the way to the geographical one at what could be considered the opposite end of a particular critical spectrum, the relation to 'world' lies at the heart of *all* pornographic desires and pornographic pleasures, one way or another.

In what follows, we will deal with certain implications of the relatively recent popularisation and conventionalisation of transnational pornographic production, distribution and reception practices. The more general machinations of globalisation underlying these developments have made it apparent that, at least in the case of all-male pornography, the literal/figurative 'World' the genre aspires to instantiating was always already the crucial imaginary (and real) horizon delimiting porn's meanings, cultural uses, and ideological functions *even before its rigorous transnationalisation*. In other words, in the wake of these recent developments in pornography – given the vantage point they provide on the forces that underlie them, and that they in turn help propel – we can now discern key tendencies even, for example, in the first wave of US 70s' feature-length, all-male hard core. In these films, a few localities – Greenwich Village and Times Square in New York, Fire Island, The Castro in San Francisco, West Hollywood in Los Angeles – are repeatedly overlaid with

the rhetorical mandate of constructing a world in which the post-Stonewall gay male can achieve coherence as a visible, recognisable entity. Yes, this world is a ghetto, in some sense. But it is also a 'place' more expansive than even the nation, especially given the already transnational nature of pornography's distribution networks. (Think for example of the history of mail-order 'French films' in the United States, or the continual influx of Swedish and German product to Western and Central European markets.) These sites are thereby charged with the duty of participating in the phantasy that the process of publicly imaging/imagining such a 'world' (its figuration) can somehow serve to install it, as imagined, in the actual (literal) World in which figurations are made material in the first place.[1]

The 'transnational turn' in gay porn that we are discussing begins with the coagulation of a recognisable sub-genre by around 1990, by which time there already exists a significant lineage of 'travelogue'-type tapes shot in the tropics, Central Europe and the Eastern bloc, and other parts of the world (including non-urban corners of the United States). In these tapes, local men and boys in and from distinct locations perform the sex for their 'patrons', who are most often implicitly or explicitly figured as Northern, Western and/or significantly older than the 'indigenous' models. The sub-genre becomes more and more marketable and profitable over time, less and less of an obscure specialty category. By the mid-90s, this flowers into the much more complex sort of more fully narrativised, more fully-blown transnational and transregional pornographic forms that we will discuss in detail. At this time, the resulting texts have a great deal to tell us about the modes of subjectivity available to the gay men in different, unevenly developed spaces of the post-Fordist empire around the globe.

The contemporary sub-genre in which this has resulted continually de-locates and re-locates its 'subject', as narrative is bound to do. This process works through the tapes' industrial, reception and phantasy contexts, as well as the significant changes in textual convention that have occurred since the more primitive, 'area-studies'-type travelogue aesthetics of earlier international pornographic forays. (This is an aesthetics whose more 'primitive' forms arguably remain, to this day, much more central in the 'heterosexual' international canon.) We will illustrate why and how these newer transnational forms make so interesting and so important the process of tracking its subject's trajectories within the world that it figures and within the World in which it literally exists. In the process, we will demonstrate some of the complications of apprehending the aesthetic astonishments and ideological effects of explicit moving-image, male–male sexual representation once these astonishments have become as self-reflexive and convoluted as they have since the all-male production apparatus went explicitly transnational – or since it began saliently acknowledging, and attempting to recuperate, the world of pornography's crucial functional entanglement with the 'World' of pornography.

1

The overarching critical and theoretical complexities germane to these issues have been outlined most succinctly by George Chauncey and Elizabeth Povinelli. In the introduction to their co-edited November 1999 special issue of *GLQ* on the transnational turn in gay and lesbian studies, they stress the importance of basing this critical endeavour on work that is 'careful not to mistake the emergence of the consciousness of a global ecumene for the emergence of the phenomenon of globalization itself'. They write:

> A troubling aspect of the literature on globalization is its tendency to read social life off external social forms – flows, circuits, and circulations of people, capital, and culture – without any model of subjective mediation. In other words, globalization studies often proceed as if tracking and mapping the facticity of economic and population flows were sufficient to account for current cultural forms and subjective interiorities – or as if an accurate map of the space and time of post-Fordist accumulation could provide an accurate map of the subject and her embodiment and desires.

For Chauncey and Povinelli, it is precisely the *non-correspondence* between discursive, psychic and practical orders that has yet to be sufficiently integrated into 'transnationalist' exegetical methods.

> How do we produce our undoing as we attempt to follow our desires? After all, in doing what we 'will to do,' we 'do a thousand and one things we hadn't willed to do,' and so 'the act is not pure.' We leave traces and, in wiping away these traces, we leave others. In Levinas's words, it is 'like an animal fleeing in a straight line across the snow before the sound of the hunters, thus leaving the very traces that will lead to its death.'.... It is this travail of the subject, fashioned far afield from itself, that globalization studies has yet to track.[2]

Clearly, then, the subject is 'fashioned as far afield from itself', both literally and figuratively, in gay pornography as anywhere else. It is for precisely this reason that we immediately run up against a serious complication even by using the word 'gay' in attempting to track this subject, however necessary that usage might be. 'Gay' shatters into an irrepressible categorical incoherence in any global analytical context that attempts to encompass North and South, East and West, and old and new. This is why we feel compelled to revert to the generic anachronism we have revived so far: 'all-male'. While the word 'gay' causes more multilayered problems in the international context than it already causes in the US one, even in the latter interpretive context the concept is, of course, hardly stable. For instance, it cannot be ignored that many of the United States' most illustrious all-male performers are continually characterised in journalistic reports and publicity materials as being merely 'gay for pay'. Unstable, provisional relationships between acts and identity characterise 'national discourse' on same-sex activity even in the places and times at which the relationship between the two is, relatively speaking, supposedly most stable and successfully reified. In other words, this instability is already clearly structured into the encounter with pornography, including its pleasures, its displeasures, and all of those aspects that are outside of a viewer's awareness. This is true even in the places and times at which the pressures towards consciously or unconsciously 'buying into' identitarian models are supposedly most irresistible.

In pornography whose essence lies between and across global regions rather than within them, the mechanisms by which closely related, though different, instabilities are structured into the encounter with pornography are themselves distinct. The difference is symptomatic of the overall affective operations of contemporary global capitalism these days, and of the whole thorny question of identitarianism's significance to the politics of non-normative sexual acts – as well as the nature of the 'social movements' that are or are not (apparently) connected to those acts in different places. In other words, thinking through transnational all-male porn as a particular globally marketable sub-genre won't let us forget, *pace* Chauncey and Povinelli, just how far afield of itself is the 'transnational gay subject' on various separate theoretical counts.[3]

These cultural artifacts, and attached discursive movements, demand in unique ways that we continually remember that the transcontextual 'gay subject' *doesn't even necessarily exist*. They demand this for their spectator as well as their critic. By definition, such a subject exists only phantasmatically, in a realm that 'shadows' its phenomenal traces. All-male pornography's dictate that we remember this results from three distinct issues, then. Each of them is attached to one of the three separate words 'transnational', 'gay' and 'subject'. Relative to the notion of the individual that is perpetually attached to the term 'subject' in media and cultural theory in various complicated, fluid, unstable and sometimes downright erroneous ways: 1) the contemporary 'transnational' doesn't necessarily exist in globally delimitable spatial or temporal terms, or as a concept we can assume is 'identical to itself' across different local contexts; 2) 'gay' doesn't necessarily exist as a delineable identity formulation unhooked from time and place, or as one that we can assume is 'identical to itself' across spatial and temporal contexts, or even present in all such contexts, and; 3) the 'subject' does not, again, exist at all – except as an 'effect' (and *through* the effects) of the propensities to assume that individuals can be 'identical to themselves' at different points in their trajectories through time and space.[4]

But again, much less abstract recent developments also drive the analysis that follows, as do a number of needed correctives to previous understandings of all-male porn as signifying practice (or *culture*), and to knee-jerk assumptions about its exact connections to the realms of the economic and the social within contemporary global capitalism. In particular, certain territorial and transterritorial economic and institutional changes in the all-male industry, the moving-image porn industry as a whole, and the social world as a whole. These changes are both the cause (e.g., the opening of various Eastern markets to Western capitalism) and the effect (e.g., all sorts of new 'ethnic' and 'national' relationships between real people, whether workers in the porn industries, fans, video store clerks) of moving-image pornography's 'going transnational' in the 90s with a theretofore unimaginable vigour, and with surprising accompanying developments in textual form.[5] Of course, many of these changes function as both causes and effects, simultaneously. In fact, the degree to which such changes have become apparent in both the global industry and its local manifestations – especially as the internet becomes an increasingly important mode of transterritorial distribution and exhibition, and one that already incorporates 'production' into distribution and reception in new ways – retroactively makes obvious the extent to which we should have *already* been rigorously thinking through film and video pornography, along with its related subject effects, in terms of the territorial, spatial and place-related dimensions that we will consider below.[6]

To more closely detail the contours of these issues, and to begin to connect certain recent textual/aesthetic movements, and the (trans)national intersections at which they arise, to the ideological workings of both all-male pornography and global capitalism in general, we will turn to the work of one particular director: Kristen Bjorn. Bjorn has been effectively presented, in the US and elsewhere, as a pioneer in, and a high auteur *par excellence* of, international all-male video porn. He's sort of the grand pooh-bah of this field, associated in particularly illuminating ways with the all-male 'quality porn' sub-genre as well as the 'international' one.

2

Bjorn is the British-born, Washington, DC-raised son of a diplomat who was supposedly sexually initiated, depending on which of the reports you believe, in Brazil or Lisbon or French Canada. Reputedly, he is now an Australian citizen, though his business is run largely out of the United States. His *nom-de-caméra-stylo* was chosen when tennis star Bjorn Borg was at the height of his popularity, while

'Kristen' himself was still a porn performer. According to one typically libidinally charged report in the US gay press, he now resides for a third of each year in Miami, Montreal and Sydney. When he's not shooting on location elsewhere, that is. As essentially a one man-with-a-Betacam shooting operation, Bjorn began turning out remarkable nation-based features in the mid-80s. He then continued at a rate of approximately three a year until, along with US pornography at large, he began taking his work into former Eastern bloc countries in around 1992. Apparently, this was exactly the right time for the consolidation of a gay specialty market that, it quickly became clear, had broader appeal than anticipated. It was just after Bel Ami really began to hit it big internationally with tapes such as the original *Lucas' Story*, which were very important in constituting Western niche markets for such works.

Having made the right industry contacts as a magazine model and moving-image performer for San Francisco's Falcon Studios in the early 80s, from the outset of his career as a director Bjorn very carefully marketed and distributed his work in the US and around the world. To this day, he has remained at the helm of marketing and distribution operations rather than signing them away to a larger distribution company, micro-managing all phases of production and carefully 'trademarking' his name through its association with 'internationalist', all-male video porn. This micro-management has been recently extended through the reach of the bjorn.com website, which boasts model portfolios, biographies of crew as well as cast, production diaries, and even monthly emails from 'Bjorn himself' to his subscribers. These email updates come from an email address that bears Bjorn's own name. They contain updates on purchase specials, forthcoming releases (especially as Bjorn's earlier work has been gradually re-released on DVD in the past few years), live shows and parties in various cities, model searches that are in progress within the company, and so on.

Bjorn's pre-1993 features are organised mostly by recourse to specific iconographies of the national. They systematically explore the spaces of the under-developed or developing world as well as those of the formerly colonised developed world, partly via the aforementioned travelogue aesthetics. Typically revealing titles include *Carnival in Rio* (1989), *Jungle Heat* (non-urban Brazil), *Tropical Heatwave*

(Dominican Republic, 1988), *The Caracas Adventure* (Venezuela, 1993), *Jackaroos* (Australia, 1991), *Call of the Wild* (Quebec) and *Montreal Men* (1993). They also occasionally explore diasporic societal pockets in cities like New York (cf. *Manhattan Latin*, 1992), an interest that is a significant harbinger of later developments. In 1993, Bjorn began to explore post-Communist Central European and Eastern bloc nations, though still in a series of primarily nation-centred tapes shot in the Czech Republic, Hungary and Russia. These works include *Hungary for Men*, *Hungarians*, *Comrades in Arms* (1995) and *A Vampire in Budapest* (1995). With the exception of the tapes produced in Australia and Canada, the phantasmatic sites around which these works are built have in common the fact that they are culturally 'Latin' and, later, 'Eastern European'.[7] This is one important key to understanding just what is important, new and finally so arresting about Bjorn's work, as well as its notable international marketability – or, to use a trickier word, 'popularity'.

His most recent tapes, from the mid-90s to the present, can be said to comprise a discrete 'transnational series', a second phase in Bjorn's oeuvre as a director. Here, heterogeneous groups – gangs, even – of national subjects interact within and across particular urban spaces. That space is Miami in the case of *Gangsters at Large* (1997), *Anchor Hotel* (1998), *Little Havana* (1999*)*, and *Wet Dreams 1* and *2* (2000/2001), Thus, this series of features is rigorously transnationalised in a very high concept way, using Miami as the key vortex for imagining Bjorn's particular brand of all-male contemporary cosmopolitanism.[8] Other features produced in this period, like *A World of Men* (1995), *Thick as Thieves* (1999) and *Manwatcher* (2001), move across several transnational spaces. *Thick as Thieves*, for instance, follows the exploits of an international ring of hunky and willing art thieves as they traverse various museum-like, deterritorialised 'zones' and 'scapes' of liminal, interlocking metropolitan bricolage.[9] What seems particularly important about Bjorn's place in contemporary gay porn during both phases of his career is not merely his work's 'international specialty' dimension, but its related – and yet not necessarily correspondent – conceptual approach to *place,* and to the overall importance of place in pornography. To be more accurate, it's a particular understanding of *location* that's on the table here. However bound this concept is to the international dimension of Bjorn's work, it also seems quite separate from it in ideological function. It is here that the idea of 'quality porn' intervenes as one mediating factor.

Indeed, 'location, location, location' had emerged as a mantra of all-male porn at some time in the early 70s. This especially blossomed into prominence during the Reagan/Thatcher era, with video. From the post-industrial sex club to the adult movie house to the Palm Springs sex resort to the West Hollywood apartment building to the desert-as-landscape and, finally, to the California sun itself as a non-representational sign of place, the construction of intertextual networks of spaces, places and sounds – e.g. the similar music mixes we hear in our Starbucks shops, video stores, sex clubs, restaurants and aerobics classes – across which gay subjectivity ostensibly enacts itself has become a crucial organisational rubric for all-male, moving-image systems of signification. Within this nexus, Bjorn's phase II work represents an impulse to move this intertextual network 'beyond' spaces that are 'American' and, more broadly, beyond places plausibly presentable as 'purely national' in the first place. The transnational in Bjorn, then, is always intricately connected to various logistical materialities of particular production locations, as well as to the overall 'system' from which these particularities emerge. This brings us to the first aesthetic question posed by his work: its continual, almost systematic deconstruction of signifiers of regionally specific, class-related taste cultures. This is registered via bodies as well as their surroundings.

How do such signifiers potentially interact with other taste hierarchies in the transterritorial reception of these tapes, as well as in their transterritorial production dimensions? To what extent do these signifiers and their interactions arise from the specificity of the culture(s) in which Bjorn immerses himself at a given moment, to what extent from his own brand of production practice as a mode of transnational sociality, and to what extent from individual sites of reception around the world?

On the production end, Bjorn's working method is highly idiosyncratic. It is described by Bjorn himself in an extended 1997 interview with his cinematographer, 'The Bear'. The interview is (re-)published on Bjorn's website. The Bear has also written and published production diaries from a few individual tapes. The cinematographer got into porn at his friend Bjorn's urging when his employer, Pan American Airlines, went bankrupt in 1991. He has since gone on to direct his own work, distributed by Bjorn's distribution companies. This includes the 2001 tape *Moscow,* a very, very interesting work that spins Bjorn's aesthetic and 'social project' in unexpected directions, and adds whole new dimensions to the questions we pose in the current essay. The idiosyncrasies of Bjorn's mode of production arise only partly from Bjorn's international focus, and cause all manner of time and energy to be spent 'acquiring' and emotionally managing models in various countries as they are grouped together in myriad combinations and paid to perform all sorts of sex acts. Most of these performers are reportedly not at all 'gay' in the North American sense.

The Bear notes, at one point in his *A World of Men* production diary, that the nicest thing about shooting the 'transnational' (phase II) features is that, when the models can't verbally communicate with each other due to language differences, the kind of complex problems among the models detailed for the other shoots can't develop in the same way. His prior example of such problems is the fierce fist fight that broke out while shooting an early feature in the Brazilian jungle, among the four Portuguese-speaking models involved in a group sex number. Such 'production documents', which are 'published' on the Bjorn website, are clearly deploying some appeal to exoticism and authenticity as a marketing strategy, however much they also record the 'truth' of various events.[10] Nevertheless, the appeal of the non-identitarian, when combined with such exoticist rhetorical dimensions, perhaps brings the Western spectatorial 'desire' for such models (as pornographic personas) in line with a desire for a sort of 'virgin' untainted by an identitarian 'gay' model that is presumed to be Northern, Western and non-indigenous to the places represented in the process. Or, a desire for a persona who has already *transcended* that identitarian model in ways that differ from the US 'gay for pay' performer.

For instance, the ethnographic status of the following excerpt from The Bear's production diaries, about interviewing potential models around the world, is made suspect (to the say the least) by its continual appeal to myriad registers of national/ transnational phantasy in decoding forms of endlessly interpretable ambiguity:

Between Kristen and myself, we can communicate with models in Spanish, Portuguese, German, and French. But Hungarian, being totally unrelated to any of these languages, made it impossible to get even the idea of what was being said. The models all walked in individually and said something like 'seeya.' Then, they gave their last names first, and departed saying 'hello!' All of them turned the pages of the magazine backwards when shown a sample photo layout. But interviews in Budapest were thirty minutes apart with models being for the most part punctual, at least in comparison to the Brazilians!

Similarly, a subsequent passage describes problems obtaining 'money shots' in Central Europe. Here, a model is described as suddenly panting that he is 'about to go' during a take, throwing the two-man shooting crew into chaos and confusion. Hungarians, according to The Bear, just do 'everything in reverse'. Indeed, this slippage between the 'authentic' and the 'orientalised' is continually at play in Bjorn, especially given the fact that the production lore used for marketing is always potentially part of the tapes' reception. Whether or not one actually believes that the Hungarian stepping forward on the set to be the one to get fucked is married in real life ('I don't mind it at all'), or that two macho South Americans were called 'fags' on the set by the other models with whom they did a number because they began to develop a strong sexual 'love' relationship over the course of a shoot (rather than just maintaining a 'functional' one that is more clearly in line with the stereotypical 'Latin tradition'), resulting in a four-man fist fight, these myths potentially structure interdiscursive transactions between viewers and these works.

One question here is the extent to which Bjorn's production methods unearth something that is already culturally present in these local spaces, and the extent to which they bring to light something that is phantasmatically imposed upon them only in the tapes themselves. Of course, this is a question of overdetermination as well as anthropological epistemology. For this reason, a plausible answer cannot be immediately evident, even by some theoretically impoverished appeal to Chauncey and Povinelli's 'facticity of economic and population flows' that serves to constitute the realm of *society* as a harder and faster realm than that of *culture*, and as a realm whose relationship to culture is far simpler and more direct than it should be, given what we already know about their relative autonomy. This sort of appeal is still all-too-common in disciplinary formations that are staunchly and/or provincially invested in certain highly circumscribed notions of 'the social'. This is especially important to note at this juncture because of the tendency in cultural studies today to automatically characterise such images as, say, 'orientalist'. Doing so will continue to impede media criticism from ever dealing with *non-correspondence* and, through it, with the really interesting ideological operations hinted at in the formal characteristics of the texts themselves – not to mention with the still important question of what ideological effects are actually engendered by the encounter with these formal characteristics in different real world contexts by different sorts of real people.

With a crew generally consisting only of himself, The Bear and one assistant, Bjorn is supposedly able to spend four to five days shooting a typical sex scene. This is partly because of the relatively big budgets made possible by both the international marketability/popularity of his work and its 'critical' success. Completing a scene reportedly involves between eight and twelve hours a day with the models, in generally remote locations. According to their production documents, Bjorn and The Bear have gone to such Herzogian lengths as bringing generators into the Brazilian jungle – and into the deep, dark, 1570-built Kiraly baths in Budapest – in order to maintain the continuity of their trademark careful lighting. Furthermore, Bjorn typically uses enormous numbers of shots in the course of an edited scene, even storyboarding sex scenes in the course of shooting them. Many of these scenes are notably complex, since formally meticulous group numbers hold an especially important position in Bjorn's oeuvre. The Bear says it this way in the diaries: 'Kristen deftly positions models into sexual bouquets, as if they were flower arrangements.' When interviewed, Bjorn himself is even given to making proclamations like 'Light! Light! Porn is all about light!'

In another notable reversal of the shooting style of the gay pornographic 'studio' system of California's San Fernando Valley, Bjorn claims always to shoot his sex scenes first. This way, he can let the dynamics that develop on the set among his actors dictate at least the tone of the narrative, and often the actual form and movement of the plot. He sees both story and discourse as very important, within and beyond the sex numbers. Bjorn's concern for narrative only reached fruition in the mid-90s, with the move towards 'transnationalism' from 'internationalism'. His earlier, episodic tapes consist mostly of series of tableaux generated by iconic aspects of a particular landscape, such as the banana boats, huts and rain-forests in *Tropical Heatwave*. But it seems that this earlier work allowed Bjorn to perfect a unique way of presenting the sex numbers. And the later, more complex narratives still derive their overall allegorical force from the ways the sex between men is already imagined within the numbers, via the following formal qualities.[11]

Bjorn's is a signature authorial style comprised of at least seven major components: 1) a wide array of complex moving camera shots within a scene; 2) group tableaux in which reciprocity in all acts is more the norm than is any individual sticking to one sexual position (top or bottom), as is more common in US gay porn; 3) a very atypical, multi-orgasmic sort of pornotemporality wherein not only is no performer seen without an erection once a sex scene has begun – which often happens in run-of-the-mill, non-'quality' pornography – but each participant in a scene generally ejaculates two or three times, and scenes don't necessarily progress onwards from 'fore-play' to 'intercourse' to ending as US studio scenes typically do, but instead alternate in novel ways between intercourse and acts often categorised as 'foreplay'; 4) a very idiosyncratic sort of 'spontaneous orgasm' shot – a money shot which is not preceded by the frenzy of penile self-manipulation character-istic of nearly all-male US porn (where orgasm is almost always preceded by a model's manual self-stimulation), but by no touching of the penis at all, or by oral or manual stimulation exclusively by one or more *other performers*, and it is generally not the ejac-ulant's penis that is primarily administered to at the moment of orgasm (for example, it may well be only his nipples that are being attended to); 5) a closely related 'penile spasm' shot, wherein the penis moves up and down of its 'own volition', often commission-ing a close-up, to signify extreme arousal in a manner that is only very ambiguously 'controlled' by its owner; 6) a particular sort of sonic envelopment in the sex scenes that involves sophisticated post-pro-duction sound processing, and whose discrete impli-

cations will be discussed later; and, finally, 7) a number of specific signature tableaux in the *mise en scène*, the most striking of which we like to call the 'big lift'. In this tableau, a group of four or five men lift up another, lower him on to the penis of a well-endowed man seated on some sort of 'throne', and then continue to move the recipient mechanically up and down while he visually enacts 'totally pure pas-sivity' for the camera, a passivity that is compounded by the fact that others simultaneously manipulate his penis and other body parts until he ejaculates. In Bjorn's fully transnational phase, a repeated variation on this is the 'international lift', wherein a group of men from various countries and regions co-operate in a UN-style synergistic provision of lifting and lower-ing power – or, alternatively, in an efficient, transna-tional conglomerate-style use of heterogeneous proletarian manpower.

How is 'foreignness' symbolised via these salient elements of authorial style, and to what effect? What is the relation of these aspects of the tapes to the ideological aspirations of cultural products within global capitalism in general, and to the social and subject effects of such cultural products – especially pornographic ones? Clearly, this version of 'foreign-ness' is designed to be as polysemic as possible, for mobilisation at myriad reception sites around the world. But that polysemy must arise from both the specificities and the generalities of ethnic, racial and national embodied difference. The result is a textual (and spectatorial) problematic whereby the spaces in which all of these scenarios are 'located' aspire to both supporting and continually undoing all concep-tions of 'gay male subjectivity', as well as all the pre- or post- 'gay' acts-based dispersions of that 'subject', that are currently in global circulation.

In the early days of gay film porn, exhibition venues almost universally advertised their product as being 'all-male'. Beyond what we have already men-tioned, we intentionally 'revert' to using that phrase here precisely because it is also a term that, however anachronistic it might seem, describes something very real that is happening not only in the porn of Kristen Bjorn, but in a host of other works produced on the transnational market. This is an appeal to a kind of universal 'brotherhood' which goes beyond any particular sort of claim to identity. To some extent, this reads as a strategy to avoid scaring off all those consumers of all-male porn around the world who, like it or not, don't fit those identity claims anyway. More interestingly, though, the 'Latin' quality of Bjorn's early work is arguably the base from which springs his entire 'world picture'. This is the acts-based conception of sexuality where the identity-based issue of 'coming out' is supposedly completely irrelevant, as we saw in the publicity discourse. This gets grafted into and onto Central and Eastern Europe in his later work and, especially in the transnational series, onto the entire phenomenological 'world of men' that Bjorn has charged himself with imaging. Of course, this Latin sense of performativity is clearly phantasmatic. As such, though, it is nonetheless the result of a 'passage through' Western-style and, as we will see in our analysis later on, even *US-style* gayness. For while identity is not, at least according to the publicity, generally the issue for Bjorn's 'models' (many of whom are, again, supposedly not at all 'gay' in any American sense of the term, but who don't necessarily mind being taken as such after having done these tapes), neither is, unusually, the binary opposition active/passive (which historically has been officially decisive in structuring 'Latin' homosexuality). This also places Bjorn's work in an intriguing symptomatic position relative to US all-male porn, where the active/passive binary rules so strongly both despite and because of the fact that most American actors ultimately perform at both ends of that binary.

In other words, the actors in Bjorn's finished works seem to have no 'problems' shifting between the positions of top and bottom. But in Bjorn's work it is as if 'Latin' (or else 'Greek') performativity has opened up the entire 'world of men' to reciprocal homosexual experience, all of which has been paradoxically enabled by the existence and dispersion of a Western politics, and by the forces of Western market expansion, that necessarily *were* at some point pinned to issues of identity – however territorially bounded either sort of sexual *ethos* and *pathos* may once have been, and however seemingly superseded either now has become within some hard to define dialectical movement that has presumably already occurred (or is, at very least, already deep in process). Put another way, if some analogue of the 'Classical' sexual imaginary asserted as 'concept' the non-existence of 'the homosexual', then US-style gayness is the negation of the concept, and Bjorn's work is a (phantasmatic) sublimation which brings the concept

back after its passage through its negation.[12] This is precisely why, when Bjorn turns his attention to the Central/Eastern European male, the 'Classical', but here particularly Latin, sexuality embedded in the sex numbers in Bjorn's earlier career continues to operate, though now across yet another set of socio-cultural divides.

Ultimately, these two figures (the Latin and the 'Eastern European') are brought together and set against each other in the transnational series. *Gangsters at Large* is somewhat representative of this series. Here the visual and sonic aesthetics delineated above are placed in a narrative context in such a way that interesting further complications arise for the analysis of such work and its real world effects. After some detailed analysis of *Gangsters*, it should be clear that Bjorn's oeuvre as a whole makes it apparent that the particular, historically determinate constructions of 'the homosexual' in the US pornographic texts that now constitute a tradition from which Bjorn's work partly arises, and which it 'critiques' as being unnecessarily narrow in its own 'tastes', are actually variants of the much more overarching fact that 'the identity in question', however conceived, must always be experienced in relation to a *public*, and thus a *world*, that has been circumscribed in ways that already contextually and temporally aim at the 'appropriability' of central segments of various related ideological lattices by making them look so doggedly different from different global perspectives.

This is why it becomes important, politically, to understand that to say that both Bjorn's work and the transterritorial dialectical understanding it (impossibly) warrants move beyond a certain identitarian or non-identitarian political position is not necessarily to devalue either such position. For, as Lauren Berlant and Michael Warner eloquently note, in a context ridden with a very different series of displacements and inversions:

> Respectable gays like to think that they owe nothing to the sexual subculture they think of as sleazy. But their success, their way of living, their political rights, and their very identities would never have been possible but for the existence of the public sexual culture they now despise. Extinguish it, and almost all out gay or *queer* culture will wither on the vine [emphasis ours].[13]

3   *GANGSTERS AT LARGE*

The salient features of Bjorn's imagined world can also be viewed as corollaries to one overarching structural trope: the eschewing of the one-on-one sexual number productive of the couple in favour of the group or orgy scene that involves from three to six men, and sometimes as many as dozens. (Though one-on-ones do of course appear from time to time in Bjorn's tapes.) The men in these group scenes are represented as multiply orgasmic. As a rule, most of them democratically assume the positions of both top and bottom. Almost all of Bjorn's sex numbers are thus not teleological. They do not pretend to bring the spectator through the temporality of 'foreplay', 'intercourse' and orgasm so common to US gay porn. The result is an improvisational – though, in production, carefully orchestrated – fluidity across zones and organs, with ejaculations occurring at myriad 'conjunctions' rather than at 'terminal' instances, and sometimes even 'spontaneously' (as described above).

We do not 'celebrate' Bjorn's work for this reason, in the worst tradition of a liberatory cultural populism, and a closely related 'democratic reformism', that assume that such work necessarily has social potential because of these characteristics. Nevertheless, we think that the 'spontaneous orgasm' is original enough to be regarded as the aspect of Bjorn's authorial signature to end all others, and that its status as symptom cuts right to the heart of pornography's visualisation of 'agency'. The spontaneity of Bjorn's conventional money shot is a derailment of the very cause and effect logic whose upholding we can now see as the central ideological 'work' of the moving-image pornography of the West. For instance, note both the similarity and difference of Bjorn's spontaneous orgasm to what Linda Williams is discussing when she theorises the function of the female voice in straight porn. The woman's voice is central to formulating a relation between cause (the man's penis, and the much broader male desire to 'penetrate' female subjectivity) and effect (the woman's orgasm as a marker of her submission to this penetration, which occurs at some mysterious point or another in the process of her being 'worked upon' from the outside). Nevertheless, the woman's voice is fundamentally decentred in relation to its 'cause' in Williams's interpretive system. A decentring of voice also provides the context for the materialisation of the orgasm in Bjorn's work, but it is a

decentring with different mechanics due to the all-male context as well as the international one.

The sexual numbers comprising the phase II tape *Gangsters at Large* illustrate this well. The tape begins in a wittily 'retro updated', art deco Miami office. Gin-swigging, hard-boiled South Beach detective 'Steve Sax' opens a piece of mail containing a letter soliciting his services and nude photographs of 'Tyler Grey'. We learn from Sax's voice-over reading of the letter that this young man is being held hostage by a Russian mob-run modelling agency. (Like 'Steve Sax', we note from the opening credits, the name 'Tyler Grey' refers to both the character and the actor.) The agency, we also learn from Sax's voice-over, is a front for illegal activities involving both drugs and 'white slaves'. It has become a crucial organisation in the Russian mob's gang war with the Colombian 'Mafia', in Miami and globally. The detective's 'studying' of the photographs promptly turns into a sexual fantasy – and the tape's first brief sexual number, a solo – as the black-and-white photograph of the kidnapped Tyler Grey 'comes alive', with Grey masturbating to climax within the shot. We then move through the following numbers:

Modelling agency: Steve Sax visits to begin his investigation and poses as aspiring model; the head of the agency asks him to pose for nude photographs after slipping a drug into his drink; the 'modelling' session turns into a (photographed) orgy with three Russian and Central/Eastern European employees and/or 'slaves'; Sax slips into unconsciousness when done.

The Colombian gangsters' compound: The head of the operation watches his younger brother actively initiate oral sex with a fellow Colombian grounds guard, and then takes control of the action by forcing the brother into a three-way by threatening, cell phone in hand, to inform their (literal) 'Papa' about his brother's pot smoking as well as this behaviour with the guard.

Makeshift 'jail' quarters: A naked, now bound Steve Sax manages to free himself. Escaping, he notices two other naked 'prisoners' on the other side of a chain link fence, one of whom is Tyler Grey. Sax 'frees' them. The three have sex.

Miami nightclub run by Russian mob: A live sex show in which dozens of masked audience members watch as a hulking, manacled Hungarian breaks his chains and proceeds to have sex with the two other Hungarian slaves on stage with him. The audience for the sex show

– about thirty men masked so that no facial signifiers of nationality/ethnicity are visible, and who wear only jeans – commences an orgy of its own.

Inside the gangsters' lair: A blond, jock-strapped American slave is brought in, hidden in a rolled-up Persian carpet. The Colombians and the Russians attempt to forge a truce through a contest to see which ethnic group can produce the largest penis. Orgy ensues, with around sixteen men.

Steve Sax's bedroom: Our detective-protagonist very gradually awakens from an apparent dream to the oral and manual ministrations of his (Anglo) lover. Surprise: it is Tyler Grey in bed with him. After being brought to orgasm while still in his semi-somnolent state, Sax tells Grey he 'just had the weirdest dream'. Grey earnestly requests that Sax tell him about it. But first they kiss. End title.

The second sex number, in the Colombian compound, immediately 'responds' to the first one – Steve Sax with the Central/Eastern European and Russian employees/slaves at the modelling agency – with the 'Latinised', performative view of male–male sexual acts that is such an important trope from early on in Bjorn's work. In the latter number, the younger brother walks into the courtyard of the house. A hunky, uniformed bodyguard (played by Tony Tarango) stands watch, armed with a submachine gun. The younger brother solicits the bodyguard. Tarango initially keeps shaking his head 'no', until he finally relents by taking out his penis and allowing himself to be fellated. During this part of the number, Tarango barely looks at the man 'servicing' him. It is as if the sexual act with one of his male 'bosses' is totally permissible as long as he doesn't acknowledge it or reciprocate.

Meanwhile, the fellator's older brother appears on the balcony overlooking the courtyard and assumes an expression of shock when he sees the action below. His dismay is apparently compounded by having smelled his younger brother's marijuana smoking moments before. (The younger of the two has been partaking of both of the underground 'markets' in which the family trafficks.) The older brother goes down to the courtyard, and – as if administering a punishment – commands the younger brother to fellate *him*. Now, however, the younger brother is the one who refuses by shaking his head 'no', as if his own masculinity will be com-

promised if he assents. He is convinced to perform the act only when the older brother takes out his cell phone and dials their father (!), explicitly threatening to break the news of his brother's double dissolution to 'Papa'.

The tape thus establishes a view of male–male sex as something having nothing at all to do with an 'identity' that looks much like the 'identity' of gayness. To boot, the sex intensifies as the three-way moves into all sorts of permutations, until the entire issue of who is 'active' and who 'passive' has been rendered mute. The word 'mute' here is deliberate. It is as if Bjorn, in 'having his cake and eating it too' – as well as in his self-conscious use of the cellular telephone connection to Papa, and his use of the 'commanding voice' to phallically structure the scene – is setting forth the utopian fantasy that the preservation of 'masculinity' that is so stereotypically central to Latinate sexuality can be achieved despite how one is positioned sexually, and solely by an ever-dissolvable pact of fraternal *silence*. (The older brother does not tell the father then or later, despite being on the verge of it here.) How and why is such a phantasy scenario doing the work of 're-fashioning' the post-Stonewall gay male of the advanced capitalist West into the overarching transnational project of which this film is an instance?

The sex number in the Russian mob-/modelling agency-run sex club helps answer that last question. This scene begins with the arresting spectacle of a manacled Hungarian body-builder brought on stage before a crowd of naked, masked spectators. Partly in a parody of 'Hercules'/'Maciste' films, he grunts and strains, and then does some very serious screaming, while looking directly into the masked eyes of the individuals in his audience. It's actually quite a potentially harrowing scene, though it's also potentially funny. He finally breaks the chains so that he can 'free' the two other slaves in the 'act' . . . though the three proceed to have sex onstage right then and there rather than to escape. All of this is intercut with the increasingly aroused group of masked spectators, among whom an orgy is ignited as a result. The first thing to note about this scene is the indistinguishability of the 'spectacle' from the 'plot', as well as the tenuous boundary between the spectacle within the plot from the spectacle outside it.

After all, the plot of *Gangsters at Large* hinges on a modelling company that is actually a front for an illicit international trafficking ring. Is the melodrama of the sex show on stage to be taken literally or not? Put another way, is the Hungarian to be taken as 'really' enchained within the film's diegesis, or is that just a necessarily shabby pretence for the nightclub sex 'act'? Are these 'real' chains, or chains designed to be broken? Also, this scene can be viewed as a repetition, now performed in public, of the earlier scene where Steve Sax, himself manacled in the agency's dungeon, proceeds to free himself and two other 'prisoners', providing the occasion for a 'pre-liberation' sexual three-way – and also providing a narrative nexus at which, since Tyler Grey is one of the freed slaves, we will later see that the text may or may not trail off into a different register of story space. If we are to take their coupling as having happened at this earlier moment, in other words, one possible interpretation of the tape's ending (the bedroom scene) is that the remainder of the plot – from the point of Sax's chain-breaking until the scene in the bedroom – is Steve Sax's 'weird dream'. Of course, another interpretation is that the whole detective identity, and the whole detection scenario that grounds that 'identity' – including the discovery of Tyler Grey as a prisoner via the photos sent to his office (i.e., the entire tape back to the beginning) – is Sax's weird dream. The conflation of character names with performer names makes this second interpretation seem an especially loaded one.

Significantly, much of both this scene and the one it repeats are staged through the barrier of chain-link fences which, in the second scene, are not really functional as boundaries. They could simply be walked around. Another question that thus arises is whether the manacle-busting Hungarian is actually a 'sex slave' in the first place. And, if so, in precisely what sense? It is the indeterminacy of this last question that deposits us most directly on the doormat of internationalised all-male pornography's most vexing contradictions.

For the essence of this sex act scene is at once self-reflexive and melodramatic. It is melodramatic in the sense that the stage show's principal device is exaggeration, from the steroid muscles of the Hungarian's over-developed body to the wild overacting and pumped-up volume characterising his screaming, and characterising the three-man show in general. But this exaggeration of 'scale' and of 'acting' is also a general characteristic of studio-produced, or non-

amateur, porn. Here, however, the sex show produces in its 'audience-within-the-scene' an idealised enactment of the reception to which all-male porn, by its own continuous admission, has long aspired. In other words, Bjorn has here constructed a scene that unmasks for us the very 'apparatus' of male–male pornographic texts by imaging one of their 'ideal' reception conditions. But the issue of pornography's *indexicality* has somewhere undergone a fundamental shift in the process. It is *a shift away from the 'come shot'* – which, in Western conceptual models of pornography, is the visible evidence establishing the text's claim to truth[14] – *and towards something else*, something at which the ambiguous overacting of the Hungarian and its orgiastic reception by the crowd only hints.

We have already noted that one of the key elements of Bjorn's authorial signature is a kind of come shot that is 'unhooked' from its standard position as temporally coincident with a scene's climax. By derailing the teleology of the sexual scenario, the Bjornian money shot presents us with a more radically fluid, or (impossibly) 'polymorphously perverse', imagining of not just all-male sexuality, but of all-male *sociality*. This is closely related to his use of the voice too. It is by now almost a truism, given the arguments laid out over the past decade by queer theory, that male–male sex is bound to be, in short, 'non-productive'. It has taken someone like Bjorn, and the transnationalist context that produces him, to develop a convention for (repeatedly) inscribing this notion into moving-image pornographic aesthetics in a context where that non-productivity gets displaced into and onto something else through the particular textual 'scandal' that results. That something else here has to do with the international.

What is it, then, that all-male porn indexes by the time it goes transnational to this extent? Wherein lie its fundamental claims to truth? Given all the above, it would seem that its truth-claims have less to do with any narrowly conceived 'experience' of embodied individuality and more to do with the 'World' that the pornographic enterprise can finally overtly understand to be the condition of that individuality. This is why the relationship between the national and the transnational has become so critical in contemporary pornography in the first place. Think again about the nightclub sex act scene. On the one hand, we have the mass of spectators in the club. They are all male, and all masked, so that they are stripped not only of their clothes but also of most potential physiognomic signs of ethnicity – except, notably, for the possibilities of the penis in this regard. On the one hand, these figures thus potentially image a fundamentally democratic, liberal humanist 'subjectivity' via quite brilliant, abstracted signifiers for the necessary bracketing of individuation that the production of such a subject entails. But meanwhile, on stage, the indubitably unique-looking/sounding Hungarian is literally breaking the chains that bind him, in what can be seen as an absurdly campy allegory of post-communist 'liberation'.[15] And possibly as one whose seriousness lies precisely in its absurdity and campiness.

The tension between the universal and the particular that here erupts is exactly the problematic underlying the emergence of the democratic nation-state for a whole tradition of theorists. In Slavoj Žižek's wry formulation, for instance, the 'Nation-Thing' is precisely that left over that allows the universal to lay claim to a given set of particulars in the first place.[16] If communism was an ideological formation that attempted to bypass the national 'left over' in the name of some transnational 'brotherhood', then it overlooked a fundamental paradox involved in the mediation of universal and particular. When the communist regimes of Central and Eastern Europe fell, what emerged in their place was the nation-state ready to take its place in the frenzy of transnational capitalism. And what these nations had to market was men, as Bjorn was one of the quickest to discover, and is still perhaps most adept at textualising. (He was followed soon by Falcon International and a host of other production companies from around the world, some of which continue to make quite interesting product in the wake of Bjorn's 'inventions'.) How could men for whom male–male sex had, supposedly, nothing to do with the gradual refinements of gay male subjectivity that had evolved in the US over the preceding twenty-five years not have been intensely marketable in such a context?

In this regard, Bjorn's work presents us with a series of homologous paradoxes. His video aesthetics aspire to a form of transnationalism, a world of men without internal or external borders, which can only be achieved by constant recourse to the realms of the specified ethnic, national and regional. Yet his work already seems to 'understand' that the breaking of the phallic mandate – i.e., the imagination of a world without the Father, which would also be a world in which the male bodies are all equally penetrable – ends up eroding the very validity of 'nation' as concept, so that what we end up with in its place is the 'gang' of one sort or another, while the rule of the Father goes on only outside the frame.[17]

Once we arrive at this conceptual neo-tribalism – which also, incidentally, explains the role of Haring paintings and other contemporary art in *Thick as Thieves* – we can understand not only what is probably most appealing about Bjorn's tapes to the contemporary US 'gay audiences' for transnational porn, but also why the sexual 'couple' is all but banished from his sexual numbers, which are dominated by group sex. We could say that Bjorn's work is investigating Jean-Jacques Rousseau's question regarding the prerequisite to democratic citizenship, which involves 'the nature of the act by which a people is a people', through analytical methods of which Rousseau himself probably never dreamed. In short, the paradoxical slippage between nation and transnational in Bjorn serves both to continually support and continually undo the 'gay male subject' via acts that, on the one hand, are the ones selected to serve this very purpose and, on the other, end up forever deferring their given goal rather than being compliant with it. In rendering that subject perpetually beyond itself, but always nevertheless attached to all-male 'practice', such image-creation systems (re-)circulate much more than just bodies into the traffic of transnational commerce.

A reminder about the 'chronotopes' of contemporary male porn in general will make our argument clearer. Daniel Harris has noted an interesting aspect not only of Bjorn's tapes, but also of gay porn in general since the 'centralisation' of its production on the outskirts of Los Angeles. Harris describes the frequent disjunction between the spaces inhabited by the characters and the characters themselves, in terms of the tangible (in the case of the spaces) as well as more intangible (in the case of the models) class signifiers that circulate both within and beyond the actual tapes.[18] The characters in the 'diegesis' simply don't seem to have the literal or figurative capital to command the spaces in which they perform. Usually, this is most evident as soon as the character/actor delivers his lines. What comes out of the mouths of these babes somehow puts the kibosh on any credibility that they could possibly have the wherewithal to own their surroundings, even those with the most astounding appearances. We see an interesting twist on this in the Colombian compound scene in *Gangsters*, where it is clearly the invisible patriarchal Father who has set the models up in the space of the compound, rather than them having ostensibly installed themselves there. Another twist on this is the sex act scene, where the Hungarian's screams are so hard to make sense of partly because the question of the voice's functionality in this capacity has been effectively short-circuited.

As opposed to the way similar disjunctions work in, say, contemporary Hollywood cinema, what gets put into play in US gay porn's particular spatial disjunctions of this sort is a different sort of *structuring absence* than that with which film studies has usually dealt. The rich men (or, at least, upper-class and/or bourgeois men) who own these spaces, and lend them out for use as porn 'sets', are hardly ever diegetically represented. In the real world, they are perhaps too old, too powerful, and/or too closeted to make themselves known. One need only think of the legendary *modus operandi* of either 'Mafiosi' absentee ownership of gay-oriented businesses or the closeted Hollywood star like Rock Hudson. The closet star's wealth reputedly enables him to send out 'scouts' in limos to West Hollywood bars, where groups of young men can be gathered up and chauffeured up to some mansion in the Hollywood Hills for a poolside orgy. Thus we see exactly why this absence running through gay porn has the status of a full-blown symptom: because of the (at least imaginary) radical 'levelling potential' of male–male sex itself. (At least as long as it remains non-monogamous, and does not aspire to mimic heterosexual marriage.) Everyone equally becomes the empty, democratic subject in this phantasmatic economy, ready to enter into any number of possible 'exchanges' for the sake of one hoped-for state of futurity or another. Why? Because 'coming out', and its endless litany of cognate 'identity procedures' – both individual and collective ones – are continual processes, rather than the discrete acts as which most versions of identitarianism still advertise them. As Jeffrey Weeks writes, transnational or not, 'The idea of sexual or intimate citizenship is simply an index of the political space that needs to be developed, rather than a conclusive answer to it.'[19]

And, as Alan Sinfield writes in the essay that partly provoked Weeks' above comment:

> The hybridity of our [gay] subcultures derives not from the loss of even a mythical unity, but from the difficulty we experience in envisioning ourselves beyond the framework of normative heterosexuality. . . . If diasporic Africans are poised between alternative homelands – in mid-Atlantic, Paul Gilroy suggests – then lesbians and gay men are stuck at the moment of emergence. For coming out is not once-and-for-all; like the Africans, we never quite arrive.[20]

We have been trying to point out the stumbling block that emerges, in Bjorn's work, around the binary opposition of the national versus the transnational. It is the obverse of this other stumbling block that emerges around the issue of sexual identity. While there is in Bjorn a clear aspiration to move beyond an identitarian model of male–male sexuality, the attempt succeeds only insofar as it, too, leaves behind a residue. It is as if the urban gay male subject both reflected in and constructed by the first wave of gay (filmic) porn is as necessary a prerequisite to Bjorn's project as all the (mostly forgotten?) swimming pool proletarians who have by now been caught on San Fernando Valley film and videotape. In a video like *Gangsters*, recourse to yet another salient characteristic of Bjorn's work is made in the process of this aspiration and the continuous slippage it initiates. It is one that repeatedly emerges in the sound-image relations characteristic of Bjorn's work.

Consider, once again, the scene in the Miami sex club. In this scene, the implantation of voice within the Hungarian takes the typically pornographic form of possibly inauthentic grunts and moans, though they aren't sexual at the start of the scene. But these 'non-representational' – and thus relatively 'cross-culturally' decodable – vocatives are dissociated from the sex act, and connected instead to the melodramatic, Herculean allegory of the breaking of the chains. This is to say that these moans are placed in the text not via the generic conventions of porn, but via an entirely different moving-image tradition: schlock epics churned out for the international subaltern. In this sense, this detail from the soundtrack makes clear Bjorn's underlying sonic proclivities: tendencies that actually look back to the earliest days of post-

Stonewall gay porn. Bjorn uses a non-synchronous track of sexual sounds in much the same way as was common in early 70s' porn, even though Bjorn is shooting and editing with a medium (video) where this is not demanded by either the production apparatus or, in his case, financial constraints.

A sex number in the tape *A World of Men* illustrates this best. As the number begins, the models speak Spanish and Russian in synchronous sound throughout the preliminaries. A repetitive, New Age score by Bjorn's regular collaborator François Girard is laid underneath. But this music track imperceptibly 'takes over' the function of synchronous sound as the number proceeds to full-blown sex. The music is pulsing and employs electronically processed percussive sounds to simulate the heavy breathing of sex. Gradually, one hears layered onto this music track 'actual' breathing and moaning sounds. In faked synch! Yet, these 'human sounds' are so seamlessly woven in and out of the percussives that it is difficult to hear, or see, the artifice of the general strategy. To use a term taken from Michel Chion's theorisation of high-budget soundtracks in the age of the Dolby mix,[21] this particular sort of 'sonic envelope' is, in Bjorn's tapes (which are obviously not mixed in Dolby), the aesthetic equivalent of such mixes. These sound strategies potentially implant within the text the same kind of aspiration towards utopian, democratic sexual space as is common in post-Stonewall filmic porn's soundtracks,[22] but for a set of publics that are more explicitly delimited by, and beyond, the (trans)national.

Oddly, then, Bjorn's work – and particularly *Gangsters at Large* – brings us back, via its citations, to a kind of 'golden age' of gay male porn. It does this even as it adopts its resolutely postmodern, transnational, and post- or pre-identitarian attitude. Miami, for instance, becomes the phantasmatic site of this fusion of old and new, and film noir becomes the overarching generic base with which *Gangsters* plays. The opening scene, in particular, is a parody of noir conventions, from the detective alone in his office to the gin he swigs to the sultry jazz saxophone on the soundtrack to the parcel that has just arrived. The ending of the tape, in yet another noir parody, has this detective – who is named Steve Sax to boot – waking up in bed beside Tyler Grey, and saying that he just had 'the weirdest dream'. Structurally, Bjorn's tape adopts as a kind of 'frame' the standard coupling trajectory of the typical American gay porn text, while the body of the film, as 'dream', can be said to reveal the hidden truths of the said text, and deconstruct its tenets in what are sometimes quite unabashedly hectic ways (cf. the sex act in the nightclub).

Taking the very different sort of temporalities of orgasm in his sex numbers together with the above, however, a very-bifurcated attitude towards, say, Michel Foucault's old quip about homosexuality seems to result. 'For a homosexual', Foucault (in)famously said, 'the best moment of love is likely to be when the lover leaves in a taxi, for the homosexual imagination is for the most part concerned with reminiscing about the act, rather than anticipating it'.[23] Indeed, memory is here being fixated upon as a key problematic of and in homosexual identity – key, perhaps, even just to all-male *acts* in the overall narrative forms of Bjorn's later works. Further evidence is the extent to which the Hungarians huddled together onstage seem engaged in a sort of ethic of 'care' for each other that is quite typical of Bjorn's group scenes, which presumably results from the trauma of either diaspora or from sudden, extreme changes in economic systems – not to mention such systems flip-flopping back and forth over time. In other words, their horrified screaming might invoke *something* that necessitates and commissions that capacity for 'care' and 'attention': nobody knows the trouble they've seen (and remember), and so on. But another question is whether this 'something' is 'hard-core' historical/(trans)national/ethnic trauma or simply the trauma of being enclosed by camp and irony and a sort of transnational displacement which functions mostly through entrapment in 'spaces' of continually snowballing *mise en abyminal* self-reflexivity.

For, on the other hand, within the sex numbers themselves, the Hungarians, for instance, don't really seem to have much to remember! How could they? The status of their memory is up for radical question, as is the very value of the act of remembrance, since futurity is pulsing in the particular directions in which it is currently pulsing, and since the past is being marketed as the particular past as which it is being marketed to younger generations. In other words, it might just be the amnesiac's imperative to look completely *forwards* rather than backwards – to capitalism, to gay identity, beyond either or both, who knows? – that is so horrifying, so productive of desire, and is currently demanding that it be some-how written into the very acts by which a people become, and remain, a people.

This is the point at which the urban space of Miami becomes crucial. Miami must here be seen as a city of 'ruins' in the Benjaminian sense, because it presents the tourist/spectator with 'dialectical images': the resort-city of a disappeared epoch now refurbished by a globalised, and largely Latinised and 'gayed', neocapitalism. Fredric Jameson has argued that art deco, the signature style of Miami Beach, should be conceived as a 'formal synthesis between modernization and modernism'. This is due to its surprising adoption of a cubist visual system in the design of a commodity, whether an appliance, an ornament or an advertisement. Such a synthesis, for Jameson, can either be inflected in an aristocratic or a populist direction, as it was, respectively, in the 20s and the 30s. Jameson concludes that the contempor-ary, nostalgic citation of art deco automatically refer-ences a *historical sequence*; a passage from the 20s to the 30s, and by extension, from aristocracy to mass politics. (And, by further extension, to the very emergence of 'late capitalism.') Art deco thus becomes a cipher for the emergence of History itself.[24]

In the case of Bjorn, both the developing Third World and the post-communist world are treated as sites for the emergence of a (utopian?) sexuality that is pre-modern and pre-capitalist: this at the very moment when these parts of the world are caught in the anarchic frenzy of 'nascent' capitalism and, con-comitantly, in the frenzy of international porn pro-duction. (Only partly, as we know, because of significant differentials in cost between, say, Prague and Los Angeles.) Yet, as Bjorn's soundtracks attest, this moment of profound historical contradiction can, in relation to the gay subject, be grasped only by reinvoking an earlier, now ostensibly 'properly Amer-ican' utopian moment – when pornography promised us, in the wake of Stonewall, the image of ourselves as 'subject' rather than just as individuals.

So it would seem that, in turning the plot into the weird dream (or journey) that has as its result the production of the presumably relatively monoga-mous, WASP couple of Steve Sax and Tyler Grey, Bjorn has chosen in *Gangsters at Large* to finally ground the whole paradoxical interplay between the nation and the transnational in one very particular

mode of appearance of male–male relations, however shaky is that grounding. This, of course, is what we still refer to in media theory as 'an ideological oper-ation'.

Yet, as we've seen, rubbing against this ideologi-cal operation is an apparent will towards something else. Both reactionary and potentially radical, it is the dream-wish for 'a world of men' that substitutes the brother for the patriarch and the 'gang' for the 'couple', and the future for the past. In these terms, it makes extensive enquiries into the permeability of the boundary between the perceptual world (and the processes of perceiving/encountering it) and the global world (and the processes of traversing/per-ceiving/encountering it). By way of their unique but also very representative 'transnationalism', Bjorn's tapes thus register that 'moment' of de- and re-territorialisation – long forgotten by advanced capi-talism, as obsessed as it is with some subsequent transformative rupture – called 'modernisation'. As a result, these cultural documents open up yet again, even in their 'basest' pleasures, the conundrum of whether or not this rupture and its regular, ritualised remembrance will bring with them some new, as yet unimagined, organisation of the social and the psy-chic. They also reopen the question of whether or not its beautiful and charmed 'models' are doomed only to vanish anyway.

Acknowledgements: For the very important contribu-tions they have made to this essay through their responses, we thank audiences at presentations of earlier versions at the Society for Cinema Studies Conference (Chicago, Spring 2000), the British Film Institute (London, July 2001), and Central European University (Budapest, March 2002).

NOTES

1. For further description of this idea and the process it describes – as well its relation to the actual look and feel of all-male, moving-image pornography at different moments in history (the 70s, the 80s and the 90s) and in different media (film and video) – see Rich Cante and Angelo Restivo, 'The Voice of Pornography', in Matthew Tinkcom and Amy Villarejo (eds), *Key Frames: Popular Film and Cultural Studies* (London: Routledge, 2001), pp. 207–28 and 'The Cultural-Aesthetic Specificities of All-Male Moving-Image Pornography', in Linda Williams

(ed.), *Pornographies On/Scene* (Durham, NC: Duke University Press, forthcoming). On the issue of visibility more generally, and that of the world attached to it, we take much from Amy Villarejo's overall argument in *Lesbian Rule: Cultural Criticism and the Value of Desire* (Durham, NC: Duke University Press, 2003).

2. George Chauncey and Elizabeth Povinelli, 'Thinking Sexuality Transnationally: An Introduction', *GLQ*, vol. 5 no. 2 (Autumn 1999), pp. 439–49.

3. Incidentally, let us be clear that our saying this has nothing at all to do with the word or movement 'queer'.

4. This is a particularly important point because of the degree to which recent media study that takes textual and formal questions seriously tends to very problematically use the term 'subject' to refer to something that veers unfortunately close to the individual. Such work ends up blithely describing things such as 'subject positions', for example, without understanding that subjectivity always transcends positionality. Despite the amount of lip service paid to the more superficial aspects of their work via buzzwords such as 'performativity' or 'governmental-ity', the important theoretical contributions of people like Butler, Žižek, Warner and Berlant, and many others (especially Foucault himself) are left pretty much unattended to in the process. Such work in media studies also typically falls back into a form of 'democratic, multicultural representationalism' that does more than a serious disservice to homosexuality and its politics. None of this is to suggest that dealing with the question of the subject is or should be easy – just that in media studies that are rigorously formal, the degree to which the attempt is even seriously made seems generally wanting these days.

5. For a summary of the global economics of pornography after video, see Joseph Slade, 'Pornography in the Late Nineties', *Wide Angle*, vol. 19 no. 3 (July 1997), pp. 1–12.

6. On general issues of gay subjectivity, identity, and citizenship which become mind-bogglingly self-reflexive with pornography – symptomatically so – see in particular two relatively recent volumes. The publication of Dennis Altman's intelligent *Global Sex* (Chicago, IL: University of Chicago Press, 2001) for a 'general readership' audience is further evidence of its timeliness, at least as perceived by educated 'non-specialist' gay male and female citizens – or

publishers' preconceptions about them. For another very good overview, see David Bell and Jon Binnie, *The Sexual Citizen: Queer Politics and Beyond* (Cambridge: Polity, 2000). For a very tough-minded and important critique of Altman's work, see Donald Morton's 'Global (Sexual) Politics, Class Struggle, and the Queer Left' in John C. Hawley (ed.), *Post-Colonial, Queer* (Albany: State University of New York Press, 2001). Morton's is an article that contains pointers to the remains of the heated internet debate that arose between Morton, Altman and others on various issues central to our own analysis. Morton's article is also an uncommonly strong critique of 'queer theory' from a committed materialist position.

7. We mean 'Eastern European' at least by Western standards, that is. For briefs on the lexicographical and geo-cultural 'problem' of 'Central Europe', which is especially relevant to Bjorn's work in Hungary, see the still very valuable early primers in the *New York Review of Books* by Milan Kundera ('The Tragedy of Central Europe', 26 April 1984) and Timothy Garton Ash ('Does Central Europe Exist?', 9 October 1986).

8. It is important to note that the way in which Bjorn's oeuvre now seems so easily breakable into distinct periods poses an important conceptual/epistemologi-cal problem in the present analysis. 'Before' we can discuss porn's way of modelling public agency – or its 'public enactments of individuality', which we can also call 'citizenship' – and its modelling of the context for all agency *vis-à-vis* the transnational 'public sphere', it might seem that we should have some understanding of the connection between pornography and the public sphere in a single nation. But, beyond any facile idea of a 'national iconography' – like jocks in red, white and blue – that's still an area that needs a lot of thought. Michael Warner comes closest to dealing with it thoroughly in the gay male case, in *The Trouble with Normal: Sex, Politics, and the Ethics of Queer Life* (Boston, MA: Harvard University Press, 2000).

9. On the significance of these spatial terms, see Arjun Appadurai's *Modernity at Large: Cultural Dimensions of Globalization* (Minneapolis: University of Minnesota Press, 1996).

10. The manner in which such documents, including the interviews and production diaries – which are posted at the website and were floated to the gay press – compress heteroauthenticity with 'foreignness', and heterosexuality with national identity in general (especially in opposing South to North America, and

East Europe to West) doesn't allow us to forget that, whatever else they are and whatever the 'truth' of their contents, these are also marketing materials carefully designed to perpetually produce precisely such differentiated realms of 'foreignness' for consumers, though to produce these distinctly in various parts of the world. Such activational texts also exemplify the 'infotainment' dimension that continues to linger around so much contemporary pornography, though now in an evidently 'cross-cultural' way. For a good start on the issue of foreignness as it relates to visuality and narrative as well as pedagogy, see Bonnie Honig, *Democracy and the Foreigner* (Princeton, N.J.: Princeton University Press, 2003).

11. It should be noted that there is a return to the episodic, 'area-studies' style in Bjorn's most recent work, the *Wet Dreams* series and *Manwatcher*. In this latest work, though, groups of international models are being used together, with the older, less narrativised nation-based aesthetics structuring the texts. So, it's a fusion between the Bjorn of phase I and the very different Bjorn of phase II. The question of why this is ultimately possible, and why it is necessary, is an interesting one.

12. For an interesting juxtaposition between this appeal to the Latin Classical and a film that, however superficially, takes contemporary homosexual traditions back to Greece, and through textual forms that are correspondingly very different from Bjorn's (they are much more characteristics of the US all-male studio porn style, though made on international location), see Falcon International's *Out of Athens* series (1998–2002). The very title, and in particular the ambiguous play of its preposition, is only the first of the many ways this video seems diametrically opposed to the position that Bjorn takes on this contemporary dialectic that we are attempting to tease out.

13. Lauren Berlant and Michael Warner, 'Sex in Public', in Lauren Berlant (ed.), *Intimacy* (Chicago, IL: University of Chicago Press, 2000), pp. 311–31. See also Michael Warner, 'The Mass Public and the Mass Subject', in Craig Calhoun (ed.), *Habermas and the Public Sphere* (Cambridge, MA: MIT Press, 1997), pp. 377–402.

14. Linda Williams's, book is, of course, the *locus classicus* of this discussion, as she is the first to have brought this issue to light. See Williams, *Hard Core: Power, Pleasure, and the 'Frenzy of the Visible'* (Berkeley: University of California Press, 1989).

15. For a similar allegorical movement that structures one of Bjorn's entire texts through its plot – and, in fact, another of the Hungarian texts – see *A Vampire in Budapest*. Here, the disappearance of an ostensibly archaic (old Hungarian?) mythological eroticised figure accompanies the appearance of a real material gay lover to facilitate the good old-fashioned identitarian coupling form. The entire plot thus transforms itself, not unlike the manner in which *Gangsters* potentially transforms itself with its *Wizard of Oz*-esque ending, from a non-identitarian framework for the envisioning of male–male sex to a (new Hungarian?) *possibly* identitarian one. Of course, the key here lies in that *possibly* – given the text's own tone, and the way it lays out its own problematic via its other characteristics.

16. Slavoj Žižek, *Looking Awry: An Introduction to Jacques Lacan through Popular Culture* (Cambridge, MA: MIT Press, 1992) pp. 162–9.

17. See Bruce La Bruce's hard-core version of *Skin Gang* (a.k.a. *Skin Flick*, 1999, All Worlds Video) for an interesting instance where 'the gang' is worked with in a different, and highly charged, (trans)national, regional and urban context. La Bruce's film, shot on Super 8 and video, is a pretty shocking all-male, hard-core 'fantasia' on neo-Nazism in contemporary Germany.

18. Daniel Harris, 'Pornography: Video', in his *The Rise and Fall of Gay Culture* (New York: Hyperion, 1997).

19. Jeffrey Weeks, 'The Sexual Citizen', in Mike Featherstone (ed.), *Love and Eroticism* (London: Sage, 1999), p. 48.

20. Alan Sinfield, 'Diaspora and Hybridity: Queer Identities and the Ethnicity Model', *Textual Practice* 10 (1996), p. 282.

21. Michel Chion, 'Quiet Revolution and Rigid Stagnation', trans. B. Brewster, *October* 58 (1991), pp. 69–80.

22. The connection between the sonic envelope, early porn and its utopian aspirations is developed more fully in our essay, 'The Cultural-Aesthetic Specificities of All-Male Moving-Image Pornography'.

23. 'Sexual Choice, Sexual Act: An Interview with Michel Foucault', *Salmagundi* 58–9 (Autumn 1982/Winter 1983), p. 11.

24. For the entire, very complex argument, see Fredric Jameson, 'The Existence of Italy', in Jameson, *Signatures of the Visible* (New York: Routledge, 1990), especially pp. 225–9.

11 Loving the Other:
Arab-Male Fetish Pornography and the Dark Continent of Masculinity

Royce Mahawatte

This chapter will explore the phenomenon of Arab fetish pornography, that is, erotic writing and images that focus on the men originating from the North African countries of Morocco, Algeria and Tunisia to Egypt and the Syrian–Arabic peninsula, as a source of sexual stimulus for other men. The interest in Arabic men has a long tradition in the West and this interest, in many different ways, pinpoints what appears to be the intrinsically libidinous nature of 'the Arab'. As absurd and incorrect as such a notion is, it has occupied a prime position in dominant Western thought, a position that has complex and far-reaching implications. Before looking at pornography, however, it might be helpful to put the material into a contemporary context.

In the days following the fall of Kandahar to the United States army in January 2002, an article appeared in the weekend edition of the London *Times*. Entitled 'Kandahar Comes out of the Closet', it outlined a supposed change that could be perceived in the region following the fall of the Taliban.

> Now that Taliban rule is over in Mullah Omar's former southern stronghold, it is not only televisions, kites and razors which have begun to emerge. Visible again, too, are men with their ashna, or beloveds: young boys they have groomed for sex. Kandahar's Pashtuns have been notorious for their homosexuality for centuries, particularly their fondness for naive young boys. Before the Taliban arrived in 1994, the streets were filled with teenagers and their sugar daddies, flaunting their relationship. It is called the homosexual capital of south Asia. Such is the Pashtun obsession with sodomy – locals tell you that birds fly over the city using only one wing, the other covering their posterior – that the rape of young boys by warlords was one of the key factors in Mullah Omar mobilising the Taliban.[1]

The tone of the article is not particularly surprising, considering the conservative inclinations of the newspaper, but what is worthy of note is the way in which, in a so-called 'current affairs' story, Arabic men are depicted. It seems that in the first instance, the liberation of Kandahar brought about the re-emergence of consumer capitalism, but it's not long before the abduction of minors is alleged to have taken place. In a beguiling rewriting of Middle Eastern politics, the Taliban are seen to exist primarily to stamp out homosexuality and their fall meant a re-emergence of a pederastic homosexual sub-culture. Using a word such as 'groomed', the vocabulary of paedophile sexual psychology, the article implies that the fall of the Taliban necessarily causes the rise of a socialised form of paedophilia endemic to Kandahar. So on the one hand, the defeat of the warlords is a triumph for the United States army, but on the other it is an alleged moral decline. What becomes quite clear by the end of the article is that a human interest piece has become a document of pure wartime propaganda. The journalist archly writes 'Despite the Taliban's disdain for women, and the bizarre penchant of many for eyeliner, Omar immediately suppressed homosexuality'. Whichever way they turn, the Afghans are presented as being morally deviant. The depiction of Arabic men as either depraved and effeminate cross-dressers, or as over-masculinised rapists, whether ruled by the Taliban or not, places this piece in a long tradition of orientalist literature that seeks to place 'the uncivilised Arab' in opposition to the Western civilised way of seeing.

How does an item in the London *Times* relate to pornography? During the relatively short period of time in which pornography has been a subject of academic study, academics, critics and commentators have tried to draw links between pornographic material and our socialised experiences. Whether the connection is negative, associating pornography with violence, or simply an acceptance of pornography as one particular thread in the tapestry of our cultural life, academic discussion presents the notion that pornography does not operate in a vacuum behind closed doors. Pornography is never without political consequences – so how, exactly, does the socio-cultural climate, at any given moment, affect subject matter and style within the genre? In answer, it is only necessary to look at adult titles released after the Lewinsky debacle and the impeachment of Bill Clinton to see how topical events can have porno-graphic appeal. But does this relationship have a more complex manifestation than offerings such as *The Porn Starr Report*? Can the codes and structures relating to the actual representation of the body and the sexuality in pornography be affected by politics? To answer this question, I would like to investigate a sub-genre of gay pornography.

What will become apparent during the course of this investigation is that the selective, ignorant depic-tion of Arabic men in the article from *The Times* quoted earlier bears a striking – though not direct – relationship to the codes and structures within Arab fetish pornography. Such a way of seeing Arabic men, however, is not simply a case of the Western gaze on the body of the Arab 'other'. This gaze is complicated by the factor of desire, not just for the model in any particular image or narrative, but more significantly, for an abstract notion of masculinity that is secreted within the idea of the other.

There has been very little discussion of the relationship between race and pornography. It is a striking omission, considering the number of titles and cultural practices in both the gay and straight markets that cater for 'racial interests'. Whether it be pornography that contains images of black, Asian or Arabic models, the selection of models for what are perceived to be racial differences is customary in the production of pornography. Kobena Mercer's pio-neering work on racial fetishism in the work of Robert Mapplethorpe and other artists brings to attention the complexity to be found in the act of looking at racialised gay pornography and, by impli-cation, at pornography *per se*.[2] One of the reasons why Mercer's work is so useful to critics and com-mentators is the split subjectivity that he injects into the analysis of pornographic images. Mercer prevents any closure around the interpretation of pornogra-phy, fundamental to his attack on the New Right, but he also crucially engages with the complexity of con-temporary audience responses. Pornography that focuses on race fetishises race, obviously, but it is worthy of further investigation because fetishes that imbue racial characteristics with sexual qualities make for a complex form of racism that can evade strict political categorisation. As reductive as it may appear on the surface, Arab fetish pornography teaches us virtually nothing about Arabic men, any more than that article in *The Times*; but what it teaches us about both the gay gaze and the 'Western' gaze is telling and intricate.

In a case study of Arab fetish pornography, this intricacy reveals much about Western codes of mas-culinity and its depiction of the 'other'. Traditionally, stereotypes of Arabic men have been presented as 'uncivilised', especially in terms of sexual impulses. Arab fetish pornography reveals that this depiction of the other is transmitted through another discourse – the perception of the working class. The represen-tation of Arabic men as being 'depraved' and danger-ous to Western civilisation aligns it with the traditional perception of the working classes or even an amorphous and threatening 'underclass' – that' dark continent' described by George Sims in *How the Poor Live* (1883).[3] This conflation between the depictions of the Arabic and the working class gives us an insight into how identifying the foreign other necessarily meant demarcating the working-class 'other' within national boundaries.

When projected into the domain of gay por-nography, these negative images are ameliorated. They become sexualised, masculine forms that are separate from a Western, middle-class and appar-ently weaker manhood. In this instance, masculinity itself is presented as a 'dark continent'. Pointing out such a difference is not, however, simply a matter of saying that in gay pornography racism is an escape for a white and middle-class audience. It is rather that the stereotype and the discrimination takes on a new meaning within a greater discourse of Western masculinity.

The strong Western interest in the sexual life of Arabic people has a long history in the somewhat dubious past of nineteenth-century anthropology, erotology and the development of racial theories. I will illustrate the way in which the making of the 'immoral Arab other' is changed into a positive and sublime exponent of masculinity when viewed as a gay fetish.

The second and third sections concentrate on texts that illustrate Arabic fetish pornography and include a discussion of a film from the series *Studio Beurs* produced by the French production company JNRC, in which the styling of the models and the production values play on a political notion that French Arabs are a part of an underclass that is, intrinsically, sexual. And the subsequent discussion of an American internet newsgroup dedicated to Western men with a particular sexual interest in Arabic men does not assume that they are directly comparable, nor that the two examples are representative of the same 'gaze'. Rather, at the risk of intercontinental leap-frogging, I seek to examine the particular, complex subjectivity found in Arab fetish pornography.

Since the attacks on the World Trade Center on 11 September 2001 and following the invasions of Afghanistan and Iraq, the already-fraught relationship between the West and Islam has reached crisis point. These tensions have found their way into pornographic practice. A posting on the newsgroup mentioned earlier articulates anti-Taliban propaganda that plays on many of the same stereotypes as those in *The Times* article. This series, 'I Was a Taliban Sex-slave', is a bizarre mix of wartime propaganda and fetish pornography. It also reveals the complexity of the subjectivity found in the gay gaze and the depiction of the foreign, enemy other.

1 'THE MATERIALIST-EGOISTIC APPROACH OF THE MUSLIM' – THE ARAB, FROM ANTHROPOLOGY TO PORNOGRAPHY

There has been a long history of the West looking at the East and Middle-East in order to define not only its cultural position, but also its moral superiority to other civilisations. Fanon, Said, Williams and Chrisman all illustrate in their very different ways that the study of the Orient was a mechanism which perpetuated the idea that the West and the East were oppositional in every way.[4] Said, influential as his work has been, has not engaged in the gay sexual element of the West's involvement with the East.[5]

Boone, however, constructs a history of the gay sexual interest in the Middle East.[6] What is clear from Boone's research is that the scientific interests of orientalist Richard Burton and sexologists Edwardes and Masters in the bodies and lives of the Arabic men operated as a rather equivocal form of study. Their anthropological work played a very important, though not exclusive, role in the formation of what came to be racial theories of the 19th and 20th centuries. Their studies of Eastern cultures focused on sexual customs and initiation rituals and deduced from these the idea that non-European and non-Christian people were necessarily immoral, promiscuous and full of desire for white Westerners. Nineteenth- and early twentieth-century travellers would leave Europe for the Orient, convinced that they were about to enter not only a new physical environment, but also a series of moral and sexual challenges. Colonial frontiers and cultural differences were dangerous, character-building, exciting and monstrous. In his documentation of the Arab people, Burton claimed that there was a 'Sotadic Zone' in which sodomy was 'popular and endemic', and such a stereotype became firmly lodged in the Western imagination.[7] In his *Personal Narrative of a Pilgrimage to Al-Madinah and Meccah* (1893) he argued that members of 'the Nilotic race, although commonly called "Arabs" are more closely related to the African black because of the size of their sexual organs'.[8] This footnote was written in Latin to ward off the non-specialist, which would indicate that there is a kind of anxiety, a sense of shame that anatomical differences represented a truth about an Arabic man's virility that needed to be controlled. Within the branch of anthropology that focused on the sexual behaviour of non-Western people, there was the underlying belief that studying these people would show the West the potency, spontaneity and freedom that had been curtailed under the gilded chains of industrialisation and the rise of the bourgeoisie. The idea that Arabs were somehow more fundamentally connected to their sexuality was on the one hand a veiled lamentation for a lost era in the West, but more importantly, it provided the licence to govern and rule these cultures on moral grounds.

Allen Edwardes and R. Masters's *The Cradle of Erotica* is a work that on the one hand purports to give a faithful account of the initiation and sexual rituals of non-Western women and men, yet unsurprisingly, it doubles up as a piece of pornography that could easily be smuggled onto respectable library stacks.[9] Outlining the sexual customs of the East, region by region, when it comes to the Middle East Edwardes and Masters write 'fabulous Araby has reeked of aphrodisiac excitement', and after very detailed descriptions of circumcision rituals, they go on to assert that: 'among the North African Arabs and Jews, many of the former being circumcised in infancy like all of the latter, the masturbation habit is not only common but customary'.[10] And following this, detailed accounts of different techniques of masturbation are given. In the closing chapter, entitled 'East and West, Concluding Remarks', the writers explain the purpose of the book:

> The dramatic loosening of sexual morals in the West is in part a product of the less developed peoples, from below, and the greater sophistication of Europe, from above, chipping and sucking at the 'puritanism' of America, have bludgeoned and drained off seditional rigidities and certainties, filling the gaps, when not leaving them yawning, with still undigestible substance, and so spawning confusion. . . . There will surely be some who will say that this is an immoral book, that such a book can only give further encouragement to the drift to demoralisation already so apparent, throughout much of the world. But the careful reader will know better. . . . It has become customary to regard the West as materialistic, and the East as idealistic – both to a fault. But in sexual matters, exactly the reverse has often been the case. What is most commendable in the Oriental approach to sexual relationships is the clear realistic understanding that the need of the flesh must and should be met. What is most commendable in the Western approach is the recognition that sexual intercourse need not be just a physical experience, that it may also involve mind and emotions, blending selfless benevolence with self-interest, the enrichment of the participants. . . . The materialist–egoistic approach of the Muslim leads to coarseness and brutality, and so necessarily fails to realise the potential value of the sexual experience.[11]

So Edwardes and Masters, through their highly sexualised prose style, present and perpetuate the idea that Muslims are brutal and insensitive in relation to sex and, lacking the supposed Western sublimity of appreciation, are incapable of a full understanding of sex. This kind of representation is predictable, but there is also the underlying idea that the 'coarseness and brutality', the sheer sensuality of the Muslim, is treated as an impulse that is outside Western civilisation. When such a notion is taken to its logical conclusion, it is not difficult to see that sensuality and unmediated sexual impulses are prohibited in Western cultures. It is this notion that forms the very basis of Arabic fetish pornography. If the Orient holds dangers for the Western man, then, it is the Orient that holds experiences for the man seeking danger. And if 'danger' means a real or imagined sexual encounter with a passionate and highly 'masculine' man, then dissidence becomes a tantalising opportunity. Jerry Zaritt writes on his experiences in Iran:

> Western gay men, like Western technology, filled a need in rapidly developing Iran . . . They had deprived lives for centuries, but now they were suddenly made aware of their frustrations. Westerners had a combined sexual, economic, and political appeal for Iranians. . . . Iran likewise had considerable appeal for us. Whatever our fantasies – cops, truck drivers, students, athletes, sailors, businessmen, gang bangs with masculine types – Iran was the place where we were likely to act them out . . .[12]

Zaritt transposes the tropes of gay pornography, the cops, sailors and masculine types, onto Iranian men. He occupies a consumerist position: masculinity is a scarce commodity, difficult to find in the West and rather abundant in the Middle East – Iran is a natural resource of unmediated masculinity. The very reasons that made Arabic men forbidden and 'other' within dominant Western thought, were the same reasons Arabic men were sexually valuable to men in search of sexual encounters and a masculinity that itself had become 'other' in the West. Since the mid-1700s, men have travelled to the East and the Middle East in search of a re-identification with their masculinity. This is not to say that they were all seeking sexual encounters with foreign men, but as historian John Tosh writes, there was little place for middle-class men to explore the limits of their masculinity in a professional or domestic environment at home.[13] Whether or not the need for young men to leave the comfort of Great Britain for the challenges of overseas was the result of an innate need to find an essential 'masculine' experience, it is clear that with respect to certain gay experiences, some men chose to discover this essential type of masculinity in the form of the Arab body.

Arabic society, which allows homosociality to be highly visible, provided an opportunity for gay men to explore relationships with men, whether they were sexual or not. André Gide, Oscar Wilde, E. M. Forster, William Burroughs, Allen Ginsberg and Roland Barthes – there is a tradition of male writers who travelled to the Near and Middle East in search of excitement.[14] The psychoanalytical revolution that fixed and drew discrete boundaries around human sexuality in the West did not make itself felt in Arab countries during most of the 20th century. And instead homosexual cultures were found in the *hammans*, beaches and streets that offered covert possibilities for Western men in search of sexual gratification. So Egypt, Tunisia and Morocco have developed a reputation for gay tourism. In recent years, however, this has been lessening due to the rise of anti-Western sentiment and the growing awareness of gay cultures in the West.

2   *STUDIO BEURS* – A CASE STUDY IN ARAB FETISH PORNOGRAPHY

So for the best part of the 20th century, men travelled to where the indigenous men were innocent of Western nomenclature and psychoanalytical history, while back home a market has sprung up that satisfies the interest in the 'other'. The production company Jean Noel René Clair (JNRC) has been a producer of pornography since the mid-80s. Based in Marseilles, it produces a range of titles to satisfy a fetish market. With titles that use sport, the military and race as sexual fetishes, the company has come to be a distinctive producer. The series *Studio Beurs* (1997–9) concentrates on, in the main, Arabic men, *beur* being a colloquialism for a man or woman of Maghrebian origin and French nationality and also the word *arabe* in *verlan*, the French slang in which a word's phonemes are transposed and spoken back to front, 'ebara' to 'beur'. Alluding to the large Arabic population in the city, the videos present a simple sequence of young Arabic men lying on a bed in a makeshift studio and masturbating in front of the camera. The presentation of both the models and the film itself tell us a great deal about not only the fetishisation of the Arabic male, but also about the discourse of race, dissidence and the crucial matter of the subjective gaze.

Studio Beurs, the first in the series, begins with a model in his early twenties sitting on the bed in what looks like a room in a ground-floor flat. The movie is made on video tape, and there is a strange mixture of natural lighting and a single harsh spotlight; a blue

sheet has been haphazardly pinned to the walls. The model wears a pair of jeans and a white tee-shirt, his hair is gelled and he has a small moustache. After introducing himself as 'Amir', he slowly and quite clumsily does a striptease. He removes his trainers and socks and the rest follow. Two cameras are used, one fixed and one hand held, and while the masturbation takes place, the jump-cuts from the man's genitals to the rest of his body and face are unsteady. The model looks at something beyond the camera, out of shot, presumably a television showing him pornography, and just before he ejaculates, he alerts the cameraman so that he does not miss the climax. After another cut, the model is shown lying on his front, so his buttocks are being filmed and he rubs himself against the bed until he climaxes again.

The video continues in the same way for six models; some are older, some speak a little more. One model, 'Arian', wearing a blue shellsuit, tells us that he wants to be a professional footballer. The style of the shots is very distinctive: there is an attempt to be as 'natural' as possible. Unlike most pornography, there is no soundtrack – instead, there is just background noise, a car engine and the barking of a dog can be heard outside. In the second sequence, a telephone rings and the model looks to the cameraman to see whether he should stop. Despite the frequent jump-cuts, there are long moments where the models do nothing but sit and watch the film that is out of shot. The director makes

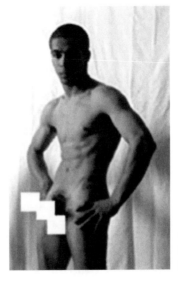

Studio Beurs (1997) (Photo by Jean Noel René Clair)

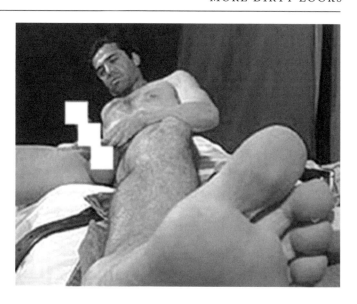

Studio Beurs (1997) (Photo by Jean Noel
René Clair)

no attempt to hide the awkwardness of the scenario:
the bed creaks, the floor seems uneven, the models
get caught up in their trousers, and their bare feet,
usually covered in porn films, come close to the
camera.

It is the extraordinary amateurishness that seems
to be a key feature of the series. In the other series
produced by the same company, the production
values are high – titles like *Wake Up* and *Another
World* use external locations and scripted dialogue –
but the *Studio Beurs* series is clearly constructed to
portray a baseness and a raw kind of simplicity. The
clothes the models wear are cheap and comfortable –
probably their own. There has been no attempt to
dress these men up as anything else but working-
class immigrants who have just walked into the
studio off the street. In fact this is, clearly, the unique
selling point of the film. The promotional copy on
the packaging reads: 'For the first time JNRC has
infiltrated the hot quarters of the dangerous suburbs
where young Arabs exhibit themselves and get pleasure in an improvised studio'. The word *'craignos'* is
used to describe the suburbs, with its connotations of
fear and bad neighbourhoods. The inference is that
these are the kind of men who are socially dangerous,
from a forbidden part of town and sexually masculine. They are a part of an underclass – this association emphasises the men's foreignness and their
sexual allure.

It is surprising, considering the title of the series,
that in the films there are no references to Arabic

culture, life in the Maghreb or to the men's lives as a
part of an Arab community in Marseilles. Instead,
what we see is a series of men with working-class
aspirations, removing their everyday clothes, and
filmed in a disarmingly amateurish way. Ethnicity
and sexual allure are, in part, conveyed by the signs of
social class. Such an act of 'class-ification' is highly
illuminating when the concept and signifiers of race
are considered.

The work of Burton, Edwardes and Masters may
well have tried to define race in terms of difference of
skin colour and body type, but the underlying discourse of moral and totalising inferiority comes from
a different source. It is a widely held belief that the
discourse of race arose out of the anthropology that
accompanied the study of the subjects gained after
the European conquest of Africa and the East. Racial
theories developed not just out of racial study of
Africa and the Orient, but also of the 'primitive
people' *within* the home country. After the guarded
enthusiasm that characterised the positivist Victorian
era, turn-of-the-century thinkers began to doubt the
power of rationalism, especially in the context of
society's 'lower orders'. George Sims's comment that
'there is a dark continent that is within easy walking
distance of the General Post Office' articulates just
how the language of geography found itself describing class.[15] As historians such as Eugene Weber and
Daniel Pick note, the colonisation of the world
began with endocolonisation, the cultural assimilation of the rural and urban lower orders within

Europe.[16] Racism begins at home; once a projection of inferiority, supposed primitivism and a lack of moral sophistication had become a discourse for thinking about the conditions of the working classes, only then was it adapted and applied to people abroad.[17]

Whether at home or abroad, it is this dark continent that is 'other' and perceived as dangerous to a social stability. In the *Studio Beurs* series, this otherness is projected through three social distinctions, the Arab, the working class and, most importantly perhaps, through masculinity. The anxiety, the darkness in this domain has a sexualised and positive quality – a unique purchasing feature for a gay consumer who chooses to hold onto such cultural constructions and resonances of masculinity.

To a large extent, the discussion of the video material has been critical – it casts Arab fetish pornography as being unrepresentative and exploitative. It presents the relationship between viewer and viewed as being dubious. Are these men no more than a blank canvas for the inscription of white ethnic angst? Such a question can never really be convincingly answered. The class-orientated reading of the video's production values is reader-dependent and that is not to render the act of interpretation amorphous or over-liberal. There is no doubt that the issues of class are as present as those of masculinity, but the practices of reading and interpretation demand some explanation of a range of complex subjectivities around the material and its consumption.

3 'WELCOME TO GAY-ARAB-SEXUALITY' – THE ISSUES OF AN INTERNET NEWSGROUP

The notion of very different subjectivities operating in relationship to the same text can be illustrated through certain internet postings. As the gay pornography market and access to it has widened, with both the commercialisation of gay identity and the expansion of the internet, there has been a proliferation of pornographic 'niche interests'. It is easy to find websites and newsgroups dedicated to men wearing different kinds of sportswear, or men photographed in different types of scenario from the office to the prison; there are sites dedicated to voyeurism, amateur pornography, medical examinations, strip-searches – and different races and ethnic groups. There have been a number of sites dedicated to Arabic and Muslim men: Arabgayworld.com, started in 2000, Arabdudes.com started in 2001. The Gay-Arab-Sexuality newsgroup onYahoo started on 28 June 2001 and TurkishDads in March 2001, and Sex-encounters-with-Arab-Men on 20 October 2000.[18]

Internet newsgroups play an important part in providing access for gay men with a demand for niche-interest pornography. Electronic newsgroups allow people to share pictures and experiences, to meet other men, to question and inform. Members have to accept the terms of group membership, which are to post information on the relevant topic, to refrain from advertising or insulting other members and to steer clear of images where the models may be under age. The Gay-arab-sexuality group opens with the greeting:

Welcome to Gay-Arab-Sexuality.

Gay-Arab-Sexuality is an uncensored yahoogroup that celebrates the range of opinions about sexuality among some of the sexiest men on this planet. Post any thing political, religious, or cultural. Post pics of nude Arab men. We are not afraid for gay bashers. The more they spew their hatred, the more it will make no sense to them. However, stay on topic! Or you will be banned. Other than that, anything goes. [. . .]![19]

On the whole the group stays true to this remit. On the site you will find, along with the numerous posts of nude Arab men, guides to videos and websites, the discussion of Arabic cultural identity and customs, Middle Eastern politics, guides for men visiting Arab countries, sexual stories about encounters with Arabic men, fierce debates on circumcision, techniques on flirting with and picking up Arabic men, and much discussion of the dynamics of homosocial Middle Eastern cultures and their relation to Western gay culture.

One of the striking features of the site is the 'academic' nature of the discussion. Postings are frequently accompanied with full bibliographies and the analysis of academic articles which then almost seamlessly segue into the discussion of sex and pornography. One posting contains an analysis of Stephen Murray's and Will Roscoe's *Islamic Homosexualities: Culture, History, and Literature*, while another, posted in August 2001 entitled 'For your political pleasure', contains information from a

United States Government department website on
Economic Support Funds for the financial year 1999
for Israel, Egypt, Jordan, the West Bank and Gaza.
Recording the range of different types of information
on the newsgroup is not simply an attempt to show
how 'credible' or 'serious' this site is. The Arab fetish
site is ostensibly an exclusively male culture – most of
the members on the site use pseudonyms or just first
names and present themselves to the site as being
male, so for the purpose of this piece I have accepted
the claim that members are 'male'. It is a place where
men who like Arabic men meet not only for sex, but
also to pursue other interests.

As can be expected, the attacks on the World
Trade Center generated much discussion on the
site; there were postings of outrage, grief and protest
against both the attacks on the American people
and the anti-Muslim responses within America. In
the days after 11 September, there were also postings which were a strange conflation of global politics and pornography, presumably intended to be
'humorous'. Although in extremely poor taste, they
provide an extraordinary insight into both the
adumbrations of global and sexual politics, and the
different subjectivities that can carve out very different political placings. One message posted on 1
October 2001 included the series of photographs of
the then suspected terrorists with the caption
underneath: '– good dick wasted – Some of these
guys should have been blowing each other instead
of buildings. . . . Blow A Dick, Not A Dynamite
Stick!!!' Such a posting makes it clear how
extremely complicated this situation is. After the
fetishisation, sexual and otherwise, of the Middle
and Near East by commentators of the 19th and
20th centuries, the Arab world is now in a vague
and insulting way homogenised, demonised and, in
the context of the newsgroup, sexualised – where
gay sex acts are seen as providing a moral corrective
to global terrorism.

Perhaps the most interesting piece was a thread
of narratives found 'on the web' and posted onto the
site in October 2001 by the narrator with the dis-
claimer: 'Beats me whether this is true or not'. Called
'I Was a Taliban Sex-slave', the narrative falls into the
genre of outlandish erotic writing, composed by college students, often found in newsgroups or circulated as email. It is a piece of supposedly 'humorous'
and homophobic propaganda framed within a 'gay'

subjectivity which makes its classification and strict
political interpretation virtually impossible. Told in
the first person, the narrative claims to be the first-
hand account of a young soldier who is captured by
the Taliban. The piece continues over three days and
is posted in instalments, complete with cliff-hanger
endings and geographical details. It plays heavily on
the homosociality of Arab culture, the definition of
masculinity and also the fear and stigma of being the
recipient of anal intercourse:

> I am not gay thanks to Allah. In fact I have no gay
> friends and until recently I would have said that I hated
> gays. . . . And this story is about what happened when
> a Taliban army captain wanted me. And the story didn't
> end there because I was forced to take heroin until I
> agreed to become a sex slave for top Taliban com-
> manders and several times I participated in 'political
> lessons' given by Osama Bin Laden to young Taliban
> fighters.[20]

As is often the norm in this type of gay fantasy, the
protagonist is supposedly heterosexual, yet finds
himself participating in brutal and non-consensual
gay sex. I have quoted this opening to show the
highly emotive, and rather literary, *Bildungsroman*
style of narration that is used as the story makes its
slow journey towards its climax. Part One is called
'The Captain' and tells of a student at the university
of Cairo with 'an adventurous and romantic inclination fortified by youthful idealism and who [was]
interested in joining the Taliban'. Travelling to
Afghanistan the protagonist and a friend find the
Taliban and begin their training. When his friend is
brutally murdered by the commander, the storyteller
finds himself the subject of abuse by the lieutenant.
After being asked to bend over an ammunition box,
he is penetrated by a rifle and is certain that he might
be killed there and then. Unfortunately the Taliban
have other plans for him – he is told that he will be
sodomised every day of his life. At this, we are told,
'I have never been so happy in all my life. Not
because I am gay but because here in his contempt
was the offer of life. The sweetest gift that can be
given.' So presented with the alternatives of dying or
being sodomised, the hero happily accepts the latter
and starts his career in the Taliban as a sex slave.
After being rescued by a senior Taliban officer, who
apologises for the inhuman treatment he has

received, he is asked to work as an engineer in Kandahar. The episode ends with the closing line: 'Little did I realize that my agreement would embark me on yet another journey into the sordid world of sex exploitation in the ranks of the sex-starved Taliban'. The next episode, intended to ridicule Arabic culture in general and the Taliban in particular, is entitled 'Osama's Confession' and sees the hero taken to a bunker in the city where he told he is to be prepared for 'Osama'. He is made to lie across a table, on top of a map of Afghanistan, and is threatened by an officer with all kinds of sadomasochistic tortures.

There then follows an extraordinary sequence carefully designed to cause maximum offence to Arab readers:

> The next moment was the most astonishing of my life. For looking down at the now naked man kneeling in front of me I instantly recognised Osama Bin Laden. . . . to see (him) on his knees in such an uncompromisingly self-indulgent submissive position was for those first few moments truly shocking.[21]

The hero is then made to shave, wear make-up, and perfume and live in a secret compound underground. 'Osama Bin Laden' likes to watch the protagonist as he takes his shower in the morning and evening. When 'Osama' finally does try to take the hero, there is a shocking revelation:

> I was shocked to discover that when Osama's hands finally took hold of my behind, that he too was trembling but despite this his grip was sure and steady. His body came closer to mine and he kissed my neck and he began to push against me with increasingly violent thrusts.
>
> But then he stopped and I heard him crying. I didn't dare move.[22]

This absurd, calculatedly offensive piece of narration is a disturbing and bizarre combination of crude pornography, jingoism and Islamophobia. Baiting the 'enemy' and trying to depict Bin Laden as a guilty and weeping fan of anal sex is a part of a tradition that attempts to depict that enemy as depraved and deviant. Is it just racist and homophobic – or more complex? As a piece of political propaganda, its intentions are clear, but its very placing in the newsgroup obscures the invective. In the first instance, it is

intended to be a piece of controversial 'humour'. Supposedly discovered elsewhere, its placing here, for a gay group, raises numerous and very complicated questions around the nature of authorship and audiences.

The location opens out the possibilities of interpretation. On the one hand, the narrative appeals to an audience who might like to read fantasies about gay rape and sadomasochistic encounters, yet on the other the piece articulates conservative fears about effeminacy, degradation, coercion and humiliation, all of which relate to the genre. Fear, titillation, political impulse and absurdity are combined in equal amounts. This piece is by far the most perplexing posting on the site and in the most exaggerated way shows how racism and homophobia can feed into individual pornographic tastes and practices.

This material takes the image of the Arab far beyond exploitation, projection and objectification. Of course all of these modes of representation are present, but there is a highly contemporary kind of political protest involved in unequivocally viewing this type of narrative as a particular type of gay pornographic one. The placing of the text into a gay site negates any kind of traditional campaign or stance against the bigoted nature of the humour, and instead converts the aesthetic for a niche group. The posting about the dynamite stick supports the idea that a pornographic perspective is a kind of political corrective – simplistic, yes, but in effect that is what could be seen as happening within these strange spaces.

4 CONCLUSION

The spectre of gay orientalism is still with us; it has simply changed its medium. Just as with its print predecessors, Arab fetish pornography is a consequence of the complex relationship that exists between the gazes of pornography-producing societies and the very nature of 'masculinity'. It reveals little about the actual lives, both sexual and real, of the men in question. Dominant patriarchal thought creates otherness by positioning foreigners and the working class as other, and through a gay fetishistic lens, which magnifies the tensions, these qualities become ciphers for an ostracised type of masculinity, a masculinity that is virtually taboo, or at least undesirable. The fetish for 'beurs' exists not because there are Arabs on the earth, but rather because the particular stereotype of masculinity, with which they are associated, is so heavily delimited in the West. In fact, a masculinity unmediated by social mores is marginalised, only to be found in gay pornography and in strip-joints. Within the mainstream, it is viewed with irony. To a certain extent, this pornography is a nostalgic yearning for an archaic and fading type of masculinity and also an acknowledgment of an abstraction that is difficult to locate because of our own supposed cultural sophistication. The abstract dimension to this type of pornography is a reflection of the physical competition that is translated into psychological competition in the workplace. There is little or no real place for the kind of physicality demonstrated in the *Studio Beurs* series or the postings on the website. Arab male fetish pornography is a global solution to a relatively modern national problem. Just as Western patriarchal views want to portray the Arabic male as anti-social threat, the gay fetish subculture wants to seek out the other in order to be released from the Western patriarchy that is so constraining.

But this is only one reading of the phenomenon. Fetishism in its widest sense seeks to imbue a physical quality or object with an abstract notion. In the case of Arabic men, fetishism pivots around a number of different meanings. The article in *The Times*, the *Studio Beurs* series and the newsgroup posting, all fetishise the Arab, but the actual meaning and implication of such fetishism is under a constant process of reinscription. Whether it be for the needs of global geopolitics or the politics of sexuality or gender, fetishism, in the examples given here, is fundamentally a representation of the West's relationship with its own discourses on masculinity and, in the most simplest cases, of the representation of 'evil'. Arabic men are merely ciphers for the arguments and exponents for abstract subjectivities.

NOTES

1. Tim Reid, *The Times*, 12 January 2002, p. 16.
2. Kobena Mercer, *Welcome to the Jungle: New Positions in Black Cultural Studies* (Routledge: New York and London, 1994), pp. 171–221.
3. P. Keating (ed.), *Into Unknown England* (Manchester: Manchester University Press, 1976), p. 14.
4. Patrick Williams and Laura Chrisman (eds), *Colonial Discourse and Post-Colonial Theory: A Reader* (New York: Columbia University Press, 1994), p. 7.
5. Edward Said, *Orientalism* (London and Henley: Routledge and Kegan Paul, 1978), p. 188.
6. J. A. Boone, 'Vacation Cruises; or, The Homoerotics of Orientalism', *PLMA*, 110 (1) (1995), pp. 89–107.
7. Ibid.
8. Richard Burton, *Personal Narrative of a Pilgrimage to Al-Madinah and Meccah*, vol. II (London: Darf Publisher Ltd, 1986), p. 83.
9. Allen Edwardes and R. E. L. Masters, *The Cradle of Erotica* (London: The Odyssey Press, 1970). D. Gilmore, *Manhood in the Making* (London and New York: Yale, 1990).
10. Ibid., p. 123.
11. Ibid., p. 166.
12. Jerry Zaritt, 'The Intimate Look of the Iranian Male', in Arno Schmitt and Jehoeda Sofer (eds), *Sexuality and Eroticism among Males in Moslem Societies* (London: Harrington Park Press, 1992), p. 59.
13. John Tosh, 'Domesticity and Manliness in the Victorian Middle Class. The Family of Edward White Benson', in Michael Roper and John Tosh (eds), *Manful Assertions: Masculinities in Britain since 1800*, (Routledge, 1991), pp. 44–73.
14. Boone, 'Vacation Cruises', p. 90.
15. Keating, *Into Unknown England*, p. 14.
16. Eugene Weber, *Peasants into Frenchmen: The Modernisation of Rural France 1870–1914* (New York: Stanford University Press, 1976) and Daniel Pick, *Faces of Degeneration: A European Disorder, c. 1848–1918* (Cambridge: Cambridge University Press, 1989).
17. Pick, *Faces of Degeneration*, pp. 38–9; Kenan Malik, *The Meaning of Race, Race, History and Culture in Western Society* (Basingstoke: Macmillan, 1996), pp. 81–2.
18. <www.Arabgayworld.com>, <www.Arabdudes.com>, <www.egroups.com/gay-arab-sexuality>, <www.egroups.com/ TurkishDads>, <www.egroups.com/ Sex-encounters-with-Arab-Men>.
19. <www. egroups.com/gay-arab-sexuality>, 28 June 2001.
20. Ibid., 24 November 2001.
21. Ibid.
22. Ibid.

12   Taste-Making: Indifference, Interiors and the Unbound Image

Alistair O'Neill

1

Confidential British Foreign Office papers, recently released by the Public Record Office in London, reveal that, in 1968, prints by David Hockney were banned from being exhibited as part of 'New Tendencies', a South American touring exhibition of new British art, staged by the British Council. The 'Cavafy Suite' prints, inspired by the work of the poet C. P. Cavafy, were removed due to the personal intervention of the British ambassador, Peter Hope, who considered the pictorial content of the prints – two men in various states of undress in an anonymous interior – as 'filthy pictures' that 'would tend to draw to the exhibition a crowd of young queens and beatniks who might create disorderly scenes there'.[1] As a 'summer filler', the story managed to make page three of the *Guardian*, a pictorial trailer at the bottom of the front page and even a comment on the leader page:

> Yet another response to the story might be nostalgia for the decade it comes from and the sharpness of attitude often on display during it. Paradoxically, censors have to believe the objects of their attention matter. Hockney, inadvertently, got to the ambassador. His pictures shocked. Art that is not dangerous is not worth censoring. In a blasé age when indifference is the norm, should we regret losing that sense of awe surrounding a new work?[2]

The notion of a left-liberal British newspaper getting maudlin over the censorious treatment of artworks of the recent past was not only amusing but strangely particular. The intention seemed to be an attempt to resuscitate the 'shock of the new' by identifying its recorded presence in the judicious paperwork of the recent past: a record of what we once possessed and what we now seemed to be losing. In mourning the loss of the awe which once surrounded a new artwork deemed 'dangerous' because of its obscene or pornographic content, the newspaper saw this as evidence of a contemporary indifference to the reception of anything 'shocking'.

If we were to consider a contemporary photograph in a similar vein that could evidence this lack of concern, it could be 'Cornel Windlin, last preparation for the book, Cologne, 1996' by the fashion photographer Jürgen Teller.[3] In the image, the editor and designer of Teller's monograph stands, utterly unconcerned, wearing only his underpants, on the telephone in a sparsely furnished room dominated by a large-scale photograph by Jeff Koons – a close-up of the artist himself engaged in penetrating La Cicciolina. In this instance, it is not the poetical associations of desire that are interesting, as in Hockney's suite of images, but a poetical quality of nonchalance in the face of the sexually explicit. Moreover, rather than sexualising the subject, there is a calculated detachment between the ostensible subject of the photograph and the sexual act depicted. In many ways it is the implication of distance that is most redolent of this contemporary condition.

This is an attempt to analyse a body of work by two contemporary photographers, Jeff Burton and Paul Graham, who are interested in the representation of the obscene and the pornographic through the condition of 'indifference'. Both employ strategies that seem reserved in comparison to the scope of what they could document, and in doing so they demonstrate a *recherché* quality in the act of looking that is ostensibly at odds with the contemporary malaise. Like Hockney's prints, both bodies of work deal with the location of sexuality and desire in the interior, and, like the British ambassador's comment, the respective subject matters are 'treated pretty clinically' by all.[4]

The mode of detachment that this treatment implies conventionally structures the resultant images with a tension strung between art and pornography, the aesthetic and the obscene; oppositions that have 'structured much modern cultural discourse',[5] particularly the foregrounding of a postwar definition of culture and the parameters of 'high' and 'low' cultural forms. So, it is the established relation between this historical discourse and the mode of detachment utilised by the two photographers that is in question.

Paul Graham's recent body of work, 'Paintings', is a series of large-scale, lavish colour photographs of close-ups of sexually obscene graffiti on public lavatory walls. In transforming the smears on lavatory walls into artistic works contemplated for their very 'painterliness', he references the Viennese architect Adolf Loos's belief in the relationship between the need to ornament being directly related to the social standing of an individual, with the degenerate as the lowest and most ardent example.[6] Yet in transforming these ornamental gestures into artistic ones, Graham cites the appropriation of primitive forms as a historical feature and fancy of modernism's rejection of canonical art.

Jeff Burton takes photographs of film sets in LA, used mainly for gay pornography, sets on which he works as a stills photographer. In the publication 'Dreamland', the sets are central to the images, while the rendering of any sexual interaction is either entirely absent or else cropped to the side, caught in a reflection or intimated by out-of-focus forms. This approach cites Barthes's idea of the erotic rather than the pornographic photograph as containing a *punctum* that 'is a kind of subtle beyond – as if the image launched desire beyond what it permits us to see'.[7] Yet, given the very polite nature of Burton's photographs, the intention is not necessarily the erotic, but the establishing of the 'blind field' of 'subtle beyond' as not necessarily being 'beyond what it permits us to see'. Rather, it is by its being secreted within what is permitted.

The notion of 'indifference' does, of course, have a historical precedent in the concept of alienation as a response to the increased industrialisation and urbanisation of the 19th century. Further, ennui as an existential pose established the condition as one which could be stylised within a postwar positioning. More recently, Amy M. Spindler, writing in the *New York Times,* identified a contemporary look of 'alienation' in an advertising campaign for Calvin Klein for spring/summer 1998, shot by Steven Meisel. Spindler traced this look of isolation as being

drawn from the 1970s' paintings of Alex Katz and Bergman's *Persona* (1966); she has contextualised it by quoting Ingrid Sischy, editor of *Interview* magazine: 'The 90s has its own very specific version of existentialism, but instead of "no meaning" it's now "no connection".'[8]

In this instance, 'disconnection' is evidenced in 'images depicting the height of isolation, figures in close physical proximity but with eyes never meeting'.[9] The affinity this statement shares with the renderings of the pornographic establishes that the alienation central to commodity exchange and sexual exchange is ever tangible yet ever distant, ever unfulfilled. The connections between these two loveless worlds will dot the enquiry, as it continues to underline the difference between organic and inorganic objects of desire as inessential – a principle that Burton and Graham elegantly realise.

The indifference to the erotic and the obscene on the part of both artists can also be understood through the aesthetic condition of disinterest in the production and contemplation of a work of art, a condition that bears distance and detachment as evident indicators. In addition, both strategies can be understood as inscribing distance and detachment, in turn, with longing and desire-appreciation forced by absence set between idea and execution, inclusion and exclusion, containment and release. They support the notion that the knowledge required to possess an object of desire is that much richer the longer one has to wait, the further one has to travel.

In visualising this passage of time as a space about to empty or a space waiting to be filled – in the rendering, say, of a toilet cubicle, a stage set – both sets of work posit the secretion of longing and desire on the surface of things by their visual consideration of the facades and details of the interior. To study this trace of sexuality in the interior is, in essence, to study the translation of the sexual act to pornographic language expressed as *mise en scène*. As such, it is a mode of enquiry analogous to Pierre Bourdieu's demonstration of *habitus*, being:

> an objective relationship between two objectivities, enables an intelligible and necessary relation to be established between practices and a situation, the meaning of which is produced by the habitus through categories of perception and appreciation that are themselves produced by an observable social condition.[10]

Bourdieu regarded the *habitus* as similar to the essential core of reproduction in literary pastiche, distinct from the saliency of parody and caricature. He evidences this by quoting Jacques Rivière, who believed that Proust's ability for pastiche generated 'the hearth of mental activity.'[11] Similarly, the photographs of Burton and Graham reproduce perceptions and appreciations secreted (although not necessarily evident or visible) in a visible social condition that articulate the mental activity of fantasy.

I was initially drawn to considering the writings of Bourdieu in this context, particularly 'Distinction: A Social Critique of the Judgement of Taste', through an observation made by Lynda Nead in her essay on erotic art, reprinted elsewhere in this book (pp. 216–23), that seemed to chime with the approaches of the two photographers, but not necessarily their intentions: 'What better way to demonstrate your cultural disinterestedness and superiority than to come into contact with the erotic and to be – practically – unmoved?'.[12] However, I am less interested in the reception of these works as evidencing superiority or disinterestedness than in investigating the subtle methods of interpretation that Bourdieu offers for such a study on the themes of distance, the stylisation of everyday practices, the impressions of objectified reality and the implication of narrative. While Bourdieu's oppositional mode of enquiry may seem mechanical and simplistic, in the studied difference, say, between warm and cold, light and dark, it actually reaps subtle results in a consideration of the nature of taste.

It is the fact that Bourdieu's study is rooted as much in interior decoration as in aesthetics that makes it seem so pertinent to an understanding of Burton's work. Burton's monograph 'Dreamland' has a fabric hardback cover that is reminiscent of those interior decoration sample manuals you find in interior decorators' showrooms. British *Vogue* recently recommended it as a book worthy of the coffee table, establishing the monograph as a decorative object in its own right, with more than enough of its own cultural capital. Further, the Italian shoe designer Ernesto Espolito commissioned Burton to shoot his advertisements for its spring/summer 2003 campaign. In this instance, Burton's technique of displaced framing in pornographic stills photography becomes a convenient mechanism through which to concentrate attention on the merchandising of the fashionable commodity, turning sexual exchange into commodity exchange.

2

In trying to undermine Kant's 'Critique of Judgement', Bourdieu established the distance between 'that which pleases' and 'that which gratifies' as an oppositional tension by which the creation and reception of a work of art could be measured. This distance between 'disinterestedness' and the interest of the senses surely implies that the measure of virtue in a work is proportionate to the measure of its resistance to vice. Bourdieu illustrated this by citing derisively the popular works of Mahler and the excessive pomp of Beethoven as taking to extremes the demonstration and elongation of resistance. His identification of this strain as becoming a pleasure in itself is important:

> The inhibition of too immediately accessible pleasure, initially the pre-condition for the experience of 'pure' pleasure, can even become a source of pleasure in itself; refinement can lead to a cultivation, for its own sake, of Freud's 'preliminary pleasure', an ever increasing deferment of the resolution of tension, with, for example, a growing distance between the dissonant chord and its full or conventional resolution.[13]

The distance between the two chords suggests a reverberation in time and space of the dissonant sound before its resolve. In a photograph by Burton, a sun-bleached, bourgeois-styled interior, with French doors leading to a garden, features a Directoire lampshade, a parlour palm and a naked woman standing by a harpsichord as if about to play music in order to accompany the sexual activity taking place on her left. With her hand poised above the sharp keys we ponder whether she will actually play, if she will pretend, or if there is indeed any pretext? The image is not so much concerned with her prospective musical accompaniment but rather with the poetic reverberations of her presence, disinterested and listless, forming a visual interlude within the frame.

In the scene, the deferment of the resolution of tension is about a different kind of reverberation. It's more about the agonisingly extended duration of pornographic sex matching the agonisingly extended duration of the Muzak soundtrack. Pleasure then, in this instance, is to be drawn from the hope of a resolution, an end to the continual reverberating movement of bodies and endless repetition of chord sequences.

Through Burton's particular framing of the scene, we are not so much interested in the action, which is displaced, but by how the woman's disinterestedness fills the space, how it reverberates throughout the intentionally harmonious surroundings. In a similar vein, the staged quality of the surroundings that Burton cites through his displaced framing calls to question the synthesis between the reverie and the setting: a synthesis that is notated (as if musically) as stylisation. J. M. Bernstein's commentary on Adorno's critique of mass culture pays similar homage to the aforementioned chord structure:

> dissonance in music, the stress on individual colours or brushstrokes in painting, or particular words, images or psychological states in the novel negatively express the false unity of the whole. ... Analogously, Adorno stresses the ersatz character of the pleasure the culture industry offers the consumer. Real pleasure is not even on offer; the promissory note, which is the plot and staging of the work, is in reality all that is on offer, thus making the original promise illusory: 'all it actually confirms is that the real point will never be reached, that the diner must be satisfied with the menu'.[14]

For Adorno, the anticipation of resolve from the promissory note is all that the culture industry offers; the resolve never sounds, just the dissonance, heard as a strange imitation. In using his metaphor of the diner, Adorno asserts that pleasure is to be found only in the cultural presentation of the menu rather than the material sustenance of the food, in the consumption of style over content. This form of everyday aesthetics, 'the primacy of forms over function, of manner over matter' is, of course, central to Bourdieu's hypothesis about the social demonstration of taste, but it is the expressed relation between the supposed *artlessness* of the activity and the *artfulness* of the setting in the pornographic tableaux as documented in Burton's photography that contradicts this bi-polar tension. Nead's observations on the 'stylelessness' of pornography need to be quoted for their comparison with literary and artistic models:

> There is of course a paradox in this conception of pornography as stylelessness, or of style reduced to the utmost degree. For language — written or visual — to give the reader a sense of stylistic absence demands extreme stylisation. It requires conventions of representation, narration, contextualisation which say to the reader or viewer: this is representation 'stripped naked',

Untitled #68 (Harpsichord) (© Jeff Burton, 1994)

which abandons superfluous details of style and form and takes you directly, without formal interference, to the realm of the sexual.[15]

To continue, one could assert that in this interpretation, the stylisation of the sex can be offset against the anonymity of the setting – the hotel room, the locker room, the poolside – yet in Burton's photographs, it is the stylisation of the setting that underscores the stylishness of the sex. In refuting the primacy of the directorial gaze, Burton not only exposes the production as collaborative, but underlines a more minor role, namely the production designer who sources such sets and then styles them.

Burton's technique of displaced framing also recalls Bourdieu's notion of the pure gaze: a feature of the act of classifying from an aesthetic disposition that invites stratification in accommodating differing competences and interpretations. So, as an example, a single film might be understood through the fame of the actor involved, or through genre, or through director, each offering a different form of engagement by the level of knowledge attained. It follows rather easily that Burton asserts even finer distinctions by pointing to the role of the production designer, but what is particularly interesting is Bourdieu's own explanation of the pure gaze, the spatial qualities he implies in relation to the concept of distance and the staging of performed action:

> The pure gaze implies a break with the ordinary attitude towards the world, which, given the conditions in which it is performed, it is also a social separation. . . . This is ounce [sic] accepted conventions (as regard scenery, plot etc) tend to distance the spectator, preventing him from getting involved and fully identifying with the characters (I am thinking of Brechtian alienation or the disruption of plot in the nouveau roman).[16]

Here, Bourdieu asserts that to detach the establishing of character from the conventions of scenery and plot is to assert formal experimentation. In doing so, he demonstrates that distance is a structural component of the modernist artwork, realised as a formal strategy. The distance implied from 'ordinariness' and 'believability' stratifies not only the performance but also the social separation, evidenced in class-orientated interpretations. As Jennifer Wicke has confirmed, 'the genre distinctions within pornography are [also] drawn on aesthetic and social grounds'.[17] However, the recent rise of *Gonzo* as a genre to match what is known as *Features*, mirrors this mode of detachment but to different ends. As Martin Amis explains:

> Features are sex films with some sort of claim to the ordinary narrative: characterisation, storyline. 'We don't show you people fucking,' said a features executive. 'We show you why they're fucking.' . . . Gonzo porn is also known as 'wall-to-wall'. It shows you people fucking without concerning itself with why they're fucking.[18]

Within the genre of *Gonzo* the detachment between character and convention is, unsurprisingly, not considered to be formal experimentation, yet the detachment forces an elision between character and convention that is almost solely informed by the setting within which the action takes place. The use of the term *wall-to-wall* thus establishes the essentialism of these surfaces as the register of detachment and the register of an implied proximity to the sexual act. In her study of *Features* porn, Gertrud Koch maintains that the establishing of characterisation and storyline through the constant change of make-up, costumes and locations, desire is structured through 'the trappings of anonymous passion' while being 'obscured in the films themselves by the hearty gymnastic primacy of genital sex'.[19]

Yet this is not to deny their centrality to desire by their obscuration, as they are often its prop. The American pornographer Ed Powers, famous for his oeuvre of *Amateur* films of young men and women often encountering a pornographer for the first time, has succeeded in turning the trappings of his studio, captured in his films as an anonymous background setting, into a recognisable visual register of *Amateur* as a genre of porn. The appropriation of this assemblage of imitation wood-laminate wall coverings and cheap peach-coloured carpets by fashion photographer Stephen Meisel for a Calvin Klein campaign of 1995 caused widespread complaint; the poses of the models, though no more pornographic than those imitated in many fashion magazines, were deemed pornographic in the context of their constructed setting. The perceived need for pornography to be staged in cheap settings is not only particular to *Amateur* film, it is central to the performative staging of desire and to the choice of trappings.

The very bourgeois arrangement of furnishings that the set designs documented by Jeff Burton's photographs ape initially engages a tension built on the oppositional values of the respectable and the obscene. A reproduction of a Gainsborough Lady casts a mannered glance over some anal sex; a rococo frame above a bedstead hangs tilted as if arching with the performer's back; the carved wooden frame of a recliner undulates in synthesis with the out-of-focus fleshy forms; twin lamps wait in symmetry and anticipation to be turned on. But it is the veneer of these things, the obviousness of their imitation, the fact that they are not what they purport to be, to which Burton draws our attention. For Bourdieu, the use of such cheap substitutes is indicative of dispossession:

> As much as by the absence of luxury goods, whisky or paintings, champagne or concerts, cruises or art exhibitions, caviar or antiques, the working-class lifestyle is characterised by the presence of numerous cheap substitutes for these rare goods, 'sparkling white wine' for champagne, imitation leather for real leather, reproductions for paintings, indices of a dispossession at the second power, which accepts the definition of the goods worthy of being possessed.[20]

By drawing our attention to these things, Burton not only references the accepted definitions and values of the dispossessed, but actually implies that the marking of the interior with the indices of dispossession is, in fact, a marking of a form of distancing from the real and the authentic to the embracing of the imaginary and artificial, both necessary foundations for the rise of fantasy. In another photograph by Burton we see a black man's foot clad in a black sock with an insignia of a Pierre Cardin signature in white. The Cardin sock is quite important here, as the signifier of a particular kind of 'designer' product and the expression of a particular kind of taste.

In the 70s Pierre Cardin was at the forefront of a trend which saw fashion designers use the cachet of their names to widen their market appeal through licensing deals. By licensing his name to a bewildering number of goods in the 70s, Pierre Cardin soon eclipsed his reputation as a modernist couturier of the 60s and instead became a by-word for a cheap and readily available kind of 'designer' item that often bore no relation to the ethos of the designer.

The lowly status accorded such 'designer' goods (particularly those licensed by Cardin) bears heavily on its very conspicuousness in the image, the way the focus highlights the misprinting of the signature on the fabric surface. Burton captures the branded signature at the level of the crotch of another man, who is sitting behind in white underpants and in so doing, renders the squiggly white form as possibly allusive to the money shot, that ocular register in pornography that pleasure has taken place. To sketch pleasure on a signature on cheap 'designer' goods, is to link the dispossession of the projected fantasies from the world of goods as a marker of artifice equal to that of the money shot, or the performed register of dispossession.

Thus, the veneer of the signature on the sock is the signature of stylisation and the signature of some kind of satisfaction. It is the grip of objects in their substitutional embrace. This interdependent relationship between things and actions in the pornographic tableaux, conveyed as the staging of fantasy is also reflected in Bourdieu's idea of social structure, 'so well put by the word taste – simultaneously "the faculty of perceiving flavours" and "the capacity to discern aesthetic values" – is social necessity made second nature, turned into muscular patterns and bodily automatisms'.[21]

This implies that the performative relation between performers and props structures subject/object relations through social distinctions; mimetic gestures received and communicated through bodily experiences that may well be unconscious. Fashion photographer Guy Bourdin crystallised this idea in a lingerie catalogue that he produced for Bloomingdales' department store in New York in the late 70s, entitled 'Sighs and Whispers'. In the catalogue a series of similar hotel room interiors interconnect through the turning of each page, a mimesis of the unconscious cyclical associations of desire and the rendering of the female model as subject and object of her own desire parallel to the projected desire of the consumer. In her study of the catalogue, Rosetta Brooks articulates the notion of distance particular to fashion photography:

> Instead of naturalising the setting, Bourdin makes the image strange, exploiting the peculiarity of the fashion photograph by imposing devices which keep the consumer at a distance from the ostensive content of the

Untitled #117 (Pierre Cardin) (© Jeff Burton, 2000)

image (the product). In the turning of the pages from slips to nightgowns, we go from reality to appearance, from the female double to the mirror reflection.[22]

Bourdieu is also taken with the slippage between subjects and objects as indicative of a form of separation, in the ability for inanimate objects to express, in dulcet tones, the condition of their subject and it is the 'whispering' quality of these utterances that is central:

If a group's whole lifestyle can be read off from the style it adopts in furnishing or clothing, that is not only because these properties are the objectification of the economic and cultural necessity which determined their selection, but also because the social relations objectified in familiar objects, in their luxury or poverty, their 'distinction' or 'vulgarity', their 'beauty' or 'ugliness', impress themselves through bodily experiences which may be as profoundly unconscious as the quiet caress of beige carpets or the thin clamminess of tattered, garish linoleum, the harsh smell of bleach or perfumes as imperceptible as a negative scent. Every interior expresses, in its own language, the present and

even past state of its occupants, bespeaking the elegant assurance of inherited wealth, the flashy arrogance of the *nouveau riches*, the discreet shabbiness of the poor and the gilded shabbiness of 'poor relations' struggling to live beyond their means.[23]

This idea of the attributes of the interior rendered as marks of social relations indicates mark-making as a possessive activity. As a mark (*ma griffe*, also the name of a perfume by Carven), it also implies that the expression bears the hand of the subject, the signature which, as already demonstrated, is invariably conditioned by stylisation. In many ways, these attributes are what visually substantiate the veneer of possession in the name of displaying individuality or ownership.

3

In the photographs of Paul Graham, the notion of mark-making on walls as a signifying practice of ownership is explored, where the unconscious attributes of the interior are overwritten by the citation of the unconscious desire of the individual. In Bourdieu's analysis it is the textural qualities of the interior that impress themselves as 'profoundly unconscious'

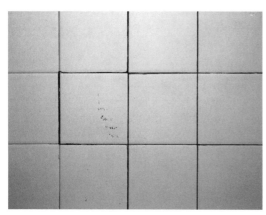

Untitled no. 14 from *Paintings* (© Paul Graham, courtesy Anthony Reynolds Gallery, London)

but expressive. In Graham's photographs, it is the textual qualities written on the surface of the interior that impress themselves as profoundly unconscious, yet expressive – but this is not to claim the textural and the textual as being mutually exclusive in this instance; rather, it is the very way in which they are bound together.

What is contradictory within Graham's photographs is that although they depict textural surfaces, they remain flat in reproduction and through this, the surface in consideration becomes, inevitably, stylised. We recognise this process as an act of distancing, an act which references not only the historical appropriation of primitive marks by modern artists, but also the concomitant modes of appreciation for essentially the same marks appearing in different situations. The catalogue that accompanied the exhibition of Graham's photographs is prefaced by the reproduction of an excerpt from a letter of intent written by the American abstract expressionists Mark Rothko, Barnett Newman and Adolph Gottlieb. By this historical citation Graham makes explicit the link between the aesthetic beliefs of these artists as set out in the letter printed in the *New York Times* in 1943 and the plainly visual fact that his images look not unlike abstract paintings when reproduced.

Thus, in the excerpt from the letter, 'We are for flat forms because they destroy illusion and reveal truth', (in Graham, 2001), the allusion to the distancing techniques of photographic practice and the picture plane becomes evident. When the abstract expressionists declare: 'Only that subject matter is

valid which is tragic and timeless. That is why we profess spiritual kinship with primitive and archaic art.'[24] Graham's quotation of this illuminates the inevitable stylisation of such subject matters through knowing and differentiated kinship – an inevitable glossing and containment of lowly forms.

As an obvious register of the oppositional tensions between high and low cultural forms in fine art practice, Graham acknowledges in his photographs that the transformation of the vulgar and the crude into artistic technique is not particularly new. But whereas for an artist like Dubuffet, where the textural surface was a necessary part of his best paintings, the absence of texture smoothed by the plane of Graham's photographic surface is *impasto-ed* with the presence of the textual. Graham's photographs problematise the definitions of exalted and base cultural forms, not only from an art-historical perspective but also from the formations of sexual identity, perhaps the more obvious sites for what we understand as 'Sighs and Whispers'.

The idea of flat forms destroying illusion and revealing truth is explored in Graham's photographs by the establishing of allusion and the concealment of reality on a vertical surface, a layering of intertextual fantasies that expand in concern beyond the surface of their inscription. The marks that confirm this are both varied and ambiguous: scrawled messages are stabs at connecting, sexual stories are open-ended in significance, sketches are never merely illustrative. They map the passing of time and the passing of desire, attempts and failures not only between those wishing to engrave desire in the pursuit of its consummation, but also with those who wish to erase it. On a stainless steel surface the chalky residual film of cleaning fluid intermingles with other white stains, the paper residue of a removed sticker on an inscribable surface becomes the only space to set the frankest of details.

In a photograph by Graham of a pink-tiled wall, graffiti has been erased to a point where the ink of the pen has stained the grouting an unappealing black, emphasising the grid-like quality to the composition of the image to offset the just-legible 'I WILL SUCK YOUR COCK' still visible on one of the tiles. The image expresses a series of parallel tensions, the hand of the inscriber against the patina of erasure, the dirt of the material contaminating the hygiene of the environment, the sugariness of the pink offsetting the mechanical quality of the statement. The strangeness of desire residing in such an austere setting is here not in question, but it leads us to Bourdieu's thoughts on the disgust of the facile from an aesthetic disposition:

> often called 'visceral' (it 'makes one sick' or 'makes one vomit') for everything that is 'facile' – facile music, or a facile stylistic effect, but also 'easy virtue' or an 'easy lay'. The refusal of what is easy in the sense of simple, and therefore shallow, and 'cheap', because it is easily decoded and culturally 'undemanding', naturally leads to the refusal of what is facile in the ethical or aesthetic sense, of everything that offers pleasures that are too immediately accessible and so discredited as 'childish' or 'primitive' (as opposed to the deferred pleasures of legitimate art).[25]

Contrary to the established relation between these varied terms that move from the viscerally innate to the virtuously inane, Graham's photographs refute the principle that 'low' necessarily means 'easy'. Although they establish the setting of desire as visceral and document primitive marks as expressive of the hope for an easy lay, they resist the reflexive refusal of aesthetic disposition. This is achieved not by the implication of the artfulness of the framing against the artlessness of the subject, but by the implication of how hard it would be to stylise or stage these found surfaces. It is their construction as surfaces resistant to stylisation that confers them as primal, a starting point from which disinterestedness distances and an end point to the drives of desire. It is their citation as visual regis-

Untitled no. 4 from *Paintings* (© Paul Graham, courtesy Anthony Reynolds Gallery, London)

ters of the primal that gives them their power and, in turn, fascination. A good case of visual comparison is the stage-set construction of spaces intended to mimic 'cottages' for gay porn films where the production quality of the applied graffiti inscribes the setting as unreal and in turn problematic, for instance, *Skin Flick* (1999) directed by Bruce La Bruce, featuring fashion photographer Terry Richardson. Jennifer Wicke has commented on the spectators' response to such details in porn films where:

> hair, body language, body morphology, bedroom props only have to be a shade off to sunder any sexual response to the pictures and to instead open up a reverie on the *punctum* of any particular image, a *punctum* which is more mass cultural than Barthes' rather ahistorical nostalgia for a past, frozen time.[26]

As already stated, the *punctum* is understood as the point at which 'the image launch(es) desire beyond what it permits us to see' but in this instance, the *punctum* becomes a blockage to this ability to access desire from the beyond; it is a *punctum* that establishes distance and in turn dispossession. Pornography is caught in this need to assert the primal through the repetitive clichés of dispossession. Graham's photographs underscore the fact that the crafting of 'low' in pornographic practice is an endless recreation of the meaning of *easy* to necessitate its very consumption. The fact that this is not necessarily easy to produce is underlined by the artist's own concern with the transformation of the details of desire by his documentation of them. Bourdieu offers the following consolation for this predicament:

> Intellectuals and artists have a special predilection for the most risky but also the most profitable strategies of distinction, those which consist in asserting the power, which is peculiarly theirs, to constitute insignificant objects as works of art, or, more subtly, to give aesthetic redefinition to objects already defined as art, but in another mode, by other classes or class fractions (e.g. kitsch). In this case, it is the manner of consuming which creates the object of consumption, and a second-degree delight which transforms the vulgar artefacts abandoned to common consumption, Westerns, strip cartoons, family snapshots, graffiti, into distinguished and distinctive works of culture.[27]

The idea of a *second-degree delight* is most profitably read when we consider it as a manner of consumption similar to that of dispossession, to secondary satisfaction, to a cheap designer sock. In aligning the artistic condition of disinterestedness to the everyday indices of dispossession, Graham's photographs connect a mode of consumption bound by indifference to one bound by the recognition that its status is secondary. By structuring these forms of consumption around the primal core of desire, he renders their attempts to connect with its 'kind of subtle beyond' as equally secondary.

In the pictorial appropriation of the lowly, Bourdieu asserts that the artist introduces 'a distance, a gap – the measure of his distant distinction . . . (by moving from content to the analysis of form).'[28] Yet in their concern with the nature of desire, Graham's photographs seem to assert that it is through this distance that something is inevitably lost rather than something gained. In many ways, it is the condition of indifference rather than the acceptance of dispossession that memorialises this loss, a state of disinterestedness that is not unmoved, but frigid, unable to engage. This is often inferred in the photographs by the harshness of the surfaces depicted. In one of these a painted black wall bounces the falling natural light off its gloss finish, while the sparse surface details destroy any sense of illusionary depth that the pictorial plane can imply. At the bottom of the image a drilled 'glory-hole' intended for visual spectatorship and engagement with someone on the other side of the wall is jammed with a wodge of white toilet paper, denying any visual depth, any further contact. Appearing almost like a white flower, the toilet paper appears almost to mourn the loss of desire that once drove the inscription next to it – which reads 'SPUNK NEEDED 2/8'.

4

For Bourdieu, exclusion is central to the refined games of taste, but it is also central to the charge of fantasy. Exclusion is a process that intends its subject to be ever more solitary; Burton's and Graham's photographs can be understood as individual takes on the solitary qualities of desire. In concentrating on surfaces and things inscribed with the *mise en scène* of desire, the photographs recognise that individual responses are conditioned by the arrangement of such things, their necessary order in a non-temporal and non-spatial scheme. In terms of its poetical ren-

dering of this idea, the following quotation from Jean Genet's *Our Lady of the Flowers* serves as a pertinent example in terms of the expressive fluidity between the real and imaginary architectures of the interior and exterior, the body and mind:

> I do not know whether it is their faces, the real ones, which spatter the wall of my cell with a sparkling mud, but it cannot be by chance that I cut those handsome, vacant-eyed heads out of the magazines. I say vacant, for all the eyes are clear and must be sky-blue, like the razor's edge to which clings a star of transparent light, blue and vacant like the windows of buildings under construction, through which you can see the sky from the windows of the opposite wall. Like those barracks which in the morning are open to all the winds, which you think are empty and pure when they are swarming with dangerous males, sprawled promiscuously on their beds.[29]

In this passage the solitary confinement of the protagonist in his prison cell becomes an active visual register in the fashioning of the things that surround him and the concomitant rise of his desire. For Genet, solitariness is the starting point – through the containment of being by fixtures and fittings. The idea of solitary containment away from the world is a theme that Norman Bryson has considered in his discussion of still-life painting, which serves as a useful paradigm to examining the trappings of desire documented by Burton and Graham.

For Bryson, the absence of the human form is the prerequisite of still-life, 'what is abolished in still-life is the subject's access to distinction. The subject is not only exiled physically: the scale of the values on which narrative is based is erased also.'[30] Bryson confirms that narrative is constructed in historical painting, in the documentation of greatness in opposition to the documentation of its absence, as evidenced in still-life. Yet peculiar to this strict opposition is the ability still-life has to demonstrate 'the commitment to the presentation of culture as circulating between luxury and necessity in a continuous cycle'.[31] In a sense, it offers a stratification system that lies beyond the generation of narrative; something whispered, as 'profoundly unconscious as the quiet caress of beige carpets'.[32]

In the work of Burton and Graham, we can now recognise the solitary quality of the depopulated space where narrative is erased and indifference rises from an inability to compose desire from such reductive elements. Importantly, it is the stylisation of these things that imparts the necessary feeling of exclusion and resistance, supported by Susan Sontag's view that 'stylistic devices are also techniques of avoidance. The most potent elements in a work of art are, often, its silences.'[33]

Contrary to the idea that narrative is erased, Susan Stewart has written in her book *On Longing* that the structuring device that surrounds desire formed from absence is, in fact, narrative, 'a structure that both invents and distances its object and thereby inscribes again and again the gap between signifier and signified that is the place of generation for the symbolic.'[34] It would seem that it is the furnishing of this gap that both these photographers point to, visualised and inscribed as provisional substitutes.

This idea of visual narratives mapping desire has recently been considered by Richard Meyer in his study of the possessions and photographs of Robert Mapplethorpe who 'pictured homosexuality not simply as a sexual act or an individual identity but also as a set of spaces, surfaces and objects, as a theatrical scene in which the backdrop and the props are no less important than the players'.[35] Meyer supports this by the example of the synthesis in a Mapplethorpe portrait of Larry Hunt between the studding of the oak bench on which he sits, one designed by the Austrian furniture maker Gustav Stickly and the lacing studs on the knee-high leather boots he wears. Meyer implies a correlation between the spartan form of the bench and the restrictive nature of the sitter's footwear conditioned by the arrangements of the photographer so as to be possessed by narrative. Lamentably, the cataloguing of his portfolio of private images, society portraits and floral pistils began a stylisation of this narrative so that:

> once leatherman and carnation inhabit the same photographic lexicon, even the most audacious of sadomasochists can be 'tamed' into elegant abstraction and the gentlest of floral arrangements freighted with a sexual charge.[36]

Here, the relentless furnishing of the gap transforms one value into the other, creating a narrative which comforts in its cultural competence, 'translating the energies of compulsion and perversion to the lofty heights of aestheticism and the language of form'.[37] Further, the symbiosis of forms (the one into the other) placates the confusion of commodities where the world of goods exchanges with the world of the sexual. However, possession of the desired objects is never realised, only their rearrangement in the movements of exchange. In her study of fantasy in film as being analogous to the fantasy of daydreams and the unconscious, Elizabeth Cowie confirms what is essential to the work of Burton and Graham:

> Fantasy involves, is characterised by, not the achievement of desired objects, but the arranging of, a setting out of, desire: a veritable *mise en scène* of desire. For of course, Lacan says, desire is unsatisfiable, much as Freud commented that there is something in the nature of sexuality which is resistant to satisfaction. The fantasy depends not on particular objects, but on their setting out; and the pleasure of fantasy lies in the setting out, not in the having of objects.[38]

For Burton and Graham, the pleasure in setting out is their pleasure in documenting. The pleasure we take from their images is derived from their qualities that are secondary, once removed. What we take from these images in our condition of indifference is not primary, only seemingly. As a proposition it is very much in keeping with Susan Sontag's view in her essay 'On Style' of our reception techniques when engaging with art: 'Which is to say that the knowledge we gain through art is an experience of the form of style of knowing something, rather than a knowledge of something (like a fact or moral judgement) in itself.'[39] All that is imparted, all that can be gathered is a sense of seeming rather than being. What we are left with is a sense of inferiority essential to the machinations of taste; a feeling that we all prefer to remain indifferent to while remaining ever conscious of its subtleties and arrangements. Continued participation then, is about keeping up with the continual rearrangement of forms. The pleasure of fantasy as a practice, then, becomes something that has more in common with the practice of a set designer for a pornographic film than the director. It's more about sofas and sheets than sequences and shots.

Both Burton's and Graham's work are examples of the pornographic desire to connect being considered by the artistic desire to resist. In this construct consumption and indifference become

entwined, stylised into unified form. Here, nonchalance in the face of the explicit is elevated to an aesthetic style position; but this isn't to suggest that the
material becomes any easier to digest, as in many
ways it becomes trickier. Genet best demonstrated
this when he heard that readers of his books could
find themselves sexually aroused by the act of reading them. In answer he replied: 'Insofar as my books
are pornographic, I don't reject them. I simply say
that I lacked grace.'[40]

NOTES

1. Alan Travis, 'How Our Man in Mexico Kept Beatniks
   at Bay', *Guardian*, 16 July 2001, p. 3.
2. 'Potent Pictures', *Guardian*, 16 July 2001, p. 17.
3. Jürgen Teller, 'Jürgen Teller' (Koln, London: Taschen,
   1996), p. 58.
4. Travis, 'How Our Man in Mexico Kept Beatniks at
   Bay', p. 3.
5. Lynda Nead, ' "Above the Pulp-line": The Cultural
   Significance of Erotic Art', in this volume, p. 216.
6. Adolf Loos, 'Ornament & Crime', in *Programme und
   Manifeste zur Architektur des 20. Jahrhunderts*
   (London: Land Humphries, 1970).
7. Roland Barthes, *Camera Lucida: Reflections on
   Photography*, (London: Vintage, 1993), p. 59.
8. Ingrid Sischy in Amy M. Spindler, 'Critic's Notebook:
   Tracing the Look of Alienation', *New York Times*,
   24 March 1998.
9. Ibid.
10. Pierre Bourdieu, *Distinction: A Social Critique of the
    Judgement of Taste* (London: Routledge, 1984), p. 101.
11. Ibid., p. 173.
12. Nead, ' "Above the Pulp-line" ', in this volume, p. 218.
13. Bourdieu, *Distinction*, p. 490.
14. J. M. Bernstein, 'Introduction to Theodor W.
    Adorno', *The Culture Industry: Selected Essays on Mass
    Culture* (London: Routledge, 1991), p. 8.
15. Nead, ' "Above the Pulp-line" ', in this volume, p. 219.
16. Bourdieu, *Distinction*, p. 4.
17. Jennifer Wicke, 'Through a Gaze Darkly:
    Pornography's Academic Market', in this volume,
    p. 180.
18. Martin Amis, 'A Rough Trade', *Guardian Weekend*, 17
    March 2001, pp. 8–9.
19. Gertrud Koch, 'The Body's Shadow Realm', in this
    volume, p. 159.
20. Bourdieu, *Distinction*, p. 386.
21. Ibid., p. xx.
22. Rosetta Brooks, 'Sighs and Whispers' in *Zoot Suits &
    Second-Hand Dresses: An Anthology of Fashion and
    Music* (Basingstoke: Macmillan, 1989), p. 186.
23. Bourdieu, *Distinction*, p. 77.
24. Both quotes are from Paul Graham, *Paintings*
    (London: Anthony Reynolds Gallery, 2001).
25. Bourdieu, *Distinction*, p. 486.
26. Wicke, 'Through a Gaze Darkly', in this volume,
    p. 183.
27. Bourdieu, *Distinction*, p. 283.
28. Ibid., p. 34.
29. Jean Genet, *Our Lady of the Flowers* (St Albans:
    Panther, 1968), p. 56.
30. Norman Bryson, *Looking at the Overlooked: Four
    Essays on Still-life Painting* (London: Reaktion, 1990),
    p. 61.
31. Ibid., p. 62.
32. Bourdieu, *Distinction*, p. 77.
33. Susan Sontag, *Against Interpretation and Other Essays*
    (New York: Farrar, Straus & Giroux, 1961), p. 36.
34. Susan Stewart, *On Longing* (Baltimore, MD: Johns
    Hopkins University Press, 1984) p. ix
35. Richard Meyer, 'Mapplethorpe's Living Room:
    Photography and the Furnishing of Desire', in *Art
    History*, vol. 24 no. 2, April 2001, p. 308.
36. Meyer, 'Mapplethorpe's Living Room', p. 301.
37. Laura Kipnis, 'She-Male Fantasies and the Aesthetics
    of Pornography', in this volume, p. 210.
38. Elizabeth Cowie, *Representing the Woman*
    (Basingstoke: Macmillan, 1997).
39. Sontag, *Against Interpretation and Other Essays*, p. 22.
40. Genet in Sontag, ibid., p. 27.

13   The Body's Shadow Realm

Gertrud Koch

ON THE HISTORY OF PORNOGRAPHIC FILMS: CINEMA IN BROTHELS, BROTHELS IN CINEMA, CINEMA IN PLACE OF BROTHELS

The history of film is also the history of its limitations, supervision, regimentation, judicial constraint, and examination of norms. Reviewing chronologies of film history, we see the extent of the censor's alarm system, which would monitor the flow of cinematographic production, classified and catalogued into acceptable and unacceptable areas:

> According to a police directive, censorship cards will be instituted and censorship jurisdiction will be transferred to the chief of police of each of Berlin's police precincts. (20 May 1908)[1]
>
> All members of the Seventh District Court appeared at Berlin police headquarters for the screening of a film which has caused a public scandal. This is the first judicial review of a film in Germany. (12 December 1909)
>
> In March, the People's Institute of New York and Dr Charles Sprague Smith established the 'National Board of Censorship' as a film review board. (1902)[2]
>
> In Sweden, film censorship is instituted at the request of the film industry. (1911)
>
> According to a German municipal ordinance, every film must be submitted for certification to the appropriate precinct office twenty-four hours before public screening. (1911)[3]
>
> Through the founding of the Hays organisation's 'Motion Picture Producers and Distributors of America', the American film industry sets up a form of voluntary self-regulation. (1922)[4]

Although these historians do not mention the rules then in effect for banning a film as offensive, we know from another source that the censorship authorities collected pornographic films:

For the most part, the supervising authorities, the police, know about this class of films, films fated to lead a humble and obscure life. We define pornographic films as the cinematic depiction in an obscene form of whatever concerns sexual life, and these include just about everything human fantasy can possibly invent in the area of sexuality. The films pass directly from the producer to the consumer, thus steering clear of the censor, and with good reason. Nevertheless, the police archives are filled with films such as chance and vigilance have brought their way.[5]

Even though the invention of cinema was soon followed by institutionalised censorship, pornographic films still had time to become widespread. Unencumbered by censorship, which wasn't established until 1908, film pornography was already in full bloom in Germany by 1904. Short pornographic films – of up to a minute in length – furthered the technical development already seen in photographic pornography in such apparatus as the stereoscope and mutascope. By 1904, such films had grown to four acts and ran twenty minutes. Early pornographic movies thus kept pace with most of cinema's developments, which raises the questions: what kind of aesthetic development did this genre undergo? Can we in fact even speak of a genre? And what would define its particular aesthetic?

To answer these questions we have to look to the few available sources describing early pornographic films and their modes of reception:

In most cases, these sotadic films were screened in private societies or in men's clubs founded for this purpose. In Germany, the entry price ranged from ten to thirty marks. The distribution of tickets was handled by prostitutes, pimps, café waiters, barbers, and other persons in contact with the clientele, who knew they could earn a tidy profit by marking up the price. Since these

vendors usually knew their clientele and their preferences, there was little danger of coming into conflict
with the police.[6]

For the most part, pornographic films were bought
and screened by brothels, which hoped to entice customers with filmic come-ons while also earning
money by charging for the screenings. At first, the
pleasure offered by pornographic films was expensive, reserved for the well-to-do customers who
frequented such establishments in European metropolises from Paris to Moscow. Abroad, both Buenos
Aires and Cairo offered international tourists the
opportunity to visit pornographic cinemas. In *Die
Schaubühne*, Kurt Tucholsky describes an experience
in a porn house in Berlin:

> Nobody spoke out loud, since everyone was a bit anx-
> ious; they only murmured. The screen turned white; a
> fragile, mottled silver-white light appeared, trembling.
> It began. But everyone laughed, myself included. We
> had expected something bizarre and extravagant. We
> saw a meow-kitty and a woof-doggy romping on the
> screen. Maybe the exporter had tacked the scene on to
> fool the police – who knows? The film ran without
> music, rattling monotonously; it was gloomy and not
> very pleasant.
>
> . . .
>
> Things remained *gemütlich* in the cinema. We didn't
> realise that even Tristan and Isolde would seem ridicu-
> lous in this setting, or that Romeo and Juliet, viewed
> impartially from another planet, would seem a comic
> and straightlaced affair.
>
> No, nothing of the sort among the patrons. The only
> reason they didn't play cards was because it was too
> dark. An atmosphere of healthy and hearty pleasure
> prevailed. You had to say to yourself – all this phony
> business – at least here you knew. . . . The ending was
> so obscure that when it was over everyone thought
> there was more to come – it just goes to show, that's
> how it is with sex. The men stood around feeling self-
> conscious and embarrassed, remarking on the lack of
> values here and in general. And then we pushed
> through narrow passageways into an adjoining estab-
> lishment where the music was loud and shrill, and
> everyone was strangely quiet and excited. I heard later
> that the proprietor had ordered twenty call girls.[7]

The atmosphere of this occasion in Berlin – with the

camaraderie of male bonding, uneasy and secret
arousal, and forced jocularity – was apparently not
unique. Norbert Jacques provides an illustration from
Buenos Aires, one that enriches the steamy Berlin-
beer flavour with sadomasochistically tinged exotic
stereotypes:

> One night in Caracas, walking along the harbour wall
> where the long low Platte River steamers slept, I
> reached a point beyond the criminal quarter. An odd
> but impressive scaffolding stopped me in my tracks. . .
> . While I was looking up into its towering height, I
> saw a boat under me with a light, tied to the harbour
> wall. A man on the boat called out something to me.
> This man and I were totally alone there. He rushed up
> to me and pointed across the harbour, saying: 'Isla
> Maciel!' and blurted out in an international language,
> 'Cinematografo. Nina, deitsch, frances, englishmen,
> amor, dirty cinematographico!' . . . A large arc lamp
> radiated harshly over a sinister-looking shack on the
> other side.
>
> The man rowed me over there past the ships. . . . I
> came to a lonely trail, and one hundred metres up
> ahead of me was the glaring arc lamp. . . . On my left
> was a hedge; on the right, an impenetrable gloom of
> dirty shacks and dark corners; and on both sides, the
> breath of sudden, quick, raw, silent criminality. . . . I
> came to the house with the arc lamp. A large sign
> declared: 'Cinematografo para hombres solo'. The scene
> at its best! Before I went in, two local police at the door
> searched my pockets. It was like a scene out of a detec-
> tive yarn.
>
> The show was in progress. It was a large hall with a
> gallery running around the sides. A screen hung from
> the ceiling, on which the cinematographic theatre
> played out its scenes. . . . While stupid pricks chased
> each other around up there, women roamed among the
> guests. They were mostly Germans. The dregs of the
> world's brothels. . . .
>
> It was so stupid, so unbelievably dull and absurd,
> these idiotic, tired and insolent wenches and the pre-
> tend vices on the screen overhead, which were sup-
> posed to enflame the customers' passions. It was all so
> insane, so nonsensically perverse. Here is this modern
> technical device, lighting up the faces of men staring up
> out of the darkness, acting as a pacesetter for a cat
> house, by speeding up the nervous, excited procession
> to the rooms. Men and hookers disappeared noisily and
> quickly up the dark steps.[8]

It seems that in viewing pornographic films one has to overcome a certain kind of shyness. Which has nothing to do with the legal or moral condemnation of pornography, nor with the obvious reason for pornographic films being suited to the brothel. Even today, when pornographic films are shown in public theatres and no longer connected to the business of a brothel, a palpable sense of shame still attaches to the experience, which cannot be fully explained by the few remaining moral taboos. The same atmosphere of uneasiness and shame, excitement and repulsion is also revealed in historical documents encountered in more recent reports. Günter Kunert, for example, describes a visit to a porn house as follows:

Kino Rondell. Silent men in darkness. No women. No throat-clearing. No coughing. Not even the proverbial pin drop could be heard. A gathering of the living dead, so it seems, sitting on folding chairs, always two at a table, whose greasy top has a list of drinks lit up from underneath, and a call bell. . . .

A trailer for next week's feature is playing: a fat, ageing 'Herr Robert', whose voice lags behind the picture, snaps his fingers out of sync, followed by quick cuts of more or less (mostly more) naked girls parading across the screen in more or less (mostly less) seductive poses, displaying out-of-proportion bodies and faces radiating an aura of stupidity.

Now a brandy! No one orders. No one smokes. No one breathes louder or heavier. In front of the rows of seats the celluloid nymphs twist and turn and seem more alive than the live audience, which, later, after the feature – a Danish production on the complexities and peculiarities of sex – leaves the Kino Rondell as silently as they had occupied it: without a laugh, without audible approval or disapproval.

A kind of erotic phantom fades away quickly and quietly, condemned to take on corporeal existence once again, when the bell sounds for the next performance.[9]

If the porn cinema clientele is made up of human beings who act like zombies, voyeuristic pleasure in these cinemas clearly must have something in common with the secrecy of the peeping tom. The voyeur likes to look, but doesn't like to be seen. Displeasure in the porn house apparently results from the displeasure in being seen while looking. Where the connection between 'cinema and brothel' still exists, and a 'modern technical device' acts as a 'pace-setter' for cat houses, then this displeasure and this shame in erotic relations will be channelled into 'healthy and hearty pleasure'. Pornographic films fulfil this function still, not only as a kind of G-rated masturbatory cinema, but also in brothels and prostitution. Along with this type, however, another type of pornographic film has developed which has no other intention, no other purpose than that of satisfying voyeuristic desire. In these films, the specialised sense of sight, regarded in the other type of pornographic cinema as fulfilling a subordinate function in foreplay, asserts its autonomy as isolated, unadulterated voyeuristic pleasure.

Only by assuming such a specialised mode of viewing can we explain the tremendous success of public pornographic movie houses, in spite of the displeasure they inflict on the zombie-like voyeur. The language of our age of visual culture, in which the active subjugating eye wins out over the passive receptive sense organs, such as the ears, finds an apt metaphor in the recent divorce of cinema from brothel, pornography from prostitution. Since the workplace has long since demanded nothing more of the body than keeping a watchful eye on the control board, perhaps the private peep-show booth will soon offer the porn theatre visitor a serviceable leisure-time retreat. It may be that over the history of pornographic cinema the films themselves have not changed so much as the organisation of the senses. It may be that films' effects are more directly related to the social environments in which the films are presented than to the films' form and content. In other words, the audience's sexual orientation defines the way the product is consumed.

Although it is not certain whether pornographic films for heterosexuals are, aesthetically speaking, better or worse than those for homosexuals, they obviously encompass different modes of reception and consumption. Kurt Tucholsky described audience response in the days when the business of heterosexual pornography was still linked to prostitution: 'Shouts, encouragements, grunts, applause, and rooting cheers rang out. Somebody compares his own private ecstasy. There was a lot of noise and yelling.'[10]

Brendan Gill rediscovered a similar scene in a New York porn theatre in the 1970s: 'A large portion of the audience at both heterosexual and homosexual blue movies is Oriental. Unlike white males, Oriental males come into the theatre by two's and three's and talk and laugh freely throughout the course of the program.'[11] Gill also describes a connection between gay porn theatres and erotic practice that is hardly ever encountered in public heterosexual porn houses:

> For the homosexual, it is the accepted thing that the theatre is there to be cruised in; this is one of the advantages he has purchased with his expensive ticket of admission. . . . Far from sitting slumped motionless in one's chair, one moves about at will, sizing up possibilities. Often there will be found standing at the back of the theatre two or three young men, any of whom, for a fee, will accompany one to seats well down front and there practise upon one the same arts that are being practised upon others on the screen.[12]

We also see that in the course of time, settings, stereotypes and characters change even in pornographic cinema in order to conform to newer fashions, especially about what is considered sexy. Early pornography, for example, attempted to please its well-to-do clientele by presenting erotic scenes involving servant girls and masters, thus capturing an everyday erotic fantasy, while in more recent pornographic films these roles give way to other trades. Newer films produced for public screening and sale also differ from older ones in that they follow the letter of the law more strictly; they avoid showing certain erotic activities that *were* shown earlier, since the early films were illegal anyway. According to Curt Moreck's description of pornographic films of the 20s and earlier, individual films could be distinguished according to country of origin and target audience:

> Pornographic films reveal something about different erotic preferences in different countries. Thus French pornography presents excretory acts with striking frequency and indulges in lengthy depictions of preparatory manoeuvres, while the sex act itself often doesn't occur at all or is shifted behind the scenes. England, which produces such films mainly for South Africa and India, favours flagellation scenes and sadistic abuse of blacks. . . . Italy, whose southern location already overlaps into the zone of 'Oriental' sexuality, cultivates the depiction of acts of sodomy as a speciality, while scenes of sexual union between humans and animals and

scenes of animals mating are also popular. It has been said that Germans sin without grace. German pornographic films lend some credence to that assumption. Without exception they show well-executed, realistic scenes of coitus. On the other hand, erotic scenes with animals are totally absent. Now and again something kinky is thrown in to broaden their appeal.[13]

Apparently, early pornographic films were also divided into those with quasi-realistic settings – thus bearing some relation to the customer's everyday life – and those set in a world of fantasy or using stock settings associated with forbidden sexuality or foreign exoticism. The 'realistic' films depicted masters and servants in bourgeois surroundings – the home of an officer, for instance. The escapist ones were acted out in harems, cloisters, and so forth. This dichotomy apparently still holds true: consider, on the one hand, the 'Housewife Reports' (pornographic serials about housewife affairs with the postman, gasman, etc.) and, on the other, racist excursions into exotic domains – Thailand in *Emmanuelle*, for example.

The blue movie genre has meanwhile obviously become more professional, unintentional comic relief and unbelievable plots having given way to a routinely crafted product. Cinematography has become more skilful and the overall construction more sophisticated, with cutting for suspense and other formal procedures turning straightforward illustrations into cinematic images. Even if we assume that some ironic observations were employed by historical commentators as defence mechanisms against their own shame and excitement, we still come to the conclusion that early porn films were awkward and amateurish, made with little thought to achieving cinematic effect:

> Now came *Scenes in a Harem*. The wallpaper in the empty room, along with the carpet and curtains, suggested that the location was a red-light district, like Schlesisches Tor in Berlin. Fatima danced. The depraved girl took off her extravagant lingerie and danced – that is, she turned around casually by herself while everyone admired her. She danced in front of her sultan, who was lolling about listlessly in other harem girls' laps. He was a bon vivant. The women fanned him with large Japanese paper fans, and on a table in front of them stood a glass of *Weissbier*. . . .

Secrets of the Cloister and *Anna's Sideline* came on next. Two 'perverse beauties' rolled around on a carpet. One of them, I found out, was a certain Emmy Raschke, who laughed continuously, probably because she thought the whole thing a bit funny. Well, they were all there, cool and very businesslike, to act out (if the audience is any guide) the most exquisite things, while the cameraman yells directions at them. . . .

The Captain's Wife was playing upstairs. It was pornography come to life. While the worthy officer cheated on his wife with the lieutenant's wife, the captain's wife made good use of the time with her husband's orderly. They are caught in the act, and it leads to blows. Say what you like, the film was true to life, even though the life of French soldiers does seem a little strange: things happen so fast. In any case, there were two or three moments where the actors played their roles to the hilt.[14]

Here, Tucholsky describes the kind of porn films that abstain from so-called perversions and limit themselves to that which Curt Moreck called typical for German blue movies: 'well-executed, realistic scenes of coitus' and 'sin without grace'.[15]

Comic moments, described by Tucholsky as unintentional, occur often in the genre. We cannot assume that these comic aspects of old porn movies are merely an effect of historical distance. Even today, many sex films function as farce, with dirty jokes, and witty commentary. So too, in popular older films, comic moments played a significant role:

The comic element naturally plays an important role in pornographic films, since most people have a humorous attitude toward certain sexual practices rather than a serious or even pathetic one. Films make use of this fact by showing people in sticky situations, interrupted or embarrassed while tending to bodily needs, or getting caught in awkward positions through some droll mishap while having sexual relations.[16]

A 'humorous attitude toward certain sexual practices' probably arises out of sexual repression and anxiety; laughter and nervous giggling are often indications that a taboo has been violated. It seems as if the persistence of comedy as a pornographic form has to do with the pleasure of looking, with voyeurism itself: we laugh at the secret exposure of others. This can also be seen in the fact that TV producers and viewers concur in considering as 'comedy' shows, such as *Candid Camera*, which involve watching people with hidden cameras.

THE KNOWING LOOK AND THE PLEASURE OF LOOKING: ON THE AUTONOMY OF THE SENSES

What is new in pornographic cinema is obviously its existence as a voyeuristic amusement park. It promises nothing more or less than it advertises: the pleasure in looking, erotic activity without social contact. This new pornographic cinema is found not only in the large industrial metropolises but also in small towns and in the daily programmes of staid resorts. Those who, with good and honourable intentions, reproach blue movies for deceiving the poor consumer – instead of delivering the genuine product, 'real' sex, these films palm off on him a phony substitute – are missing the point. Such critics assume the primacy of genital pleasure over that which arises out of the 'component instincts', one of which is voyeurism, visual sensuality, *Schaulust*.

The consumer who buys his ticket at the door doesn't expect and probably doesn't even want to experience sexual gratification with another person. Like Mr Chance in Hal Ashby's film comedy *Being There* (1980), the porn movie patron is 'just looking'. Criticism of pornography thus misses the mark when it assumes that the customer has been cheated because he expects and pays for something he doesn't get. Customer fraud would hardly explain the success of pornographic movies. While having improved on their heavy-handed and awkward predecessors, the quality of today's porn films explains this success even less, since these films do not begin to come up to the formal standards of other genres. Recent attempts to have porn 'taken seriously' by enhancing the genre with stars, festivals and directors should probably be seen not so much as a gimmick to attract a wider audience as an effort by an association of craftsmen to gain credibility. Meanwhile, even apart from the hype, the porn film trend keeps on growing. The bids for credibility may help overcome the last bastions of resistance to pornographic films, but they won't do much for box office.

In my view this trend toward pornographic movies involves a more far-reaching development in society's organisation of our senses. Porn houses are not the motor but the chassis. An explanation for the growth of pornographic cinema can be found in its function within prevailing sexual organisation. Walter Serner, overwhelmed by this new invention of cinema, already proposed such an idea in *Die Schaubühne* in 1913:

> All the likely reasons somehow don't add up to an explanation of the movies' unprecedented success everywhere one looks. The reason must lie deeper than we think. And if we look into those strange flickering eyes to find out why people spend their last penny to go to the movies, they take us way back into the history of humankind. There we find, writ large: *Schaulust*. It is not merely harmless fascination with moving images and colour, but a terrifying lust, as powerful and violent as the deepest passions. It's the kind of rush that makes the blood boil and the head spin until that baffling potent excitement, common to every passion, races through the flesh. . . .
>
> This ghastly pleasure in seeing atrocities, violence and death lies dormant in us all. It is this kind of pleasure which brings us, hurrying to the morgue, to the scene of the crime, to every chase, to every street fight, and makes us pay good money for a glimpse of sodomy. And this is what draws the masses into the cinemas as if they were possessed. Cinema offers the masses the kind of pleasure which, day by day, is eroded by the advance of civilisation. And neither the magic of the stage nor the tired thrills of a circus, music hall or cabaret can attempt to replace it. In cinema, the masses reclaim, in all its former glory, the sensuousness of looking: *Schaulust*.[17]

Serner prophetically anticipates that cinema's appeal lies in a Nero-like diversion: being able to participate from the bleachers in the atrocities of an epoch. Acknowledgment of this aspect of the pairing within popular culture of 'sex and violence', as the critics call it, has been suppressed. While societies have long permitted the depiction of brutal violence, hatred, war, crime, destruction and death, this has not applied to the presentation of naked bodies and sexuality. It is no wonder that, with the relaxing of sexual taboos, cinema has now seized upon sexuality as a voyeuristic object. Up to now you could see just about every possible way of killing a person. Now we can also see 99, or 150, or 'x' ways of making love. *Schaulust*, which Serner describes as a violent, volatile passion, and to which he ascribes an ultimately corruptive influence, is itself neither outcome nor origin.

Rather it arose and took shape on its own out of the processes involved in the establishment of a highly rationalised and thoroughly organised society. The success of the porn house in its present form is the expression of this cultural-historical development rather than of a primal passion:

> The eye is an organ constantly under stress, working, concentrating, always unequivocally interpreting. The ear, on the other hand, is more diffuse and passive. Unlike an eye, you don't have to open it first.[18]
>
> The eye has adapted to bourgeois rationality and ultimately to a highly industrialised order by accustoming itself to interpreting reality, a priori, as a world of objects, basically as a world of commodities; the ear has achieved nothing similar.[19]
>
> Such a division of labour between the various receptive faculties of human beings, a specialisation of the senses, was necessary for a particular stage of capitalist production, the same stage of the production process that is singled out by 'Taylorism'.[20]

In the age of Taylorism, a dramatic rise in the dissemination of pornography was observed in Victorian England. It remains to be demonstrated that this sudden interest is strictly the result of the notoriously repressive Victorian society, that is, that it was conceived as an outlet for dammed-up passions. Rather, the dissemination of pornography is connected to specific social aspects of modernisation, as well as to parallel changes in the perceptual apparatus and intrapsychic mechanisms. In a certain respect pornographic cinema is both the symptom of this development and its expression. Training the eye means adapting the sense of sight to strategies of rationalisation and modernisation. An expansion of voyeurism at the level of the organisation of the drives corresponds to this social/perceptual development, thereby bringing sexuality in line with it.

The connection between power, control and sexuality can only be made through changes in sexuality itself. Pornography may be one of those sieves through which power seeps into the inner regions of sexuality while sexuality flows out and becomes a part of this power. Michel Foucault analyses the intermeshing of power and sex in the first volume of *The History of Sexuality*, without, however, viewing the matter in terms of a simple oppressor/victim relationship of repression:

This implantation of multiple perversions is not a mockery of sexuality taking revenge on a power that has thrust on it an excessively repressive law. Neither are we dealing with paradoxical forms of pleasure that turn back on power and invest it in the form of a 'pleasure to be endured'. The implantation of perversions is an instrument-effect: it is through the isolation, intensification, and consolidation of peripheral sexualities that the relations of power to sex and pleasure branched out and multiplied, measured the body, and penetrated modes of conduct. And accompanying this encroachment of powers, scattered sexualities rigidified, became stuck to an age, a place, a type of practice. A proliferation of sexualities through the extension of power; an optimisation of the power to which each of these local sexualities gave a surface of intervention: this concatenation, particularly since the nineteenth century, has been ensured and relayed by the countless economic interests which, with the help of medicine, psychiatry, prostitution, and pornography, have tapped into both this analytical multiplication of pleasure and this optimisation of the power that controls it. Pleasure and power do not cancel or turn back against one another; they seek out, overlap, and reinforce one another. They are linked together by complex mechanisms and devices of excitation and incitement.[21]

The history of sexuality, according to Foucault, is inscribed in the 'will to knowledge', meaning power. Pornography thus becomes nothing other than the 'will to knowledge' – the night school for sex education – where, by means of voyeurism's cognitive urge, the discourse of power is begun. In fact, some studies of the social history of pornography offer evidence that these films were only too happy to be thought of as a contribution to research on sexuality and its various forms. Then came the recent wave of porn films whose opening credits declared their intention to offer practical advice for living, to be purveyors of knowledge. Examples of these are the Oswald Kolle series, or *Helga*. The classification of formal knowledge by category still attaches to an unending series of 'Film Reports', often presenting sexual behaviour according to various occupations. Even early porn films displayed a lexicographic tendency, as an eyewitness noticed:

A special flavour is given to obscene films through the scrupulously realistic presentation of every imaginable

perversion. Although life itself very often offers the connoisseur a view of simple vice, the chance to enjoy real perversity as a spectator is much rarer; in this case, film tries to fill the void. There are some films in this genre which seem to have been staged directly from Krafft-Ebing's *Psychopathia Sexualis*, as a manual of abnormal sexual operations for civilised man.[22]

All the vices of man flickered by on the screen. Every one of the hundred and fifty ways from the old *Treatise on the Hundred and Fifty Ways of Loving* was demonstrated, with occasional interruptions for lesbian, pederast, and masturbation jokes. All that was harmless. Sadists and masochists waved their instruments, sodomy was practised, coprophagous acts were on display. Nothing was held back, everything occurred in a banal reality, all the more infuriating for its technical crudity.[23]

The 'will to knowledge' activates the eye, which in turn casts its gaze upon sexuality – *Schaulust* as an instrument of cognition, cognition as *Schaulust*: pornography discovers its social role. Psychoanalytic theory established the notion of a relationship between curiosity, cognitive activity and voyeurism in the developmental history of the individual even before pornography revealed this connection by becoming a typical product of our society. The optical organisation of reality implies control, from the vigilant eye of the hunter to 'the great eye of the government' (Foucault). Jean-Paul Sartre notes in *Being and Nothingness*:

In addition the idea of discovery, of revelation, includes an idea of appropriative enjoyment. What is seen is possessed; to see is to *deflower*. . . . More than this, knowledge is a hunt. Bacon called it the hunt of Pan. The scientist is the hunter who surprises a white nudity and who violates by looking at it. Thus the totality of these images reveals something which we will call the *Actaeon-complex* . . . : a person hunts for the sake of eating. Curiosity in an animal is always either sexual or alimentary. To know is to devour with the eyes.[24]

Let us assume the correctness of Foucault's thesis that the history of sexuality is based on a will to knowledge and concede that pornography is a conduit for this transmission of sex and power. If, in addition, we consider another point made by Sartre, we might be able to explain why pornographic cinema today is a medium for conveying knowledge (in Foucault's sense) rather than a medium for aesthetic experience. Sartre assumes a difference between art and cognition that is based on their different relationships to appropriation. Works of art resist appropriation: 'The work of art is like a fixed emanation of the mind. The mind is continually creating it and yet it stands alone and indifferent in relation to that creation.'[25] Cognition, on the other hand, is constituted as an act of appropriation, thus incorporating the object of cognition and assimilating it: 'Knowledge is at one and the same time a *penetration* and a *superficial* caress, a digestion and the contemplation from afar of an object which will never lose its form.'[26]

Sartre analyses cognition as assimilation, whose end is reached when desire destroys its object, rather than preserving it through appropriation – you can't have your cake and eat it too! It seems to me that Sartre's analysis of cognition as penetration and as detached observation also characterises the appropriation process in pornographic films. If the viewer allows himself to be carried away by the desire to possess – thus relinquishing the position of a detached observer – he must sacrifice his *Schaulust* in order to take in a specific moment or image; in the meantime, subsequent images and sensations have already appeared on the screen. Thus the viewer is caught between two modes of appropriating: perception and cognition. It is like Buridan's hungry ass of old caught between two tasty piles of hay:

> When I look at a porn magazine, I don't care about the way the scene is visualised, even if the men and women are ugly or something else isn't quite right. In my fantasy they exist in a way that excites me. Besides, it's up to me which picture I choose to look at, and I can always turn the page or go back to a certain picture... . The viewer of a porn film always remains alienated from the situation he's observing, because he has to keep his clothes on and can't touch, even though the pictures arouse him. He becomes confused.[27]

This description of a user experience points to the key difference between the two pornographic mediums and raises the question: why, despite such a frustrating situation, have so many people developed a distinct preference for pornographic movies? Perhaps

the reaction of the regular viewer of porn films is not one of confusion at all; maybe the person like Mr Chance, who only wants to look is quite common. It is possible that inside the porn theatre desire actually becomes transformed into the fetishism of the aficionado, who only needs to know what is available, then sits back down to watch – the ultimate triumph of the eye over the body.

This theoretical notion seems to be supported by the evidence of amateur pornographic films, like those that Robert van Ackern includes with other kinds of home movies in his scathing compilation film *Germany in Private* (1980). The films, though formally far inferior to commercial porn films, nevertheless draw on them for their fantasies. Pornographic ideas and *mise en scène* are recorded by a Super-8 camera in a totally naturalistic fashion; in fact, in contrast to more polished professional porn, one has the distinct impression that the events are taking place only for the sake of the camera. An agitated woman sprawls out on a kidney-shaped coffee table in a living room; another models sexy underwear. Pleasure in the actions themselves seems minimal; the liveliest thing about these bodies is their lascivious gaze into the camera. The recording camera creates the show. It's like Mr Chance thinking he can turn off unpleasant reality with a flick of his TV remote control. Once again the assimilation of filmed pornographic fantasies becomes alienated from erotic practice. What is assimilated is not the sexuality that is represented but the representation of sexuality. Pornographic movies beget pornographic movies.

THE REALM OF THE PORNOGRAPHIC FILM: SHADOWS, SHOCK, SCARCITY, AND PLENTY

In the beginning of this essay I discussed the ways in which liberalisation through penal code reforms led, in most Western countries, to the emergence of a varied system of pornographic cinemas. This development was understood as the result of the permeation of sexuality by social power. It was also suggested that in pornographic cinema instrumental reason tailors sensuality to its own measure. The image of the human being in pornographic films is one of the body as a mechanism for experiencing and maximising pleasure, and of the person as monad – as defined by bourgeois ideology in its strictest sense

– as one whose actions are guided by self-interest, specifically, in experiencing as much pleasure as possible.

The perpetual motion of desire is choreographed for us in pornographic cinema, and is constituted out of its arsenal. Everything becomes an instrument for sensual pleasure: the body, a hair brush, a dildo, a banana. Every situation leads to sex: a flat tyre, the beach, the carwash, or an office party. Bodies are linked with one another according to mathematical equations; orgies are conducted like a game of dominoes. What Horkheimer and Adorno have to say about Sade also applies to porn movies.

> What Kant grounded transcendentally, the affinity of knowledge and planning, which impressed the stamp of inescapable expediency on every aspect of a bourgeois existence that was wholly rationalised, even in every breathing-space, Sade realised empirically more than a century before sport was conceived. The teams of modern sport whose interaction is so precisely regulated that no member has any doubt about his role, and which provide a reserve for every player, have their exact counterpart in the sexual teams of *Juliette*, which employ every moment usefully, neglect no human orifice, and carry out every function.[28]

In fact, newer pornographic films demonstrate significant advances, especially in the area of gymnastic-artistic formations. Technique has evolved from presentations of 'perverse beauties rolling around on a carpet' to orgies of group sex that demonstrate athletic control of the body along with simultaneous sexual feats. The aesthetic of the pornographic film relies on an underlying metaphor of the body as a machine: editing makes it possible to replace tired bodies with fresh ones, or with those that have been replenished in the interim. Or else in a pinch, when nothing more can be exhorted from these sexual athletes, editing can be used to create movement artificially. The performers' interchangeability and anonymity function as a material correlative to the ideology they express. There's no longer room for the old-fashioned clumsiness of a giggling Emmy Raschke. Now we have high performance professionals who, in the manner of Taylorisation, contribute specialised physical skills to the completion of the final product. Meanwhile, maintenance crews with spare parts stand ready to take care of breakdowns. These production manoeuvres are of no interest to the viewer, who pays as little notice to the rapid relay of aroused penises, wide-open mouths, spread thighs, and drawn labia as he or she does when the female performer changes wigs – from a blonde equestrienne to a red-headed lesbian.

The most sophisticated porn films are structured in such a way that the keyhole perspective of the voyeur is built right into the film. This device allows for several 'numbers' at the same time, shown through parallel editing, and helps counteract the fatigue that invariably sets in when an entire coition is presented without interruption in a single take. The latter usually gives the impression of being hard work rather than pleasure. Pornographic cinema emerges at the end of a developmental process in a society of specialisation and differentiation. Pornography itself contributes to this specialisation by promoting the autonomy of *Schaulust*. The differentiation of pornography as a product parallels developments in society, as producers speculate on the consumer's current and projected needs and taboos. Male homosexuality doesn't turn up in a heterosexual porn house and vice versa, anal eroticism only takes place between men and women, and the only way a man comes close to another man is when a woman, who lies between them, is entered both vaginally and anally. Lesbian sex does not appear either; when women caress each other, it is only because they are waiting for a man or performing for a male voyeur.

But criticism of pornography is still clearly ill at ease with its newer forms, especially its filmic forms. Despite the routine way in which the socialisation of sexuality is pursued, some quality still clings to pornographic cinema which places it into the category that Siegfried Kracauer called 'phenomena overwhelming consciousness':

> Elemental catastrophes, the atrocities of war, acts of violence and terror, sexual debauchery, and death are events which tend to overwhelm consciousness. In any case they call forth excitements and agonies bound to thwart detached observation. No one witnessing such an event, let alone playing an active part in it, should therefore be expected accurately to account for what he has seen. Since these manifestations of crude nature, human or otherwise, fall into the area of physical reality,

they comprise all the more cinematic subjects. Only the camera is able to represent them without distortion. . . .

The cinema, then, aims at transforming the agitated witness into a conscious observer. Nothing could be more legitimate than its lack of inhibitions in picturing spectacles which upset the mind. Thus it keeps us from shutting our eyes to the 'blind drive of things'.[29]

Kracauer suggests that only through the alienation of the image is it possible to imagine a reconciliation with objects and their recuperation from mere functionalism. The one-dimensionality of the optical appropriation of the world is mirrored in the flat screen of pornographic cinema, and somehow makes it even more scintillating and enticing than any ideological criticism – no matter how well-intentioned or well-founded – has been able to account for.

One must learn to read between the lines of gaping flesh and labia, as if these constituted a code of prohibition and denial. . . . But the whole iconography of unlived life, of anti-eroticism in capitalist systems, is only revealed to the person who remains sensitive to pornography's debasement, dirtiness, vulgarity and brutality, who has seen its leering grin.[30]

Those who, like Peter Gorsen in the above quotation, learn to read pornographic films against the grain will find not only a 'code of prohibition and denial' – in the sense that the cinema supplies what reality denies. They will also recognise the wounds that the 'code of prohibition and denial' have inflicted on desire itself – wounds that are not external to but within the iconographic system, a system that expresses rather than represses. Even with the machine-like availability and interchangeability of bodies in pornographic films, their crude naturalism harbours a wish for a realm beyond renunciation where milk and honey flow. In his study of sexuality and pornography in Victorian England, Steven Marcus traces the historical context of the era's imagery to its economy:

The fantasies that are at work here have to do with economics; the body is regarded as a productive system with only a limited amount of material at its disposal. And the model on which this notion of semen is formed is clearly that of money. . . .

Furthermore, the economy envisaged in this idea is based on scarcity and has as its aim the accumulation of its own product. And the fantasy of pornography, as we shall have ample opportunity to observe, is this idea's complement, for the world of pornography is a world of plenty. In it all men are limitlessly endowed with that universal fluid currency which can be spent without loss. Just as in the myth Zeus descends upon Danae in a shower of gold, so in pornography the world is bathed, floated, flooded, inundated in this magical produce of the body.[31]

The Victorian pornographic fantasy of abundance complemented real poverty in the external world. The wealth that pornographic cinema commands today had yet to be amassed. Thus, now, the endless flow of semen, the bodies of women doused in sperm, allude to one particular scarcity: that of the body itself. Pornographic fantasy invariably refers us back to the world of machines, of interlocking systems and cogs, in which everyone, ultimately, is caught up. But the fantasy alludes, above all, to the subjugation of the body, which suffers from want in the midst of material plenty.

Today pornographic film no longer refers to meanings lying outside its own subject matter; it refers primarily to itself by relying on what can be seen on the screen: bodies and their passions. Now we must reconsider the problem of voyeurism addressed above and pose the question: What is it that is seen? What aspects of sexuality can be visualised? I will attempt to answer this question in the next section, which deals with the iconography of the visible (the phallus) and the invisible (the vagina) in gender-specific pornographic imagery. But first I want to examine further that distance between observer and observed which, according to Kracauer, is created by the camera.

Kracauer believes distance is necessary to lessen the shock that would result from the spectator's direct confrontation with certain phenomena. Pornography obviously plays off a certain fear of crudity, coarseness, and undisguised, unsublimated sexuality. Only through the image can the observer confront that which would otherwise frighten him or her. The same process occurs within the individual in the dream-work. In the case of pornographic cinema, the camera becomes a device for creating distance and the medium of a harmless voyeurism:

Like a camera, I observe but am not involved. In a narrow place in a dark cave I look through the camera and film a scene. I see a huge scorpion, while somebody outside tries to kill it. It's four or five feet long. The guy outside uses his hands and feet to throw sand into the cave, moving it fast, back and forth – so sexual. He hurls a cold, poisoned lobster's tail as bait, so the scorpion won't bite him. Jesus, what a dream! I filmed the battle between these two jokers. It's dangerous and disturbing.[32]

This dream, as related by a patient to his psychoanalyst, provides a good description of the discharge mechanism inherent in this camera-voyeurism. The dream is interpreted by the psychoanalyst as fear of sexuality. (The camera played a role not only in the dreams of this patient, but also in his actual sexual life. He made slides from photos that he took of his girlfriend during their sex games.) Parallels with the procedures of pornographic voyeurism can thus be found at the level of individual psychology. Such everyday examples demonstrate just how deeply embedded are these organisational forms of the perceptual apparatus. Thus the idea of a bad 'influence' originating in the simple content of pornographic cinema – an idea often used by political conservatives as an argument for censorship – is not a viable one.[33]

Looking, as a form of sexual curiosity that probes an undiscovered sexuality, requires distance in order to mitigate the fear of the unknown – the Kracauerian shock. Some literary works employ shadow metaphors to create the necessary distance between observer and observed. The following example from literature demonstrates, from a different perspective, the same need for distance in sexual looking that we see in pornographic cinema:

The shadow of the housekeeper's legs, as she lay with her back on the table, rose up with bent knees over the coachman's creeping shadow, and the shadow of the coachman, resting on his knees, rose above the shadow of the housekeeper's stomach. The shadow of the coachman's hands reached under the shadow of the housekeeper's skirts, the shadow of the skirt slipped down and the shadow of the coachman's abdomen burrowed into the shadow of the housekeeper's exposed thighs. The shadow of the coachman's arm dug into the shadow of his crotch and pulled out a polelike shadow, which in its shape and position matched his tool; he

thrust this protruding shadow into the big well-rounded shadow of the housekeeper's belly after the shadow of the housekeeper's legs had raised themselves above the shadow of the coachman's shoulders.[34]

The schematic, the stereotypical, the elaboration of persons and identities through the movements of their bodies – thus does Peter Weiss capture the voyeuristic experience in a literary form in which the action dissolves into endless genitives. As a characteristic of pornographic film, the voyeuristic experience is presented at face value and is not problematised. The transformation of persons into patterns which comport themselves according to a preconceived design refers even in pornographic cinema to the longing for a sexual life that is not predicated on the identity of 'mature personality' and 'genital sex':

One experiences a glimpse of sexual utopia when one doesn't have to be oneself, and when one doesn't merely love one's lover for herself: it is the negation of the ego principle. It undermines that invariable aspect of bourgeois society, in its broadest sense, which defines identity as integration. . . .

The advancing social reinforcement of genitality brings about greater repression of the component instincts, as well as their representative forms in genital relations. What remains of those instincts is cultivated only in the socialised voyeurism of foreplay. Voyeurism exchanges union with one person for observation of all, and thus expresses sexuality's tendency to socialisation, which is itself an aspect of sexuality's deadly integration.[35]

The constant change of locations encompassed in the domain of the porn movie, the make-up and costumes that are the trappings of anonymous passion, are perhaps the last traces of a search for non-identity in sex. The appearance in a porn movie of a proletarian captain of a steamer on the Elbe promises a two-fisted ingredient in *Firm Grip*. In *The Duchess of Porn* a black evening gown offers a touch of French decadence; and *Convent Girls* hints at sado-masochistic flagellation orgies in hair shirts. The component instincts conceal their desires in the secret code of the films' settings, desires obscured in the films themselves by the hearty gymnastic primacy of genital sex.

THE SECRET OF THE MISSING PHALLUS AND WOMAN'S OTHER PLACE

Criticism of pornographic cinema, originally levelled by conservatives on moral grounds, is now exercised, after widespread easing of controls and liberalisation, primarily in feminist political action and analysis. But the feminist critique of pornographic film is fundamentally distinguished from that of conservative moralists in its intent. Feminists see in pornographic cinema not the erosion of existing norms but rather their expression and confirmation. Pornographic cinema reduces sexuality to the measure of a male perspective, one grounded in patriarchal myths about female sexuality and the phallus. In short, pornographic cinema is sexist. Feminists argue that sexism prevents the emancipation of sexuality, an emancipation that would liberate women's sexual fantasies and prepare the way for a well-deserved end to a phallocentric primacy in the prevailing sexual order. The intent of these arguments is, therefore, not a conservative preservation of existing values but revolutionary change. The arguments arise out of the strategies of the women's sexual and political liberation movement.

The disturbing state of sexuality today makes it difficult to object to the goals of feminist criticisms of pornographic film. One can, however, object to arguments that posit a direct connection between viewing pornographic films and engaging in certain sexual acts, the argument, for example, that whoever views sadistic porn movies sees in them a possible way of behaving and an invitation to rape and sadistically torture women; or that whoever sees phallic fantasies of omnipotence endorsed on the screen will hardly be prepared to act differently in reality. It has never been proven that filmed events have a direct effect on human behaviour. It is my conviction that we can only conceive of such a connection in a broad, collective sense, not as a direct relationship as defined by behavioural psychology. In contrast to the above argument, I assume that pornography is less an expression of prevailing male sexual *practice* than an expression of its deficiency, the rehabilitation of damaged fantasies. Although legislative and executive regulation and prosecution are no longer widespread, the subculture of pornographic movies still maintains an aura of the secret and forbidden, the sensational and the never-before-seen; it is therefore promoted

not as something ordinary or potentially ordinary, but as something 'extraordinary'. A porn house in London displayed the following notice in front of the theatre: 'WARNING: This cinema is showing pornographic films depicting close-ups of sexual intercourse, oral sex, and male and female masturbation and is not for the easily shocked.'[36]

The shock, the sense of alarm used here as a promotion, recalls Kracauer's 'phenomena overwhelming consciousness'. This element of shock seems to be a constituent of voyeuristic pleasure in pornographic cinema. But what is it that is so terrible to see? Are sex organs and copulating couples really terrifying? Where does this terror that leads to fascination come from? Feminist arguments overlap with psychoanalytical ones in answering this question, because both proceed from the assumption of the primacy of male sexuality in pornographic films.

According to Freud's analysis, there is a close connection between *Schaulust* and fear of castration: a male child who sees a woman's sex organ for the first time in his life is amazed that no penis is attached. Disturbed by the fact than an object so important for him is missing from the female organ, he imagines a number of equally anxiety-laden possibilities: a) the female organ is the result of castration, or b) the woman is hiding her penis. The second possibility, 'b', is already a working through of the fears aroused by the possibility of 'a'. It is this aspect of the castration complex that gives rise to the persistent voyeuristic mania to look at the female organ, constantly and as closely as possible, in order to uncover the secret of the missing penis. The adult viewer of pornographic films seeks a confirmation of his childhood sexual theory – the phallic myth about the female organ. Because this mania is the result of the castration complex, seeing lots of penises confirms their durability and intactness; castration anxiety is also reduced by inducing the feeling of phallic omnipotence. The restless search for something that can't be found – the woman's penis – is compensated by an appeasing display of erections and potency. The endless merry-go-round of sex orgies, the reduction of a person to his or her sex organs, the mechanical, compulsive repetition in the action of pornographic films thus arise out of the male sexual organisation, rather than from a lack of imagination on the filmmaker's part. A secret rite conjures up a naked body at any moment and around every corner. The fantasy world of the adult is like the magical, archaic world of the child, where time and space are freed from the constraints of physical reality. It is as if, with a magic word, an ordinary place becomes a secret site of sexuality. The world of pornographic films builds pyramids of gymnasts on an archaic foundation: on a childhood sexual theory.

John Ellis has shown that in the voyeuristic realm of pornographic films the invisible female phallus must be transformed into a visible fetish, so that pleasure can overcome the fear of castration:

> The fetish offered by these representations is no longer a fragment of clothing, or even the deceptively smooth body of the phallic woman, it is now the woman's sexual pleasure. The woman nevertheless has the phallus in sexual pleasure; the woman's lack of a phallus is disavowed in her orgasm. . . . In orgasm woman no longer is the phallus, she has the phallus. Films currently produced within the pornographic sector gain their impulsion from the repetition of instances of female sexual pleasure, and male pleasure is perfunctory in most cases. The films (and photographs) are concerned with the *mise en scène* of the female organs; they constantly circle around it, trying to find it, to abolish the spectator's separation from it.[37]

The transformation of the empirical penis into a mythic, symbolic phallus, into a fetishistic image signifying the existence of female orgasm, also signifies the process of transformation whereby something invisible becomes visible in the fetish. It is true that many pornographic films give particular weight in their *mise en scène* to signifiers of female orgasm. But this raises another problem in the relationship of visible and invisible. For the place where the woman 'possesses' a phallus and is supposed to have the orgasm is no more visible than the phantom phallus the man seeks to find in her.

Because of the expressive poverty of its naturalistic style, pornographic film necessarily reaches its limit literally *ante portas*, before achieving its goal of seeing the secret place where woman's pleasure resides. Dennis Giles outlines this problem in a psychoanalytic essay on pornographic films:

> The interior space she encloses (identified as the woman *in essence*) is an *invisible place* . . . it cannot be possessed by visual knowledge. In order to emphasise its separation from the *known* space of the pornographic film, I call this central interior the Other place.[38]

The invisible, other place, affirmed by pornographic films without showing it, can be made visible through pornographic language. Steven Marcus impressively affirms it in a description of the female body as a landscape, rendered in a Max Weberian construction of an ideal-typical 'Pornotopia':

> Farther down, the scene narrows and changes in perspective. Off to the right and left just two smooth snowy ridges. Between them, at their point of juncture, is a dark wood – we are now at the middle of our journey. This dark wood – sometimes it is called a thicket – is triangular in shape. It is also like a cedar cover, and in its midst is a dark romantic chasm. In this chasm the wonders of nature abound. From its top there descends a large, pink stalactite, which changes in shape, size and colour in accord with the movement of the tides within. Within the chasm – which is roughly pear-shaped – there are caverns measureless to man, grottoes, hermits' caves, underground streams – a whole internal and subterranean landscape. The climate is warm but wet. Thunderstorms are frequent in this region, as are tremors and quakings of the earth. The walls of the cavern often heave and contract in rhythmic violence, and when they do the salty streams that run through it double their flow. The whole place is dark yet visible. This is the centre of the earth and the home of man.[39]

In film this literary, utopian other place remains invisible. Woman's pleasure is not only signified, it is also simulated by external signs; only the penis is visible in pornographic films, and it must bear the burden of proof. We hardly ever see a coition that doesn't end with a penis ejaculating on a woman. The abundance of sperm once again becomes a sign of inadequacy, an inadequacy of representation. Still, the sight of an ejaculating penis seems to be pleasurable for the straight male viewer, because to him it is a sign of intactness, an assurance that the vagina, imagined as insatiable and dangerous, has once again yielded its victim, unscathed, to see the light of day. Another reason for the choice of a naturalistic style of depiction in pornographic films is that it confers perceptual certainty on the films' guarantee of 'uncastratedness'. This convention therefore sacrifices the woman's pleasure, since the actress has to simulate orgasm after the penis is no longer inside her.

The psychic codification of sexuality can thus be seen even in the naturalistic habits of pornographic films. Films are never transparent, pure images, they are always a symbolic structuring of that which is portrayed. Thus we can now extend the definition encountered above – pornographic cinema as an instrument of the 'will to knowledge' – to the intrapsychic level: pornographic cinema is the night school of the sexual theories of children. Even though, ultimately, any such definitions remain inadequate, an analysis that measures pornographic films with the yardstick of psychopathology and concludes they involve infantile, perverse male sexual fantasies is, in a clinical diagnostic sense, entirely correct. This argument offers the feminist critique of pornographic film its strongest support.

Yet psychopathological analyses, based exclusively on a reconstruction of the male sexual perspective, cannot explain the fact that, 'with disgusted and fascinated gaze',[40] and in spite of well-founded moral and critical indignation, women are fellow travellers on the road to 'Pornotopia'.[41]

The pleasure of looking, as an exploration of a strange sex as well as one's own, is certainly a pleasure common to both sexes. Likewise, it is not only male desire that is expressed in the longing to return to the womb and in narcissistic fusion and exchange fantasies. The idea of promiscuous abundance, which saturates the images of pornographic films, is present not only at the level of symbolic abstraction – in the sense that all those visible, concrete penises and vulvas represent only a single symbolic phallus. Although always bound within a symbolic, social discourse, film images never quite free themselves from the resistance offered by the concrete world of objects, which those images transfer to the world of symbols.[42] If all these genitalia and individual bodies symbolise a single meaning, it may be because they are experienced through the abstract, generalising mania of male perception – that is, only within the systematic context of the symbolic organisation of a phallocentric world. Nevertheless, they still also exist as images of particular things whose substantiality is also real and empirical, as the naturalistic style of pornographic film never tires of reminding us. It may

be that female perception is not actually integrated within a phallic discourse which can never be woman's own. It may be that women, through their own more concrete organisation, can undo the fantasy in order to move about outside the inscribed symbolic discourse.

Pornotopia would become a world of fragments, disclosing the gap between the sexes, something the phallus nervously denies. Pornotopia then becomes the empire of a phallic ruler, who is powerless against the woman's gaze at specific objects; it partitions his empire according to its own preferences. The woman's gaze at pornographic films, 'disgusted and fascinated', doesn't have to search for and find a phallus behind every penis. The fact that women react ambivalently to pornographic films, torn between fascination and disappointment, may not always be because of a prudish upbringing, which forbids an open view and leads to repulsion and a defensive attitude towards sexuality. It may still be possible for women, in spite of their criticism, to take a utopian view of Pornotopia. This may come to pass if they are able to recognise that utopian plenitude is not to be found in a phallocentric generalisation, but rather in the details of a quivering world of objects; and if, with their gaze, they manage to create, out of the shadow world, bodies of flesh and blood. Concrete criticism and reception of pornographic cinema, as demonstrated in interviews conducted with women by Marie-Françoise Hans and Gilles Lapouge,[43] indicate something more than merely women's insufficient understanding of the objective content of pornographic movies; the concrete approach also turns up a different kind of appropriation, one which is reflected in fragments. Even when women smash pornographic cinema into pieces, they bring more to light in these fragments than the whole can possibly offer: an alternative sexuality, which is as much a part of the radical feminist negative critique of pornographic movies as it is of the 'uncritical', appropriating gaze of its female patrons.

This article was initially published in *Lust und Elend: Das Erotische Kino* (Munich and Lucerne: C. J. Bucher, 1981), a collection of essays on erotic film. In the period between its writing and its English-language publication, the increasingly liberal attitudes towards pornography that the essay discusses have been reversed by the coming to power of conservatives in both Germany and the US. Moreover, the changes in pornography's production, distribution and reception brought about by the advent of the home video market also occurred during this intervening period.

Translated by Jan-Christoper Horak and Joyce Rheuban. Reprinted from *October* 50, Autumn 1989, pp. 3–29, by permission of the MIT Press, Cambridge, Massachusetts.

NOTES

1. Heinrich Fraenkel, *Unsterblicher Film. Die Grosse Chronik von der Laterna Magica bis zum Tonfilm* (Munich: Kindler, 1956), p. 380.
2. Ibid., p. 382.
3. Ibid., p. 385.
4. Ibid., p. 408.
5. Curt Moreck, *Sittengeschichte des Kinos* (Dresden: Paul Aretz, 1956), p. 173.
6. Ibid., p. 175. (The adjective *sotadic* derives from Sotades [323–247 BC] who wrote coarse satires and travesties of mythology in a peculiar metre which bears his name.)
7. Ibid., pp. 178–80.
8. Ibid., pp. 180–2.
9. Günter Kunert, *Ortsangaben* (Berlin [East]: 1970), pp. 123–4.
10. Moreck, *Sittengeschichte des Kinos*, p. 179.
11. Brendan Gill, 'Blue Notes', *Film Comment*, vol. 9 no. 1, 1973, p. 11.
12. Ibid.
13. Moreck, *Sittengeschichte des Kinos*, p. 183.
14. Ibid., pp. 178–9
15. Ibid., p. 183.
16. Ibid.
17. Walter Serner, 'Kino und Schaulust', *Die Schaubühne* 9, 1913. Quoted in Anton Kaes (ed.), *Kino-Debatte* (Munich: Deutscher Taschenbuch, 1978), pp. 53–4.
18. Theodor W. Adorno and Hanns Eisler, *Komposition für den Film* (Munich: Roger and Bernhard, 1969), p. 43.
19. Ibid., p. 41.
20. Oskar Negt and Alexander Kluge, *Öffentlichkeit und Erfahrung. Zur Organisationsanalyse von bürgerlicher und proletärischer Öffentlichkeit* (Frankfurt am Main: Suhrkamp, 1972), p. 237. Frederick Winslow Taylor developed a system of rationalising the work process, a conception which was widely adopted and applied to shape industrial design and management practices.
21. Michel Foucault, *The History of Sexuality*, trans. Robert Hurley (New York: Vintage Books, 1980), p. 48.
22. Moreck, *Sittengeschichte des Kinos*, p. 182.
23. Ibid., p. 181.
24. Jean-Paul Sartre, *Being and Nothingness. An Essay on Phenomenological Ontology* (New York: Philosophical Library, 1956), p. 578.
25. Ibid.
26. Ibid., pp. 579–80
27. Beate Klöckner, 'Hörst du mein heimliches Rufen? Die 'gute' und die 'böse' Lust', *Strandgut*, no. 26, March 1980, p. 17.
28. Max Horkheimer and Theodor W. Adorno, *Dialectic of Enlightenment* (New York: Continuum, 1987), p. 88.
29. Siegfried Kracauer, *Nature of Film* (London and New York: Oxford University Press, 1960), pp. 57–8.
30. Peter Gorsen, *Sexualästhetik. Zur bürgerlichen Rezeption von Obszönität und Pornographie* (Reinbek: Rowohlt, 1972), p. 104.
31. Steven Marcus, *The Other Victorians. A Study of Sexuality and Pornography in Mid-Nineteenth Century England* (London: Weidenfeld and Nicolson, 1966), p. 22.
32. Leon L. Altman, *Praxis der Traumdeutung* (Frankfurt am Main: Suhrkamp, 1981), p. 121.
33. In connection with these problems compare Volkmar Sigusch's summary of the *Pornography Report*, quoted in Gorsen, *Sexualästhetik*, pp. 108–10.
34. Peter Weiss, *Der Schatten des Körpers des Kutschers* (Frankfurt am Main: Suhrkamp, 1964), pp. 98–9.
35. Theodor W. Adorno, 'Sexualtabus und Recht heute', in *Eingriffe. Neun kritische Modelle* (Frankfurt am Main: Suhrkamp, 1963), pp. 104–5.
36. John Ellis, 'On Pornography', *Screen*, vol. 21 no. 1, Spring 1980, p. 103.
37. Ibid. Ellis's analysis takes its cue from Laura Mulvey's 'Visual Pleasure and Narrative Cinema'.
38. Dennis Giles, 'Pornographic Space: The Other Place', 'Film-Historical Theoretical Speculations', *The 1977 Film Studies Annual* (Pleasantville, N.Y.: Redgrave Publishing Company, 1977), Part II.
39. Marcus, *The Other Victorians*, pp. 274–5.
40. Marie-Françoise Hans and Gilles Lapouge, *Die Frauen – Pornographie und Erotik* (Neuwied: Luchterhand, 1979), p. 204.
41. If one strictly defines pornographic cinema as a medium oriented solely toward the depiction of male sexuality, then one still has to explain why women are

not necessarily turned off by such depictions. They
will hardly find an image of their own sexuality, unless
we accept Freud's assumption of penis envy, which
presupposes that the heterosexual, phallically oriented
female identifies with the penis and its pleasure. The
penis envy thesis, so vehemently opposed by feminist
theoreticians, will not be discussed further here,
although I'm inclined to accept its historical, if not its
universal, anthropological validity. It might be helpful
to look at Freud's assumption regarding a
constitutional bisexuality, which characterises not only
men but also women. In his late works Freud went so
far as to state that biological bisexuality might
contradict his penis envy theory. If we imagine that
the strict schism between male/female, phallus/vulva
is actually a relationship, whereby each sex
incorporates repressed elements of the other, then we
might have an explanation of why women can
discover at least a portion of themselves in
'Pornotopia'. Viewing a penis would then also imply a
degree of pleasure for women, and would thus not
only mean subjugation by phallic power or
identification with the oppressor. This would of
course mean that we women would have to free
ourselves from such constructs as 'evil', 'destructive',
and 'misogynist' perversions, while at the same time
attempting to study the utopian and anti-
establishment contents of these perversions before
clinically disqualifying them.

42. Compare Kracauer, *Nature of Film*, pp. 57–8.
Kracauer's essentialist film theory, based as it is on
phenomenology, is centrally concerned with the idea
of film as a redemption of physical reality, as found in
the 'flow of life'. Even if one doesn't agree with
Kracauer's philosophical precepts, one can hardly
disregard Kracauer's having defined one of the basic
tenets of film aesthetics: the preservation of the
physical representation of objects, which film captures
as a physical image, not an imaginary image as, for
example, painting might. According to Kracauer, film
is – and this definition seems to me to hold true for
pornography – 'the shimmering sky reflected in a
dirty puddle'.

43. See note 40. Compare Gertrud Koch, 'Von der
weiblichen Sinnlichkeit und ihrer Lust und Unlust
am Kino. Mutmassungen über vergangene Freuden
und neue Hoffnungen', in Gabriele Dietz (ed.), *Die
Überwindung der sprachlosigkeit* (Neuwied:
Luchterhand, 1979), pp. 116–38. (Koch's theoretical
essays on women's responses to film have been
published in English in *Jump Cut*. See 'Why Women
Go to the Movies' [no. 27] and 'Female Sensuality:
Past Joys and Future Hopes' [no. 30].)

14   Second Thoughts on *Hard Core*:
American Obscenity Law and the Scapegoating of Deviance

Linda Williams

When the editors of this volume asked me to contribute an essay that would collect my thoughts about hard-core film pornography a few years after writing a book on the subject, they jokingly listed my contribution as 'The Afterglow of *Hard Core*'. Having long ago learned that *any* sexual pun or innuendo was to be vehemently eschewed in the attempt to write as neutrally as possible about the volatile genre of hard-core pornography, I changed the title. Afterglow, with its suggestion of smug satisfaction, I do not have; afterthoughts, even second thoughts, I have in abundance and some will be developed in what follows.

First, however, I would like to address the overarching issue that lurks beneath and motivates many of the jokes and innuendoes – including afterglow – that arise so frequently around discussions of sexual representations. When Paul Reubens (a.k.a. Pee Wee Herman) was arrested in a Florida Adult Theatre for exposing himself, he was publicly embarrassed for doing in a public place what many viewers of pornography do in private. Pee Wee's sad fate of banishment from children's television suggests just how explosive is the question of a genre-induced arousal and satisfaction, especially when linked to an effeminate public personality with an influence on children.

Pornography is a volatile issue not simply because it represents sexual acts and fantasies, but because in that representation it frankly seeks to arouse viewers. Perhaps more than any other genre its pleasures are aimed at the body. Indeed, pornography fails as a genre if it does not arouse the body. *Hustler* magazine's 'peter meters', which measure the quality of a porn film or video in terms of degrees of erection of the male organ, are just one, blatantly phallic, example of this expectation. Arousal, which is not always controlled by proper aesthetic or moral constraints, can be publicly embarrassing. Hence one reason for the sometimes defensive, sometimes

aggressive humour around it; hence my own reason for resisting the implication that I had enjoyed the progression from arousal to satisfaction in the title 'afterglow'.

For example, attorneys involved in prosecuting obscenity cases report that jury members who see the works in question are sometimes unexpectedly sexually aroused, especially if permitted to see works in their entirety. Prosecutors oppose the showing of the contested works in their entirety because once jurors have so responded it becomes harder for them to declare a work obscene.[1] In other words, when jurors find a piece of pornography arousing to *them*, the old division – if it turns the other person on it's obscenity, if it turns me on it's erotic – doesn't hold.

An older era of American jurisprudence could more simply dismiss a range of sexual representations that were presumably only 'for sex's sake' – that is, just for purposes of arousal. 'Pure lust' was once the very definition of obscenity, and that, so it seemed, was that. But this definition has gradually changed as 'sex' has become an increasingly important motive force, so entwined with all aspects of human desire and endeavour as to be difficult to isolate in an absolutely pure state of obscenity. Thus, while the very word obscenity has been interpreted by many to mean that which is or should be off (*ob*) the stage (*scene*) of representation, and while confused concern about obscenity has been mounting steadily in the wake of the Meese Commission report, National Endowment for the Arts defunding of artists, Senator Jesse Helms' legislation forbidding the spending of federal funds on 'obscene' art, and the Robert Mapplethorpe and 2 Live Crew trials, sexual representations are now so much *on the scene*, even in the arguments about these representations, that they cannot be easily dismissed as *ob scene*.[2]

In this essay I would like to explore the repercussions of what I am calling this historically unprecedented on/scenity in the context of current attempts to define and prosecute an elusive 'hard core' of obscenity. My main argument is that Americans are experiencing a remarkable on/scenity of sexuality which, in pornography no less than in all the arts, has become an important means of representing a wide range of sexual identities once labelled deviant – gay, lesbian, bisexual, sadomasochist, not to mention the female sexuality which has functioned throughout Western civilisation, and certainly in much pornography, as the basic deviation from a male 'norm'. Paradoxically, however, this new on/scenity, which has been remarkably liberating for previously closeted and repressed sexualities, has also provided the means for a new form of scapegoating of which the tendency to blame pornography for a wide range of crimes is the most insistent example. For in the wake of the greater presence on/scene of diverse sexualities as a motive force in all human endeavour and identity, there has also been a tendency to blame 'sex' and especially sexual 'deviants' for such diverse societal ills as AIDS, child molestation, rape and sexual harassment. My goal in what follows, then, is to trace a major change taking place in American obscenity law and the prosecution of sex crimes as they have moved away from the notion of explicit sex and towards the targeting of scapegoatable 'deviants'.

Since we are no longer able to claim, as sexual libertarians could once claim, that sex is a private matter, since sex has, in effect, become so very public a matter, even to those who would argue to keep it private, we have not attained the 'end of obscenity' predicted in the late 1960s by Charles Rembar.[3] Rather, we have seen an increasing politicisation of represented sexualities in a context of proliferating sexual discourses, and an intensified 'speaking sex'. Anti-pornography feminists have vociferously engaged in this intensified speaking sex. Not only do the novels and the critiques of pornography written by Andrea Dworkin themselves qualify as pornography, but the critique of pornography offered by Catharine MacKinnon is not, as has sometimes been assumed, that pornography *causes* harm to women, but that pornography *is* in its very representation of (heterosexual) sex harmful to women.[4] What MacKinnon and Dworkin, and the legal attacks on obscenity they have fostered, object to is not the bad influence of pornography on susceptible 'others', but what they see as the essence of pornographic speech:

'Pornography is exactly that speech of men that silences the speech of women'.[5] To MacKinnon, pornography is the essence of the power exercised by men over women through sexuality. That pornography could be a form of the sexual speech of heterosexual women, gays, lesbians and others who have been suppressed by male heterosexuality is to MacKinnon unthinkable. I hope to show the cost of this unthinkability in the context of the changing meaning of obscenity.

THE MILLER TEST

The event in American jurisprudence which marks the most important shift towards the new awareness that sex cannot easily be relegated to a place off-scene is paradoxically a 1973 case tried before the American Supreme Court. In *Miller v. California*, the court arrived at a three-pronged legal test designed to clarify, once and for all, what was and what wasn't obscene. The Miller Test, as it has come to be called, asks whether a work, taken as a whole, appeals to *prurient interest*, whether it depicts or describes sexual conduct in a *patently offensive* way, and whether it lacks '*serious literary, artistic, political or scientific value*' (emphases mine).[6] If lacking all these qualities a work may, according to *prevailing community standards*, be judged obscene.[7]

In recording the 1973 decision that presented the Miller Test, Justice Warren Burger asserted the concept of a non-socially redeemable prurience, a 'hard core' of mere 'sex for sex's sake', defined as explicit or graphic representations that went 'substantially beyond customary limits of candour'. Burger attempted to offer some 'plain examples' of hard-core depictions. These were 'patently offensive representations or descriptions of ultimate sexual acts, normal or perverted, actual or simulated, including patently offensive representations or descriptions of masturbation, excretory functions, and lewd exhibition of the genitals'.[8] The case was designed to reassure the public that the law could define – and thus keep 'off/scene' – the obscene, but in practice the very vagueness of the Miller Test, coupled with the undeniably growing importance of sexuality as an overt and 'on/scene', not a hidden, force in contemporary society, meant that unprecedentedly wide varieties of sexual representation increasingly found their way on to the scene of representation. Even X-rated film pornography, which aims to be prurient, was acknowledged to be more than mere prurience.

Another difficulty was how to determine what these words – prurient interest, patently offensive – really meant. In a 1985 case that attempted to clarify the definition of prurient as that which 'incites lasciviousness or lust' the Supreme Court decided that 'lust' referred to 'normal' while 'lascivious' referred to 'abnormal' sexual responses.[9] Thus prurience was supposedly 'clarified' as containing both abnormal and normal sexual response. In other words, some level of prurience was admitted on/scene and the line was now drawn at a lasciviousness considered abnormal.

From Justice Burger's original attempt to clarify the definition of obscenity in the Miller Test, we can see a shift in attitude: in 1973 the censorable hard core included, at least in theory, depictions of 'ultimate sexual acts, normal and perverted'; by 1985, in the ruling mentioned above, the line between acceptable and censorable was drawn between a normal lust and an abnormal lasciviousness. 'Hard core' depictions of ultimate sexual acts, by which Burger seemed to mean 'normal' heterosexual acts, were no longer perceived by the court as the place where the line would be drawn. Gradually, in the wake of proliferating sexual representations, a new line was being formulated. We can see the emergence of this line in a later ruling which noted, for example, that while some depictions of heterosexual intercourse may be obscene, 'most hard-core pornography emphasises various *other sexual practices*, such as homosexuality, bestiality, flagellation, sadomasochism, fellatio, cunnilingus, and the like'.[10]

Once it was no longer mere sexual explicitness that could be used to define an unacceptable obscenity, American courts were often compelled to specify which sexual acts were obscene. The Miller Test itself did not so specify. This lack of specificity has been its value in establishing freedom of speech in sexual expression. And it is important to remember, as Carol Vance points out, that the Miller Test still stands as the predominant legal definition of obscenity. Yet I would point out that the ruling that justified it, as well as many subsequent rulings, have frequently tried to provide some 'plain examples' of what constitutes obscenity. And not surprisingly, when these 'plain examples' are invoked they turn out to be 'other sexual practices'. Thus in the definition of obscenity, explicitness has given way to the deviant sexuality of the 'other', defined in relation to a presumed heterosexual, non-sadomasochistic norm that excludes both fellatio and cunnilingus. Presumably these specified 'other sexual practices' would turn the 'normal' juror off. Burger's specification thus shifted obscenity from mere explicitness to the representation of 'ultimate sexual acts' – for example, heterosexual intercourse[11] – to a paradoxical lack of the 'ultimate' – an absence of an end goal or direct gratification – that is often the hallmark, and the literal meaning of perversion.

What Burger was grappling with in his original attempt to define the elusive 'hard core' was the paradox of the existence of some sexual acts that epitomised (to *his* heterosexual male norm) an alien perversion, and the fact that such acts do not necessarily depict the sexual organs and genital actions whose simple visibility had previously sufficed to define obscenity. Because they are not 'direct' or 'ultimate sexual acts' they are difficult, under the earlier standard of 'pure lust', to define as obscene. In what precise sense, for example, is flagellation obscene?

Burger's definition, as opposed to the Miller Test itself, thus already left open the possibility that obscenity is not limited to explicit sexual acts (typically but not exclusively male and female genitals in coitus), but actually leans towards more 'deviant sexualities – those sexual acts and fantasies that 'prevailing community standards' do not want to admit to be arousing. In the intervening years *these* perverse sexual acts have been targeted as the most important obscenities. We may note, for example, as both Carol Vance and Judith Butler have done,[12] the wording of Jesse Helms's NEA bill forbidding the spending of federal funds in the arts if the works proposed for funding 'promote, disseminate or produce obscene materials, including but not limited to depictions of sadomasochism, homoeroticism, the exploitation of children, or individuals engaged in sex acts'.[13]

Helms's bill (Public Law 101–121, passed in the Senate in September 1989 but subsequently softened in a House–Senate compromise bill that reverted to the Miller definition of obscenity) has been seen by Carol Vance as a contradiction and betrayal of the Miller Test which did not specify which sexual acts could be considered obscene. I agree with Vance's point that the Miller Test, which has paradoxically functioned to admit diverse sexual representations, was undercut by Helms's attempt to attach a 'sexual laundry list' to the word obscenity. Interpreters of the bill could all too easily understand it to mean that any depiction of sadomasochism or homoeroticism is obscene.[14]

However, if we compare Helms's amendment to the language with which Burger tried to explain, and specify, the 1973 Miller Test (as opposed to the Miller Test itself), then we can see that Helms's bill was not so much a contradiction of Burger's original intent as an attempt to reorder the list of the censorable. Burger's original 'sexual laundry list' included at the top heterosexual genital acts and then mentioned various 'perversions'. In contrast, Helms places the 'perverts' at the top and 'individuals [presumably heterosexual] engaged in sex acts' at the bottom, almost as an afterthought. The difference between 1973 and 1989 is striking. A wholesale reversal of the hierarchy of obscene sexual acts has taken place with the installation of sexual perversion, especially sadomasochism, at the top of the list. Despite the failure of Helms's amendment, its text remains significant for its indication of how variants of sadomasochism or homosexuality have gradually grown to become the most prominent of the obscenities in popular consciousness.

Jesse Helms says, in effect, look at how disgusting these deviant sexual acts and fantasies are. Yet in pointing the finger to condemn, he brings the representation on/scene just as surely as any pornographer.[15] He gambles that readers and viewers will share his disgust. But the risk he runs is that they won't. Like the risk to the prosecutors who must show contested works in, rather than out of, context, the danger is that the more sexual representations of all sorts are on/scene, the more they contribute to the recognition, by jurors and casual viewers alike, that it is possible to be turned on by very irrational things, indeed by some very 'patently offensive', 'obscene' things that are exciting precisely because they are transgressions of reason and 'normality' and a 'properly' aesthetic, heterosexual, non-sadomasochistic erotics.

We have seen that debates over eroticism and pornography tend to prove only that one person's erotica can be another's porn and, somewhat similarly, that one person's perversion can be another person's norm. Though we can point in general to pornography's tendency towards the explicit depiction of 'ultimate sexual acts' and the existence of a more aestheticised, less explicit erotic, there simply

isn't any hard and fast line to be drawn between the two. In fact, if we look closely at Helms's language we see that he has tossed 'depictions of homoeroticism' which could be entirely non-explicit into his list of obscene materials. What does emerge, however, is the way the line has tended increasingly to be drawn between a normal and a perverse rather than a non-explicit and an explicit representation, and how these two poles depend on one another for definition. Pornographers, just as surely as Jesse Helms, need the idea that there is a line. The history of pornography, like the history of censorship, shows how variable that line has been and how paradoxically on/scene the various obscenities of pornography have been.

THE McMARTIN PRESCHOOL TRIAL

My second example of the 'on/scenity' of obscenity only indirectly concerns pornography. Yet it probably would not have occurred without the public hysteria over the putative harms of pornography that came to a head in the convergence of 'moral majoritist' activism against sexual representations with anti-pornography feminists in the 1986 Meese Commission hearings. In 1983 Raymond Buckey, an employee at the McMartin preschool in Manhattan Beach, California, was accused by a mother of molesting her two-and-a-half-year-old son at the school. Buckey was arrested, then released for lack of evidence. But during their investigation police sent letters to 200 parents naming Buckey as a suspect in child molestation. Nearly 400 children were subsequently interviewed by Children's Institute International, a Los Angeles agency that cares for abused children. The interviews were videotaped by an unlicensed therapist and eventually introduced as evidence in the trial of Buckey and his mother, Peggy McMartin Buckey, administrator of the preschool. Both were accused of sexually molesting forty-one children and of making 'kiddie porn' with them.[16]

The trial began in April 1987, after Buckey and his mother had already spent five years in jail before being able to raise the $1.5 million bond. It ended in January 1990 with the Buckeys' acquittal on fifty-two counts and a mistrial on all thirteen others. At two and a half years, the trial was the longest and costliest criminal proceeding in American history. Though no one will ever know for sure what actually transpired between the Buckeys and the children, in the end jurors could not separate fact from fantasy in the controversial videotaped interviews with the children admitted as testimony in the trial. If the Buckeys did the deeds they were accused of doing, they certainly committed not only obscene speech but, much more importantly, illegal, abusive and harmful acts. The jury could not determine, however, whether these illegal, abusive sexual acts occurred or whether they were transmitted to children via the videotaped interviews.

Sexual crimes of the most fantastic sort were recounted by the child witnesses in these interviews. But since the only way the children could be made to describe acts for which they had no words was for adults to give them the words, there was no guarantee that the children were not contaminated by adult sexual fears and fantasies. In these interviews the children were given anatomical dolls and urged to show how they were molested. As one juror put it, 'The children were never allowed to say in their own words what happened to them'.[17] Another juror said it appeared the children were coaxed into charging that the Buckeys had raped and sodomised them and touched their genitals.[18] The entire trial could thus be a remarkable demonstration of what Foucault has called our modern compulsion to 'speak sex' and to incite sex – to bring sexuality on the scene even where we most fear it: in the lives of children.[19]

For example, in an interview with one seven-year-old boy, Kee MacFarlane, the social worker who conducted the videotaped interviews, asked what the 'stuff' from Buckey's penis tasted like, explaining to the child, in an attempt to speak the child's language, that they were 'trying to figure out if it tastes good'. The boy replied, 'He never did that to [me], I don't think.' MacFarlane then asked a puppet – one of the anatomical dolls used by CII – if it knew what the 'stuff' tastes like, 'if it tastes good like candy?' The boy then replied, 'I think it would taste like yucky ants.' MacFarlane: 'Oh. You think it would be sort of – you think that would be sticky, like sticky, yucky ants?' A clinical psychologist who was a witness for the defence commented that prior to MacFarlane's introduction of the idea of ejaculation no mention of it had been made by any of the children. But once the acts were brought on/scene in the interviews with the children, as one clinical psychologist witness for the defence put it, it did not take 'a great leap to identify [Buckey] as the potential person who was involved in all those other things that have already been placed on stage'.

We can note, of course, just who had done this placing 'on stage'. It was the adult social worker, responding to what may have been the delusions of the original accuser (this mother died of alcohol-related illness before the case was brought to trial), who provided the explicit word, 'sticky'. Jurors who were originally inclined to believe that some of the children may have been molested, if not by the Buckeys then 'in some sense, by someone', finally objected to the 'no holds barred' fantasies incited by a publicity-hungry prosecution.[20] In the end, probably the most tangible evidence of molestation in this case was that of the prosecuting parents and social workers who brought sexual obscenities so dramatically on/scene.

MacFarlane and the mother who instigated charges that a sadistic devil-worshipping Raymond Buckey had anal intercourse with the children of the preschool offer a prime example of the new importance of certain obscene fantasies in which, as with Jesse Helms, 'homoeroticism' functions as a key transgressive content. In order to prosecute the case MacFarlane had, in effect, to become the very kiddie pornographer she suspected Buckey to be. If Buckey and his mother are innocent, then it was MacFarlane who corrupted the children with her incitement to discourse via videos and dolls.

Trials such as the McMartin molestation case have been increasing in the wake of public hysteria about the harms of pornography ever since the Meese Commission hearings – hearings which were themselves a dramatic display of the 'on/scenity' of pornography. These sex panics are a remarkable demonstration of the fact that the more we look for obscenity in order to ban it, the more we do not so much find it – as if it were an objectively existing cause of harm – as produce it in our own, and in this case in our children's, subjective fantasies. No evidence was ever found that the Buckeys were making kiddie porn, though the FBI, the US Customs Service and Interpol all sought it and the parents in the case offered a reward of $25,000 for photos that would prove pornography had been made. Nothing was found.[21] Yet the attempt to link alleged sexual crimes of child molestation with pornography continued. For pornography is public in a way that the elusive crimes of sex offenders (most of which take place not in schools and not in pornography but privately in the home) are not. Because of this public, exhibitionist quality it is often pornography, and those who can be vilified through its use or production, rather than real sexual harassers, who end up being blamed and punished.

I do not want to minimise the existence of sexual harassment and molestation; indeed, my point is that these actual crimes are too often minimised while on/scene displays of sexual representations take their place as convenient objects of blame. This is undoubtedly why in the McMartin case police and FBI looked so long and hard for pornography. The familiar image of a perverse, obscene deviant forcing a powerless victim to satisfy his sexual whims needs to be recognised for what it is: a sex-negative fantasy which blames bad sex on the perversions of a villainous other. Perhaps the most fantastic thing about this fantasy is the melodramatic idea that bad, obscene, perverse sex can be so conveniently identified in the persona of a conventional villain – that is, someone 'other' than 'us'. We saw above how that villain has increasingly been defined as a homosexual sadomasochist stalking defenceless children. This villain is convenient, Judith Butler has noted, because he can be located outside the home.[22] We do well to remember, however, that not too long ago the villain was a heterosexual man in a raincoat whose enjoyment of pornography was considered harmful to the civil rights of women.

I have traced the elusive concept of obscenity in American law in order to suggest the mixed blessings of the loss of mere explicitness as a measure of obscenity. On the one hand, this loss of explicitness as a criterion has meant the arrival on/scene of many different kinds of sexual representation. On the other hand, it has meant the increasing politicisation of those representations. While this politicisation has in many ways been beneficial to feminism and to sexual minorities, it has also led to the finger-pointing condemnations of the bad sexualities of 'others' and to a mood of sexual hysteria that can erupt into witch-hunts and trials such as the McMartin case. Feminist anti-pornographers have participated in this process even though their goal has not been to attack either obscenity or deviancy. Their attack is on male power. While they have not directly intended to blame deviancy, the result of their efforts has been to aid the work of Jesse Helms. I will cite a very recent, and to me very disturbing example of how anti-pornography feminists collude with this blame-the-deviant method of opposing pornography.

A ruling by the Canadian Supreme Court was hailed as a victory of 'world historic importance' for feminism by Catharine MacKinnon,[23] who with Andrea Dworkin devised the city ordinances formulating a 'harms' approach to pornography defined as the sexual subordination of women by men. In this ruling, the court decided that obscenity is to be defined by the harm it does to women's pursuit of equality. Canadian Justice John Sopinka wrote: 'If true equality between male and female persons is to be achieved, we cannot ignore the threat to equality resulting from exposure to audiences of certain types of violent and degrading material.'[24]

The court rejected a free-speech appeal by a Winnipeg porn video dealer who had been convicted in 1987 for violating Canada's obscenity law. Obscenity had been previously defined in Canada, which has a weaker tradition of free speech than the US, as 'undue exploitation of sex' violating (undefined) 'community standards'. The court's 'clarification' of obscenity no longer includes issues of morality and taste, but it relies heavily on the idea that violence and degradation can be the determination of obscenity. A threat to women's equality is thus now an acceptable ground for placing limits on freedom of speech in Canada. The court decided that pornography does harm to the self-respect and safety of women. It was not even necessary to prove a direct cause between pornographic representations and harms, since there is a 'reasoned apprehension' that pornography's 'gross misrepresentations' may lead to 'abject and servile victimization'. In other words, as *Ms Magazine* triumphantly summarised: 'Porn lies, and it hurts.'[25]

But what is this pornography that lies and hurts and so clearly reveals harm to the self-respect and safety of women? It turns out to be the scapegoatable deviant sexuality of the 'other' and not at all an example of masculine power over women. Kathleen F. Mahoney, professor of law at the University of Calgary, who represented the women's Legal Education and Action Fund which successfully argued the case, told *Ms Magazine* that their group won because 'We showed them the porn – and among the seized videos were some horrifically violent and degrading gay movies'. Mahoney claims that the reason these films worked to convince the court was that the 'abused men in these films were being treated like women – and the judges got it. Otherwise, men can't put themselves in our shoes.'[26] Although Mahoney argues that showing gay porn allowed the male justices to identify with the position of 'victim' – as if identification in sexual fantasy were a simple matter of identifying with one's sexual like[27] – I think she really won the case for the same reason Jesse Helms first succeeded in passing his version of the NEA amendment: the ability to point the finger at that same homosexual sadomasochist 'other', rather than to offer any real challenge to male power and authority in sexual representations.

This Canadian decision is of special interest to Americans since it may be a harbinger of a new harms-oriented American approach to obscenity. A bill was put to the Senate, the Pornography Victims Compensation Act, which would allow civil damage suits against publishers, producers and distributors of pornography under the assumption that these representations can cause sex crimes. The author of the bill, Senator Mitch McConnell, maintains that hard-core pornography is a 'form of group libel, principally aimed at women and children. Its techniques echo the propaganda that others have used to cultivate hatred toward specific groups: it is typically degrading, distorted, dehumanising and brimming with misogynist malice.'[28]

This new 'harms' approach to pornography would permit plaintiffs in civil suits to collect damages if they can show that obscene materials 'caused' the crimes committed against them by third parties. As Henry Louis Gates, Jr has argued, 'Criminals, like the rest of us, are happy to attribute their bad behaviour to an external agency (mother, Hostess Twinkies, demon rum, *Playboy*), thus diminishing, in some measure, their own culpability.'[29] As I have argued above, and as the pattern of prosecution by the Justice Department over the last few years reveals, it is not pornography depicting rape and violence against women that has been most consistently prosecuted. Indeed, as I have argued elsewhere, there is today comparatively little pornography depicting rape when one considers the amount of rape and abuse depicted in many more mainstream forms of mass-market representations, and sadomasochistic consensual violence can be very tricky to analyse as straightforward abuse.[30] Rather, it is the scapegoatable sexualities of sexual deviants that are prosecuted. In a recent Oklahoma case, for example, a video produced by the Pink Ladies, a support group for

women in the adult video industry, was charged with obscenity. In this video, entitled *Sorority Pink*, there was no violence, rape or degradation of women. There was, however, a lesbian orgy.[31]

AFTERTHOUGHTS/SECOND THOUGHTS

The above is a roundabout way of getting to my most pressing 'afterthought' regarding my 1989 book, *Hard Core: Power, Pleasure and 'the Frenzy of the Visible'*: the unfortunate result of my concentration on heterosexual hard-core pornography. At the time of writing, the Meese Commission and anti-pornography feminists had themselves concentrated on the aggressive nature of the heterosexual masculine 'norm'. It seemed natural, therefore, to address this notion of pornography even if that meant ignoring other pornographies that were also on/scene – the vast market of gay pornography; the emerging, tentative markets of lesbian and bisexual porn. I did make a gesture towards the more diverse forms of pornography in a chapter on sadomasochistic pornography and in another on new forms of heterosexual pornography by women. But I now recognise that my focus on the 'mainstream' as constructed by the then dominant discourse on pornography was too reactive, and too prone to the main error of all condemners of pornography who view it as a monolithic example of whatever seems 'bad' to them in sexuality. The reaction led, unfortunately, to my own 'containment' of deviancy in a single chapter on sadomasochism, when the more useful political move would have been to map the remarkable decentring effects of proliferating sexual representations.[32]

Another reason for my failure to address the diversity of sexual desires was that, as a heterosexual, I felt I had no right or authority to analyse gay and lesbian porn. Speaking from what I now recognise to be a false sense of fixed sexual identity – an identity theoretically wedded to a sexual binary divided neatly into masculine and feminine heterosexual desire – I was unable to see then that what I was learning from the book was actually how easy it was to identify with diverse subject positions and to desire diverse objects. Indeed, how polymorphously perverse the genre of pornography could be. One did not necessarily have to be lesbian or gay to enjoy these 'other' pornographies. Nor did one have to be heterosexual to enjoy the more 'normal' ones. I had far too rigid a sense of the proper audience for each sub-genre.

Another problem related to the diversity of desires articulated by pornography was pornography's challenge to the feminist film theory dictum that the 'gaze is male'. I had already suggested this challenge with respect to heterosexual porn in *Hard Core*, but gay, lesbian and bisexual pornographies presented an even greater challenge to this oversimplified Lacanian formula. For gay porn could not be reduced, as it would seem the Canadian feminists did try to reduce it, to an aggressive male gaze at a feminised object. Nor did new lesbian porn with its butch/femme dichotomies and S/M orientation fit expectations of the 'kinder, gentler', more nurturing sexual pleasures of women. And bisexual porn, which makes a point of articulating a female gaze at male couples, is even more confounding of heterosexual presumptions of the workings of desire. With the best of intentions, then, my book's focus on the heterosexual mainstream may have actually strengthened the idea of a monolithic pornography that I wanted to challenge. I regret this now, especially in the context of the above shift in line-drawing from explicit to deviant.

Yet another 'second thought' has to do with the question of the researcher's gendered relation to his or her object of study, in particular: *what is a 'proper' female relation to the classically bad object of pornography?* Feminist engagement with pornography arose from a critique of the most masculine and misogynist of genres. Yet the more I looked at the genre, the more it seemed that previous discussions of pornography had been tainted by descriptions of films and videos supercharged with the emotions of the critic's own reactions. Looking at the short tradition of critical writing about pornography of all sorts, I knew I did not want to emulate any of the already established reactions to pornography. These included: Steven Marcus writing the whole of *The Other Victorians* while seemingly holding his nose; Susan Sontag in a more celebratory mode giving the avant-garde literary, high-serious French treatment to the Sadean-Bataille tradition; Andrea Dworkin offering the most meticulous descriptions of pornographic writing or images in tones of monumental outrage yet still complicit with the word's and the image's power to arouse.[33]

Neutrality of tone seemed the obvious solution to these condemnations or overly defensive appreciations. I therefore resolved to skip the nervous jokes and the easy condemnation of aesthetic or moral shortcomings and to avoid condemnation of defensiveness. I would ask instead what the genre does, how it does it, and I would remove myself from pro or con arguments as much as possible. Yet this objective, distanced stance of the reasoned observer, neither partisan nor condemner, placed me in a position of indifference, as if above the genre. Was it right, or even useful to analysis, to assume to be indifferent to, or unmoved by, these texts? Or, if I was moved, as I was sometimes to either arousal or offence, what was the proper place of this reaction in criticism? While I attempted, ever so neutrally, to simply describe, wasn't something of my personal reaction already embedded, in a coded way, in the attention I gave to certain texts and sub-genres and not to others? Donna Haraway once said in passing that one should not 'do' cultural studies of objects to which one is not vulnerable. In my case I had begun with what I thought to be an invulnerability, even a disdain for the texts of pornography, but was then surprised to find myself 'moved' by some works. What was the place of this vulnerability in writing about the genre? I don't know the answer to this question, but I grow increasingly convinced that there must be some place for this in writings about mass culture.[34]

There is a related problem in that, as a woman writing about a traditionally male genre, my interest in the genre is, at this historical conjuncture, more acceptable to many readers than a man's might be. For example, I was once asked if my contribution to the understanding of pornography would have been as well received if it had been written by a Larry instead of a Linda. The question was somewhat hostile, implying that men, who are too readily condemned by a politically correct feminism for enjoying porn, must condemn it or be condemned in turn, while I could 'get away' with having a scholarly interest in pornography. There is a certain justice to the criticism: masculine sexuality has been under siege by feminism for its very real abuses, and has often been forced into a rather cringing and unproductive *mea culpa* for its aggressive fantasies.[35] Yet if, as I have tried to argue both here and elsewhere, pornography is not the monolithic expression of phallic misogyny that it has been stigmatised as being, then there is good reason even for heterosexual men to explore the pleasures of the genre without having to admit too many *mea culpas*.

My final 'second thought' concerns the methodology of the study of pornography, in particular the question of *what theories best explain the genre*. Freud and Lacan are indispensable theorists of sexuality, fantasy and desire, yet to adopt them is on some level to ignore both history and the social, to accept a hermetically sealed explanatory system based on the woman's 'lack' of a penis and the hegemony of heterosexual desire. Foucault and new historians of sexuality are indispensable theorists of the historical contingencies of material bodies caught up in competing discourses of knowledge, power and pleasure, yet to adopt them is to lose an ability to account for the driving force of desire and fantasy so important in pornography. In addition, both theories are remarkably silent about women's sexuality, fantasies, desires and experience.

My solution to this problem is an admittedly makeshift and sometimes inconsistent oscillation between psychoanalytic and Foucauldian theories tempered and corrected by feminist critique. The key area of difficulty in the application of both psychoanalysis and Foucault is the status of perversion within their notions of sexuality. On one level both theories see all sexuality as inherently perverse. Freud theoretically accounts for this inherent perversion, but there is still a sense in which adult sexual perversion remains for Freud. . . . well, perverse (that is, Freud's use of the term often exists in contrast to a proper heterosexual and heterogenital norm). Foucault, on the other hand, sees the history of sexuality as the 'implantation' of one perversion after another. Perversions are, for him, in a sense the norm. This is a more progressive attitude but it does not adequately account for the apparent dynamic between norm and perversion in the texts of pornography, where the excitement of the genre lies, at least partly, in the transgression of whatever sexual norms happen to be in effect.

CONCLUSION

The question that now faces both feminists and sexual minorities is the political one of whose sexual desires and pleasures will be permitted on/scene now that we no longer conceive of sex as containing a 'hard core' of obscenity. For our current sexual politics can no longer be that begun by Kate Millett and continued by anti-pornography feminists.[36] This politics of condemning the evil masculine 'other'

feeds all too easily into the condemnation of the deviant sexualities of 'perverse others'. Now that these perverse others take their place, not simply as freak contrasts to a dominant norm, but as authoritative subjectivities, both explicit *and* erotic, on the scene of sexual representation, the anti-pornography feminist vilification of a reified masculine lust backfires as a strategy for the furtherance of feminist goals.

In *Hard Core*, I described what seemed to me to be the uneasy bargain struck between the 1986 Meese Commission on Pornography and the anti-pornography feminists who joined forces with the Commission to condemn pornography. It seemed to me then that the Meese Commissioners gained the radical feminist critique of phallic pleasure as a violent form of male power, but at the cost of curbing their own desire for an equally strong critique of gay or lesbian pornography or sexual practice. The rhetoric of violence against helpless victims could not be mobilised against this pornography because women were not its victims. In this tacit bargain, the Meese Commission gained new leverage against some forms of obscenity but not the gay and lesbian deviancy it also targeted. In turn, anti-pornography feminists got to assert the abnormality of a graphically depicted phallic power that had once been considered a natural aspect of (hetero)sexual pleasure. However, unless these representations could be construed as violent they could not be condemned.

Thus, although the two interests had very different notions of what the norms of sexual behaviour should be, in the end they condemned only those they could agree to hate. Today, as we have seen in both the changing notion of obscenity and the new pattern of blaming deviant sexuality for sexual abuses that are deeply embedded in patriarchal culture, there is greater agreement to hate homosexuals. If we do not want to be in the business of condemning the sexuality of villainous others, we need a better sexual politics. This sexual politics must be aware of the diversity of sexual fantasies which cannot be simplified into an easily scapegoatable aggression, perversion or evil. One way to explore this diversity would be to become aware that pornography is no monolith, that it has a history, and that in that history it has appealed to many more 'bodies and pleasures' than are dreamt of in any feminist anti-pornography philosophy.

NOTES

1. Donald Alexander Downs, *The New Politics of Pornography* (Chicago, IL: University of Chicago Press, 1989), p. 21.

2. One possible etymology of the word obscene is the literal Latin meaning of 'off scene' – those things which are, or should be, kept off (ob) the scene (scena) or stage of public representation. Andrea Dworkin, in *Pornography: Men Possessing Women* (New York: Perigee Books, 1979), p. 9, has noted this etymology along with the alternative Latin meaning of filth or excrement.

3. See Charles Rembar's influential work, *The End of Obscenity: The Trials of Lady Chatterley, Tropic of Cancer, and Fanny Hill* (New York: Random House, 1968).

4. See Dworkin's *Pornography* and *Intercourse* (New York: Macmillan Press, 1987); and Catharine MacKinnon's *Feminism Unmodified: Discourses on Life and Law* (Cambridge, MA: Harvard University Press, 1987).

5. MacKinnon, *Feminism Unmodified*, p. 209.

6. I take the text of the Miller Test, as well as much of the following discussion of the vagaries of the attempt to define obscenity, from Alexander Downs's very helpful *The New Politics of Pornography*. This book offers a meticulous assessment of the changes taking place in the politics of pornography since the rise of anti-pornography feminism. Downs is a liberal who defends free speech and objects to the intolerance of pornography's attackers and defenders. While I do not always agree with his liberal stance, his book, along with Walter Kendrick's *The Secret Museum: Pornography in Modern Culture* (New York: Viking Press, 1987), offer the two best surveys of the legal battles over the definitions of obscene sexual speech. Another recent book is Edward de Grazia's *Girls Lean Back Everywhere: The Law of Obscenity and the Assault on Genius* (New York: Random House, 1992).

7. Downs, *The New Politics of Pornography*, p. 17.

8. De Grazia, *Girls Lean Back Everywhere*, p. 567.

9. Downs, *The New Politics of Pornography*, p. 29.

10. Frederick Schauer, *Law of Obscenity* (Washington, DC: Bureau of National Affairs, 1976).

11. Downs, *The New Politics of Pornography*, p. 17.

12. Carol Vance, 'Misunderstanding Obscenity', *Art in America*, February 1990, pp. 49–55; Judith Butler, *Gender Trouble; Feminism and the Subversion of Identity* (New York: Routledge, 1990), pp. 105–25.

13. Vance, 'Misunderstanding Obscenity', p. 51.

14. Ibid.

15. While running for re-election in 1990, Helms quite literally performed a prurient finger-pointing that was reminiscent of a men-only stag smoker. At a barbecue in Burlington, North Carolina, Helms invited, as he had already done on the floor of the Senate, only the men in the audience to examine three portfolios of Robert Mapplethorpe nudes, guarded by his assistants. The photos were from the 'Perfect Moment' exhibit whose National Endowment for the Arts funding Helms opposed (*Time*, 10 September 1990, p. 17). His point was to outrage voters that taxpayers' money funded the exhibit. His method – to bring the offending photos to the barbecue but only to let the men see them – participates in the very titillation he opposes. (On the Senate floor Helms asked 'all the pages, all the ladies, and maybe all the staff to leave the Chamber so that the male Senators 'can see exactly what they're voting on' (de Grazia, *Girls Lean Back Everywhere*, p. 637).

16. *New York Times*, 19 January 1990.

17. *Los Angeles Daily Journal*, 19 January 1990.

18. *New York Times*, 19 January 1990.

19. I owe thanks to Elizabeth Losch, whose unpublished essay on videotaped testimony of children in sexual abuse cases alerted me to the question of adult incitement of children to sexual discourse, and to Kee MacFarlane and Jill Waterman's book about the techniques of coaxing child witnesses, *Sexual Abuse of Young Children* (New York: The Guilford Press, 1986).

20. *New York Times*, 19 January 1990.

21. *Playboy*, June 1990.

22. Butler, *Gender Trouble*, p. 116.

23. I have learned of this recent ruling just as this essay goes to press and have therefore not had time to research the details of what would appear to be a quite dangerous precedent.

24. Michele Landsberg, 'Canada: Antipornography Breakthrough in the Law', *Ms Magazine*, May–June 1992, p. 14.

25. Ibid.

26. Ibid.

27. Since it has taken feminist film theory a long time to break from the assumption that desire as articulated by the various 'looks' of cinema can be anything but heterosexual and male, it is perhaps not surprising that the operating assumptions of anti-pornography

feminists have, in so far as they have theorised desire at all, also deployed a masculine heterosexual model of desire.

28. McConnell's statement is quoted in the newsletter written by Bobby Lilly, *Californians ACT against Censorship Together* (14 May 1992).

29. Henry Louis Gates, Jr, 'To "Deprave and Corrupt" ', *The Nation*, 29 June 1992, p. 902.

30. Both these points are discussed at length in Linda Williams, *Hard Core: Power, Pleasure, and the 'Frenzy of the Visible'* (Berkeley: University of California Press, 1989), pp. 164–6, 184–228.

31. Lilly, *Californians ACT against Censorship Together*, p. 2.

32. I map these proliferating forms of gay, lesbian, bisexual and sadomasochistic pornographies in a recent essay: Linda Williams, 'Pornographies on/scene, or "diff'rent strokes for diff'rent folks" ', in Lynne Segal and Mary McIntosh (eds), *Sex Exposed: Sexuality and the Pornography Debate* (London: Virago, 1992).

33. Steven Marcus, *The Other Victorians: A Study of Sexuality and Pornography in Mid-Nineteenth Century England* (London: Weidenfeld and Nicolson, 1966); Susan Sontag, 'The Pornographic Imagination', in *Styles of Radical Will* (New York: Dell, 1969), pp. 35–73; Dworkin, *Pornography*.

34. Constance Penley has recently spoken to this problem in a fascinating account of her own involvement as student and fan of amateur fan magazines that offer explicit sexual relations between the two main male characters of the *Star Trek* series: 'Feminism, Psychoanalysis, and the Study of Popular Culture', in Lawrence Grossberg, Cary Nelson and Paula Treichler (eds), *Cultural Studies* (New York: Routledge, 1992). Since the fans of these 'zines' tend to be women, and since women's desires are articulated through these apparently gay representations, Penley, unlike the Canadian feminists who used such representations to stigmatise a deviant other, asks about her own implication as a fan, a feminist, a critic and a voyeur of such texts (p. 484).

35. See, for example, Michael Kimmel's interesting but guilt-ridden, even self-pitying, *Men Confront Pornography* (New York: Crown, 1990).

36. Kate Millett, *Sexual Politics* (New York: Doubleday, 1969).

15 Through a Gaze Darkly: Pornography's Academic Market

Jennifer Wicke

Adventuring in the skin trade: pornography is one of the most salient new critical domains of interest, compelling an orgy of publication and commentary that maps and mimics the equally unstoppable flood of pornographic materials into all cultural interstices. While this second tier of pornographic exploration is not represented in the racks at the 7-Eleven, say, along with the discourse which it feeds on, there is a discernible increase in the academic pornography market. Casual browsing through the programme bulletin of the yearly MLA meeting – to take just one academic barometer as an index – yields a sudden profusion of 'Pornography and . . .' topics, the generic noun usually being linked to rather unwonted proper nouns, like 'Milton', a yoking actually to be found in the 1990 bulletin. Courses are being offered, seminars suggested, books emerging apace, and even the instinctive feel one acquires for what will radiate as hot and imperative in a book or essay title is shifting to 'pornography', having supplanted the early 80s' thrill of 'power' and the delights later in the decade of 'sexuality', perhaps because pornography so neatly conflates the two.

The dimensions of pornography are much larger than the parochial corner of academic discourse I am going to patrol, but the very immensity, and the intensity, of the social discourse on pornography precludes its consideration; better the tip of the iceberg one can actually see. Moreover, the extreme interest in pornography on academic fronts at the moment – and I include not only strictly institutional venues but the intellectual journals, magazines, journalistic debates, television opinion shows and independent film-making efforts – has created a metapornography well worth investigating for its symptomatic meanings. Such an investigation does not imply that all these takes on pornography are somehow equally deluded, or contaminated, or beside the point; rather, it asks what value pornography has in our current academic exchanges, and how it plays its role in the academic marketplace.

Pornography plays a major, if sometimes invisible, role in academic discussion because it represents the flip side of the argument about what texts or representations can hope to accomplish in general. Pornography is the dark side of this particular moon, the segment of social discourse whose effects are almost entirely agreed to be negative. I propose that the focus on pornography in academic circles often stems from a corresponding and more taboo fear – that 'good' or 'serious' works in fact will not save us. Stripped to barest premises, it is thought that pornography is a form of representation whose perusal will cause people, read men, to devalue women even more than they already do, and encourage them to express this in violent ways; the strongest statement of this position is that perusing the pornographic image or words already constitutes such violence, that the act of reading or looking is intrinsically demeaning and violent in its 'objectification' of the women, or, less likely, the men represented. Pair this with its partner in social discourse, the fate of representation in general. Normally, pornography is not linked to the debates on the worth of studying particular texts, except in those rare instances where crossover texts emerge, and Joyce's *Ulysses*, for example, has to pass a legal challenge to disabuse itself of the pornographic label before qualifying as a work of serious merit, a classic. Because these realms are then usually so disjunct, it may seem peculiar to claim that an animating impulse for the debate on pornography is the seemingly much more rarefied, or even incontrovertible, status of great books and/or great works of art.

There is a hinge connecting these two realms of discourse, however. Pornography is a secret sharer in the canon debate, and a hidden partner of the high art/mass culture conflict that rages beyond the perimeters of the canon. Ultimately, pedagogy in general is involved, or 'paideia', to give it its Greek etymology and correspondingly enlarged social sense: pornography peeps out from its brown paper wrappers and asks how a culture reproduces itself, in and through the images and texts it disseminates, in a paideia at large. Pornography confutes and scandalises and banalises the intensely held beliefs of a text-based culture that people are what they read. The politics of this belief do not break down neatly into right and left camps, and this is perhaps why pornography is so insidiously stimulating as an academic subject – behind the complexities of the arguments about pornography often lies a philosophical discourse about representation and education, seeing and knowing. It is more than possible to want to guard against any censorship of pornography, and nonetheless to feel that good books make people good along the same lines of reasoning that help to buttress pornography's enemies. As a consequence, pornography strikes very deep into the sociocultural formation of education, knowledge and cultural awareness, arousing a profound need to write about pornography, almost as an act of exorcism. This is the largest of the embedded circles of my argument, and one to which I will return.

The current profusion of works about pornography also stems from the unique interdisciplinary and intratheoretical role pornography as a subject is capable of playing at the moment. Pornography is 'hot' now, or at least galvanising in academic circles, because it serves a variety of discursive and political purposes no other subject area can quite encompass at this juncture. These arenas are several, and can only be mapped rather fuzzily, since they have ways of blending into one another quite promiscuously. The primary amalgam, though, is the meshing of an ahistoricist, apolitical American feminist criticism with certain discrete and selectively chosen pieces of (psychoanalytic and Althusserian) feminist film theory, giving it enough theory to posit an 'objectifying gaze', in collision with the deep social conservatism of so-called 'radical' feminism; this mixture operates in tandem with or sometimes parallel to an unexamined attitude toward the complexity of mass cultural formations, or the perpetuation of a Frankfurt School culture-industry disapprobation. This is a heady stew, and, moreover, not every text on the topic shares these features. Some diverge strikingly and profoundly, but my point in assaying the mixture in the first place is to account for the hectic frenzy surrounding the topic and the marketability of responses to pornography.

For feminist critics who are women, the article or the book on pornography has taken on a *de rigeur* status, since pornography is the latest inflection of feminist discourse and appears to have a genuinely extra-academic reality – giving such messages on pornography a political piquancy, activist overtones that are played with the solemnity of organ chords by some (here one would list all the radical feminist texts of Andrea Dworkin, Catharine MacKinnon, Robin Morgan, *et al.*, and works like Joan Huff and Susan Gubar's *For Adult Users Only*[1] and Susanne Kappeler's *The Pornography of Representation*),[2] and in a more playful and tolerant tenor by those opposing censorship of pornography, particularly in the name of feminism (like the *Caught Looking* collective,[3] gay male feminist theorists such as Scott Tucker and Jeffrey Weeks, and literary and social theorists like Andrew Ross and Walter Kendrick, for example). In the back of any feminist's head the little ditty 'pornography is the theory, rape is the practice' is always sounding, whether as mental inspiration or annoyingly reductive Muzak. Answering to the real, incontrovertible facts of the rape and battering and murdering of women (the ever-rising statistics that comprise women's actual social lives) more and more has needed to be done by taking a stand on pornography, in part because feminism and pornography have come to be intertwined in the public and political realms. At the risk of simplifying, there is a laudable desire to write about arenas that seem to have genuine political impact, and pornography, as a primarily visual and textual manifestation, can be 'read' by those best trained in critical reading, to the benefit of concrete social policy. That bottom line position also is mirrored in professional terms by the turf wars over feminist theory and the desire to stake out domains for the exercising of feminist critique. Sexism and misogyny having been thoroughly uncovered in the major works of the male authors and painters and so on, it remains to go back over them to find specifically pornographic modes of expression and representation.

It is imperative to deal one's hand early on in any essay on pornography, because positions are always being crystallised in such works, despite the ironically limited number of positions available, in a field whose metier is proliferating positionality. That being the case, it should be said that this article rests on the bedrock foundations, or the missionary position, that pornography is not, perforce and *tout court*, violence to women, that pornography should not be censored or prohibited, except quite obviously in the case of child pornography, where what is being regulated is the abuse of children by adults, and that pornography is not what is wrong with everything, especially not the cause of the hierarchical social relations of domination that obtain between men as a group and women as a group. The social reality of the ongoing domination of women by men can be so frustrating that it is tempting to isolate pornography as the sole basis for its perpetuation, and in some feminist circles it even defies common sense to say that pornography is not violence towards women, so ritualistic has that equation become. Nonetheless, to deny this is to step outside a circle drawn claustrophobically close by mistaken theoretical assumptions and accidents of intellectual and academic history, into a more ambiguous, historical and indeed social understanding of pornography.

My assumptions are general and unwieldy and could be superimposed on theoretical and political premises very different from those I will try to develop here, but in the climate of Jesse Helms and the Reverend Wildmon words cannot be minced. What is intriguing is how often the second proposition against censorship is, albeit reluctantly, conceded, and how rarely the other two claims, that pornography is not simply violence against women and that it is not the root of all gender hierarchy, are stated with vigour, at least in writing about pornography by women. The feminist historian Christine Stansell, for example, has given talks based on her brilliant research into the history of pornography and in particular its ambivalent and even vital relation to American social and sexual change, only to be met with some hostility because the sacrosanct position about 'violence' cannot, in her analyses, be preserved; for perhaps obvious reasons of gender, reactions to Andrew Ross's proposal that pornography has a complicated and important place in social life have been even more severe. In other words, it costs real feminist points to deny that 'pornography' is the appropriate appellation for the social pathology of gender hierarchy and violence; even where the climate is not as frosty to considerations of female desire and sexual fantasy as it is in radical feminist areas of the academy, it is still hard to be unadulteratedly 'for' pornography. The grid of certain feminist theoretical and critical

vectors has discovered pornography at the centre of its discursive concerns. It is difficult, but necessary as well, to agree that pornography is important while disagreeing with the constraints on the discussion of it. To displace pornography from the centre by (self-) reflecting on the reasons for its centrality may also dislodge the received ideas about pornography and how it should play in academic/feminist/theoretical/political inquiry.

One leaves those precincts upon entering a book like the off-puttingly named *For Adult Users Only*, edited by Susan Gubar and Joan Huff, with an introduction by the former. To report my own feelings honestly, this book makes almost any seedy tabloid indecency look like a refreshing excursion into normal, carnivalesque perversity, not because all of its contributed essays are so bad, although a number of them are, but because the book smacks of crass bad faith and unbearable academic pretension. The opening essay situates us in this queasy territory, by explaining how the book came to exist, which we are meant to take as a more serious and urgent matter than the publication of, say, another collection of essays on Renaissance literature or a philosophical Festschrift. After a paean to the bucolic and middle-class joys of Bloomington, Indiana, where no one had apparently any worries, even during the Reagan era, and academic complacency proceeded without a qualm, Gubar narrates the intrusion of two horrific murders of women upon the peace of the town. The first murder involves a son killing his mother, with whom he has long resided in a trailer home, while the second is described with even more detail because, sadly enough, the victim was a former graduate student in the English department who, after apparently suffering a breakdown, had begun an eccentric life with numerous cats in a depressed area of town, where she was ultimately violently killed.

These tales are very grim, under any circumstances; what defies belief is that they are adduced as the reason a 'task-force' discussion group on pornography was eventually formed on campus, leading to the publication of the book. This gives the text a self-important 'white paper' or Kerner Commission overtone that comports ludicrously with the contents. An essay by Gubar on Magritte as, basically, surrealist pornography and an essay by Mary Jo Weaver on religion and sexuality are so rhetorically academic and specialised that the notion that a reader is meant to be continually reading with the image of poor dismembered Mrs Adams or the tragically violated graduate student haunting the pages comes to be very disturbing. The frisson of terror and pity elicited by the introductory recital of these murders is then used to segue seamlessly into the 'realm' of pornography, as if the murders had any connection, obvious or abstruse, with the topic. One wonders whether psychopathology, or economic decline, or alcohol- or drug-related violence, or any number of other social problem areas might not have suggested themselves first for study, but no, pornography it is, and any balking at this connection implies a lack of concern for the victims hovering before us.

What pornography might be meant, then – (extremely rare) snuff material? Mother/son bondage duos? Not at all. Pornography, it turns out, is the David Lynch film *Blue Velvet*. The segue is dizzyingly fast: from a pair of distressingly familiar murders a diagnostic case is made.

In *Blue Velvet* (1986), a crazed man tortures a woman whose child he has kidnapped and whom he calls 'mommy' when he repeatedly batters and rapes her. Pumping himself up by breathing through a sinister oxygen mask, the character portrayed by Dennis Hopper reduces his 'mommy' to a fleshy thing presumably because he is still traumatised by the otherness of the first woman in his life, his mother.

And lest *Blue Velvet* account only for the murder of the mother, Mabel Adams, it has gruesome relevance to the killing of Ellen Marks.

Both *Blue Velvet* and *Angel Heart* evince a fascination with bloody parts that permeates the letter written by the man who may have spent three years planning to dismember Ellen Marks: in the first case, the ears that the psychopath slices off his victims as well as the mouths which he stuffs with pieces of blue velvet . . .

Gubar follows this assessment with a carefully nuanced treatment of the aesthetic features of the film(s) in question, even including the point made by many that such films can be read as critiques of masculine socialisation. But Gubar can't finally buy that: 'How different, then, are these comparatively ambitious films from *Deep Throat* or *Debbie Does Dallas*?' And later, 'All of the essays in this volume necessarily engage the problem of defining pornography to determine its relationship to violence against women.' The circularity of the argument

means that only violence will be found, or that only violence will be found to be the common denominator that allows *Blue Velvet* to be the equivalent of *Debbie Does Dallas*. Of course, it is just as wrong to suppose that the latter film is responsible for the two murders Gubar cites; her manoeuvre goes in two directions and each is equally factitious.

Pornography jumps many disciplinary boundaries and critical barriers in its translation into metapornography, a discourse for all seasons. Many of the implicit assumptions about pornography in feminist theory and criticism have affinities with debates further afield, especially with considerations of consumption and mass culture often unacknowledged in what seem to be much more pressing matters of sexual politics. The subterranean connections are there, however, in myriad guises, especially when pornography is set up as an objectifying and commodifying form of patriarchal expression, and when more subtle differences between pornography and artistic practices are probed.

At the bottom of the so-called pornography debate lies a mystified relation to the conditions of mass culture, and this problem infects the very interpretation of what is pornographic. The visceral energies directed 'at' pornography by social forces concentrate on its visual aspects, on the film, video and photographic incarnations of pornography, largely to the exclusion of its literary modalities, which don't seem to exercise people as thoroughly, except in the academic debates, which often privilege the textual and find 'pornography' in texts many others would consider too dreary to read. While pornographic books and magazines are also massproduced and consumed, they are less visible as targets of critique or analysis because the prevailing figure for pornographic consumption lies so squarely in the arresting of the visual, in the enthralled spectatorship of the eye, where pornographic images seem to fuse themselves directly to the eye, rather than taking the more circuitous route of the mediation of print. To many commentators, the ease and rapidity of mass cultural consumptive visual strategies is appallingly emblematised by pornography itself, where the languor and voluptuousness of consumption in general gets raised to its apotheosis. As a consequence, visual pornography seems not only worse, but more typical, especially because new visual technologies are rapidly enlisted for pornography production along with the entire range of mass cultural forms and representations.

The model of consumption most often culturally proffered is that of simple assimilation, of the taking in of the consumed object in a mindless or insensate state, the engorgement of pleasure. When this construction or understanding of consumption is simply mapped onto the pornographic scenario of consumption, the metaphorical understanding appears to become doubled and thereby literalised by what pornography actually does – arouse. In other words, if all acts of consumption bear some relation to a mindless infusion of hedonic frenzy, then pornographic consumption adds the quotient of physiological arousal to the intoxicated state of consumer possession in general, which already mimes sexual abandon, at least in these descriptions of it. All the valences of affect used to discuss consumer states of mind come into play with redoubled fervour and seeming relevance when translated into the arena of pornography consumption – satiety, passivity, absorption. Thus part of what is suspect about pornography stems from its ubiquitous availability, and from the proliferation of its visual and verbal forms.

Pornography needs to be understood as a genre, indeed a genre of consumption, with many branches, in order to break down the monolith of 'pornography' that can only serve to turn it into an allegory. To view pornography as a genre would immediately make suspect (in my view, rightly) the tendency to assimilate Milton's *Paradise Lost* or Dante Gabriel Rossetti's poems or Magritte's surrealism to pornography. Pornography might be said to be a quintessentially mixed genre, but not mixed in the sense that it can easily assimilate works like those just cited – instead, mixed in that while a genre of pornography exists, defined in large part by its production and distribution and consumption strategies, which are all *sui generis*, it has internal divisions and distinctions that follow their own laws of genre over time. For example, the mildly pornographic magazines concentrating on enormous breast size to be found at many newsstands are caught up primarily in extending the genre of the sexual pun. Yes, breasts and their photographic representation are involved, but the magazines exist to establish erotic connections between language and image in the form of somewhat tedious puns – 'Yvonne pours her jugs for you', and so on. This is a far generic cry from the intricate confessional/medical mode of a publication like *Forum*, and both are at a great remove from the genre constraints of *The Police Gazette*. The genre distinctions within pornography are drawn on aesthetic and social grounds; the punning of 'jugs' is related to a working-class British tradition of pun and rhyme melded to sexual content, while *Forum* builds verbal fantasy worlds out of middle-class managerial and professional milieux, interlaced with a vocabulary of the aesthetically upscale, or 'beautiful'. Some genres of pornography have vast historical lineages and equally complex codes; others spring up when a commercial space is suddenly made available in the plenum of capitalised opportunities, like miniature pornographic pictures sold in condom machines newly placed in truck stops.

An objection can be made to this array of genres, of course, by saying that in heterosexual pornography, at least, they all depend on the woman's body, on the objectification of that body for the male subject of desire. It is precisely at that spot that the discourse of objectification – what John Berger memorably calls 'the woman as the to-be-looked-at' – crosses over into the discourse of the object or the commodity, and the result, in discussions of pornography, is to embed objectification, itself conceived of as an either/or, entirely negative phenomenon, in the thickets of consumption, as these objects are invariably seen as something to then be consumed by a subject. The critical geometry is drawn tight, and q.e.d., in pornography the woman is an object to be consumed by the man.

In a sophisticated and trenchant essay, 'The Antidialectic of Pornography', in *Men Confront Pornography*,[4] Joel Kovel takes on this difficulty with mass culture from a Frankfurt School, leftwing perspective that leads him to differentiate pornography and eroticism on the grounds that the former is contaminated by mass culture – in short, that it is mass culture. Eroticism, on the other hand, typified by works by de Sade and Bataille, engages the metaphysical aspects of sexuality untainted by the culture industry, whose adventures into eroticism inevitably produce pornography. Kovel is very careful not to base the pornography/eroticism distinction on moralism, as is so often done; he wants instead to provide an ontological difference between them that will not rest on whether eroticism is 'nicer' to women or more 'reciprocal'. Nonetheless, a moralism of another sort creeps in through the Horkheimer and Adorno back door of culture industry analysis. What is wrong with pornography is that it is a ruthless, totalising system of mass cultural entrapment, freezing its consumers in postures of reification rather than the sportive sexual positions it ostensibly favours. 'From another angle, pornography is the captivity of the erotic within mass culture. It is the erotic less its negativity, less its ambivalence, its association of sexuality with death, and, finally, its truthfulness.' Eroticism makes people think, it offers the autonomy of negative critique, whereas pornographic material is such a slippery consumer slope it can give no purchase to critical thought. As Wittgenstein wrote, 'We need friction. Away from the smooth ground!' Pornography is thus on a par with the depredations of advertising or the induced delusions of television narrative; what it gives proof of is the penetration of capital into yet another legitimate conduit of desire – the desire for sexuality, here trammelled by, made less serious by, its usurpation by mass cultural forms.

This notion of the fallenness of pornography, mass culture's stranglehold on sexuality, requires the avant-gardism of Adorno's theses about the work of art in the modern age, a defiant object of negative critique. If one assumes a less programmatic 'culture industry' capable of brainwashing its consumer victims, and looks instead at mass cultural forms as produced also by their consumers, used and transformed and redeployed, the image of consumption alters considerably. I'm not proposing anything utopian about this transfigured pornographic consumption, nor making the familiar claim that sexuality is always and everywhere transgressive and consequently liberatory. Rather, I want to direct attention to what is usually left out of the equation in discussing consumption, let alone pornographic consumption, which is the work of consumption. Pierre Bourdieu and Michel de Certeau have each helped to theorise this aspect of consumption, Bourdieu by referring to 'that production which is consumption', and de Certeau in his emphasis on the 'tactics of the weak', examining popular culture for its infinite capacity to reorder dominant social hierarchies. John Fiske's *Using Popular Culture* makes explicit this shift, drawing on these two theorists as well as others to sketch out the domain of popular, as opposed to mass, culture – popular culture being what it becomes at the user's end.

Without romanticising the pornographic *per se*, a similar shift needs to be undertaken in gauging its cultural scenario. In other words, it needs to be accepted that pornography is not 'just' consumed, but is used, worked on, elaborated, remembered, fantasised about by its subjects. To stop the analysis at the artefact, as virtually all the current books and articles do, imagining that the representation is the pornography in quite simple terms, is to truncate the consumption process radically, and thereby to leave unconsidered the human making involved in completing the act of pornographic consumption. Because of the overwhelming focus on the artefacts or representations of pornography, such 'making' has been obscured in favour of simply asserting that these artefacts have a specific or even an indelible meaning, the one read off the representation by the critic. That act of interpretation is at a far remove from what happens in pornographic consumption itself, where the premium is on incorporating or acquiring material for a range of phantasmic transformations. When the pornographic image or text is acquired, the work of pornographic consumption has just begun. Some may feel that by labelling such activity 'work' an overly valorising appraisal is set up; without investing that act of fabrication with any special grandeur, I want to insist that some real consuming 'labour' transpires here too.

What is the nature of this work? Without being facetious, it is not the undoubted minor physical labour needed to complete the arousal, but instead the shuffling and collating and transcription of images or words so that they have effectivity within one's own fantasy universe – an act of accommodation, as it were. This will often entail wholesale elimination of elements of the representation, or changing salient features within it; the representation needs to blur into or become charged with historical and/or private fantasy meanings. To insist on this for pornography flies in the face of one's interest in seeing the mechanical, repetitive or even the alienating qualities of pornography, which are manifest. People in many, if not most, cases do not get the pornography they deserve, or the pornography one might imagine. Still, the pornography debate must move beyond the supposed transparency or univocity of the pornographic artefact to ask highly specific questions about the consumption of pornography by actual persons in radically different situations. One wing of the pornography discussion does, of course, already move beyond the artefact, by assuming that the consumption of pornography injects men with violence towards women, which they then act out, if only in the very fantasy entailed by looking at the pornography. So much historical and social analysis renders this dubious that it may not need to be rehearsed here; a particularly incisive rejoinder is to ask why then pornography does not have the same effect on everyone who reads it or sees it, or how to account for violence against women in its relative absence. Moving beyond that impasse, the crucial issue is to explore how what we now call 'sexuality' is imbricated with pornography's work of consumption, how integrally and intricately and unpredictably pornography figures in the *phantasmic* sexual constructions men and women both engage.

Linda Williams's recent study of pornography, *Hard Core: Power, Pleasure, and the 'Frenzy of the Visible'*,[5] is distinguished by its meticulous focus on genre, and by its dispassionate intertextual untangling of the history of the hard-core film. By zeroing in on a generic realm of pornography, she avoids entirely the impulse to totalise the pornographic that is so endemic to feminist analyses; by taking seriously the conventions, constraints and historical specificity of hard-core film, Williams can show its internal development and its sensitivity to cultural changes and consumer markets. Free-floating 'misogyny' or historically omnipresent 'violence towards women' drop away as explanatory vehicles as the book speculates that pornography intersects with the technologically induced 'frenzy of the visible', mass culture's need to bring to sight what technology can allow to become visible. A key crux of this analysis involves the hard-core film as an instrument for forcing the 'confession' of female sexuality, a demonstration which, ever since Diderot's *Les Bijoux indiscrets* as cited by Williams, is doomed to founder on the invisibility and the unknowability of female sexual pleasure. The visual elaboration of this lack runs up against the paradox of invisibility, even in the hardest-core scenario. Williams makes deft use of her thesis, which also happens to mesh with a desire to see pornography as structured around the presiding absence or invisibility of female pleasure.

Williams's adherence to the tenets of feminist film theory produces a fascinating result when set up against the strictures of film pornography. Her thesis overcomes the paralysing limits of Laura Mulvey's original formulations of the objectifying nature of the male gaze as transferred to the film camera, because Williams breaks down that paradigm through finely tuned historical and generic investigation; what remains is the mass cultural/avant-garde binary so deeply embedded in the theoretical practice of film theory. As played out in much of film theory, including Mulvey's seminal essay, narrative is the ideological villain, and the politically progressive film text must be anti-narrative, resisting visual closure at every turn, so that the alienation effects of anti-narrative can do their revelatory work of demystification.

Williams finds her version of this Brechtian cinema within hard core in the sadomasochistic genre, because it is here that sexual identities appear to be less fixed, more labile and mobile. By her own premises Williams is forced to privilege one particular sector of pornographic production over the others, in a sense painted into this corner by the belief that 'unfixed' sexual identities may provide the epiphany such consumers need – the moment of negative critique that will strip away the illusions of sexual hierarchy. What is intriguing is that labile sexual identities are not assumed to inhere in any and all of these representations; this could only be realised by Williams and other prescriptive avant-gardists if the work that consumption pornography, and other mass cultural forms, entails were also recognised. At this moment in her analysis, Williams takes a position of distance from the presumed viewers of such hard-core films, the same rather precious stance of political enlightenment that tends to mar the avant-gardist aesthetic strain of film theory (and its affiliated discourses).

Williams will wait patiently in the audience for this group of pornography consumers to encounter the rupturing moment of gender disidentification and receive their revelation, an epiphany about gender Williams already knows, and which she has not needed pornography to allow her to experience. The problem with this is not that Williams or others have hopes for a utopian overcoming of politically rigid gender identities, but that the hopes rest on a fairly hidden assumption that mass culture is a degraded form within which embryonic avant-garde progressive texts are struggling to get out. Because sadomasochism is performative and theatrical, because it is a mode of 'play', it segues neatly into theories that need to stress the performative and the constructed. This is far, far preferable to the literalist reading so prevalent in the pornography-obsessed world of Andrea Dworkin *et al.*, where sadomasochism is anathema, impossible to view even as representation. If anything, one would wish to have it valorised if only to circumvent such misunderstandings. Still, the uncanny fit between film theory's favourite 'perversion' and the practice of hard core too readily makes for an evolutionary narrative, and then the contingency and the historicity drop out. The pornographic film becomes an exercise in estrangement for its presumably naive viewers, who can build on the revelatory shock of recognition that gender identities are mutable. Julia Kristeva hopes people will read *Finnegans Wake* to find out the same thing; *chacun à son goût.*

If one problem with theories of pornography is that they in fact disdain consumption, or presume that the real work is done somewhere else, then attention should be paid to the practices of consuming pornography and its nature as an activity. The collection of pornographic images and accompanying essays gathered under the title *Caught Looking* is meant to offer actual pornography to consume, but it turns out to be exemplary of the role of historicity and sheer accident in desire, and can serve as a cautionary document in the forgetting of, the repression of, the work of fantasy entailed by the consumption of pornography. This delightful and cogent compilation, interlaced with acute brief essays and on-target polemics against censorship, testifies not only to the embeddedness of desire in time, but also, in the modern era, to its embeddedness in fashion, style and image, in patterns of consumption.

A riveting picture of a man rather desultorily having intercourse with a woman on what looks like a cafeteria table before some slightly bemused onlookers is riveting not for the act in progress, the flashes of buttock and pubic hair, but for the incredible sideburns he is sporting, as well as the insouciance of the ribbed poor-boy turtleneck he hasn't had the energy to doff. The turn-of-the-century photo of a woman easing down on a man's penis is remarkable not for its hearty, graphic genital frankness but for the accoutrements of these organs, the outmoded lingerie styles, the moustache, the grainy texture of the photographic technique and the assessment of how long the participants must have had to hold their poses in obedient tumescence. The entire book is alluring not as a pornographic volume, although one or another of these pictures might possibly 'speak' to someone in that voice, but instead as a gloss on the imbrication of mass cultural styles in the pornographic response of modernity. Hair, body language, body morphology, bedroom props only have to be a shade off to sunder any sexual response to the pictures and to instead open up a reverie on the *punctum* of any particular image, a *punctum* which is more mass cultural than Barthes' rather ahistorical nostalgia for a past, frozen time. An image of two men getting it on on a beach somewhere is difficult to date except for the jeans pulled down to halfmast – those jeans occasion almost infinitely proliferating meditations on James Dean, California, an age of grace.

Caught Looking is an empowering book in that it dares to offer these images under the rubric of feminism itself, a bold move in the Meese Commission climate of its publication (and even bolder under current conditions). What it suggests, too, is the difficulty of intervening in the pornography debates with anything like 'real' pornography, pornography produced out of the academic discourse itself, since the album version of *Caught Looking* is extremely compelling but immediately self-cancelling as pornography. What it violates is the mass cultural contextuality so essential to contemporary pornography. In other words the reassemblage of 'pornographic' photographic images under the imprimatur of critical consciousness empties out the pornographic moment, a moment that is experienced on the continuum of such pornographic exposures. The pornographic artefact lodges in the meshes of a mass cultural pornographic discourse, and it does not 'mean' or 'read' as pornographic outside those necessary nets. By singling out images garnered over relatively vast historical and sexual expanses, and then making an inventive bricolage of the resulting singularities, pornography is vitiated.

This is not to preclude someone's finding one of these images such a treasure that they felt compelled to scissor it out and put it to pornographic (masturbatory) use; what it does mean, though, is that the collection isn't pornography and never will be. Pornography registers *in relation*; each pornographic 'item' speaks the name of its fellows, distinguished along lines of genre, activity, character or medium. When that relation is violated by creating a pornographic miscellany, a type of art is formed or posited – each piece of the collection is given singular, auratic status by virtue of how we look at it. This is not how mass culture functions, and as a consequence, pornography withers in its absence.

The academic surfeit of texts on pornography does not arise uncontextually itself; it has been fostered by or is reactive to the intense cultural concern with pornography, which it echoes. This context is not always explicitly about pornography, and requires another term to locate it on the social spectrum. Social pornography is the best phrase I can muster for the substitutive collective pornographies our culture produces; social pornography is the name for the pornographic fantasies the society collectively engenders and then mass culturally disseminates, usually in the cause of anti-pornography. The past decade's fascination with explicit and imaginary child sexual abuse is the best example, although there are many others, not the least of which is the public discussion of pornography, which allows for pornographic enactment in the most explicit if mediated forms. (The Wildmon attacks on what it calls 'gay pornography' are stunning creations of gay pornography; Wildmon et fils ignore legal and explicit gay pornography, i.e. magazines, to rant about a gay pornography they discern in various art works or films, necessitating their arcanely hermeneutic explanations, social pornography to perfection.) The graphic replication in the media of the acts alleged to have been committed in the McMartin preschool trial, for example, allowed an astonishing social fixation on sexual acts and sexualised children's bodies to flow into public discourse unimpeded, in the guise of a repudiation of these acts.

A most unintentionally amusing contribution to the social pornography discourse is offered by David Mura in *A Male Grief*.[6] These latter-day confessions of a pornography eater are remarkable for the way they consolidate the incipient discourses that flutter about pornography and suck from its stem, to wit, addiction, sexual abuse, male feminism and confessional mania. While Mura has written a very interesting book on his visit to Japan as a Japanese American, has contributed to the Greywolf multicultural annual, and so on, *A Male Grief* is highly problematic, and can help to demonstrate the uneasy place of mass culture in the profusion of discussion on pornography, because it is lodged so tightly within various mass cultural forms and yet considers itself a *cri de coeur*, a departure from the pornographic. Pornography is shown to be a disease; like heart attacks or alcoholism it is a disease that strikes the already vulnerable, those made vulnerable by the perversion of family bonds through alcohol abuse.

This criticism is not meant to minimise the devastating impact of the sexual abuse of children, nor to question the importance of its exposure; what must be addressed is the slippage of an addiction theory into a singular explanation for interest in pornography. The etiology of pornography 'addiction' is traced directly to several rather murkily presented acts of abuse by an uncle figure; ironically, these sections are the most 'poetic' in form and, in this text filled with solecism and ungainly writing, are the best-written and most evocative interludes, presumably because they reflect the fact that Mura, a poet, is on shaky ground in more sustained modes of exposition. The notion that other men might read, look at or be otherwise absorbed in pornography for different reasons, or with less haunted and urgent sensations than those he reports, seems never to strike him; the 'secret' of pornography is revealed, and its Rosetta stone is child sexual abuse. Mura embraces woman-against-pornography attitudes with wholehearted approval – yes, he is one of those men who have done violence to women in their thoughts by the very act of rushing home from the convenience store and burying themselves in *Hustler*.

No doubt an actual addiction to pornography can exist, and can be infinitely painful and poignant. The answer to such addictions is not to define all pornography as such an addiction, nor to claim that what was unfortunate about the addiction in this case was 'violence towards women'. Mura portrays himself in the piece as out of touch with women altogether, and instead incredibly eager to have some time to read his magazines. There are few male commentators more eager to embrace the views of Andrea Dworkin and Catharine MacKinnon, *et al.*, with a disconcerting, enthusiastically hysterical cry of 'mea culpa, mea maxima culpa!'

In this particular case, the argument that pornography is 'natural' ignores the fact that there are men who have given up their obsession with pornography and who have not died. . . . Even if men's desire for pornography is natural (i.e., genetically determined), this does not mean we must recognise it as good or inevitable. We do not turn to the diabetic and say, there is nothing you can do, you must enjoy your disease.

It's true what they say, Mura concurs, and, moreover, it can't be helped – men have a tragic addiction to pornography arising out of the dysfunctional family, and the solution will require its own version of a twelve-step programme and abstention from pornography for life. Would that this last were even possible: alcohol can be avoided, with some difficulty, by staying away from bars and package stores and ordering alternative beverages; pornography will wink out at you from every billboard and husting, from matchbook covers and *Life* magazine covers and mainstream TV. Women, of course, have nothing to do with pornography; they are uninterested in it, and even if abused they express their victimhood in less damaging, or more victimlike, ways. One wonders if Mura's wife was buying romance novels at the supermarket to counter his men's magazines; what Ann Snitow refers to as 'pornography for women' might give Mura a turn if he read some of it. The judicious exclusion of women from the torments of pornographic addiction is partially due to Mura's notion that they do not possess an 'objectifying' sexual desire, or maybe any desire, but also springs from his certainty that women are not as connected to this form of consumption.

The disease model of pornography denies phantasmic necessity for pornographic representation at all; there is no safe 'level' of consumption, helpfully linking pornography with the new American view of drug use, where even that one puff of marijuana inhaled at a party in 1973 has left discernible scars on the internal moral soul. However, men are not to blame – they are victims, compensating for the scourge of sexual abuse with the elixir of pornography. An ecstatic round-robin is set up, a sort of circle jerk of social pornography, which helps to show how deeply implicated pornography is at all levels of mass culture, even those levels that would fervently deny such complicity. It is more typical to assume that these discursive forces are conflictually engaged; for example, that the upsurge in trials of daycare operators for child sexual abuse is a counter-swing of the pendulum that has pornography at its nether end, so to speak. The phenomena seem more intimately tied than that; the enlarging and eager audience for the recital of child sex abuse details has more to do with making the everyday pornographic in its familiar sites, those of the home, the school, the daycare centre. In any such discussion one has to take enormous pains to acknowledge that the silence that formerly prevailed on the frequency of sex abuse, especially within the home, and the silencing of its many victims, preponderantly but not exclusively female, was of course an atrocious wrong. To imagine that the audience for all the hyperbolically embellished sexual descriptions in the Hilary Foretich case had as its primary interest the salvaging of the child's life, though, is quite absurd. 'Hilary', as a media construct, was a deliciously harrowing Alice in Wonderland of social pornography.

The nadir of arguments about pornography could be said to have been reached with Susanne Kappeler's book, *The Pornography of Representation*. This excruciatingly reductive work fills the slot allocated to a seemingly 'Marxist' feminist critique of pornography, since Kappeler throws out words like 'commodity' and 'capitalism' at strategic junctures, a critique which by extension includes all of representation. Simplistic arguments and poor reasoning aside, *The Pornography of Representation* bears scrutiny because it fascinatingly demonstrates the farther, wilder shores of the feminist pornography battle; ultimately, all representation becomes, or is, suspect. Whatever this text may think it is doing, it is really a book about the perils and dangers of representation, which of course includes not only art in every form, but the very representational nature of human language and psychic structure. Pornography is imbricated in every representation, because representation is 'the reification of the message'. Kappeler wishes to sweep this away with one broom, so that in place of complicitous representation of any and all stripes, women could set 'communication'.

If anything is to be done about pornography, if a cultural shift in consciousness (revolution, not *coup d'état*) will eventually move away from pornographic structures of perception and thought, then the arts themselves will necessarily also have to change, Art will have to go.

That final admission is the one Kappeler has been avoiding throughout the book, while its *sotto voce* muttering has been implicit under the text's breath. Somehow, women will produce new forms of communication practices, not what we now know is suspect – Art. How is it that women will be exempt from or immune to the omnipresent regime of pornographic representation? A touching and befuddled Marxism provides the answer: women – all women, even Margaret Thatcher – are outside the hegemonic power structure, and they are just waiting for the chance to escape its nets and begin the perceptual millennium.

If women, black people, workers, listeners were allowed to contribute to the culture's description of 'its' condition, Hegel might be challenged, the dominant versions of the partial collectivities of the family, of the brotherhood, of the mafia, of the nation, of the first world, might be rejected as unacceptable models of groups that are based on self-interest rather than solidarity.

All oppression is homologous in Kappeler's analysis, and all dominations run together: capitalists are pornographers are wife-beaters are slave-owners who keep pets. (Kappeler devotes a chapter to a delirious historical free-for-all that links the bourgeois keeping of pets to the commodification of women as sexual 'pets', seemingly unaware that in that case she has failed to consider the vast proportion of women not so favoured by class or whose gender oppression is poorly modelled on the paradigm of the family pet or even the imprisoned zoo animal, Kappeler's other indictment of the nineteenth-century male.) Aesthetic endeavours of any kind are simply part of this large conspiracy, men's demonic attempts to use women as sex objects or 'speech' objects (men do all the talking in Kappeler's universe). 'Pornography' is really Kappeler's name for the conspiracy of patriarchy; it is the quintessence of domination, hegemony's substrate, the reified, metaphysical form of power itself.

Kappeler's argument has the virtue of being deeply symptomatic, a ground-zero representation of the pornographic. Ironically, what Kappeler wants to deny, to expunge, to vilify and to overthrow is representation; to achieve this end, within analysis at least, women become the purest victims of a pornographic regime, the very name for gender hierarchy. *The Pornography of Representation* has a goofy dignity achieved through its haphazard amalgam of quasi-Marxist analysis and aesthetic *ressentiment*. What it ignores is that there is nothing outside representation, including language, the eminently representational. Kappeler's book is deeply symptomatic of the intimate tie between pornography and the representations of culture in general, especially those of literature and the plastic arts. Her slash-and-burn thesis cannot sustain its own logic, but one remembers how tenuous maintaining the differences between cultural objects proves to be. Allan Bloom locates the downfall of American civilisation in the ravishments of Mick Jagger's pelvic gyrations, sufficient to thrust

aside the greater merits of Plato and Nietzsche. His position is simply ludicrous, predicated as it is on his own fantasy of and desire for the cultural power of those protean hips, and his certitude that without mass culture the young would be safely ensconced in the library; still, it points to an undercurrent in the academic pornography market. Pornography is sexy, and so is writing about it; pornography can't and won't replace political philosophy, but it does bring to the fore all the worries our culture has about representation and its lack of guarantees.

A central difficulty in adjudicating this debate, or even in participating in it, is the essentialisation of 'sexuality' that is the often invariable accompaniment. Sexuality in this reified form gets parcelled out over the population, atomised as individuals with 'a sexuality'. At times this refers to the broad division hegemonically made by society in characterising heterosexual and homosexual behaviour, in order to legally proscribe the latter and to police the forms of the former. At other moments, sexuality refers to the supposed essence of one's sexual being, one's sexual feelings or orientation or particular slot on the spectrum of speciality tastes. These macroscopic definitions are necessary and inevitable, but they also serve to skew discussions of the place of the pornographic and its role in sexuality. A more supple and elastic conception of sexualities – not, however, the forfeiting of sexual identities or discrete practices linked to those identities – such as is suggested in the dispersal of sexuality across several ambiguous 'types' of its practice in our everyday lives, could help to dislodge the essentialised sexuality of contemporary discourse, which gives rise to, among other noxious things, the Dworkin view of male sexuality, where intercourse is, simply, rape.

Sexuality might better, or more richly, be conceived as discontinuous or adjacent practices, many or most of which are not enacted, multiple formations with loose, instead of rigid, psychosocial affiliation. A possible metaphor for the interaction of these sexualities might be sedimentation, or, more conceptually put, overdetermination again, although one could also, in order to preserve a singular sexuality, describe this as a sexual economy with numerous simultaneous circuits. Among these layers, there is a sexuality emanating from family relations, a family romance that never disappears and is not simply absorbed into 'adult' sexuality. Childhood sexuality remains as more than a residue or a sublimated resource; it is not 'outgrown' or transformed only, but continues to exist as a rich social dimension of sexual practice, even where it is seemingly forgotten. A vector of sexuality is concerned with animals and the natural world; here I'm not speaking of bestiality or of anything considered perverse, but of the utterly familiar and undeniably sexual relations people exhibit with their pets and their sexual attraction to other animals. A specific sexuality belongs to the realm of images and phantasmic representations; these highly charged relations are a practice unto themselves. A considerable amount of the sexual economy can be given over to this circuit, which tends then to seem to be 'sexuality' emerging in some straightforward preference for particular images. Here is where pornography enters in, showing why it is too simple to annex pornography to one invariant sexual mode of being, or to one invariant attitude towards women. Pornography consumption is or can be one quite distinct realm of sexual behaviour as transcribed onto images, words, memories, repetitions. It is only a part of an ensemble or a constellation of sexual possibilities and realities, and its isolation in most current discussions is formidably at odds with its highly particular, material, and contingent places in the spectrum of individually constructed sexualities.

Scott Tucker's recent essay, 'Gender, Fucking and Utopia',[7] makes a beautiful and idiosyncratic argument for the necessity of representation and the multiple iconographies of pornography, and offers a powerful statement against sexuality as a pure 'social fiction'. Tucker is not willing to dispense with nature quite so easily, not in the form of a 'natural' sexuality, but as a determinant of and a limitation on all human existence. Gay pornography is the most telling revision of the thesis that pornography is violence against women; certain theorists have had to turn cartwheels to assimilate gay male pornography to the dire objectification thought to run rampant in heterosexual pornography. Tucker's stance on this – himself a gay male pornography star, among other professional accomplishments – reverberates with the truth: 'I don't doubt our current identities are too restrictive; I also don't doubt that definable identities will emerge even in utopia.'[8]

To conclude is to mediate on the perilous nature of the object. The academic market is hot for pornography because pornography is both the object and the subject of desire, the representation and the reader, the consumer and the consumed, in one inextricable package. We need to resist the reification of pornography into one singular phenomenon or social form, to acknowledge its multiplicity, to accept that people transform the mass cultural objects that come before them in a variety of ways, to admit that men and women develop their own pornographic lexicons, whether through entirely home-made images or in purchased form, and to see that 'objectification' need not be in itself a violent act. Objectification in the liminal form of images or words encountered in private may in fact be a *sine qua non* of desire; how this is translated into social relations of equality and justice is a pressing issue, if not *the* pressing issue, but about pornography it can fairly be said 'you can't get there from here'. The charge of 'pornography' has again become a potent cultural weapon, and at this moment it is more crucial to support the potential for transgression and critique still inherent in pornography as an outlaw discourse, than obsessionally to pursue the hidden inner secret of the pornographic as violent or objectifying. In our lust to pronounce on pornography, we measure our envy of the truly consumable, and consuming, text.

Reprinted from *Transition*, issue 54, pp. 68–89, by kind permission of Oxford University Press, Inc.

NOTES

1. Susan Gubar and Joan Huff (eds), *For Adult Users Only: The Dilemma of Violent Pornography* (Bloomington: Indiana University Press, 1989).

2. Susanne Kappeler, *The Pornography of Representation* (Cambridge: Polity Press, 1986).

3. Kate Ellis *et al.* (eds), *Caught Looking: Feminism, Pornography and Censorship* (Seattle, WA: Real Comet Press, 1988).

4. Joel Kovel, 'The Antidialectic of Pornography', in Michael S. Kimmel (ed.), *Men Confront Pornography* (New York: Crown Publishers, 1989).

5. Linda Williams, *Hard Core: Power, Pleasure, and the 'Frenzy of the Visible'* (Berkeley, CA: University of California Press, 1989).

6. David Mura, *A Male Grief* (Minneapolis, MN: Milkweed Editions, ca. 1987).

7. Scott Tucker, 'Gender, Fucking and Utopia', *Social Text* 27 (1991).

8. Ibid.

16   Complicity: Women Artists Investigating Masculinity[1]

Liz Kotz

INTRODUCTION

Some of the most powerful work being done today around sexuality and the body inhabits a messy, ambiguous space where pathology meets pleasure, where what we most fear is what we most desire. Such a strategy is not about the critique of 'misrepresentation' – from the presumed plain of greater enlightenment – but about a cautious entry into the discourses of entrapment and subjugation as fields of fantasy or sites of exploration.

This space of potentially complicitous fascination offers a provocative, and provocatively dangerous, site for contemporary feminist art-making. Recent work by media artists Lutz Bacher and Abigail Child probes what it means for women artists to appropriate and obsessively explore specific discourses, representations and stances conventionally regarded as 'masculine' – particularly those involving misogynist or pornographic representations. Though pornography, with its highly charged narratives of subjugation and entrapment, constitutes a key site in their investigations, the strategies they employ could not be more different from those of anti-porn feminists. For while Bacher and Child acknowledge that these registers of fantasy and desire are indeed troubling, they dive headlong into this moral morass in all its grotesque hilarity, seduction and horror, insisting that this terrain should be obsessively explored rather than proscribed.

Working at the edges of feminist theories of sexual representation, these artists challenge a kind of 'first stage' feminism often predicated on constructing an identification with female characters and subject positions and a critique of male or 'masculinist' ones. Instead, they investigate the kinds of *instabilities* and *ambivalences* elicited when female artists invite female spectators to identify with conventionally male subject positions – enacting and exploiting instabilities and ambivalences which recent feminist theoretical models suggest are already structured into the very project of gender identities.

Echoing the radical readings of Freudian and Lacanian psychoanalysis undertaken by North American theorists such as Judith Butler and Kaja Silverman, Bacher's and Child's interests in moments of fractured psychic identification point to the very transversality and instability of gender categories. In questioning rigid categories of 'sexual difference' established in more traditional psychoanalytic feminist theory, both Butler and Silverman have emphasised the intense ambivalence at the heart of mimetic incorporations, and the complex interpenetrations of desire and identification which make fixed, stable or unified gender positions difficult at best. Investigating psychic mechanisms of obsession and repetition, these writers suggest how the very 'compulsion to repeat' that seemingly structures and consolidates gender identities can perhaps be made to subvert and disperse them as well.

Taken seriously, these radically reconfigured theoretical projects mark a critical shift in practices and assumptions, one which revolves around the articulation of feminist strategies which do not rely on the fiction of an authentic female subject. Indeed, the very questioning of what counts as 'feminist', once categories of gender are envisioned as neither stable nor self-evident, is central to this shift. Since both Silverman's and Butler's theoretical projects have important consequences for understanding Bacher's and Child's appropriation and repetition of problematic images and materials to shift and disperse gender positions, I will outline some of these theorists' key insights before returning to a discussion of the two artists' work.

In her book *The Acoustic Mirror*, film theorist Kaja Silverman has probed the relationship of women film-makers to their 'masculine' characters and materials, proposing the idea that women artists must first assume masculine identities in order to dismantle or disperse them. Silverman has written on the films of Liliana Cavani which, in her analysis, work to erase some of the boundaries separating male from female subjectivity, positing highly transversal and unstable heterosexual relationships.[2] Probing this project of what she terms 'phallic divestiture', Silverman identifies 'the psychic transfer at the centre of Cavani's cinema: the transfer from female to male and back again',[3] positing a preoccupation with femininity and with masochism paradoxically mediated through male representations. Just as, for male artists, intense identification with female characters or personas may challenge culturally enforced regimes of gender and sexuality (although not unproblematically, Silverman is quick to note), the female exploration of male subjectivity offers a potentially productive, if easily misunderstood, site for feminist art-making.

Tracing female authorial desire and subjectivity in a number of avant-garde texts, Silverman articulates an implicitly performative theory of authorial gender, one which locates authorship in the 'libidinal coherence' of a body of films, in a reading of 'the desire that circulates there' as organised around a primal fantasmatic scene or scenario. In order to challenge reductive readings of authorial gender (which presume authorial identification along stable gender lines, or rely on normative readings of authorial intention), Silverman focuses on texts by female authors which operate precisely along series of problematic or deviant identifications, texts in which authorial gender 'within' and 'outside' the text must often be read against each other, relationally, rather than assuming their straightforward correspondence.[4]

Butler's own project, articulated in her book *Gender Trouble* and more recent critical essays, has focused on strategies of 'parodic imitation' and 'gender insubordination' evident in many lesbian and gay cultural practices. Butler's emphasis in fact is precisely on the destabilising and denaturalising effects of such problematic identifications, effects which, she argues, serve to destabilise the very naturalness or self-evidence of the more normative psychic processes (for example, male identification with male figures) they ostensibly mimic or imitate.[5] Her key insight that 'the copy of the origin *displaces the origin as origin*'[6] offers a compelling account of why female

artists might choose to copy or re-enact male representations rather than romantically attempt to create their 'own'.

Such strategies of gender insubordination are not incompatible with Silverman's insight into the potential transgressivity of female imitations of male models, so aggressive as to verge on impersonation, which potentially challenge the stability of both 'male' and 'female' terms. Yet by insisting that all gender is structured on mechanisms of repetition and imitation, Butler's performative theory of gender implicitly extends this notion of 'impersonation' to include diverse cross-gender and intra-gender imitations as well.[7] Countering the feminist epithet that some women are 'male-identified', Butler's work contends that in this symbolic system we are all to some extent 'male-identified', and that the feminist pursuit of some mythic state of authentically female identification is illusory at best and often rigidly exclusionary and regulatory in effect.[8]

By emphasising the possibility of multiple identifications, and putting the kinds of 'subversive and parodic convergences that characterise gay and lesbian cultures' at the centre of her analysis, Butler questions the stability of any form of gender identity constructed on a strict binary framework.[9] An understanding of radically dispersed and disorganised gender identities, and of the body as the surface upon which gender is inscribed, leads Butler to a consideration of a possibly radical *disjuncture* between body and identity, and the possible confusion and redistribution of the various attributes upon which gender identification constructs itself. Noting that 'transsexuals often claim a radical discontinuity between sexual pleasures and bodily parts', Butler suggests such disjunctures between 'real' and 'imagined' bodies are hardly limited to clear-cut instances of gender dysphoria. Pleasures and desires are always imaginary, representing fantasmatic processes with complex relations to the real. Rejecting a heterosexual matrix which would naturalise illusions of continuity and causality between sex, gender and desire, Butler insists on the many possible disjunctures, excesses and confusions operating among these terms, including the very role desire plays in fantasmatically constructing the body: 'the phantasmatic nature of desire reveals the body not as its ground or cause but as its *occasion* and its *object*. . . . This imaginary condition of desire always exceeds the physical body through or on which it works.'[10]

Such rigorous interrogations of the relations between gender, identification and desire are indeed critical to a more complex understanding of pornographic representations, since they serve to question, for instance, the pervasive tendency to conflate fantasy and the real which produces all-too-familiar readings of porn. Even progressive analyses of heterosexual porn, such as Andrew Ross's[11] (and, arguably, Linda Williams' [but see pp. 164–74 of this volume]), which argue in favour of 'pornography from a woman's point of view' – varying sexual scenarios and offering more 'equality' of representation, such as portraying the woman on top – rest on a completely naturalised reading of gender relations, in which it is assumed that readers or viewers identify along predictable male/female lines – a binary model of gender which, as Butler demonstrates, naturalises and restabilises gender within a heterosexual matrix. A very different reading, primarily derived from lesbian and gay cultural practices, would emphasise the possibility for multiple and contradictory gender identifications which shift and disperse within the scene, so that the woman viewer, in effect, can be anywhere. Challenging more normative feminist readings of female authorial desire and spectatorial identification, both Butler and Silverman help us to tease out the consequences of these fractured psychic identifications, and to embrace the proliferation of possible gender identities. Thus they offer ways of theorising the diverse strategies of resignification, imitation and repetition at play in the work of artists such as Lutz Bacher and Abigail Child.

THE COMPULSION TO REPEAT: MINIMALISM AND PORNOGRAPHY

Lutz Bacher is a Berkeley-based conceptual artist who has worked in photography, video and installation formats since the mid-1970s, when she formed part of the Bay area group 'Photography and Language'.[12] Her work is critical in its excavation of masculinity, from her early photo projects such as *Men at War* (1975) to her current installation projects and feminist reappropriations of canonical male art works.[13] Throughout her career, Bacher has investigated the twisted representations of sexuality and desire found in pornographic books, pulp sociology, medical texts, televised trials and the art-historical canon, among other sources, enacting the warped relationship of a female viewer to such perverse historical documents.

These interests link Bacher's work with that of Abigail Child, a New York-based experimental film- and video-maker.[14] In recent years, Child's work has been exhibited internationally, including screenings at the 1989 Whitney Biennial and the New York Film Festival. Her seven-part series *Is This What You Were Born For?* (1981–1989) combines found footage and recreated elements of film noir, pornography, soap opera, early cinema and home movies relentlessly to probe gesture and the body. While her work, as film, employs very different means to engage and disturb its viewer, Child, like Bacher, delves into this obsessive interrogation of gender and sexuality as sites of pleasure and unease. In her short, dense and highly poetic films, Child teases out the moments of rupture and excess in cinematic melodrama and popular cultural forms.

Ambivalent, obsessive, and focused on materials which are somehow 'not okay', Bacher's and Child's works are controversial within traditional feminist contexts. This controversy may in part reflect their interest in the excavation of masculinity, particularly normative male heterosexuality, as a site of female analysis and obsession. Yet while their use of pornographic texts is clearly a key issue, the difficulties their works pose may have less to do with the *kinds* of found materials they work with than the *ambiguity* with which they approach them. There's a kind of camp axiom that 'you have to love the materials you're working with'[15] which suggests something of the ambivalence, the inseparability of horror and fascination, built into the relationship of women artists towards their borrowed images and materials – and to the borrowed artistic and formal traditions within which they work.

Animating both artists' work is the use of serial structure (or in Child's work, the sequencing possibilities of film) to undo the stability of gender positions, and of repetition to produce and proliferate these unstable identifications: by relentlessly denaturalising the content of representations and constantly shifting the subject position of the viewer.[16] Indeed, despite its often aggressively pop content, almost all of Bacher's work is structured along devices derived from classic minimalism: duration, repetition, serial structure, sequencing, attention to scale, etc. These strategies also inform earlier works by Child, such as her 1985 film *Covert Action*, which selectively fractures and repeats sequences from found 1950s' home movie footage of two men and two women on vacation; as with Bacher, the repetition functions to put the viewer in a constantly shifting and ambivalent relation to the material, and to shift attention from the incidentally topical material to the basic structures of gender, gesture and the corporeal theatrics of the body.

As the centrality of these formal strategies of repetition and proliferation suggests, Bacher's work constructs a relation to minimalist art analogous to Child's relation to structural film-making.[17] Both represent feminist projects located partially within the legacies of historically male artistic practices, which adapt their rigorous attention to structure and materiality and reinscribe these from a conviction that the cultural meanings of images and materials *do* matter.[18] Working in a visual vocabulary that references minimalist forms and strategies (typified by the serial presentation of large, often industrial, objects), Bacher has a strategic interest in pushing art towards the everyday, in exploring the charge which art can produce as a bearer of the real.[19] Her obsession with the serial presentation of messy pop cultural materials suggests an intersection between pop and minimalist concerns. In a series of projects which, over the past sixteen years, have focused variously on found photographs, porn images and texts, self-help narratives, medical devices and other everyday materials, Bacher seems to suggest that all these things are minimalist objects now.

As this curious conjuncture of sexually charged, scavenged materials and minimal strategies attests, both Bacher's and Child's projects suggest a joining of the tropes of pornography and minimalism. As oddly matched as these two spheres appear to be – one canonical and art-historical, the other everyday and sexual – their intersection is critical to understanding how both artists work these formal strategies of repetition and accumulation to unsettle the kinds of stable subject positions that would produce predictable, predetermined responses to these materials.[20] For just as both minimalism and pornography undeniably offer sites for the female investigation of masculinity, both also tend to be structured around repetition, one psychically and the other materially.

As the critic, Hal Foster has argued, minimalist art practices historically operated to 'push art toward the quotidian, the utilitarian, the non- or anti-

artistic'.[21] Rejecting a traditional art-historical account of 1960s' art movements of minimalism and pop as *opposing* practices, Foster sees them as united through their common embrace of serial structure and their response to a new order of serial production and consumer culture. This embrace of seriality serves to sever art not only from the subjectivity of the artist but also from the very representational paradigm that has structured post-Enlightenment art production. While conventional histories have focused on the challenge to representation posed by the negation of content in abstract art, Foster suggests that the simulacral nature of seriality and repetition, derived from the commodity structures of late capitalist society, may be far more significant. Indeed, he argues, 'in any serious social history of paradigms, repetition, not abstraction, may well supersede representation'.[22]

Rather than contesting representation in terms of content – as criteria of 'truthfulness' or 'positive representation' in effect do – strategies of repetition and proliferation offer means of subverting the referential logic that underpins representation, of emptying the referent of its meaning, of its status *as* representation. Such a strategy animates both Bacher's and Child's use of mass cultural materials, one which operates by repeating certain highly charged images or sequences until they effectively implode, rather than attempting to judge their veracity in relation to some original truth. This strategy, derived from a conjuncture of pop and minimalist practices, is perhaps most visible and most powerful in their redeployment of pornographic materials, since it allows them to exploit instabilities of fantasy and identification that are always already embedded in pornographic representations.

In his revisionist, psychoanalytically informed reading of minimalism and surrealism, Foster privileges the simulacral effects of both repetition and fantasy as modes which, debased within high modernism's perpetual 'search for origins', now offer potentially useful postmodernist mechanisms for superseding a representational paradigm. Citing Gilles Deleuze on *Difference and Repetition* (a key text for Butler as well), Foster suggests that in a commodity-saturated culture it is largely difference, artificially produced, that we consume, and claims this structure as what unites pop and minimalism. Arguing for the structuring role of this logic of 'difference and repetition', in all aspects of modern culture, Foster considers its potentially contradictory effects:

More than any other mass cultural content in pop, or industrial technique in minimalism, it is this logic, now general to both high art and popular culture, that redefines the lines between high and low culture. Though involvement with this logic must ultimately qualify the transgressivity of minimalism and pop, it is important to stress that they do not merely reflect it: they exploit this logic, which is to say that, at least potentially, they release difference and repetition as subversive forces.[23]

This effect, of releasing difference and repetition as potentially subversive forces, can be seen as what links Bacher's and Child's engagements with minimalism with their relentless interrogations of gender. Their tendency to combine tropes of pornography and minimalism stands in for what is an overarching strategy: the obsessive repetition and proliferation of problematic images in order effectively to undo their referential logic – a project in which, to reprise Butler's key formulation, 'the copy of the origin *displaces the origin as origin*'.

Yet, among all the possible forms of pop and mass cultural representation, certain instabilities inherent to pornography as a genre make it particularly susceptible to such mechanisms of repetition and recontextualisation. As Abigail Solomon-Godeau has argued, pornography tends to offer a set of 'limit texts' for the study of sexuality and representation, embodying certain functions at their most extreme and most visible. 'The very nature of the subject,' she asserts, 'functions to elicit the investigator's own stake in an explicitly sexual visual field.'[24] As such, pornography represents a place where distance breaks down, where subjectivity is insistently engaged, even uncomfortably so. Even its incorporation into a project of critique is notoriously unstable, since even the most determined efforts to reframe pornographic representations as objects of a politically motivated examination can go deeply awry, subverting authorial intention in fascinating if problematic ways.[25]

As Judith Butler has written, pornographic representations, as a register of fantasy, have a notoriously complex relation to the real.[26] Butler is responding to the realist and mimetic readings of porn offered by North American feminists such as Andrea Dworkin and Catharine MacKinnon (and rightwing American politicians like Jesse Helms), which conflate the fantasmatic and the real, and rely on the kinds of straightforward, unproblematised gender identifications that both Butler and Silverman, along with others, have relentlessly questioned. Butler uses psychoanalytic theory to emphasise the displacement and multiplicity of the very 'I' that fantasises, already split inside and outside the fantasmatic scene. Citing Laplanche and Pontalis's contention that 'fantasy is not the object of desire, but its setting', Butler notes that fantasy entails a proliferation of identifications distributed among the various elements of the scene, its dispersal including setting, all characters, and all actions.[27]

While I agree with Butler's assertion that fantasy disperses identification throughout the scene (and with the anti-censorship politics with which she aligns her analysis), her framework appears to neglect precisely what Dworkin and MacKinnon cling to all too single-mindedly: the notion that while one may identify with the scene as a whole, one may well also experience a particularly compelling identification with a certain specific position, figure or role (an identification that need not, as Silverman's work clearly demonstrates, always align itself along fixed gender lines, although the weight of compulsory heterosexuality indeed forcefully acts to compel such identifications). The very elegance of Butler's rebuttal of Dworkin and MacKinnon seems to rest on a politically motivated systematicity that appears to disavow these very kinds of contradiction (a theoretical consistency and rhetorical elegance for which MacKinnon's writing is well known, disavowing as she does any contradictory information or experience). For if identifications can be dispersed in fantasy, they can also be consolidated and reconfigured.

Both Bacher and Child enact a more complex and ambiguous strategy, one which acknowledges the power of both analyses, and the instability of a practice that cannot be elegant because it must work from these implicitly messy contradictions and discontinuities. Neither conflating nor severing fantasy and 'real life', they seem to work from a position that acknowledges the undeniable *tension* between the fantasmatic and the real embodied in pornography, a tension which plays on both the oscillation between the subject 'inside' and 'outside' the scene, and between a diffuse identification with the 'scene' as a whole and a particularly compelling identification with a specific position or figure – an identification that need not rest on the gender or 'actual' physical body of the viewer.

This tension seems located precisely in the very filmic and photographic media with which these artists work. As Solomon-Godeau notes, in her inquiry into the history of pornographic photography (a history which appears to be co-extensive with that of photography as a technology), photography imparts to visual representation, however problematically, an undeniable 'aura' of the real. In her examination of the shift from pre-photographic practices (erotic paintings, engravings, drawings, and so forth) to the introduction of erotic photography, Solomon-Godeau suggests that, far from involving a mere change in media or materials, this particular conjuncture – pornographic representations and photographic technologies – initiates some kind of paradigm shift, one which invokes a very different, more indexical relation to the real. The effects of such a shift, it seems, cannot fully be accounted for by relying on analogies between intra-psychic mechanisms of visual fantasy and actual visual representations.

Both Bacher and Child effectively exploit this inherent instability and tension in filmic and photographic pornographic representations, and use techniques derived from minimalism to push it to greater extremes: to fragment further and shift viewer identifications, to engage and displace the fears and desires such representations provoke, and to heighten the potential diffusion of attention, not only between male and female subject positions, but more formally, from act to frame, or sequence to sequence. Proliferating instances of repetition, fragmentation and excess within these borrowed materials, their interventions exploit the very kinds of distraction and disruption that pornographic conventions attempt, however unsuccessfully, to contain, and produce very different kinds of pleasure in the process.

In a key project, *Sex with Strangers* (*Obscenity, Misogyny, Desire*) (1986), Bacher presented a series of large photographic images with accompanying captions, taken from a 1970s' porn book thinly disguised as a sociological text. The black and white images, of 'rape' and fellatio, are disturbing and eerie, awkward and explicit. Shot in very high contrast, the images take on an edge of abstraction. Yet their effect is made all the odder by the captions, which veer between registers of parody, porn narrative, and the faux-scientific in their lurid accounts of female nymphomania and wayward hitchhikers. One reads,

'In countless oral adventures some girls are overreacting to a restrictive lifestyle that was imposed on them by parents.' By crossing disciplinary languages, such texts bring out the perverse voyeurism embedded in porn narratives and sociological discourses alike. Whereas in much 80s' text/image art the verbiage effectively repressed the visual, in *Sex with Strangers* the preposterous, high-blown captions fail to 'anchor' the images: graphic, repetitive and obsessive, they spin hopelessly out of control.

With its predilection for such 'limit texts' embodying relations of power and sexuality at their most densely congealed, disturbing and humorous, Bacher's work asserts the necessity for women to explore these messy spaces of culture and desire. *Sex with Strangers* is about power *and* the erotic, about their very inseparability. By blowing the images up on a gallery wall (the mural-like prints are 72″ x 40″), but refusing to alter, reframe or comment on them in any other way, Bacher forces the viewer to confront a potential instability of responses: a constant slippage between positions of 'looking on' and identification, between psychic dispersal and fixity, and between feelings of pleasure and unease, attraction and repulsion. While the scenes depicted are heterosexual, the subject positions they construct need not be – particularly since the abstraction and scale of the images elicits identification with the scene or with actions more than the specifically gendered participants. The image/texts are offered up not only as objects of analysis (a by now familiar trope, one that would attempt to stabilise a univocal reading), but as objects of an aesthetic, indeed an aestheticising, gaze. As Bacher has suggested, in her statements about the project, her use of these debased materials is as much about reconfiguring the sublime as addressing questions of sexuality and gender; indeed, her engagement with these deeply visceral images suggests the very inseparability of the two projects:

> I don't think about whether something is pornographic or obscene. This is just not the approach I take. I mean I don't look for the most inflammatory or controversial approach to any subject either. Rather I look for images and texts that embody a certain complex of ideas in the most visceral and direct way. Now the image/texts from *Sex with Strangers* are representative of that complex nexus where gender, sex, and language meet – which

seems like something preposterous to say about a bunch of pictures of sucking. . . . I always return to the enormous feeling of desire and subjugation in the images.

My use of [the images from *Sex with Strangers*] has as much to do with reconfiguring the territory both of what images can be looked at as art, and what a woman as an artist would need to look at if she's seriously concerned with questions about the sublime and about sex and gender and language and that nexus.[28]

Bacher has continued to elaborate this project in her most recent work, some of which returns to explicitly sexual materials.

Evincing a continued preoccupation with male subjectivity, Bacher's work engages Silverman's suggestion that women artists usurp masculine identities in order to dismantle or disperse them. Both her early installation *Men at War* (1975) and her more recent project *Men in Love* (1990) involve Bacher as the female author re-enacting, and implicitly watching, male group rituals of submerged aggression – a repeated trope that echoes Cavani's repeated filmic re-enactments of male divestiture and masochism, which Silverman reads through the Freudian 'beating fantasy'.[29] What is at stake when a female artist

stages scenes of threatened or impaired masculinity? What is her relation to this 'scene', and more importantly, what positions does she construct for the viewer? Or, as Silverman poses the question, 'What desire finds expression through this constant return to and preoccupation with male subjectivity?' and 'why [does] that preoccupation require the support of a male representation?'[30]

In *Men in Love*,[31] a collection of confessional narratives taken from a quasi-instructional, quasi-pornographic male masturbation manual, Bacher assembles an idiosyncratic collection of impaired or pathetic masculine subjectivities.[32] Alternately funny and grotesque, and sometimes arousing, the installation offers a mini-catalogue of perversions, in which such familiar topics as exhibitionism, voyeurism and paedophilia are joined by far more obscure and unnamed practices – which range from getting off on the warm vibrations of a washing machine to the pleasures of jerking off onto the mirrors in fancy men's rooms. By presenting the thirty-one texts on 12″ mirrors, the installation foregrounds both the baroque qualities of the first-person stories – the incredible variation within the sameness – and the intense self-consciousness they both display and provoke. There's an unavoidable element of narcis-

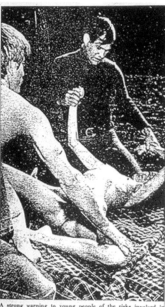
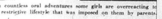

In countless oral adventures some girls are overreacting to a restrictive lifestyle that was imposed on them by parents.

Rapists who may appear normal on the surface often mask their true impulses until they have the victim where they want her.

A strong warning to young people of the risks involved in hitchhiking is indicated in the events of this case history.

Sex with Strangers (Lutz Bacher, 1986)

sism in reading them, with your face staring back at you, which draws the reader into some kind of identification, however awkward, with the men whose names provide the titles of each piece.[33]

The paradox Bacher works with is that these documents are both deeply twisted *and* deeply conventional. By seizing on the odd text or the extreme moment, Bacher analyses how these 'language systems' themselves create and produce the very masculine desires they record and circulate. The key question, in Bacher's installation pieces, is what it means for a female artist to be doing such work, to be 'taking on' the male voice so forcefully.[34] Porn in this analysis is an apparatus of male subjectivity, a technology of gender; yet by focusing on such 'marginal' texts – porn books, a masturbation manual, texts in the generic interstices of sociology, 'self-help' and pornography – Bacher insists on the inseparability of pornographic representations from other, more 'acceptable' but equally normative cultural practices.

Obsessively exploring these sites of misogyny (all culture is a site of misogyny – porn, *pace* MacKinnon and Dworkin, has no special status), Bacher insists on the impossibility of actually transcending or exiting these warped registers of desire. Explicating the untenability of 'sex positive' or naively intimate images of sex which would claim to evade or undo the complex implication of sexuality, power and representation, Bacher has stated, in reference to *Sex with Strangers*:

> As a woman, I pretty much understand that sex is not a safe situation, that the occasion of sex, the speaking of sex, the way in which sex comes up, is always in effect with strangers, always in that area of pleasure and danger. . . . If I was setting up my friends or myself and taking pictures and so on, that would be about some notion of totally free sex, the innocent body, an innocent image world that doesn't exist. This work assumes that bodies aren't innocent, images aren't innocent and language isn't innocent. As for what they're about – who(ever) owns these images gets to say that and make use of them.[35]

What strikes home about *Sex with Strangers* is not just the intense awkwardness of the images, but the *oscillation* between desire and subjugation they embody, and the unstable subject position they invite – a strategy which animates much of Child's work as well. Of course, one reading would be simply to see the materials as completely repellent, and to refuse to accept that any viewer, male or female, could find them a turn-on. Yet what Bacher seems interested in is precisely such moments of *problematic identification* – especially when women take up the position designed for male spectators.

In Bacher's case the masculinity being appropriated is both homo- and heterosexual, representing a complex response not only to straight male misogyny but also to a gay male aesthetic itself sometimes modelled on the refiguring of culturally normative 'femininity'. Positions of 'masculine' and 'feminine', Bacher's work seems to insist, are themselves unstable and transversal, capable of generating an intense back-and-forth movement. Rather than attempt to enforce the stability and autonomy of these positions – invoking the 'authenticity' of 'identities' as one strain of both feminist and gay politics would advocate – Bacher's 'extreme examples', joining minimalist and pornographic tropes, work to unfix these positions through obsessive repetition and displacement. For it is through this repetitive cataloguing of awkward instances of male fantasy and desire that Bacher explores heterosexuality as what Butler has termed 'an incessant and panicked imitation of its own naturalised idealisation'. As Butler notes, 'That heterosexuality is always in the act of elaborating itself is evidence that it is perpetually at risk, that is, that it "knows" its own possibility of becoming undone.'[36] Intuitively honing in on these instances of risk and rupture, Bacher picks apart some of the artifices and instabilities of male subjectivity, in effect appropriating them for the female viewer. The point is not to close down or consolidate these positions of 'male' and 'female' but to keep them open to new and unanticipated significations.[37]

In a project linked to Bacher's critical excavation of male subjectivity, Abigail Child's series *Is This What You Were Born For?* probes how 'masculinity' and 'femininity' are figured in Western cinematic representation. Like Bacher, Child works with the destabilising of familiar images, sequences and tableaux, insistently exploring the artifices which structure narrative for moments of rupture and excess. Her focus is on the body, not as narrated in the confessional discourse, but as visually and corporeally enacted through gait, gesture, rhythm and repetition. Influenced by the strategies of language poetry and the avant-garde musical work of John Zorn, Christian Marclay and Zeena Parkins (all of whom have collaborated on her films), she uses rapid editing, disjunctive juxtaposition and multilayered sound-cutting to reframe and reposition highly charged images and materials. Contrapuntally rechoreographing these fragments of action, gesture and ritualised movement (what Butler has termed 'the array of corporeal theatrics understood as gender presentation'[38]), Child makes a kind of music out of this 'noise'.[39]

Mayhem, the penultimate film of the series, focuses on film noir, teasing apart its complex threads of sexuality and violence, narrative and voyeurism. Drawing on a rich collection of archival footage and historical materials, Child fragments and intercuts sequences to confuse and disorder contemporary regimes of gender and sexuality, playing up the troubling interpenetration of male and female (and heterosexual and homosexual) desires embedded in her dizzying array of borrowed and recreated materials. As Child describes the film:

> Perversely and equally inspired by de Sade's *Justine* and Vertov's sentences about the satiric detective advertisement, *Mayhem* is my attempt to create a film in which sound is the character and to do so focusing on sexuality and the erotic. Not so much to undo the entrapment (we fear what we desire, we desire what we fear) but to frame fate, show up the rotation, upset the common, and incline our contradictions towards satisfaction, albeit conscious.[40]

The film opens with a classic noir scenario. A woman in 40s' attire waits in a darkened room. Her face is barred by diagonal shadows, created by the light through a Venetian blind. The music suggests fear, foreboding. She looks up, startled, awaiting an intrusion. It then cuts to a scene of two men peering menacingly, suggesting malice – except that the sequence is lifted from a postwar spy thriller. Veering between historical periods and locales, the film catalogues types of action, codified gestures, ways of presenting the body, as men and women shift positions constantly. Two men pursue a woman through an urban landscape; just when things look menacing, she turns to watch them as they suddenly embrace, introducing slippages between heterosexual and homosexual desires that reverberate through the text.

Yet simply describing sequences cannot do the film justice, for *Mayhem* is a deeply kinetic experience, one in which the images slip from the viewer's grasp before being fully registered – a strategy which heightens their almost subliminal apprehension, their capacity for slippage and deferred action. As it repeatedly sets up and then redirects its melodramatic encounters, *Mayhem* plays on the fine line between threat and fascination; rather than attempting to separate out pleasure and danger (or straight and gay scenes), the film reworks what is fearful or pathologised as a turn-on.

As film scholar Madeline Leskin has noted, '*Mayhem* meticulously employs the language of noir: the lighting, the camera angles, even the latent sadism, but takes noir to the next level by drawing the connections between sex and violence.'[41] With its frenzied cataloguing of allusive glances, awkward

Mayhem (Abigail Child, 1987) (above and opposite)

pursuits, disguised identities and threatened poses, all forced into a breathless pitch, Child's film suggests a world in which such melodramatic gestures, while full of meaning, do not lend themselves to any sure decoding.[42] Instead, they form an endless series of detours and diversions, disruptions and deviations, as their intimations of violence and suspense take on delayed impacts, detonating at different moments within the film instead of setting up linear continuities of cause and effect.[43]

As the film embraces sexual ambiguity and the relationality of sexual identities, it combines a multiplicity of gazes and forms of desire; the collisions between them give *Mayhem* density and movement. There is a loose progression in the film, from sequences of fear and foreboding towards more playful and comic scenes; this is paralleled by a movement from strictly heterosexual scenes to more mixed encounters, but the film does not lend itself to a reductive or utopian reading about lesbian or gay sexualities. Instead, like the collage and theft-based strategies of the gay fanzines that critic Matias Viegener has written about,[44] Child's found footage and reconstructed materials offer a strategy of appropriation and erotic reinscription of pleasurable *and* problematic images from an array of (sometimes deeply misogynist) mass cultural sources – a strategy based on reconstructing and refiguring these images, rather than trying to produce an 'affirmative image' of female sexuality.

In so doing, Child's representational strategy engages a more critical, contemporary understanding of sexual identity, one not based on somehow 'celebrating' gay identity but actively exploring and interrogating it. Drawing on the historical articulation of

gay identities as inseparably liberatory *and* regulatory, work by Judith Butler, Diana Fuss, Jeffrey Weeks and other gay theorists has compellingly argued that any efforts to produce stable, unified identities – even marginal ones – will inevitably be regulative. Attempts to ground lesbian and gay politics or cultural practices in a similarly conceived model of stable, autonomous and 'authentic' sexual identities all too easily fall into the same trap, reactively defined in relation to their heterosexual opposites which they must continually seek to exclude (and based on gender identities that are themselves products of a heterosexual matrix). Instead, theoretical projects such as Butler's propose that the imitative and parodic effects of lesbian and gay cultural practices, by embracing and exploiting their implicit relation with heterosexual norms and practices, can indeed unwrite the very 'originality' of their heterosexual models – the idea that such 'repetitions' and 'reinscriptions', rather than reproducing or reinforcing existing regimes of identity and gender, may potentially act to disrupt and subvert them.[45]

The potentially threatening ambiguity with which this process of reinscription works can be seen in the porn sequence that ends *Mayhem*, and which provides a sort of epilogue or coda to it. These final scenes, taken from a 1920s' porn film of unknown origin, feature two women furiously making love; vaguely oriental, it is shot with apparently mock-Japanese setting and characters, but because of the degradation of the image the particulars are difficult to make out. The pair are interrupted by a thief who masturbates to the women's lovemaking and is then discovered by them and 'forced' at gunpoint to join it. As the voyeuristic dimensions of noir are enacted, very literally, the conventions linking sex, violence and control are stripped bare. Yet as a representation of lesbian sexuality, the sequence is far from reassuring. It offers no safe place, no nostalgic retreat, from the voyeurism and entrapment of dominant cinematic codes. Instead of offering reassurance or the illusion of an uncorrupted sphere of representation, the sequence instead seems to propose a series of questions which reflect back on the film as a whole. Who was this meant for? Who is turned on? What kinds of images are disturbing? What is erotic?

By closing on such a 'corrupt' lesbian image, one not 'free' but completely embedded in histories of oppression and resistance, *Mayhem* implicitly questions the production of sexual identities that are 'stable, natural and good'[46] – as well as questioning the privileged position of a feminist 'critique' which seeks to authorise its own status as rational analysis, somehow outside such histories of distortion, entrapment and desire. Instead it presents a kind of alternative map through its idiosyncratically assembled film history, offering a *proliferation* of sexual identities, pleasures and dangers. As the film constructs a range of positions from which to identify with its male *and* female characters, homo *and* hetero desires, Child, like Bacher, explores just what happens when these limits are tested, when these identities are confused or made ambiguous.[47]

CONCLUSION

Reflecting a deeply immersed fascination with popular genres, styles and devices, these projects of course participate in a wider tendency within contemporary feminist art-making, one which involves the entry of comic books, soap opera, photo-novella and pornography into high art practice. Yet I want to make a distinction, one which seems critical, between works which use such pop cultural or pornographic images as material, as the surface for yet another critical reading – a strategy which seems all about reassuring the viewer in her own superiority and distance – and works which, like Bacher's and Child's, appropriate these warped documents on a much more structural level, engaging with their mechanisms of entrapment and probing the notoriously restless operations of desire and identification.[48]

In their refusal – perhaps even suspicion – of the clarity and authority of a more avowedly critical art, both Bacher and Child explore an admittedly ambiguous position for feminist representation, one committed to exploring the subjugation, inhabiting the distortions, engaging and perhaps even identifying with the sense of pathology. It is work about complicity, and for good reasons it may make some viewers uncomfortable. In threatening our own position as spectators, our forever thwarted desires to escape the entrapments of our culture, these artists enact a deep-seated engagement with psychic mechanisms of fantasy, obsession and obsessive repetition.

Exploring sites of trauma and exploiting the very instability inherent in repetition, Bacher and Child tap into the power of this psychic 'compulsion to repeat' which can work towards potentially conserva-

tive or profoundly destabilising ends. In this, the political valency of their work is not always clear. Yet it is perhaps precisely this psychically and politically charged ambivalence that gives their works their aesthetic power. For, as Hal Foster notes, writing on the contradictory nature of the surrealist image in terms that could well be used to describe Bacher's and Child's art-making, this very structural ambivalence can be seen as 'an effect of a repetitive working over of fantasmatic scenes by a mobile subject, a working over that is never purely involuntary and symptomatic *or* controlled and curative'.[49]

NOTES

1. Sections of this article have been published in 'Lutz Bacher: Sex with Strangers', *Artforum*, September 1992; and 'An Unrequited Desire for the Sublime: Looking at Lesbian Representation across the Works of Abigail Child, Cecilia Dougherty, and Su Friedrich', in Martha Gever, John Greyson and Pratibha Parmar (eds), *Queer Looks* (New York and London: Routledge, 1993). Thanks to John Archer, Jennifer Kabat, Matias Viegener and Alys Weinstein for commenting on drafts of this article, and to the artists for extensively discussing their works with me.

2. Kaja Silverman, *The Acoustic Mirror: The Female Voice in Psychoanalysis and Cinema* (Bloomington: Indiana University Press, 1988).

3. Ibid., p. 227. Silverman goes on to elucidate what she sees as the usefulness, or even necessity, of relying on male characters to express certain fantasies of gender dismantling:

This (desire for discursive power) is a necessary desire for the female subject, even as it dreams of a moment beyond it: of the moment when, having acceded to power, the female subject can divest herself of it. . . . Cavani is obliged to rely on male characters to express this dream because they alone occupy a position from which divestiture is possible. Her constant return to male subjectivity speaks to the desire to participate in a renunciation which is not yet possible for the female subject (which indeed can only be seen as a dangerous lure at this moment in her history) – the renunciation of power in all its many social, cultural, political and economic guises (p. 231).

4. Ibid., p. 217. However, she cautions that these two terms – gender 'within' and 'outside' the text – can neither be conflated nor completely severed. While Silverman wants to claim such moments of slippage

as at least potentially transgressive (implicitly arguing against feminist analyses that would ascribe to such strategies purely colonising or complicitous operations), she does not disavow their problematic status, but instead points to the *complexity* of such unstable gender identifications, which are by no means limited to straightforward reversals or substitutions:

At the same time, this libidinal masculinity or femininity must be read in relation to the biological gender of the biographical author, since it is clearly not the same thing, socially or politically, for a woman to speak with a female voice as it is for a man to do so, and vice versa. All sorts of cultural imperatives dictate a smooth match between biological gender and subject position, making any deviation a site of potential resistance to sexual difference.

5. In *Gender Trouble: Feminism and the Subversion of Identity* (New York and London: Routledge, 1990), Butler performs a series of provocative readings of Lacan, Freud and Joan Riviere, among others, analysing their competing versions of how gender identifications work – 'indeed, of whether they can be said to "work" at all.' Butler queries the viability of any unitary, univocal 'gender identity':

Can gender complexity and dissonance be accounted for by the multiplication and convergence of culturally dissonant identifications? Or is all identification constructed through the exclusion of a sexuality that puts those identifications into question? In the first instance, multiple identifications can constitute a non-hierarchical configuration of shifting and overlapping identifications that call into question the primacy of any univocal gender attribution (p. 66).

6. Judith Butler, 'Phantasmatic Identification and the Question of Sex', presented at the Fifth Annual Lesbian and Gay Studies Association Conference, 1–3 November 1991, Rutgers University.

7. Like Butler, Silverman conceives of gender as perpetually troubled, perpetually endangered. Yet while Butler's reading will focus on the kinds of *pleasure* produced by the instability of these categories, Silverman instead seems to focus on gender as a kind of *anxiety*: as a series of displacements, a set of relationally defined terms uneasily resisting an enormous amount of anxiety, which perpetually threatens to undo these very terms.

Such a model of gender as anxiety, as perpetually unfinished 'work', is by no means unique to

Silverman, and indeed underpins many feminist readings of Lacan and of the oedipalised 'acquisition' of gender. See, for example, Juliet Mitchell, *Feminism and Psychoanalysis* (London: Allen Lane, 1974) and Jacqueline Rose, *Sexuality in the Field of Vision* (London and New York: Verso, 1986). The often British-based, Lacanian-inflected, psychoanalytic feminist theories radically diverge from more sociologically based and empirically oriented American feminist models, such as those of Nancy Chodorow (in *The Reproduction of Mothering: Psychoanalysis and the Sociology of Gender*, Berkeley: University of California Press, 1978), which tend to rest upon the assumption that the acquisition of gender actually *works*, that it actually achieves any stability and normativity.

8. Butler, *Gender Trouble*, pp. 30–1.

9. Arguing against a more traditional Lacanian reading of the Law of the Symbolic as fixing identity in a rigid and universal determinism, Butler notes:

The alternative perspective that emerges from psychoanalytic theory suggests that multiple and coexisting identifications produce conflicts, convergences, and innovative dissonances within gender configurations, which contest the fixity of masculine and feminine placements with respect to the paternal law. In effect, the possibility of multiple identifications (which are not finally reducible to primary or founding identifications that are fixed within masculine and feminine positions) suggests that the law is not deterministic and that 'the' law may not even be singular (*Gender Trouble*, p. 67).

10. Butler, *Gender Trouble*, p. 71. Such a disaggregation of what 'counts' as gender then in turn underpins Butler's discussion, in subsequent work, of the potential disaggregation and dispersal of the elements of what appear to us as consolidated sexual identity categories. Questioning the possibility of such identities to be adequately constituted and expressed through strategies of disclosure such as 'coming out', Butler asks:

If a sexuality is to be disclosed, what will we take as the true determinant of its meaning: the phantasy structure, the act, the orifice, the gender, the anatomy? And if the practice engages a complex interplay of all those, which one of these erotic dimensions will come to stand for the sexuality that requires them all? ('Imitation and Gender Insubordination', in Diana Fuss (ed.), *Inside/Out: Lesbian Theories, Gay Theories* [New York and London: Routledge, 1991], p. 17).

11. Andrew Ross, *No Respect: Intellectuals and Popular Culture* (New York and London: Routledge, 1989), pp. 171–208.

12. See Lew Thomas (ed.), *Photography & Language* (San Francisco, CA: Camerawork Press, 1986).

13. Loosely titled 'A Birth of the Reader', the project will involve female-authored 're-creations' of canonical male art pieces, from a Robert Morris process piece to a series of Warhol paintings.

14. Critical writings on Child include Marjorie Keller, 'Is This What You Were Born For?', and Charles Bernstein, 'Interview with Abigail Child', *X-Dream* (Autumn, 1987); Maureen Turim, 'Childhood Memories and Household Events in the Feminist "Avant-garde"', *Journal of Film and Video*, no. XXXVIII (Summer/Autumn, 1986); Barbara Hammer, 'The Invisible Screen: Lesbian Cinema', *Center Quarterly* (Spring, 1988); Dennis Barone, 'Abigail Child', *Arts Magazine* (September, 1990); as well as Child's book of experimental writings, *A Motive for Mayhem* (Hartford, CT: Potes & Poets Press, 1989).

15. See, for instance, Susan Sontag's 'Notes on Camp', for a depoliticised and yet in some instances quite useful reading of camp, in *Against Interpretation* (New York: Farrar, Straus & Giroux, 1966). For critiques of Sontag by theorists emphasising the critical, denaturalising, or defamiliarising strategies embedded in camp practices, see Michael Moon, 'Flaming Closets', *October*, no. 51 (Winter, 1989) and Andrew Ross, 'Uses of Camp', in *No Respect: Intellectuals and Popular Culture* (New York and London: Routledge, 1989).

16. This function can be seen across very different works: the video installation *My Penis* (1992), a two-hour tape loop of a short utterance from William Kennedy Smith's televised trial testimony, uses both duration and repetition to keep shifting the viewer's reception and apprehension of the utterance. On her relation to cinematic minimalism, specifically structural film-making, Bacher herself has noted that her earlier work *Huge Uterus* (1989), a six-hour video installation, 'could not have been made without Michael Snow's *Wavelength*' (conversation with the author, December 1991). Overall, Bacher's disparate projects could be unified through their use of topical materials in structures derived from minimalism; in turn, it is this use of minimalist repetition, serial structure, and duration that tends to distance them radically from more conventional 'topical' or 'political' art, since these strategies orient the viewer off the specific event onto basic structures.

17. Structural film-making, a movement associated with Michael Snow, Peter Gidal, Hollis Frampton, Paul Sharits, Ernie Gehr, the early work of Tony Conrad, and others, constitutes an analogous movement of minimalism within experimental film culture (just as the earlier 'expressionistic', 'poetic', and 'personal film-making' of Maya Deren, Stan Brakhage and others saw itself as roughly allied with abstract expressionism). According to an early assessment of structural film by P. Adams Sitney, 'Theirs is a cinema of structure in which the shape of the whole film is pre-determined and simplified, and it is that shape which is the primal impression of the film' (*Visionary Film: the American Avant-garde 1943–1978* [New York and London: Oxford University Press, 1979], pp. 369–97).

18. As Anna Chave has suggested in her controversial article, 'Minimalism and the Rhetoric of Power', high minimalist art of the 1960s, in its engagement with the visual vocabulary of industry and technology, can indeed be read as a paradigmatic discourse of power and of masculinity. As critically reassessed in the 1980s, minimalism at times came to stand for a quintessentially straight male practice (often defined in opposition to Pop art, many of whose major practitioners were gay men) in its evisceration of content, politics, emotion or pleasure, as conventionally understood, from visual art-making. See Anna C. Chave, 'Minimalism and the Rhetoric of Power', *Arts Magazine*, January 1990, pp. 44–63. For a response to Chave, see Brian Wallis, 'Power, Gender and Abstraction', in *Power: Its Myths and Mores in American Art 1961–1991* (Indianapolis, Indianapolis Museum of Art/Indiana University Press, 1991). For a look at contemporary, more politicised reinscriptions of minimalist practices, see Kathryn Hixson, 'The Subject is the Object: Legacies of Minimalism', *New Art Examiner* (May 1991) and ' . . . and the Object is the Body', *New Art Examiner* (October 1991).

19. And, as her recent piece 'Menstrual Extraction Kit' (1991) suggests, the charge produced by the possibility that this relation is itself transversal, that art could slip out of the frame and back into use – 'menstrual extraction' being of course a euphemism for home-made abortion devices.

20. As Silverman notes, in her exploration of the unstable relation of female 'authors' to their male characters:

> Foucault is correct to suggest that there is a more crucial project than determining the relation between the author and what he or she says, and that is to establish the position which the reader or viewer will come to occupy through identifying with the subject of a given statement. That position is indeed 'assignable' (or reassignable). All of this is another way of saying that the reader or viewer may be captated by the authorial system of a given text or group of texts (*The Acoustic Mirror*, p. 233).

21. Hal Foster, 'The Crux of Minimalism', in Howard Singerman (ed.), *Individuals: A Selected History of Contemporary Art, 1945–1986* (Los Angeles, CA: Museum of Contemporary Art/Abbeville Press, 1986), p. 163.

22. Ibid., p. 179. Foster elaborates: 'It is not the 'anti-illusionism' of minimalism that 'rids' art of the anthropomorphic and the representational, but its serial mode of production: for abstraction *sublates* representation, preserves it even as it cancels it, whereas repetition, the (re)production of simulacra, *subverts* representation, undercuts its referential logic.'

23. Ibid., p. 180.

24. Abigail Solomon-Godeau, 'Reconsidering Erotic Photography: Notes for a Project of Historical Salvage', from *Photography at the Dock* (Minneapolis: University of Minnesota Press, 1991), p. 220.

25. This accusation, that feminist projects critiquing pornography inevitably invite the very pruriently interested forms of spectatorship they endeavour to condemn, has plagued many undertakings, with anti-porn critics almost routinely claiming that supposedly anti-porn films, such as the Canadian documentary *Not a Love Story*, will bring in the 'raincoat crowd' – not to mention the perversity of a document such as the Meese Commission report, itself an amazing compendium of pornographic scenarios. While in anti-porn discourse this phenomenon is clearly seen as a problem, to me it presents a provocative instance of the instability and indeterminacy of subject positions, the very multivalency of porn that Child and Bacher both exploit to more artistic, and to my mind more politically useful, ends.

    I was struck by this phenomenon while recently reading, in Susan Suleiman's *Subversive Intent*, a section on Andrea Dworkin's rewriting of Bataille's 'The Story of the Eye'. While Dworkin's rewrite, as Suleiman rather predictably asserts, flattens Bataille's 'exquisitely' elegant French prose and the 'frisson' produced by bringing it to such coarse and vulgar subject matter, Suleiman completely misses what to me is a far more interesting effect: Dworkin's rewrite, in its direct, crude, street-smart way, reminds me of nothing so much as mid-1970s' Kathy Acker. That *Pornography: Men Hating Women* and *The Childlike Life of the Black Tarantula*, two apparently opposed 1970s' feminist projects, should exhibit such hidden, and probably unintentional, intertextuality strikes me as very interesting. Acker has in fact stated that she admired Dworkin's work prior to Dworkin's current political commitment to anti-porn censorship; various commentators have noted how the very anti-porn legislation Dworkin has advocated could ironically be used to suppress some of her own books.

26. Judith Butler, 'The Force of Fantasy: Feminism, Mapplethorpe, and Discursive Excess', *differences*, vol. 2 no. 2, 1990.

27. Ibid., pp. 109–10

28. Lutz Bacher, Statement, 6 July 1990.

29. Phase three of the fantasy: 'Some boys are being beaten (and I am watching)' – being the primary psychoanalytic narrative of female masochism. As Silverman poses the relation: 'For what is the exchange that occurs between Cavani as the author "outside" the text and those male characters who represent her within the text if not a restaging of that fantasmatic drama whereby a girl turns herself into a group of boys only in order to position them as female, i.e. to "castrate" them?' (*The Acoustic Mirror*, p. 232).

30. Silverman, *The Acoustic Mirror*, pp. 220 and 225.

31. See Maria Porges, 'Lutz Bacher', *Artforum*, March 1991, pp. 136–7; Liz Kotz, 'Lutz Bacher, *Men in Love*', *Shift*, Spring 1991, pp. 62–3; and Robert Mahoney, 'Lutz Bacher', *Arts Magazine*, January 1992.

32. This terrain – the mapping of masochistic, marginal or impaired masculinities as a site of resistance to phallic norms – has been a crux of radical male art-making as represented by Vito Acconci and others, since the early 1970s. See Kathy O'Dell, 'The Performance Artist as Masochistic Woman', *Arts Magazine*, June 1988, and her PhD dissertation, 'Toward a Theory of Performance Art: An Investigation of Its Sites' (The Graduate Center, City University of New York, 1992), and my own 'Pathetic

Masculinities', *Artforum*, November 1992. For critical readings of masculinity in contemporary art, see Wallis, 'Power, Gender and Abstraction', note 18, and Laura Cottingham, 'Negotiating Masculinity and Representation', *Contemporanea* (October 1989). See also Kaja Silverman, *Male Subjectivity at the Margins* (New York: Routledge, 1992).

33. Hung somewhat low, at 5 feet, I was the right height to read them without stooping – Bacher implicitly positions these narratives for a presumed female viewer. Such stories, she correctly assumes, are not particularly transgressive when framed (in the porn manual) for private male consumption, but become so when reframed, in the gallery, for public female consumption – an intuition borne out more empirically by observing viewers at two installations of the project, one in San Francisco and one in New York: when women entered, men would often leave the room, as if co-occupying this formerly 'private' space of fantasy with female viewers provoked discomfort and embarrassment.

34. One risk is a potentially straightforward reappropriation by the male. Bacher's work, long neglected by many feminist critics, was later frequently promoted by gay male artists and curators and purchased by gay male collectors – a phenomenon that potentially short-circuits the complex female-to-male-to-female circulation of desire in the work, producing a situation instead where the female artist becomes the mediator between masculine positions of production and consumption.

35. Renny Pritikin, 'Interview with Lutz Bacher', San Francisco, 6 July 1990.

36. Butler, 'Imitation and Gender Insubordination', p. 23.

37. Working from an examination of drag as a sometimes controversial practice of gender imitation, one which 'enacts the very structure of impersonation by which *any gender* is assumed', Butler has asserted the importance of abandoning 'proprietary' notions of gender, and argues instead that *all* gender identities operate by processes of imitation and impersonation. Proposing that 'there is no "proper" gender, a gender proper to one sex rather than another, which in some sense that sex's cultural property,' Butler asserts that 'where that notion of the "proper" operates, it is always and only *improperly* installed as the effect of a compulsory system' ('Imitation and Gender Insubordination', p. 21).

38. Butler, 'Imitation and Gender Insubordination', p. 28.

39. In this investigation of gesture and the body, Child is of course deeply influenced by post-Judson Church dance, and the early work of Yvonne Rainer, Simone Forti, and other choreographers who abandoned the classical 'dance' body to turn towards everyday movements (walking, vacuuming, shutting a door, etc.) as an inspiration for modern dance. See Yvonne Rainer, *Works 1961–73* (Halifax: The Press of the Nova Scotia College of Art and Design, and New York: New York University Press, 1974).

40. Child, 'Program Notes', San Francisco Cinematheque, 22 February 1990.

41. Madeline Leskin, 'Interview with Abigail Child', from *Skop* (West Berlin, February 1988), reprinted in *Motion Picture*, vol. 3 nos 1/2, Winter 1989–90 (New York: Collective for Living Cinema).

42. As Peter Brooks has noted, 'Melodrama operates by an *overdetermination* of signs, it tends towards "total theatre", its signs projected sequentially or simultaneously on several plains' (Brooks, *The Melodramatic Imagination: Balzac, Henry James, Melodrama and the Mode of Excess* [New Haven, CT: Yale University Press, 1976, p. 46]). These signs are then played across a number of registers – music, acting style, costumes, décor, visual tableaux – which can reinforce and also relay each other. In *Mayhem*, Child uses such overdetermination to play her registers against each other, more contrapuntally, to open up or scatter the meanings they create.

43. In his article 'Convulsive Identity' (*October*, no. 57, Summer 1991) Hal Foster, drawing from Dominic La Capra and Peter Brooks, suggests the importance of understanding how effects of 'deferred action' operate within and between texts, in order 'to complicate readings of influence, the effectivity of the present on the past' (p. 21). See also Peter Brooks, *Reading for the Plot: Design and Intention in Narrative* (New York: Vintage Books, 1984).

44. Matias Viegener, 'There's Trouble in That Body', *Afterimage*, January 1991. Reprinted in David Bergman (ed.), *Camp Grounds* (Amherst: University of Massachusetts Press, 1993).

45. In Butler's model, identity does not pre-exist such performance but is constituted by it; there is, she remarks in *Gender Trouble*, 'no doer behind the deed'. Instead, in 'Imitation and Gender Insubordination', she conceives of the psyche itself as *compulsive repetition*:

If gender is drag, and if it is an imitation that regularly produces the ideal it attempts to approximate, then gender is a performance that *produces* the illusion of an inner sex or essence or psychic gender core; it *produces* on the skin, through the gesture, the move, the gait (that array of corporeal theatrics understood as gender presentation), the illusion of an inner depth. . . . To dispute the psyche as *inner depth*, however, is not to refuse the psyche altogether. On the contrary, the psyche calls to be rethought precisely as a compulsive repetition, as that which conditions and disables the repetitive performance of identity (p. 28).

46. See Viegener, 'There's Trouble in That Body', p. 12.

47. In her final film of the series, *Mercy* (1990), Child focuses on the endangered *male* body, bringing together 'encyclopedic ephemera – industrial, promotional, tourist films of the 60s, military training films, etc. – to explore the body in social landscape, and particularly, through these images of men, in machine-like poses, the kind of masculinity formed around mimesis of the machine' (artist's statement, 1990).

48. For an analysis of the inseparability of 'lesbian' and 'heterosexual' identifications as they operate in North American fashion photography, see Diana Fuss, 'Fashion and the Homospectatorial Look', *Critical Inquiry*, vol. 18 no. 4 (Summer 1992), pp. 713–37.

49. Hal Foster, 'Convulsive Identity', p. 52.

17 She-Male Fantasies and the Aesthetics of Pornography

Laura Kipnis

In Chicago, where I live and where, like most places, pornography is a thriving business, it's illegal to sell magazines such as *Guys in Gowns, Gender Gap, Transvestites on Parade, Feminine Illusion, Masquerade, Petticoat Impostors, Great Pretenders, Femme Mimics* and *She-Male Rendezvous*. Adult book stores are crammed full with all variety of what is often referred to as perversion: sadomasochism, for example, is freely traded, but you cannot buy magazines which eroticise female dress worn by men.[1] You can sell magazines showing naked men, naked women, and any combination of them doing very acrobatic, unexpected or violent things to each other, but if one of the men is wearing a garter belt you would be subject to arrest and prosecution in the state of Illinois.

The nuances and the microdistinctions of this state's obscenity code (you can sell transvestite [TV] newspapers and videos, but not TV magazines, for example) might suggest that it is the act of regulation and deployment of state power over sexuality rather than the specifics of what's regulated that is crucial.[2] And, as is frequently pointed out, anti-pornography feminism shares a highly questionable alliance with the Right and the state to the extent that both see sexual representation as a potential site of regulation and law, and work to criminalise consumers of pornography (whether juridically or through feminist condemnation and ignominy). I had to cross the border into Wisconsin to purchase TV magazines and did, in fact, transport them across state lines to Illinois. I probably committed a crime in order to write this article – against the state, and before I'm through, some might say, against feminism. You may be abetting one by reading this.

The more pornography I look at, though, the less feminist certainty I have about what exactly it is and what, if anything, defines it. There's been general feminist consensus that pornography concerns gender relations. Susan Gubar, for example, defines

pornography as 'a gender-specific genre produced primarily for men but focused obsessively on the female figure' and distinguished by its dehumanising effect.[3] So what pornography both portrays and endeavours to perpetuate is the deployment of male power over female bodies; while violating women through representation is just one instance of the male desire to violate women generally, it is the sole purpose of porn.

But what about the pornography of male bodies? There seems to have been a reticence on the part of both pro and anti-porn feminist theorists to discuss, for example, gay male porn, as either not concerned with and not addressed to women, thus none of our business (Linda Williams),[4] or because it is heterosexuality and its institutions that are the problem (Andrea Dworkin).[5] Perhaps one of the reasons there's been a certain under-theorisation of pornography of male bodies is that it might throw that certainty about what pornography as a category is, and does, into question. Yet the vast market share of pornography of male bodies makes this form of the genre not merely not anomalous, but central. Take transvestite porn. The majority of the bodies portrayed are male, a large number are even *fully clothed*. And while gender is certainly at issue, it doesn't follow any of the standard presumptions of how porn works and at whose expense. Yet this material is unproblematically classed, even criminalised in some areas, as pornographic.

These magazines are fairly generic in form – I'll describe a typical one for my non-TV readers. Each issue generally features one or two short stories, in which typically an unwilling man is forced through a variety of circumstances to dress in women's clothes, which are described in elaborate detail. Sometimes this leads to sex in various configurations with either another man or a dominant woman. There are also advice columns in which similar narratives are presented in the guise of letters. Then there are, of course, pictorials of crossdressed men, usually a posed male or (pre-operative) transsexual model in female outfits or articles of clothing, often lingerie.[6] Some display their genitals, others are fully clothed. Sometimes the models are engaged in sex, alone or with others, sometimes the partners are other men, other transvestites, or sometimes women. Some are in a sadomasochistic vein and sometimes other types of fantasy scenarios are enacted – the French maid, the sexual novice. While clinical literature typically insists that TVs are heterosexuals (transvestism is distinguished by fetishism of the female clothing, as opposed to gay drag), bisexuality tends to be the sexual norm in these magazines: pictorial captions or short stories might insist that a man is heterosexual, but he often finds himself enticed by a beautiful transvestite or transsexual.[7] There seems to be a fairly casual back and forth between males and females as sex partners, with the use of hormones by some men additionally blurring the distinction.

Then there are numerous advertisements: for hormone supplements, make-up and dress advice, sexual services, videos and other pornography, an array of expensive and probably useless products like breast enhancement cream, vitamin tablets formulated from various glands which claim to soften skin, and a myriad of prosthetics, supplements and depilatories. As in traditional women's magazines, there appears to be a large market in female anxiety, whatever the sex of the subject experiencing it, and wherever it can be aroused there's soon a product to capitalise on it. It's clear from advice columns and stories that many of the readers experience great anxiety over not being (or imagining they're not) successful as women – that is, seamlessly feminine. As in women's magazines, femininity is viewed as something to be worked at and achieved. Any creeping traces of masculinity – unwanted hair growth, rough skin, figure problems – or harsh judgments by others about one's clothes, appearance or demeanour, or even worse, not being thought universally sexually attractive, comprise the everyday trauma of womanhood. It's quite an interesting cultural indicator that regardless of biological sex, femininity and anxiety are so closely allied.

Perhaps it's also worth mentioning that the TV community seems to have assimilated a number of the forms of contemporary women's culture (much of

which I'd interpret historically as the residue of early feminism). These tend to be non-politicised versions of consciousness-raising (C.R.) that have trickled down to the culture at large as strategies for dealing with female anxiety, and are now in their second incarnation as commercial forms. If that other staple of commodified female culture, the daytime talk show, can be seen as the media-commodity annexation of the C.R. group, these magazines, too, advertise a number of for-sale versions of what were once local types of female coping and sublimating mechanisms and are now products – self-help and self-acceptance literature; advice columns; and special telephone lines for make-up and clothes advice, networking, introductions and support.

And lastly, the magazines contain a large number of photographic personal ads. In fact, some of the magazines have no editorial content at all, but consist solely of advertisements and photo classifieds. It's this last aspect of these magazines, the photo classifieds, which I want to discuss here. I'd add that with such a large and growing number of these photos in circulation – around 50–75 photos in each issue of, currently, perhaps twenty-five different magazines just in the US – they clearly have to enter into any discussion of pornography, as one of its *disparate practices*.

These personal ads are basically amateur self-portraits. Many seem to be taken with time-lapse devices or remote shutter cables (which can sometimes be seen in the photos), although it's usually not possible to say when the photo might have been taken by a second person. Most are reproduced in grainy black and white, although some are in colour. They're most often of a single figure, a man, in a variety of dress and undress, almost always articles of female clothing or lingerie. Most of the men face the camera frontally, gazing into the lens, although expressions and poses vary considerably. The majority are full figure. Sometimes genitals are showing, sometimes an erection is prominent, sometimes the man makes a point of concealing his genitals between his legs and feminising himself. In many cases the man is dressed completely as a woman and strikes a pose suggestive of various feminine stereotypes – the movie starlet, the slut, the matron, the shy virgin, the maid, 'the good ole girl'.

Unlike most pornography, however, these images aren't produced for monetary gain: the posers and/or

Transvestite and Transsexual
PERSONALS

'GIRL' ON FIRE
CA-TV With passion and desire - wants
to fill your nights with heavenly delights
and sexual pleasure we both will
treasure. All answered. See photo.
T905182-CA

Personal ads

photographers aren't paid (although publishers and distributors of the magazine are obviously profiting). So a question might be asked immediately about the status of these images as pornography in relation to feminist analyses of the porn industry as exploitative of women. The relations of production of these images involve no exploitation that I can discern, and generally no biological women either (though there are scattered ads by professional female dominatrixes who grudgingly admit to being willing to consider applications from submissive men who need training and discipline).[8] One of the generally undiscussed issues in the porn debates is how or why sexual images of men work differently from sexual images of women – and clearly there's an assumption that men are positioned differently because, to my knowledge, it's solely images of women that have been the

focus of feminist anti-pornography efforts. All the anti-pornography legislation that feminists are attempting to enact across the US and Canada speaks of the violation of *women's* civil rights. So if these TV self-portraits or gay male porn images are not seen as exploitative or degrading to the male models, and are not seen as causing detrimental effects to men at large, it would seem to be due to a somewhat tautological line of reasoning: porn is seen as genericising women alone; men as a class don't suffer ill effects from male pornographic images because porn victimises women.

The ostensible purpose of these photos is to meet other people (they all list box numbers and the state the poser hails from, along with a brief caption and description), often for explicit sexual purposes, but at times simply requesting friendship, advice or correspondence. Often what the poser claims to be advertising for, however, seems highly unlikely to meet with a response. For example, some ads consist simply of a torso, a body part, or the poser from behind, and in some the language is so vague – 'Write and tell me about yourself' – that it is unclear who and what sex, is meant to respond. Some of the photos seem, to me anyway, deliberately comic, or at least carnivalesque, with garish make-up jobs and precariously top-heavy outsize prosthetic breasts. My speculation is that, to some degree, these ads are forms of self-display rather than, necessarily, attempts to meet others. But instead of trying to guess at the motives behind the practice, I'd like to consider some other, similar forms of bodily display as a device to approach the transvestite classifieds and, through them, larger questions about pornography generally. How might it disturb and perhaps unsettle the category 'pornography' if I were to wrench these photos out of definitional certainty by bringing other discourses to bear on them, if I were to consider them, say, within the category of the self-portrait, a sub-genre of Western art and aesthetics with antecedents in painting as far back as the 15th century, which as critic and historian Barbara Rose puts it, records:

the artist's subjective feelings about himself – his conception of how he is perceived by his world and how he experiences himself within a specific social, political, economic, moral and psychological context. Self-portraits often include revealing subconscious clues to the artist's emotional state and inner drama.[9]

So what if I were to conjecture that the motive of transvestite self-portraiture is, as our culture tends to understand self-portraiture in general, an aesthetic act of self-definition, and to suggest that we might come to these images with the same kinds of anticipation we bring to the museum or gallery: of aesthetic shocks and visual pleasures, of a descent into symbolic language, of access to another consciousness, or a revealing exposure of our own lives and culture.

To establish the case for so treating TV self-portraiture, I'd like to detour through the work of a well-known contemporary artist who has herself made a career of photographic self-portraiture, or at least of recirculating its codes. Cindy Sherman

became known in the early 1980s for a series of photographs called 'Untitled Film Stills'. In them, she transforms herself into a variety of female types – 'The Girl Detective, America's Sweetheart, The Young Housewife, The Starlet, The Whore with a Heart of Gold, The Girl Friday, The Girl Next Door' *et al.* – posed within the *mise en scènes* of non-existent B-movies. To call them self-portraits raises an immediate dilemma: although they are all 'of' Sherman, who the 'self' is, is open to question. As Arthur Danto puts it in his definitive critical essay on Sherman's work, the introduction to a coffee table-size book of her photographs: 'They are portraits at best of an identity she shares with every woman who conceives the narrative of her life in the idiom of the cheap movie.'[10]

At first glance, the similarities between Sherman's work and the TV self-portraits are striking: both put categories of identity into question by using the genre of the self-portrait to document an invented 'self'. And both are centrally and crucially concerned with femininity and its masquerades. Danto, however, as aesthetician and critic, is concerned with categories and classifications in the arts. Although he doesn't bother with the regulation question, 'Is it art?', instead he asks 'Is it photography?' Sherman isn't particularly concerned with the standard concerns of the art photograph – print quality, and so on – and further, the genre she chooses to appropriate, the film still, is what Danto labels 'working photographs', that is, photographs which have a *purpose*, are meant to perform some labour, and are 'subartistic'. Danto finally concedes on two different grounds, however, that Sherman *is* a photographer. First because the camera is central to her work; it doesn't 'simply document the pose: the pose itself draws on the language of the still'. Secondly, Danto admits that the prejudice against 'working photographs' is the basis of a *class system* in photography with an 'aristocracy of proto-paintings allowed into the precincts of high art, and a proletariat of working photographs playing productive roles in the facilitation of life'.

It was the upheavals of the 60s (Danto confines himself to upheavals in art, by which he means Warhol) that allowed the working photo to be perceived as a vehicle of meaning, and allowed 'photographs of common life [that] had little to do with the artistic ambitions of fine photography . . . to find their way into the space of art'. These commonplace photos – baby pictures, graduation photos – carry a 'powerful charge of human meaning'; they 'condense the biographies of each of us', and it was the 60s that taught us to be able to 'recognize the deep human essence with which these lowly images were steeped, aesthetics be damned'. So by extension, Danto seems to imply that refusing to perform critical labour on non-aristocratic, non-high art photographs, or refusing to work at extrapolating the same kinds of meaning and affective impact from, say, TV self-portraiture as from, say, Sherman's work, would mean that one was both forgetting the lessons of the 60s, and imposing a class system on the field of photography – perpetuating inequalities which presumably reverberate through other social spheres as well.

Having established to his satisfaction that Sherman can be considered a photographer, Danto plumbs the work for meaning, not in terms of its aesthetic qualities, but in its thematics and relation to its culture and audience. Through her photographic self-reflexivity, Sherman achieves

> a oneness with her means, a oneness with her culture, a oneness with a set of narrative structures instantly legible to everyone who lives this culture, and so a oneness with her presumed audience. The stills acquire consequently a stature as art which draws together and transcends their artistic antecedents. . . . [They] condense an entire drama.[11]

Given the licence Danto has established to look more deeply at non-art photography, I have to ask: in what sense is his assessment of how Sherman's photos operate on an audience not true of TV self-portraiture as well? Don't their photos resonantly (and self-reflexively) call up in each of us a deeply internalised cultural memory-bank of images and codes of 'feminine' poses – in that these photos are only 'legible' to the extent that the viewer recognises and shares the gender and dress codes in operation? Within Western culture they're instantly legible as an act of defiance against the 'naturalness' of the set of arbitrary signifiers – dress, hair, make-up – which tend to be taken as evidence of the equivalence of sex and gender, and legible as an assault on the almost universal assumption that you can tell a person's sex by looking at their clothes and gender presentation.

So the viewer of these photographs – even more so than in Sherman's work – is made critically aware

of the cultural construction of the feminine, in that the poser, the bearer of the codes of femininity, is (and often explicitly displays the fact that he is) biologically male. Doesn't this work very evocatively 'condense an entire drama' – most obviously, the drama of gender assignment, a universal and sometimes disastrous drama, as is brought home by TV self-portraiture's brief glimpses into the occasional yet recurring schism between biological sex and binary gender? Sherman's work, Danto tells us, 'rises to the demand on great art, that it embody the transformative metaphors for the meaning of human reality.' Could we actually refuse transvestite self-portraits the opportunity to embody transformative metaphors? Or is it that the transformations embodied here actually surpass the threshold of what Danto names and values as 'disturbatory art', which seeks 'real transformations through charged artistic enactments', 'requires great courage' and 'set[s] up perturbations across a social field.' (Or when great art seeks 'real transformations', are these expected to be confined to art institutions and their specific audiences?)

And as a postmodern critic, I have to add that we would also want to consider the TV self-portraits, like Sherman's work, in their contemporaneity, in the context of other examples of postmodernist representational practices that appropriate and recirculate genres and idioms – the self-portrait, in these cases – of previous styles and epochs. In that contest I might be led to deduce that the 'self' presented in these self-portraits *is* just that, a self in quotation marks rather than the stolid Cartesian self-certainty displayed in the self-portraiture of a Rubens or a Rembrandt. The ceaselessness of all this transvestite self-representation, read in the aggregate, seems not dissimilar to certain other relentless preoccupations and repetitions of postmodernist representation which return, like Sherman's work, again and again to the same sore tooth, probing those no longer viable humanist fictions of self, nature and truth.

Sherman's work, somewhat surprisingly, propels Danto into a tizzy of humanist hyperbole rather than post-humanist gloom: 'I can think of no body of work at once so timeless and yet so much of its own time as Cindy Sherman's stills, no oeuvre which addresses us in our common humanity . . . no images which say something profound about the feminine condition and yet touch us at a level *beyond sexual difference* [my emphasis].' Perhaps Danto is so cheery about Sherman's work only because he seems to be in a certain state of denial about its sexual and gender politics, because he prefers to think he's being addressed 'at a level beyond sexual difference' in his 'common humanity'. While Danto seems unable to take sexual difference seriously as a category, the psychoanalyst Louise Kaplan, who does, points out that the transvestite *also* desires a position beyond sexual difference.

Kaplan's general view of perversions in both men and women is that rather than being sexual pathologies, they're pathologies of gender role identity – an inability to conform completely to the gender conventions and gender stereotypes of the dominant social order. Kaplan defines perversions as mental strategies that use

> one or another social stereotype of masculinity and femininity in a way that deceives the onlooker about the unconscious meanings of the behaviors she or he is observing. Were we to think about perversion solely in terms of manifest behaviors without going into the motives that give meaning to those behaviors, we could simply conclude that the male perversions are quests for forbidden sexual pleasures and nothing more.[12]

So Kaplan would tend to overlook the sexual motives of the TV personals to look at their narratives of gendering. All 'perverse scenarios', for Kaplan, are ways of triumphing over childhood traumas; male perversions allow men to cope with forbidden and humiliating feminine strivings and longings. Perversions are a series of deceptions: the perverse strategy is to give vent to one forbidden impulse as a way of masking an even more shameful or dangerous one. The desire that is out in the open distracts the viewer from the thing that's hidden. So a male transvestite, in Kaplan's view, doesn't want to *be* a woman, but is coping with forbidden feminine longings and the insurmountable anxiety they cause by demonstrating that he *can* be a woman, but a woman with a phallus, a woman who hasn't been castrated. Cross-dressing is a performance of a *script* that allows the man to allay the anxiety of his feminine wishes, and of his incomplete assimilation to the social gender binary of masculinity. So, as with Danto, transvestites are attracted to elaborate, theatrical forms of feminine display (I'm speaking of Danto's choice of Sherman's work as subject matter) as a way of *denying* sexual difference. This is no aspersion on the estimable

Arthur Danto: one of the things I hope we'll begin to see is that wherever there is art, or even art criticism, there is also perversion, or as Kaplan would put it, perverse *strategies*.

Much of Kaplan's study is devoted to defining and detecting female perversion (perversion has generally been thought to be a male domain) in behaviours that exaggerate femininity, behaviour often seen as 'normal' female behaviour. So, for example, were Cindy Sherman's adoption of stereotypically feminine behaviours, poses and clothing presented outside the distancing device of the art gallery, the clinical term 'homovestism' – a gender impersonation of the same-sex person – might apply, a term coined by Canadian psychoanalyst George Zavitzianos to describe gender conflicts expressed through dressing in exaggerated or ritualised versions of same-sex clothing.[13] Sherman, in her repetitive return to the same 'script', and without the art world, outside the gallery, would seem as perverse in her preoccupations as any cross-dresser.

According to psychoanalyst and gender researcher Robert Stoller, the 'scripts' behind the perverse scenarios are similar to *all* instances of sexual excitation. Behind every erection, male or female, are fantasies . . .

> . . . meanings, scripts, interpretations, tales, myths, memories, beliefs, melodramas, and built like a playwright's plot, with exquisite care, no matter how casual and spontaneous the product appears. In this story – which may take form in a daydream as one's habitual method of operation for erotic encounters, in styles of dress and other adornments, in erotic object choice, and in preference in pornography (in brief, in any and all manifestations of erotic desire) – I shall keep insisting that *every detail counts.*[14]

So for Stoller, sexual excitation, whether perverse or quotidian, has an *aesthetics* which is as complex, coded and meaning-laden as other forms of narrative, theatre or art. And perverse scenarios are particularly tightly constructed, with every detail and element fraught with narrative significance.

We might note, interestingly, that the language used to delineate the aesthetics of perversions, to trace their etiologies and describe their psychobiographical raw materials, is almost identical to the type of psychocritical language used to describe the aesthetic and creative process of the modern artist. Artistic activity, and the specific repetitions within an individual artist's oeuvre that constitute style, thematics, even medium, are often said to have their formation in unconscious, unresolved conflicts, traumas and torments that are expressed, returned to and repeated in art and literature. It may be something of a critical cliché in the age of the 'death of the author', but the artist as suffering neurotic is still one of the most prevalent discourses of artistic production. This art historian's analysis of Mondrian's abstractions is typical:

> Mondrian's aesthetic choices emerged from his unconscious conflicts; as he translated these choices into his painting, wielding his ruler and applying his brush, these conflicts guided his hand. He found sensuality so frightening that it was his dread of desire, rather than the desires themselves, that ultimately shaped his abstract designs. No sentiment, no curves, no touching – that is how he lived and that is what his paintings proclaim.
> . . . [They] offer impressive evidence just how much beauty the talented can wrest from fear. . . . Painting was, for Mondrian, the aesthetic correlative for his repressions, his way of coming to terms with himself – at once an expression of his problem and an embodiment of his solution.[15]

And who among us hasn't made some sort of casual inference about an artist, writer or film-maker's unconscious life and preoccupations read through the symptom of his or her work? One has only to think of say, Hitchcock, and the cottage industry in linking his psychosexual quirks to the thematics of his films. So *sublimation*, which in its pop psychology form means 'working something out' through other means, is tacitly acknowledged by both professional and casual critical enterprise as the key to artistic production: socially unacceptable impulses and contents are channelled through and buried in the artistic work for future critics and historians to elicit and decode. As perversion starts to appear more aesthetic – 'every detail counts' – don't aesthetics, conversely, start to seem more perverse?

In Freudian theory proper, the *what* that gets channelled elsewhere, into more socially valued forms, is sexual energy. And for Freud, too, the connection is explicitly made *between art and perversion*:

'The forces that can be employed for cultural activities are thus to a great extent obtained through the suppression of what are known as the *perverse* elements of sexual excitation.' These are what Freud called the component instincts which are anarchic, polymorphous and infantile, and which, when they fail to achieve successful integration into normal adult sexuality, are most likely to become sublimated into other aims.[16] (And the connection between the terms 'sublimation' and the sublime shouldn't be forgotten.) So art and perversion are similar in origin, dissimilar in that art rechannels the same impulses and energies into a socially acceptable or elevated idiom: aesthetic language.

So clearly this rechannelling will mean that, at a surface level, art tends to *look* different from perversion, or its media form, hard-core pornography. Stoller defines pornography as material that intends to be pornographic, that is to produce a certain response – arousal – in its audience. But for Stoller, art and pornography are formally similar: erotic response is as complex a phenomenon as aesthetic response, and the distinctions between the two come down to differences in their respective contents.[17] But as we've seen, the two are also quite proximate: art is also libidinal, perverse; perversions have their aesthetics, and both are structured according to the imperatives of the unconscious. It's perversion which, having undergone transformation through the psychic processes of sublimation, then *elicits, produces* aesthetic response.[18] The energy devoted to keeping aesthetics and perversity – art and pornography – so discursively sequestered begins to make more sense when you see that the aesthetic response is actually completely *dependent* on perversity, only produced in the alchemy of sublimation.

What Stoller also neglects to mention are the class aspirations behind these content differences – that the competence necessary to do the work of translating the energies of compulsion and perversion into the lofty heights of aestheticism and the language of form is, to a large degree, an educated response, a cultural competence.[19] It presupposes a degree of intellectualisation and the 'distance from the world' which, Pierre Bourdieu writes, is the basis of the bourgeois experience.[20] There may be upper-class aesthetes using porn or lower-class abstract artists producing gallery art, but as Bourdieu puts it:

The aesthetic disposition, understood as the aptitude for perceiving and deciphering specifically stylistic characteristics, is thus inseparable from specifically artistic competence. The latter may be acquired by explicit learning or simply by regular contact with works of art, especially those assembled in museums and galleries.[21]

This aesthetic competence, produced largely through the vehicle of what Bourdieu calls 'educational capital', is a form of cultural capital, a mechanism for enforcing class distinctions. So also at stake in maintaining the absolute discursive distinction between art and pornography are the class divisions that a distinctively high art works to maintain, as well as the necessity of reproducing the requirement for sublimation – so crucial for the bourgeois project of producing distance from the body, the unconscious and the materiality of everyday life.[22]

And perhaps there's another stake: art's potential *as* 'disturbatory', *as* political. For art historian Francis O'Connor, also writing about self-portraiture, Mondrian's translation of his conflicts into *abstraction* 'from symbol to sign . . . denies the aesthetic a world other than itself'. A similar argument has been advanced by Peter Burger, also writing of the twentieth-century avant-garde, that in modernism and twentieth-century art generally art lost any political edge as it became increasingly self-referential, increasingly mediated by art institutions, and increasingly cordoned off from praxis and everyday life.[23] O'Connor adds that what Mondrian has done is to relegate art to 'a mode of moral etiquette'. So both writers appear to be saying that the work of translation and transmogrification of perversion, neurosis, social conflict and artistic rebellion into self-referential art – into *gallery art* – is precisely what strips art of social meaning: for Burger, of its political potential; for O'Connor, of the possibility of being something other than mere moral etiquette. So this seems to be an argument *against* sublimation, against aesthetics as an exercise in decorousness and the social niceties. It seems to be an argument, then, for pornography over art.

If the discursive distinctions between art and pornography come largely down to issues around sublimation and the class imperative to produce and reproduce it, the problem with pornography appears to be its failure to translate one set of contents into another. The problem is that it produces a body of images that are too *blatantly* out of the unconscious, too *unaesthetically* written in the language of obsession, compulsion, perversion, infantile desires, rage, fear, pain and misogyny; too literally about sex and power rather than their aesthetically coded forms in the works of any number of famous and adulated artists and writers who treat similar themes (or the socially coded but equally ritualised forms through which they're expressed at gallery openings and academic conferences). Too *potent* for art. It might appear that the interest of the state in regulating pornography is that it *meets* the criteria for 'disturbatory art', as Danto calls it, which seeks 'charged artistic enactments' and sets up 'perturbations across a social field'. And as art has moved to appropriate – or return to – pornographic idioms, in the work of Robert Mapplethorpe, Karen Finley, Holly Hughes, to name a few, the government has been very quick to step in.

As the distinctions between art and perversion begin to unravel, perhaps some of the certainty about what pornography is and how it functions does so too. This isn't necessarily an argument for moving pornography into the art galleries and museums. Aesthetics may rely on perversity, perversity may be aesthetically complex, but sublimation isn't imaginary: the pornographic response is still viscerally and experientially distinct from aesthetic response. It *is* an argument, however, for regarding pornography (when we regard it theoretically) *as* we do artistic production rather than as discursively distinct, and for applying the same degree of critical, interpretive acumen to it; for understanding porn, as Stoller suggests, as imbued with theatrical and semiotic complexity, far from lacking in nuance. It's not *only* a naked woman, it's not *transparently* a pair of lace panties, it's a condensation of narratives of the entry into the social order, the passage from infancy to childhood to adulthood, the prison-house of binary gender role assignment, of mother-dominated childbearing *and* the oppression of women. But as Kaplan indicates, the woman in the porn pictorial is as likely to represent the female side of the male viewer he wants to subjugate as it is to express, in some literal way, his desire to oppress me. There's no reason to assume that pornographic images function any more literally (or produce more literal effects) than other more socially elevated images that we're accustomed

to reading for their symbolic and latent meanings –
no reason other than class prejudice against 'working
photographs' or pure censoriousness against sexual
pleasure.

So as I began trying to look as closely at TV self-
portraiture as the art establishment would at Cindy
Sherman's work, I began to examine the *mise en scène*
of the photos: the spaces around the bodies instead of
the distracting flash of the bodies themselves. Rather
than posing themselves against a blank wall or backdrop (although a few do), most of the men choose to
pose themselves within their domestic space, afford-
ing a voyeuristic glimpse into its décor and environs.
The juxtapositions of the body and its social geography condense, in tableau, the lived experience of
gender distress and its familial melodramas: the

burden of liminality and otherness and their by-
product secrecy and shame. They force the viewer
onto intimate terms with the small forms of social
tyranny and the too often, too taken-for-granted
policing of everyday life that none of us – however
putatively gender-normative – ever escapes.

These self-portraits are very much dramas of the
home. They tell stories. Living rooms and bedrooms
are both popular scenarios, but a lot of men choose to
pose themselves in their kitchens as well – perhaps in
their minds the most feminine space in the house.
The image of a glamorous yet virile blond in four-
inch heels perched seductively on the kitchen counter
– the shiny kitchen appliances, dish soap, cute spice
rack and harvest-motif wallpaper competing visually
with her erect penis – suggests the American sit-com

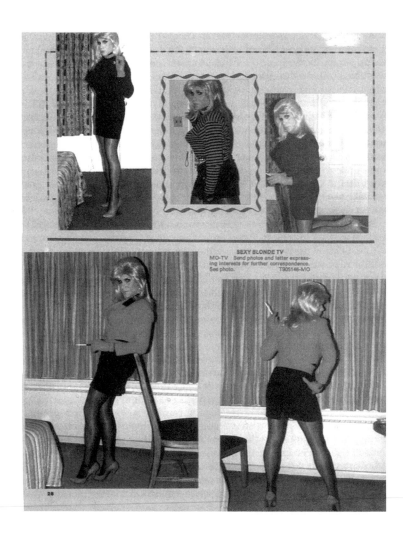

Personal ads

suburban mom as imagined by David Lynch or perhaps John Waters, and the absent presence of a 'real' wife as well. The wife-impersonator, gazing impudently into the camera, usurping the rightful occupant (and her narrative), verifies the complaints of many TV wives that their husbands are competitive as women: spending more time on looks, more money on clothes, making the wives feel dumpy and inferior as women. The kitchen as a gendered turf conveys that both the wife we see and the wives we don't are equally padlocked into social gender stereotypes and their domestic spaces.

The image of a beefy man in lingerie pouting into the camera, posed in front of a Swedish-modern breakfront displaying a neatly arranged collection of *Time-Life* books and china figurines – with perhaps even a wedding photo in the background – says everything about carefully compartmentalised secrets and the fantasy of seamless 'normal' surfaces, with this insistent display of all the props and set-pieces of happy American home life. It's an image that almost makes you understand the popularity of Ronald Reagan – the carefully constructed, pomaded and overproduced surface, that cynical (and of course completely fictive) promise of sit-com family normalcy, of docile mothers and strong fathers who will bomb us out of perversity and back to the fantasy of God-given sex roles and their respective, separate, wardrobes.

Sometimes the self-portraitist will send in not just one photo, but an entire layout in which he poses himself in every room of the house, giving you the guided tour – the formal dining room, the rec room with the CD collection and component stereo system, the master bedroom suite. As is common throughout the history of portraiture, he pictorially surrounds himself with his property and possessions. What mute assertion or appeal is being made here? Schooled by John Berger in 'ways of seeing' early oil painting, we're alerted that these objects supply us information about the poser's position in the world – his class status and material wealth obviously – but also about what *possession* itself implies: entitlement, citizenship, the assertion of a right.[24] Given what we know about the disdain heaped on the male transvestite in our society, this self-protective gathering of one's possessions around oneself seems sadly talismanic. (Interestingly, for Berger, pictorial qualities such as these are gendered: a man's presence is

dependent on displayed forms of external power and possessions, whereas a woman's presence is in her physical appearance. These TV self-portraits, not surprisingly, walk right down the middle. Even Berger has no aesthetic analysis that isn't binary in its gender assumptions.)

The more of these photos I looked at, the more curious I began to be about why so many transvestites seem to have matching bedspreads and curtains in their bedrooms. Had I stumbled onto the missing link in the etiology of transvestism through my close reading of transvestite home décor? Something about matching fabric? I finally realised that what I was looking at were motel rooms, and began to notice the further clues (most of these photos are quite grainy): a suitcase in a corner, those backbreaking slab-of-wood headboards that no one would dream of putting on their own bed, an occasional rate card on the door, the motel-type plumbing fixtures in the bathrooms.

These *mise en scènes* narrate a fairly obvious tale of secrecy – a compulsion to cross-dress that the man has managed to keep secret from a wife and family. So, a small drama, a brief glimpse into what fear and pain must accompany the deception of being unable to reveal the most central thing about yourself to your mate, and the catastrophe that exposure would mean in a life carefully constructed around a sexual secret.

One thing to add about this evident sexual secrecy is that it flies completely in the face of Robert Stoller's account of the essential role of women in the causation and maintenance of transvestism. According to Stoller, who has written extensively about transvestites and transsexuals, 'the women of transvestites . . . all share the attribute of taking a conscious and intense pleasure in seeing males dressed as females. All have in common a fear of and a need to ruin masculinity.' The cooperation of women is essential for 'successful' transvestism – and the fact that some men are able to pass as women is 'almost invariably due' to women and girlfriends – 'succorers', Stoller calls them, who, because of their own concealed rage at men devote themselves to teaching the transvestite how to dress, walk and use make-up.[25]

These motel room photos stand in silent rebuke to the clinical literature and, of course, to its blame-the-woman line. As with feminist art, which consciously appropriated the power to define and narrate women's lives against dominant and dominating discourses – including, frequently, the male-dominated medical and psychiatric professions – so may these TV self-portraits be forms of defiance and self-empowerment for another oppressed minority.

I've chosen to discuss a form of pornography that may seem, to a certain extent, anomalous. TV classifieds are something of a folk practice, hand-crafted and artisanal in relation to other more mass-produced forms of porn. And I've chosen to discuss a form of pornography that doesn't depict biological women's bodies either – largely in order to be able to talk about porn without all the usual red flags going off, and to avoid reproducing all the usual gender assumptions of the porn debates. But in conclusion I want to suggest that perhaps in reading all pornography more closely we might uncover other histories, other narratives, perhaps crudely written, and perhaps, as Kaplan says of perverse scenarios exposing one thing to distract you from thinking about another. The perverse strategy hides *through* exposure, it works overtime to deflect your attention from what's really at stake. Pornography exposes a lot of naked bodies, but perhaps this is as distraction: the repetitions of all pornography, the return again and again to the same scenarios and scripts, have the compulsive character that is the mark of material emanating from the unconscious.

In seeing pornographic images of women as so transparently about male erections and female disempowerment, what remains hidden? As with the TV self-portraits, closer reading may provide glimpses into the forgotten (repressed) histories that all gendered subjects share, and from which some have emerged more unscathed than others. Perhaps there is some understanding to be gained – for women, and maybe men too – that will be the wedge into male power, perhaps a realisation that so often what looks like power is props, compensatory mechanisms and empty signifiers. I suggest that in looking at pornography we should not be so distracted by surfaces, and that like art critics, we're alert for meaning, to what we don't yet know, are threatened by, or may have forgotten.

NOTES

1. My use of the word 'perversion' throughout this essay should not be read as derogatory. I've retained the term primarily because it's used throughout the clinical literature I refer to; however, it will become clear that my attitude towards that literature is ambivalent. The word perversion obviously implies its distinction from so-called 'normal' sexuality, but this should be understood as referring to social norms, and not implying some form of natural or a priori sexuality.

2. For example, bestiality is another such regulated area. This means you can freely slaughter and eat animals, you just can't photograph sex with them, which is surely not any *less* humane.

3. Susan Gubar, 'Representing Pornography: Feminism, Criticism, and Depictions of Female Violation', in Susan Gubar and Joan Huff (eds), *For Adult Users Only* (Bloomington: Indiana University Press, 1989), p. 48.

4. Linda Williams, *Hard Core: Power, Pleasure, and the 'Frenzy of the Visible'* (Berkeley: University of California Press, 1989), p. 6.

5. See Andrea Dworkin, *Intercourse* (New York: Macmillan Press, 1987).

6. The term 'transvestite' refers to men (I don't discuss female transvestism here) who dress in women's clothing. The term 'transsexual' denotes men who through hormones or surgery have physically changed their primary or secondary sexual attributes, most typically in these magazines men who have developed breasts through hormone use. For clinicians, the difference additionally is that transvestites see themselves as men and want to be men, albeit men dressed occasionally as women; transsexuals actually want to be women.

7. It's not my purpose here to try to distinguish between heterosexual and homosexual transvestism, or otherwise categorise practices, but I do want to point out that these magazines do seem to belie the clinical literature on transvestism, which defines transvestism as heterosexual. Both Stoller and Kaplan define male transvestism as a man fetishising female clothing as a path to arousal but in which the sexual object choice is a woman; both define homosexual drag as non-fetishistic cross-dressing. What the magazines indicate, though, both in the stories and in the personal ads which I discuss here, is that many men who cross-dress and define themselves as heterosexual *are* interested in sex with other men or cross-dressed men when they themselves are cross-dressed (though they may see themselves and even their bodies and genitalia as female in those encounters), and that their

sexuality, at least as far as the biological sex of their object choice goes, is much more multivalent than the clinicians suggest. There also *does* seem to be homosexual fetishism of female clothing. But I make no assumption that any of these images or writings represent actual practices, but that, as with all porn, this may strictly represent fantasy.

8. It should be noted, though, that feminists have repeatedly expressed resentment of the fact that the transvestite male may foray into femininity while in no way relinquishing any of the prerogatives of male power. It has also often been said of transvestites that they caricature the 'worst' aspects of femininity and are, deep down, actually hostile to women; so some analysts may be inclined to read some degree of coded misogyny in these images. For a feminist analysis of transvestism, see Annie Woodhouse, *Fantastic Women: Sex, Gender and Transvestism* (New Brunswick, NJ: Rutgers, 1989), which, as the author says, 'is not a study which is particularly sympathetic to transvestism' (p. xiii). See also Marjorie Garber, *Vested Interests: Cross-Dressing and Cultural Anxiety* (New York: Routledge, 1992), which, though primarily concerned with the figure of the transvestite across Western culture, also analyses the gender and sexual politics of transvestism from a feminist vantage point.

9. Barbara Rose, 'Self-Portraiture: Theme with a Thousand Faces', *Art in America*, January–February 1975, pp. 66–73.

10. Arthur Danto, 'Photography and Performance: Cindy Sherman's Stills', in Cindy Sherman, *Untitled Film Stills/Cindy Sherman* (New York: Rizzoli, 1990), pp. 5–14.

11. Ibid.

12. Louise Kaplan, *Female Perversions* (New York: Doubleday, 1991), p. 9.

13. See also Joan Riviere, 'Womanliness as a Masquerade', in Cora Kaplan (ed.), *Formations of Fantasy* (New York: Methuen, 1986), pp. 35–44.

14. Robert J. Stoller, MD, *Observing the Erotic Imagination* (New Haven, CT: Yale University Press, 1985), p. 49.

15. P. Gay, *Art and Act: On Causes in History – Manet, Gropius, Mondrian* (New York: Harper & Row, 1976), pp. 225–6. Quoted by Francis V. O'Connor, 'The Psychodynamics of the Fronted Self-Portrait', in Mary Mathews Gedo (ed.), *Psychoanalytic Perspectives on Art* (New Jersey: The Analytic Press, 1985), p. 197.

16. J. Laplanche and J.-B. Pontalis, *The Language of Psychoanalysis* (New York: Norton, 1973), p. 432.

17. Stoller, *Observing the Erotic Imagination*, chapter 2, 'Erotics/Aesthetics'. The content argument actually gets harder to support as more and more artists appropriate pornographic idioms. For example, as I write, novelist Nicholson Baker's new book *Vox*, which is composed entirely of a two-way phone sex conversation, is third on the *New York Times Book Review* hard-cover bestseller list.

18. See also Janine Chasseguet-Smirgel, *Creativity and Perversion* (New York: Norton, 1984), p. 89.

19. On the class basis of anti-pornography sentiments see Laura Kipnis, '(Male) Desire and (Female) Disgust: Reading *Hustler*', in Lawrence Grossberg, Cary Nelson and Paula Treichler (eds), *Cultural Studies* (New York: Routledge, 1992), pp. 373–91.

20. Pierre Bourdieu, *Distinction: A Social Critique of the Judgment of Taste* (Cambridge, MA: Harvard University Press, 1984), p. 54.

21. Ibid., p. 51.

22. See Norbert Elias, *The History of Manners* (New York: Urizen Books, 1978).

23. Peter Burger, *Theory of the Avant Garde* (Minneapolis: University of Minnesota Press, 1984).

24. John Berger, *Ways of Seeing* (London: Penguin, 1972).

25. Robert J. Stoller, MD, *Sex and Gender: On the Development of Masculinity and Femininity* (New York: Science House, 1968), pp. 206–17.

18 'Above the Pulp-line': The Cultural Significance of Erotic Art[1]

Lynda Nead

INTRODUCING THE EROTIC

Up to the point of obscenity, art consecrates and purifies all it touches.

(Charles Augustin Sainte-Beuve, as quoted by Peter Webb, 1975)[2]

The advantage of erotic art over the common run of hard-core pornography is that . . . like all good art . . . it quietly *educates* while it entertains. It may arouse our senses and stimulate desire – it is meant to do so and would fail if it didn't – but it will do so by making us *think* as well as feel.

(Drs P. and E. Kronhausen, 1973)[3]

These quotations introduce the central terms of this discussion: obscenity, pornography, art and the erotic. Both are drawn from publications which appeared in the early to mid-1970s, a moment when, as will be argued at the end of this essay, the attempt to draw meaningful distinctions between these terms and to assert the value of erotic art had a particular urgency. Webb and the Kronhausens represent different aspects of sexual liberalism, itself only one voice within the polyphony of sexual discourses in the 1970s. Webb uses the words of Sainte-Beuve to assert the mutual exclusivity of art and obscenity. Obscenity appears as a given or intrinsic quality of an object or representation; it is the point at which the sacred powers of art are rendered useless. If art represents here the domain of pure culture, then obscenity symbolises the profane, where culture disintegrates and the subject is strictly beyond representation.

The Kronhausens express a more pragmatic view. Hard-core pornography lacks cultural distinction, its function is merely and solely that of sexual arousal and sensual gratification. Erotic art, on the other hand, takes on the didactic role of high art and lifts the depiction of desire to a higher cultural plane.

Desire is thus contained and controlled by the aesthetic. Erotic art arouses, but it is a reflective and enriching form of arousal.

The opposition of art and pornography, or the aesthetic and the obscene, is one which has structured much modern cultural discourse. It has worked to classify acceptable and unacceptable forms of culture and to differentiate the licit and the illicit, the ennobling and the forbidden. In 1972, Lord Longford, one of the main British campaigners of the period for the restoration of 'traditional' moral values and the family, organised an investigation of pornography and its effects on contemporary British society. The report of the Longford Committee was published in the form of a mass-market paperback and launched in a blaze of publicity. Among the many expert witnesses called before the committee was Lord Kenneth Clark, a key figure within British arts administration and one of the Western world's best-known art historians through his presentation of the television series *Civilisation* (1969–70). His formulation of the art/pornography opposition usefully summarises the view inherited from Enlightenment aesthetics:

To my mind art exists in the realm of contemplation, and is bound by some sort of imaginative transposition. The moment art becomes an incentive to action it loses its true character. This is my objection to painting with a communist programme, and it would also apply to pornography.[4]

For art to be art it has to engage the mind rather than the body; it has to involve the faculty of imagination and bring about a still, contemplative state in the viewer. Propaganda and pornography shatter the unified subjectivity of the viewer and incite, or more accurately excite, the body to action. What is clear from this kind of formulation is that the artistic and the pornographic are not simply properties of any given representation, but are also, and perhaps more significantly, classifications of those who view the images; they are social, cultural and moral designations of people as well as objects.

Clark's definition recalls the work of Steven Marcus, whose classic study of Victorian pornography, *The Other Victorians*, was published in 1966. For Marcus, literary writing is characterised by multiplicity, narrative complexity and a concern with human relations; but pornography is essentially repetitive, literal and unmetaphoric, and interested in organs rather than people.[5] Although this is primarily an account of formal characteristics, it too may be taken as a description and ranking of audiences as well as texts.

As views such as these demonstrate, pornography is seen to be essentially non-creative; in its urgency to bring about sexual arousal in the viewer, its singular onanistic intention, it sweeps aside all the formal and imaginative preoccupations which are seen to be at the heart of artistic creativity. But perhaps the terms of this cultural debate need to be recast or refocused. What about other categories within this system, categories such as the erotic? Within both mainstream and alternative cultural politics the focus has been on producing objective criteria for the designation of pornography. Although this has produced competing definitions, involving both the extension and narrowing of the boundaries of the pornographic, essentially this exclusive preoccupation with pornography, seen as a discrete cultural category rather than as part of a broader system of cultural distinction, perpetuates the view of cultural production and consumption polarised between art and pornography, the pure and the profane. It fails to recognise the significance of the mid-terms within this system which, as I will argue, are the principal means by which meaning is produced.

It is easy to conceive of art and pornography in their most extreme forms, forms which we might situate securely at the centre of each category; it is harder, though, to specify where one category ends and the other begins, and yet this is surely the critical place of judgment. It is at the limit, at the framing edge of the category, where differences are most emphatic and where the finest distinctions between

inclusion and exclusion, acceptability and unacceptability are made. So we might begin to alter the focus, away from the polarisation of art and pornography and towards a re-examination of erotic art, where art most nearly succumbs to the pornographic and brushes up against the obscene. Erotic art defines the boundaries of allowable sexual representation in modern Western culture and is where the depiction of sex can be given moral and social value. How, then, is the erotic differentiated from the pornographic or the obscene?

The etymology of pornography is from the Greek words for harlot and writing; the *Oxford English Dictionary* therefore gives the primary definition as writings of or about prostitutes and their patrons. The word has subsequently taken on the additional meaning of the expression of obscene or unchaste subjects. The derivation of erotic is from the Greek 'eros', sexual love – its *OED* definition is given as 'of or pertaining to the passion of love'. Significantly, one of the references given in the *OED* is from George Steiner's *Language and Silence* (1967): 'Above the pulp-line . . . lies the world of erotica, of sexual writing with literary pretensions or genuine claims.' The pulp-line is an apt metaphor for the boundary between illicit and licit sexual representation. Pulp connotes unbounded matter, possibly the body reduced to unformed flesh, the body as it is addressed by pornography, void of moral or intellectual regulation. Erotic art then, is above the pulp-line, for it implies a form of contained cultural consumption which, while carrying the exciting risk of failure, succeeds in addressing the viewer as a unified and rational subject. Clearly there are significant areas where the two terms dissolve into each other, for if pornography is the domain of forbidden sexual representation, then erotic art must always carry the traces of this possibility in order to retain its distinctive identity and not simply be absorbed into the realm of art.

As we can see from the etymology of pornography, the term has always connoted a form of commodified sex; sex for a mass market and sold for a profit. The erotic, however, carries none of these associations; its etymological roots are with love. Erotic art seeks to transcend the marketplace, and it is this absence of concern with commercialisation and money which makes the concept of 'erotic art' possible.

CULTURAL DISTINCTION

> Taste classifies, and it classifies the classifier. Social sub-
> jects, classified by their classification, distinguish them-
> selves by the distinctions they make, between the
> beautiful and the ugly, the distinguished and the vulgar
> . . .
>
> (Pierre Bourdieu, 1984)[6]

The judgment of erotic art should be seen, in Bourdieu's terms, as an act of cultural distinction which
carries particular social significance. Bourdieu's
survey of taste takes the form of a critique of Kantian notions of the aesthetic. Kant sought to distinguish the condition of disinterestedness, which is the
only guarantee of aesthetic contemplation and which
differentiates it from the interests of reason and the
senses. Bourdieu suggests that the Kantian notion of
the detached and pure gaze asserts a life free from
economic necessity which functions at all levels of
society:

> Although art obviously offers the greatest scope to the
> aesthetic disposition, there is no area of practice in
> which the aim of purifying, reforming and sublimating
> primary needs and impulses cannot assert itself, no area
> in which the stylisation of life, that is, the primacy of
> forms over function, of manner over matter, does not
> produce the same effects.[7]

Although Bourdieu could justly be accused of having
a romanticised perception of an uncorrupted, honest
working-class culture, his general theoretical framework offers a particularly helpful way of understanding the cultural significance of erotic art. For
Bourdieu, the cultural sphere is maintained by the
evacuation of vulgar, coarse and venal pleasures and
the assertion of pure, disinterested and sublimated
ones. This hierarchy is commonly expressed by the
prioritising of form over function and of manner over
matter. According to Bourdieu, those who are satisfied by purified pleasures are assured social superiority; cultural consumption thus fulfils the function of
legitimating social differences.

When this model is applied to the judgment of
erotic art, we can see that this form of classification
might yield a special legitimating force. If the sacred
sphere of culture is characterised by the expulsion of
the appetite, then what could be more risky, but
potentially more rewarding than to classify the venal,

sex, itself? What better way to demonstrate your cultural disinterestedness and superiority than to come
into contact with the erotic and to be – practically –
unmoved? Erotic art legitimises the representation of
the sexual through the assertion of form which holds
off the collapse into the pornographic. Erotic art
takes the viewer to the frontier of legitimate culture;
it allows the viewer to be aroused but within the
purified, contemplative mode of high culture.
Arousal and contemplation – erotic art must remain
for ever between these two conditions for it to function as the point of distinction between art and pornography. This flirtation with the sexual can be seen
at work in Kenneth Clark's evocation of the eroticism
of the painted nude:

> No nude, however abstract, should fail to arouse in the
> spectator some vestige of erotic feeling, even although
> it be only the faintest shadow. . . . The desire to grasp
> and be united with another human body is so funda-
> mental a part of our nature, that our judgment of what
> is known as 'pure form' is inevitably influenced by it;
> and one of the difficulties of the nude as a subject for art
> is that these instincts cannot lie hidden, as they do for
> example in our enjoyment of a piece of pottery, thereby
> gaining the force of sublimation, but are dragged into
> the foreground, where they risk upsetting the unity of
> responses from which a work of art derives its inde-
> pendent life. Even so, the amount of erotic content
> which a work of art can hold in solution is very high.[8]

The publishing success of Clark's *The Nude*, from
which this extract is drawn, makes it worth looking at
in detail. The text takes us through a series of steps
which negotiate the issue of erotic art. The uneasiness
of its tone is apparent, particularly towards the end
where Clark describes the way in which sexual
instincts are 'dragged' into the open by the nude and
'risk upsetting' the purity of the aesthetic faculty. In
fact throughout the extract Clark emphasises the mag-
nitude of the risk which faces the intrepid connoisseur.
Beginning with vestiges and shadows of erotic feeling,
the sexual body makes itself ever more present until,
towards the end, the response verges on the kinaes-
thetic. But the entire passage asserts the mastery of the
body, the triumph of the mind over the baser senses
and instincts. It is the enactment of cultural distinction, announcing the social and cultural superiority of
the connoisseur art historian and the putative reader.

THE PRIMACY OF FORM AND SOUND ECONOMICS

We have seen that to maintain its function as arbiter of the pulp-line, erotic art must be seen to foreground the concern with form. Whereas pornography is believed to reduce language to its most basic forms or to cliché and stereotype, erotic art pursues the dual preoccupations of love and linguistic exploration. In Steiner's essay on contemporary erotic writing, he describes pornographic vocabulary as the ' "stripped naked' of language', brought about by the reduction of privacy and individual imagination within a mass consumer society. 'Where everything can be said with a shout,' he observes, 'less and less can be said in a low voice.'[9] Pornography is presented as the genre of function and necessity, the language of the sexual body, for which style is simply an obstacle to its primary task of arousal. Good erotic art, on the other hand, is the genre of individualism, of the subtle and enchanting whisper rather than the yells of the mob.

There is of course a paradox in this conception of pornography as stylelessness, or of style reduced to the utmost degree. For language – written or visual – to give the reader a sense of stylistic absence demands extreme stylisation. It requires conventions of representation, narration, contextualisation which say to the reader or viewer: this is representation 'stripped naked', which abandons superfluous details of style and form and takes you directly, without formal interference, to the realm of the sexual. Erotic art cannot easily take this risk with style but has to neutralise obscenity through a range of creative forms. As one aesthetician puts it:

> The erotic elements may be treated metaphysically. In this case sex is regarded as the absolute or related to some other absolute. ... Second, the sexual may be poeticized, that is, invested with emotional charge. ... Third, the description of sex may be intellectualized through a distancing of the characters from their behavior. ... Finally, the most frequent method, aestheticization, that is, the accenting of such values as sound, color, shape, movement etc.[10]

In all these cases the content undergoes a formal manoeuvre which distances the sexual and transforms it into culture. Of course, this transmutation cannot be guaranteed or permanently secured, the erotic may devolve into pornography and all these classifications are subject to competing and historically specific claims. What is most constant is the connotation of eroticism as style made manifest, even if it is parodic style which mimics the stylelessness of pornography. Style is a signifier of the aesthetic and necessitates an engagement which is non-sensual and unconcerned with gratification.

Within the discipline of art history this process of aestheticisation of the sexual has been explored to the point at which the medium itself, regardless of content, is seen as an expression of sex. Comparing a female nude and a landscape by the painter Pierre Bonnard, Janet Hobhouse writes:

> The landscape is by far the sexier painting, with its trees and leaves pulsating in the wild, emotive colouring of Bonnard's palette. Nature is voluptuous, enticing, opulent, beckoning the painter in the same manner as did his early nudes.[11]

The aesthetic disposition is thus able to purify and sublimate the sexual to the extent that form and medium alone are able to convey the wild, expressive sexuality of the painter. The language of connoisseurship ensures that this does not become a vulgar display; instead, the response serves as an indication of the viewer's refinement and taste.

The concepts of art, pornography and the erotic are constituted through moral and cultural discourses, and they are also economic categories. Pornography is the product of mass culture; it is, as we have seen, sexual representation made solely for the purpose of profit. But pornography represents a wayward form of economics; it circulates covertly, 'under the counter', and seems to transgress the system of differential value established in the field of culture. In 1972 the report of the Longford Committee emphasised the huge sums of money being made through trading pornography and the disparity between its cost and its cultural value:

> Glossy art books sell for £6 or £7 a time, and *Private*, an internationally notorious erotic magazine – printed in four languages – costs no less than £5 an issue in Britain. From the same source colour pictures cost £4 for a set of eight, or £80 for 'all 27 sets'.[12]

What kind of economic system is this, in which a porn magazine costs nearly as much as a well-produced glossy art book and in which 'pin-ups' go for the price of masterpieces? Pornography is thus characterised by disparity between economic and cultural value, whereas erotic art is altogether a sounder product which confirms the parity between these two fields of value. Erotic art never evades the question of market value altogether, however; rather it occupies a particular place within the specific economic conditions of the art market.[13] Art as a commodity is priced according to quality and rarity, and as a part of this system erotic art is set apart from other commodities and the trash of mass-produced porn.

Pornography testifies to the loss of economic management which is an apt paralleling of the loss of moral management. This relationship comes together most forcefully in the notion of 'permissiveness', a metaphor which emerged in the political context of the 1960s and 1970s.[14] Used most frequently by the advocates of traditional and authoritarian morality, permissiveness was a term which connoted loose moral standards and sexual promiscuity leading to a general decline in social life. From the perspective of legislation, permissiveness encapsulates a series of legal reforms concerning issues such as obscenity and censorship, abortion, contraception and divorce. But in its wider context permissiveness can be applied to a much more generalised set of social changes arising from the boom in the world capitalist economy following World War II. The 1960s, then, seemed to be an age of economic affluence and moral liberalism. There is a long and complex association between transformations in the economic field and in sexual morality; in the mid-19th century the metaphor of 'spending' carried the sense of both economic and sexual expenditure and implied the need for careful self-management in both spheres. In terms of the development of this metaphor in the 1960s, Jeffrey Weeks comments: 'There is no doubt that the prolonged boom depended in part upon a switch in moral attitudes away from traditional bourgeois virtues of self-denial and saving ("prudence") towards a compulsion to spend.'[15]

Perhaps the most visible feature of this growth in economic and sexual consumption was pornography. Although there was undoubtedly an increasing eroticisation of social life in the major cities of Western Europe and the United States and a manifest expansion in the pornography industry, it is equally true that pornography – or, more precisely, the represen-

tation of the sexual – took on symbolic importance in the 1960s and early 1970s. It became the battleground for competing definitions of sexual and social acceptability, and it was precisely in this historical context that attention was turned to erotic art as the site where new ground might be won for sexual freedom within legitimate culture, or which confirmed the corruption of traditional public life through permissiveness. In order to exemplify some of the issues discussed so far, it is worth looking in more detail at the formation of erotic art during the historical moment of the late 1960s.

THE FIRST INTERNATIONAL EXHIBITION OF EROTIC ART

This exhibition of erotic art opened in a public gallery in Sweden on 3 May 1968, more or less to the day when student revolts in Paris and in campuses across Britain and the USA reached a peak. From Sweden, the show moved on to a gallery in Denmark and then sought a private venue in the USA. The exhibition was largely the work of two people, the Drs Phyllis and Eberhard Kronhausen, psychologists who had pioneered new techniques in psychotherapy and had published on various aspects of sexual psychology, sex and censorship. The Kronhausens also had an extensive personal collection of erotic art, which formed the nucleus of the show. The exhibition received substantial publicity in Sweden and in other European countries and the implications of public funding for the display of sexually explicit material were fought out by various moral and political factions.

As well as the exhibition itself there was an accompanying catalogue, two substantial volumes which included an essay by the Kronhausens on the nature and value of erotic art, transcribed interviews with visitors and experts and illustrations of the exhibits. Both the show and the catalogue promoted the Kronhausens's view of the liberatory and therapeutic effects of erotic art and of sexual behaviour freed from the conventions of bourgeois authoritarianism and repression:

> Erotic art expresses the demand for sexual freedom – a freedom vital to individual happiness and mental wellbeing. In that sense, erotic art carries a truly revolutionary message: it demands no less than extension of freedom, not only in the sexual area, but in every sphere of social life.[16]

For the organisers, the significance of the exhibition was that it gave the public an opportunity to look at pictures about sex without looking at pornography, without feeling embarrassed or ashamed. Indeed, although it is not specified, the implication of their position is that the pornographic and the erotic are largely defined in terms of their means of distribution and consumption and their place within the cultural spectrum. If representations of sex are placed on the walls of a public art gallery, they are more likely to be understood within the discourse of art than that of pornography.

> In the case of pornography, most people will feel that they are looking at something they shouldn't perhaps be looking at. But here in the museum they can look at erotic pictures that are beautiful and artistic and they can do so in an atmosphere of social acceptance, social approval.[17]

This partial recognition of the discursive formation of pornography is perhaps the most lasting radical aspect of the exhibition; otherwise the commentary and exhibits are marked by an exclusive concern with heterosexuality and a romantic view of sexual freedom as a state of pre-Fall bliss.

The poster which advertised the exhibition begins to demonstrate how the primacy of form is deployed by the Kronhausens (see opposite). This poster raised particular problems for the organisers since, by its very function, its circulation was less circumscribed than the exhibition and it was more likely to transgress the boundaries of acceptable and unacceptable public display. Although the exhibition included a wide range of Western and non-Western art, contemporary and historical, the image used on the poster is a seventeenth-century Japanese woodcut. This image exemplifies the concept of primacy of form, discussed earlier; the depiction of pattern and surface decoration is visually at least as important as the representation of sexual intercourse. Formally the bodies are a continuation of the lines and shapes of the surrounding drapery. Moreover, the woodcut is historically and geographically distant and, wrenched from its cultural specificity, it can become a timeless, aesthetic evocation of sexual love. Elsewhere in the catalogue, this process of aestheticisation is repeated:

We had occasion, in fact, to watch the transformation of pornography into art before our own eyes when Hans Bellmer one day worked in our presence, making a complicated and highly erotic engraving from a series of common pornographic photographs.[18]

The erotic artist is thus perceived as an alchemist who transmutes the base matter of pornography into the gold of high culture.

According to the organisers, erotic art is a force for liberation, aesthetically valuable and a better product than pornography. Bringing sexual representation out into the open as legitimate culture would, they claimed, produce more discerning consumers who, in turn, could impose their taste and choice on the pornography industry. Denmark and Sweden could thus lead the way in the production of erotic art, 'as they once did with modern furniture and household design'.[19]

'The First International Exhibition of Erotic Art' was made possible by the lifting of censorship laws in

From P. and E. Kronhausen, *Erotic Art: A Survey of Erotic Fact and Fancy in the Fine Arts*, vol.1 (New York: Grove Press, 1968), p. 9

Sweden and Denmark during the second half of the 1960s. In 1967 Denmark removed all restrictions on written forms of pornography, and what became known as the 'Danish experiment' was assessed on both sides of the Atlantic as part of the reshaping of obscenity and censorship legislation. In September 1970 the report of the American 'Commission on Obscenity and Pornography' was published, rejecting any clear correlation between pornography and acts of sexual violence and advocating a liberalising of sex education in order to foster 'healthy' sexual development. The report resulted in a split between members of the Commission and was rejected by the Senate and President Nixon. In June 1970 an interim report was produced which contradicted the conclusions of the Commission. The 'Obscenity Report' came down strongly on the side of moral authoritarianism and, in a brash dismissal of cultural distinction, situated images of the unclothed body in high art on a sexual continuum with pornography:

> In galleries from Washington, D.C., to San Francisco, pictures of naked people are regularly displayed and in Europe the situation is even more deplorable. Sometimes these pictures masquerade as culture – for example the projected Kronhausen tour through the United States of notorious erotic paintings from Europe. But a naked body is naked, whether it be in oil or in the flesh.[20]

In Britain there was a cluster of prosecutions for obscenity in the early 1970s; the National Viewers and Listeners Association organised a popular campaign against immorality in broadcasting, and in 1972 Lord Longford published his report on pornography. Longford concluded that exposure to pornography did adversely affect social behaviour and moral standards, and cited the Danish and American situations as evidence that the state alone could not be relied upon to protect moral standards.

What we find during this period is a number of different interests trying to redraw the lines around forms of sexual representation. To look at this situation solely from the perspective of pornography is to misunderstand how these debates occupy the whole of the cultural sphere rather than one discrete area. I have been arguing that in many ways erotic art, as the boundary of legitimate culture, is a more significant site of judgment and contestation than pornography,

a view which is borne out by more recent debates. In 1989, in the United States, Senator Jesse Helms spearheaded a campaign to prohibit the use of public funds from the National Endowment for the Arts for work which might be deemed obscene. During his campaign, Helms targeted an exhibition by the photographer Robert Mapplethorpe, denouncing his photographs of 'homosexual erotica' as pornographic and obscene.[21]

In these cases the entire spectrum of culture is recast; to redefine erotic art is necessarily to redefine art and pornography. So one way out of the current impasse within discussions of pornography is to reintegrate our examination of culture and sexual representation, to bring together the high and the low, the world of the aesthetic and the pornographic, precisely at the point of the erotic. And it may be that with a careful and critical re-examination of this category, there is a way forward for a progressive and exciting form of sexual representation.

NOTES

1. The quotation in the title is from George Steiner, *Language and Silence: Essays 1958–1966* (London: Faber & Faber, 1967), p. 91.
2. Charles Augustin Sainte-Beuve (1804–1869), literary critic, novelist and poet; as cited in Peter Webb, *The Erotic Arts* (London: Secker & Warburg, 1975), p. 1.
3. Phyllis and Eberhard Kronhausen, *The International Museum of Erotic Art* (New York: Ballantine, 1973), p. 6.
4. Quoted in Lord Longford, *Pornography: The Longford Report* (London: Coronet, 1972), pp. 99–100.
5. Steven Marcus, *The Other Victorians: A Study of Sexuality and Pornography in Mid-Nineteenth Century England* (London: Weidenfeld and Nicolson, 1966), pp. 278–80.
6. Pierre Bourdieu, *Distinction: A Social Critique of the Judgement of Taste*, trans. Richard Nice (London and New York: Routledge, 1984), p. 6.
7. Ibid., p. 5.
8. Kenneth Clark, *The Nude: A Study of Ideal Art* (London: John Murray, 1956), p. 6.
9. Steiner, *Language and Silence*, p. 89. The essay, 'Night Words', from which these quotes are taken, is in fact a critique of modern American erotic fiction. The details of this argument about the 'Great American Novel' cannot be addressed within the scope of this article.

10. Stefan Morawski, 'Art and Obscenity', *Journal of Aesthetics and Art Criticism*, vol. XXVI no. 2 (Winter 1967), p. 204.

11. Janet Hobhouse, *The Bride Stripped Bare: The Artist and the Nude in the Twentieth Century* (London: Jonathan Cape, 1988), p. 44.

12. Longford, *Pornography*, p. 37.

13. See, for example, discussions such as 'A Passion for Collecting: Erotic Art Comes out of the Closet and into the Auction Rooms', *Economist*, no. 302 (10 January 1987), p. 82.

14. This discussion is particularly indebted to the account given in Jeffrey Weeks, *Sex, Politics and Society: The Regulation of Sexuality since 1800* (London and New York: Longman, 1981), pp. 248–72. See also John Selwyn Gummer, *The Permissive Society: Fact or Fantasy?* (London: Cassell, 1971).

15. Weeks, *Sex, Politics and Society*, p. 250.

16. Phyllis and Eberhard Kronhausen, *Erotic Art: A Survey of Erotic Fact and Fancy in the Fine Arts*, vol. 1 (New York: Grove Press, 1968), p. 8.

17. Ibid., p. 16.

18. Ibid., p. 3.

19. Ibid., p. 7.

20. *The Obscenity Report: The Report to the Task Force on Pornography and Obscenity* (New York: Stein and Day, 1972), p. 32. See also 'Report of the Commission on Obscenity and Pornography, September 1970' (Washington, DC: Government Printing Office, 30 September 1970).

21. For further discussion of the Helms amendment, see Carol S. Vance, 'Misunderstanding Obscenity', *Art in America* (May 1990), pp. 49–55.

19 The Seduction of Boundaries: Feminist Fluidity in Annie Sprinkle's Art/Education/Sex

Chris Straayer

Annie Sprinkle's post-porn modernist art surpasses revision and crossover via an autoerotic straddling of fences. Her fusional play engages multiple discourses from pornography, feminism, art, spirituality, sex education, advertising, political activism, performance art, body play, and the self-help health, prostitutes' rights and safe sex movements. As a 'nurse' she prescribes sex as an analgesic; as a porn star she sells pubic hair, soiled panties and urine; as an artist she exhibits her cervix; as a slut-goddess she pisses/ejaculates. Offering her wrist to Spider Webb on the steps of the Museum of Modern Art in 1981, Sprinkle successfully defied Manhattan's prohibition against tattooing. Despite an arrest in the late 70s for 'conspiracy to publish obscene materials, conspiracy to commit sodomy, and sodomy', Sprinkle has prospered as a photographer, performer, writer and producer of erotic art. Her Sprinkle Salon in Manhattan has been touted as the 1990s' version of Warhol's factory. Her book *Annie Sprinkle: Post Porn Modernist*, which provides the personal history in this essay, is an autobiographical artwork in which self-actualisation relies on artifice as much as origins.[1]

Within this multiplex creativity, numerous boundaries are licked clear. Art melts into porn, porn accommodates life, life becomes art. Breathing orgasms into non-genital sex, and spirituality into orgasms, Sprinkle seduces deconstruction. Exercising a 'queer' ideology arising from contemporary gay and lesbian subculture, she confounds pornography's boundaries, transgresses ours, and wraps us in her own. Pornography's naturalist philosophy spreads outward, merging private and public realms, simultaneously intensifying and diffusing the pornographic sensibility. I'll track these multiple confluences in Sprinkle's social intercourse to their denaturalised climaxes. In her self-conscious photography, performance art and film/video work, I will locate a demystification of sexiness, an affirmation of

fluid identity, and a visualisation of female orgasm. Finally, I will argue that Annie Sprinkle's sex-life-art challenges the hegemonic categories of 'heterosexual' and 'male'.

First, I want to underscore the intersection of feminist art and porn discourses in Sprinkle's 'arthole' activities. My juxtaposition of two photos graphically suggests Sprinkle's vital link to 70s' feminist performance art, no doubt augmented by her summer camp training with life-artist Linda Montano.[2] The first photo shows Carolee Schneemann in a 1975

Interior Scroll performance by Carolee Schneemann, 1975 (Photo by Anthony McCall)

Annie Sprinkle douching in her one woman show, *Post Post Porn Modernist*

performance asserting the propriety of personal experience as content for art by reading a diary scroll withdrawn from her vagina. The second photo shows Annie Sprinkle in 1991 douching on stage in preparation for her 'public cervix announcement' in which, aided by speculum and flashlight, she allows audience members to look at her cervix (see opposite and above). Just as feminist artists such as Montano, Schneemann, Suzanne Lacy, Judy Chicago and many others injected women's everyday experience (from housework to menstruation) into art, Annie injects the everyday into porn. Like Schneemann, Sprinkle uses her body to unsettle gendered knowledge. Ultimately, Sprinkle foregrounds gender as the performance of roles.

In 'Anatomy of a Pinup Photo' (1991), Sprinkle dissects another form of body art to display the constructed 'nature' of sexiness (see p. 226). This demystification of the sexual object is a motif in Sprinkle's work from her admission that she can't walk in her six-inch heels to her design for a paper-doll Annie with cock, finger and tampax accoutrements. In her

Transformation Salon photos, Sprinkle demonstrates the coexisting potentialities of 'regular person' and 'sex star' in a series of before/after snapshots/portraits. Sluts and sex goddesses are readily 'revealed' in a variety of ordinary women via make-up, costume, studio lighting, and direction. As Sprinkle explains to her female audience, 'Maybe there's a little porn star in you. Maybe not. But I can tell you from experience . . . there's a little of you in every porn star'.[3] The codes of soft porn constitute a Pygmalion discourse which women can deploy as strategically as men.

In 'The Most Prevalent Form of Degradation in Erotic Life', Freud explains how the psychology of male love commonly necessitates a good-bad binary opposition for women:

> In only a very few people of culture are the two strains of tenderness and sexuality duly fused into one; the man almost always feels his sexual activity hampered by his respect for the woman and only develops full sexual potency when he finds himself in the presence of a lower type of sexual object; and this again is partly conditioned by the circumstance that his sexual aims include those of perverse sexual components, which he does not like to gratify with a woman he respects. Full sexual satisfaction only comes when he can give himself up wholeheartedly to enjoyment, which with his well-brought up wife, for instance, he does not venture to do. Hence comes his need for a less exalted sexual object, a woman ethically inferior, to whom he need ascribe no aesthetic misgivings, and who does not know the rest of his life and cannot criticize him. It is to such a woman that he prefers to devote his sexual potency, even when all the tenderness in him belongs to one of a higher type.[4]

In addition to the implicitly classist dichotomisation of sex and ethics in this statement, the sequestration of sexuality from the rest of life draws a protective line between private and public. For this reason, I submit the quotation here as a symptomatic text rather than a theoretical foundation. In the essay, Freud describes psychoanaesthesia, a behaviour (in love) of the psychically impotent type, widespread in civilised society. He offers a number of factors contributing to a man's dependence on a lower object for full sexual gratification, for example the early incestuous fixations of childhood (the original impetus for

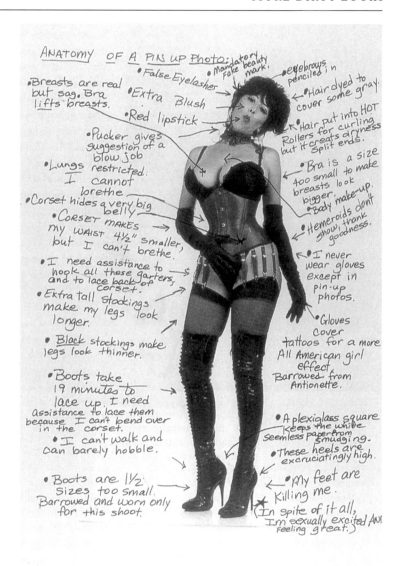

Anatomy of a Pin-up by Annie
Sprinkle, 1991 (Photo by Zorro,
1981)

phantasies in which boys 'degrade the mother to the level of prostitute'); the nearly equal prohibition of sex with persons outside the family during adolescence; the tension between animal excitation, arising from the contiguity of erotic and excremental organs, and its necessary sublimation into cultural achievement. What remains less clear is the etiology of a woman's lower status. Is her ethical inferiority God-made or man-made?

Where such men love they have no desire and where they desire they cannot love. In order to keep their sensuality out of contact with the objects they love, they seek out objects whom they need not love;

and, in accordance with the laws of the 'sensitivity of complexes' and the 'return of the repressed', the strange refusal implied in psychical impotence is made whenever the objects selected in order to avoid incest possess some trait, often quite inconspicuous, reminiscent of the objects that must be avoided.

The principal means of protection used by men against this complaint consists in *lowering* the sexual object in their own estimation, while reserving for the incestuous object and for those who represent it the overestimation normally felt for the sexual object. As soon as the sexual object fulfils the condition of being degraded, sensual feeling can have free play, considerable sexual capacity and a high degree of pleasure can be developed.[5]

In Freud's argument, (a) woman's lower status is both attributed and assigned to her. This corresponds to the relation of unchastity to both impurity and defilement identified by Gail Pheterson in 'The Social Consequences of Unchastity', a critique of the gendered stigma of 'whore'.[6] Women of colour and working-class women (with dirty hands) are especially vulnerable to the 'whore' stigma. But experience also, especially that which veers away from virginity and monogamy whether by desire or abuse, can defile girls and women and condemn them to the 'whore' stigma. Whether their own or men's, sexuality degrades women.

In 'Speaking the Body: Mid-Victorian Constructions of Female Desire', Mary Poovey argues that mid-Victorian debate over prostitution inadvertently provided opportunity for the discussion of female sexuality.[7] Contradictory discourse simultaneously positioned 'the prostitute' as wanton and fallen, as revelling in sexual delight and victim of her originally passionless, positive love of self-sacrifice. The prostitute is understood as innately sinful and made sinful by her desperate actions. This discordant representation was deployed for middle-class interests to allow, but regulate, prostitution. At the same time, however, it became available for use by women differently positioned in the social formation. As Poovey states, 'If the limits of female self-representation were initially set by the dominant representation of women, however, this representation could not finally dictate how individuals with a different investment in it would elaborate the contradictions it contained'.[8]

These views of prostitution and women's sexuality remain today ready for an exploitation of their 'contrariness'. Within her creative porn discourse, Annie Sprinkle certainly retains a feminine 'heart of gold'; but she inextricably fuses it with active female sexual desire and audacious sex positivity. Furthermore, she seeks and values personal change through sexual encounters. Through her assertion of desire, she consciously claims prostitution and pornography as her own sexual experiences. The tricks, the experiments, the knowledge, the exhibition, the pornographic discourse, the pleasure belong to her. Her aim to please the client is not in conflict with her other sexual aims.

Typically, the pornography genre deploys the articulation of female desire in the service of a reassuring address to male viewers. Such address circumvents anxiety over masculine performance and competition; the viewer need only be male to be desirable. Sprinkle both exploits and extends this effect. In his essay 'When Did Annie Sprinkle Become an Artist?', Chuck Kleinhans describes Sprinkle in her early porn performances as already a performance artist, who constructs simultaneously generous and ironic personae: the teacher, the nurse, the mother.

> In (decidedly non-Lacanian) Oedipal terms: she enacts the nurturing mother who encourages sexual exploration: a figure who allays performance anxiety while encouraging voyeurism as part of the acquisition of knowledge that can create a new straight male sexual subject. In brief, she prepares boys (i.e., an infantile/juvenile/adolescent unconscious formation in all adult males) to be (het or bi) men that (het or bi) women can (at least tolerably) live with and have sex with.[9]

This subject position, Kleinhans argues, offers a positive alternative to 'the aggressive sadist voyeur model which has dominated discussion of heterosexual male spectatorship of pornographic imagery'. Freud's mother vs. prostitute dichotomy, therefore, is effectively collapsed in the 'mothering prostitute'.

In Monika Treut's independent feature film *My Father Is Coming* (Germany, 1991), in which a bisexual's straight father arrives for a visit from Germany, it is Annie Sprinkle who initiates the older generation in the pleasures of New York City's Lower East Side/Times Square sexual culture. Annie's character enthusiastically and genuinely seduces this older man, who is not conventionally attractive in either physical appearance or narrative agency (see p. 228). Although unusual for mainstream cinema, this is not unusual for pornography. But, as Kleinhans has suggested, Sprinkle's performance is as much nurturing as reassuring. As such, her pan-sexuality displays a challenging array of sexual desires, activities and objects.

In her 'personal' life, which frequently occurs on screen, Sprinkle pursues even less conventional sex partners: a gay man, a female amputee, a 43-inch-tall man. In her tape *Linda/Les and Annie – The First Female to Male Transsexual Love Story*, Annie enjoys sex

Alfred Edel and Annie Sprinkle in *My Father Is Coming*
(Monika Treut, 1991)

with her lover Les, a lesbian separatist-turned-macho transsexual who has a constructed penis but also retains his female genitals – a male hermaphrodite with a clitoris enlarged by excessive hormone ingestion. In 1989, Annie exhibited Les as a freak show at Coney Island. People could enter the hermaphrodite's tent with flashlight in hand and examine the genitalia. This exposure of 'the curiosity' as a mirror for our own curiosity was too much for the Coney Island management, who closed it down. Sprinkle has also photographically transformed Les into a 'sex slut'; supposedly it took three hours of transformative (cross)dressing to 'bring out [Les's] femininity to the hilt'.

Sprinkle exercises a polysexual desire which ultimately foregrounds traditional desires as codified. The male viewer who accepts Annie's unconditional positive regard is grouped implicitly with her other objects of desire and hence complies with her confrontation of these codes. When he knows of her life/art/work, he cannot simply appropriate her reassuring discourse for himself; this discourse also calls for rethinking the economy of desire.

In 'A Provoking Agent: The Pornography and Performance Art of Annie Sprinkle', Linda Williams[10] analyses in detail Sprinkle's 1981 porn film *Deep Inside Annie Sprinkle*. She describes a scene in which Annie fingers a man's anus while addressing the (extradiegetic) viewer with 'dirty talk' instructions. Here, Williams argues, Sprinkle raises new questions about the gendered nature of address.

Is she telling and showing a hypothetical 'him' how to finger another man's ass? If so, the film insidiously transgresses 'normal' heterosexual taboos against males penetrating males. Is she telling and showing 'him' how *she* likes to finger a man's ass? If so, the pleasure depicted casts her in the role of the active penetrator and him in the role of penetrated, again a switch in expectations for the conventionally posited heterosexual male viewer. Or is she perhaps telling and showing a hypothetical 'her' how to finger a man's anus? After all, this is 80s porn and women are included in its address. If so, the original rhetoric of the female-whore addressing the male-client breaks down. Any way you look at it, Annie has played with the conventions of who gives pleasure to whom.[11]

I agree with Williams but also believe that the above viewer, male or female, is encouraged to identify with Annie *as a woman* – with her heterosexual activity and female sexual pleasure – as well as with the on screen man. In other words, Sprinkle is not only reversing traditional subject-object sexual and viewing positions, but is also engaging us in what will become, in her later video work, a virtual identity orgy.

By now it seems mandatory to claim Annie Sprinkle as an exemplary proponent of 'queer' aesthetics, sexualities and politics. Indeed, she deserves the compliment. In contemporary sexual politics, 'queer' embraces a population far larger than lesbians and gay men: bisexuals, transsexuals and various non-straight heterosexuals; transvestites, S&M enthusiasts, fetishists, and so on. In theory, more than in practice, 'queer' also embraces diversity in race, class and ethnicity. When conceptualised most radically, the category 'queer', to my mind, does not necessarily contain all lesbians and gay men. In other words, I endorse a 'queer' politics which is deconstructive *as well as* non-normative. Although 'queer' has been praised and berated for its (potential) inclusiveness, I feel its theoretical framework allows a more critical stance. Annie Sprinkle puts 'queer' theory into practice. And, in representations of herself and her younger and older queer-peers and partners, she demonstrates that 'queer' mentality is not the sole jurisdiction of youth. Most importantly, Sprinkle extends a 'queer' celebration of differences to contest the very straight-and-narrow referent itself – that illusory but nonetheless pure heterosexual.

In 'Misreading Sodomy: A Critique of the Classification of "Homosexuals" in Federal Equal

Protection Law', Janet E. Halley describes how US sodomy laws, which in almost half the states determine anal intercourse, fellatio and cunnilingus to be criminal behaviour for heterosexuals and homosexuals alike, are discriminately applied to homosexuals only.[12] Felony sodomy virtually becomes homosexual sodomy. The act of sodomy is conflated with and comes to define homosexual status. Homosexuals, then, are those identified by this act while all others remain unmarked and presumed heterosexual.

> Sexual orientation identities are produced in a highly unstable public discourse in which a provisional default class of 'heterosexuals' predicates homosexual identity upon acts of sodomy in a constantly eroding effort to police its own coherence and referentiality.[13]

Inadvertently containing both sexually inactive homosexuals and secretive homosexual sodomites, the default category of non-homosexuals, or heterosexuals, encourages closeted behaviour and internalised homophobia. Of course this category also contains heterosexuals who engage in anal intercourse, fellatio and cunnilingus, but, as Halley states, 'The criminality of sodomitical acts involving persons of different genders is simply assumed out of existence' (p. 357). Within these terms, the unity of heterosexual identity relies on both the knowing of homosexual sodomy and the unknowing of heterosexual sodomy.

In *Epistemology of the Closet*, Eve Sedgwick ascribes as much potency to unknowing as to knowing.

> I would like to be able to make use in sexual-political thinking of the deconstructive understanding that particular insights generate, are lined with, and at the same time are themselves structured by particular opacities. If ignorance is not – as it evidently is not – a single Manichaean, aboriginal maw of darkness from which the heroics of human cognition can occasionally wrestle facts, insights, freedoms, progress, perhaps there exists instead a plethora of *ignorances*, and we may begin to ask questions about the labor, erotics, and economies of their human production and distribution. Insofar as ignorance is ignorance *of* a knowledge – a knowledge that may itself, it goes without saying, be seen as either true or false under some other regime of truth – these ignorances, far from being pieces of the

originary dark, are produced by and correspond to particular knowledges and circulate as part of particular regimes of truth.[14]

Annie Sprinkle reinscribes sodomy into heterosexuality. By expanding the understanding of heterosexuality to acknowledge innumerable and diverse desires and practices (including certain activities shared by homosexuals and bisexuals), Sprinkle effectively contests the equation between homosexuality and deviance as well as the boundaries between homosexual, heterosexual and bisexual.

Sprinkle's contestation of boundaries is further elaborated by her creative participation in four avant-garde film/video texts: *Annie* (Monika Treut, US/West Germany, 16mm, 1989), *25 Year Old Gay Man Loses His Virginity to a Woman* (Philip B. Roth, US, video, 1990), *Linda/Les and Annie* (Albert Jaccoma, John Armstrong and Annie Sprinkle, written by Sprinkle, US, video, 1990), and *The Sluts and Goddesses Video Workshop, or How to Be a Sex Goddess in 101 Easy Steps* (Maria Beatty and Annie Sprinkle, written by Sprinkle; Spiritual Advisor, Linda Montano; Inspiration, Carolee Schneemann; dedicated to Joan of Arc, US, video, 1992). In these films/videos Sprinkle combines and integrates numerous subcultural figures and widely diverse discourses. This constructs a liberationist sexual ideology in complex relation to and against notions of identity. Annie's explicit visual presence is complemented by her intense diaristic, instructional and seductive verbal activity. Pornography's naturalist presumption must make way for crucial teaching and sharing of sexual information. Tantric symbols and anatomical diagrams are integrated with porn iconography to conjoin what Foucault has distinguished as *ars erotica* and *scientia sexualis*.[15]

With slides and re-enactments, *Annie* 'documents' one of Sprinkle's performance art works in which she combines codes from feminist body art, diary, science, pornography and erotic stripping. Encouraging the sexual dimension of voyeurism but discouraging distance, Sprinkle creates a performance arena in which audience members (film viewers as well as the diegetic audience) can look at the female body with both desire and curiosity. Annie relates her personal history, plays 'Tit Art' with her large bare breasts, bends over and spanks her ass, lectures on the female reproductive system, and shows the audience her sex. 'Isn't it beautiful,' she says over a close-up of her cervix. 'I have my period today so it might be a bit bloody. But that's OK. Isn't it great!'

25 Year Old Gay Man Loses His Virginity to a Woman documents video-maker Philip Roth and Annie Sprinkle having sex. The tape begins with Philip confessing his fear; he's afraid that a heterosexual experience might alter that part of his identity which is gay. Annie advises him simply to decide to stay gay regardless of their upcoming intercourse. For herself, fluid identity holds no threat. 'I just became a lesbian myself. . . . It's a real adventure to change your identity, I think.' Later Philip adds, 'I wouldn't ever want to give up men.' 'No,' Annie replies. 'I wouldn't either.' Annie proceeds to demonstrate how a tampax is used, engages Philip in wrestling, teaches him how to stimulate her clitoris, and initiates various positions for intercourse. During all this, they affectionately discuss their emotional and physical feelings, Annie explains who Grafenberg was, and they both occasionally look at and talk to the cameraperson. Wishing Philip love and prosperity, Annie then presents him with a small box for his

altar in which they place his condom and one of her pubic hairs.

Linda/Les and Annie begins with Annie sitting in a wooded location wearing a girlish outfit and writing in her diary. In voice-over, she expresses her excitement about her new lover. 'He's really different than the other guys,' she says as the image cuts to Les Nichols in black jeans and tank top, with long side-burns and tattooed arms, drinking beer and smoking a cigarette. As the lyrics to 'Best of Both Worlds' suggest and the delayed title confirms, Les is a female-to-male transsexual. 'I'm a big man on the outside but you know he was a she. Yes you know I'm hard and nasty, but I'm sweet and sassy too.' Later we see Les neatly groomed in a pressed blue workshirt and red tie. 'This is America,' he states. 'And I made the choice.' We learn that his choice cost $50,000 and multiple surgery. Medical pictures accompany Annie's voice-over explanation of phalloplasty procedures. We also see Les making his penis erect first by inserting a plastic rod and then by inserting his thumb. Despite humorous contrary narrative evidence, Annie declares, 'It felt free not to worry about getting it up

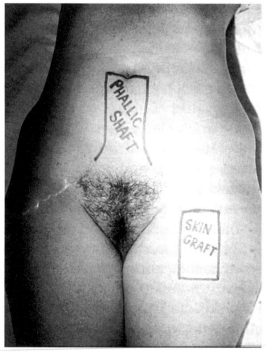

Linda Nichols

Mapping transexuality

Les Nichols

Linda/Les and Annie

and keeping it up.' Both Les's male and female geni- tals are explicitly demonstrated during the love- making that follows (see opposite and above).

Les reports that as a male now he has more priv- ilege and gets more respect – as if he were 'born to ask'. He refers to his male genitalia as phallus rather than penis. This framework, perhaps inadvertently, lends attitude and meaning to his description of his earlier female body as 'nothing down there'. By con- trast, Annie cleverly credits hermaphroditism to Les's body when writing and narrating their story: 'He had large succulent nipples – the kind made for feeding babies. . . . When I informed Les that I was having the last day of my period, he just said, "No problem". What man could be more understanding and less intimidated by a little blood than a man who used to menstruate? . . . His skin was soft and smooth like a woman's, yet he had hair on his chest. His hands were small and delicate with a woman's touch, yet he wore men's rings.' Annie finds sex with Les a positive mind-fuck as she sucks both 'his clit' and his 'new sex toy'.

In *The Sluts and Goddesses Video Workshop*, Annie acts as host with seven facilitators who are trans-

formed for our instruction into ancient sacred pros- titutes via facials, clay baths, make-up, masks, wigs, hair ornaments, body jewellery, false fingernails, body paint, tattoos, piercings, high heels, new names, new clothes, sexercises and sex. High-tech video effects create natural and cosmic backgrounds, provide graphs and illustrations for sex education, and allow Annie to 'emerge' full body from a close-up vulva. Later, these newly constructed sacred prostitutes facilitate two orgasms 'of, by, and for' women (of Annie, by them, and for us). Both these orgasms are visually evidenced, the first by female ejaculation (which the subtitles name 'Moon Flower Drops of Wisdom'), the second by a running orange line superimposed over live footage of Annie which charts her five-minute ten-second orgasm. In the latter, orgasmic codes of pornography such as the woman's face and open mouth are combined with indexical sweating and a didactical tracing of subjec- tivity. Of course, these visual representations can only provide problematic evidence. Representation always remains inconclusive. Although Annie feels her experience, we do not. Nevertheless, the mixing of sexology/porn/feminist discourses in these ejaculation and graphed orgasm scenes adds considerable envy to any remaining doubt (see below).

In her book *Hard Core: Power, Pleasure, and the 'Frenzy of the Visible'*, Linda Williams locates within the genre a quest for a visible truth of female pleasure.[16] Although a productive reading of pornography texts, this does not adequately explain the industry's scarce use of female ejaculation as a possible signifier of orgasm. The current shock wave resulting from representations of female ejaculation in tapes such as Blush Entertainment/Fatale's *Clips* marks this quest in the bulk of pornographic texts as self-imposed and pseudo. Obviously, many pornographers actually avoid available visible evidence. Censoring the image of female ejaculation, one might argue, maintains a male standard by a deliberate unknowing that consciously re-produces female 'lack'.

In 'Feminist Ejaculations', Shannon Bell cites sporadic references to female ejaculation from Hippocrates in 400 BC to Grafenberg in 1950, then notes that it was ignored by dominant scientific discourses defining female sexuality from 1950 to 1978.[17] Sexologists and physicians either denied its existence altogether or (mis)diagnosed it as urinary stress incontinence. In 1978, J. L. Sevely and J. W. Bennett published 'Concerning Female Ejaculation and the Female Prostate', upon which Bell relies heavily.[18] In this article, the authors use historical and anatomical texts to assert that: a) both males and females have active prostates; b) a wide variation in size and distribution of this gland occurs among women; c) that male prostate produces much of the fluid expelled during ejaculation (the testes contribute only a small volume which contains the pro-

creative sperm); and d) at least in some women, the female prostate (also known as the para- and peri-urethral glands) allows for ejaculation through the urethral meatus of a fluid not identical with urine. They argue that the erasure of female ejaculation is supported semantically by: a) the often improper use of adjectives such as 'vestigial' and 'atrophied' to describe the less developed homologue of an organ found in both sexes, a naming which serves to emphasise sexual bipolarity, and b) the Aristotelian discovery that female ejaculate, which Galen and Hippocrates had called 'semen' and assumed procreative, was in fact not.

> With the resolution of the Aristotelian argument, the language that had been previously used to describe the fluids of both sexes was allocated in the scientific literature to the male alone. Since female ejaculatory fluids did not contain 'seed', these fluids were left without a word to describe them. The apparent solution was to drop the notion of a female 'semen', which simultaneously meant the loss of the concept of female ejaculation.[19]

Language misuse and insufficiencies therefore produced an ironic invisibility of female ejaculation.

Shannon Bell suggests a more interested reason for the continuing invisibility of female ejaculation despite significant research and debate following Sevely and Bennett's article. Specifically, she questions why feminists have failed to speak about female ejaculation, and postulates the reason to be that female ejaculation challenges the fundamental assumption in feminism of sexual difference.

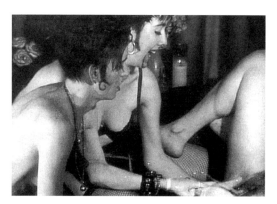

From *The Sluts and Goddesses Video Workshop* (Maria Beatty/Annie Sprinkle, 1992)

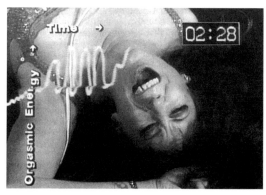

From *The Sluts and Goddesses Video Workshop* (Maria Beatty/Annie Sprinkle, 1992)

The ejaculating female body has not acquired much of a feminist voice nor has it been appropriated by feminist discourse. What is the reason for this lacuna in feminist scholarship and for the silencing of the ejaculating female subject? It has to do with the fact that the questions posed, and the basic assumptions about female sexuality, are overwhelmingly premised on the difference between female and male bodies. . . . The most important primary differences have been that women have the ability to give birth and men ejaculate. Women's reproductive ability has been emphasized as a central metaphor in feminist critiques of partriarchal texts and has been theorized into a 'philosophy of birth' and an economy of (re)production. Feminists, in their efforts to revalorize the female body usually devalued in phallocentric discourse, have privileged some form of the mother-body as the source of écriture féminine: writing that evokes women's power as women's bodily experience. . . . The fluids, reappropriated in feminine sexual discourse and theorized by French feminist philosophers such as Luce Irigaray and Julia Kristeva, have been the fluids of the mother-body: fluids of the womb, birth fluids, menstrual blood, milk: fluids that flow. Ejaculate – fluid that shoots, fluid that sprays – has been given over to the male body. To accept female ejaculate and female ejaculation one has to accept the sameness of male and female bodies.[20]

Although I agree that equating motherhood with womanhood is dangerous, I strongly disagree with Bell's monolithic representation of feminism. Not all women are or want to be mothers, nor do all women ejaculate; but scholarship and political practices relating to both these (and many other) experiences have been intellectually provocative, perhaps even earth-shaking. We can see that the use of maternity as an essential metaphor for womanhood sustains the historical elision of female sexual desires and pleasures. However, even cultural feminism (which best describes the subgroup of feminists attacked by Bell) has always included women who deployed 'sexual difference' for purposes other than mythologising women's birthing capacity, for example to idealise lesbian sex. Bell's articulation of her argument reinforces a currently popular although reductive dichotomisation of sex-positive women and feminists. I would argue that not only does the category 'feminist' contain an enormous range of intellectual and political practices and positions on motherhood,

sex, sexuality and gender, but the contemporary stance of sex-positivity was made possible by, and builds on, feminism's reclaiming of women's bodies to empower women. In other words, the current sexual rebellion, depending on, as much as attacking, feminism's investigation of sexual difference, is a *feminist* sexual rebellion of benefit to and properly credited to 'both sides'. (From the 'feminist' in her title 'Feminist Ejaculations', I doubt that Bell and I totally disagree about this.) Certainly Annie Sprinkle finds no incompatibility between feminism and active female sexuality, between menstrual blood and ejaculate. Her slut-goddess, divine prostitute and mothering sex partner exemplify such (non-re) productive discursive intercourse. Feminism must be and is an expanding discourse that responds to and initiates critical self-reflection and continuing political debate.

Nevertheless, although I would replace her term 'sameness' with 'similarity', I agree strongly with Bell's primary argument. Female ejaculation pierces a culturally constructed and enforced boundary between 'males' and 'females'. It is not just that its existence corrects the mistaken assumption that only men have prostates. It is one leak that solicits further inspection of the more generally leaky system of binary sex. For starters, we might consider the article immediately following Sevely and Bennett's in *The Journal of Sex Research*, entitled 'Multiple Orgasms in Males'.[21] Here, Mina Robbins and Gordon Jensen describe multiple orgasms in men which they note correlate physiologically to multiple orgasms in women. These orgasms, which are generally non-ejaculatory except for the final one in a series, establish an independence between orgasm and ejaculation and, moreover, can probably be learned. Annie Sprinkle's exaltation of multiple orgasms in Les Nichols may not be so (positively) 'freaky' as she supposes. We might also consider a 1984 essay on female ejaculation by Desmond Heath in which embryological and histological research supports a consideration of the anterior vagina, urethra, glands, vulva and clitoris as a single organ, a concept more 'naturally' associated with male sexuality.[22] (This of course is subject to attack as in Irigaray's critique of men's projection of sameness – that is, unitary sex – onto women.[23] However, as the following discussion of Laqueur's work demonstrates, a system of difference can erase women's eroticism as much as sameness can.)

In his book *Making Sex*, Thomas Laqueur identifies a shift in knowledge occurring in the 18th century from a one-sex to a two-sex human model, a shift not scientifically determined but rather resulting from an epistemological and social-political revolution.[24] Galen's description in the 2nd century AD of women as essentially the same as men, having the same genitalia inside their bodies that men's bodies held visibly outside, has been upstaged by a now dominant understanding of women as men's opposite (and of woman as 'lack'). Laqueur argues that near the end of the Enlightenment, the noted irrelevance of female orgasm to human reproduction opened the way for a new concept of female passionlessness. 'The presence or absence of orgasm became a biological signpost of sexual difference'.[25] Scientific progress is not to be credited for this shift in conceptualising sex. For example, the embryological homologies of penis and clitoris, labia and scrotum, ovaries and testes, which were not identified until the 1850s, could have supported a one-sex model as much as adult genital anatomy might earlier have supported a two-sex model. As Laqueur states, 'To be sure, difference and sameness, more or less recondite, are everywhere; but which ones count and for what ends is determined outside the bounds of empirical investigation'.[26]

What we know does not necessarily derive from what we see. But neither can language contain all possible knowledge. Female ejaculation, experienced by some women and perhaps often wrongly known, witnessed by many women and men but perhaps wrongly named, challenges hegemonic difference but cannot replace it with totalising sameness. What it can do is happen. And for those who 'know' (or even consider) this, female ejaculation invites a recollection of 'feminist conceptions' in all their nurturing, erotic and intellectual dimensions.

I would like to conclude by examining one more blurring in Annie Sprinkle's feminist-porn-art. This concerns a 'confusion' between golden showers and female ejaculation. According to Sprinkle, a golden shower is 'the art of erotic urination during sex-play', a creative scene for which she is well known. She elaborates: 'Women can pee while getting fucked, and it's an incredible sensation for both partners.' Although in her film *Deep Inside Annie Sprinkle* she calls it 'squirting pussy juice', Annie reports that the film is no longer available for sale because of a 'peeing

scene'. This scene, which Linda Williams refers to as a female 'money shot', was read (at our 1992 Society for Cinema Studies conference panel) by Linda Williams and myself as ejaculation, but by Chuck Kleinhans as urination. In marketing her mail-order Golden Shower Ritual Kit 5019 (in *Love Magazine* 83, co-edited with Veronica Vera), Annie again uses the term 'pussy juice'. And in the accompanying text that guides the user through a fantasy ritual, she writes, 'I'd like to slide your finger up into my hole so you can feel it before it comes out.' Although, I'm frankly at a loss as to *which* hole she means and what *it* is, this confusion hardly seems problematic under the conditions of mail-order sex. The term 'golden showers' comes from porn discourse and itself functions to excite. However, despite all her feminist demystification, I feel Annie's slippery discourse can support an erasure of female ejaculation. Viewers are given the authority to interpret these scenes to service their own pleasure and comfort. But perhaps this is just the point. Once again, representation allows rather than ensures any 'preferred' readings.

To my knowledge, the only explicit reference to women ejaculating in Annie's published work occurs in a utopian vision of the future.

> I have a vision for the future, of a world where all the necessary sex education will be available to everyone, thus, there will be no more sexually transmitted diseases. . . . Fetish lingerie and sex toys will be freely distributed to all people. People will be able to make love without touching if they choose. Men will be able to have multiple orgasms without ejaculating, so that they can maintain erections for as long as they want. Women will ejaculate. It will be possible to make love anywhere in public, and it will not be impolite to watch. . . .
>
> On second thoughts; the world is really PERFECT just the way that it is.[27]

When I presented an earlier version of this article at the Society for Cinema Studies conference, I concluded that Sprinkle's blurring of 'golden showers' and ejaculation effectively contributed to the medico-scientific erasure of female ejaculation. Since that time I have expanded my position to recognise also that Sprinkle's discourse contains a subtextual attack on one more binary. Discussing my project with Sprinkle while selecting the photos to accompany

Deep Inside Porn Stars by Club 90 and Carnival Knowledge
(Photo by Dona Ann McAdams)

this piece, I learned that she actually does *not* see a distinct line between ejaculation and urination – a position that resonates significantly with the anatomical-physiological descriptions outlined earlier and graphically illustrated in the Federation of Feminist Women's Health Centers' *A New View of a Woman's Body*.[28] Sprinkle describes (and prescribes) at least four kinds of erotic female fluids: vaginal secretions, 'golden showers', the squirting or dribbling of non-urine fluid through the urethral opening (which can occur with or independently of orgasm), and erotically induced urination. The fourth type, which falls into the overlap of the second and third, Sprinkle finds most clearly evident when, after a group discussion on sexuality (or a performance by Annie, I might add) the women's restroom is 'flooded'. At the LUST Conference ('Lesbians Undoing Sexual Taboos', 17 November 1992, New York, attended by approximately 500 women), Sprinkle asked those women in the audience who ejaculated to raise their hands. Approximately one third did so. She reported that in 1982 she ejaculated in a porn movie but had assumed it was a 'golden showers' scene. Acknowledging that female ejaculation is all the rage, she announced that she is currently more enthusiastic about 'energy orgasms', for which she proceeded to provide instructions.

It has not been my purpose here to defend or critique sex-liberationist ideology but rather to analyse the ends towards which Annie Sprinkle develops and deploys a particular brand of it. In her post-porn modernist art, Sprinkle not only attempts to break down

barriers among people but also challenges the arbitrary and assumed boundaries among/between pornography, art and everyday experience, spirituality and sexuality, queer and straight, homosexual and heterosexual, male and female, desirable and undesirable, slut and goddess, prostitute and mother, 'golden showers' and female ejaculation. She effects this purposeful aesthetics by 'self'-exposure, by displaying her tools and methods for sexy encoding and her unconventional attitudes, desires, practices and pleasures. She enacts a fluidity in which lesbian and heterosexual identities are not mutually exclusive. Exhibiting sodomy within heterosexuality, she probes the legal/semantic basis by which heterosexuality is constructed as a default class in opposition to 'sodomites'. Her demonstrations of lengthy, multiple and ejaculating orgasms cross-examine pornography's generic 'transcendental' money shot, a signifier that I would argue relies on an interpretive editing of man's 'little death'.

Whether Annie Sprinkle is acting (and/)or experiencing orgasms in her performances cannot be determined by us. Similarly, the possibility of non-ejaculating orgasms in men allows that we may not always have (or want) visible evidence of male orgasm. In video porn, fluid has been injected into vaginas to produce images of female ejaculation (*The Grafenberg Spot*), and realistically functioning penis-like prostheses have been used (on women) to image male ejaculation convincingly (*Bi and Beyond*). Nevertheless, it is interesting that the current visibility and widespread discussion of female ejaculation have resulted from films and videos made by women. The refusal to read signs can produce misrecognition as much as can 'lying' signs. To utilise Sedgwick's terminology, with regard to its elision of female ejaculation and its continuing investment in the invisible female orgasm, the regime of pornography has exercised a long-standing 'privilege of unknowing'.

NOTES

1. Annie Sprinkle, *Annie Sprinkle: Post Porn Modernist* (Amsterdam: Torch Books, 1991).

2. Linda Montano, 'Summer Saint Camp 1987', *Drama Review*, vol. 33 no. 1 (Spring 1989).

3. Sprinkle, *Annie Sprinkle*, p. 91.

4. Sigmund Freud, 'The Most Prevalent Form of Degradation in Erotic Life (1912)', in *Sexuality and the Psychology of Love* (New York: Collier Books, 1963, p. 64).

5. Ibid., p. 62.

6. Gail Pheterson, 'The Social Consequences of Unchastity', in Frédérique Delacoste and Priscilla Alexander (eds), *Sex Work: Writings by Women in the Sex Industry* (Pittsburgh, PA: Cleis Press, 1987), pp. 215–30.

7. Mary Poovey, 'Speaking the Body: Mid-Victorian Constructions of Female Desire', in Mary Jacobus, Evelyn Fox Keller and Sally Shuttlewo (eds), *Body/Politics: Woman and the Discourses of Science* (New York: Routledge, 1990), pp. 29–46.

8. Ibid., p. 43.

9. Chuck Kleinhans, 'When Did Annie Sprinkle Become an Artist? Female Performance Art, Male Performance Anxiety, Art as Alibi, and Labial Art', paper presented at the Society for Cinema Studies conference, University of Pittsburgh, May 1992.

10. Linda Williams, 'A Provoking Agent: The Pornography and Performance Art of Annie Sprinkle', in Pamela Church Gibson and Roma Gibson (eds), *Dirty Looks: Women, Pornography, Power* (BFI, 1993), pp. 176–92.

11. Ibid., p. 185.

12. Janet E. Halley, 'Misreading Sodomy: A Critique of the Classification of "Homosexuals" in Federal Equal Protection Law', in Julia Epstein and Kristina Straub (eds), *Body Guards: The Cultural Politics of Gender Ambiguity* (New York: Routledge, 1991).

13. Ibid., p. 352.

14. Eve Kosofksy Sedgwick, *Epistemology of the Closet* (Berkeley: University of California Press, 1990), p. 8.

15. Michel Foucault, *The History of Sexuality Vol. 1*, trans. Robert Hurley (New York: Vintage Books, 1980).

16. Linda Williams, *Hard Core: Power, Pleasure, and the 'Frenzy of the Visible'* (Berkeley: University of California Press, 1989).

17. Shannon Bell, 'Feminist Ejaculations', in Arthur and Marilouise Kroker (eds), *The Hysterical Male: New Feminist Theory* (New York: St Martin's Press, 1991), pp. 155–69.

18. J. Lowndes Sevely and J. W. Bennett, 'Concerning Female Ejaculation and the Female Prostate', *The Journal of Sex Research*, vol. 14 no. 1 (February 1978), pp. 1–20.

19. Ibid., p. 17.

20. Bell, 'Feminist Ejaculations', pp. 162–3.

21. Mina B. Robbins and Gordon D. Jensen, 'Multiple Orgasms in Males', *The Journal of Sex Research*, vol. 14 no. 1 (February 1978), pp. 21–6.

22. Desmond Heath, 'An Investigation into the Origins of a Copious Vaginal Discharge During Intercourse: "Enough to Wet the Bed – 'That' Is Not Urine" ', *The Journal of Sex Research*, vol. 20 no. 2 (May 1984), pp. 194–215.

23. Luce Irigaray, *This Sex Which Is Not One*, trans. Catherine Porter with Carolyn Burke (Ithaca, NY: Cornell University Press, 1985).

24. Thomas Laqueur, *Making Sex: Body and Gender from the Greeks to Freud* (Cambridge, MA: Harvard University Press, 1990).

25. Ibid., p. 4.

26. Ibid., p. 10.

27. Sprinkle, *Annie Sprinkle*, p. 117.

28. Federation of Feminist Women's Health Centers, *A New View of a Woman's Body* (West Hollywood, CA: Feminist Health Press, 1991), pp. 46–57.

20   Maid to Order: Commercial S/M and Gender Power

Anne McClintock

In *Sex*, Madonna has her wits, if not her clothes, about her. The scandal of *Sex* is the scandal of S/M: the provocative confession that the edicts of power are reversible. So the critics bay for her blood: a woman who takes sex and money into her own hands must – sooner or later – bare her breasts to the knife. But with the utmost artifice and levity, Madonna refuses to imitate tragedy. Taking sex into the street, and money into the bedroom, she flagrantly violates the sacramental edicts of private and public, and stages sexual commerce as a theatre of transformation.

Madonna's erotic photo album is filled with the theatrical paraphernalia of S/M: boots, chains, leather, whips, masks, costumes and scripts. Andrew Neil, editor of the London *Sunday Times*, warns ominously that it thus runs the risk of unleashing 'the dark side' of human nature, 'with particular danger for women'.[1] But the outrage of *Sex* is its insight into S/M as high theatre.[2] Demonising S/M confuses the distinction between unbridled sadism and the social subculture of consensual fetishism.[3] To argue that in consensual S/M the master has power, and the slave has not, is to read theatre for reality; it is to play the world forwards. The economy of S/M is the economy of conversion: slave to master, adult to baby, pain to pleasure, man to woman, and back again. S/M, as Foucault puts it, 'is not a name given to a practice as old as Eros; it is a massive cultural fact which appeared precisely at the end of the eighteenth century, and which constitutes one of the greatest conversions of Western imagination: unreason transformed into delirium of the heart'.[4] Consensual S/M 'plays the world backwards'.[5]

In *Sex*, as in S/M, roles are swiftly swapped. At the Vault, New York's amiable S/M dungeon, the domina Madonna archly flicks her whip across the glistening leather hips of a female 'slave'. The domina's breasts are bare; the slave is armoured. Contrary to popular stigma, S/M theatrically flouts the edict that manhood is synonymous with mastery, and submission a female fate. Further into the album, a man genuflects at Madonna's feet, neck bound in a collar, the lash at his back. But the domina's foot is also bound, and the leash straps her hand to his neck. The bondage fetish performs identity and power as twined in interdependence, and rebuts the Enlightenment vision of the solitary and self-generating individual. The lesbian with the knife is also the lover; scenes of bondage are stapled to scenes of abandon, and *Sex* makes no pretence at romantic profundity but flaunts S/M as a theatre of scene and surface.

Hence the paradox of consensual S/M. On the one hand, it seems to parade a servile obedience to conventions of power. In its clichéd reverence for formal ritual, it is the most ceremonial and decorous of practices. S/M is 'beautifully suited to symbolism'.[6] As theatre, S/M borrows its décor, props and costumery (bonds, chains, ropes, blindfolds) and its scenes (bedrooms, kitchens, dungeons, convents, prisons, empire) from the everyday cultures of power. At first glance, then, S/M seems a servant to orthodox power. Yet, on the contrary, with its exaggerated emphasis on costume and scene S/M performs social power as *scripted*, and hence as permanently subject to change. As a theatre of conversion, S/M reverses and transmutes the social meanings it borrows, yet also without finally stepping outside the enchantment of its magic circle. In S/M, paradox is paraded, not resolved. This chapter is pitched at the borders of contradiction.

AGAINST NATURE: S/M AND SEXOLOGY

In 1885, the sexologist Richard von Krafft-Ebing coined the terms sadism and masochism, and medicalised them both as individual psychopathologies of the flesh.[7] Sadism, for Krafft-Ebing, was an aberrant and atavistic manifestation of the 'innate desire to humiliate, hurt, wound or even destroy others in order thereby to create sexual pleasure in one's self'.[8] Nature was the overlord of power, that had, in its wisdom, seen fit to ordain the aggressive impulse in men, not women. 'Under normal circumstances man meets obstacles which it is his part to overcome, and for which nature has given him an aggressive character.'[9] 'Normal' sexuality thus merely enacts the male's 'natural' sexual aggression and the female's 'natural' sexual passivity: 'In the intercourse of the sexes, the active or aggressive role belongs to man; woman remains passive, defensive. It affords man great pleasure to win a woman, to conquer her.'[10] Yet women, for Krafft-Ebing, are indirectly to blame for male sadism, for their very shyness provokes male aggression: 'It seems probable that this sadistic force is developed by the natural shyness and modesty of women towards the aggressive manners of the male.'[11] Happily, however, Nature designed woman to take a refined pleasure in man's rough victory: 'Woman no doubt derives pleasure from her innate coyness and the final victory of man affords her intense gratification.'[12]

The task for medical sexology was to police a double boundary: between the 'normal' culture of male aggression and the 'abnormal' culture of S/M, and between 'normal' female masochism and 'abnormal' male masochism. The first contradiction – between 'natural' heterosexuality and the 'unnatural' perversions – was primarily managed by projecting the 'perversions' onto the invented zone of race. Sexologists like Krafft-Ebing demonised S/M as the psychopathology of the atavistic individual, as a blood-flaw and stigma of the flesh. S/M, like other fetishisms, was figured as a regression in time to the 'prehistory' of racial 'degeneration', existing ominously in the heart of the imperial metropolis – the degeneration of the race writ as an individual pathology of the soul.

Thus for Krafft-Ebing, decent doses of male aggression are a *fait accompli* of nature. Genuine sadism, however, exists in 'civilised man' only in a 'weak and rather rudimentary degree'.[13] While sadism is a natural trait of 'primitive' peoples, atavistic traces of sadism in 'civilised man' stem, not from environment or social accident, but from a primordial past: 'Sadism must . . . be counted among the primitive anomalies of the sexual life. It is a disturbance (a deviation) in the evolution of psychosexual processes sprouting from the soil of psychical degeneration.'[14]

Action in early eighteenth-century flagellant brothel; frontispiece of the 1718 London edition of Meibom's treatise. Note the voyeurs at the window. (Courtesy of the British Library Board).

Like Krafft-Ebing, Freud agrees that the aggressive impulse is 'readily demonstrable in the normal individual'.[15] Again, the 'normal individual' is male: 'The sexuality of most men shows an admixture of aggression, of a desire to subdue.'[16] For Freud, the difference between aggression and sadism is one of degree, not of kind: 'Sadism would then correspond to an aggressive component of the sexual instinct which has become independent and exaggerated and has been brought to the foreground by displacement.'[17] Masochism, however, presents a more subtle riddle. For Krafft-Ebing, since it is simply Nature's way of saying that women are destined for a passive role in society, masochism is natural to women but not to men. Freud, however, sees the 'most striking peculiarity' of sadomasochism as the fact that 'its active and passive forms are regularly encountered together in the same person'.[18] Male masochism, moreover, is by no means an uncommon phenomenon. Freud, however, manages this contradiction by identifying male masochism as, more properly speaking, 'feminine'.[19] The heterosexual distribution of 'male' aggression and 'female' passivity is sustained, if precariously.

By contrast with unbridled sadism, however, consensual and commercial S/M is less a biological flaw or pathological variant of natural, male aggression and natural female passivity, than it is a historical subculture that emerged in Europe alongside the Enlightenment. Far from being a primordial manifestation of racial 'degeneracy', S/M is a sub-culture organised primarily around the symbolic exercise of social risk. Indeed, the outrage of S/M is precisely its hostility to the idea of Nature as the custodian of social power: S/M refuses to read power as fate or destiny. Since S/M is the theatrical exercise of social contradiction, it is self-consciously *against* Nature, not in the sense that it violates natural law, but in the sense that it denies the existence of natural law in the first place. S/M *performs* social power as both contingent and constitutive, as sanctioned neither by fate nor by God, but by social convention and invention, and thus open to historical change.

Consensual S/M insists on exhibiting the 'primitive' (slave, baby, woman) as a *character* in the historical time of modernity. S/M stages the 'primitive irrational' as a dramatic script, a communal performance in the heart of Western reason. The paraphernalia of S/M (boots, whips, chains, uniforms) are the paraphernalia of state power, public punishment converted to private pleasure. S/M plays social power backwards, visibly staging hierarchy, difference and power, the irrational, ecstasy, and the alienation of the body as at the centre of Western reason, thus revealing the imperial *logic* of individualism, but also irreverently refusing it as *fate*. S/M manipulates the *signs* of power in order to refuse their legitimacy as *nature*. Hence the unstinting severity of the law in policing commercial S/M.

NOTHING TO USE BUT YOUR CHAINS: FETISHES IN THE LAND OF FEM-DOM

Some feminists demonise heterosexual S/M as the sanctioned exercise of male tyranny: 'Patriarchy and heterosexuality attempt to freeze power, to make one side always passive. . . . It is the origin of masochistic and sadistic positions.'[20] For other feminists, even lesbian S/M is 'self-debasement on all levels that renders wimmin unable to execute truly feminist goals'.[21] Kathleen Barry in *Female Sexual Slavery* denounces S/M as 'a disguise for the act of sexually forcing a woman against her will'.[22]

It is also commonly thought that men who pay for commercial S/M pay to indulge in the sadistic abuse of women. Yet the testimony of dominatrixes reveals precisely the opposite. By far the most common service paid for by men in heterosexual S/M is the extravagant display of submission. In most commercial B & D (bondage and discipline), men are the 'slaves', not women. As the dominatrix Lindi St Clair says, far from being the vicious unleashing of male dominance, S/M is typically 'the other way round'.[23] Allegra Taylor agrees:

> Amber can call on the services of a couple of 'submissive' girls who themselves enjoy being beaten, to service the needs of the few 'dominant' men who want to dish it out rather than take it, but the majority of her clients come and pay a lot of money in order to submit, to relinquish themselves, to suffer.[24]

Who are these men? 'Proper gentlemen who know how to behave.' Amber's regulars include 'solicitors, Harley Street doctors, senior police officers, business executives and churchmen. They come to be punished, humiliated, frightened and tormented to the limits of their endurance.'[25]

Kelly, an Australian B & D specialist, claims her clients are 'mostly businessmen, middle-age upwards. They were all well dressed, you wouldn't pick them in the street, they could be your boss at work. B & D seems to attract that kind of clientele, as though people in authority want that taken away from them.'[26] As Lindi St Clair testifies:

> An awful lot of men . . . want to dress up in what we call rubber-wear, or leather, or they want to be tied up, and put into bondage, or spanked, or caned, or they want to dress in ladies' clothing, or they want to be urinated on, or they want to be abused by a dominant female . . . and none of this involves straight sex. . . . All these men are married, with families. . . . They'd never admit it to anyone.[27]

Far from male sadism being the norm, she says: 'There's a few of what are called 'masters', who want submissive girls, but I've never come across that. It's very, very small. It's the other way round.'[28] Bonnie, an Australian prostitute writes: 'In New Zealand and here it's much the same, usually they're guys who want to get a beating.'[29] Says Kelly: 'There are those who are just happy grovelling around the floor begging for mercy.'[30] This verdict is confirmed again and again: 'In the world of the sadomasochist, there is nothing "abnormal" about a male being passive and submissive.'[31] Indeed, male passivity is by far the most common phenomenon. What is the meaning of this conversion?

THE DOMESTIC SLAVE

Prostitutes testify that men frequently enact scripts framed by the 'degradation' of domesticity: paying large sums of money to sweep, clean, launder and tidy, under a female regime of verbal taunts and abuse:

> 'Domestic' slaves want to be drudges and set to work cleaning, shopping, ironing, etc. . . . One elderly gentleman of seventy does the best domestic work I have ever seen. Another slave tried to get rid of him, and they would bicker over who would wash up, peel the potatoes, or sweep the floor.[32]

Some dominas keep 'pets', who pay regularly to do their housework for them. During her trial in 1987, Madame Cyn Payne calmly confessed to the court: 'Well, I've had one or two slaves. It's someone who does all the housework and painting and decorating, and in return he likes a little bit of caning, insults and humiliation.'[33]

Similar testimonies abound. Lisa, an Australian prostitute, remembers a domestic 'slave' who liked nothing so much as 'to crawl around the floor doing the vacuum with a cucumber up his bum'.[34] Kelly remembers: 'Another guy came around each week and paid to do our laundry.'[35] Another paid to empty the bins of condoms and tissues. The eighteenth-century prostitute, Ann Sheldon, records in her memoirs 'a person of very gentleman-like behaviour' who had a fancy for being roundly beaten with dishcloths while doing the washing up:

> Looking over the kitchen-door, I saw the good man, disrobed of his clothes and wig, and dressed in a mob cap, a tattered bed-gown, and an old petticoat belonging to the cook, as busy in washing the dishes as if this employment had been the source of his daily bread – but this was not all; for while he was thus occupied, the mantua-maker on one side, and the cook on the other, were belabouring him with dish-clouts; he continuing to make a thousand excuses for his awkwardness and promising to do the business better on a future occasion.[36]

What are we to make of these rituals, belonging as they do in the realm of the fetish?

In their secret society of the spectacle, male 'slaves' enact with compulsive repetition the forbidden knowledge of the power of women. In cultures where women are the child-raisers, an infant's first identification is with the culture of femininity, which enters the child's identity as its first structuring principle. But in these same societies, boys are tasked with identifying away from women, that is, away from a founding dimension of their own identity, towards an often abstracted and remote masculinity – identity not through recognition, but through negation. Masculinity thus comes into being through the ritualised disavowal of the feminine, predicated on a host of male rites of negation. Nonetheless, identification with the culture of women survives in secret rites – taboo and full of shame.

By cross-dressing as women or as maids, by paying to do 'women's work', or by ritually worshipping dominas as socially powerful, the male 'slave' relishes the forbidden, feminine aspects of his own identity, furtively recalling the childhood image of female power and the memory of maternity, banished by social shame to the museum of masturbation. In Freudian psychoanalysis, as in Western culture at large, male identification *with* the mother figure is seen as pathological, perverse, the source of arrest, fixation and hysteria, rather than as an inevitable aspect of any child's identity. For Freud, the mother is seen as an object the child must try to possess and control, rather than a social ideal *with whom* to identify. For boys, active identification is allowed only with men, thus splitting complex, dynamic patterns of identity into two distinct, gendered categories. For men, the disjunction between women as object-choice and women as desirable to identify *with* is split and unresolved, policed by social shame and stigma.

It is not surprising, then, that cleaning rituals figure so often in the land of Fem-Dom (Female Domination). Male floor-washing, laundering, foot-licking and boot-scrubbing rituals fill the fantasy columns of Fem-Dom magazines such as *Mistress, F-D Xtra* and *Madame in a World of Fantasy*. Perhaps these expiation rituals symbolically absolve the 'slave' of sexual and gender shame, in elaborate absolution scenes that are replete with Christian overtones. Sex can be indulged if guilt can be atoned for, through the ritual washing of floors, feet and lingerie – 'masochism as expiation for the sin of sexuality'.[37]

The domestic fetish brings into crisis the historic separation of the 'male' sphere of the market and the 'female' sphere of the home. By paying handsomely to perform household services that wives are expected to perform for free, male 'slaves' stage, as outrageous display, the social contradiction between women's paid work and women's unpaid work in the home. If the middle-class cult of domesticity disavowed the economic value of housework, and exalted the home as the space for the elaborate display of leisure and consumption, domestic S/M does the opposite. In the ritual exchange of cash and the reversal of gender roles, domestic S/M stages women's work as having both *exhibition and economic* value. The social disavowal and *undervaluation* of domestic work is reversed in the extravagant *overvaluation* of women's dirty work, and the remuneration of *women* for the supervision of *men's* labour.

The domestic-slave fetish – inhabiting as it does the threshold between private and public, marriage and market – embodies the trace of both historical and personal memory, exhibiting, without resolution, the social contradiction between the historical disavowal of women's labour and the personal memory of women's power. Male 'slaves' throw into question the liberal separation of private and public, insisting on exhibiting women's work, women's *value* in the home: that space putatively beyond both slave labour and the market economy. Exhibiting their 'filth' as value, they give the lie to the disavowal of women's work and the middle-class denunciation of sexual and domestic 'dirt'. At the same time, the slave-band brings into the bourgeois home the memory of empire: the clanking of chains and the crack of the whip. The fetish slave-band, mimicking the metal collars worn by black slaves in the homes of the imperial bourgeoisie, enacts the history of industrial

capital as haunted by the traumatic and ineradicable memory of slave imperialism.

Male TV (transvestite) 'slavery' thus veers between nostalgia for female power, embodied in the awful spectacle of the whip-wielding domina, and the ritual negation of female power, embodied in the feminised male 'slave' as the nadir of self-abasement. In the process, however, the spectacle of the male 'slave' on his hands and knees, naked as a newt and scrubbing the kitchen floor, throws radically into question 'Nature''s edict that differences in gender entail natural divisions of labour.

Some men play the submissive role only when dressed as women, doing 'women's work' costumed as housemaids or nannies. A question then arises: do men indulge in submission only when dressed as women and slaves, dogs and babies? Would heterosexuality be flung into confusion if men performed domestic work in Dacron suits and Leonard From Paris ties? After the *via dolorosa* of the S/M session, the domina bears witness to the resurrection of manhood: 'Finally, it was all over. . . . Dennis got up and gingerly put his pants on. He was instantly transformed into a normal confident, assertive man. . . . We all stood around chatting and having a cup of tea.'[38] Is the heterosexual male thus left finally unimpaired, to be reassembled again in boardroom and bedroom?[39]

Yet not all 'slaves' cross-dress when doing domestic work. As one writer grumbled in *Madame in a World of Fantasy*: 'Dear Candida, I know you like to give all tastes a share in your magazine, but the portion given to those interested in men that are feminised is way over the top.'[40] Many 'slaves' retain their male persona and perform domestic work as an elaborate reversal of gender *agency*, but not of gender *identity*. It is therefore important to stress that S/M does not constitute a single subculture, but rather comprises a cluster of circulating genres, some of which are distinct, some of which overlap.

In S/M, social identities shift libidinously. In her ground-breaking book *Vested Interests*, Marjorie Garber invites us to take transvestites on their own terms, not as one sex or gender but as the enactment of ambiguity itself: not even so much a 'blurred sex', as the embodiment and performance of social contradiction.[41] She contends that the 'specter of transvestism' throws into question the very notion of a fixed and stable identity, challenging any easy binary of 'female' and 'male'. The cross-dresser represents the 'crisis of category itself'. Garber thus sets herself against the 'progress narrative' theory of cross-dressing, which attempts to uncover a 'real' desired identity, either 'male' or 'female' beneath the transvestite mask. Rather, the transvestite is the figure that inhabits the borderland where oppositions are permanently disarranged.

Cross-dressing celebrates the peculiar freedoms of ambiguity, rather than the fixity of one identity. For many the allure of transvestism is not the transformation of man-to-woman, or woman-to-man, but the subversive parade of man-*as*-woman, woman-*as*-man. Cross-dressers often desire, not the security of a perfect imitation, but rather the delicious impersonation that belies complete disguise: the hairy leg in the lace suspender, the bald pate in the bonnet. In 'tranny' (transvestite) publications such as *The World of Transvestism*, a man's hirsute calf protrudes beneath the silken skirt, the shadow of an erection is pressed against the lacy lingerie. One TV writes:

> I agree with what you have said, Brian, about contrast – male with female. Long black fishnet stockings, frilly suspender belts, pretty frocks and finally see-through panties that when one raises one's frock, the big erect penis bulging through the silky flimsy material can clearly be seen.[42]

THE DIRT FETISH

Domestic S/M is organised in complex and repetitive ways around the fetish of 'dirt'. Why does 'dirt' exert such a compulsive fascination over the S/M imagination?

The dirt fetish embodies the traces of both personal and historical memory. Dirt may recall, as personal memory, punishment during toilet training for being out of control – of one's faeces, one's urine, one's erections and ejaculation, one's wandering, desirous fingers. Faecal dirt smeared by children on themselves, their walls, their cots or their siblings can embody a variety of inchoate passions: rage, curiosity, an attempt to reach out and influence the world, frustration and loneliness. If unaccountably punished for such acts, the emotion may be arrested, destined to recur compulsively for ritualistic re-enactment. In the dirt fetish, the fetishist takes control of perilous memory, playing memory backwards, in an excess of desire, and disarranging the social compact between

sexual transgression and dirt. If fetishists, as children, were punished for being out of control of their 'dirt', in the rebellious circus of fetishism they re-enact, in reverse, an *excess* of control over 'dirt'. If, as children, an obscure logic of parental rebuke equated erotic pleasure with 'filth' and 'smut', meriting swift retribution, then, as adults, the S/Mers invert the logic, equating dirt with an exquisite excess of erotic pleasure, re-enacting 'toilet training' in an exhibitionist parody of the domestic economy of pleasure and power.

S/M also embodies a historical memory trace. Since the 19th century, the subculture of S/M has been denounced by reference to the bestiary and the iconography of 'filth'. But nothing is inherently dirty; dirt expresses a relation to social value and social disorder. Dirt, as Mary Douglas suggests, is that which transgresses social boundary. A broom in a kitchen closet is not 'dirty', whereas lying on a bed it is. Sex with one's spouse is not 'dirty', whereas the same act with a prostitute is. Boxing is not 'dirty', but S/M is.

During the 19th century, the iconography of 'dirt' became deeply integrated in the policing and transgression of social boundary. In Victorian culture, the bodily relation to 'dirt' expressed a social relation to labour. The male middle class – seeking to dismantle the aristocratic body and the aristocratic regime of legitimacy – came to distinguish itself as a class in two ways: it earned its living (unlike the aristocracy), and it owned property (unlike the working class). Unlike the working class, however, its members, especially its female members, could not bear on their bodies the visible evidence of manual labour. Dirt was a Victorian scandal, because it was the surplus evidence of manual work, the visible residue that stubbornly remained after the process of industrial rationality had done its work. Dirt is the counterpart of the commodity; something is dirty precisely *because* it is void of commercial value, or because it transgresses the 'normal' commercial market. Dirt is what is left over after exchange value has been extracted. Dirt is by definition *useless*, since it is that which belongs outside the commodity market.

If, as Marx noted, commodity fetishism exhibits the *overvaluation* of commercial exchange as the fundamental principle of social community, then the Victorian obsession with dirt marks a dialectic: the fetishised *undervaluation* of human labour. Smeared on trousers, faces, hands and aprons, dirt was the memory trace of working-class and female labour, unseemly evidence that the production of industrial and imperial wealth lay fundamentally in the hands and bodies of the working class, women and the colonised. In this way dirt, like all fetishes, expresses a crisis in value, for it contradicts the liberal dictum that social wealth is created by the abstract, rational principles of the market, and not by labour. For this reason Victorian dirt entered the symbolic realm of fetishism with great force.

As the 19th century drew on, the iconography of dirt became a poetic of surveillance, deployed increasingly to police the boundaries between 'normal' sexuality and 'dirty' sexuality, 'normal' work and 'dirty' work, and 'normal' money and 'dirty' money. 'Dirty' sex – masturbation, prostitution, lesbian and gay sexuality, S/M, the host of the Victorian 'perversions' – transgressed the libidinal economy of male-controlled, heterosexual reproduction within monogamous marital relations (clean sex which has *value*). Likewise, 'dirty' money – associated with prostitutes, Jews, gamblers, thieves – transgressed the fiscal economy of the male-dominated, market exchange (clean money which has *value*). Prostitutes stood on the dangerous threshold of work, money and sexuality, and came to be figured increasingly in the iconography of 'pollution', 'disorder', 'plagues', 'moral contagion' and racial 'filth'.

MEN BABIES IN THE LAND OF FEM-DOM

S/M is haunted by memory. By re-enacting *loss* of control in a staged situation of *excessive* control, the S/Mer gains symbolic power over perilous memory. By reinventing the memory of trauma, S/M affords a delirious triumph over the past, and from this triumph an orgasmic excess of pleasure. But since the triumph over memory is symbolic, however intensely felt in the flesh, resolution is perpetually deferred. For this reason, the fetish, the scene, will recur for perpetual re-enactment, and compulsive repetition emerges as a fundamental structuring principle of S/M.

By many accounts, babyism is a common fetish in commercial S/M. As Allegra Taylor says: 'There's a whole area of deviant behaviour called babyism where the client likes to dress up in a nappy, suck a giant dummy or one of her [the domina's] breasts and just be rocked.'[43] In trade parlance, a 'babyist' or

'infantilist' pays large sums of money to be bathed, powdered, put in nappies, sat in playpens, or wrapped tightly in swaddling clothes. The fem-dom magazine *Fantasy* explains: 'We often have requests for stories of poor (un)willing creatures who wish to return to the beginning of their existence and be completely babyfied, dominated entirely.'[44] Ann Sheldon's eighteenth-century gentleman who fancied being beaten while doing the dishes liked the two women who beat him then 'to skewer him up tight in a blanket, and roll him backwards and forwards upon the carpet, in the parlour, 'till he was lulled to sleep'.[45]

Enough men like to be rocked and 'nursed' to give dominas a steady trade. As St Clair attests: ' "Babyists" need mummy Lindi to dress them in nappies, bibs, bonnets and booties, to powder their bottoms and breastfeed them.'[46] Another domina runs a two-storey building: at lunchtime, businessmen arrive, discreetly take off their clothes, don giant-size nappies with giant-size nappy pins, and spend large sums of money to sit for an hour in giant-size playpens, sucking bottles, before redressing and returning to the hurly-burly of high finance.

Babyist scenes in F-D magazines feature grown men in outsize frilly baby wear, strapped into baby cots, or gazing wide-eyed at the camera from behind their dummies. A typical magazine fantasy runs as follows:

> He began to feel, not just his mummy's child, but his total dependency on her. . . . He sighed contentedly. Babba had been his childhood name. . . . Now he was to be Babba again. . . . From the next day, all baby hair was removed. Mummy bathed him, dried him, put baby-oil between his legs. . . . Bobby, at home, has become a baby again.[47]

Male babyism holds up to society a scandalous, accusatory hybrid: not so much man-into-baby but man-*as*-baby, baby-*as*-man. Contradictions are exhibited but not resolved. In these scenes, men surrender deliriously to the memory of female power and their own helplessness in their mother's or nurse's arms. If men are socially tasked with upholding the burden of rational self-containment, perhaps in the babyland of fem-dom they can fleetingly relinquish their stolid control, surrendering responsibility and authority in an ecstatic release of power.

Babyism may also grant men retrospective control over perilous memories of infancy: nightmares of restraint, rubber sheets, helplessness, inexplicable punishments, isolation and grief. The rubber fetish seems associated, for some, with inchoate memories of rubber diapers, wet beds and mortification. F-D magazine fantasies reveal aching images of childhood as a bewildering limbo of denial, discomfort, parental rage and neglect. One babyist muses:

> The problem probably stemmed from my early childhood. I was an only child and my mother left home. . . . My father was away fighting the war . . . and I was thus brought up by an aunt. . . . She would cuff me round the ear at the slightest excuse.[48]

Another fetishist recalls:

> But in the depths of my mind there lurked a more sinister side of myself, an obsession to be dominated and humiliated as a child, forced back to the cradle by beautiful, cruel women, normally nurses or nannies.[49]

This writer's masochism began at boarding school, when he was ridiculed for bed-wetting. When punishment failed to cure him, the school nurse subjected him to a public circus of mortification:

> She gathered all the boys around . . . while she removed my shorts and underpants. With a captive audience, she pinned me into a bulky nappy. . . . 'There,' she beamed, 'baby has a nappy on at last.' . . . My humiliation was complete.[50]

Now, however, as an adult, in his F-D theatre of conversion, the babyist converts the *incapacity* to control bodily functions and the failure to preserve the boundaries between child and adult into the *imperative* to lose control, and to blur the boundaries between adult and child. Through the control frame of cash and fantasy, perilous memory of *loss* of control is re-enacted under circumstances of a scrupulous *excess* of control.

In their secret nursery for Goliaths, babyists ritually indulge in the forbidden, nostalgic spectacle of the power of women. The land of Fem-Dom is frequently described by men as a 'feminist' utopia, a futuristic paradise in which women are 'fully liberated and universally recognized as the Superior

Sex'.[51] The voices of martinets, scolds and governesses crack through the pages of these magazines: ' "This is exactly what you *deserve*, my boy. A good smacked *bottom*!," she said sternly, *just* like a strict governess.'[52] The agony aunts of F-D columns are similarly vituperative: 'Disgusting creature though you are, you have my permission to write again,' snaps one.[53] 'You sound a miserable worm to me . . . and deserve all you get,' barks another.[54]

The 'naughty husband' fantasy, in which callous men are punished for various domestic infringements, appears frequently. A STRICT BOTTOM-SMACKING WIFE writes: 'A little wifely discipline is often necessary. I am sure that many wives have often felt like turning a misbehaving young husband over a knee and smacking his bottom – the thing is to do it.'[55] 'I am a firm believer,' writes another 'wife', 'in petticoating and nursery treatment as a means of reminding a troublesome husband that he is still subject to maternal rule.'[56]

Perhaps in these expiation rituals, men pay not only to surrender gender responsibility, or to gain control of perilous memories, but also to be symbolically absolved of guilt for the everyday abuse of women – only to resume their authority once more as they return restored from babyland. As Gebhard suggests: 'The masochist has a nice guilt-relieving system – he gets his punishment simultaneously with his sexual pleasure or else is entitled to his pleasure by first enduring the punishment.'[57] Moreover, the 'feminist' utopia exalted by these men is a paradise arranged and organised for male pleasure. In the private security of fantasy, men can indulge secretly and guiltily their knowledge of women's power, while enclosing female power in a fantasy land that lies far beyond the cities and towns of genuine feminist change.

CRIMINAL JUSTICE: THE POLICING OF S/M

On 28 January 1987, at the height of the celebrated trial of Madame Cyn Payne, Sergeant David Broadwell dragged into court a large plastic bag and exposed to the titillated courtroom the taboo paraphernalia of S/M: whips, belts, chains, a dog collar, and assorted sticks and leather items.[58] For days, police and witnesses described the 'naughtinesses' at Payne's party: spankings, lesbian shows, elderly gentlemen cross-dressed in women's evening clothes, policemen in drag, and lawyers, businessmen and even a peer of the realm waiting in queues on the stairs for sex.

The sex trial, conducted in a blaze of publicity, exposes its own structuring paradox, staging in public, as a vicarious spectacle, what it renders criminally deviant outside the juridical domain. Ordering the unspeakable to be spoken in public, the sex trial takes shape around the very fetishism it sets itself to isolate and punish. Through the prostitution trial, transgressions in the distribution of money, pleasure and power are isolated as *crimes*, and are then performed again in the theatrical ceremony of the trial as *confession*. The judiciary is a system of ordered procedures for the production of 'Truth'. It is also a system for disqualifying alternative discourses: the disenfranchised, feminists, prostitutes, fetishists. By being obliged to speak

'forensically' in the courtroom about their illicit activities, prostitutes rehearse, as spectacle, the taboo body of the woman who receives money for sex. The more she speaks of her actions in public, however, the more she incriminates herself. But in its obsessive display of 'dirty' pictures, filmed evidence, confessions and exhibits, the sex trial reveals itself as deployed about the archival exhibition of the fetish. Under his purple robes, the judge has an erection.

The sex trial and the flagellation scene mirror each other in a common liturgy. There is, first of all, the Chamber. In the trial, this is the Court; in S/M it is the Vault, the Dungeon or the Schoolroom. The first rite is exposure – in the trial, the accused is exposed before the crowd; in the flagellant scene the 'slave''s buttocks are bared. The Judge, like the Dominatrix, is theatrically costumed, while the judge's

" I'M AFRAID THERE'S A QUEUE ON THE STAIRS AGAIN, OLD BOY ! "

'This time, Madam Cyn, I thought we'd come in uniform to celebrate...'

© Mel Calman

wig, like the prostitute's wig, guarantees the separation between self and body, and thereby the 'impartiality' of the trial. Both Judge and Dominatrix are paid money to exercise the right to punish, while fetish elements are common to both: theatrical costumery, stage, gavels, whips, handcuffs. The second rite is restraint: the accused is penned in the dock; the 'slave' is tied, or bent over the block. The third element is the charge, for which it is also necessary that there be spectators, voyeurism being an indispensable element in both scenes. Next, it is crucial that both accused and 'slave' participate verbally in their trial, in the plea, the interrogation, denials and

confession. Warnings are given, sentence is pronounced, and execution takes place. Only then is the logic of pleasure and punishment reversed: the trial displays illicit pleasure and power for punishment; S/M displays illicit punishment for pleasure and power. The trial exists to produce the sentence of rational Truth, while in S/M Truth becomes orgasm, and the word is made flesh. S/M thus emerges as a private parody of the public trial: public punishment converted to private pleasure.

If the sex trial isolates 'deviant' sexual *pleasure* for *punishment*, commercial S/M is the dialectical twin of the trial, organising the *punishment* of sexual deviance for *pleasure*. If the sex trial redistributes illicit female money back into male circulation through fines, commercial S/M enacts the reverse, staging women's sexual work as having economic value, and insisting, strictly, on payment.

Consensual S/M brings to its limit the liberal discourse on consent. In 1990, the notorious Spanner investigation became an estimated £2.5 million showcase for the policing of gay S/M in Britain. On 19 December 1990, fifteen men were sentenced at the Old Bailey by Judge James Rant for willingly and privately engaging in S/M acts with each other for sexual pleasure. Eight of the men were given custodial sentences ranging up to four and a half years. On 19 February 1992, five of the men failed to have their conviction overturned by the Court of Appeal.[59] The presiding Lord Chief Justice, Lord Lane, ruled that the men's consent and the privacy of their acts were no defence, and that S/M libido did not constitute causing bodily harm 'for good reason'.

By contrast, activities such as boxing, football, rugby or cosmetic surgery apparently constitute, in the eyes of the law, well-recognised cases of licit, consensual bodily harm, for they are conducted for 'good reason', that is, for the profitable, public consumption of 'natural' female vanity, 'natural' male aggression and the law of male, market competition – for the proper maintenance, that is, of heterosexual difference. In violent contact sports, men touch each other in furious and often wounding intimacy, but the homoerotic implications are scrupulously disavowed.

Perhaps even more revealingly, Feminists Against Censorship, the gay rights group Outrage, Liberty (formerly the National Council of Civil Liberties), and others, have pointed out that the sentences meted out by Judge Rant for consensual S/M exceed,

We find the
defendant NOT
GUILTY – but
we'd like to
hear
all the
EVIDENCE
again ...

calman

© Mark Boxer Ltd

in many cases, those for the violent, non-consensual rape or battery of women or for cases of lesbian and gay bashing. As Alex Kershaw notes: 'In 1988, for example, a man was fined £100 at Carlisle Crown Court for sadomasochistic assaults on women.'[60] Suzanne Moore sums it up: 'In other words when a heterosexual woman says "no" she really means "yes", but when a homosexual man says "yes", the law says that is not good enough.'[61] The Spanner trial throws radically into question the law's putative impartiality in the adjudication of consent.

The outrage of consensual S/M is multiple. It publicly exposes the possibility that manhood is not *naturally* synonymous with mastery, nor femininity with passivity. Social identity becomes commutable, and the boundaries of gender and class open to invention and transfiguration. Men touch each other for pleasure and women wreak well-paid vengeance. Perhaps most subversively of all, eroticism is sundered from the rule of procreation: the erotic body

expands beyond the genitals to include non-procreational sites – ears, feet, nipples – of life-saving potential in the era of AIDS.[62] At the same time, the power dynamics and erotic implications of social ritual are visibly and flagrantly explored. As Califia says: 'In an S & M context, the uniforms and roles and dialogue become a parody of authority, a challenge to it, a recognition of its secret, sexual nature.'[63] In S/M's house of misrule, woman is judge and jury, man is penitent, the master does the slave's bidding, and the sacred is profane.

S/M is the most liturgical of forms, sharing with Christianity a theatrical iconography of punishment and expiation: washing rituals, bondage, flagellation, body-piercing and symbolic torture. Like S/M, the economy of Christianity is the economy of conversion: the meek exalted, the high made low. Mortifying the flesh exalts one in the eyes of the Master. Through humility on earth, one stores up a surplus stock of spiritual value in heaven. Like Christianity, S/M performs the paradox of redemptive suffering, and like Christianity, it takes shape around the masochistic logic of transcendence through the mortification of the flesh: through self-abasement, the spirit finds release in an ecstasy of abandonment. In both S/M and Christianity, earthly desire exacts strict payment in an economy of penance and pleasure. In S/M, washing rituals and the pouring of water effect a baptismal cleansing and exoneration of guilt. These are purification rituals, a staged appropriation of Christian pageantry, stealing a delirious, fleshly advance on one's spiritual credit – a forbidden taste of what should properly be exaltation in the hereafter.

THE RIGHT TO PUNISH

The historic subculture of S/M emerged within the Enlightenment, alongside what Foucault has identified as a new technology of the power-to-punish.[64] During the Enlightenment, as Foucault argues, penal reform shifted the right-to-punish from the whimsical, terrible vengeance of the sovereign to the contractual 'defence of society'.[65] The spectacle of punishment no longer lay in the sumptuous rage of the monarch, which had taken effect as a series of ostentatious mutilations of the criminal's flesh – floggings, brandings, beheadings, flayings, quarterings and so on. Punishment now lay in the visible *representation* of an abstract, bureaucratic power, which took effect as a series of ritual restraints – detention, incarceration, regulation, retraining, restrictions, fines and, in some cases, rationalised and limited corporal punishment. An array of techniques was devised for adjusting punishment to the new social body, and a host of new principles was laid down for refining the art of punishing.[66] In the hands of an elite bureaucracy, punishment became legitimised, not as personal revenge, but as civic prevention. Punishment became the rationally calculated, causal *effect* of the crime, and the administrators of punishment were figured as no more than the dispassionate ministrants of rational law.

Penal reform, as Foucault sees it, had the centrifugal effect of multiplying and dispersing punishment as an 'art of affects': the penalty must have its most intense effects on those who have not committed the crime.[67] The link between crime and punishment must be publicly *seen* to coincide causally with the operation of rationally administered Truth. The Enlightenment technology of punishment thus had two aims in view: to get all citizens to participate in the 'contractual' punishment of the social enemy, and to render the power to punish 'entirely adequate and transparent to the laws that publicly define it'.[68] Punishments became less ritual marks violently gouged into the flesh, than *tableaux vivants* designed to be witnessed by the general public as representative of the mechanics of natural law.

Under this regime, schools came to serve as miniature penal mechanisms, with forms of discipline borrowed directly from the juridical model: solitary confinement, flagellation, petty humiliations and an extravagant attention to rule. Public mortification was meted out according to a theatrical liturgy of floggings, restraints and deprivations, with the undeviating precision of machinery.

The scandal of S/M, however, is that it borrows directly from the juridical model, while radically disarranging the right-to-punish. S/M stages the right-to-punish, not for the civic prevention of crime, but for pleasure, parading a scrupulous fidelity to the *scene* and costumery of the penal model while at the same time interfering directly with the rules of *agency*. Hence the intolerable affront embodied in the dominatrix and her client. How can punishment be established in the minds of the public as a logical calculus of criminal *cause* and penal *effect* – the rational execution of Truth – if members of the general public can take up, on whim, the birch, the rod, the hand-

cuffs, the whipping block, and declare sentence not for the prevention of crime, but for the delirious excess of pleasure? For it is as subversive of the modern penal economy to commit an unpunished crime as it is to enjoy a punishment without having first committed a crime.

Hence the unstinting severity of the law in policing consensual S/M. Penal reform, despite its egalitarian, civic-minded cast, placed the restricted exercise of the penal right in the hands of a few elect institutions and a few elect actors: judges, prison warders, schoolteachers, army courts and parents, as proxies of natural law. Whatever else changed, however, punishment remained a male right: the judge, the jury, the prison governor and the executioner were, until very recently, all men. Wives of elite men might punish slaves, servants and children, but only as proxies of male law.

By contrast, heterosexual, commercial S/M flagrantly subverts the gendered economy of the right-to-punish, putting the whip and the money in the woman's hand, and exhibiting the man on his knees. With even greater effrontery, lesbian and gay S/Mers parade punishment, not as the dutiful exercise of civic prevention, but as a recreational theatre of power, denying the state its penal monopoly and provocatively exposing the right-to-punish, not as Reason's immutable decree, but as the irregular product of social hierarchy.

The legal denunciation of consensual S/M flies out, then, not as a human cry from the heart, a refined shrinking from the infliction of pain and the spectacle of torment, but as the jealous wrath of the penal bureaucracy challenged in its punitive monopoly. In sentencing S/Mers to bondage and discipline, floggings and ritual humiliation in Houses of Correction, the law, far from exhibiting defined disgust at the exhibition of pain, is merely asserting its jealous right over the penal regime.

S/M AS A THEATRE OF SOCIAL RISK

Most consensual S/M is less 'the desire to inflict pain', as Freud argued, than what John Alan Lee calls 'the social organisation of sexual risk'.[69] One can also call S/M the *sexual* organisation of *social risk*, for one of S/M's characteristics is the eroticising of scenes, symbols, context and contradictions which society does not typically recognise as sexual: domestic work, infancy, boots, water, money, uniforms and so on.

Contrary to Robert Stoller's notion that S/M sex is the 'erotic form of hatred', a great deal of S/M involves neither pain nor hatred.[70] The ritual violations of S/M are less violations to the flesh than symbolic re-enactments of social violations of selfhood, which can take a myriad of shapes and emerge from a myriad of social situations. S/M publicly performs the failure of the Enlightenment idea of individual autonomy, staging the dynamics of power and interdependency for personal pleasure. As such, S/M rituals may be called *rituals of recognition*. In these rituals of recognition, participants seek a witness – to trauma, pain, pleasure or power. As Lee puts it: 'Each partner served as an audience to the other, and in the process, *contained* the other.'[71] The prevalence of voyeurism and spectators comes to represent a transposed desire for social recognition. In commercial S/M, the domina acts as an official, if forbidden, witness – to private anguish, baffled desires and the obscure deliriums of the flesh.

In many respects, S/M is a theatre of signs, granting temporary control over social risk. By scripting and controlling the circus of signs, the fetishist stages the delirious loss of control within a situation of extreme control. For many S/Mers, *loss of control* as *memory* is mediated by a show of *excess* of control as *spectacle*. As a result, S/Mers depend deeply on what Goffman calls 'control frames', by which to manage the staging of social risk.[72] In an important article, John Alan Lee explores the ways in which gay S/M culture attempts to limit the 'great potential dangers involved' in S/M: through the screening of partners, the shared understanding of costume signals, colour coding, the reciprocal negotiation of scenarios and ground rules, scripting, the use of signal words or 'keys' to indicate limits, and the confirming of consent during the scenario.[73] Mastering the control frame – the scene, the script, the costume, the magazine, the fantasy, the exchange of money – is indispensable to the sensation of mastery over what might otherwise be terrifying ambiguities.

Indeed, it is often not so much the *actuality* of power or submission that holds the S/Mer in its thrall but the *signs* of power: images, words, costumes, uniforms, scripts. The self-styled sexual therapist Sara Dale says her clients want often only to hear the snap of her whip through the air.[74] Lindi St Clair writes: 'Men wanting a fantasy liked to be in kinky "theme rooms" and "pretend": for example they

would *talk* about certain props or scenarios, although in reality they wouldn't be interested in *doing* such things at all.'[75] Many clients are helplessly fascinated by fetish images of authority – handcuffs, badges, uniforms – and most dominas have rackfuls of costumes: ' "Uniformists" desire to wear or be serviced by someone wearing uniform – military, medical, police, traffic warden, or any other persuasion. The most popular are schoolgirl's and French maid's.'[76] Allegra Taylor, visiting a Dungeon, recalls:

> I was still amazed by the sheer volume of props and costumes. It was like a theatre warehouse or a film set. Hanging on pegs on all the walls and corridors were hundreds of outfits – nurse's and policewomen's uniforms, gymslips, black rubber knickers, dozens of pairs of boots . . . anything you can imagine having a fetish about.[77]

Other clients are enthralled by the verbal *representation* of desire, and like nothing so much as to send their 'literary Mistresses' letters, fantasies and scripts: 'Dear Madame Candida, If you find you have the space, would you kindly print the following humble letter. . . . Madame, may long you reign.'[78] In one Fem-Dom magazine, large white spaces are left beneath photographs of male 'slaves', accompanied by the schoolmarmish instruction: 'I am asking you to write beneath each photo what you imagine Madame Sheena is saying to her slave.'[79] Here, does the voyeur identify with Madame Sheena, her slave, or both? Identity shifts libidinously.

Hence the importance of scripts and initiation rituals in consensual S/M. Far from being the tyrannical exercise of one will upon a helpless other, consensual S/M is typically collaborative, involving careful training, initiation rites, a scrupulous definition of limits, and a constant confirmation of reciprocity.[80] As Paul Gebhard writes: 'The average sadomasochistic session is usually scripted. . . . Often the phenomenon reminds one of a planned ritual or theatrical production.'[81] Clients and dominas typically agree on key words, which the 'bottom' uses to intensify, change or stop the action. Many S/M fetishists claim that it is thus the 'bottom' who is in control.

Havelock Ellis was the first to point out that much S/M is motivated by love. Since S/M involves the negotiation of perilous boundaries, mutual fidelity to the pledge of trust can create intimacy of a very intense kind. The bond of collaboration binds the players in an ecstasy of interdependence: abandonment at the very moment of dependence. Far from ruthlessly wreaking one's sadistic will upon another, 'the sadist must develop an extraordinary perceptiveness to know when to continue, despite cries and protests, and when to cease'.[82] Here, 'enslavement' is ceremonial rather than real, a symbolic gift that can be retracted at any moment. For this reason, Pat Califia calls S/M 'power without privilege'.[83]

Yet at the same time, any violation of the script is fraught with risk. If, at any point, control is lost, or the rules of the game transgressed, either of the players can be plunged into panic or rage. Dominas therefore stress the emotional and physical skill, as well as the dangers, involved in commercial S/M: '[It] does take a special kind of person who can do B & D properly because it can get right out of control. You have to keep your cool all the time.'[84] Untoward changes in the script or collapse of the control frame can plunge clients into extreme distress or ferocious rage. The magic spell can be violently broken, and at such moments dominas face great danger.

For this reason, I remain unconvinced by the libertarian argument that all S/M lies in a cloud cuckoo land safely beyond any real abuses of power. The libertarian view all too easily conflates sexual repression with political oppression in a Reichian celebration of unlimit. But as Califia says, 'I do not believe that sex has an inherent power to transform the world. I do not believe that pleasure is always an anarchic force for good. I do not believe that we can fuck our way to freedom.'[85] S/M's theatre of risk inhabits the perilous borders of transgression, power and pleasure, where emotions can slip, identities shift, inchoate memories surface out of control, or everyday inequities be imported unexpectedly into the scene. As Sophie, a prostitute, says:

> People need to be pretty sure what they're doing. I don't want to make it sound like an elitist pastime, but you're dealing with such deep and potent forces that there is a risk of getting out of your depth. This happened with my previous lover. The sex we had brought up loads of stuff for her about being abused as a child which would have been a lot better coming through slowly and gently in therapy. I don't begin to have adequate

resources to deal with that with a lover. I think S/M sex is good and it can be great, but I'd only want to do it with someone who has extensive self-knowledge.[86]

To recognise the theatrical aspect of S/M does not diminish the risks that may be involved. S/M inhabits the anomalous border between the theory of mimesis and the idea of catharsis, neither replicating social power nor finally subverting it, veering between polarities, converting scenes of disempowerment into a staged excess of pleasure, caricaturing social edicts in a sumptuous display of irreverence, but without substantially interrupting the social order.

In my view, the extreme libertarian argument that S/M *never* involves real anger or hate runs the risk of disavowing the intense emotional voltages that can be S/M's appeal.[87] Some dominas confess to potent expressions of feminist anger, outrage and power when they work: 'In bondage you have the power and control,' says Zoe, a parlour and escort woman, 'and it's quite refreshing to be in that position of total power getting a little anger out and let(ting) your expression out, and it wasn't threatening to the guy asking for it. . . . I gained a lot of confidence out of it.'[88] Kelly explains that she became a bondage specialist because she 'enjoyed beating up men'. Some dominas, she said,

> like inflicting pain perhaps because they have been hurt in their private lives, or where they are suppressed in their home life it is a role reversal, just like the guys the other way around. It is a reversal of the patriarchal system in which they have been suppressed all their lives; they are home doing the washing and ironing for their husbands in the day and they go out of a night and whip guys, and get paid for it.[89]

While such emotions may be unrepresentative, they cannot be wholly dismissed.

An important theoretical distinction therefore needs to be made between *reciprocal* S/M for mutual pleasure, and *consensual* S/M organised as a commercial exchange. Whatever else it is, commercial S/M is a labour issue. While all S/M is deeply stigmatised and violently policed, the criminalising of sexwork places dominas under particular pressure. Sexworkers argue that the current laws punish rather than protect them. In Britain, if a domina shares a flat with a friend, she can be convicted for running a brothel. If she pays towards the rent or upkeep of her flat, her friend can be convicted for living off immoral earnings. Yet working alone can be fatal. Moreover, where sexwork is a crime, a domina cannot seek police or legal aid if she is raped, battered or robbed. Clients know this, so commercial S/M's theatre of risk can, at times, become risky indeed, losing some of the collective safeguards that characterise much reciprocal S/M. Nonetheless, sexworkers insist that it is not S/M or the exchange of cash that endangers them, but the laws and the context in which the exchange is made. Whatever else it does, commercial S/M throws into question the myth of all sexworkers as unambiguous victims. Dominas, like all sexworkers, are calling internationally for the decriminalising of their profession, so that they can collectively organise to transform the trade to meet their own needs.[90]

On its own, then, S/M does not escape its own paradoxes. Within its magic circle, social and personal contradictions can be deployed or negotiated but may not be resolved, for the sources and ends of these paradoxes lie beyond the individual, even though they may be lived with exquisite intensity in the flesh. S/M thus brings to its conceptual limit the libertarian promise that individual agency alone can suffice to resolve social dilemmas. In order to understand more fully the myriad meanings of S/M, it is necessary to distinguish between the social cultures from which it takes its multiple shapes, and against which it sets itself in stubborn refusal. The sub-culture of collective fetishism is an arena of contestation and negotiation, which does not teach simple lessons in power and domination.

NOTES

1. Andrew Neil, Channel 4, 16 October 1991.
2. In this paper, I use the term S/M in its broad sense, to refer to the general subculture of organised fetishism. The term S/M thus includes a wide variety of fetishes: B & D (bondage and discipline), CP (corporal punishment), TV (transvestism), babyism, Scat, body piercing, foot fetishism and so on. These fetishes should be seen as sometimes overlapping, sometimes distinct subgenres in a general subculture of collective fetish ritual. Moreover, within these genres there may be distinct forms: there are different forms of transvestism, for example, and different forms of B & D. Indeed, understanding and

negotiating these distinctions serves as a crucial source of the pleasure, intimacy, identity and communality that can be engendered by consensual S/M.

3. The subculture of S/M is not synonymous with the non-consensual inflictions of violence, pain, abuse or terror. A man does not usually don leather gear, fetish costumes and make-up before battering his wife. At times, however, the boundaries may blur and distinctions falter.

4. Michel Foucault, *Madness and Civilisation: A History of Insanity in the Age of Reason*, trans. Richard Howard (London: Tavistock Publications, 1965).

5. Erving Goffman, *Frame Analysis* (New York: Harper and Row, 1974), quoted by Thomas S. Weinberg in 'Sadism and Masochism: Sociological Perspectives', in Thomas S. Weinberg and G. W. Levi Kamel (eds), *S and M: Studies in Sadomasochism* (Buffalo, NY: Prometheus Books, 1983), p. 106.

6. Paul H. Gebhard, 'Sadomasochism', in Weinberg and Kamel, *S and M*, p. 39.

7. Richard von Krafft-Ebing, *Psychopathia Sexualis*, trans. Franklin S. Klaf (New York: Stein and Day, 1965). See Jeffrey Weeks, *Against Nature: Essays on History, Sexuality and Identity* (London: Rivers Oram Press, 1991), and Jonathan Dollimore, *Sexual Dissidence: Augustine to Wilde, Freud to Foucault* (Oxford: Clarendon Press, 1991), for analyses of the discourses on 'perversion'.

8. Krafft-Ebing, *Psychopathia Sexualis*, p. 53. Quoted in Weinberg and Kamel, *S and M*, p. 17.

9. Ibid., p. 53. Quoted in Weinberg and Kamel, *S and M*, p. 27.

10. Ibid.

11. Ibid., p. 25.

12. Ibid., pp. 25–6.

13. Ibid., p. 26.

14. Ibid.

15. Sigmund Freud, *The Basic Writings of Sigmund Freud*, trans. and ed. A. A. Brill (New York: Modern Library, 1938), p. 569. Excerpted in Weinberg and Kamel, *S and M*, p. 30.

16. Ibid.

17. Ibid.

18. Ibid., p. 31.

19. 'I have been led to recognise a primary erotogenic masochism from which there develop two later forms, a feminine and a moral masochism.' Sigmund Freud, 'Das Ökonomische Problem des Masochisten', Int. Zeit. F. Psa, 10, 121, 1924. Translated in *Collected*

Papers (London: Hogarth Press, 1953–74), vol. 2, p. 255. Quoted in Weinberg and Kamel, *S and M*, p. 32.

20. Juicy Lucy, 'If I Ask You to Tie Me up, Will You Still Want to Love Me?' in Katherine Davis *et al.* (eds), *Coming to Power: Writings and Graphics on Lesbian S/M* (Boston, MA: Alyson Publications, 1983), p. 32.

21. Vivienne Walker-Crawford, 'The Saga of Sadie O. Massey', in Robin Ruth Linden *et al.* (eds), *Against Sadomasochism: A Radical Feminist Analysis* (San Francisco, CA: Frog in the Well, 1982), p. 149.

22. Kathleen Barry, *Female Sexual Slavery* (New York: New York University Press, 1979), p. 209.

23. Interview with Anne McClintock, London, 3 July 1991.

24. Allegra Taylor, *Prostitution: What's Love Got to Do with It* (London: Macdonald Optima, 1991), p. 42.

25. Ibid., p. 41.

26. Roberta Perkins and Garry Bennett, *Being a Prostitute: Prostitute Women and Prostitute Men* (Sydney: Allen and Unwin, 1985), p. 127.

27. Interview with Anne McClintock, London, 3 July 1991.

28. Ibid.

29. Perkins and Bennett, *Being a Prostitute*, p. 142.

30. Ibid., p. 128.

31. Thomas S. Weinberg and G. W. Kamel, 'S/M: An Introduction to the Study of Sadomasochism', in Weinberg and Kamel, *S and M*, p. 21.

32. Lindi St Clair with Pamela Winfield, *It's Only a Game: The Autobiography of Miss Whiplash* (London: Piatkus, 1992), pp. 65, 74.

33. Gloria Walker and Lynn Daly, *Sexplicitly Yours: The Trial of Cynthia Payne* (London: Penguin, 1987), p. 66. One slave, Payne explained, came every Monday and let himself in with his own key, setting about his housewifely chores wearing only a wristwatch.

34. Perkins and Bennett, *Being a Prostitute*, p. 87.

35. Ibid., p. 128.

36. Quoted in Neil Philip, *Working Girls: An Illustrated History of the Oldest Profession* (London: Albion Press, 1991), p. 112.

37. Gebhard, 'Sadomasochism', in Weinberg and Kamel, *S and M*, p. 37.

38. Taylor, *Prostitution*, p. 45.

39. See Weinberg and Kamel, *S and M*, p. 109. Also Leyvoy Joenson, ' "Erotic Blasphemy": The Politics of Sadomasochism', unpublished paper.

40. *Madame in a World of Fantasy*, vol. 15 no. 8, p. 19.

41. Marjorie Garber, *Vested Interests: Cross-Dressing and Cultural Anxiety* (New York: Routledge, 1992), pp. 11, 10. See my essay 'The Return of the Female Fetish and the Fiction of the Phallus', in *New Formations*, issue 19 (1994), pp. 1–21, for a sympathetic critique of Garber's theory of fetishism.

42. *The World of Transvestism*, vol. 1 no. 5, p. 10.

43. Taylor, *Prostitution*, p. 39.

44. *Madame in a World of Fantasy*, vol. 14 no. 10, p. 5.

45. Philip, *Working Girls*, p. 112.

46. St Clair, *It's Only a Game*, p. 64.

47. *Madame in a World of Fantasy*, vol. 15 no. 8, p. 49.

48. Ibid., p. 51.

49. *Madame in a World of Fantasy*, vol. 14 no. 10, p. 7.

50. Ibid., p. 9.

51. *Mistress* 28, p. 48 (n.d.).

52. *Madame in a World of Fantasy*, vol. 15 no. 8, p. 61.

53. *Mistress* 28, p. 47.

54. Ibid.

55. *Madame in a World of Fantasy*, vol. 15 no. 8, p. 17.

56. Ibid., p. 37.

57. Gebhard, 'Sadomasochism', in Weinberg and Kamel, *S and M*, p. 37.

58. See Walker and Daly, *Sexplicitly Yours*, p. 66.

59. See Clare Dyer, 'Sado-masochists Guilty Verdict Upheld', *Guardian*, 20 February 1992. Also Alex Kershaw, 'Spanner in the Works', *Guardian Weekend*, 8–9 February, 1992, pp. 12–13; and Kershaw, 'Love Hurts', in *Guardian Weekend*, 28 November 1992, pp. 6–10.

60. Kershaw, 'Spanner in the Works', p. 13. See also Helena Kennedy, *Eve Was Framed: Women and British Justice* (London: Chatto and Windus, 1992), for a searing account of the miscarriage of justice.

61. Suzanne Moore, 'Deviant Laws', *Marxism Today*, February 1991, p. 11.

62. Anthony Brown, one of the men sentenced in the Spanner case, suggests: 'Perhaps there's a tendency for S & M activity to have increased, particularly among homosexual men, as a result of the threat of AIDS. To a degree it's a displacement activity.' Quoted in Kershaw, 'Spanner in the Works', p. 13.

63. Pat Califia, quoted in Kershaw, 'Love Hurts', p. 7.

64. Michel Foucault, *Discipline and Punish: The Birth of the Prison*, trans. Alan Sheridan (London: Penguin, 1977).

65. Ibid., p. 91.

66. Ibid., p. 81.

67. Ibid., pp. 93, 95.

68. Ibid., p. 129.

69. John Alan Lee, 'The Social Organisation of Sexual Risk', in Weinberg and Kamel, *S and M*, pp. 175–93; Sigmund Freud, *Three Essays on the Theory of Sexuality* (New York: Basic, 1962), p. 23.

70. Robert Stoller, *Perversion: The Erotic Form of Hatred* (New York: Dell, 1975).

71. Lee, 'The Social Organisation of Sexual Risk', p. 189. See also Goffman, *Frame Analysis*, p. 135.

72. Goffman, *Frame Analysis*.

73. Lee, 'The Social Organisation of Sexual Risk', p. 178.

74. Interview with Anne McClintock, London, October 1992.

75. St Clair, *It's Only a Game*, p. 64.

76. Ibid.

77. Taylor, *Prostitution*, p. 38.

78. *Madame in a World of Fantasy*, vol. 15 no. 8, p. 18.

79. Ibid., pp. 42–3.

80. As Weinberg and Kamel argue: 'S & M scenarios are *willingly and cooperatively* produced: more often than not it is the masochist's fantasies that are acted out'. Weinberg and Kamel, *S and M*, p. 20.

81. Gebhard, 'Sadomasochism', in Weinberg and Kamel, *S and M*, p. 37.

82. Ibid.

83. Pat Califia, 'Unravelling the Sexual Fringe: A Secret Side of Lesbian Sexuality', *The Advocate*, 27 December 1979, p. 22. Quoted in Jeffrey Weeks, *Sexuality and Its Discontents: Meanings, Myths and Modern Sexualities* (London: Routledge, 1985), p. 238.

84. Kelly, 'It's Not a Right or Wrong Issue, It's up to the Individual', in Perkins and Bennett, *Being a Prostitute*, p. 130. ('Kelly' is a working pseudonym.)

85. Pat Califia, *Macho Sluts: Erotic Fiction* (Boston, MA: Alyson Publications, 1988), p. 15.

86. Quoted in Taylor, *Prostitution*, p. 31.

87. See Donald McRae's brilliant account of the power struggle between a domina and a client in *Nothing Personal: The Business of Sex* (Edinburgh: Mainstream, 1992).

88. Zoe, 'The Only Way I Can Be Independent', in Perkins and Bennett, *Being a Prostitute*, p. 108.

89. 'I had by this stage recognised myself as a lesbian. I was also on a male hate trip and I thought all men were useless at that stage of my life.' Kelly, quoted in 'It's Not a Right or Wrong Issue', in Perkins and Bennett, *Being a Prostitute*, pp. 127, 130. For others, the imaginative demands are fatiguing, and they prefer the greater detachment that comes with giving brisk sexual services. As Margaret, an Australian prostitute says, 'I did bondage sometimes, but it was so damn exhausting I would prefer to do sex than bondage. Some of them wanted to be hit hard and that took it out of me physically and mentally.' In *Being a Prostitute*, p. 121.

90. See my expanded analysis of the legal issues facing sexworkers in Anne McClintock, 'Screwing the System: Sexwork, Race and the Law', in *Boundary 11*, Autumn 1992.

Index

LIST OF ILLUSTRATIONS

Untitled #115 (Measuring Tape) © Jeff Burton; *Bareback Rider*, © Douglas Kent Hall; *Desperado*, MAD; *Man of the West*, Ashton Productions; *Hannie Caulder*, Tigon British Film Productions/Curtwel Productions; *Studio Beurs*, © Jean Noel René Clair; *Untitled #68 (Harpsichord)*, © Jeff Burton; *Untitled #117 (Pierre Cardin)*, © Jeff Burton; *Untitled no. 14* from *Paintings*, © Paul Graham, courtesy Anthony Reynolds Gallery, London; *Untitled no. 4* from *Paintings*, © Paul Graham, courtesy Anthony Reynolds Gallery; *Sex with Strangers (Obscenity, Misogyny, Desire)*, Lutz Bacher; *Mayhem*, Abigail Child; 'The First International Exhibition of Erotic Art' from P. and E. Kronhausen, *Erotic Art: A Survey of Erotic Fact and Fancy in the Fine Arts*, vol. 1; *Interior Scroll* performance by Carolee Schneemann (photo by Anthony McCall); *Post-Post Porn Modernist, Anatomy of a Pin-up* (photo by Zorro), © Annie Sprinkle; *My Father is Coming*, Hyäne Filmproduktion; *Linda/Les and Annie*, Annie Sprinkle; *The Sluts and Goddesses Video Workshop*, Maria Beatty/Annie Sprinkle; *Deep Inside Porn Stars* by Club 90 and Carnival Knowledge (photo by Dona Ann McAdams); Frontispiece of the 1718 London edition of Meibom's treatise (Courtesy of the British Library Board); 'I'm afraid there's a queue on the stairs again, old boy!', © Rex Features Ltd; 'This time, Madame Cyn, I thought we'd come in uniform to celebrate...', © Mel Calman; 'We find the defendant NOT GUILTY – but we'd like to hear all the EVIDENCE again...', © Mark Boxer Ltd.